CADOGANguides

ROME

DANA FACAROS & MICHAEL PAULS

About the authors

Dana Facaros and **Michael Pauls** have written over 30 books for Cadogan Guides, including all of the Italy series. They lived for three years in Umbria but have now moved to a farmhouse surrounded by vineyards in the Lot Valley.

About the updaters

Jon Eldan baked bread and studied history in Berkeley, California, before buying a one-way ticket to Europe to bake his way across the continent. His road led to Rome, where he met **Carla Lionello**, a pastry chef from Venice. In 1995, they set up quarters in the Eternal City and began writing guide books. Jon now lives in Oakland, California, but returns to Rome several times a year. Carla still lives in the heart of the city, where she teaches cooking to interested travellers (*md2063@mclink*).

Deborah Soria (Nightlife and Entertainment chapters) runs a children's bookshop in Rome and enjoys going out in her native city.

Cadogan Guides
Network House, 1 Ariel Way, London W12 7SL
cadoganguides@morrispub.co.uk
www.cadoganguides.com

The Globe Pequot Press
246 Goose Lane, PO Box 480, Guilford, Connecticut
06437–0480

Copyright © Dana Facaros and Michael Pauls 1989, 1993, 1999, 2002
Updated by Jon Eldan and Carla Lionello 2002
Nightlife and Entertainment updated by Deborah Soria 2002

Series design: Andrew Barker
Series cover design: Sheridan Wall
Art Director: Sarah Rianhard-Gardner
Cover photo: © Joe Beynon/Axiom,
Photography: © Kicca Tommasi
Maps: © Cadogan Guides, drawn by Oxford Cartographers
Map Co-ordinator: Angie Watts

Editorial Director: Vicki Ingle
Series Editor: Claudia Martin
Editors: Christine Stroyan and Georgina Palffy
Proofreading and indexing: Judith Wardman
Grid-referencing: Linda McQueen
Production: Book Production Services
Printed in Italy by Legoprint
A catalogue record for this book is available from the British Library
ISBN 1860118542

Contents

Introduction

The ancestor of the book in your hand, the 12th-century *Mirabilia Urbis Romae*, was perhaps the first real travel guide of the modern era. Its English author described a city that was the wonder of the world, built by a race of men that seemed superhuman to the Middle Agers. To account for its marvels, the *Mirabilia* is full of legends and fairy tales; the truth, had its author known it, would often have been even stranger. Rome is one city where the improbable is a regular occurrence, constantly renewed – as in the Renaissance papacy's attempt to recapture the ancient magic, or Cola di Rienzo's, or Mussolini's. Or the Treaty of Rome, creating the European Union. Nothing is new under the sun, but especially under the *sole romano*.

Two thousand years ago Rome the Predator brought the first unity and peace to Europe, while evolving into a new urban life form: the Eternal Parasite. It bullied, battled and excommunicated itself into this unique position, and the city still lives with complacency off the pennies of the faithful, the travellers' cheques of tourists, and the euros of grudging Italian taxpayers. Yet its kitsch-colossal architecture, its enormous appetites, its modern maelstroms of traffic and misbegotten redevelopment throw into focus its moments of nobility and beauty: Michelangelo's *Pietà* becomes all the more poignant for its setting in The World's Biggest Church.

Why go to Rome? Go to see the Pantheon, to have your picture snapped in front of the Colosseum, to visit the bones of the saints; go for a glass of Frascati and a plate of *saltimbocca alla romana*; go to browse the designer shops around Piazza di Spagna or to stroll the streets at night, stopping off for an ice cream or a drink alongside Rome's fashionistas and lowlifes; go clubbing in the former abattoir in Testaccio or in one of the city's smarter *dolce vita*-era clubs – where the men still wear jackets and ties.

But besides all the usual reasons, let us add another: go to Rome to understand how the western world must outgrow its excesses for its own survival; see how Rome has transcended its inheritance of imperial brutality and exploitation, religious megalomania and endless, insatiable greed – and revived itself many times over, creating an intriguing spontaneous cubism of time and space, layer upon layer, where ancient temples jostle medieval brothels next to your neighbourhood grocer. James Joyce said that Rome was like a man who made a living by putting his grandmother's corpse on display. But what an amazing corpse it is – although goodness knows, it's high time for an autopsy. This book will sharpen your scalpel.

The Neighbourhoods

1 St Peter's and the Vatican Museums, p.199

Vatican City and St Peter's

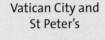

Tridente

Campo Marzio

5 Piazza Navona, p.82

Capitoline Hill and Tiber Banks

Trastevere and the Janiculum

3 Pantheon, p.87

7 Campo de' Fiori, p.79

8 Bocca della Verità, p.127

4 Capitoline Hill and Museums, p.124

9 Piazza del Popolo, p.102

In this guide, the city is divided into the eight neighbourhoods outlined on the map below, each with its own sightseeing chapter. This map also shows our suggestions for the Top Ten activities and places to visit in Rome. The following colour pages introduce the neighbourhoods in more detail, explaining the distinctive character and highlights of each.

Quirinale, Viminale and Esquiline Hill

Forums, Colosseum and Palatine Hill

6 Trevi Fountain, p.113

Caelian Hill and the Aventine

10 Appian Way, p.237

2 The Forums and Colosseum, p.133

4

Campo Marzio

To enjoy your stay in Rome to the full, you'll be spending a lot of time here, in the big bend of the Tiber that encloses the *Campus Martius* of the ancient Romans. In the Dark Ages, what was left of Rome's population straggled down here from the hills. Since then they have turned the Pantheon into a church for the faithful and Domitian's stadium into Piazza Navona for lovers of fashion and ice cream. Lively Campo de' Fiori and its market are here, and the little streets in every direction lead off into delightful piazzas, each a setting for an ancient relic, a frothy Baroque church or an elegant *palazzo*.

Clockwise from top right: Santa Maria della Pace, Pantheon dome and interior, Campo de' Fiori market, Piazza della Rotonda, Four Rivers Fountain, Campo Marzio rooftops.

Campo Marzio
Campo Marzio chapter p.79
Hotels p.284 Restaurants p.299 Bars p.318

Tridente

Even in this most photogenic of cities, such a neighbourhood stands out. Three of Rome's most familiar sights – the Spanish Steps, the Trevi Fountain and Piazza del Popolo – provide the backdrop; politicians, shoppers and tourists share the stage. Italy's parliament is here at Montecitorio, along with the swish shops of Via Condotti. Around Via del Corso, the main stem of this district, you'll also find fine art collections in the *palazzo*-museums of the Galleria Doria-Pamphili and Galleria Colonna.

Clockwise from top: Piazza Colonna, Keats-Shelley House, Pincio gardens, Spanish Steps, Via Condotti, designer shoe shop.

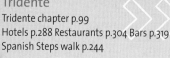

Capitoline Hill and Tiber Banks

This entire neighbourhood is one of Rome's more gratifying little secrets. Hidden behind the city's kitsch leviathan, the Altar of the Nation, the Capitoline Hill holds Michelangelo's lovely Piazza del Campidoiglio, and hoards of ancient art in the Capitoline Museums. Down below, along the Tiber, is a peaceful quarter (when the traffic permits) covered in a patina of red ochre and antique grace. Here, where Romulus and Remus hit the shore, are ancient Rome's only surviving temples and the Teatro Marcello, the Bocca della Verità, the peaceful Tiber Island and the old Jewish quarter around the Portico d'Ottavia.

Clockwise from top: Piazza Bocca della Verità, Tiber Island, Capitoline Museums, Teatro Marcello.

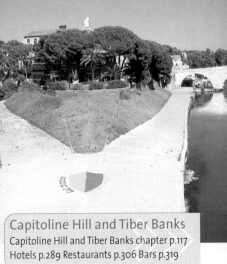

Capitoline Hill and Tiber Banks

Forums, Colosseum and Palatine Hill

Nobody lives in this neighbourhood now except scruffy cats and Roman ghosts, but you'll have to come and join them for a while if you want to see the centre of the ancient world. Everybody wants a look at the Colosseum. As for the rest, two millennia of popes gradually carted away most of the stone to build other vanities. What is left was carefully cleared and dusted off for you by Mussolini; it isn't the ruins themselves that make it all worthwhile, but the stories along the way.

Clockwise from top: Temple of Vespasian, Arch of Constantine, Colosseum, Roman Forum, the navel of Rome.

Forums, Colosseum and Palatine Hill

Caelian Hill and the Aventine

The Caelian Hill is the big green space at the bottom of the maps, a neighbourhood that was one of the busiest in the ancient city, but has been pretty much empty since the time of Totila the Goth. But don't think that there's nothing here worth your time; on the contrary this hill offers some of Rome's nicest surprises, in a green setting under Roman pines: San Clemente, with its three levels of walk-in history underneath, and the Baths of Caracalla. Above all, this area specializes in little-known but fascinating ancient churches. You'll find more of these on its neighbour to the west, the Aventine, along with a view of St Peter's through a keyhole.

Clockwise from top: Pyramid of Gaius Cestius, Baths of Caracalla, Porta San Sebastiano, Circus Maximus.

Caelian Hill and the Aventine

Caelian Hill and the Aventine chapter p.155 Hotels p.292 Restaurants p.311 Bars p.319

Quirinale, Viminale and Esquiline Hill

These are three of Rome's less magical hills, with a population that ranges from the lowlifes around Termini Station to the President of Italy. Baroque masterpieces of Borromini and Bernini are the main attractions. The Via Veneto is just nearby, come down in the world a bit since it was the headquarters of Roman *dolce vita* in the 1950s. Like every other neighbourhood of the city, this one has two important museums: one of the great patrician galleries in the Palazzo Barberini, and the Museo Nazionale Romano, set in the middle of what was once the Baths of Diocletian. The Esquiline Hill was one of the rougher parts of Rome in Augustus' day, and it hasn't changed much. But you shouldn't miss the ancient basilica of Santa Maria Maggiore, or the Byzantine mosaics in Santa Prassede.

From top: Porta Pinciana on Via Veneto, Tritone Fountain, Palazzo del Quirinale.

Trastevere and the Janiculum

Just over the Tiber is Rome's Brooklyn or Left Bank, a proud community with a spirit all its own. Everyone in Rome crosses over on a summer's night, to enjoy the quiet medieval lanes and some of Rome's most convivial trattorias. There is pure, concentrated *Romanità* at the centre, in the wonderful piazza and church of Santa Maria in Trastevere. Right around the corner is the Romans' own museum, the Museo di Roma in Trastevere.

Clockwise from top: Trastevere corner, Ponte Sisto, view from the Janiculum, street scene.

Trastevere and the Janiculum

Vatican City and St Peter's

Clockwise from top: Colonnade of Piazza San Pietro, façade of St Peter's, dome and interior of St Peter's.

The biggest piazza, signed by Bernini, welcomes you into the biggest church, signed by half the architects of the Renaissance (and they still couldn't get it right). The Vatican is a tremendous super-concentrated time capsule, a place where things are not always what they seem, stuffed to the ceiling with great art and dubious history. Tacked on to the side is the biggest museum, where the Sistine Chapel has to fight for attention with a few million other wonders, ancient and modern. Special tours offer a look at the pagan tombs underneath St Peter's altar, and the popes' cabbages in the Vatican gardens. Back on Italian soil, there's the Borgo, the Anglo-Saxon home-from-home in the Middle Ages, and the grimly fascinating stronghold of the papacy, Castel Sant'Angelo.

Vatican City and St Peter's

Days Out in Rome

Roma dei Romani p.14

Peace and Quiet p.16

Medieval and Renaissance Rome p.22

Unexpected Rome p.18

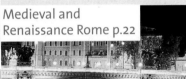

Baroqueorama p.20

Ancient Rome p.24

ROMA DEI ROMANI

To really live like a Roman, you'd be spending the day stuck in traffic in your Fiat on the Gran Raccordo Anulare (Rome's ring road). But in spite of mass tourism, high rents and suburban exodus, Rome's old centre persists in having a life of its own.

One

Start: Campo de' Fiori.
Breakfast: A cappuccino and a classy *cornetto alla crema* at **Bar Farnese**, in neighbouring Piazza Farnese.

Morning: The **Campo de' Fiori market** (*photo bottom left*), and a walk through the side streets to the **Museo di Roma a Palazzo Braschi**, with mosaics from old St Peter's.
Lunch: **Grappolo d'Oro**, a neighbourhood favourite – one of the best places to sit outside and feast on Roman home cooking. Try the *bucatini all'amatriciana*.
Afternoon: Cross the Tiber to see old Rome come to life in the rival **Museo di Roma in Trastevere**, and stroll around this characteristically Left Bank district.
Dinner: **Checco er Carettiere**, with its *romanaccio*-dialect name, is one of Trastevere's oldest inns. It serves popular Roman specialities and is famous for making even *trippa alla romana* (tripe) taste good.
Evening: Hang out for hours over a drink at **Bar San Calisto**, Trastevere's most authentic, scruffy, no-frills watering hole.

Two

Start: Corso del Rinascimento.

Breakfast: **Bar Sant'Eustachio** is known by Romans as the best place for coffee in the capital.

Morning: Stroll down the swish streets around **Piazza di Spagna** window-shopping for designer clothes (*photos below*).

Lunch: Head to Testaccio for home-style Roman cuisine – *rigatoni con pajata* (pasta with veal intestine) – at **Da Felice**. Expect brusque service.

Afternoon: From May to September, Romans take off for the beach whenever they can. Do as the Romans do: hop on a train at Piramide and spend the afternoon sunbathing at the **Lido di Ostia**. Don't forget your suntan lotion.

Dinner: Trendy, younger Romans – especially students – head for the gritty zone of San Lorenzo in the evenings. **Tram Tram** is particularly popular for its lighter meals and salads and also has a bar for pre- and post-dinner drinks.

Evening: End the night cruising the city for ***cornetti caldi*** – hot crois-sants – sold direct from the oven by overnight bakeries.

Food and Drinks

Sights and Activities

Nightlife

PEACE AND QUIET

It's easier than you might think to find peace and quiet in Rome. Unless the police or the paparazzi are after you, you'll find as many quiet corners in this city as in any metropolis. There aren't many parks, although Villa Borghese, Villa Celimontana and Villa Doria-Pamphili make a trio of urban graces, but Rome has so many churches and small piazzas that even the tourists can't find them all. In a city of endless sights you can track down all the tranquillity you need in the ones they miss: ancient churches, aristocratic art galleries and little-known ruins.

Three

Start: Piazza del Popolo.

Breakfast: **Ciampini al Café du Jardin**, in the **Pincio** gardens (*photos top left and this page bottom right*), is the perfect spot for a peaceful cappuccino in summer. In winter retreat to the genteel salon of **Canova** on Piazza del Popolo.

Morning: The **Villa Borghese** (*photos top right and bottom left*), central Rome's biggest park, will be all yours on a weekday morning.

Lunch: Picnic in the park or enjoy the pleasant hush at **Relais le Jardin**, Rome's top restaurant.

Afternoon: A walk around the Campo Marzio, avoiding main streets, can show you Rome at its most serene and likeable: **Piazza Farnese** (*photo centre left*) and **Via Giulia**, **Via dei Coronari** and **Via dell'Orso**, **Piazza Collegio Romano** and **Via del Portico d'Ottavia** all offer havens.

Dinner: The intimate veranda of the elegant **Taverna Antonina**.

Evening: Watch the sunset over an *aperitivo* at **Bar Gianicolo** and check the schedules of the **Associazione Musicale 'Il Tempietto'** for chamber music in a fine medieval church.

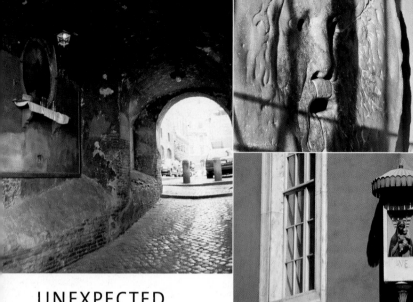

UNEXPECTED ROME

The Eternal City has far more of the singular, the spooky and the down-right bizarre than a city really needs. Any church crypt might come up with a little surprise, but it isn't all underground: this category also includes the world's silliest wax museum, the Mussolinian pomposity of the Foro Italico and EUR, and the mystic alchemical ceiling of Santa Maria in Domnica. Rome's environs can offer as much of the unexpected as the city itself: consider a day trip to the strangest of all Renaissance follies, the Monster Park of Bomarzo, taking in the pentagonal Villa Farnese in Caprarola.

Four

Start: Largo di Torre Argentina.
Breakfast: **La Dolceroma**, owned by an Austro-Italian couple, bakes un-Italian cakes. Boost your blood-sugar levels with American brownies or Austrian Sachertorte.
Morning: Continue the day cheerfully among the bones of 4,000 dead monks at the **Convento dei Cappuccini** on Via Veneto; skip to the bulls' blood-soaked *mithraeum* beneath **San Clemente**; and, if there's time, take in one of the **catacombs** on the Appian Way.
Lunch: For a change from Roman cuisine, try **Court Delicati** – Chinese and Thai specialities including nasi goreng, satay chicken and fish soup.
Afternoon: Tour the pagan tombs in the **Necropolis of St Peter's**, the dungeons of **Castel Sant'Angelo** (*photo top left*) and the **Museum of Purgatory**, pausing to look at the shops displaying religious tat (*photo opposite page bottom right*).
Dinner: **La Cantina Tirolese** proudly displays more than 30 Tyrolese fabric calendars on the walls.
Evening: Try the unusual fruits of the forest sangria at **Il Piccolo**.

Five

Start: Piazza del Popolo.

Breakfast: Get a morning cuppa at **Babington's Tea Rooms**, opened in 1896 by an English spinster who thought what Romans needed most was a cup of tea, scones, crumpets and English breakfast.

Morning: Visit the **Foro Italico**, with its 60 colossal stone athletes, for pure Fascist kitsch entertainment.

Lunch: **Sogo Asahi**, a wonderful Japanese restaurant seldom frequented by Westerners, has an excellent-value sushi lunch menu.

Afternoon: Carry on the trip at **EUR**, with Fascist street names like the Boulevard of Humanism, and the De Chirico-esque metaphysical

Palazzo della Città del Lavoro – known as the Square Colosseum.

Dinner: **Jaya Sai Ma** – 'Victory of Mother Earth' in Sanskrit – serves no meat or alcohol and bans smoking. It's a healthy haven where you can linger over a herbal tea.

Evening: Check out what's going on at the **Villaggio Globale**, Rome's former abattoir, in Testaccio, or at **Forte Prenestino**, an atmospheric squat in an impressive old fort.

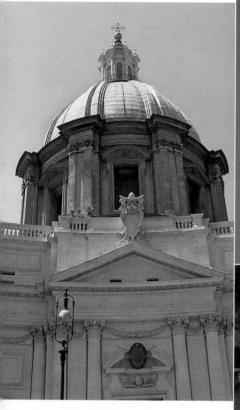

BAROQUEORAMA

Two centuries with all those curlicues and foofaraws and emoting marble saints – what was that all about? The Baroque was invented in Rome, so there's no better place to find out. Nearly all the greatest works of its inventors are here – Bernini, Borromini and Pietro da Cortona. In addition to architecture, Rome has a remarkable collection of private art galleries, with painting and sculpture of the time still in the palaces of the families that collected them.

Eight

Start: Metro Termini.

Morning: Tour the Baroque beauties of the Quirinale: **Santa Maria della Vittoria**, with Bernini's remarkable *Ecstasy of Saint Teresa* – five seconds away from climax for 300 years; the

two rival churches of **Sant'Andrea in Quirinale** (Bernini) and **San Carlo alle Quattro Fontane** (Borromini); the twin staircases by Bernini (square) and Borromini (oval) at **Palazzo Barberini**; and the **Trevi Fountain** – often falsely attributed to Bernini, but still a Baroque gem.

Lunch: **Al Piccolo Arancio**, in a narrow lane behind the Trevi Fountain.

Afternoon: Continue the tour with another fountain, Bernini's **Four Rivers Fountain** in Piazza Navona, and **Santa Maria della Pace**, its clever interplay of concave and convex forms creating the 'stage set' effect the decorous Baroque age strove for.

Dinner: Extend your experience of the Baroque by dining alongside Vatican vsitors at **L'Eau Vive**, run by the Christian Virgins of Catholic Missionary Action through Work.

Evening: Join Rome's poseurs in the Baroque setting of **Bar della Pace**.

MEDIEVAL AND RENAISSANCE ROME

In the Middle Ages, Rome's native artists created their own styles in frescoes and mosaics, while in the Renaissance the popes called in the best from all over Italy to surpass them. There is more to art in Rome than just Michelangelo and Raphael in the Vatican Museums, more in fact than you could see in a week. In this city of 901 churches (or 923, or 1,001 – nobody really knows), you'll be relieved to know that a serious culture tourist need visit only a hundred or so. On top of that, in the shadow of the great museums there is a flock of smaller ones matched by few cities in the world.

Six

Start: Piazza Venezia.
Breakfast: **Bar Ara Coeli**, steps from San Marco's medieval mosaics.

Morning: Start at the **Museo del Palazzo Venezia**, a fine collection of early Renaissance paintings housed in Rome's first important secular building of the Renaissance. Walk up Michelangelo's **Cordonata** to his **Campidoglio** (*photo above*). Take a stroll up **Via Giulia** (*photo opposite page right*), example of a subtler Renaissance aesthetic, to the High Renaissance **Piazza Farnese**.

Lunch: **Taverna Giulia** serves tasty Ligurian dishes in a 15th-century house just off Via Giulia.

Afternoon: Spend the afternoon indoors looking at the Renaissance paintings of the **Galleria Doria-Pamphili** – from Raphael to Caravaggio – and **Galleria Colonna**.

Dinner: **Camponeschi** sets its tables out in front of Tuscan Renaissance architect Antonio da Sangallo the Younger's Palazzo Farnese.

Evening: **Bartaruga** overlooks the tortoise fountain of Giacomo della Porta *et al*. It's a lively place to stop off for a cocktail after dinner.

Seven

Start: Piazza Santa Maria in Trastevere.

Breakfast: **Caffè di Marzio** has a terrace on this pretty piazza.

Morning: Take a tour of Trastevere, stopping at **Santa Maria in Trastevere**, the church in Rome that has best retained its medieval appearance, and **Santa Cecilia**, with fragments of medieval mosaics in its 12th-century *quadroporticus*. For a contrast, walk up the Janiculum to see **Il Tempietto**, the most characteristic work of the Roman High Renaissance, tucked away inside San Pietro in Montorio.

Lunch: **Hostaria La Canonica**, just behind Santa Maria, serves good seafood in a mock-rustic setting with a medieval atmosphere.

Afternoon: Head across town for two Patriarchal basilicas. **Santa Maria Maggiore** has preserved 12th-century mosaics from its medieval façade telling the legend of the church's founding. **San Giovanni in Laterano** conceals a medieval jewel of a cloister. Finish off with Rome's Carolingian Renaissance masterpiece, **Santa Prassede**.

Dinner: Dine at **Cannavota**, across the piazza from San Giovanni's gems.

Evening: Catch some medieval choral singing at the **Oratorio del Gonfalone**.

ANCIENT ROME

You could spend 20 days visiting
the remains of ancient Rome.
Besides the best-known sights – the
Forums, Colosseum and Palatine Hill
– there are fascinating relics in every
corner of the city.

Nine

Start: Via dei Fori Imperiali.
Breakfast: Have a good one at your
    hotel before starting out.
Morning: Begin with the obvious:
    the **Roman Forum** (*photo this page
    bottom right*), **Palatine Hill**, **Imperial
    Fora** and **Capitoline Museums**.
Lunch: You're unlikely to find an
    imperial feast in this part of Rome
    today. For a kitsch alternative, head

down the road to San Giovanni and
Pizza Forum, kitted out as a theme-
park version of an ancient forum.
Afternoon: Complete the tour of core
sights with the **Colosseum** (*photo
this page top right*) and the **Domus
Aurea** – Nero's Golden House – then
catch a bus up Via Cavour to the

Museo Nazionale Romano in the Baths of Diocletian and the Aula Ottagona, packed with Roman relics of every sort.

Dinner: Sadly no nightingales' tongues in this part of town either, but **Agata e Romeo** is perfectly sited for dinner near the Museo Nazionale Romano.

Evening: Why not see if *Giulio Cesare* is playing at the **Teatro dell'Opera**?

Ten

Start: Piazza del Popolo.

Breakfast: Sit out on the terrace of **Tempio Bar**, in full view of the Pantheon, with a cappuccino.

Morning: A walk through the centre will pass sights like the **Ara Pacis** of Augustus, the **Column of Marcus Aurelius**, the **Pantheon**, the **Portico d'Ottavia**, and the **Temple of Vesta** (*photo p.26 top right*) and **Temple of Fortuna Virilis** (*photo this page bottom left*) on the Tiber banks. Stop at Palazzo Altemps for more of the Museo Nazionale Romano.

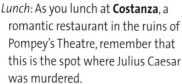

Lunch: As you lunch at **Costanza**, a romantic restaurant in the ruins of Pompey's Theatre, remember that this is the spot where Julius Caesar was murdered.

Afternoon: Take the short trip out to **Ostia Antica**, or stay in the city for a walk on the **Caelian Hill** (Celio), with its early Christian churches (San Clemente, Santo Stefano Rotondo, Santi Giovanni e Paolo), then carry on down to the **Baths of Caracalla** and the **Appian Way**.

Dinner: If you've made it as far as the Appian Way, dine at **Cecilia Metella**.

Evening: In summer, watch *Gladiator* or *Spartacus* under the stars at **Cinema Massenzio**, against a backdrop of the Colosseum at night.

Roots of the City

The strongest poison ever known
Came from Caesar's laurel crown.
                                    William Blake

According to the Romans' own legends, volcanic eruptions forced them down to the Tiber valley some time about 1000 BC. And that is a perfect introduction to the problems of Roman history – like a million other legends concocted in antiquity, it isn't true. The real beginnings of their city are lost in a Tiber mist. Some finds of pottery around the Capitol go back to 1200 BC. By 900, scattered settlements had sprouted all over Rome's hills. Culturally, these Romans were at the back of the class, but they had two very accomplished neighbours to learn from: the Greeks, and more importantly, the Etruscans. In the 8th century the Greeks began founding the rich and magnificent cities of Magna Graecia (southern Italy and Sicily) whose merchants traded everywhere along the Tyrrhenian coast. Accounts of the powerful Etruscan nation, which covered modern Tuscany and parts of Campania and northern Italy, usually include the adjective 'mysterious'. No one can say for sure where the Etruscans came from, although a possibility is Asia Minor, about 900 BC; their language has yet to be fully deciphered, and their political history and complex, secretive religion have vexed scholars for centuries.

In the 8th century BC, the Etruscan confederation of city-states was an empire that dominated the Italian peninsula. Rome, lying on its main route of communications, was strategically crucial. The Etruscans ruled it for much of the 7th and 6th centuries, welding the little villages on the hills into a city; tradition gives the date of its founding as 753 BC.

Behind the Myths

In later centuries, Romans would create an elaborate mythology to account for the founding of their city and its early history (see 'Legends', below). Making sense of it is a problem. The first 'kings of Rome' and other legendary figures may or may not have really

Legends of Early Rome

To understand Rome, the city's own myths of its beginnings are as important as the elusive historical facts. For a detailed account, there is Livy, the 1st-century BC historian who provided the most complete account (and himself invented some of it), and his contemporary, Virgil. Rome's greatest poet, under the spell of Greek culture, sought to give the new mistress of the world a proper classical background in his *Aeneid*, embellishing the tale of Aeneas, who fled the sack of Troy and found his way to Latium after dallying with the Carthaginian Queen Dido. Livy wanted to emphasize Rome's difference, and also embellished its origins to provide a divine ordination for the city's tremendous destiny.

Livy begins in the ancient Latin capital, *Alba Longa* (founded, according to Virgil, by Aeneas' son Ascanius), with Numitor, a Latin king whose throne was usurped by his brother Amulius. To preclude contending heirs, Amulius forced Numitor's only daughter, Rhea Sylvia, into service as a Vestal Virgin. Destiny intervened when the god Mars appeared in the Vestals' chambers, leaving her pregnant with twins **Romulus and Remus**. Following one of the world's best-known fairytale motifs, Amulius found out and packed the baby twins away in a little basket, like Moses, adrift on the waters. The gods steered them up the Tiber to safe harbour in the Velabrum, the marshes under the Capitoline Hill, where the famous she-wolf looked after the twins until a kindly shepherd took them home. Years later, Mars appeared again to explain to the grown-up twins their origins and destiny. They travelled to Alba Longa to settle accounts with Amulius, then returned to found the city Mars had commanded. According to Livy, the year was 753 BC.

In another enduring fairytale motif, the brothers soon fell out, like Cain and Abel (for Remus' demise, see Palatine Hill, p.151). Romulus invited one and all to join with his combative new city. The episode of the lived; the traditional date of 509 for the founding of the Republic was probably fixed later to coincide with the expulsion of the last tyrant from Athens. Servius' Wall, according to the archaeologists, really went up over a century and a half after his reign, in the 370s. And despite the famous tale of Horatius at the bridge, some historians believe that the Etruscans did retake Rome soon after the expulsion of King Tarquin. Whenever the Romans did break away, they took a powerful Etruscan heritage with them, including their alphabet (with a later Greek influence) and much vocabulary – many English words derive from Etruscan, by way of Latin: 'person' comes from an Etruscan word meaning the mask of an actor. The Etruscans also gave the Romans gods and rituals, divination and auspices, the circus and gladiatorial games. Even the lictors' rods (later Mussolini's fasces) were an Etruscan symbol of magistrates' authority .

But this growing, half-Etruscan city was already beginning to develop a strong personality of its own. Usually, the Romans expressed their young and carefree souls by waging unending warfare against their neighbours. In the 5th century BC the city became a formidable rival to its economically declining Etruscan neighbours (the city of Veii was only 12 miles away) while fighting constant campaigns to subjugate the rest of the Latins and tribes even further afield. At home, the militarist fathers of the Republic had to deal with unrest among the lower classes, who did most of the fighting and got to keep few of the spoils. In 494, the plebeians established a magistracy called the tribunate to look after their interests. In 450, they pulled off perhaps history's first general strike, or 'secession', resulting in codification and publication of the laws, which previously had been held as a religious secret among the patricians. The result was the famous **Twelve Tables**, in a sense Rome's constitution, drawn up by a temporary junta of ten called the Decemvirate (450) and published on bronze tablets displayed in the Forum.

Sabine women came soon after, when the Romans, lacking females, resolved to steal some from their neighbours. Romulus was the first of Rome's legendary seven kings. The next, **Numa Pompilius**, was a prophet, who visited a learned nymph named Egeria to learn how to lay down the rules for Rome's cults, priesthoods and auguries. After him came **Tullus Hostilius**, who extended Rome's rule over most of Latium, and **Ancus Martius**, who founded the port of Ostia. The next king, **Tarquinius Priscus**, was an Etruscan, who built Rome into a true city, erecting the Circus Maximus and digging the Cloaca Maxima to drain the area around the Forum.

His successor, according to Livy, was a Latin, **Servius Tullius**. He began the class division of Roman society into patricians (the senatorial class) and plebeians, and built his great wall to keep the Etruscans out. Apparently it did not work as planned, for the next king, **Tarquinius Superbus** (about 534 BC), was an Etruscan, and another great builder. His misfortune was to have a hot-headed son,

Tarquinius Sextus, who imposed himself on a virtuous Roman maiden named Lucretia (*cf.* Shakespeare's *Rape of Lucrece*). She committed public suicide the next morning, and the enraged Romans, led by **Lucius Junius Brutus** (later to be the first consul), chased out Tarquin and the Etruscans, and established the Roman Republic before the day was out.

For the next episode, you can follow an even better storyteller than Livy – Macaulay – in his stirring epic *Horatius*, about the brave fellow who defended the bridge when Lars Porsena of Clusium and the Etruscan allies came down to recapture the city. As the young republic went from success to success, the patriotic legends continued to multiply: old Cincinnatus accepting the title of Dictator to defeat the neighbouring Aequians, then returning quietly to his farm; the sack by the marauding Gauls in 390, when the cackling of the geese saved the Romans bottled up in their citadel on the Capitol (see p.123); and so on.

Rome Conquers Italy, and a Bit More

A brief interruption to Rome's march of conquest came around 390, when an army of nomadic **Gauls** from the north swooped down on one of their regular raids. When the Romans put up a hard-nosed resistance, the angry Celts took and sacked Rome itself, agreeing to leave only after payment of a stiff tribute. But Rome soon recovered its momentum. Already its arch-enemy Veii had been conquered and razed to the ground. The rest of southern Etruria was Rome's by mid-century, but the Romans needed another 50 years to swallow up the powerful **Samnites** in the mountains to the east. By 250, they had subdued the **Greek** cities to the south.

Other cities lived by trade or manufactures; Rome, disdaining any sort of honest living, found that constant conquest was necessary to keep its military machine oiled, and province after province was sucked dry to feed Roman avarice and meet the army's budget. The system was working so well that class conflict remained muted, although never completely extinguished, and Rome was always able to face its victims with unbroken determination. Its success in the next century was beyond anyone's dreams. In the **Punic Wars** (264–146) the total defeat of rival predator **Carthage** gave Rome the entire western Mediterranean. Looking east, politically-divided **Greece** was digested by 168. The equally disunited remnants of Alexander the Great's empire in the east proved easy targets, and by AD 64 Rome's legions were camped on the Cataracts of the Nile, in Jerusalem, and halfway across Asia Minor.

But every success only tended to confirm Rome in the worst side of its character. Roman rule under the republic meant an organized, systematic looting that never stopped. An endless stream of money and slaves flowed into the city. Taxation ceased for the relatively small number of Roman citizens, and cheap requisitioned imports of grain ruined most of the farmers, allowing the Roman elite to buy up most of their land and turn Italy into a nation of landed barons and helpless sharecroppers. Many Italian cities actually withered and died in this period, especially those of the Greeks and Etruscans. Many rural districts were abandoned, their populations fleeing to Rome, where the new rich always could use more help to look after the household, while they themselves learned the delights of orgies, gladiatorial combats, and being carried about in the streets by slaves.

Not that Rome's victims utterly failed to resist. A **Popular Party** did its best to effect reforms, but the new rich of the landed nobility, the **Optimates**, managed to have every one of their leaders murdered. In 133 BC, a remarkable politician named **Tiberius Gracchus** was elected tribune; his plans for land reform earned him assassination the following year. Brother **Gaius Gracchus** went even further, attempting to turn Rome into a genuine democracy, but the Senate had him murdered too. After more of the same, and a disappointing interval of mildly popular rule under a military strongman named **Gaius Marius** (c.100–91), all Italy rose in revolt. The **Social Wars** (92–89) and the famous slaves' rebellion of **Spartacus** (73) both ended as grisly proofs of the Roman elite's monopoly of force. Their privileges were saved, at the cost of permanently deranging the institutions of the Republic.

From Republic to Empire

Optimates and Populists alike realized that the only real power lay with the army, and the last vestiges of the rule of law soon disappeared. After Marius, a reactionary general named **Sulla** made a military coup with the aid of the Senate (82), establishing the bloodiest dictatorship Rome had ever seen. After his death, power passed to the immensely vain but apolitical and intelligent general **Pompey**, who shared it after 59 in the **First Triumvirate** with a crooked building magnate named **Crassus** and a young upstart who went into politics to pay his debts, **Julius Caesar**. Like any aspiring Roman politician, what Caesar wanted was not a meaningless title in the city, but a military command abroad. He got it, conquered Gaul, crossed the Rubicon in 50 (the worried Senate had forbidden his return to Italy), and defeated Pompey two years later to become unchallenged master of Rome.

Despite repression and incessant civil war, a gradual transformation was coming over the old pirates' nest. The rough and ready appearance of the metropolis slowly began to blossom into marbled urbanity, as both Pompey and Caesar began building. Both built theatres, an indication of how Greek culture was finally making its way into Rome. Romans began to reflect on the meaning of their republicanism, and the responsibilities that came with power. This Rome of the 1st century BC could produce a man like **Marcus Tullius Cicero**, who represented what was left of the Italian middle classes – but too late. His dreams of a stable, constitutional republic came to naught in the end, caught between his own political ineptitude and the rapacity of his opponents.

And the age produced Caesar, who took up the popular cause in better style than anyone before, and reformed everything in Rome, even the calendar. His just, decisive government did much to heal the scars of oppression, but his murder in 44 by a clique of senatorial bitter-enders brought another spell of war. When the dust settled 13 years later, Caesar's adopted son Octavian came out on top, and continued his reforms, liberally dispensing Cleopatra's expropriated treasure to grease the way. Personal rule was nicely institutionalized; keeping up the forms of the dead Republic, Octavian occupied most of the offices, modestly referring to himself as princeps ('first citizen'). Less modestly, he had Caesar declared a god, and renamed himself **Augustus**. For the city, the grandeur of which had long lagged behind its power and wealth, his rule was golden. Augustus transformed 'a city of brick into one of marble'; imposing new temples, basilicas, and theatres sprang up everywhere.

Rome's population may have passed the million mark at this time, surpassing Antioch and Alexandria as the greatest city in the world. Augustus' Rome, governmental and financial metropolis of the West, was also the city of **Horace** and **Virgil**, for the first time a cultural centre in its own right. The reigns of future emperors, good or bad, had little effect on the city except to give Romans something to talk about at dinner parties. One big event was the great fire of 23 April 64 AD, under Nero, in which a quarter of the city went up in flames. Another was the completion of the Colosseum in 81, the definitive monument to Rome's conspicuous consumption, not only of money, but blood.

Still the ultimate predator, Rome produced nothing and consumed everything. No one with any spare *denarii* would be foolish enough to go into business with them, when the real money was to be made from

From Early Roman Republic to the End of Empire

Appian Way, to see the 'queen of roads', the ancient Roman route to Gaul, lined by tombs and catacombs, p.237 and p.247

Baths of Caracalla, for a symbol of Roman opulence, baths which could service 2,000 bathers at a time, p.162

Capitoline Hill and Museums, for the legendary origins of Rome and the best-kept and richest collection of Roman art, p.125

Colosseum, to see the ruin to beat all ruins, built by Vespasian to scourge the memory of Nero's excesses, p.149

Imperial Fora, for the emperors' vision to reduce crowding in the Roman Forum – five imperial shopping malls, p.136

Museo Nazionale Romano, for perhaps the greatest collection of Roman art and relics anywhere, p.181

Palatine Hill, to see the site of the imperial residences that gave 'palace' to nearly every European language, p.151

Pantheon, for the most perfect major monument of the ancient world, p.87

Roman Forum, for what was once the centre of the Mediterranean world, p.139

Rome's Seven Hills

Originally they were much higher. Centuries of building, rebuilding and river flooding have made the ground level in the valleys much higher, and at various times emperors and popes shaved bits off their tops in building programmes. The **Capitoline Hill**, smallest but most important, now has Rome's City Hall, the Campidoglio, roughly on the site of ancient Rome's greatest temple, that of Jupiter Greatest and Best. The **Palatine**, adjacent to it, was originally the most fashionable district, and eventually got entirely covered by the palaces of the emperors – the heart of the Roman Empire. The usually plebeian **Aventine** lies to the south of it, across from the Circus Maximus. Between the Colosseum and Termini Station, the **Esquiline**, the **Viminale**, and the **Quirinale** stand three in a row. The Quirinale was long the residence of the popes, and later of the Italian kings. Finally, there is the **Caelian Hill,** south of the Colosseum, now a charming oasis of parkland and ancient churches in the centre of Rome. The Urbs of course has other hills not included in the canonical seven: Monte Vaticano, from which the Vatican takes its name, Monte Pincio, including the Villa Borghese, Rome's biggest park, and the Gianicolo, the long ridge above Trastevere that was called the Janiculum by the ancient Romans.

government, speculation, or real estate. At times most of the population was on the dole – not necessarily because they were poor, but because of the time-honoured tradition of buying citizens' loyalty with 'bread and circuses'. No city has ever been so unabashedly obsessed with money and the things it can buy. Some poets, like **Horace**, devote much of their attention to accounts of banquets and new luxuries from the east, while the more honest ones, like **Juvenal**, paint an insatiable Rome of unnatural vices and brazen crimes, intrigues and poisons, where 'every street is thronged with gloomy-faced debauchees'.

The empire, in the unparalleled prosperity of the 1st and 2nd centuries, could afford to indulge its wayward capital. While the last monstrous heirs of Augustus – **Tiberius**, **Caligula** and **Nero** – outdid their subjects, Augustus' disciplined civil service managed to keep the ship of state on an even keel. In the 2nd century, an unbroken string of good emperors – **Trajan** and **Hadrian** (both from Spain, both gay) and **Antoninus Pius** and **Marcus Aurelius** (the Antonines) – gave the empire sympathetic, effective government and victorious peace, while bestowing on Rome many of its finest monuments. When times got rougher, with the military setbacks and economic crises of the 3rd century, the Mediterranean world began to see that it could no longer support Rome in the manner to which it had become accustomed. And in 275, the threat of invasions caused **Aurelian** to give Rome a wall, the first in over 600 years. By that time, the city was already an irrelevant, bloated backwater and emperors spent most of their time in the east, or up at army headquarters in Mediolanum (Milan). Army recruiters stopped taking conscripts from the city some time in the 2nd century – the centurions all said real Romans were too sick and debauched to make decent soldiers.

By 300, Rome's empire had become a shabby, impoverished totalitarian state, a nightmare of roughhouse police and taxmen run by the army and all but abandoned by its rotten ruling classes. **Constantine**, a cruel but energetic emperor (304–37), did Rome the double indignity of moving the imperial capital to his new base, Constantinople, and tossing aside the city's ancient religious traditions by promoting the wealthy and influential cult of the **Christians**. The last great imperial builder, Constantine included an impressive programme of Christian basilicas in his works. By 400, with the economy and the military in a state of utter collapse, the barbarians were knocking politely at the door. Few Romans could be found to defend the state, and barbarian generals guarded the western empire, while its emperors hid out in the impregnable new capital, Ravenna.

Alaric the Goth, invading Italy in 410, did not get the tribute he had been promised by the Romans, so he simply broke in and treated the city to a cautious, respectful sacking. Alaric did little damage, but the news of the sack resounded across the Roman world like the Trump of Doom.

The next visitor, in 452, was **Attila the Hun**. There were no armies to stop him, but the real leader of Rome – Pope Leo I – somehow talked him into leaving the city in peace. **Genseric the Vandal** passed through three years later, a conscientious sacker the long-dead Roman heroes would have appreciated – he stole everything that wasn't nailed down. In 475, **Odoacer the Goth** pensioned off the last western emperor; Italy became a Gothic kingdom. Under **Theodoric**, his successor, it was a peaceful and prosperous place, popular mythology notwithstanding. In Rome, chariot races were still on the bill at the Circus Maximus, new churches were built, and the decadent nobility still held on to its immense wealth and privileges. No longer a capital (Theodoric ruled from Ravenna), the city shrank; the Gothic King had to pass laws to keep the Romans from dismantling their own monuments for building stone, and from stealing the gilt and bronze statues. With no new prey to batten on, Rome was beginning to devour itself.

Rome's Middle Age

The serious disasters came not at the hands of barbarians – but of Romans. Eastern Emperor **Justinian** invaded Italy in 538 and plunged the entire peninsula into chaos and misery. Rome changed hands several times during the long wars. During King Totila's siege of Rome in 546, when the population may have been down to a few hundred, the aqueducts were cut and never after repaired; their water flooded the surrounding districts, turning them into malarial swamps. People were forced to abandon homes on the hills, to camp out among the decaying ruins of the Campus Martius, and to drink the infected waters of the Tiber. Recurring plagues and

famines, along with the invasion of the truly barbaric **Lombards** (567), kept the city on the skids, although a number of able and energetic popes did their best to ameliorate the situation – especially **Gregory the Great** (590–604), who brought much relief to the starving Romans, and laid the foundations for the papacy as a temporal power.

Gregory was the heir of Rome's richest family. It is not often realized that the well-run and thriving Roman Church of these times was almost entirely a creation of the Roman nobility, and remained so for centuries. Strangely, almost miraculously, this class managed to shed the drowsiness of its imperial decadence, recapturing the iron resolve of the brave days of old. Pooling their resources by donating vast properties to the Church, the nobles exchanged togas for surplices and cassocks, and survived.

Thanks to them, Dark Age Rome never went entirely dark. Crowds of pilgrims still came every year. New churches were built, and decorated with glittering Byzantine

Rome's Middle Age

San Clemente, to see the the change from *mithraeum* to Christian basilica in 375, p.158

San Giovanni Laterano, for Constantine's octagonal baptistry and Scala Santa, brought here by his mother St Helen, p.166

San Lorenzo fuori le Mura, to see another 4th-century basilica of Constantine's, where St Lawrence got a grilling for his faith, p.235

Sant'Agnese fuori le Mura, for Constantia's memorial to the martyr of modesty, whose hair grew to cover her nakedness, p. 234

Santa Costanza, for the mausoleum of Constantine's daughter Constantia, p.235

Santa Croce in Gerusalemme, founded on St Helen's fragment of the True Cross, p.236

Santa Maria Maggiore, for the the 12th-century mosaics from the medieval façade, telling the legend of its 352 founding, p.186

Santa Prassede, for Theodora's 'Garden of Paradise' mausoleum, completely covered with gold-ground mosaics, p.187

Santa Pudenziana, its sister, for the apse adorned with a 390s Christian mosaic, p.188

Rome's Layers

Look at any good map and you begin to see the classical city hiding beneath the modern one. Straight streets like Via delle Botteghe Oscure, Via dei Cestari or Via dei Coronari, have survived intact from the **ancient city**, while the winding lanes betray medieval origins. Oddities on the map give away every sort of old secret: the block east of Campo de' Fiori follows the curves of Pompey's Theatre; the course of Domitian's stadium is preserved in Piazza Navona; the semicircle of Piazza della Repubblica follows the line of the *exedra* of Diocletian's Baths.

In the Campo Marzio, where most Romans lived after the 500s, you can explore the **medieval city**, one of Italy's most complete: no cathedral, no centre, but a lesson in medieval planning, not as careless as it first appears. Here the basic unit is not the street, but the piazza – over a hundred of them between the Corso and the river; the streets simply connect them. It's a contrast with modern cities – the difference between getting somewhere and being somewhere, and the essential background for Rome's *dolce vita*. Medieval cities do not give you obelisks to find your way around. They make your eyes and brain work harder – spend some time walking around this old quarter, and you'll get the point. A simple exercise: almost every street corner in old Rome has a view worth a picture – the busy engravers of 18th-century prints never exhausted the subject. Stop now and then, and look around to find it; look up, if traffic permits. Roofs, towers and domes offer surprises and the clues that an old Roman used to find his way.

The rest is easy. A new Rome balanced between **Renaissance** and **Baroque**, with long straight boulevards punctuated by obelisks, appeared around the fringes, an innovation in urban design that has influenced the work of all planners since.

mosaics. There were libraries, and scholars to use them. Especially in the 8th and 9th centuries, under able popes like **Adrian I** and **Leo III**, both great builders, a rebirth of culture and unity seemed to be under way. The popes found new protectors in the powerful Frankish kings, and when Leo placed an Imperial crown on the head of **Charlemagne** in St Peter's, on Christmas Eve in 800, a partnership was sealed that would change Europe. Oddly enough, Charlemagne wasn't expecting it: the Pope sneaked up behind him with the crown while he was praying. Nevertheless, he could not or would not undo the *fait accompli*, and the idea was born that Holy Roman Emperors had to get their crown from a Roman pontiff. Caesar's ghost was stirring once more.

The rapid decline of Frankish power after Charlemagne brought big troubles to Italy. **Muslim** raiders occupied parts of Latium and Campania and raided Rome itself in 846, looting St Peter's. In the strife of the terrible 9th century, power in Rome fell to a remarkable pair of ladies, **Theodora** and daughter **Marozia**. Theodora, who after 880 assumed the title Senatrix, attempted to found a little state, with her family as dynasts. Marozia, an even more formidable woman, has suffered sensational character assassination by male chauvinist historians (her career may be one of the sources of the legend of 'Pope Joan'). She dominated Rome, making her lovers and children into popes, until 932, when her son **Alberic** performed a neat coup d'état.

For the first time, under Alberic Rome stood independent and secular. He reformed both Church and state, and pointed the way for Rome to become a free republican *comune* like other Italian cities. The situation became more complicated after his death. In fact the 10th and 11th centuries were anarchy, with nobles like the Crescenzi seizing Castel Sant'Angelo and declaring themselves 'Consuls', German emperors making regular sorties over the Alps to sort things out, and popes and anti-popes sprouting almost every year. In the 10th century alone, nine popes managed to get themselves murdered.

The banana papacy did not get back on the track until the 1070s; then it was due largely to the strenuous efforts of a reforming cleric named **Hildebrand**, who eventually became pope as Gregory VII in 1073. Rome's power returned, enough to humble the German emperors and to proclaim the First Crusade in 1097. Along the way, in 1084, the popes' supposed Norman allies under Robert Guiscard treated the city to its worst ever sacking. Although the popes were strong enough to meddle in the affairs of all Europe, the 12th century proved almost as confusing and bloody as those before. The 1140s, for example, witnessed the spectacle of a Jewish pope – **Anacletus II**, head of Rome's powerful Pierleoni family – while the mighty city of the Caesars was making war on its little neighbour Tivoli, and losing. A sincere monkish reformer appeared, **Arnold of Brescia**, preaching democratic ideals and the divorce of the Church from temporal power. In 1145, his supporters re-established the Roman Republic, complete with Consuls and Senate. Ten years later, he was captured by Emperor Frederick I, and given over to Pope **Adrian IV** (Nicholas Breakspear, the only English pope) for torture and hanging.

At the century's close, the occupant of St Peter's throne was **Innocent III**, perhaps the most powerful of all popes, able to make his will obeyed everywhere in Europe – excepting occasionally Rome. In the 1200s, popes had to contend not only with deter-mined emperors like Frederick II, and feudal, virtually sovereign Roman families like the legendary **Colonna** and **Orsini**, but also with the Roman people, still trying to keep some-thing of Arnold's Republic alive. For all the troubles, it was a brilliant age for art in Rome, and a time of great prosperity. An especially vile pope, **Boniface VIII** (1294–1303), spoiled it. His high-handed behaviour, trying to fill the shoes of Innocent III, lost the papacy what-ever friends it had in Europe. After he died, the French King purchased the election of a French pope, **Clement V**, who packed the Vatican with French cardinals, and then, in 1305, moved the whole show to Avignon.

For Rome, the effect was war, plague and depression all in one. The parasite city that had been living off the pennies of Europe's faithful for so long now found itself cut off from its only source of income, while Orsinis, Colonnas and imitators raged unchecked in the streets. Much of the city began to look abandoned, as the population dropped to its lowest level in 800 years. To fill the vacuum, there appeared the improbable figure of **Cola di Rienzo**, the self-educated son of a washer-woman, whose musings among monuments and inscriptions of antiquity fired him with an obsessive passion for returning his city to its former greatness. Bending the ears of anyone who would listen, the young orator literally talked Rome into declaring Republic once more, in May of 1347; the nobles, for all their gangs of warriors, could not stop it.

Unfortunately, history has shown few examples of power corrupting so quickly, and so absolutely. Rienzo ruled with near insane conceit and arrogance, claiming dominion for Rome over the entire world. Although the Republic's citizen militia defeated the noble forces, a complete loss of popular support forced Rienzo to abdicate in November of the same year. In 1354, obese and decayed, he returned and seduced the Romans again. The result was the same, and Rienzo met his end later in the year, torn to pieces by a mob of once-loyal citizens. Thanks largely to another great persuader, St Catherine of Siena, **Pope Gregory XI** finally returned to Rome in 1377 – although anti-popes remained in Avignon and Pisa for decades. A successful Jubilee Year in 1390 paid for some needed repairs, and Rome was back in business.

The New Rome

The old papacy, before Avignon, had been a simple instrument of the Roman nobility. In the more settled conditions of the 1400s, a new papacy emerged, richer and more sophisticated. **Martin V** (a Colonna) and **Nicholas V** (1447–55) contributed perhaps the most to re-establishing it. Under **Julius II** (1503–13), the papal domains for the first time were run like a modern state; Julius also laid plans for the rebuilding of St Peter's, beginning the great building programme

The New Rome

Palazzo Farnese, the most magnificent of High Renaissance palaces, named after rapacious predator Alessandro Farnese, p.93

St Peter's, to see the basilica commissioned by Pope Julius II and built by Bramante, Michelangelo, Raphael and others, p.204

San Pietro in Vincoli, to see Michelangelo's *Moses* on the Tomb of Julius II, p.184

Sistine Chapel, to see Rome's most popular tourist sight ever since a weary Michelangelo opened its doors in 1512, p.218

Via Giulia, laid out by Julius II and designed by Bramante to cut straight from central Rome to St Peter's, p.95

that was to transform the city. New streets were laid out, especially the Via Giulia and the grand avenues radiating from the Piazza del Popolo. Buildings that had survived substantially intact for 1,500 years were cannibalized for their marble; Julius' main architect, **Bramante**, knocked down medieval Rome with such gay abandon that Raphael nicknamed him 'Ruinante'. Over the next two centuries, the work continued at a frenetic pace. Besides St Peter's, hundreds of churches were either built or rebuilt, and cardinals and noble families lined the streets with new palaces, imposing if not always beautiful.

In the general prosperity of the time, and despite the **Reformation** – caused partly by the increased sale of indulgences and Church offices by **Leo X** (1513–22) – money poured into Rome as never before. The Renaissance popes have a wonderful reputation as enlightened men of the world and patrons of arts and letters that is largely deserved. On the other hand, most of them rank among the most cynically corrupt and murderous popes of all time. More than ever, the papacy became a private club among the leading Italian noble houses, devoted entirely to their enrichment. In the papal auction, it cost millions to get elected – but you knew you would get it back with interest. When the Church's money no longer sufficed for their appetites, they began taxing the economy of the Papal States out of existence.

Through the previous century, last vestiges of Roman civic liberty had been gradually extinguished. Now, the popes allied themselves alternately with Spain, France or the Emperor to extend their power, decisively contributing to the gradual enslavement of all Italy by foreign powers. In doing so, they reaped a bitter harvest in the **1527 Sack of Rome**. An out-of-control imperial army of Spaniards, Italians and German Lutherans occupied the city for almost a year, causing tremendous destruction, while the calamitous **Pope Clement VII** looked on helplessly from Castel Sant'Angelo. Afterwards, the popes were happy to become part of the Imperial-Spanish system. Political repression was fiercer than anywhere else in Italy; the **Inquisition** was refounded in 1542 by **Paul III**, and book burnings, torture, and executions became more common than in Spain itself.

The End of Papal Rule

By about 1610, there was no Roman foolish enough to get burned at the stake; at the same time workmen were adding the last stones to the cupola of St Peter's. It was the end of an era, but the building continued. A thick accretion of Baroque, some coral and some barnacle, collected over Rome. **Bernini** made his Piazza Navona fountain in 1650, and the Colonnade for St Peter's 15 years later. The political importance of the popes, however, disappeared with surprising finality. Having turned Italy into a political backwater, and exhausted the moral capital of their Church, they drifted into irrelevance in the power politics of modern Europe during the **Thirty Years' War** and after. Rome was left to enjoy a decadent but pleasant twilight, while the papacy remained as venal as ever – nearly all the popes managed a grand palace or two for their families. Carnival and fireworks shows were never better. No one in Rome starved, as religious charities began to take the character of the ancient imperial dole, and the worldly Romans learned to polish their lives into the *dolce vita* of a city that had seen it all.

This was the Rome that proved so irresistible to northern Europeans at the start of the **Grand Tour**. Even Protestants had a good time, and found it easy to slide around the religious laws and sleepy Inquisitors. A brief interruption to this pleasant state of affairs came when **Napoleon** invaded in 1796, carting off much of the city's wealth and tons of its art treasures to Paris. Papal rule was restored in 1815; the reaction was complete, although not harsh, and Romans seemed not too unhappy about sliding back into the 18th century. But when a **Roman Republic** appeared in February 1849, at the crest of the 1848 revolutionary wave, the populace responded with fervour. The great revolutionary intriguer, Giuseppe Mazzini, took charge, and a Ligurian sailor named Giuseppe Garibaldi, with experience in South American guerrilla wars, came to lead the militia. A French army besieged the city; despite a heroic resistance they had the pope propped back on his throne by July.

Napoleon III maintained a garrison to look after the pope, and consequently Rome became the last part of Italy to join the new Italian kingdom. When the Prussians sorted out France in 1870, the opportunity was clear. Italian troops blasted a hole in the old

Aurelian Wall near the Porta Pia and cake-walked in. Pius IX, who ironically had decreed Papal Infallibility just the year before, locked himself in the Vatican and pouted; the popes were to be 'prisoners' until the Concordat of 1929. The Italians confiscated most of the monasteries and the pope's Quirinale Palace, knocked down the walls of the Jewish ghetto, and freed the last three woebegone prisoners of the Inquisition.

Capital City, Open City

As capital of the new state, Rome underwent another building boom; new streets like Via del Tritone, Via Vittorio Veneto, and Via Nazionale made circulation a little easier around the seven hills, and the lovely villas and gardens that once encircled the city disappeared under endless blocks of tawdry speculative building (everything round Termini Station, for example). The new Italian kingdom strove mightily to impress the world with gigantic, absurd public buildings and monuments, such as the Altar of the Nation and the Finance Ministry on Via XX Settembre, as big as two Colosseums. More damage was done under Mussolini, who drove wide automobile roads through the picturesque city centre, isolating and sanitizing innumerable ancient ruins.

From the **Italian armistice** in 1943 until 5 June 1944, Rome found itself on short rations under a rough **German occupation**. The city's Resistance acquitted itself bravely; as many as 200,000 people – Jews, escaped Allied prisoners and anti-Fascists – were hidden in homes and convents, while Socialist and Communist guerrillas did their best to sabotage the Germans. Their success provoked vicious reprisals like the **Fosse Ardeatine massacre**, when 335 prisoners from the Regina Coeli prison were murdered in retaliation for a guerrilla bombing. Serious destruction of the city was averted by the careful aim of the Allied air forces (of all the churches, only S. Lorenzo was badly damaged, although homes, hospitals and even the Vatican were occasionally hit), and

The End of Papal Rule

Colonnade of St Peter's, for Bernini's 284 massive columns and statues of 140 saints, that symbolize 'the arms of the Church embracing the world', p.203

Keats–Shelley Memorial House, to see where the two poets lived and Keats died, at the heart of the 'English Ghetto', p.106

Palazzo del Quirinale, to see where the Roman Republic of 1848 was declared and Mazzini took up residence after booting out the popes, once and for all, p.176

Piazza Navona, for the Baroque coral of Bernini's *Four Rivers Fountain*, recoiling from Borromini's Sant'Agnese in Agone, p.83

Protestant Cemetery, to see where consumptive and accident-prone Grand Tourists were buried – including both Keats and Shelley, p.171

Capital City, Open City

by the good graces of Adolf Hitler and Feldmarschall von Kesselring, who pulled out their armies and declared Rome an Open City as soon as the Allies approached it.

In the charmed '50s, Rome caught the imagination of the world, if only for the brilliant films of Fellini, de Sica, Visconti and the rest, pouring out of Cinecittà. Mass tourism arrived, and the city continued to dilate unattractively in all directions. By the '70s, the magic illusion of *La Dolce Vita* was only a memory – with the collapse of the Italian film industry, the government briefly considered selling off Cinecittà for building lots. As Rome's urban problems increased, Italy's **Anni di Piombi** (years of lead) made the city a reluctant centre stage for a decade of political sleaze and terrorism, fostered by radical right-wing elements in the government and intelligence services, which reached its climax with the kidnapping and murder of Prime Minister Aldo Moro in 1978.

Rome Today

Rome is inhabited by know-nothings who do not want to be disturbed. They are perfect products of the Church, the type of people who have become so gangrenous in their own secular condition that they believe they can and must live only like this. The Roman is like a grotesque, overgrown child who has the satisfaction of being continually spanked by the Pope. Rome's own newspapers have called it the 'anti-città', a 'mega-factory of poisons', a rancid, uninhabitable city, close behind Naples in the race towards complete social and environmental collapse.

Allowances must always be made for Italian journalistic exaggeration. At first glance, Rome's problems do not seem overwhelming. Despite massive improvements, parked cars and traffic still choke the medieval alleys and foul the air. Crime has gone down substantially in the late 1990s, along with the general economic upturn throughout Europe. Drug addiction is still a problem, but no more than in any other large city with social divides. You may find Termini Station and some of the less salubrious streets around it full of desolate junkies if you look hard enough. Rome is very slowly becoming more multicultural, as immigrants and refugees from Africa, the Philippines, Bangladesh, Sri Lanka and Eastern Europe flock to the city. Membership of neo-fascist groups such as the Fronte del Gioventù and Naziskins has swelled, but to nothing like the extent that has occurred in northern Italy, with its separatist, rightwing parties.

Delinquency in Rome is hardly the sole preserve of the poor. Political kickbacks have been a Roman tradition since the days of the Caesars, but no one suspected the depth of depravity the early '90s *tangentopoli* (kickback city) investigations uncovered, among the big shots in Rome and Sicily, but perhaps more surprisingly in Milan. Nearly all the major vampires of the nation's old political class have at one point been in hiding, on trial, or at least under suspicion for diverting funds, mafia connections and even worse – although after a spate of high-profile suicides of suspects in prisons, the investigations ultimately petered out under pressure from the usual forces. Until *tangentopoli*, the Christian Democratic Party was an allegory for Divine Inevitability, in a class with death, value-added tax and blocked drains. The

Some Facts to Get You Started

You'll find Rome at 41.53 degrees latitude (about the same as Madrid, New York and Beijing) and 12.29 degrees longitude. It has an officially registered population of 2,800,000, and an estimated real population of 3,700,000. The lowest point, at 13m above sea level, is the square in front of the Pantheon; the highest, at 120m, is Monte Mario. In between are not seven, but twenty hills of varying height.

Rome is the capital of two sovereign states, Italy and the Vatican, and one sovereign order, the Knights of Malta. It is among the most densely populated cities anywhere, but within its extensive boundaries it grows more agricultural products than any local government unit in Europe. Psychiatrists, and neurotics, are extremely rare, even though the most recent studies make Rome the noisiest city on the continent, averaging some 20 decibels louder than the EU standards say is good for your health. In the city of the popes, only 3 per cent of the population goes to mass – perhaps the lowest number in Christendom. Of the great capitals of Europe, it has the most rats and the fewest cockroaches. Rome's birthday is 21 April, and at the time of writing it is officially 2,754 years old.

government-mafia alliance collected the cream, while creating local regimes that were so boring and kafkaesque that no one could even think of trying to impose any serious reforms on them. For decades, useful initiatives were smothered in a damp caress of *democristiani* good intentions, bureaucratic obfuscation and avuncular incompetence, while funding vanished down the plug-hole of corruption.

Before 1993, city government had been largely managed by the state. Reforms in that year, part of the reaction to *tangentopoli*, brought a new leftwing city government under the first-ever elected mayor, Green Party candidate Francesco Rutelli. In his eight years in office, Rutelli worked to improve the quality of city life in many ways, albeit slowly and cautiously. Culture was a priority, with big projects like the reopening of the Galleria Borghese, the Museo Nazionale Romano and the Domus Aurea. Although the city failed in its bid for the 2004 Olympics, it did host a successful Jubilee Year in 2000, attracting over 23 million pilgrims and visitors. Having become the bright young hope of the Italian left, Rutelli led the Olive Tree coalition in the 2001 national elections; he lost to Silvio Berlusconi and Forza Italia, but now leads the centre-left coalition of opposition parties. Romans were happy enough with his administration to elect as his successor Walter Veltroni, a close political ally who had previously been the national Minister of Culture – and is now considered by many to be the man of the future in Italian politics.

Rome has some big plans. One old dream of the city's planners is to turn much of central Rome – the largely undeveloped area of ancient monuments from Piazza Venezia to the Via Appia Antica – into an urban park. The funds are there, the plans have been drawn up, but the delays and arguments have been continuing for years, with no end in sight. Meanwhile, land speculation has begun in suburbs, like Saxa Rubra, destined some day to become satellite towns of government offices.

In part, Rome's problems are a side effect of its queer destiny, a papal Gormenghast fated to become capital of a modern European state. The city that craves continual papal spankings, thrown into the First Division with London, Paris and Berlin, found itself constrained to become a cultural capital after 300 years of somnolence. Rome, already the capital of Italian *bella figura*, could handle the packaging, but never the content. Cultural life, as in the 18th century, is stimulated by the large communities of foreigners and visiting artists.

Meanwhile, a bit of old Rome still lives on in the centre: the sarcastic old codger behind the bar, the saucy market ladies and the weary gents in varnish-stained vests who

Rioni

On the older streets of Rome, you will see small travertine plaques with odd symbols: a pine cone, a griffin, a standing column. Pope Benedict IV had these put up, some time in the 1750s, to mark the boundaries of the *rioni*, the wards into which Rome has been divided since a decree of Augustus. After the fall of the Empire they survived as political bodies, and offered their people some degree of protection even in the worst of times. Today, with the toadstool growth of the city, there are many more *rioni*, but the ones you will see, bounded by Benedict's plaques, are the originals:

I Monti: its symbol, three stylized hills; includes all the western fringes, almost everything east of the Capitol.

II Trevi: three horizontal swords; Trevi Fountain, most of the Quirinale.

III Colonna: a column; everything between Piazza Colonna and Via Veneto.

IV Campo Marzio: a crescent moon; the upper Corso and Pincio.

V Ponte: a bridge; western tip of old Campus Martius, opposite Castel Sant'Angelo.

VI Parione: a griffin; Piazza Navona.

VII Regola (means 'fine sand', like Via Arenula): a stag; south of Campo de' Fiori.

restore gaudy Baroque furniture in tiny shops west of Campo de' Fiori. But most of the real Romans have been shunted off to the newer districts, like those around Via Trionfale and Via Appia Nuova. In a city that has increased in population twentyfold in the last century, authenticity is at a premium. 'I'm a real Roman of the Romans ...' someone tells you; later you find out what he means is that his grandfather came here from Sicily.

Rents are nothing like as high as in London or New York, but the old folks do feel under siege in the limited space of the quarter between the Corso and the Tiber, as speculation drives up land values relentlessly. Everyone wants to live around Piazza Navona, or in Trastevere; leading the invasion is a remarkable sort of Roman yuppie, perhaps an entirely new species of humanity. You'll see them in the cafés, nursing a scotch for two hours while they peek through their sunglasses to see if anyone is looking at them. A city with a cast of characters like this will continue to shake off the whims of its overbearing rulers as it has done already for millennia.

Art and Architecture

Perhaps a better title would be 'Art and Architecture in the Service of Rome'. There are three ways of decorating a city: doing it yourself, stealing other people's art outright, and taxing or tithing captive provinces to death and hiring away their artists with the proceeds. Rome, through almost all of its eternal story, has preferred the last two.

The Etruscans

Although Rome and Latium stood on the fringes of the Etruscan world, the young city could hardly help being overwhelmed by the presence of a superior culture almost on its doorstep. Along with much of its religion, customs, and its engineering talent, early Rome owed its first art to the enemies from the north. Not that there was ever much of it. For the first five centuries of the city's history, the high point undoubtedly came under the rule of the Etruscan kings: the Tarquins' monumental building programme, including the first **Temple of the Capitoline Jupiter**, in its time the biggest in Italy. Reconstructions show this lost building as a typical Etruscan work, deriving its form from the Greek temple but with a more ornate decoration on the frieze and pediment, and perhaps statues along the roofline. Other Etruscan temples, with projecting pediments steeper than the Greek, and an emphasis on the exposed ends of beams and rafters, must have seemed an odd cross between a classical temple and an oriental pagoda.

Thanks to the **Museo Etrusco Nazionale di Villa Giulia**, with finds from all over Etruria, and the wonderful tombs in nearby

Cervéteri, Rome can show you much of the best of Etruscan art. Enigmatic, often fantastical, and always intensely vital, Etruria's artistic magpies were able to steal from every style and technique that came out of Greece – from the Archaic, through the Classical and Hellenistic eclecticism – and turn it into something uniquely their own. In their remarkable portrait sculpture (usually in terracotta), they often excelled even the Greeks. For this, for their love of fresco painting, and for their distinctive 'grotesque' decoration, embodying the Etruscan fancy for the excessive and outlandish, every period of later Roman art is in their debt.

The Romans Learn Building and Can't Stop

The greatest builders of antiquity, no less – although even in late imperial times, when it was a question of aesthetics they would usually hire a Greek. In architecture, ancient Roman practicality found its greatest expression. They did not invent the arch, concrete, or the aqueduct; they learned how to build roads and bridges from the Etruscans. Nevertheless, they perfected all these serviceable things to build works never dreamed of before, combining beauty and utility for their most significant contribution to western culture. Speaking strictly of design, the outstanding fact of Roman building was its conservatism. Under the Republic, Rome adopted Greek architecture wholesale, with a predilection for the more delicate Corinthian order (and a weeding out of Etruscan styles). When the money started rolling in, the Romans began to build in marble; the 2nd century BC **Temple of Portunus**, still standing by the Tiber, was one of the first examples. But for 400 years, until the height of empire under Trajan and Hadrian, very little changed.

As Rome became the capital of the Mediterranean world, its rulers introduced new building types to embellish it: the series of imperial fora, variations on the Greek agora, the first of which was begun by Julius

The Etruscans

Cervéteri, Civitavecchia, Tarquinia and Tuscania, to see Etruscan necropolises, built for eternity, p.262

Museo Etrusco Nazionale di Villa Giulia, for the terracotta *Sarcofago degli Sposi* from Cervéteri (6th century BC), p.231

Museo Nazionale Tarquinia, for the Winged Horses, from the 'Altar of the Queen' temple, and other archaeological finds, p.264

Caesar; public baths, a custom imported from Campania; colonnaded streets, as in Syria and Asia Minor; and theatres. Unlike Greek theatres, these were enclosed (but not covered), with a semicircular orchestra and columned stage buildings. Theatre buildings were illegal in Republican Rome; Pompey and Caesar got around the law by adding temples, quadrangles and meeting halls, and claiming the whole as a religious sanctuary. Rome's own contribution was the basilica, a large rectangular hall supported on columns, impossibly noisy as a courtroom but still the perfect stage for Romans in their togas to act out their boisterous public life.

In a city of over a million and a half people, some advances in planning and design could be expected. The **Forum of Trajan** (AD 107–12, by Apollodorus of Damascus) makes the work of many modern planners look primitive. Besides providing noble buildings and open space in the crowded city centre, the Forum skilfully combines widely divergent land uses – temples, libraries, government, and a big market – to create the first and finest of large-scale civic centres.

Concrete may not seem a very romantic subject, but in the hands of imperial builders it changed both the theory and practice of architecture. Volcanic sand from the Bay of Naples, used with rubble as a filler, allowed the Romans to cover vast spaces cheaply. Roman concrete lasts almost for ever; it's better than anything in use now. First in the palaces (such as Nero's Golden House), and later in the **Pantheon**, with its giant concrete dome (AD 128), and in the huge public baths (those of Caracalla and Diocletian were the largest and most elaborate), an increasingly sophisticated use of arches and vaults made the old Greek architecture of columns and lintels obsolete. Concrete seating made the **Colosseum** and the vast theatres possible, and allowed *insulae* – Roman apartment blocks – to climb six storeys and more.

Near the Empire's end, the tendency towards gigantism becomes an enduring symptom of Roman decadence; the clumsy forms of late monsters like **Diocletian's Baths**

(298–306) and the **Basilica of Maxentius** (306–10) show a technology far outstripping art, while the nascent Christian Church was failing in its attempts to find an original architectural inspiration for its worship. When **Constantine**, the last of the big builders, financed Christian foundations around Rome, they all took the form of the basilica – an interesting comment on the early Roman church, that it would choose not a contemplative temple for its gatherings, but a form that to any Roman mind signified temporal authority.

Roman Sculpture, Painting and Mosaics

In the beginning, Romans couldn't have cared less for such stuff. Even after the conquests of the 2nd century BC followed by the methodical looting of the cultured East, it was a long time before Rome produced anything of its own. As in architecture, the other arts were dependent for centuries on the Greeks, either by importing artists or by copying classical works. Portrait sculpture, inherited from the Etruscans, is the notable exception, with a tradition of almost

Roman Sculpture, Painting and Mosaics

photographic, warts-and-all busts and funeral reliefs extending well into the imperial centuries. Augustus, who did so much else to decorate Rome, first exploited the possibilities of sculpture as a propaganda tool; the relief scenes of his reign on the **Ara Pacis** (13 BC) exemplify the clarity and classical restraint Romans preferred. Neither state policy nor private tastes encouraged experimentation. Rome's sculptors churned out endless copies of celebrated Greek works, even when the originals were on display in the emperors' gardens and temples.

As in architecture, sculptors began to consider new departures only in the confident, self-assured age of the Flavian and Antonine emperors. Some scholars have called the new style in reliefs 'impressionism', with a greater emphasis on effects of light and shadow, at times creating the illusion of depth, and more dynamic, 'unposed' compositions (as on the Arch of Titus or Trajan's Column). More than any other art, sculpture provides a compelling psychological record of Rome's history. In the 3rd century, as that confidence was undergoing its first crisis at the hands of German and Persian invaders, sculpture veers slowly but irreversibly towards the introverted and strange. Already under the late Antonines, the tendency is apparent, with the grim, realistic battle scenes on **Marcus Aurelius' column**, or the troubled portraits of that emperor himself.

Later portraits become even more unsettling, with rigid features and staring eyes, concerned more with psychological depth than outward appearances. Third-century reliefs can be either vigorous and queerly contorted, tending towards the abstract, or awkward and stiff, as in the large number of imperial propaganda reliefs on the **Arch of Constantine**, where emperors on campaign or distributing gifts appear in static arrangements of figures, hardly more than symbols, a trend that presages the hieratic Church art of Byzantium and medieval Italy.

In any case, during the 3rd and 4th centuries there was little public art at all. In its brief revival under Constantine, we see how far the process of decay had gone. No work better evokes the Rome of the totalitarian late empire than the weird, immense head of Constantine in the **Capitoline Museums**. Gigantism, as in architecture, survived the disappearance of individuality and genuinely civic art and the imperial portraits freeze into eerie icons.

Painting and mosaic work were never exposed to the same storm and stress as sculpture. Although both were present from at least the 1st century BC, Romans considered them little more than decoration, and only rarely entrusted to them any serious subjects. Both are a legacy from the Greeks, and both found their way to Rome by way of talented, half-Greek Campania to the south. Painting, in the days of Caesar and Augustus, usually meant wall frescoes in the homes of the wealthy, with large scenes of gardens, or architectural fantasies in the form of window views, making small Roman rooms look brighter and bigger. Mythological scenes were also popular (the careers of Hercules and Dionysus remained favourite subjects for centuries), and there are mentions of 'battle paintings', an early sort of propaganda brought home by victorious generals ready to go into politics; none of these survive. Like the Etruscans, although less ambitiously, Romans liked to paint the walls of their tombs; you can see some in the **Necropolis of St Peter's**.

No important advances ever occurred in Roman painting. Skill and grace gradually deteriorated over the centuries; few of the paintings in the Christian catacombs, for example, are anything more than primitive. Mosaics, another import, had their greatest centre at Antioch, in Hellenized Syria, and only became a significant medium at Rome in the 2nd century AD, as painting was declining. Rome is full of simple black and white floor mosaics, but occasionally a virtuoso would turn out a marvellous small scene (like the debris of a banquet in the Vatican's Museo Gregoriano Profano) for a wealthy patron; the *tesserae* used could be as small as 1/32 inch. Sparkling mosaics of tinted glass chips were also used in fountains and the bottoms of pools, although unfortunately none of this survives. If Rome, too, had been buried under volcanic lava, at whatever period, it is unlikely that much would be found to surpass the 2nd and 1st century BC art discovered at Pompeii.

Early Christian and Medieval Art

Almost from the beginning, Rome's Christians sought to express their faith in art. The cartoon scrawls in the catacombs are no indication of the sophistication they often reached. Dozens of finely carved *sarcophagi* and statues, dating from the third century on (many are in the Vatican Museums), represent the figure of Christ the 'Good Shepherd', a beardless youth with a lamb slung over his shoulder. Occasionally he wears a proper Roman toga. Familiar New Testament scenes are common, along with figures of early martyrs. Constantine's 4th-century building programme filled Rome with imposing Christian basilicas, although little of the original work remains. The **Lateran Baptistry**, begun in the 320s, is Christendom's oldest; its octagonal shape was copied in baptistries all over Italy for over a thousand years. Sculpture and architecture may have been in decline, but 4th-century mosaic artists were still able to create graceful syntheses of

antique art and Christian symbolism, as in **Santa Pudenziana** church, or the imperial mausoleum, now **Santa Costanza**.

Through the 5th and early 6th centuries, Christian art – the only art now permitted – changed little in style but broadened its subject matter, including scenes from the Old Testament, as in the **Santa Maria Maggiore** mosaics, and the Passion of Christ – the Crucifixion on the wooden doors of **Santa Sabina** may be the oldest one in existence. The new symbolism included the representation of Christ as the Lamb, as in **Santi Cosma e Damiano**, the animal symbols of the four Evangelists, and the four rivers, representing both the 'four rivers of Paradise' and the four Gospels. There was little money to continue after destructive wars but the elegant chancel of **San Lorenzo**, really the original church, begun in 579, shows how the Romans built even in the worst of times.

Another monument from the advent of the Dark Ages is the mosaics of **Sant'Agnese** (638). The profound, unearthly gaze of the beautiful St Agnes, and the rich gold background, introduce the Byzantine influence into Roman art. Ravenna, not Rome, was now the artistic centre of Italy, and through it came the formal, mystical art ('hieratic', the Italians call it) of Byzantium. Greek dominance increased in the next three centuries, with an influx of artists fleeing Antioch and Alexandria after the Arab conquests, and from Constantinople itself during the persecutions of the Iconoclast emperors.

An impressive revival of Roman building came in the late 8th century, with peace, relative prosperity, and the enlightened reigns of popes like Hadrian, Leo III and Paschal I. New churches went up – **Santa Maria in Cosmedin, Santa Prassede, Santa Maria in Domnica** – all decorated with mosaics by Greek artists. The return of hard times after the collapse of the Carolingian Empire put an end to this little Renaissance, and very little was done in Rome until the 1100s.

When Rome began building again, it was largely with native artists, and stylistically there was almost a clean break with the past. The **Cosmati**, perhaps originally a single family of artisans, but eventually a name for a whole school, ground up fragments of coloured glass and precious stone from Rome's ruins and turned them into intricate pavements, altars, paschal candlesticks, pulpits and other decoration, geometrically patterned in styles derived from southern Italy, and ultimately from the Moslem world. Some of the Cosmati school eventually became accomplished sculptors, architects and mosaicists, such as Pietro Vassalletto, who may have been involved in building the the cloisters at the Lateran (late 12th century) and **Iacopo Torriti** (mosaic of the *Coronation of the Virgin* at Santa Maria Maggiore; late 13th century). One of the Cosmati artists, Pietro Oderisi, made it to London, to design Henry III's tomb in Westminster Abbey.

Perhaps the greatest medieval Roman artist was **Pietro Cavallini** (*c.*1250–1330), whose new freedom in composition and brilliant talent for expressive portraiture make him a genuine precursor of the Renaissance, equally at home in mosaics (Santa Maria in Trastevere) and fresco (Santa Cecilia). Further

nudges towards the Renaissance came from outsiders, often Tuscans, such as the sculptor and architect **Arnolfo di Cambio**; although more famous for Florence's Cathedral and Palazzo della Signoria, he also left considerable work in Rome (in San Clemente, San Paolo, St Peter's). Giotto also visited Rome, but almost none of his work at St Peter's survives. Outside influences even went so far as to give Rome a Florentine Gothic church (Santa Maria sopra Minerva, 1280), the one exception to Rome's haughty, almost neurotic avoidance of what at the time was Europe's International Style.

Then came the so-called Babylonian Captivity, in 1305. With no popes to order the work, and no money from tithes or pilgrims to pay for it, Rome's promising career as a leader in Italian art came to an abrupt end.

The Renaissance in Rome

Rome had nothing to do with the beginnings of the Renaissance – its first century belonged to Tuscany and to Venice – but with yet another revival of the papacy the city was to have the last word. Almost every Tuscan Renaissance master is represented somewhere in Rome (minor works of Donatello at St Peter's and the Aracoeli, Ghirlandaio, Botticelli and Perugino in the Sistine Chapel, Masolino at San Clemente, Pinturicchio in the Vatican, Aracoeli and Santa Maria del Popolo, Melozzo da Forlì in the Vatican and Santa Croce, among others); they came as cultural missionaries to a city that had been a backwater since 1308. **Pius II**, the most artistic of the early Renaissance popes, preferred to expend most of his patronage on his native Tuscany. **Paul II** (1464–71) commissioned many works, including Rome's first proper Renaissance palace, the Palazzo Venezia. **Alexander VI** (1492–1503), an intelligent papal patron, ordered Pinturicchio frescoes in his Vatican apartments.

Rome's High Renaissance, though, begins with **Julius II** (1503–13). **Michelangelo Buonarroti** (1475–1564) had already arrived, to amaze the world of art with his *Pietà* in St Peter's (1499), but the true inauguration of Rome's greatest artistic period was the arrival of **Donato Bramante** (1444–1514), an architect who had already made a name in Milan. In Rome, where the example of the ancients impressed him deeply, he immediately left off the busy, somewhat eccentric style of his youth and began creating a refined classicism that seemed to exemplify the aspirations of the Renaissance more completely than anything that had gone before. This new marriage of the Renaissance and ancient Rome can best be seen at Bramante's **Tempietto** at San Pietro in Montorio (1503), or at his cloister for **Santa Maria della Pace** (1504). The round Tempietto, the first modern building to depend entirely on the proportions of the classical orders (the Doric, in this case), was the most sophisticated attempt at creating a perfect 'temple', fusing the highest conceptions of faith and art, an ideal taken from the architectural fantasies of early Renaissance paintings (for example, in Perugino's *Donation of the Keys* in the Sistine Chapel).

For painting and sculpture, the High Renaissance meant a greater emphasis on emotion, dynamic movement, and virtuosity. Following in Bramante's footsteps was **Raffaello Sanzio of Urbino** (1483–1520), who arrived from Florence in 1508. Learning the grand manner from antique sculpture and the ancient approach to decoration from the paintings in Nero's recently unearthed Golden House, he applied these lessons in the frescoes of the Vatican **Stanze** (begun 1509), one of the definitive achievements of the age. A versatile artist, Raphael excelled at portraiture, painted mythological frescoes (as in the Villa Farnesina), and was at times capable of almost visionary religious work (the *Liberation of St Peter* in the Vatican Stanze). He was the most influential painter of his time, with an easy virtuosity and sunny personality that patrons found irresistible. He would have been mortified to know that his weakness for sweet Madonnas, clouds, putti, and floating holy celebrities was

introducing a kitsch element that plagued European sensibilities for three centuries.

Michelangelo, unwashed and overworked as ever, spent much of his time sulking over the successes of these two men, who he claimed stole all their ideas from him. Pope Julius kept him busy enough, with the gargantuan project for his papal tomb that was to bother the artist for much of his life, finally scaled down to a small ensemble, including the famous *Moses*, at San Pietro in Vincoli. Michelangelo tried to flee his terrible patron in 1506, but Julius snatched him back and put him up on the ceiling of the **Sistine Chapel** two years later. The artist responded to the unusual commission (ceilings are not exactly the best place for great art, although this one started a fad that would last for centuries) with the most profound and imaginative synthesis of art and faith Renaissance Rome would know.

After Julius came the Medici pope, **Leo X**, open-handed to artists, though greatly overrated as a patron – thanks to Voltaire, who wrote of the 'Age of Leo X' as an unsurpassed golden age of culture. Michelangelo and Raphael kept at their work (until 1520, when the latter died and the former returned to Florence). Poetry and humanist scholarship were still fostered at the papal court, but through his reign and that of **Clement VII**, the other Medici, nothing in art appeared as revolutionary as the works done under Julius.

The End of the Renaissance

The Sack of Rome in 1527 brought a rude interruption to artistic endeavours of all kinds. Many of the most promising artists left Rome for ever, including **Rosso Fiorentino** and **Giulio Romano** (one of the rare native Romans, a man who had worked for years as assistant to Raphael). Recovery was swift, although the creative intensity of the years before 1527 was never recaptured. Among the artists who returned to Rome, there was of course Michelangelo, who began the *Last Judgement* in the Sistine Chapel in 1536. Its sombre tones, not to mention its subject matter, illustrate more clearly than any other work the change in mood that had come over Roman art.

In his later years, Michelangelo produced little sculpture or painting. **Pope Paul III**, one of the more serious patrons to occupy the papal throne, appointed him architect of St Peter's in 1547 – when he was 72. Other late works include the **Campidoglio** civic centre (1547) and **Santa Maria degli Angeli** (1563). His antagonist, taking up Bramante's old job, was **Antonio da Sangallo the Younger**, most accomplished of a family of Tuscan architects. A less flamboyant architect than Michelangelo, Sangallo continued the High Renaissance tradition, giving Rome some of its finest buildings (Farnese Palace, 1546).

Tuscan **Mannerism**, the often eccentric, avant-garde tendency that rebelled against the Olympian high art of the Renaissance, found a place in Rome for its less shocking exponents: painters such as **Francesco Salviati**, **Perin del Vaga** and **Baldassare Peruzzi of Siena** (1510–63), who besides his paintings contributed original architectural creations like the **Villa Farnesina** and **Palazzo Massimo alle Colonne** on Corso Vittorio Emanuele (1536). Two other distinctive architects of this period created fanciful buildings with a touch of Mannerist restlessness – at least in their secular commissions – **Giacomo da Vignola** (Villa Giulia, Villa Farnese at Caprarola) and **Pirro Ligorio** (Casino of Pius IV in the Vatican Gardens, 1558; Villa d'Este at Tivoli, 1550). Their works, some of the most delightful and challenging buildings of the Roman cinquecento, found no one to follow their example in the tough years that followed. The inspiration of the Renaissance was gradually becoming exhausted, just as political conditions were constraining artists to be very, very careful.

The Art of the Counter-Reformation

Decades of rampant Counter-Reformation and the advent of the Inquisition put a chill on the Italian imagination that would never really be dispelled. In 1563, the final documents of the **Council of Trent** decreed the new order for art; it was to be conformist and naturalistic, a propaganda tool entirely in the service of the new totalitarian Church, with a touch of Spanish discipline and emotionalism to remind everyone where the real power lay. Largely under the direction of the Jesuits, a costly building programme was undertaken, with large, extravagant churches to overawe the faithful and provide an opulent background for the pageantry and bombastic sermons of the new Catholicism: the **Gesù church** (1568), **Santa Maria in Vallicella** (1575), and **Sant'Andrea della Valle** (1591), all on Corso Vittorio Emanuele, remain the chief works of the transitional order which past centuries called the 'Jesuit Style'.

The leading architect of the age, **Giacomo della Porta** (Sant'Andrea, façade of the Gesù, Palazzo della Sapienza), earns a place as the last of the Renaissance tradition, with a coolly classical style immune to the artistic decay and political stresses of the time.

By the end of the 1500s, painting and sculpture were in a bad way, with technically proficient but terminally dull artists like the **Cavaliere d'Arpino** (frescoes in St Peter's dome) holding sway among Roman patrons. **Taddeo Zuccari** and brother Federico rank among the serious men who thought Mannerism would last for ever, and sought to steer it towards a stiff academicism.

Rome itself was ordained to become the urban symbol of the Church resurgent, the most modern, most beautiful city in the world. Under the papacy of **Sixtus V** (1585–90), **Domenico Fontana** and other architects commenced an epochal planning scheme, uniting the sprawling medieval city with a network of long, straight avenues sighted on obelisks in the major piazzas. Fontana's attempts at architecture, such as the drab **Lateran Palace** (1586), were less fortunate, but other architects were pointing the way towards the dawning Baroque. **Carlo Maderno**'s façade for **Santa Susanna** (1603) was one of the first symptoms, although the more conventional façade he designed for St Peter's 10 years later has been universally condemned ever since as one of the missed opportunities of Roman art.

Times were right for a change. The militant, intolerant atmosphere of the early Counter-Reformation could never last long among the worldly aristocrats of Rome, no matter how much mischief they were causing to the rest of Europe. Hedonism and artistic innovation resurfaced under a thin veneer of piety and propriety. Many of the first challenges came from painters: first **Annibale Carracci**, who reintroduced mythological subjects, taboo in the early Counter-Reformation terror, along with an intense, dynamic style that harks back to Michelangelo's Sistine ceiling (Palazzo Farnese gallery, begun 1597). His greatest follower, whose dramatic altarpieces and ceilings contributed much to the birth of the Baroque, was **Guercino** (Casino Ludovisi frescoes, 1621, and the sensuous *Venus* in the Accademia di San Luca).

Carracci's artistic rival, **Michelangelo Merisi da Caravaggio**, worked in Rome at roughly

The Art of the Counter-Reformation

Il Gesù, to see the pinnacle of the Jesuit style and St Ignatius' lapis lazuli tomb, p.98

The **Galleria Borghese**, **San Luigi dei Francesi** and **Santa Maria del Popolo**, for the startling *tenebroso* light and dark of Caravaggio's paintings, breaking the High Renaissance mould, p.86, p.102 and p.233

the same time (1590–1603) before leaving town over the little matter of a homicide. Rome's first bohemian might have been the last person to pick a fight with at the tavern, but he was all business at painting. Impeccable draftsmanship, combined with a revolutionary, *tenebroso* use of light and shadow and a new, naturalistic manner of portraying biblical subjects (San Luigi dei Francesi, Santa Maria del Popolo, Galleria Borghese), inspired others to find their own approach to breaking out of the High Renaissance straitjacket.

To Roman opinion, however, dry, academic painting of the expiring Renaissance was a pinnacle of artistic achievement. And to many later critics, especially in the 1700s, **Guido Reni** (in Rome about 1604–14) and **Domenichino** (1613–31) ranked with Raphael and Michelangelo as the greatest of all time; today the former's brilliantly coloured but often lifeless art and the latter's vapid classicism hardly ever get a second glance from visitors to Rome's museums.

The Age of Baroque

No one is sure where the word 'Baroque' originated. One possibility, according to Luigi Barzini in *The Italians*, is the irregular, over-sized pearls still called *perle barocche* in Italy. Barzini goes on to explain how 'the term came to be used metaphorically to describe anything pointlessly complicated, otiose, capricious and eccentric.' Such, anyway, is the reputation Baroque has acquired in our time. The opprobrium is entirely deserved. Italy was subjected to reactionary priests and despotic tyrants, and art was reduced to mere decoration, forbidden to entertain any thoughts that might be politically dangerous or subversive to Church dogma. But in this captive art there was still talent and will enough for new advances to be made, particularly in architecture.

Plenty of churches, fountains and palaces were going up in Rome, and there was every opportunity for experimentation. A second landmark, after Maderno's Santa Susanna, was the **Fountain of the Acqua Paola**, which was probably designed built by **Flaminio Ponzio** in 1610. However, the real break-through came in the 1630s, with three great masters who inaugurated the Roman High Baroque and determined the course of European architecture for the next century: first **Pietro da Cortona**, with his intricate, flowing façade and dome for **Santi Luca e Martina**; then **Francesco Borromini**, with his earliest, most memorable works, **San Carlo alle Quattro Fontane** (1646) and **Sant'Ivo** (1642), and finally **Gianlorenzo Bernini**, who began the famous colonnades in front of **St Peter's** in 1656, and the church of **Sant'Andrea al Quirinale** two years later.

These three men came to architecture from diverse backgrounds, exposing something of the range of talents and ambitions of the Baroque movement. Cortona, from the town of Cortona and steeped in the tradition of Florentine Mannerism, began as a painter and designer, already famed for his ceiling frescoes in the **Palazzo Barberini** (1633–9). Borromini, a profound architect and the son of an architect, came from Lombardy, and

brought to Rome the centuries-old tradition of Lombard building skills. The exotic geom-etry of his two great churches, mentioned above, was a medieval throwback, repudi-ating the classical Vitruvian architecture of the Renaissance. He used it to create sophis-ticated forms and spaces. Few architects were able to match this tortured soul's grasp of the art, or the sincere piety that informed it – Borromini himself, in his later career, created nothing as interesting as those first two churches – but everyone who followed did his best to conjure up even more striking and unusual combinations of shapes.

Among the first to catch the fever was Bernini. Neapolitan by birth, with experience as a playwright and stage designer, Bernini always thought of himself as a sculptor first, and in fact his best-known and most original works are decorations, occupying the vague ground between sculpture and architecture: the St Peter's colonnades, the essential state-ment of Baroque flourish and grandiosity, and the **Fountain of the Four Rivers** in Piazza Navona (1651). As architect of St Peter's from 1629 on, and the most popular artist in Rome for decades thereafter, Bernini had an oppor-tunity to transform the face of the city afforded to no other man before or since; his churches, palaces and fountains can be seen all over Rome. Other distinctive contributors to the High Baroque are **Martino Longhi** (Santi Vincenzo ed Anastasio, 1646) and **Carlo Rainaldi** (Santa Maria in Campitelli, 1663–7).

In sculpture, the Baroque meant a new emphasis on cascading drapery and exagger-ated poses – emotion, saintliness or virtue typecast in a way Renaissance artists would have found slightly trashy. Here Bernini led the way, with such works as his early *David* in the **Galleria Borghese** (1623), the florid papal tombs, equestrian statue of Constantine, and bronze baldaquin, all at St Peter's, and the incredible *Ecstasy of St Teresa* in **Santa Maria della Vittoria** (1652). His careful, eloquent portrait sculptures seem hardly to come from the same hand – for apparently the less this self-assured and somewhat arrogant artist was able to follow his fancy, the better.

The Age of Baroque

Galleria Borghese, for Bernini's virtuoso *figura serpentinata Daphne and Apollo*, p.233

San Carlo alle Quattro Fontane and **Sant'Ivo**, Borromini's early architectural masterpieces, p.177 and p.86

San Luca e Santa Martina, for Da Cortona's subtle Roman High Baroque, p.139

Sant'Andrea al Quirinale, for Bernini's Baroque pearl of a church, p.176

Santa Maria della Vittoria, to see Bernini's *Ecstasy of St Teresa*, p.180

Bernini proved a hard act to follow; the other Roman Baroque sculptors worthy of mention are sober Alessandro Algardi, and Francois Duquesnoy, from Brussels, whose modest works, scattered around Rome's museums, recall something of the freshness and lack of affectation of the early Renaissance.

Painting was on a definite downward spiral, although one usually had to look up to see it. Decorative ceiling frescoes, such as those of Pietro da Cortona, were all the rage, though few artists could bring anything like Cortona's talent to the job, **Andrea Sacchi**'s *Divina Sapienza* fresco (1633) in the Palazzo Barberini being a notable exception. After this, preciosity and tricky illusionism rapidly gained the upper hand, most flagrantly in G. B. Gaulli's ceiling for the Gesù church (1679) and the Jesuit Andrea Pozzo's *trompe l'oeil* spectacular in Sant'Ignazio (1694). Serious painting was breathing its last, but while you are in Rome's galleries keep a look out for the works of **Pier Francesco Mola** (1612–68) and two of the more endearing genre painters: the landscapes of **Salvator Rosa** (1615–73) and scenes of Roman life and ruins by **Michelangelo Cerquozzi** (1620–60).

The Last of Roman Art

From Rome, the art of the High Baroque reached out to all Europe – just as the last traces of inspiration were dying out in the city itself. The death of Pope **Alexander VII** (1667) is often mentioned as a turning point, after which there was less money, and less intelligent patronage. But as the Baroque trudged slowly off to its grave, bad paintings and sculptures were cranked out by the hundreds. Ironically, at the time when Rome's artistic powers were reaching their lowest ebb, the popes chose to restore dozens of churches in the degraded tastes of the age, destroying much of Rome's early Christian and medieval artistic patrimony.

At the tail end of the Baroque, Rome's most popular architect was **Carlo Fontana** (San Marcello in Corso, 1683, plenty of undistinguished palaces, and unrealized plans for

> ## The Last of Roman Art
> **Palazzo Montecitorio**, for Giulio Aristide Sartorio's frescoes on the walls of the parliament chamber, p.110
> **Piazza Sant'Ignazio**, for the interesting stage-set ensemble of this square, p.111
> **Spanish Steps**, for the rippling Rococo theatrics of the famous stairway, p.105
> **Trevi Fountain**, for one of the most lovable creations of the cynical, relaxed Rome of the papal twilight, p.113

extending Piazza San Pietro, even worse than the one finally built by Mussolini). After him, though, Roman architecture bounced back for a brief flurry of surprisingly creative work, beginning with Francesco de Sanctis' **Spanish Steps** of 1725, and Filippo Raguzzini's lovely, arch-Rococo San Gallicano hospital in Trastevere (1724). Raguzzini also designed the intimate, stage-set ensemble in **Piazza Sant'Ignazio** (1728). Another accomplished architect to embellish Rome in the 18th century was Ferdinando Fuga, who designed the Palazzo della Consultà (1739) and rebuilt Santa Maria Maggiore (1743). Some things had not changed; all these works continued the Baroque love of the grand gesture – and a hint of stage decoration, nowhere more so than in Nicola Salvi's endearing and utterly Roman **Trevi Fountain** of 1762.

By this time, a more introspective Rome was looking backwards. Meaningful sculpture and painting were gone for ever, and antiquarianism became a major concern of the few remaining Roman artists, most notably in the endless engravings of G. B. Piranesi (1720–78) and in the sketches, drawings, measurements and monologues of the hordes of Grand Tourists from the north. Another symbol of the age was the founding of the Vatican Museums in 1769. By the century's end, what passed for artistic life in Rome was entirely in the hands of foreigners, such as the German Johann Winckelmann, who became the pope's Superintendent of Antiquities in 1763, Swiss painter Angelica Kauffmann, French sculptor Jean-Antoine Houdon and Icelandic sculptor Thorvaldsen.

In the train of Napoleon came two Gallicized Italians, the architect **Valadier**, who gave **Piazza del Popolo** its present form, and the neo-classical sculptor **Antonio Canova**.

In the 19th century art in Rome continued to lose ground. The fathers of the new Italy, after 1870, knew in their hearts that liberation and Italian unity would unleash a wave of long-suppressed creativity, and they spent tremendous sums to help it along. They were mistaken. The sepulchral, artless monuments and ministries they imposed on Rome helped ruin the fabric of the city, while providing an enduring reminder of the sterility of the **Risorgimento** and the corrupt regimes that followed it. The modest revivals of Italian painting – the **Italian Impressionists**, the Tuscan **Macchiaioli** and the 20th-century **Futurists** – can all be seen in Rome's Galleria d'Arte Moderna, but few of the artists involved in these movements had anything to do with Rome itself. One exception to this dismal picture is the Roman artist **Giulio Aristide Sartorio** (1860–1932), influenced equally by Michelangelo and contemporary poster art; his masterpiece is the series of frescoes in the parliament chamber at Palazzo Montecitorio. Another exception is the delightful, eccentric neighbourhood of Art Nouveau fantasy houses and flats around Via Dora, just off Piazza Buenos Aires, or in the Garbatella district.

Mussolini too wanted his revolution to have its artistic expression. The sort of painting and sculpture his government preferred is best not examined too closely, but his architecture, mashing up Art Deco simplicity with a historical pomposity fit for a Duce, now and then reached beyond the level of the ridiculous (the municipal buildings on Via Petroselli). Rome today is relatively moribund as an art centre, and even architecture has not recovered from the post-Risorgimento, post-Mussolini hangover. There are no first-rate contemporary buildings in Rome. Not few – none. Efforts at planning the city's postwar growth, with satellite towns and housing schemes, resulted in confusion and concrete madness, and the hideous apartment and office blocks of the suburbs (a particularly vile nest of them can be seen along the road to the airport, around Via Magliana). Until recently it seemed impossible that Rome could ever again produce inspired architecture. However, controversial as it is, Paolo Portoghesi's mosque, a playful postmodern extravaganza out near the Villa Ada, could be a sign that the tide is turning.

Travel

GETTING THERE

By Air

There are plenty of flights to Rome. Prices vary, depending on when you travel, how far in advance you book and the availability of special fares. If you can be flexible there are good deals. Rome has two international airports, Leonardo da Vinci, commonly known as Fiumicino, and Ciampino, a military airport used by the low-cost airlines and charters.

From the UK

As well as direct scheduled flights on airlines such as BA or Alitalia, you may be able to pick up cheap tickets on Ethiopian Airlines, which flies north-south via Rome, or on a low-cost airline. Scheduled flights range from just over £100 return economy fare to £600 business class, with many flights in the £120–140 range. Low-cost deals may start as low as £10, but you can end up paying £50–100 one way too.

Scheduled Flights

Rome is served by several scheduled airlines from the UK – there are around 25 flights daily from London Heathrow, five a day from London Gatwick, and one flight daily from Birmingham and Manchester. APEX fares can be good value: they have to be booked seven days ahead, include a Saturday night, and cannot be changed or refunded.

Alitalia: t *0870 544 8259,*
w *www.alitalia.co.uk.* Five flights daily to London Heathrow, one a day to Gatwick.

British Airways: t *0845 773 3377,*
w *www.british-airways.com.* Five flights daily to London Heathrow, four daily to Gatwick, one daily to Manchester and Birmingham.

British Midland: t *(01332) 854 000,*
w *www.flybmi.com.* Four flights daily to London Heathrow.

Ethiopian Air Lines: t *(020) 8987 7000.* Flies several times a week to London Heathrow.

Lufthansa: t *0845 7737 747,*
w *www.lufthansa.com.* Four daily flights to London Heathrow.

Flights on the Internet

These days the best place to start researching your flight may be the internet. Some of the following websites are a good starting point.

In the UK and Ireland

w *www.airtickets.com*
w *www.cheapflights.co.uk*
w *www.flightcentre.co.uk*
w *www.lastminute.co.uk*
w *www.skydeals.co.uk*
w *www.sky-tours.co.uk*
w *www.thomascook.co.uk*
w *www.trailfinder.com*
w *www.traveleshop.com*
w *www.travelocity.com*
w *www.travelselect.com*

In the USA and Canada

w *www.air-fare.com*
w *www.expedia.com*
w *www.flights.com*
w *www.orbitz.com*
w *www.priceline.com*
w *www.travellersweb.ws*
w *www.travelocity.com*
w *www.xfares.com (carry-on luggage)*
w *www.smarterliving.com*

Low-cost Airlines

The cheap no-frills low-cost carriers offer good prices either if you book well ahead, or if you look out for last-minute special offers. Prices quoted are one-way and tend to go up closer to departure date, as allocations of cheap seats sell out. You can book directly over the internet for a discount.

Go: t *0870 607 6543,* **w** *www.go-fly.com.* Go is currently the only low-cost airline that flies direct to Rome from the UK. It flies from London Stansted four times a day and from Bristol once a day to Rome Ciampino.

Student Travel

Several agencies offer special flights and deals for students. You may have to show a student ID card to get the discounts.

CTS Travel: t *(020) 7290 0630,*
w *www.ctstravel.co.uk, and branches on UK university campuses.*

Europe Student Travel: *t (020) 7727 764.*
NYS Travel: *t (01904) 433 233.*
STA Travel: *t (020) 7361 6145, w www.sta-travel.com, and branches at UK universities.*
Travel CUTS: *t (020) 7255 1944, w www.travelcuts.co.uk.*
USIT Campus: *t 0870 240 1010, w www.usitcampus.co.uk, and UK campus branches.*

From the Republic of Ireland

Fewer direct flights are available from the Republic of Ireland. Alitalia and Aer Lingus offer scheduled services from Dublin. Prices range from €150–600. The cheapest option may be to fly via the UK.

Scheduled Flights

Aer Lingus: *t (01) 886 8888, w www.aerlingus.ie.* One flight daily.
Alitalia: *t (01) 677 5171, w www.alitalia.co.uk.* One flight most days.

Student Travel

Budget Travel: *t (01) 661 1866.*
United Travel: *t (01) 288 4346/7.*
USIT Now: *t (01) 679 8833, w www.usitnow.ie, and branches across Ireland.*

From the USA and Canada

Several carriers serve Rome from North American cities, but it may be worth catching a cheap flight to London (fares can be very competitive), Frankfurt, Paris or Amsterdam and flying on. Prices are higher from Canada. Fares ranges from $400 to $700.

Scheduled Flights

Air Canada: *(Canada) t 888 247 2262, w www.aircanada.ca.* Direct from Toronto.
Alitalia: *(USA) t 800 223 5730, w www.alitaliausa.com; (Canada) t 800 361 8336, w www.alitalia.ca.* Direct flights from New York, Detroit and Toronto.
American Airlines: *(USA) t 800 433 7300, w www.aa.com.* Flights to Milan and London.
British Airways: *(USA) t 800 AIRWAYS, TTY 877 993 9997; (Canada) t 800 403 0882, w www.britishairways.com.* Flights via London from many US and Canadian cities.
Continental: *(USA) t 800 231 0856; (Canada) 800 525 0280, w www.flycontinental.com.* Direct flights from New York.

Delta: *(USA) t 800 241 4141, w www.delta.com.* Flies direct from Atlanta and New York.
Northwest Airlines: *(USA) t 800 225 2525, w www.nwa.com.* Direct flights from New York and Detroit.
United Airlines: *(USA) t 800 241 6522, w www.ual.com; (Canada) t 800 241 6522, w www.united.ca.* From many US cities via Dusseldorf, Munich and other destinations.
US Airways: *(USA and Canada) t 800 6222 1015, w www.usairways.com.* Flies direct from Philadelphia.

Cheap Flights

For discounted flights, try the small ads in newspaper travel pages (e.g. *New York Times, Chicago Tribune, Toronto Globe & Mail*). Travel clubs and agencies also specialize in discount fares, but may require a membership fee.

Travel Clubs

USA

Air Brokers International: *t 800 883 3273, t 415 397 1383, w www.airbrokers.com.*
Air Courier Association: *t 800 282 1202, w www.aircourier.org.* Members club.
Airhitch: *t 212 864 2000, w www.airhitch.org.* Last-minute tickets from around $170.
Flight Center: *t 877 967 5347, w www.flight-center.com.* Centres in southern California.
Last Minute Travel Club: *t 800 527 8646, w www.lastminuteclub.com.*
New Frontiers USA: *t 800 677 0720, w www.newfrontiers.com.*
Now Voyager: *t 212 431 1616, w www.nowvoyagertravel.com.*
Travel Avenue USA: *t 800 333 3335, w www.travelavenue.com.*
Travel Discounts: *t 831 626 1212, w www.traveldiscounts.com.* Members club.
Travelers Advantage: *w www.travelersadvantage.com.* Members only.

Canada

Flight Centre: *t 888 967 5331, w www.flight-centre.ca.* Centres around the country.
Last Minute Travel Club: *t 877 970 3500, w www.lastminuteclub.com.* Standby deals.
New Frontiers: *t 514 871 3060, w www.newfrontiers.com*

Airline Offices in Rome

Aer Lingus: *t 06 481 8518.*
Air Canada: *t 06 655 7117.*
Air New Zealand: *t 06 4201 1166, t 06 4201.1200, (freephone) t 800 876 126.*
Alitalia: *t 06 65641/2/3, t 848 865 641.*
American Airlines: *(Milan) t 02 679 141.*
British Airways: *t 848 812 266.*
British Midland: *t 06 6568 4004.*
Continental Airlines: *t 06 6605 3030, (freephone) t 800 296 230.*
Delta: *(freephone) t 800 864 114.*
Ethiopian Airlines: *t 06 4201 1199.*
Go, *t 848 887 766.*
Lufthansa: *t 06 6568 4004.*
Meridiana: *t 06 478 041.*
Northwest Airlines: *(Milan) t 02 218 981.*
Qantas: *t 06 5248 2725.*
US Airways: *t 848 813 177.*

Student Travel Agencies

Council Travel: *(USA) t 212 822 2700, w www. counciltravel.com.* Specialist in student and charter flights; branches across the USA.

CTS Travel: *(USA) t 212 760 1287, e info@ctstravelusa.com.*

Educational Travel Centre: *(USA) t 608 256 5551, t 800 747 5551, e edtrav.com.*

STA Travel: *(USA) t 800 781 4040, w www. statravel.com.* Branches at most universities.

Travel Cuts: *(Canada) t 416 979 2406, w www.travelcuts.com.* Canada's largest student travel specialists, with branches in most provinces.

By Train

You can still travel by train and ferry from London to Rome; it takes the best part of 20 hours and costs around £176 second-class return (including the couchette). Or you can take a Eurostar to Paris and a high-speed train to Italy, which cuts the journey time to 15½ hours, but costs around £225.

In an age of low-cost airlines rail travel is not much of an economy unless you are able to take advantage of student, youth, families and young children and senior citizen discounts. Interail (UK) or Eurail (USA/Canada) passes give unlimited travel for all ages in Europe for one or two months. A month's full Interail pass covering France, Switzerland and Italy costs £275, or £199 for the under-26s; for France and Italy only it costs £239, or £169 for the under-26s.

The Eurail pass can be bought in the USA, for 15, 21, 30, 60 or 90 days. It saves the hassle of buying numerous tickets, but will only pay for itself if you use it every day, everywhere. It's not valid in the UK or outside the EU. Two weeks' travel is $388 for under-26s; those over 26 can get a 15-day pass for $554, a 21-day pass for $718, or a month for $890.

Rail Europe: *(UK) t 0870 5848 848, w www.raileurope.co.uk; (USA) t 800 438 7245, w www.raileurope.com.* For tickets on Eurostar and Interail/Eurail passes.

Eurostar: *(UK) t 0870 160 6600; (USA) t 800 EUROSTAR, (Canada) t 800 361 7245, w www.eurostar.com.* For reservations on Eurostar from London to Paris.

By Coach

One major company, Eurolines, offers departures daily in summer (three times a week out of season) from London to Rome; the journey takes 33½ hours. Single fares are about £75; return fares around £115. Peak-season fares from 22 July to 4 September are slightly higher. There are discounts for anyone under 26, senior citizens and children under 12. In summer, the coach can be the best bargain for anyone over 26; off-season you'll probably find a cheaper flight.

Eurolines: *t (020) 7730 8235, w www.gobycoach.com.* Times and tickets.

By Car

Italy is the best part of 24 hours' driving time from the UK, a good three days to Rome, even if you stick to fast toll roads.

Eurotunnel trains: *t 0870 535 3535.* Shuttles cars and their passengers through the Channel Tunnel from Folkestone to Calais on a simple drive-on-drive-off system (journey time 35mins). Payment is made at toll booths (which accept cash, cheques or credit cards). You can reserve in advance, or just turn up and take the next available service. In peak summer it is worth booking. Eurotunnel runs 24 hours a day, all year round, with a service at least once an hour through the night. Return fares range from £177 to £369, but special offers can bring them as low as £99.

If you prefer to take your car over by sea there are several options. Prices range from £58 return for a foot passenger to £418 return for a vehicle with two passengers, but cheaper APEX fares are available if you book in advance.

Brittany Ferries: *t 0870 5360360, w www.brittany-ferries.co.uk.* Sail from Poole to Cherbourg and St-Malo, Portsmouth to Caen and St-Malo, and Plymouth to Roscoff.

P&O: *t 0870 242 4999, w www. poportsmouth.co.* Sail from Dover to Calais and to Le Havre and Cherbourg.

P&O Stena: *t 0870 600 0600, w www.posl. com.* Sail from Dover to Calais, Southampton to Cherbourg and Newhaven to Dieppe.

Hoverspeed Fast Ferries: *t 0870 524 0241, w www.hoverspeed.com.* A new Super Seacat that goes from Newhaven to Dieppe in 2hrs.

The most scenic and hassle-free route into Italy is via the Alps but if you take a route through Switzerland expect to pay for the privilege (around €15.50 or 40 Swiss Francs for motorway use).

In winter the passes may be closed and you will have to stick to those expensive tunnels, if they are open after a series of fires (one-way tolls range from about 40–70 Swiss Francs or €15–30 for a small car).

You can avoid some driving by putting your car on the train. There are Motorail links from Denderleeuw in Belgium to Rome.

Rail Choice: *t (020) 7939 9915, w www. railchoice.co.uk.* Information and reservations on Motorail.

Italian Auto Club (ACI): *t 06 4477.* Once you have made it over or under the Alps or disembarked from your train, ACI offers reasonably priced breakdown assistance.

To bring a UK-registered car into Italy, you need a vehicle registration document, full driving licence and insurance papers (these must be carried at all times when driving). If your driving licence is an old-fashioned one without a photograph you are also strongly recommended to apply for an international driving permit (available from the AA or RAC). Non-EU citizens should have an international driving licence, preferably with an Italian translation incorporated. Your vehicle should display a nationality plate indicating its country of registration. Red triangular hazard signs and headlight converters are obligatory; also recommended are a spare set of bulbs, a first-aid kit and a fire extinguisher. Spare parts for non-Italian cars can be difficult to find, especially Japanese models. Before crossing the border, fill up; *benzina* is very expensive in Italy.

AA: *t 0990 500 600, t 0800 444 500, w www.theaa.com.* '5-star' breakdown cover.

RAC: *t 0800 550 550, w www.rac.co.uk.* A similar service to the AA.

AAA: *(USA) t 407 444 4000, t 800 222 5000, w www.aaa.com.* The American Automobile Association.

However, a car will be more of a liability than anything else in Rome. It is quite difficult to find your way around if you don't know the roads, and once you get close to the centre parking is a nightmare. Although Romans still park brazenly pretty much anywhere, restrictions are enforced in unexpected sweeps, with cars being towed away. Watch for people rushing to their cars.

SPECIALIST TOUR OPERATORS

Countless specialist tour operators offer package deals, city breaks, cultural tours, art and architecture tours, archaeological tours, painting holidays, cookery courses and so on. A selection are listed below. Not all are necesssarily ABTA-bonded.

In the UK and Ireland

Abercrombie & Kent, *Sloane Square House, Holbein Place, London SW1W 8NS*, t *(020) 7559 8500*, f *(020) 7730 9376*, e *info@abercrombie kent.co.uk*, w *www.abercrombiekent.co.uk*. City breaks and a range of other holidays.

Ace Study Tours, *Babraham, Cambridge CB2 4AP*, t *(01223) 835 055*, f *(01223) 837 394*, w *www.study-tours.org*. Cultural tours.

Alternative Travel, *69–71 Banbury Road, Oxford OX2 6PE*, t *(01865) 31578*, f *(01865) 315 697*, e *info@atg-oxford.co.uk*. Walking, garden and cycling tours.

American Express Europe, *Destination Services, 19–20 Berners St, London W1P 4AE*, t *(020) 7637 8600*, f *(020) 7631 4803*. City breaks and fly-drive.

British Airways Holidays, *Astral Towers, Betts Way, Crawley, West Sussex RH10 2XA*, t *0870 24 24 243*, t *(01293) 723 100*, f *(01293) 722 702*, w *www.britishairways.com/holidays*.

Brompton Travel, *Brompton House, 64 Richmond Road, Kingston-upon-Thames, Surrey KT2 5EH*, t *(020) 8549 3334*, f *(020) 8547 1236*, w *www.BromptonTravel.co.uk*. Tailor-made and opera tours.

Citalia, *Marco Polo House, 3–5 Lansdowne Road, Croydon CR9 1LL*, t *(020) 8686 0677*, t *(020) 8681 0712*, e *ciao@citalia.co.uk*. Italian city breaks.

Cox & Kings, *4th Floor, Gorden House, 10 Greencoat Place, London SW1P 1PH*, t *(020) 7873 5027*, f *(020) 7630 6038*, w *www. coxandkings.co.uk*. Short breaks, gourmet and escorted cultural tours with guest lecturers in Rome.

Euro Academy, *77/a George Street, Croydon CRO 1LD*, t *(020) 8686 2362*, f *(020) 8681 8850*, w *www.euroacademy.co.uk*. Art, cookery and language courses.

Italiatour, *9 Whyteleafe Business Village, Whyteleafe Hill, Whyteleafe, Surrey CR3 0AT*, t *(01883) 621 900*, f *(01883) 625 255*, e *italia tour@dial.pipex.com*, w *www.italiatour.co.uk*. City breaks, *agriturismo* and opera.

JMB, *Rushwick, Worcester WR2 5SN*, t *(01905) 425 628*, f *(01905) 420 219*, w *www.jmb-travel.co.uk*. Opera holidays.

Kirker, *3 New Concordia Wharf, Mill Street, London SE1 2BB*, t *(020) 7231 3333*, f *(020) 7231 4771*, e *cities@kirker.itsnet.co.uk*. City breaks.

Magic of Italy, *227 Shepherd's Bush Rd, London W6 7AS*, t *(020) 8748 7575*, f *(020) 8748 3731*, w *www.magictravelgroup.co.uk*. City breaks.

Martin Randall Travel, *10 Barley Mow Passage, Chiswick, London W4 4PH*, t *(020) 8742 3355*, f *(020) 8742 7766*, e *info@martin randall.co.uk*, w *www.martinrandall.com*. Cultural tours with guest lecturers.

Page & Moy, *135–140 London Road, Leicester LE2 1EN*, t *(0116) 250 7000*, t *0870 010 6212*, f *(0116) 250 7123*, w *www.page-moy.co.uk*. City breaks and escorted tours.

In the USA and Canada

Abercrombie & Kent, *1520 Kensington Rd, Oak Brook, IL 60523 2141*, t *(630) 954 2944*, t *(800) 323 7308*, w *www.abercrombiekent. com*. City breaks.

Archaeological Tours Inc., *Suite 904, 271 Madison Avenue, New York, NY 10016*, t *(212) 986 3054*. Expertly led archaeological tours for small groups focusing on ancient Rome.

CIT Tours, *15 West 44th St, New York, NY 10173*, t *(800) CIT-TOUR*, w *www.cit-tours.com*; *(Canada) 80 Tiverton Ct, Suite 401, Markham, Ontario L3R 0GA*, t *(800) 387 0711*. City breaks.

Esplanade Tours, *581 Boylston St, Boston, MA 02116*, t *(617) 266 7465*, t *(800) 426 5492*, w *www.specialtytravel.com*. Art and architecture itineraries.

Italiatour, *666 5th Ave, New York, NY 10103*, t *(USA) (800) 845 3365*, w *www.italiatour. com*; t *(Canada) (888) 515 5245*. Sightseeing tours organized by Alitalia.

Maupintour, *1421 Research Pk Drive, Kansas 66049*, t *(785) 331 1000*, t *(800) 255 4266*.

Trafalgar Tours, *11 East 26th Street, New York, NY 10010*, t *(212) 689 8977*.

Travel Concepts, *307 Princeton, MA 01541*, t *(978) 464 0411*. Wine and food.

Worldwide Classroom, *P.O. Box 1166, Milwaukee, WI 53201*, t *(414) 351 6311*, t *(800) 276 8712*, w *www.worldwide.edu*. Database listing worldwide educational organizations.

ENTRY FORMALITIES

Passports and Visas

EU nationals with a valid passport can enter and stay in Italy as long as they like. Citizens of the USA, Canada, Australia and New Zealand need only a valid passport to stay up to 90 days. If you need a visa for a longer period, apply to an Italian consulate.

By law you should register with the police within eight days of your arrival in Italy. In practice this is done automatically for visitors when they check in at their first hotel. If you plan to stay longer than three months you will need a *permesso di soggiorno*, which can be obtained from the Ufficio Stranieri at the Questura Centrale on Via Genova (*see* 'Practical A–Z', p.76).

Customs

Since July 1999, duty-free goods have been unavailable on journeys within the European Union but this does not necessarily mean that prices have gone up, as shops at airports do not always choose to pass on the cost of the duty. It does mean that there is no limit on how much you can buy, as long as it is for your own use. Guidelines are issued and, if they are exceeded, you may be asked to prove that you are going to consume it all. The current suggested limits are: spirits, 10 litres; cigarettes, 800; smoking tobacco, 1 kg; wine, 90 litres (of which only 60 can be sparkling wine), fortified wine (e.g. sherry), 20 litres.

Dogana Sezione Viaggiatori: *Aeroporto Leonardo Da Vinci (Fiumicino), 00054, t 06 6995 4343.* For information while in Rome contact the customs office at the airport.

Non-EU citizens visiting the EU can buy duty free on their way home, but face restrictions on how much they can take back. If they have been away for more than 48 hours, Americans over the age of 21 can take 1 litre of alcohol, 200 cigarettes and 100 cigars home with them. They can take $400 worth of goods duty-free, and pay 10% tax on the next $1,000 worth of goods. After that, the tax is worked out on an item by item basis.

US Customs: *PO Box 7407, Washington, DC 20044, t (202) 927 6724, w www.customs. ustreas.gov.* For more detailed information, look at the website or call the office and request the free booklet *Know Before You Go*.

Canadians can bring back 200 cigarettes, 50 cigars, 200 tobacco sticks, 220 grams of manufactured tobacco, 1.5 litres of wine or 1.14 litres of spirits or 8.5 litres of beer. They have a $750 duty-free limit if they have been away for more than 7 days ($200 for trips between 2 and 6 days long).

Revenue Canada: *2265 St. Laurent Blvd., Ottawa K1G 4KE, t 800 461 9999, t (613) 993 0534, w www.ccra-adrc.gc.ca.* Canadian customs also provides a free booklet, *I declare,* with further information.

ARRIVAL

Arriving by Air

Fiumicino: *t 06 65951.* The main airport, Leonardo da Vinci, is usually referred to as Fiumicino. It has ATMs, bureaux de change, a post office, pharmacy, lost and found, baggage deposit, nursery, shops and cafés.

Ciampino: *t 06 794 941.* The secondary airport (principally a military air field) and base for a few passenger flights. It has all the main facilities too, open to coincide with the infrequent flight arrivals.

Aeroporti di Roma: *w www.adr.it.* Runs both airports. The website has timetables, airline and flight details, information on how to get to and from the airports, and links to tourist office and hotel reservation websites.

From the Airports to Rome

Taking a **taxi** from Fiumicino into Rome costs about €40, plus a €1 supplement for each piece of luggage and a €3 supplement at nights, on Sundays and holidays. There are two **rail links** from the airport to the city: to Stazioni Trastevere, Ostiense, Tuscolana and

Tiburtina (every 20mins; €5) and a direct service to Stazione Termini, Rome's main rail station (every 30mins; €10). Between 1.15 and 5am, COTRAL **buses** run from outside the arrivals hall to Stazioni Tiburtina and Termini. The train takes 30mins from Fiumicino to Tiburtina or Termini; the bus at least 50mins.

A COTRAL **bus** runs from Ciampino to the Anagnina stop at the southern end of the Metro A line, then it's about 20 minutes to Stazione Termini, or you can continue to Piazza di Spagna (daily 6.50am–11.40pm; €1).

Arriving by Train

Almost all trains arrive and depart from Termini Station, chaotic, but modern and efficiently run. The rail information booth is usually crowded, but you can try to find times and destinations (within Italy) on one of the clever multilingual computer screens installed in the lobby.

Keep an eye out for pickpockets. There is a taxi stand right in front, car-hire booths, buses to most points in Rome from Piazza dei Cinquecento in front of the station, and two underground stations in its belly. The left luggage (€3 per item for 12 hours) is along the first track, on the far left of the station. There are two international telephone offices, one in the lobby and one downstairs, a post office, several bars (the bar downstairs is less nerve-racking), a pharmacy, bureaux de change, internet points and a bookshop with English-language books.

Rome's other stations are Tiburtina, on the east of town, Ostiense, on the south side, and Trastevere to the west.

Rail information: t 06 848 88088.

GETTING AROUND

Looking at the map, Rome seems to be made for getting around on foot. This may be true in the *centro storico*, but elsewhere it is deceptive: city blocks in the newer areas are huge, and it will always take you longer than you think to walk anywhere. The hills, the outsize scale and the traffic also make Rome a tiring place, although there is pleasant strolling to be had in the old districts either side of the Corso, around the Tiber Island, in old Trastevere and around the Caelian Hill. At some point you will need to use other forms of transport – especially bus and tram.

Public transport information: t 06 800 431 784, w www.atac.roma.it.

By Metro

Rome's underground system is not convenient, as it seems to avoid the historic parts of the city; imagine trying to dig any sort of hole in Rome, with legions of archaeologists ready to pounce. The two lines, A and B, cross at Stazione Termini and will take you to the Colosseum, around the Aventine Hill, to Piazza di Spagna, San Giovanni in Laterano, San Paolo fuori le Mura, Piazza del Popolo or within eight blocks of St Peter's. Single tickets (€1) are also good for city buses – valid for 75mins from obliteration in the turnstile – and available from machines in metro stations and tobacconists, bars and kiosks.

By Bus and Tram

Buses and trams are by far the best way to get around. Pick up a map of the bus routes from the ATAC (city bus company) booth outside Stazione Termini. Bus tickets (€1) are good for travel on any ATAC city bus or tram and one metro ride within 75mins of the first use of the ticket, which must be stamped in the machines in the back entrance of buses or trams. Spot-checks are made and there is a €52 fine for travelling without a ticket. Tickets can be bought at any terminus, at news-stands, tobacconists and bars.

There are also special-price full-day tickets called BIG (which include the metro too), for €3, as well as weekly passes (CIS, €12.50) and monthly passes, available from tobacconists. Most routes run frequently, and are often crowded. There are also reliable night bus services to many areas.

Some Useful Bus Routes

19 (tram) Piazza Risorgimento (near the Vatican)–Viale delle Milizie–Villa Borghese–Viale Regina Margherita–Porta Maggiore–San Lorenzo and Via Prenestina.

23 Musei Vaticani–Castel Sant'Angelo–Tiber banks–Porta San Paolo–S. Paolo.

3 (tram) Villa Borghese–Viale Regina Margherita–San Lorenzo–S. Giovanni in Laterano– Colosseum–Viale Aventino–Viale Trastevere (a fun trip, taking in many sights; *see* 'Walks', p.252).

36 Termini–Via Nomentana (Sant'Agnese).

46 Piazza Venezia–Corso Vittorio Emanuele–Vatican.

63 Largo Argentina–Via del Corso–Via del Tritone–Via Vittorio Veneto.

64 Termini–Via Nazionale–Corso Vittorio Emanuele–Vatican (the main bus route from the centro storico to the Vatican).

116T Piazza della Repubblica–Via Nazionale–Via del Tritone–Via del Corso–Piazza Venezia–Largo Argentina–Mausoleo di Augusto (8pm–1.30am).

116 Via Veneto–Piazza Barberini–Via del Tritone–Piazza del Parlamento–Corso Rinascimento–Corso Vittorio Emanuele–Campo de' Fiori–Piazza Farnese–Via Giulia (a circular minibus, weekdays 8am–9pm, Sat 8am–midnight).

119 Piazza del Popolo–Via del Babuino–Piazza di Spagna–Piazza Barberini–Via Veneto–Porta Pinciano (and back).

218 S. Giovanni in Laterano–Porta San Sebastiano–Via Appia Antica–Via Ardeatina (passing the catacombs and tombs).

By Taxi

Official taxis (painted white) are plentiful, and easier to get at a rank in one of the main piazzas than to flag down. They are quite expensive, with surcharges for luggage, on Sundays and after 10.30pm. Fares are clearly explained in English inside every taxi. Don't expect to find one when it's raining.

Taxi: *t 06 3570, t 06 4994.* You don't pay extra for calling a cab, but expect to pay for the time it takes for it to reach you.

By Car

Absolutely not recommended! Rome isn't as chaotic as Naples, but nearly so. Driving in Rome means frustration, rude drivers, double and triple parking, thefts and break-ins, and having your car towed away. Much of the old centre is closed to unauthorized traffic, and ought to be avoided altogether (you should be walking anyway in this compact area). This includes the Tridente south of Piazza del Popolo, the Via del Corso and nearly all the Campo Marzio outside the main streets, around the Pantheon, Piazza Navona, Campo de' Fiori and the Tiber. Petrol is expensive too, at €1.15 a litre, although lead-free (*benzina verde*) is widely available.

There are few guarded parking lots in Rome. The largest and most convenient is Parcheggio Ludovisi, on Via Veneto. Parking in the *centro storico* is for residents only (blue-marked zones). The larger, more expensive hotels offer garage parking. You may need to reserve it in advance.

Vigili Urbani: *Via della Consolazione 1, t 06 67691.* If you park on the street and return to find your car is missing, phone or drop by at the Vigili Urbani and ask the Ufficio Rimozione if it's been towed away before you go to the police. Cars picked up in the centre usually end up in the Villaggio Olimpico, on Via G.B. Valente (off the Via Prenestina) or on Via dei Cocchieri (near Ponte Marconi). If it's been clamped, the fine is €75 or more, depending on the offence. The number you need to phone will have been left on the car.

ACI (Italian Auto Club): *t 116.* If you have a breakdown, call the ACI and they will have your car towed to the nearest garage. If you have an accident, call the police (*t 113*).

Automobile Club di Roma: *t 06 4998 2389.* Runs an extremely useful helpline (*open 8am–8pm*), which monitors road conditions across Italy as well as in Rome (they speak English too).

All the major car hire firms in Rome have booths in Termini Station and at Fiumicino and Ciampino airports. There are some good local firms too.

Car Hire Firms

Avis: *Via Sardegna 38/a,* **t** *06 4282 4728,* **t** *199 100 133,* **w** *www.avis.com.*

Criss: *Via dei Prati Fiscali 273,* **t** *06 886 1920; Via Ostiense 89,* **t** *06 574 3003,* **w** *www.criss.it.*

Europcar: *Via Lombardia 7,* **t** *06 487 1274, (freephone)* **t** *800 01 4410; Via del Fiume Giallo 196,* **t** *06 5208 1244,* **w** *www.europcar.it.*

Hertz: *Via del Galoppatoio 33,* **t** *06 321 6831,* **t** *199 112 211,* **w** *www.hertz.com.*

Maggiore-Budget: *Via Tor Cervara,* **t** *06 2293 5356,* **w** *www.maggiore.it.*

Tropea: *Via S. Basilio 60 (Piazza Barberini),* **t** *06 488 1189,* **t** *06 488 4682.*

By Bicycle or Scooter

Be careful cycling among the crazies on Rome's streets – you'll note that few Romans ever risk it. The outer sections of Via Appia Antica, however, are a good route to pedal, or if you're more energetic, cycle to Veii or along the Tiber to Ostia Antica. In summer you can also rent bicycles on Largo dei Lombardi and in the Pincio Gardens.

Rome is not the place to learn how to ride a scooter, but if you've done it before, it's your chance to see Rome the way the Romans do, with a real buzz. To rent a bike, you must bring your passport; to rent a scooter you must be over 18, no driver's licence required. Expect to pay around €30 per day for a bike, and €45 for a small scooter; prices include two helmets.

Happy Rent: *Via Farini 3,* **t** *06 481 8185.* Scooters only.

I Bike Rome: *Parcheggio di Villa Borghese (underground car park with entrance off Viale delle Magnolie),* **t** *06 322 5240.*

Rent a Scooter: *Via Filippo Turati 50,* **t** *06 446 9222.*

St Peter Motor Rent: *Via di Porta Castello 43,* **t** *06 687 5714.*

Scoot a long: *Via Cavour 302,* **t** *06 678 0206.*

Scooters for Rent: *Via della Purificazione 84,* **t** *06 488 5485.*

By Carriage

The famous *carrozze* of Rome have gone the way of gondolas and are now used only by tourists. Carriage stands are at Piazza di Spagna, St Peter's Square, Piazza Navona, Via Veneto, Piazza Venezia, and by the Colosseum. Negotiate times and rates before you begin.

Practical A–Z

Climate

Rome typifies what Italians call 'bel tempo', an essentially mild climate, blue skies and moderate breezes (strong winds are rare), with occasional clouds that turn sunsets into spectacles of pink, yellow, orange and purple over the rooftops and cupolas of the city.

The abundant, typically Mediterranean vegetation of Rome's parks and terraces – oleander, bougainvillaea, palms, jasmine, geraniums and olive trees – makes it apparent that winters are not harsh (the last snowfall in Rome was in 1984).

In late July and August the thermometer frequently reaches 38°C – bring a hat, sunglasses and sunscreen if you have fair skin – but it cools down considerably at night. Year round, rain is the exception, but when it does rain it rains sul serio. From March to October, intense thunderstorms fall across the city, clearing the air. The sight of Piazza Navona after a storm is worth the cold you risk: glistening empty and silent at last; you can hardly see the far end through the cascades of water.

Spring is the prettiest time to go, when the flowering trees are in bloom, tubs of azaleas grace the Spanish Steps, and the Roman campagna is full of wild flowers. It is also the most crowded time of year, as people pour into the city for its Holy Week and Easter rituals, and the Italian school trip season gears up, so the main sights tend to be constantly crowded by bus loads of kids. Pack your sense of humour. Summer can be stifling hot and the Forum becomes a barbecue pit. Although the Romans themselves traditionally abandon the city en masse in August, and many restaurants and shops close down, an increasing number of locals now stay behind, willing to put up with the heat for the luxury of traffic-free streets. If you do come in the summer, always start your day as early as possible, and consider taking a siesta after lunch, during the hottest hours, so you can take in the night-time activities of the Estate Romana. Autumn brings both perfect days, cool and dry, and day after day of rain; sights are rarely very crowded, and there's the advantage of wine festivals in the Castelli Romani. The worst thing about winter is the shortness of the days, but it is probably the best time to see more Romans and fewer foreigners, and have the museums and churches to yourself.

The chart of average temperature and rainfall (see opposite) will give you an idea what to expect and what to pack.

Crime and the Police

Every stone [of Rome] has tasted blood, every house has had its tragedy, every shrub and tree, and blade of grass and wildflower has sucked life from death, and blossoms on a grave.

F. Marion Crawford

Rome, like the rest of Italy, is far safer than comparable urban areas in the UK and USA. Petty theft is the worst crime risk and it can be avoided with a little common sense. Don't leave luggage in your car. Don't travel with expensive jewellery. Don't flash your cash. Leave valuables in a hotel safe when you can. Otherwise watch out for pickpockets and bag-snatchers, especially in crowded areas and the usual blackspots around the station and tourist sights. There are a few Roman variations to watch out for in particular:

Romanies ('gypsies'). The hard core that used to be the main menace to tourists in Rome has pretty much gone but some still

	average temp in °C	rainfall in mm
Jan	7.4	74
Feb	8.0	87
Mar	11.5	79
Apr	14.4	62
May	18.4	57
June	22.9	38
July	25.7	6
Aug	25.5	23
Sept	22.4	66
Oct	17.7	123
Nov	13.4	121
Dec	8.9	92

hang around. Some 'gypsy' children move in swarms, carrying pieces of cardboard. When they sight their prey, some of the kids shove the cardboard under the victim's nose, pretending to ask for alms. The smaller ones, meanwhile, duck under the cardboard and pick your pockets. Favourite haunts for this game are Via del Tritone, Via Veneto, anywhere around the Colosseum, Via dei Fori Imperiali and Largo Argentina. 'Gypsy' children are never shy about putting their hands in your pockets to see what they can find, but will be prepared to give it back if it's of more value to you than to them. The best defence is to keep your valuables in a closed bag or inside pocket. You can resist if there is a crowd of citizens about. All Romans (especially honest Romanies) hate thieving ones like the plague.

Magic Fingers. These appear in any crowd (Wednesdays and Sundays in St Peter's Square, for instance) and especially on crowded buses, like the legendary 64 (from Termini Station to the Vatican). Women may find magic fingers in other places where they don't belong – the infamous *mano morta*. If you can identify the culprit, grinding your heel into his foot or elbowing him sharply in the stomach is the best redress.

Car thefts. Don't leave anything of value in a car, even in the boot.

Bag strippers. These are by and large the stuff of Alberto Moravia's tales of Rome in the '50s – young guys from the suburbs who come on motor scooters, rip off the straps of your handbag with a knife, and are gone in a second.

Muggers. This is mainly a suburban problem. As a tourist you are unlikely to venture into the dark suburban streets favoured by muggers. Any place with few people about at night is a prime hunting ground. The Termini Station area is not particularly salubrious at night, but you are unlikely to come to harm.

Reporting crime. To get the police on your case in a crisis, call the **emergency number, t** 113. Don't expect them to chase down the thieves, although if your purse or wallet is stolen, chances are good that

someone will turn it in (minus your valuables, but often with your ID intact). Once you've been robbed the only thing to do is *denunciare* (register) the fact at the **Questura** (Divisione Stranieri), Via Genova 2, **t** 06 4686. This will provide you the statement you need to make a claim from your insurance company.

Police. As Rome is Italy's capital and home to embassies from many countries to both Italy and the Vatican, there are several types of uniformed officers maintaining order. **Carabinieri** are the national police force (run by the military); they wear handsome dark uniforms with a red stripe down the side of the leg and drive dark Alfa Romeo sedans. You will see them in front of government buildings and embassies. **Vigili urbani** handle traffic and parking and enforce the city code; they are unarmed and drive small white Fiats. **Polizia** fill the gap.

Disabled Travellers

Rome is not very progressive in providing for anyone with limited mobility. In large part this is due to the centuries' old infrastructure in the parts of the city that tourists come to see, which is often protected at the expense of installing ramps and elevators.

The streets and sights of Rome present the most difficulty. Propelling yourself along the uneven, cobbled alleys is, to say the least, tiring, and you need considerable stamina to scramble on and off buses and trams. Few churches or museums are without steps. The following sights present few problems: the Forum, the Pantheon, S. Giovanni in Laterano, S. Sabina, S. Prassede, Baths of Caracalla, the Galleria Nazionale d'Arte Moderna, and the Zoo. A bit more difficult are the Colosseum, Museo Nazionale Romano, Museo Nazionale Etrusco di Villa Giulia, Museo Nazionale d'Arte Orientale and S. Lorenzo fuori le Mura.

As part of the Holy Year 2000 renovations, ramps were added to most kerbsides in the *centro storico* and around the Vatican. In addition, a special pedestrian-only path was created between the Trevi Fountain and

Pantheon, easily navigable in a wheelchair and with a tone-signal crossing of Via del Corso for the blind. St Peters and the Vatican Museums are wheelchair accessible.

Anyone in a wheelchair could have problems even in the more expensive hotels, as many are housed in historic *palazzi*, with flights of steps (without ramps) leading to entrances and even to the lifts. There are, however, tour operators who specialize in holidays for the disabled. For information about these, along with guides containing details of facilities for disabled people at sights, in hotels and at airports, write to one of the organizations listed below.

In our 'Eating Out' chapter we list those restaurants with wheelchair access. In the 'Where to Stay' chapter we list those hotels that are wholly or partly accessible.

Specialist Organizations

In Rome

In Rome, look out for the snappily titled *Guida di Roma: accessibilità, e barriere architectoniche, turismo, cultura, tempo libero* on sale at good bookshops and some newsstands. It has information on the accessibility (or otherwise) of hotels, restaurants, cafés, public transport, museums and churches.

Accessible Italy, *Promotur-Mondo Possibile, La Viaggeria, Via Lemonia 161,* **t** *06 7158 2945,* **f** *06 7158 3433,* **w** *www.tour-web.com/ accessibleitaly.* A travel agency that provides valuable, detailed information on access in Italy, including coverage of tourist spots, transport and accommodation in Rome.

Anthai, *Corso Vittorio Emanuele II 154,* **t** *06 6813 5117,* **w** *www.anthai.org.* A range of advice on accessibility.

APT (Azienda Provinciale per Il Turismo di Roma), *Via Parigi 5,* **t** *06 4889 9253.* The official tourist information office. Provides some information for disabled travellers.

Centro Informazione Documentazione Handicap, **t** *06 238 2210.* **Open** *Mon–Fri 9–5.* For information on accessibility, sports, transport and so on.

CO.IN (Consorzio Cooperative Integrate), *Via Enrico Giglioli 54/a,* **t/f** *06 2326 7504,*

(freephone) **t** *800 271 027.* Offers COINtel (**t** *06 2326 7695*), a 24-hour daily helpline in English, and publishes *Roma Accessibile*, a guide which you can obtain by post (charge for p+p), or from the APT. Also assists guided tours with transport (**t** *06 7128 9676*).

Enjoy Rome, *Via Varese 39,* **t** *06 445 1843,* **f** *06 445 0734,* **w** *www.enjoyrome.com.* Unofficial tourist service which offers some advice for travellers with disabilities.

In the UK

Holiday Care Service, **t** *(01293) 774 535,* **f** *(01293) 784 647,* Minicom **t** *(01293) 776 943,* **w** *www.holidaycare.org.uk,* **e** *holiday.care@ virgin.net.* Information sheets on travel.

RADAR (Royal Association for Disability & Rehabilitation), **t** *(020) 7250 4119,* **w** *www.radar.org.uk.* For information and books on travelling abroad.

Tripscope, **t** *0845 758 5641,* **f** *(020) 8580 7022,* **w** *www.justmobility.co.uk/tripscope/.* Practical advice on travel and transport for elderly and disabled travellers. Information can be provided by letter or audio tape.

In the USA and Canada

Access America, **w** *www.accessamerica.gov.* Information on facilities for disabled people at international airports. The US government website (**w** *www.dot.gov/airconsumer/ disabled.htm*) also has useful information.

Alternative Leisure Co, **t** *(718) 275 0023,* **w** *www.alctrips.com.* Organizes vacations abroad for disabled people.

Mobility International, **t** *(541) 343 1284,* **f** *(541) 343 6812,* **w** *www.miusa.org.* Advice, information and tours; $35 annual fee.

MossRehab ResourceNet, **w** *www.moss resourcenet.org/travel.htm.* Good resource for all aspects of accessible travel.

SATH (Society for the Advancement of Travel for the Handicapped), **t** *(212) 725 8253,* **w** *www.sath.org.* Advice on all aspects of travel for the disabled, for a $3 charge, or unlimited to members ($45; concessions $25).

On the Internet

The Able Informer, **w** *www.sasquatch.com/ ableinfo.* On-line magazine with tips for the disabled abroad.

Access Tourism, w *www.accesstourism.com.*
Pan-European website with information on
hotels, agencies and tour operators aware of
access issues affecting disabled travellers.

Emerging Horizons, w *www.emerging
horizons.com.* On-line travel newsletter for
people with disabilities.

Global Access, w *www.geocities.com.* On-
line network with information and links to
travel guides for disabled travellers.

Mobility International, w *www.mobility-
international.org.* An international body.
Produces an access guide for all EU countries,
covering transport, hotels and sights.

Electricity, Weights and Measures

The current is 225AC or 220V, the same as in
most of Europe. Americans will need
converters, and the British will need two-pin
adapters for the different plugs. Take one
with you, as they are hard to find in the city.

Italy uses the metric system. Clothing sizes
are tailored for slim Italian builds. Shoes, in
particular, tend to be narrower than in other
Western countries.

Clothing Sizes

Women's Shirts/Dresses

UK	10	12	14	16	18	
USA	8	10	12	14	16	
Italy	40	42	44	46	48	

Sweaters

UK	10	12	14	16		
USA	8	10	12	14		
Italy	46	48	50	52		

Women's Shoes

UK	3	4	5	6	7	8
USA	4	5	6	7	8	9
Italy	36	37	38	39	40	41

Men's Shirts

UK/USA	14	14.5	15	15.5	16	16.5	17
Italy	36	37	38	39	40	41	42

Men's Suits

UK/USA	36	38	40	42	44	46
Italy	46	48	50	52	54	56

Men's Shoes

UK	5	6	7	8	9	10	11	12
USA	7.5	8	9	10	10.5	11	12	13
Italy	38	39	40	41	42	43	44	45

Embassies and Consulates

In Rome

Canada: *Via G.B. De Rossi 27,* **t** *06 445 981
(Off maps;* **bus** *36, 60, 84, 90).*

Ireland: *Piazza Campitelli 3,* **t** *06 697 9121
(H9;* **tram** *8,* **bus** *H, 30, 40, 46, 62, 63, 64, 70, 87,
204, 492).*

UK: *Via XX Settembre 80/a,* **t** *06 4220 0001
(M–N5;* **bus** *38, 61, 62, 84, 86, 90, 92, 490,
491, 495).*

USA: *Via Veneto 119/a,* **t** *06 46741 (K5–6;*
metro *Barberini,* **bus** *52, 53, 63, 80, 95, 116, 116T,
119, 204).*

Abroad

Canada: *275 Slater St, Ottawa, Ontario K1P
5HG,* **t** *(613) 232 2401,* **f** *(613) 233 1484,*
e *ambital@italyincanada.com,* **w** *www.italy
incanada.com.* Consulates in Toronto,
Montreal and Vancouver.

Ireland: *63/65 Northumberland Road,
Dublin 4,* **t** *(01) 660 1744,* **f** *(01) 668 2759,*
e *italianembassy@eircom.net.*

UK: *14 Three Kings Yard, London W1Y 4EH,*
t *(020) 7312 2200,* **f** *(020) 7312 2230,*
e *emblondon@embitaly.org.uk,* **w** *www.
embitaly.org.uk.* Consulates in Edinburgh,
Manchester and Bedford.

USA: *3000 Whitehaven St, NW Washington
DC 20008,* **t** *(202) 612 4400,* **f** *(202) 518 2154,*
e *stampa@itwash.org,* **w** *www.italyemb.org.*
Consulates in most major cities.

Etiquette

A no bare shoulders, no bare knees code is
strictly enforced at St Peter's. Respectful
attire while visiting other churches will
reflect well on you. Large hats should be
removed, mobile phones switched off, and
smoking, kissing, eating and loud talking
avoided. Romans tend to be both more
charming and more assertive than British
people who should be prepared to adjust
their style a little to get along and to get
served in shops, restaurants and the like.

Health and Insurance

UK and Irish Nationals

Nationals of the **European Economic Area** – the 15 member states of the EU plus Iceland, Liechtenstein and Norway – are entitled to free or reduced-cost health care in any EEA country, on the same terms as its own nationals. Make sure you fill out an E111 form (free from a post office) before you go. One E111 covers an individual, spouse and children under 16, or under 19 and in full-time education.

In Italy, the E111 entitles you to the same medical benefits as Italian citizens, which, in an effort to decrease the country's national deficit, are being cut back. Italians have to buy a 'ticket' for all services. At the time of writing a 'ticket' for a prescription costs €1–5. Some medicines are not included in national medical coverage and have to be paid for at full price. If you are ill, either take your E111 to the foreigners' office (*stanza estero*) of the local state health centre (USL), where you will be given a temporary resident's form and a list of doctors, or go to a hospital accident and emergency unit (*pronto soccorso*). If you have to pay on the spot, you can usually claim a full or partial refund.

You may nonetheless, even if just to avoid the bureaucracy, deem it best to carry medical insurance. Check policies before you go as there can be lots of exclusions. Many credit card companies offer some degree of travel insurance when they are used to book a package holiday or aeroplane/train tickets. It is worth looking for a policy which covers not only health, but stolen or lost baggage, and cancelled or missed flights.

Health Literature Hotline, t *(freephone) 0800 555 777,* **w** *www.doh.gov.uk/travel advice.* Information on health when travelling from the UK can be obtained from this Department of Health number or website.

US and Canadian Nationals

Visitors from the **USA and Canada** who have private health insurance should check what medical coverage it provides overseas. If it does provide coverage abroad, make sure you take your insurance policy identity card and a claim form with you. The American social security Medicare programme does not provide any coverage for medical care abroad. Canadian provincial health plans provide some overseas medical coverage, but are unlikely to pay the full cost of treatment.

Hospitals in Rome

To call an ambulance, dial **t** 118.

The following public hospitals provide 24-hour first aid and medical services.

Fatebenefratelli, *Tiber Island,* **t** *06 68371 (H10;* **bus** *H, 23, 63, 280, 630, 780).*

Policlinico Umberto I, *Viale Policlinico,* **t** *06 49971 (N5;* **metro** *Castro Pretorio,* **bus** *61, 490, 91, 495).*

Rome American Hospital, *Via E. Longoni 69,* **t** *06 22551 (Off maps;* **bus** *058, 112, 312).*

San Camillo, *Circonvallazione Gianicolense 87,* **t** *06 58701 (Off maps;* **tram** *8,* **bus** *H, 228, 710, 719, 773, 774, 786, 871).*

Sant'Eugenio, *Piazzale dell'Umanesimo (EUR),* **t** *06 51001 (Off maps;* **metro** *EUR Fermi).*

San Filippo Neri, *Via Martinotti 20,* **t** *06 33061 (Off maps;* **bus** *546, 991).*

San Giacomo: *Via Canova 29,* **t** *06 36261 (H5;* **bus** *117, 119).*

Santo Spirito, *Lungotevere in Sassia 1,* **t** *06 68351 (E7;* **bus** *23, 34, 40, 62, 280).*

George Eastman Dental Hospital, *Viale Regina Elena 287,* **t** *06 844 831 (P6;* **metro** *Policlinico,* **tram** *3, 19).* For dental disasters. With an E111 a consultation 'ticket' is €13.50.

Istituto Materno Regina Elena Ostetrico, *Viale Angelico 28,* **t** *06 372 4085 (E4;* **metro** *Ottaviano,* **bus** *32).* Reliable maternity hospital.

Salvator Mundi International Hospital, *Viale delle Mura Gianicolensi 66,* **t** *06 588 961 (E11;* **bus** *44, 710, 870, 871).* A private hospital where English is spoken. For a list of English-speaking doctors phone your embassy.

Pharmacies

For minor complaints, or if you know what medicine you need, you can often go straight to the pharmacy, but without a prescription you'll have to pay full price for the remedy, and it may be hard to find English-speaking pharmacists. Medicines may be commercialized under different names, so you'll need to know the 'generic' name.

Pharmacies stay open after hours on a rotating basis; you can find a list of them in the window of every pharmacy and in *La Repubblica* and *Il Messaggero* or by ringing **t** 06 228941 for a recorded listing.

The following are pharmacies that regularly stay open all night.

Internazionale, *Piazza Barberini 49, t 06 482 5456 (K6; metro Barberini).*

Piram: *Via Nazionale 228, t 06 488 0754 (L7; metro Repubblica, bus H, 40, 60, 64, 70, 117).*

Cola di Rienzo: *Via Cola di Rienzo 213, t 06 324 3130 (E–F5; bus 81, 590).*

Brienza: *Piazza Risorgimento 44, t 06 3973 8166 (D6; tram 19, bus 32, 81).*

Arenula: *Via Arenula 73, t 06 6880 3278 (H9; tram 8, bus H, 63, 630, 780).*

Internet

Internet points are on the increase in Rome. Check rates before you log on.

EasyEverything *(K6), Via Barberini 2, t 06 4290 63388; metro Barberini, bus 52, 53, 61, 62, 63, 80. Open daily 24 hours.* Prices depend on crowding – the more crowded the more expensive. 'Happy hour' midnight–9am. Email, internet, telnet, scanning, printing and webcam on 350 PCs. English spoken. Café.

Internet Caffè *(K9), Via Cavour 213, t 06 4782 63051; metro Cavour, bus 5, 84, 204. Open daily 9am–1am.* A range of services on 25 PCs: email, internet, telnet, scanning, printing and webcam. English spoken.

The Netgate *(H7), Piazza Firenze 25, t 06 6893 6445, bus 116, 116T. Open Mon–Sat 10.30am–9pm, Sun 4–8pm.* Email, internet, telnet, scanning, printing and webcam on 27 PCs. English spoken.

Trevinet Place *(K6), Via in Arcione 103, t 06 6992 62320; metro Barberini, bus 52, 53, 61, 62, 63, 117, 119. Open Mon–Sat 10.30am–10.30pm, Sun 3–10.30pm.* Email, internet, telnet, scanning, printing and webcam facilities on 35 PCs. Happy hour from 10.30–11.30am – two hours for the price of one. English spoken.

Rome on the Internet

The Eternal City isn't exactly on the cutting edge of cyberspace but there are a few sites that may be of interest.

APT, w *www.romaturismo.com.* Rome's official tourist office website is excellent.

Enjoy Rome, w *www.enjoyrome.it.* English website offering practical information, especially for young travellers on a tight budget.

InfoRome, w *www.inforoma.it.* Weekly bulletins in English on current topics and events in Rome (and strike warnings, too!).

Roma c'è, w *www.romace.it.* The online version of Rome's weekly listings magazine publishes details of cinema, theatre, nightlife, concerts, art exhibitions and so on.

Vatican, w *www.vatican.va.* Even the Pope has a homepage, new and well-designed, in many different languages (including Polish, of course) and with very good graphics.

Launderettes and Dry Cleaners

There are hundreds of dry cleaners (*lavasecchi*) and laundry services (*tintorie*) in Rome, but very few self-service launderettes. The cost of service washes is high, especially in the *centro storico*. Enquire about laundry services at your hotel, as it may work out much less hassle and little more costly to get your laundry done in-house. Dry-cleaning prices start at around €1.50 per item.

Onda Blu, *Via Principe Amedeo (M–N8; metro Termini); Via Ottaviano (D5; metro Ottaviano); Via della Chiesa Nuova (G8; bus 40, 46, 62, 64), t 06 474 4647. All open daily 8am–10pm.* Rome's main laundromat chain is called 'Blue Wave'. A standard load costs €3.50 for wash only, about double for drying too. Soap is €0.80 a shot, or bring your own.

Lost Property

Municipal Lost Property *(F14), Via Bettoni 1, t 06 581 6040; tram 3, 8, bus H, 780. Open Mon–Fri 8.30–1, Wed and Thurs also 2–5.30.*

If you lose something in the city or on a bus, try the municipal lost property office.

Media

Radio

Vatican Radio airs the news in Italian, French and English at 8am and noon Mon–Sat (526AM/93.3/105 FM). The US Armed Forces comes in after sunset at 1107 AM, with major league baseball games nightly during the season, beginning around 2am local time.

Newspapers

Rome's daily newspaper, *Il Messaggero* (*w www.ilmessaggero.it*), is a concentrate of national and local news. Like all Italian newspapers, it has a section with TV, cinema and theatre listings. National newspapers include the independent centrist daily *La Repubblica* (*w www.repubblica.it*), with a good insert about Rome's news and cultural life, and the reliable Milan-based *Il Corriere della Sera* (*w www.cds.it*) and Turin-based *La Stampa* (*w www.lastampa.it*). Minority national newspapers *L'Unità* and *Il Manifesto* are left-leaning; *Il Quadrifoglio* leans to the right. In central Rome, all major foreign newspapers and magazines are available from most news- stands. The well-stocked kiosks on Piazza di Spagna and Via del Corso at Via del Tritone are open 24 hours a day and sell English-language newspapers, including the *International Herald Tribune*.

For classified ads in Italian buy *Porta Portese* on Tuesdays and Fridays or look on its website (*w www.portaportese.it*). You can find anything from rooms to let to second-hand scooters or furniture. *Wanted in Rome* and *Metropolitan*, both in English and available from English bookstores, offer a mixture of features on city life, reviews and ads.

TV

Italian television features three government-owned channels: **RAI 1**, **RAI 2** and **RAI 3** – the last covering regional news and with a good reputation for cultural programmes and interesting movies, especially late at night, rather than just the quiz shows, soap operas, talk shows and variety shows that are the staples of Italian TV. Prime Minister Silvio Berlusconi owns several media outlets, including **Canale 5**, **Rete 4** and **Telepiù Due** (a football channel). For TV news in English your best bet is to tune in to **CNN** or **BBC World** if you can get them in your hotel room.

Money, Banks and Taxes

After an eternity of deliberation and debate, a single European currency is finally becoming a part of everyday life in Italy and most EU countries other than the UK. These countries will also share a single interest rate, set by the European Central Bank (ECB).

The **euro** has already been in use for some time, but from 31 December 2001 all non-cash transactions are in the euro and from the end of February 2002 the euro is the only currency for the countries involved.

The euro notes themselves, introduced on 1 January 2002, are used alongside eight denominations of coin, ranging from 1 cent to 2 euros (100 cents in each euro). The rate fixed for exchange of the Italian lira to the euro is Lit 1936.27 to €1. At the time of writing, the euro is worth approximately £0.60, $0.90 and 1.40 Canadian dollars.

Changing Money

The most convenient way to change money is with your debit or credit card at one of the ATMs dotted around the city. There are also exchange offices at airports and at Termini Station, in most banks and around the city centre. Check rates and commission before making any transaction. Banks tend to give better rates than kiosks. If you have foreign banknotes there are an increasing number of automatic exchange machines in the city.

If you have American Express or Thomas Cook travellers' cheques it's worth going to the company's offices in Rome to save yourself €2.50 commission.

American Express *(15), Piazza di Spagna 38,* **t** *06 67641;* **metro** *Spagna,* **bus** *117, 119.*

Thomas Cook *(k6), Piazza Barberini 21/d,* **t** *06 482 8082;* **metro** *Barberini.* **Open** *Mon–Sat 8–6; (E7) Via della Conciliazione 23;* **bus** *62.* **Open** *Mon–Sat 8–6 and Sun 8–5.*

Credit and Debit Cards

Most banks and bureaux de change will give you cash on a credit card or Eurocheque with a Eurocheque card (taking little or no commission). ATMs (Bancomats/Cashpoints) at nearly every bank spout cash if you have a PIN number (Visa, Cirrus, Mastercard and Eurocard are the most widely accepted). Read the instructions carefully – you usually get a choice of English and other languages – so the machine does not devour your card.

Large hotels, expensive or tourist-oriented restaurants, larger shops, car hire firms and petrol stations will accept plastic as well; check the signs on the door.

Lost/stolen cards

American Express, *(international collect)* t 06 336 668 5110.

Visa/Eurocard, *(freephone)* t 800 018548.
Diners Club, *(freephone)* t 800 864 034.

VAT Refunds

Value-added tax (VAT, or IVA in Italy) is charged at 20 per cent on clothing, wine and luxury goods. On consumer goods it is already included in the amount shown on the price tag, whereas on services it may be added later. Non-EU citizens are entitled to a VAT refund on certain items under the Retail Export Scheme. You can claim a tax refund as long as you have not been in the EU for more than 365 days in the 2 years before the date you buy the goods and you leave the EU with the goods within 3 months of buying them. Items excluded from the scheme are motor vehicles, boats you intend to sail to a destination outside the EU, goods for business purposes, goods that will be consumed in the EU, bullion and unmounted gemstones. You cannot get a refund on hotel and restaurant bills, except for business.

To get your refund, shop with your passport and ask for an invoice itemizing the article, price and tax paid. When you depart Italy, take the goods and invoice to the customs office at the point of departure and have the invoice stamped. You need to do this at your last stop in the EU. Once home, and within 90 days of the purchase date, mail the stamped invoice (keeping a copy) to the shop or store, which is legally required to send you a VAT rebate. You'll get around 16.5 per cent back once post and admin are deducted. Shops that do not advertise tax-free services may be reluctant to get involved with official invoices, but the law entitles you to a refund.

For anyone who spends more than €150 at a go, many stores participate in the Tax Free Shopping scheme – you'll recognize the sign displayed in shop windows – which will do all the admin for you for a small fee. Get your invoices stamped at customs as above, then take them to one of the counters conveniently located at airports and your money will be refunded in cash on the spot, or as a refund to your debit or credit card.

Opening Hours and Public Holidays

Banks: Hours vary from bank to bank, but as a rule they open between 8 and 9am, close around 1.30pm, and open again for an hour mid-afternoon. Most bureaux de change open daily 9–7; a few stay open later in tourist areas.

Churches: Most churches open from 7.30 until midday and from between 3.30 and 5 until 6 or 7pm. Minor or *non parrocchiali* churches are rarely open.

Museums: Romans are notoriously fickle about keeping opening hours, even when strikes or restoration schemes aren't causing mayhem. The authorities are trying to standardize and extend them. Telephone ahead to avoid disappointment. Vatican Museums are free on the last Sunday of the month.

Post offices: The main post office, at Piazza San Silvestro 19, is open Mon–Fri 8.30–6.30 and Sat 8.30–1.

Shops: *See* 'Shopping' chapter.

Public holidays: Shops, banks, offices and schools in Rome are closed on:
1 January (New Year)
6 January
Easter Monday
25 April (Liberation Day)
1 May (Labour Day)

2 June (Festa della Repubblica)

29 June (SS. Pietro e Paolo)

15 August (Assumption of the BVM, better known as Ferragosto)

1 November (All Saints' Day)

8 December (Immaculate Conception of the BVM)

25 December (Christmas Day)

26 December (Santo Stefano).

Packing

Romans like to dress up, slaves to fashion rather than formality. Shorts, tee-shirts, halter tops, leisure suits, and funny hats incite Roman disdain. Comfortable shoes are absolutely essential when pounding the pavements. In summer bring a hat, sunglasses and mosquito repellent. If you plan to attend a papal audience, bring the proper clothes.

If you're a light sleeper, ear plugs may help you survive creaky hotel floors and traffic noise. Be warned that film and books in English cost twice as much as at home. Binoculars and a small torch may come in handy in gloomy churches – or hotels.

Photography and Video

Photographic film is readily available in all the usual formats. In tourist areas the price of film is high, so it's a good idea to stock up before you go. Rome is full of one-hour processing shops, privately owned rather than the chains common in the UK and USA.

Photography is permitted in most churches, but not in museums and art galleries. Flash photography is widely prohibited, as it damages the very paintings and frescoes that you are trying to capture. Clear signs indicate when photography is forbidden.

VHS videotapes are readily available, but Italy uses a different system to that used in the USA (the same as in other European countries), so your Italian videos won't be much good back home on your American NSTC standard VCR.

Post and Fax

The Italian postal system is the worst in Europe, and if you're only spending a week or two in Rome, you'll almost certainly be home before your letters and postcards. However, **Posta Prioritaria** and the more expensive **Postacelere** are new special-delivery services from the post office that guarantee delivery within 24 hours in Italy and 3–5 days abroad. Light letters up to 20 g sent as Posta Prioritaria to the USA and Canada cost €0.80, to anywhere in the EU €0.60. Make sure you buy the special gold PP stamps. Postacelere rates to the USA and Canada range from €24 for parcels under 500g (1lb) to €185 for 20kg (45lb) packages (within the EU €15.50 and €76.50 respectively). Otherwise mail them at the historically more efficient Vatican post office. Stamps may be purchased at post offices or at tobacconists' shops (at the sign of the T). If you don't know where you'll be in Rome you can have post sent General Delivery (Fermo Posta) to the Central Post Office (**Posta Centrale**, *Piazza San Silvestro 19, 00186. Open Mon–Fri 8.30–6.30, Sat 8.30–1*). Call (freephone) **t** 06 160 for information in Italian about rates and local post office opening hours, (freephone) **t** *800 009 966* for information about Postacelere. Poste Italiane's website (**w** *www.poste.it*) has information in Italian about post codes, rates, PO addresses, and a parcel-tracing service. You can send a telegram from any post office, or by ringing **t** 186 (24-hour line).

There are more fax machines per head in Italy than in any other European country. Even some one-star hotels have them, and virtually all hotels that have a fax will send messages for guests. Alternatively you can send or receive a fax at one of the city's many *copisterie* (photocopy centres).

Posting parcels home can take the better part of the day; Italian postal regulations are sometimes so complex and petty that even postal employees are confused. Your best bet is to show up with your box, and ask where to find the nearest *cartolibreria* that wraps parcels, or send it by a private company.

Several major couriers have drop-off points in central Rome (Via Barberini and Via del Traforo). For information on rates or to schedule a pick-up, call the following freephone numbers:

Federal Express, t *880 123 800.* **Open** *Mon–Fri 8am–7pm.*

DHL, t *800 345 345.* **Open** *daily 24 hours.*

SDA, t *800 016 027.* **Open** *Mon–Fri 8.30am–7.30pm and Sat 8.30am–1.30pm.*

Most couriers guarantee overnight delivery Mon–Thurs to most destinations.

Religious Affairs and Vatican Information

Rome – it is said – has 901 churches and is 99 per cent Catholic, even if only 3 per cent of Romans regularly attend Mass. Since the third century, Jews have tenuously hung on to second place, followed now perhaps by Anglicans. The most recent newcomers are Muslims, who have a new mosque by Villa Ada, designed by postmodern architect Paolo Portoghesi.

The four Patriarchal basilicas (St Peter's, S. Paolo fuori le Mura, S. Maria Maggiore, S. Giovanni in Laterano) are open all day. Every other church closes for several hours in the afternoon (at least 12–3.30). As a rule, don't enter if a service is in progress at the high altar; otherwise be discreet and walk round the chapel in use. If the sacristan opens a chapel or crypt for you, give him a small tip. Coin-operated light machines illuminate the most important works; often a pair of opera glasses or binoculars comes in handy to see a lofty mosaic or fresco.

When globe-trotting John Paul II is in Rome, general papal audiences are held on Wednesdays at 11am in the Vatican auditorium; in July and August the audiences are usually held in Castel Gandolfo. To attend in either place, write ahead for tickets from the **Prefettura della Casa Pontificia** (*Città del Vaticano, 00120*), with not more than one month's or less than two days' notice. Include name, nationality, proposed date, and your address in Rome.

Vatican City Information, t *06 6988 4466.* **Open** *Mon–Sat 9–5.* For information about Vatican or Catholic affairs.

Confession in English is heard at the Patriarchal basilicas as well as at S. Ignazio, S. Sabina, S. Anselmo, S. Clemente, S. Maria sopra Minerva, and at the Gesù. Mass may be heard in English at:

San Clemente, *Via di S. Giovanni Laterano 45–47,* **t** *06 7720 2932 (Irish; 10am on the 3rd Sunday of the month).*

Sant'Isidoro, *Via degli Artisti 41,* **t** *06 488 5359.*

San Silvestro, *Piazza San Silvestro,* **t** *06 679 7775 (English).*

Santa Susanna, *Via XX Settembre 14,* **t** *06 4201 4554 (American).*

San Patrizio, *Via Boncompagni 31,* **t** *06 488 5716 (Irish).*

San Tommaso di Canterbury, *Via di Monserrato 45,* **t** *06 686 5808 (English).*

Santi Martiri Canadesi, *Via G. B. De Rossi,* **t** *06 855 2115 (Canadian).*

Other faiths and denominations in Rome:

Adventist, *Lungotevere Michelangelo 7,* **t** *06 321 0200.*

Anglican, *All Saints, Via del Babuino 153/b,* **t** *06 3600 1881.*

Baptist/Waldensian, *Piazza S. Lorenzo in Lucina 35,* **t** *06 687 6652.*

Episcopalian, *St Paul's Within the Walls, Via Napoli 58,* **t** *06 488 3339.*

Islamic Centre, *Via della Moschea 22,* **t** *06 808 2167.*

Jewish, *Lungotevere dei Cenci 9,* **t** *06 684 0061.*

Methodist, *Ponte Sant'Angelo, Piazza Banco S. Spirito 3,* **t** *06 686 8314.*

Mormon, *Gesù Cristo dei Santi, Via Cimone 103,* **t** *06 8680 0111.*

Presbyterian, *St Andrew's of Scotland, Via XX Settembre 7,* **t** *06 482 7627.*

International Evangelists, *Via Chiovenda 57,* **t** *06 721 6400.*

Russian Orthodox, *Via Palestro 69,* **t** *06 445 0729.*

Salvation Army, *Via degli Apuli 40,* **t** *06 446 2614.*

Smoking

Although smoking is not permitted in public spaces like hospitals, post offices, airports, stations and food shops, Italians have a tendency to disregard no-smoking laws, which are seldom enforced. If you ask someone not to smoke, even in an officially-designated no-smoking area, don't expect your request to be respected. Your best bet for a smoke-free environment is out of doors. All FS trains have no-smoking carriages. Specify when you reserve.

A packet of 20 cigarettes costs from €2.20 for domestic MS to €4.40 for imported brands. They can be purchased from tobacconists and bars with a T sign. Il Castellino on Piazza Venezia is open 365 days a year, 24 hours a day.

Strikes

Official strikes (the word to look out for is *sciopero*) are usually listed in newspapers, but lightning strikes are pretty common – so don't be surprised if you turn up at a bus stop, metro or railway station and discover there is no public transport.

Students and Senior Citizens

Citizens under 18 and over 60 with ID have free entrance to Rome's state museums (Museo Nazionale Romano, Museo Nazionale Etrusco di Villa Giulia, Museo Nazionale d'Arte Orientale, Castel Sant'Angelo, Palazzo Barberini's Galleria Nazionale d'Arte Antica, and the Museo d'Arte Moderna).

Students with international ID cards have several cheap housing options (*see* 'Where to Stay') and can get some travel discounts by becoming members of student associations.

Associazione Turismo Giovanile (ATG), *Corso Vittorio Emanuele 108*, *t 06 560 1905*. Another travel agency specializing in youth and budget fares.

Centro Turistico Studentesco e Giovanile (CTS), *Via Genova 16*, (freephone) *t 06 4782 4297*; *Corso Vittorio Emanuele 297*, *t 06 687 2672*. €10 membership fee.

Enjoy Rome, *Via Varese 5*, *t 06 445 1843*. Also very helpful to young travellers.

Rome's main university, La Sapienza, is at Castro Pretorio, near Termini Station. There are many popular student hang-outs in the area of San Lorenzo nearby, but Italian students tend to live with their parents and often work too, so student life is not as concentrated as in the UK and USA.

Telephones

When making calls in Italy, always dial the city's area code. To call a local number in Rome dial 06 followed by the number. For Italian mobile phones dial the prefix without a zero in front. On business cards you may find old-style mobile numbers with a zero.

Directory enquiries, *t 12.*

Pagine Gialle, *t 06 892 424.* For full business details including business addresses, the yellow pages are more efficient. Both services cost around €0.50. If you strike lucky you may get an English-speaking operator.

As a whole Rome is well supplied with telephones – seek them out on noisy street corners, in post offices, hotels, bars or around Termini. Nearly all take coins or phone cards (*schede telefoniche*) available in roughly €2.50, €5 or €7.50 amounts at tobacconists or newsstands; stock up for a long international call. Local calls are most expensive on working days between 8am and 6.30pm. Once you call long distance, the phone becomes a hog. For reverse charges (*a erre*) dial *t 172* followed by the country code, which will connect you with the appropriate operator, e.g. 1720044 for Britain. The telephone prefix for the UK is 0044, Ireland 00353, for the US and Canada 001, for Australia 0061, New Zealand 0064.

International information, *t 176. Open Mon–Fri 8am–9pm.* For help in English on international calls or to get a translation into Italian and vice versa. Calls are charged at €2 a minute plus €7.50 tax plus 20% VAT.

If you're calling Rome from abroad, dial *t 39*, then 06, then the number.

Time

Italy is always one hour ahead of Greenwich Mean Time, and generally six hours ahead of Eastern Standard Time in the USA. Summer Time (*ora legale*) starts on the last Sunday in March at 3am – when clocks are put forward one hour – and ends on the last Sunday in October at 3am – when clocks are set back one hour. Summer and winter opening hours of major tourist sights are usually changed at the same time as the clocks, unless Easter is very early.

Tipping

Service is almost always included in restaurant bills, but Italians customarily tip waiters unless the service gives them reason not to. Rather than a percentage of the bill, a tip of €2 per person for a meal at a moderately priced restaurant is enough to convey appreciation, less at cheaper places and pizzerias, more at fancy restaurants. A €0.20 coin on the bancone with your scontrino will help to get your coffee served faster if standing at the bar. Tip a generous 10 per cent if sitting at a café. Italians tip taxi drivers and theatre ushers only if they are notably helpful. At a hotel, you might leave your chambermaid €15 for a week's stay, the bellhop €2–3 per trip. Tip the concierge only for personal services.

Toilets

Emperor Vespasian permitted fullers to place jars in public places to collect the urine they needed for their trade, in return for a small tax. When his son complained that the tax was beneath the imperial dignity, Vespasian held a gold coin to his nose. 'What, does it stink?' he asked.

The sad fact is that the visitor in ancient Rome had a much easier time finding a loo in the city – convenient, marble-seated, flushing *forica*, or latrines, could be found wherever you went, for a penny. Nowadays you have to seek them out in bars, where the byword is grotty and paper a surprising

luxury (technically you don't have to buy anything to use the facilities, although if the bar staff are in a bad mood they will claim the toilet is out of order until you buy a drink); loos tend to be cleaner in restaurants, museums, St Peter's Square, and the smarter cafés; but the rare public lavatories are the best, tended lovingly by their attendants. There are public loos on Piazza S. Silvestro, Piazza del Colosseo, Via Zanardelli, and at the 64 bus terminus near St Peter's.

Tourist Offices

Azienda di Promozione Turistica (APT), *Via Parigi 11, 00185, t 06 488 991, f 06 4889 9238. **Open** Mon–Fri 9.30–12.30, Mon and Thurs also 2.30–4.30.* The central office, near the Baths of Diocletian. The APT offices are the best source of information about what's on in Rome and its province.

APT, *(Fiumicino airport), t 06 6595 6074. **Open** Mon–Sat 8.15–7.* A useful branch office if you arrive by plane.

Comune di Roma Tourist Information Office, *Termini Station. **Open** daily 8–8.* Inside Rome's main train station. You'll find more information about the city of Rome here than at APT. You can ask for free city maps and brochures in English about the city's tourist attractions, including museums, archaeological sites and parks. The free ATAC public transport map is very useful.

The Comune di Roma also has 10 tourist information kiosks near attractions. All are well-stocked with free maps and brochures, and open daily 9–7. They are located at Via del Corso at Largo Goldoni (near the intersection with Via Condotti), and at Via Marco Minghetti (near the Trevi Fountain); on Piazza San Giovanni in Laterano; on Via Nazionale in front of the Palazzo delle Esposizioni; on Piazza delle Cinque Lune (near Piazza Navona); on Piazza Pia (near Castel Sant'Angelo); on Piazza del Tempio della Pace (near the Fori Imperiali); on Piazza Sonnino (in Trastevere); on Via dell'Olmata (near Santa Maria Maggiore); and on Piazza dei Cinquecento (outside Termini).

Discount Tickets

Combined discount tickets are available for clusters of museums. They can be bought at any of the museums or tourist offices.

Ticket one, which costs €15.50, is valid for five days and gives admittance to the Colosseum, Palatine, Baths of Caracalla, Museo Nazionale Romano (Palazzo Massimo, Palazzo Altemps, Aula Ottagona and Terme di Diocleziano).

Ticket two, which costs €7.50, is also valid for five days but gives admittance only to the Museo Nazionale Romano (all sites).

Comune di Roma helpline, t *06 3600 4399 (select 2 for an English-speaking operator).* **Open** *daily 8–7.* For similar information over the phone, contact the efficient and helpful call centre or visit the website (**w** *www.roma turismo.com*), which has useful information.

Neither APT nor the Comune di Roma offices make hotel reservations, but they can supply you with a free list of hotels and authorized B&Bs.

Women Travellers

Any young English-speaking lady who isn't on her guard will eventually find a special someone in Rome. If you want to, tell him to leave you alone (*'lasciami in pace'*). Hurling abuse is not recommended, as swearing with a foreign accent is considered rather sexy. Whenever you meet an interesting male, keep your hand on your wallet at all times.

Working and Long Stays

'Rome is a world,' wrote Goethe, 'and it would take years to become a true citizen of it. How lucky those travellers are who take one look and leave.' Nevertheless, an estimated 50,000 English-speaking foreigners do live in Rome, so if work, study, or caprice conspire to move you to become a resident you certainly won't be alone. The secret is not going crazy the first two months getting your papers in order. Many expats, keen to preserve their sanity, don't bother. If you prefer to be legal, here's the procedure.

Registration and Residency

If you are planning to stay in Italy long term without working, and are not an EU citizen, you should register with the police within eight days of arrival and apply for a *permesso di soggiorno* from the Ufficio Stranieri at the Questura Centrale on Via Genova. The Questura is open only in the mornings, like all state offices, so aim to get there early. The *permesso* lasts for three months, after which time you will need to renew it. If you can prove you have enough money to live on, permission is usually granted. You should do all you can to appear calm and remain polite through the ordeal.

Anyone who wishes to be registered as a resident should apply to their local Anagrafe (registry office). The one at Via Luigi Petroselli 50 serves Circoscrizione I. If you are in Italy for work, your employer should help you with the red-tape. Many small businessmen will only take unregistered foreigners (that way they don't have to declare them and pay tax).

Business Trips to Rome

The larger hotels that serve business travellers offer a range of business facilities including internet linkup and fax. Hotel listings in the 'Where to Stay' chapter indicate which hotels these are.

Students

Students attending courses at Italian universities or private colleges must obtain a declaration from the Italian Consulate in their home countries before their departure, certifying their 'acceptability'. If you want to study in Rome, especially to do post-graduate work, ask your embassy about scholarships offered by the Italian Ministry of Foreign Affairs (many are never used for lack of requests); or write directly to the Ministry of Foreign Affairs, Direzione Generale per la Cooperazione Culturale Scientifica e Tecnica, Piazzale della Farnesina 1, Rome.

Studying in Rome

The APT's booklet *Young Rome* has lists of universities, institutes, libraries, and workshops in the city that may be of interest for anyone on an extended stay. The Dante Alighieri Institute, Piazza Firenze 27, specializes in Italian culture and literature for foreigners, and offers reputable Italian classes. There are scores of language schools, but **Italiaidea** (*Piazza della Cancelleria 85, t 06 6830 7620*) gets good reports. Musicians should inquire about courses at the **Italian Music International Studies Centre** (*Conservatorio di S. Cecilia, Via dei Greci 18*). The University of Rome's Faculty of Architecture has courses in art restoration for foreigners, from January to June, or alternatively there's the **Scuola Restaura** (*Viale Porta Ardeatina 108, t 06 575 7185*).

Finding a Job

Finding a job in Rome can be hard. EU residents may register at the nearest Ufficio di Collocamento (Manpower Office). Teaching English is the most obvious source of income; qualifications or some experience, while not always essential, may make the difference. *Wanted in Rome, Metropolitan*, and the Roman papers are a good place to look for openings, but it never hurts to show up at a language school and ask for an interview. Some secondary schools take on mother tongue assistant teachers for their language classes.

English-speaking au pairs are also in demand: try the papers or place an ad on the PDS noticeboard on Via dei Giubbonari. The large community of artists and art students means there's always a demand for life models: again, place an ad in *Metropolitan* or *Wanted in Rome* or contact one of the schools directly. If you prefer to work with your clothes on, there are often jobs for skilled secretaries and professionals at FAO, the UN Food and Agriculture Organization.

Other secretarial and catering jobs are generally available but your chances are slim with only English. As international as Rome is, you'll miss nearly all the fun (and the good jobs) without Italian. If you're still learning, a copy of the annual English Yellow Pages (available in most bookshops) may come in handy.

Finding a Flat

Renting

Once you've become a resident, you may suddenly discover it is rather difficult to find a flat to rent. Over half the flats you'll see advertised in the *centro storico* state that tenants have to be non-residents: this does not indicate an unusually high incidence of philoxenic landlords: simply that non-residents are not covered by the same legislation as residents and are less likely to become sitting tenants. As far as you're concerned it's not an insurmountable problem. Just lie.

One important piece of advice if you come looking for a place to stay is to bring lots and lots of money. Rents are very high in Rome (at the time of writing studio and one-bedroom flats in the centre go for at least €750–1,000 per month). If you want to fix up accommodation before you go, contact International Property Network (*Via del Babuino 79, t 06 3600 0018*). Alternatively, look for a flat (or place an ad yourself) in *Metropolitan*, *Wanted in Rome* (*Via dei Delfini 17, t 06 679 0190*), available at English bookshops, and *Porta Portese* (*Via degli Orti della Farnesina 82, t 06 3638 1477*) from the news-stands, which is full of classifieds, or ask for one of the many publications that specialize in renting/buying an apartment, such as *Mille Case*; also check the Thursday and Sunday editions of *La Repubblica* and *Il Messaggero*, or the noticeboards (which often have flats to share or a single room in a house) at All Saints' Church in Via del Babuino and the Lion Bookshop in the Via dei Greci; or try the bakery La Renella, Via del Moro 15, in Trastevere; or upstairs at Centro Susanna, Via XX Settembre 14; or the American Academy, near Porta S. Pancrazio, Via Angelo Masina 5; or outside the ex-PDS centre on Via dei Giubbonari. Most landlords insist on a deposit of two, and sometimes three, months' rent in advance, and it can be the devil to get it back when you leave, even if you give the required three months' notice. If you find a flat through an estate agent their commission is usually 10 per cent of a year's rent. Rental leases are signed through a *commercialista* or *notaio* who represents both you and the landlord and is paid to know all the complicated legal niceties (land-lords often have their lawyers along, so you may want to have one, too, in case they try to pull a fast one because you're a foreigner). The lease (usually for one year) may specify that you are not to become a resident.

Buying

Of course all of the above isn't a problem if you want to buy your own flat or *palazzo* (current prices are around €5,000–7,000 a square metre in the centre). When you contact one of Rome's estate agencies (Gabetti is the largest) they will want to know right out how much you are prepared to spend and the neighbourhoods you prefer (if you have school-age children who will be attending one of Rome's several English or American international schools, life will be much easier for your child if you live nearby). Once you find a place you like, make an offer, and if the seller accepts it, you'll be expected to pay 10–15 per cent on signing an agree-ment called the *compromesso*, which penalizes either you or the seller if either party backs out. The paperwork is handled by a *notaio*, who works for you and the seller, though many people also hire a *commercial-ista* to look after their affairs. A payment schedule is worked out; Italian mortgages are usually for 50 per cent of the selling price, payable over a 10-year period. Foreigners pay 10 per cent more than Italians, but never have to pay rates. Always transfer payment from home through a bank, taking care to save certificates of the transactions so you can take the money out of Italy easily when you sell.

Finding a School

Finding the proper school for your children in Rome can be difficult – there are some 20 international schools, listed in the *Rome International Schools Booklet* – a good place to start your search, and available at all the schools and at English bookshops. The British Council, Via delle Quattro Fontane 20, also has information about schools. Some schools offer programmes to integrate children into the Italian system, if you mean to live in Italy for more than three years; others prepare students for exams and universities in Britain, the USA, or Italy. Italian state schools offer a good, rounded education, free to all children living in Italy (after you get all the proper documents translated into Italian and stamped, that is), and sending a young child to a *scuola elementare* or *asilo* (nursery school, run by the *comune* or nuns) will have him or her fluent in Italian in a matter of months. Foreign children adapt amazingly fast because teachers and their peers are irresistibly *simpatico* and helpful.

Cars

You have to be a resident to buy one second-hand and drive it in Italy; non-resi-dents are only allowed to purchase a new car on the condition that they get a special EE plate (*escursionista estero*), valid for 365 days. Sales staff should be able to help with the papers. The law says residents have to change their driving licences over to Italian ones as soon as they become residents. Non-EU citizens are required to have an international driving licence. Non-residents are only allowed to keep a foreign car in Italy for 365 days.

Campo Marzio

Campo Marzio

A broad bend in the Tiber surrounds what, for lack of a better name, is often called simply 'old Rome'. It's hardly the oldest part, but a typical irony in this venerable city is that its brightest, most alive, most ingratiating quarter should be the crumbling old medieval flatlands.

To ancient Rome this bend in the river was the *Campus Martius*, the field of Mars, where the first citizens of the republic drilled and practised swordplay, and where they came to stand up and be counted on election day. The growing city covered it with theatres and temples, public buildings and *insulae*; in the 600s, with the aqueducts out of service, what was left of Rome's population straggled down here, where drinkable (barely!) water from the Tiber was readily available.

There's no neighbourhood like this one, not in Rome or any other city. The seat of the Italian government is here, and you may find your tour interrupted by speeding blue Lancias full of diplomats and ministers, accompanied by a gaggle of Carabinieri. The Pantheon is here too, and a score of other monuments; politicians, journalists, cats, artists, trendies, fruit vendors, Dominicans and Jesuits, tons of tourists, all heaped together in what would otherwise be a peaceful residential quarter. There's room for everyone; the tight web of narrow medieval alleys and pint-sized piazzas, inscrutable and almost indecipherable to the first-time visitor, makes the neighbourhood seem bigger (and more tranquil) than it really is. The only blemish is the Corso Vittorio Emanuele, a grim, treeless boulevard bloated with traffic, exactly the sort of street you would want to avoid.

But in the 1870s, when the planners of the new Italy extended this street through the chaos of old Rome out towards the Vatican, they aligned it carefully to gobble up some old streets, and create a new address for several Renaissance and Baroque landmarks.

1 Lunch

Il Convivio, *Vicolo dei Soldati 31*, *t 06 686 9432*; *bus 30, 81, 116, 116T, 204*. *Open Tues–Sat 1–2.30 and 8–10.30, Mon 8–10.30; closed 1 week in Aug. **Expensive***. Some of the most innovative cuisine in Rome: chilled fruit soups, baked *zucchini* flowers and pastries.

2 Coffee and Cakes

Tazza d'Oro, *Via degli Orfani, just off Piazza della Rotonda*; *bus 116, 116T; wheelchair accessible. Open Mon–Sat 7am–8pm*. The latest contender for Rome's best cup of java (and coffee granita topped with cream).

3 Drinks

Bar della Pace, *Via della Pace 5; bus 46, 62, 64. Open Tues–Sun 10am–2am*. Snooty fin-de-siècle bar in a fine setting; elitist in the evenings, a pleasant retreat during the day.

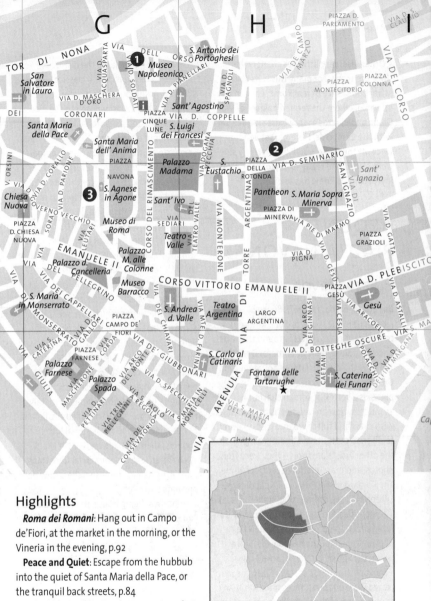

Highlights

Roma dei Romani: Hang out in Campo de'Fiori, at the market in the morning, or the Vineria in the evening, p.92

Peace and Quiet: Escape from the hubbub into the quiet of Santa Maria della Pace, or the tranquil back streets, p.84

Ancient Rome: The Pantheon, most perfect monument of the ancient world, p.87

Medieval and Renaissance: S. Maria sopra Minerva brings together the best of both, in a unique, for Rome, Gothic structure, p.89

Baroqueorama: Four Rivers Fountain, in Piazza Navona, Bernini's masterpiece, p.82

Unexpected Rome: Track down criminals at the Museum of Criminology, p.95

Otherwise, very little has changed here since the 1500s. For many this is its great attraction: a slice of real Rome, easy and informal, where the refined palaces of Via Giulia and Piazza Farnese exist side by side with the Campo de' Fiori market vendors. Once off the Corso, you'll be relatively safe from traffic, and ready to explore the most joyful corners Rome has to offer.

AROUND PIAZZA NAVONA

Piazza Navona G7–8

Bus 40, 46, 62, 64, 116, 116T, 186, 492.

Laid out in the 1640s by Pope Innocent X, this elegant piazza covers ground that was once a stadium, built by Emperor Domitian. Today, with Bernini's famous fountains and the dim, old-fashioned street lighting, the piazza is a vortex of Roman charm, favoured as much by Roman trendies as tourists, lined with cafés and full of weary artists waiting to do snap portraits of all comers. Many of the other artists are fakes – they trace from photos, and mass-produce scenes of Rome. The Romans insist they're all Neapolitans. Often you'll see the cherubic smiles of Italian TV celebrities, filming a 'spot' in front of the fountains, or pallid, scrawny models being photographed for the fashion ads. Still a circus, though of a different sort.

Most of the streets that lead into the piazza were once entrances into Domitian's stadium; one of them, Via Agonale, recalls the athletes who entered through it for the races (the name of the piazza itself was origi-nally 'in Agone', from the Greek for athlete, and later 'n'Agona'). All that is left of the orig-inal building can be seen at **Via di Tor Sanguigna 16** (G7), the little alley which follows the curve of Piazza Navona to the northeast. The remains include one of the gates, excavated from under later buildings.

On entering the piazza the distinctive shape is readily apparent, a classical Greek stadium, 900ft long, with a curve at one end. Genuine athletics, as opposed to the bloodier chariot races and gladiatorial games, never really caught on in Rome. And the deranged Domitian seems hardly the sort of emperor to have promoted them. Nevertheless, he began the work, in AD 85, for the annual games he planned to hold in honour of Capitoline Jove. By the Middle Ages, the 'field of athletes' was a rather empty corner of Rome, with vineyards and barns among the still substantial ruins. With Rome's rebirth in the 15th century it became a marketplace (later moved to Campo de' Fiori); not until the time of Pope Innocent X (1644–55) did it become the elegant square we see today.

The piazza saw more than its share of Baroque spectacles. Its construction allowed it to be flooded for mock sea battles, or for skating in the coldest winters. It has long been the home of the Toy Fair, lasting through Christmas until Epiphany. In Italy, traditionally, the old witch called the Befana brings children (and the national lottery winners) their presents on Twelfth Night. With the advent of commercial Christmas, most little Italian crumbsnatchers now get presents twice.

Innocent's dream house, the 1644 **Palazzo Pamphili** (G8), occupies the southwest corner of the square. Now the Brazilian Embassy, it has an interior by Borromini and frescoes by Pietro da Cortona – but the only part you are likely to see is the annexe, where frequent cultural exhibitions are held.

Sant'Agnese in Agone G8

*Piazza Navona. **Open** Mon–Sat 4.30–7, Sun 10–1 and for Mass.*

This church, intended to be one of the showpieces of the Baroque, never really came together as planned. The original centralized Greek cross design, by the Rainaldis, would have projected into the piazza. Borromini, called in to revise the work, solved the problem by shortening the apses on the main axis – his subtle illusionistic effects make some people leave here thinking the round dome above them is really elliptical. His façade, squeezing all this in to make it look good from the piazza, is a quiet triumph; the convex front makes a perfect setting for the dome and towers. It is perhaps the way the façade of St Peter's should have been built, a thought not lost on architects of the time.

If you pass by when Sant'Agnese is open, step inside its bold interior, full of Borrominesque artifice; the distribution of pillars makes the shallower apses appear equal to the longer ones. Many of the structural elements are hidden by a jungle of decoration, including the funeral monument of Innocent X (see 'Worst Pope', p.217). Underneath are the uninteresting remains of the original Dark Age Oratory of St Agnes, built into Domitian's stadium, where the pious virgin was flung naked into a brothel – her punishment for refusing to marry – and grew long tresses to hide her charms.

Bernini's Fountains G8

For many Piazza Navona is simply the background for these fountains, one of the peaks of Baroque sculpture and sensibility. The central **Fountain of the Four Rivers** (1651), with its massive sculptures and obelisk, has become one of the symbols of Rome. As in much of Bernini's work, there is some flaccid allegory behind the composition: besides an allusion to the four rivers of Paradise, the anthropomorphized rivers (Nile, Ganges, Danube and Rio de la Plata) represent the four corners of the world enlightened and dominated by Pope Innocent X; the dove atop the obelisk was a family symbol. In the sculpture itself, though (executed by his students), Bernini for once transcends the bombast and simple-mindedness of the Baroque. The powerful, expressive figures growing out of the jagged mass of travertine, the vivid portrayal of natural elements – rocks, tropical plants, seashells – and the brilliant use of the water itself as a sculptural

element (a trick Bernini probably invented) combine to make this something unique in the chilly, awful 1600s – a sign of life in the land of the dead.

The supposed rivalry between Bernini and Borromini plays a big part in Roman artistic folklore. Tour guides always tell their credulous charges how Bernini made the figures of the rivers seem to be recoiling in horror from Borromini's Sant'Agnese across the street, and how the angels on top of the church return the compliment by refusing even to look at the fountain. Another story has Borromini spreading the rumour that his enemy's obelisk was improperly erected, and about to fall. When the authorities put the question to Bernini, he led them to the fountain, climbed up, and tied a piece of string around the obelisk; after attaching the other end of the string to a nearby building, he went laughing all the way home.

The obelisk comes from Domitian's Temple of Isis (see p.250). Roman emperors commissioned obelisks nearly as often as they stole them; the hieroglyphics on this one record Domitian's devotion to the goddess (he built another such temple in Benevento, where there is a wonderful statue of the Emperor in Egyptian costume). Isis herself, or at least the cult image from the temple, can be seen in front of San Marco, just off Piazza Venezia; discovered during the Renaissance and placed there, she became a political talking statue, 'Madama Lucrezia' (see p.84, p.122).

Of the two smaller fountains, the northern one (G7) is 19th century. The southern fountain, however, is another dramatic design by Bernini, the **Fontana del Moro** (G8) – not really a Moor at all, but a sort of marine divinity chasing a dolphin.

Pasquino G8

*Piazza di Pasquino; **bus** 40, 46, 62, 64, 116, 116T, 186, 492.*

Just outside the southwestern corner of the piazza is another small square with a quiet, forlorn protagonist of Rome's history,

Pasquinades

If you ever cross over the Tiber on Ponte Garibaldi, take a look at the monument to Gioacchino Belli, the top-hatted Roman dialect poet who stands in his piazza welcoming you to Trastevere. On the back of the pedestal you'll see a relief with a group of old-time Romans, gathered excitedly around a queer broken statue. What makes this shapeless marble lump different from the other ten thousand in Rome is that it is a talking statue. His name is Pasquino, and you can see him today behind Palazzo Braschi, just southwest of Piazza Navona.

Political graffiti, and particularly the habit of making statues talk by hanging placards on them, has been a Roman speciality since ancient times. During the siege of AD 545, friends of King Totila set up such placards by night to chastise the Romans for their treachery towards the Goths. In the Renaissance it was big business; Pasquino could hold running dialogues with Rome's other 'talking' statues – 'Marforio', an old marble river god who now resides in the courtyard of the Capitoline Museum, and 'Madama Lucrezia', a cult figure of Isis moved in front of San Marco. One of their favourite subjects, understandably, was the insane acquisitiveness of the popes and cardinals – Pasquino once appeared with a tin cup, begging 'alms for the completion of the Palazzo Farnese', and when the Barberini pope, Urban VIII, robbed the Pantheon of its bronze ceiling, Pasquino remarked 'What the Barbarians didn't do, the Barberini did' ('Quod non fecerunt barbari fecerunt Barberini'). One irritated pope was ready to toss the statue in the Tiber, but thoughtfully refrained when a subtle counsellor warned him that it would 'infect the very frogs, who would croak pasquinades day and night'.

Pasquino, best known for 'talking statues' that have contributed witty 'pasquinades' on current affairs since ancient times. Scholars believe this talkative, though faceless fellow was originally a statue of Menelaus or some other Homeric hero that once decorated Domitian's circus. Apart from the occasional teenage revolutionary manifesto plastered to his base, and graffiti sprayed on the wall behind, Pasquino hasn't had much to say lately – just when Rome needs him most.

Santa Maria della Pace G7

Vicolo del Arco della Pace 5, t 06 686 1156. *Open Mon and Fri 10–4, Tues–Thurs 9–12.*

On a quiet alley just west of Piazza Navona is one of the most original architectural projects ever attempted (and never finished) in Rome. Santa Maria della Pace contains great works by Raphael galore, recently restored.

The church was founded by Sixtus IV in 1484. In 1656, Pope Alexander VII commissioned Pietro da Cortona to redo the façade and the surrounding piazza; the exuberant ceiling painter gave him a plan that was startling, even eccentric. The asymmetric piazza was never completed, but the church façade itself, with its clever interplay of concave and convex forms, is enough to give an idea of Da Cortona's intentions. The small space in front of S. Maria succeeds as well as any church in Rome in creating the 'stage set' effect the decorous Baroque age strove for. The cloister was Bramante's first work in Rome, cool, restrained and quintessentially Renaissance. Inside, Raphael's *Sibyls* grace the Chigi chapel and delicate stuccoes by Da Sangallo the Younger frame the Cesi chapel. Above the high altar is a fresco of the *Virgin with SS. Bridget and Catherine* by Peruzzi.

Santa Maria dell'Anima G7

Via della Pace 24, t 06 686 4160; bus 116, 204, 492. Open 7.30–1 and 2–6.

Just around the corner from S. Maria della Pace, the German national church in Rome sports a ponderous façade by Giuliano da Sangallo, uncle of the more famous Antonio. Being German did not save it from the Lutheran Landsknechten during the sack of

1527; the church was burned, only a few years after Sangallo finished it, and most of what you see now was done in the 1800s. To get inside, go around the back to no.20 Via della Pace, where a door leads into a small courtyard; the church entrance is across it.

This church, too, has one real attraction: Baldassare Peruzzi's excellent Renaissance *Tomb of Hadrian VI*, the dour reforming pope from Utrecht who delighted the Romans by lasting only one year. It stands just to the right of the altar, near a faded fresco of the *Holy Family* by Giulio Romano; almost all the rest of the interior is from the 19th century.

NORTH OF PIAZZA NAVONA

Via dei Coronari F–G7

Bus 30, 70, 81, 87, 116, 116T, 186, 204, 492, 628.

Lined with antique and artisans' shops selling everything from Baroque cherubs to Tiffany lamps, this ancient street, redesigned (like the Via Giulia) under Julius II, is worth a look. Like the other streets leading to the Tiber and the Vatican City in this neighbourhood, it has its share of Renaissance buildings, including the one at no.122 that once belonged to the painter Raphael. Halfway down this street, **San Salvatore in Lauro** (F7) has a strikingly original late Renaissance design (1584) and a fine cloister; its later interior shows gilded featherish capitals and a black *Madonna and Child* wrapped in an embroidered gown.

Via dell'Orso G–H7

Bus 70, 86, 87, 116, 116T, 204, 492.

One of the most picturesque corners of old Rome is Via dell'Orso, with the medieval Frangipane Tower (G7) and its trailing vines. The tower is better known in the neighbourhood as the **Torre della Scimmia**, or 'Monkey Tower', after a pet chimp of the 18th century who picked up his master's newborn baby

and climbed to the top. The family promised the Virgin Mary a candle burning for ever if only she would talk this midget King Kong into coming down – of course she did, and you can see the candle today on the little shrine up on the tower.

The church in the middle of this narrow lane is **Sant'Antonio dei Portoghesi** (H7), with one of Rome's most lavish Baroque interiors, heavily encrusted with precious marbles and ornate gilding. Along Via dell'Orso, note the antique sculptural fragments – lions and hares – built into the old houses. At the end of the street, a restaurant called the **Osteria dell'Orso** (G7) keeps up the name and occupies the building of what long ago was Rome's best-known hotel, host to many famous figures in the 17th and 18th centuries; the building dates from 1460, and it has been imaginatively restored.

Piazza di Ponte Umberto (G7), up the steps, has a view across the Tiber of the extravagantly awful Palazzo della Giustizia and up towards the Vatican and Castel Sant'Angelo.

Museo Napoleonico G7

Piazza di Ponte Umberto 1, t 06 6880 6286; bus 70, 81, 87, 186, 492. Open Tues–Sat 9–7, Sun 9–1; adm €2.50.

This palace home of one of Rome's smallest museums contains a weird collection of family memorabilia and neoclassical bric-a-brac, including portraits by David and Gerard, sculptures by Canova and Thorvaldsen, political cartoons, gowns, cameos, board games sent to the Emperor on St Helena, and a hopeful drawing of 'St Napoleon' made for his mum, who like any Italian mother knew her son deserved canonization at the very least. The little imperialist, for his part, found the concept of Rome as irresistible as its art treasures were portable; he dubbed his baby eaglet the King of Rome, and you can see his milk teeth here, along with some sketches donated by a later owner to Mussolini. One room is dedicated to the family Venus, Pauline Bonaparte Borghese. It displays her little shoes and a cast of her shapely breast.

PIAZZA NAVONA TO THE PANTHEON

Palazzo Madama G–H7

Corso del Rinascimento, t 06 67061,
w www.senato.it/senato.htm; bus 70, 81, 87,
116, 186, 204, 492. Open for guided visits in
Italian first Sat of the month 10–6; adm free.

The history of this big frowsy block is typical of a Roman palace; a papal treasurer bought up the property in the late 1400s, including a tower fortress of the ancient Crescenzi family, and converted the whole into a single structure. Later the Orsini picked it up, and lost it as part of the dowry when Lorenzo de' Medici married Clarice Orsini. Their son, Giovanni, lived here briefly before becoming Pope Leo X (a Roman mob sacked it upon news of his election). Emperor Charles V parked one of his illegitimate daughters here, Margaret of Parma; as a love child, the only title this girl had was Madama – hence the palace's name. Later owners, in the 1700s, tacked on the inevitable assembly-line Baroque façade (facing Corso del Rinascimento), though the part overlooking Via della Dogana Vecchia sports natty hula-hooped columns and miserable masks. As with most Roman palaces, nobody gives it a second look today, except maybe to admire the overdressed Carabinieri at the entrances. For Madama's palace was the property of the Pope in 1870, and the new Italian state was happy to snatch it up. It's been the home of the Italian Senate ever since. If you do venture inside, you can see some of the richly decorated rooms the senators use, and the senate library, which holds 500,000 volumes.

Sant'Ivo G–H8

Palazzo della Sapienza, Corso del
Rinascimento 40, t 06 686 4987; bus 70, 81, 87,
116, 186, 492. Open Sept–June Sat 9–12 and
5–7; Sun am for Mass.

The Palazzo della Sapienza, next to the Palazzo Madama, was home to Rome's old papal university, founded in 1303 as the 'Archiginnasio Romano'. Tourists have been overlooking it for 300 years, little suspecting that one of the most imaginative pieces of Baroque excess in Italy is concealed in its Renaissance courtyard: Borromini's master-piece, the church of Sant'Ivo (1642–50).

Giacomo della Porta designed the court-yard, and also contributed the façade of Sant'Ivo, at its far end, but everything behind it is Borromini's; a unique, hexagonal chapel topped by a swirling spiral lantern. There's a little obscure symbolism: the hexagon is supposed to recall the bee symbol of the Barberinis, in honour of Borromini's employer, Urban VIII. In its present state, painted a uniform dull white, Sant'Ivo loses much in first impressions. What remains is the bare bones of Borromini's remarkable geometrical conception, a complex space unified by a repetition of rhythms in threes – architecture in waltz time.

San Luigi dei Francesi H7

Piazza di San Luigi dei Francesi, t 06 688 271;
bus 81, 87, 116, 186. Open Fri–Wed 7.30–12.30
and 3.30–7, Thurs 7.30–12.30 only.

The French national church in Rome, designed, like the exterior of Sant'Ivo, by Giacomo della Porta (c.1520), was begun at the time when France was contending the domination of all Italy with Spain, and both nations were working hard to expand their influence in every sphere. A thorough plas-tering of late Baroque inside leaves little but historical associations to attract a visit; there are French memorials everywhere, including Renaissance frescoes on the conversion of Clovis and the Franks, and a big slab in the south aisle for the troops who fell attacking Garibaldi and the Roman Republic in 1849 (Rome never bears grudges).

Like so many of Rome's smaller churches, this one has one real attraction: three paint-ings by Caravaggio on the *Vocation,* *Inspiration and Martyrdom of St Matthew,* all recently restored. As always, when you hear the name Caravaggio you should check your pockets to see if you have change for the lighting machine. These works were done late in the artist's career, about 1600; only a few islands of light in the surrounding blackness are enough to make the austere figures into something magical (especially the *Vocation*, in which Matthew hears the call while collecting taxes).

Sant'Agostino H7

Piazza Sant'Agostino, t 06 6880 1962; bus 70, 87, 116, 186, 204. Open 7.45–12 and 4.30–6.30.

The plain Renaissance Sant' Agostino (1480s) is a church with two great works. On the third column of the left nave, the portrait of *Isaiah* is one of the most powerful works of Raphael (1512). The other prophets, and most of the rest of the abundant frescoes, are by a 19th-century Roman artist named Gagliardi. Beneath Isaiah, there is a fine statue of the *Madonna with St Anne* by Sansovino, and the first chapel on the left aisle has another fine Caravaggio, the *Madonna of Loreto*. Before you leave, don't miss the Junoesque *Madonna del Parto* against the back wall, credited with the power to help women conceive and give birth. It's inevitably surrounded by glinting ex-votos and vases of fresh flowers from those she's helped.

Sant'Eustachio H8

Piazza Sant'Eustachio, t 06 686 5334. Open 9–12 and 3.30–8.

The church of Sant'Eustachio, with the bronze stag's head on top, suffered a Baroque makeover in the 1700s, but keeps its campanile of 1196. One of the first Roman martyrs, St Eustace was a soldier who, while hunting, had a vision of the Holy Cross – between the antlers of a stag, like St Hubert of France.

The giant **fountain basin** on the western edge of Piazza Sant'Eustachio came from the Baths of Caracalla. It may seem sleepy enough now, but in the Middle Ages this piazza was a busy market right in the centre

of Rome. Sometime in the 1300s the area became headquarters for the English community in Rome. Sant'Eustachio was one of their churches; the other, its outlandish cupola peeking over the square, was Sant'Ivo.

PIAZZA DELLA ROTONDA

The Pantheon H8

Piazza della Rotonda, t 06 6830 0230; bus 64, 70, 75, 119. Open Mon–Sat 8.30–7.30, Sun 9–6.

Originally the centrepiece of one of the first and largest imperial building complexes, the Pantheon survives as the best-preserved, most perfect major monument of the ancient world.

In Republican days, the *Saepta* (roughly the area between the Pantheon and Via Sant'Ignazio) was the part of the *Campus Martius* where citizens came to cast their votes in the annual elections. The building complex, begun in the reign of Augustus by his great general Cornelius Agrippa, included the Baths of Agrippa (south of the Pantheon), basilicas, porticos and temples, as well as a part of the *Saepta* preserved as an enclosed park.The emperors made it into Rome's favourite promenade, with famous gardens and a lagoon, surrounded by a portico that sheltered Rome's classier art auctioneers and antique dealers, and opened into the Temple of Minerva, libraries and the Temple of Isis.

Despite the inscription mentioning Agrippa on the pediment, the Pantheon as we see it today was almost entirely reconstructed under Hadrian in AD 128. The 2nd-century writer Dio Cassius leaves us a rather cryptic anecdote concerning Hadrian: as a youth, the future emperor could not resist butting in with his opinions whenever Trajan and Apollodorus were discussing their new building programmes. On one occasion, the great architect from Damascus is reported to have told Hadrian to 'go off and draw pumpkins'. Perhaps this is exactly what he did –

tradition has it that Hadrian contributed the basic plan for the remodelled Pantheon.

Though certainly built to last, its survival to our day is a result of two strokes of good luck: first, being converted to a Christian church in 609 (the first time a pagan temple was converted in Rome) and second, in 734, when Pope Gregory III had the good sense to plate the concrete dome with lead.

Originally, the dome was glittering gilded bronze inside and out. Byzantine Emperor Constans II, passing through in 667, stole the exterior plating and most of the rest of the bronze statues and fittings in Rome – to be melted down into coins in Constantinople.

In the Dark Ages, when so much else was lost, the Pantheon became an important symbol to the Romans of their ancient greatness; the popes always took good care of it, even in the worst of times. Today, though hardly ever used for services, the Pantheon is still officially a church – S. Maria ad Martyres.

Before going inside, consider the virtuoso architectural tricks incorporated by Hadrian's architects. At first sight, the building may seem perilously unsound; there is no way a simple brick cylindrical wall could support such a heavy, shallow dome; obviously the whole thing should have tumbled down long ago. The explanation lies in the uniquely elegant design; the exterior dome really isn't a dome at all – the real one is hiding underneath, a perfect hemisphere of cast concrete that rests on a solid ring wall over 22ft thick. It was the biggest piece of concrete ever attempted before the 20th century. The ribbed dome you see outside consists of simple courses of cantilevered brick, effectively almost weightless.

A portico of colossal granite columns (used as a fishmarket in the Middle Ages) leads to a pair of equally huge bronze doors – Hadrian's originals, restored in the 1560s. No matter how many times you've seen it in pictures, the interior of the Pantheon remains one of the most astounding sights of Rome, between the immense dome (140ft, slightly larger than St Peter's), the sunlight pouring through the oculus at the top, and the rich coloured marble fittings below. No other ancient building in Italy has kept its interior so perfectly preserved. All that is missing are the original statues.

The building was planned as a meditation on the 12 Olympian gods of classical Greece; their images stood in the niches spaced along the circular wall, along with statues of Augustus and Hadrian, and in the centre, illuminated by the sun every afternoon around midsummer, that of Jove Ultor, the Avenging Jupiter, patron of Augustus' methodical revenge for his adoptive father Caesar. (If this book were being written in Hadrian's time, we would call attention to the statue of Venus, wearing two great English pearls that Caesar once gave to Cleopatra for earrings.)

As it is, the interior has enough to say about Roman opulence in the palmy days of empire – one suspects that every director of Roman costume epics since Cecil B. De Mille has drawn some inspiration from it.

After Constans, the Pantheon's worst enemy in its nearly two millennia of existence was Gianlorenzo Bernini, who talked Pope Urban VIII into letting him loot the bronze ceiling for the gaudy baldachin he was planning for the high altar of St Peter's – supposedly there was enough left over to make the Pope 60 new cannons. As if that were not indignity enough for the old temple, Bernini was sure he could improve the work of Hadrian's architects by adding a pair of Baroque spires flanking the dome; 'Bernini's asses' ears', as they were known to generations of Romans, were removed in a restoration of 1883.

Not much inside the Pantheon would make you think it was still a church, although there is an *Annunciation* attributed to Melozzo da Forlì to the left of the entrance. Over the years there was a half-hearted plan to make the place into a pantheon of famous Italians; around the walls you will see the tombs of Raphael, Baldassare Peruzzi, and Italy's first kings, Vittorio Emanuele II and Umberto I.

Outside the Pantheon, in one of old Rome's prettiest and most characteristic squares, there are two popular cafés where you can contemplate the famous façade. The obligatory **obelisk** in the centre, erected in 1575, was another find from that Temple of Isis – originally the complex may have had a dozen of them. Isis, the transcendent Egyptian goddess, always had plenty of devotees in Rome (Apuleius' *Golden Ass* was written in her honour); one of the most fervent was the Emperor Domitian, who built the temple, roughly where nearby Piazza del Collegio Romano is today.

Santa Maria sopra Minerva H8

*Piazza della Minerva, t 06 679 1217; **bus** 62, 63, 81, 85, 95, 117, 175, 204, 492. **Church open** daily 7–7; **cloister open** Mon–Sat 8–1 and 4–7.*

Just south of the Pantheon off Via dei Cestari, this was the Florentine church in Rome, and the dowdy austerity of its exterior is as evocative of the Florentine sensibility as the quirky Gothic inside. Fra Ristoro and Fra Sisto, architects of Florence's great S. Maria Novella, built it in the same style, beginning in the 1280s.

The church's name refers to the temple of Minerva that occupied the spot before the original Santa Maria was built, in the 9th century. Besides its Florentine links, this was the church of the Dominicans, and of the Inquisition; the 'monks of the Minerva' were as dear to the Romans as toothache, and on several occasions in the 1500s the church and its adjacent monastery (where Galileo was tried) only narrowly escaped destruction at the hands of a mob.

The Gothic interior should not be taken too seriously; much of it was redone in a fanciful 1840s restoration. In any case it's almost unique in Rome, a city that has entertained no Gothic thoughts since Alaric and Totila.

In the left aisle, third chapel, is a small altarpiece, perhaps the work of Perugino. The best art is in the transepts, with solid ranks of chapels along the east wall in the Florentine manner: in the 2nd left of the altar, the delicate *Tomb of Giovanni Arberini*, by that much-neglected quattrocento

sculptor Agostino di Duccio; the central relief, a battle of Hercules with the Nemean lion, is thought to be an ancient Roman work. Just left of the altar is the **Tomb of Fra Angelico**, Dominican monk and great Florentine artist who died in Rome in 1455.

Leo X and Clement VII, the Medici popes, are buried in the apse, although unless you dare pass behind the altar, you can only just glimpse their tombs. Both contributed much to the decoration of this church, and not surprisingly at least one of their commissions went to Florentine Michelangelo; his *Christ Bearing the Cross*, near the altar, is a memorable work, with Michelangelesque intensity and none of the neurotic excess.

Under the altar is buried St Catherine of Siena, who persuaded Pope Gregory XI to return to Rome from Avignon in 1377, ending the 'Babylonian Captivity' and rescuing Rome from its most serious period of decline.

In the 2nd chapel of the right transept, the Carafa Chapel, you can pay your respects to the foulest, bloodiest pope of them all, Paul IV (1555–9), father of the Inquisition. Besides the pope's tomb, there is some fine quattrocento decorative sculptural work by Mino da Fiesole and Verrocchio (both Florentines) and above all the great series of frescoes on the *Life of St Thomas Aquinas* by Filippino Lippi (1480s), his best work outside Florence.

On the wall to the left of the chapel, Giovanni Cosmati contributed one of the loveliest – and seemingly most comfortable – tombs any cleric has ever enjoyed. But for the golden mosaic of the Madonna, it would be easy to mistake this precocious work, the *Tomb of Guillaume Durand* (1296), for something from the best of the Renaissance.

Outside the church, in Piazza della Minerva, is a work of Bernini (1667), a winsome, grinning elephant supporting on its back a modest Egyptian obelisk (H8), found in the ruins of the Temple of Isis (another of its relics is the little stone cat perched high on a building around the corner, giving Via della Gatta its name). Supposedly this elephant is Bernini's tribute to the wisdom of his patron, Pope Alexander VI.

CORSO VITTORIO EMANUELE

Sant'Andrea della Valle G8

Piazza Sant'Andrea della Valle, t 06 686 1339; **bus** *40, 46, 62, 64.* **Open** *8–12 and 4.30–7.*

This Counter-Reformation showpiece was begun in 1591. A number of architects had a hand in it before its completion in the 1660s: Carlo Maderno designed the dome, Rome's second-tallest, and also the fountain across the way, while the general plan was by Giacomo della Porta. The rhythmic façade from the 1660s is by Carlo Rainaldi, perhaps after Maderno's original design.

Under Maderno's big dome, Giovanni Lanfranco pointed the way to the ceiling pyrotechnics of later Roman churches with his frantic fresco of the *Virgin in Glory* (1625–7). Few of the hundreds of contorted figures in it can still be made out. At about the same time, Domenichino contributed the *Four Evangelists* at the dome's pendentives, and scenes from the *Life of St Andrew* (whose innovative crucifixion contributed the saltire cross to the Union Jack) around the apse. Two popes are buried here, Pius II (d.1464) and III (d.1503), both of the Piccolomini family in Siena, and both great patrons of the arts – after the work they commissioned all over Tuscany, their simple tombs on the walls at the end of the nave seem hardly fitting.

Around the corner, on Piazza Vidoni, one of Rome's four 'talking statues', **Abate Luigi**, is dwarfed by the wall of the church.

Palazzo Massimo alle Colonne G8

Corso Vittorio Emanuele 141; **bus** *30, 40, 46, 62, 63, 64, 70, 81, 87, 186, 492, 628, 810, 916.* **Open** *16 Mar only 7–1;* **adm** *free.*

Baldassare Peruzzi's masterpiece of 1536 follows the curve of what was once the Odeon, built by Domitian as part of his stadium complex (*see* Piazza Navona, p.82). Blackened as it is by the traffic soot, it's hard to appreciate this unusual design, created for a haughty, murderous family that claimed to trace its nobility back to ancient Rome. The squat Doric columns around the entrance, and the ornate windows, make this one of the most idiosyncratic palaces in Rome, one more admired than really influential in its time. It's open once a year to celebrate the anniversary of a miracle of San Filippo Neri in the 16th century. Inside the palazzo there's a chapel dedicated to the saint with a painting by Pomarancio which recounts the miracle.

San Pantaleo G8

Corso Vittorio Emanuele (opposite Via dei Baullari); **bus** *30, 40, 46, 62, 63, 64, 70, 81, 87, 186, 492, 628, 810, 916.* **Open** *for Mass.*

The church with the blank 19th-century façade next to the Palazzo Massimo is dedicated to San Pantaleo (or Pantaleone), Rome's answer to Naples' famous patron, San Gennaro. Like Gennaro, Pantaleo left a phial of his blood that miraculously liquefies and boils every year, on 27 July; you can see it inside the church. But what really makes Neapolitans envious is Pantaleo's habit of giving out lottery numbers. Pray to the saint alone, in your bedroom, for three nights; on the third night, leave a pencil and paper on the nightstand, and during the night the portly saint will climb through your window and write down a winning number – but being the prankster he is, he'll hide it carefully somewhere in the house.

Museo di Roma a Palazzo Braschi G8

Piazza San Pantaleo 10, **t** *06 687 5880;* **bus** *40, 46, 62, 64, 116.* **Reopens** *after more than 10 years of restoration in 2002; call for times.*

The collection in this recently restored museum is a fine one, and includes portraits, old views of the city, and pieces of demolished buildings (including such surprises as mosaics from the original St Peter's). The building that houses the museum, the

Palazzo Braschi (c.1795), is notable only as the last big family palace to be built on the profits of the papacy. By the early 1700s, large-scale papal graft was a dying tradition, but Gianangelo Braschi of Cesena, as Pius VI, revived the old style just in time for the French Revolution; his comeuppance came in 1798, when Napoleon's troops packed him off to exile in France. Exhibitions are frequently held here; watch for posters at the entrance.

Piccola Farnesina e Museo Barracco G8

Corso Vittorio Emanuele 166, t 06 6880 6848; bus 40, 46, 62, 64, 116, 116T. Open Tues–Sun 9–7; adm €2.50.

The heraldic lilies on the decoration of this elegant, complex building by Antonio da Sangallo the Younger (an excellent Tuscan Renaissance architect, who also gave Rome the nearby Palazzo Farnese – *see* below), similar to those on the arms of the Farnese, gave the palace its familiar, entirely mistaken name, the Piccola Farnesina – in fact they are emblems of the French cardinal who had the place built in 1523.

Today the building is the Museo Barracco, an important collection of classical sculpture, assembled by a private collector, Senator Giovanni Barracco, who gave it to the city. It contains more great sculpture from ancient Greece than any other in Rome (except the Vatican), along with Egyptian works, Assyrian reliefs, Roman and early Christian art.

Palazzo della Cancelleria G8

Corso Vittorio Emanuele at Piazza della Cancelleria, t 06 6989 3405; bus 40, 46, 62, 63, 64, 70, 81, 87, 186, 492. Open for visits by reservation at least one month in advance.

Many have judged this palazzo, which dates from the 1480s, to be the best palace in Rome, though no one knows for sure which architects should have the credit; it is believed Bramante had some hand in designing the stately double arcade of the courtyard. Cardinal Raffaele Riario, nephew of Pope Sixtus IV, won the money to build it in one night's card playing. His luck must have turned on him; a later pope acquired the place soon after, and used it as a home for the papal government bureaucracy; the Cancelleria still houses Vatican offices, and can be visited only by special arrangement, although you can have a peek at the courtyard from Piazza della Cancelleria.

Chiesa Nuova or Santa Maria in Vallicella F–G8

Corso Vittorio Emanuele at Piazza della Chiesa Nuova; bus 40, 6, 62, 64, 98. Open 8–12 and 4.30–7.

Gregory XIII, in 1575, had this church rebuilt for St Philip Neri, the unconventional, irascible holy man who has been declared Patron Saint of Rome. Founder of the Roman Oratory, Philip was quite a character, with something of the Zen Buddhist in him, a remarkable contrast with the iron clerics and inquisitors who dominated Rome in that grim age. He forbade his followers any sort of philosophical speculation or dialectic, instead making them sing and write poetry. Two of his favourite pastimes were insulting the pope and embarrassing initiates, making them walk through Rome with foxtails sewn to their coats to learn humility.

Inevitably, Philip's sincere faith and modesty were translated into Roman monumentality. Neither the church nor its decoration is especially noteworthy, except perhaps the ceiling frescoes by Pietro da Cortona: the *Life and Apotheosis of Aeneas*, of all subjects, in diaphanous Baroque pastels. The sacristan might show you more works by Da Cortona, as well as Rubens and Guido Reni, in the sacristy and in St Philip's rooms nearby. This church perhaps represents the gentler side of the Counter-Reformation, a proto-Baroque version of the spacious, simple Franciscan buildings of the 1200s, built for praying and singing; the most prominent features are the two glorious gilt organs on either side of the nave.

Murder at the Vanities

The oddly shaped block at the south-western end of Campo de' Fiori is built directly over the ruins of **Pompey's Theatre**, the first permanent theatre building in Rome, and part of a complex that stretched all the way to Largo Argentina.

There's nothing to see of it, unless you dine in the cellar of Da Pancrazio or stay at the Hotel Teatro di Pompeo, both built among the foundation stones. Via di Grotta Pinta, bounded by a tall, curving wall, was roughly the *orchestra*, and the curve around Via del Biscione follows the outer boundary of the *cavea*, the semicircle of seats, with room for perhaps as many as 40,000.

Greek theatre was still something of a novelty when Pompey returned from the east after mopping up the Cilician pirates in 61 BC. But drama could wait – apparently the opening of the place included games where 500 lions were slaughtered. Some drama was undoubtedly seen, although in the later empire novel abominations were developed for the delectation of the well-to-do crowds: one-man celebrity shows with a little cross-dressing, nudity and stylized live sex, eastern music and grand panache at the finale; or perhaps the ancient snuff shows, plays where condemned criminals took the part of those about to die and were really killed on stage. One of the few plays that could still draw an audience in imperial times was Catullus' *Laureolus*, if only because the villain got tortured and crucified at the end. Usually the drama was chopped down to mere vignettes, to allow more time for the torturing. When wealthy refugees from the first sack of Rome, in 410, arrived at Carthage, their first thought, according to the chroniclers, was of what was on at the theatres.

In Pompey's time, the prudish Republic had an ordinance against permanent theatres. Pompey got round it by dedicating the entire construction as a temple; in fact, he built a small **Temple of the Victorious Venus** right on top of the seats, above the site where the modern Farnese Theatre (on Campo de' Fiori) grinds out its second-run thrillers. The complex included a quadrangle that extended as far as the Republican temples on Largo Argentina. Somewhere in this complex (perhaps where the Teatro Argentina stands now, or around the corner at Via del Sudario and Via Monte della Farina), Pompey built a small meeting hall. In the spring of 44 BC, while the Senate House in the Forum was undergoing restoration, the Senate met here – it was the spot where Caesar was murdered.

Adjacent to the church, most of the large complex of the Philippine fathers was designed by Borromini, including a pretty clock tower and the idiosyncratic façade of the **Philippine Oratory**, where Philip's congregation held its concerts and where the musical form known as the oratorio was developed. Today the complex houses the **Biblioteca Vallicelliana**, the greatest library for Rome's history and antiquities.

CAMPO DE' FIORI

The lower half of the *Campus Martius*, south of Corso Vittorio, is a cheerful warren of twisting, ochre alleys, crowded with market barrows and Baroque baubles, noisy children, convivial trattorias and antique restorers sanding frilly old tallboys in front of their tiny shops. It's one of the liveliest parts of Rome, although the serene and aristocratic environs of the Piazza Farnese and Via Giulia are just a minute away.

Campo de' Fiori G8

Bus 116, 116T.

It's 7.30am, as the slick Italian TV interviewer sticks his microphone into the face of a tired old woman, asking cheerfully: 'What are these you're selling, signora?' 'Christ!,' she replies, 'they're tomatoes; haven't you ever seen tomatoes before?' It isn't easy being the last bastion of reality in a deranged town like Rome, but Campo de' Fiori carries on as best it can. The food is good and fresh, and the neighbourhood folk – young trendies, foreigners, honest workmen, or 10th-generation Roman poor who only hang on here because of rent control – really appreciate it. Negotiate some mussels and spiralling Roman broccoli, if you've got a kitchen, or else watch the locals do it.

This is a good democratic piazza, although in the bad old days the popes used it as the site for the execution of heretics. In its centre stands a statue of **Giordano Bruno**, the foolhardy scholar, alleged spy and avowed natural magician, one of the first to take the new Copernican system to its logical extremes. After travelling through Europe, thoroughly confusing the English and French, he allowed himself to be captured by the Catholic secret police, and was burned at the stake in this square in 1600. It wasn't his scientific credo that got Bruno into trouble, contrary to popular belief, although they were mentioned in the indictment. The Church incinerated him for proposing a 'natural religion' that included both Christianity and magic. But as the hero of Italian freethinkers, he earned a monument from the new Italian kingdom directly after the liberation of Rome from papal rule.

Palazzo Farnese G9

*Piazza Farnese 67; bus 116, 116T. **Open** for group visits by arrangement with the cultural section of the French Embassy, **t** 06 6860 1414.*

Piazza Farnese, with its twin fountains spurting from giant Farnese lilies into ancient tubs taken from the Baths of Caracalla, is a perfect setting for the most magnificent of all High Renaissance palaces in Rome. Since the 1870s this has been the French Embassy, and special permission is required to get in.

Street, square and palace are all named after the most spectacularly rapacious predators that ever ruled papal Rome. Alessandro Farnese, the scion of an obscure noble family from northern Lazio, worked his way up through the church hierarchy in the late

1400s. His great good fortune was to have a willing and irresistible sister, Giulia (she of the famous nude statue in St Peter's). Alessandro set her up with Pope Alexander VI (the fellow buried around the corner) and the family's fortune was made. Unlike most of the families that built palaces with Church money, Farnese managed to begin his even before his election as Pope Paul III – on the income from his 16 absentee bishoprics.

When Alessandro became pope, Antonio da Sangallo had to modify the plans a bit; now there was booty enough to make the family hideaway the grandest palace in Europe. No expense of other people's money was spared; the builders looted tons of building stone from the Colosseum and other ancient ruins, while Pasquino and the other 'talking statues' were hung with endless *pasquinades* mocking a greed unheard of even in Rome. When Sangallo died, the vast pile was entrusted to Michelangelo, who continued the imperiously elegant design on the upper storey and added the heavy cornice.

Among the works of art inside that you may never get to see is a famous series of mythological frescoes by Annibale Carracci, one of the masterpieces of late Mannerism (finished 1603). These vigorous scenes, variations on the theme of all-conquering love, were considered by Italians of the Baroque centuries to be among the greatest paintings of all time. If you look up from the square on evenings when the French Embassy is entertaining, you can glimpse the frescoes through the illuminated first-floor windows.

The little **archway** over Via Giulia (G9) at the back of the palace is also Michelangelo's, an approach to the bridge Farnese intended to build across the Tiber, connecting the palace with Villa Farnesina in Trastevere.

Not content with two sumptuous palaces in Rome, Alessandro and his successors planted others all over Italy, including a truly colossal one in Caprarola, north of Rome. They also extracted a duchy for themselves out of the Papal State, that of Parma. This particular Farnese palace was not complete until 1589; after 1635 there were no Farnese around to enjoy it, and the place passed into the hands of the Bourbons.

While the Farnese inhabited it, this palace and square were the epicentre of aristocratic Rome; the family staged every sort of spectacle for the entertainment of the Romans: masques and mock triumphs, bullfights, water pageants, even races of carnival floats pulled by water buffaloes. It still looks the part – the most elegant Renaissance backdrop in Rome.

Palazzo Spada G9

Piazza Capo di Ferro 13; **w** *www.galleria borghese.it;* **bus** *23, 116, 116T, 280.* **Open** *Tues–Sat 9–7.30, Sun 9–6.30;* **adm** *€5.*

For anyone who feels obliged to see just one of the patrician art collections of Rome, this might be the one. Built in 1540 for a wealthy cardinal, the palace was picked up by an even wealthier one in the 1600s: Bernardino Spada, who left the collection and gave the building its current name. Most of the palace is now home to the Italian Council of State.

You can't miss this palace – it has the most outrageously ornate façade in Rome, guarded by a row of statues representing antique Roman worthies, interspersed with reliefs of dogs gazing fondly at posts. The lovely courtyard is decorated by some excellent, fanciful reliefs of mythological scenes (maybe the work of an undeservedly obscure Renaissance artist named Giulio Mazzoni) and by bored Carabinieri posing for each other. Look official enough, and you can walk right past them, up the stairway on the right to Cardinal Spada's state rooms: a corridor with more stucco reliefs by Mazzoni, some delightful ceiling frescoes by Bolognese artists A. Mitelli and M. Colonna, and one room with decoration entirely devoted to a complex ceiling sundial that gives the time around the world, decipherable perhaps only if you have a good working knowledge of physics and Latin, but enjoyable in any case. **The Grand Council Chamber** has a statue of Pompey, according to legend the one from

Pompey's Theatre at the foot of which Julius Caesar was assassinated (*see* 'Murder at the Vanities', p.92).

In the garden courtyard just outside the entrance to the museum, Cardinal Spada's friend Borromini added the best visual trick of the century – better than Sant'Ignazio's *trompe l'oeil* ceiling – worth making a detour for even if the art collection leaves you cold. An opening in the walls reveals a long colonnade leading to a garden – walk down it and you will see that the passage is a quarter the length it appeared, and the statue at the vanishing point a fraction of the size you thought when you first saw it.

If you make it to the museum they may seem surprised to see you; visitors are often as rare as new acquisitions. The works are not labelled, but each room has a small stack of photocopied guides that can identify them for you. **Room I** is rather tiresome, with portraits more often than not of Cardinal Spada. **Room II** has more portraits, with a fine *Visitation* by Andrea del Sarto (which makes a fascinating comparison with the more famous *Visitation* by his pupil, Pontormo), some works of Renaissance painters from Umbria (rare in Rome) and a Titian or two.

Room III has the Baroque art, more portraits of Spada and ancient Roman sculpture; much more interesting, though, are the terrestrial and celestial globes of the famous Dutch astronomer and geographer Caelius (1622), a complete compendium of the increased knowledge gained from Galileo and the Age of Exploration. **Room IV** holds the best pictures: the classicizing work of Orazio Gentileschi and his precocious daughter Artemisia (a follower of Caravaggio who contributes a fine *Santa Cecilia*); some naive but historically informative paintings by an earnest Baroque genre painter, Michelangelo Cerquozzi (*Masaniello's Revolt in Naples*); and best of all a relief of *Divine and Profane Love* by François Duquesnoy, an artist to look out for, one of the few in Rome to maintain the early Renaissance's common sense and line in the miasma of the Baroque.

Via Giulia F7–G9

This street provides a lesson in the subtler mood of the Renaissance aesthetic. Pope Julius II laid it out in 1508 and naturally named it after himself; long before Corso Vittorio Emanuele was dreamed of, Via Giulia was intended to be the main route from the centre of Rome to St Peter's. Bramante planned it, straight and narrow, in contrast to the winding lanes of the medieval city, and every future architect kept closely to the restrained, classical air of the developing streetscape. Via Giulia's landmark is the archway from the Palazzo Farnese, covered in vines and neatly dividing the street in two.

Santa Maria dell'Orazione e della Morte G9
Via Giulia, t 06 6880 2715; bus 23, 116, 116T, 280, 870. Open Sept–June Sun 4–7.

Near the arch, you'll see this church with its lovely 1737 façade by Ferdinando Fuga, the Rococo follower of Borromini. The Compagnia della Buona Morte, a confraternity dedicated to burials of the poor, had its headquarters here. Near the entrance, with its cheerful sculptural work, notice the *sgraffito* plaque with the coin slot and the leering skeleton; the inscription invites contributions for 'the poor snatched up in the Campagna' during the plague of 1694.

Fountains, Palaces and Prisons
Museum of Criminology open Tues, Wed and Fri 9–1, Tues and Thurs 2.30–6.30; adm €2.

A little further down the street is the outlandish fountain called the **Mascherone**, with a big grotesque face and basin recovered from an ancient fountain.

Many among the newly rich of the papal elite built palaces along Via Giulia, along with some of the more fashionable artists, such as Raphael. At **no.79** is the house Sangallo the Younger built for himself; before the unification of Italy it served as Tuscan Embassy. Like the other palaces, **no.52** (corner of Via del Gonfalone) has iron grilles on the windows – a fashion that probably came from Spain. This one, however, has some

excuse for them, being the Model Prison built in the 1650s. There is a **Museum of Criminology** inside (G9), full of old papal torture instruments and suchlike.

Sant'Eligio degli Orafi F8
Via di Sant'Eligio 8/a, t 06 686 8260; bus 23, 280. Open Mon and Tues 10–12.30, Thurs and Fri 3–5; ring bell at no.7 or no.9 to visit during these hours.

Still the property of the Roman goldsmiths, who built it in 1516, this church's original design, an austere Greek-cross plan, is attributed to Raphael, perhaps his only foray into architecture. Baldassare Peruzzi and others saw it through completion.

Santa Maria di Monserrato F8
Via di Monserrato, t 06 688 9651; bus 116, 116T. Open during Mass on Sunday.

The Spanish Borgia pope, Alexander VI, is buried in this work by Sangallo the Younger, along with Alfonso XIII, the king who went into exile when the Spanish Republic was declared in 1931.

San Giovanni dei Fiorentini F8
Largo dei Fiorentini, t 06 6889 2059; bus 23, 116, 116T, 280, 870. Open daily 7–7.

As the name suggests, this was the Florentine church in Rome. It was begun by the Medici Pope Leo X. Now that the restoration of the façade is complete, be sure not to miss the jiving ecclesiasts balancing on its cornice. It's a stately enough building, though something of a hotchpotch of all the architects who had a hand in it: Jacopo Sansovino, Sangallo the Younger, and Della Porta among others spent time trying to satisfy their fickle papal patrons. Ironically, for all that Florentine artists contributed to Rome's High Renaissance, this church has not one work worth a detour inside.

Casa Crivelli F8
Via dei Banchi Vecchi 24; bus 40, 46, 62, 64.

This small palace, on a street lined with antique shops, is familiarly known to Romans as the 'Doll's House' for its decorations: relief grotesques and trophies – armoured torsos on sticks, the sort of bizarre, arrogant imperial art you would associate with the reign of Charles V. And indeed, the owner of the house decorated it in honour of the emperor's visit to Rome in 1538.

LARGO DI TORRE ARGENTINA AND PIAZZA DEL GESÙ

Largo Argentina H8

Tram 8, bus 40, 46, 62, 63, 64, 70, 81, 186, 204, 492.

A tidy row of **Republican-era temples** was unearthed and partially restored in this square in the 1920s. It is a good pile of ruins to explore with your eyes, entirely visible below you, although never open. It isn't hard to see the difference between the pavement of travertine, added by Emperor Domitian after a fire in AD 80, and the earlier surface of brownish tufa from about 240 BC.

Looking west down Corso Vittorio towards the Vatican, and starting from the right by the bus stops: a temple of Juturna, dedicated during the Punic Wars, and converted to a church of St Nicholas in the Middle Ages (now demolished); behind it are ruins of a monumental public latrine of the Imperial age (toilets like this had plenty of marble, but no stalls; the uninhibited gentlemen of ancient Rome liked to relax and talk over business while they unburdened themselves); next, a small building with the offices of the water authorities and the *Annona*, the distributors of public grain; then a round temple of Fortune, dedicated after the defeat of the last Celtic raiders in 101 BC; next, furthest to the left, is the oldest, a small temple of Feronia from the 4th century BC; lastly, a modest domestic temple to the Lari Permarini dedicated in 179 BC. Part of it is still buried under adjacent Via Florida.

The **Torre Papita**, a medieval tower fortress, was discovered among the old buildings demolished in the 1920s, restored and rebuilt on the edge of the site.

On the west side of the square, the **Teatro Argentina** H8, built in 1732 and much restored since, has witnessed the first performances of many great operas. Rossini's *Barber of Seville* flopped badly here on the first night, in 1816, driving the composer to despair in his nearby lodgings; he didn't know that his enemy, Pauline Bonaparte, had packed the house with hecklers. The second night, however, the audience changed its mind, and went in a body to Rossini's house, in a torchlight procession, to tell him how much they liked it. The Argentina hasn't been used for opera for years, but it plays an important role in Rome's theatre scene as the home of the Teatro di Roma repertory company.

Across Corso Vittorio Emanuele, you can have a look at the latest in clerical fashions and liturgical apparatus on **Via dei Cestari**. This has been the street of religious goods shops since the Middle Ages, although the smiling bambi-eyed mannequins dressed as nuns and the displays of the latest in convent nightwear are more recent innovations.

Fontana delle Tartarughe H9

Piazza Mattei; tram 8, bus 40, 46, 62, 63, 64, 70, 186, 204.

One of the prettiest and best-loved fountains of Rome. Too many cooks couldn't spoil this turtle broth; from an original design by Della Porta, Taddeo Landini sculpted the central figure; Bernini added the tortoises.

Santa Caterina dei Funari H9

Via dei Funari, t 06 678 5883; bus 40, 46, 62, 63, 64, 70, 186, 204. Open Mon 10–12, Thurs 2–4, Sun 10–12.30.

The outside of Santa Caterina boasts one of the most ornate of all 16th-century façades (by Guidetto Guidetti, 1564); inside are fancy frescoes to match, by Federico Zuccari and other virtuoso artists.

In a way, this neglected church is a landmark; better than any other in Rome, it can show you the fizzling out of the Renaissance, in a period when virtuosity came so easily that inspiration, even if such a thing were possible, was no longer much of a concern.

Theatre of Balbus H9

Via dei Caetani 6/c; **bus** *40, 46, 62, 63, 64, 70, 186, 204.*

On this quiet street, off Via delle Botteghe Oscure, a doorway leads into a courtyard with displays and archaeological plans of this 1st-century BC theatre complex, perpetually under excavation. Parts of the stage building are currently visible. Just south of

this on Via dei Caetani, you'll see a big bronze **plaque in honour of Aldo Moro,** the progressive prime minister kidnapped and murdered by the Red Brigades – perhaps on the orders of his Christian Democrat colleagues. The car containing Moro's body was discovered here in May 1978 after 55 days of captivity.

Il Gesù I8

Piazza del Gesù, **t** *06 697 001;* **bus** *40, 46, 62, 63, 64, 70, 81, 186, 492.* **Open** *7–12 and 3–7.30.*

This church, and the buildings on the piazza around it, were the original nerve centre of the Jesuits. An old Roman story has the Wind and the Devil out walking this way. In front of the Gesù, the Devil announces he

---

Mother of Harlots

Reading most historical accounts of the early Empire and the *pax Romana* – especially if written by an Italian – you would get the impression that Rome was doing the Mediterranean world a favour by conquering and looting it. For a dissenting opinion on the real nature of Rome, there's no one better than St John the Divine. In AD 95, John escaped the Emperor Domitian's persecution of Christians by fleeing from Ephesus to the island of Patmos. Living in a cave there, he had the memorable visions that resulted in the Book of the Revelation, the Apocalypse; an indispensable aid to fire-eating preachers ever since, with an infinity of do-it-yourself interpretations, the Apocalypse, in its time, was intended and widely understood (at least on the earthly level) as a prophecy of the fall of Rome:

... Fallen, fallen is Babylon the great, she who made all nations drink the wine of her impure passion. (14.8)

Besides the persecuted Christians, John spoke for all the captive nations of the Empire, for the victims of the insatiable Roman tax collector, for the millions of slaves, for serious men who hated the abomination of Emperor-worship, for the great cities like Carthage and Corinth that Rome had wiped from the face of the earth.

In Revelation 17, John develops the unforgettable image of the Harlot:

... arrayed in purple and scarlet, and bedecked with gold and jewels and pearls, holding in her hand a golden cup full of abominations and the impurities of her fornication; and on her forehead was written a name of mystery: 'Babylon the great, mother of harlots and of earth's abominations.' And I saw the woman, drunk with the blood of the saints and the blood of the martyrs of Jesus. (17. 4–6)

An angel explains to John that the seven-headed beast the Harlot rides represents seven hills, and the surrounding waters the 'peoples and multitudes and nations and tongues' over which she has dominion. Like most prophets, John has an easier time with present realities than with the future. Fallen Babylon was laid waste, 'a dwelling place of demons, a haunt of every foul spirit,' but not nearly as soon as he would have liked. The 'new heaven and a new earth' (21.1) appeared in the fullness of time. For the holy city, the New Jerusalem, we're still waiting.

Anyone who knows Rome well will sense that the old harlot is still with us – even God couldn't kill her. She's reformed; no longer a bloodthirsty parasite, or a pious and holy parasite, but still, as any Italian taxpayer will tell you, a parasite.

has an errand inside with the subtle brothers; going inside, he is never seen again, and the Wind waits for him to this day, swirling vacantly around the dreary piazza. Appropriately enough, the successors of the Jesuits, the Christian Democratic Party, had their national headquarters here too until their long-overdue implosion in the 1990s; now the buildings house successor parties the Cristiani Democratici Uniti (CDU) and Partito Popolare Italiano (PPI) – both part of Berlusconi's 2001 right-wing coalition.

Alessandro Farnese, great-grandson of Paul III, footed the enormous bills for the church between 1568 and 1575. Its precedent-setting design (the façade by Della Porta, the interior by Vignola) took the most dramatic elements from High Renaissance architecture and distilled them further into a confectionery style that perfectly expressed the theatrical, anti-intellectual approach to Christian ritual born in the Counter-Reformation terror. Contemporary observers called it the 'Jesuit style'; ephemeral as it was, it proved to be an important stepping-stone to the Baroque.

For many years, this dirty façade contributed much to making the piazza one of Rome's gloomiest. It has now been cleaned, but to see the builders' intentions you'll have to imagine the still-gloomy interior full of candles and flowers, with a Renaissance congregation echoing hosannas to the sounding brass of a polished Jesuit sermon. Look at the *trompe l'oeil* ceiling by Baciccio (Gian Battista Gaulli) where writhing plaster bodies pasted on the corners complement the vertiginous painted angels above, all seemingly in the process of being vacuumed up into heaven through a hole in the clouds. The title of this work is the *Adoration of the Name of Jesus*, and it proved to be one of the most influential frescoes of the Roman High Baroque. Little of the painting in the side aisles is of interest, blackened and waiting for restoration.

In the left transept, the **Tomb of St Ignatius**, founder of the Jesuits, exults in its panoply of marble, gold and bronze. The original statue of Ignatius was melted down by Napoleon's men, but its replacement, under a sculptural group of the Trinity, includes a globe that is said to be the largest piece of lapis lazuli on this planet.

Tridente

Tridente

Look at the map and you'll see how this district gets its familiar name – from the three straight streets, branching out like a three-pronged fork from the great stage set of the Piazza del Popolo. On the ground, these three streets welcome you into a corner of Rome that is entirely theatrical, dream-like, and delighting in artifice – Roman architecture and high fashion in a marriage made in Italy. The neighbourhood around Piazza di Spagna has Rome's swishest shopping district and two of its most delightful piazzas. The architectural *bella figura* reaches an irresistible climax in the Spanish Steps, a sensuous cascade of travertine with a luminous sunken boat at the foot, a grandstand of fallen empire, where young pilgrims from around the world posture like hopeful starlets in a Hollywood diner – or extras at Cinecittà – waiting for something that never happens.

Running through the middle of the area is the Via del Corso. This famous street goes back to ancient Rome, when its name was Via Lata – Broad Street – an important thoroughfare that led north to the Via Flaminia, spanned by the triumphal arches of Tiberius and Claudius (both gone, the latter demolished in the 1500s). After acquiring some kinks and narrows in the Middle Ages, it was made broad and straight once more by the Renaissance popes, beginning in the 1450s.

The Corso – and all the other boulevards in Italy named after it – got its name in the last three centuries of papal rule, when the wild horse races of the Roman Carnival thundered down it towards the finish at Piazza Venezia. Nowadays the street is closed to cars, although buses, taxis and those with special permits still do their best to muscle pedestrians onto the narrow pavements.

Crowds of foreigners are nothing – not since the Renaissance: Spanish and French have long had institutions around Piazza di

1 Lunch

Pollarolo, *Via di Ripetta 5, t 06 361 0276; bus 81, 117, 119, 204. Open Fri–Wed 12–4 and 7–11; closed two weeks in Aug. Inexpensive.* Popular among TV and theatre people for excellent family-style Roman cooking.

2 Coffee and Cakes

Bar Europeo, *Piazza S. Lorenzo in Lucina 33; bus 117. Open daily 7am–9pm.* Treats for the sweet-toothed such as Sicilian *cannoli* with sweetened ricotta.

3 Drinks

Fratelli Roffi Isabelli, *Via della Croce 76; metro Spagna, bus 117, 119. Open Mon–Sat 12–10.* A beautiful 19th-century-style wine shop, where you can buy by the bottle or by the glass at the bar.

Highlights

Roma dei Romani: Piazza Colonna, shared by shoppers and politicians, p.109

Peace and Quiet: Pincio gardens, *the* place to watch the sun set over the city, p.105

Ancient Rome: The Temple of Hadrian, behind the Rome Stock Exchange, a good example of the best 2nd-century style, p.110

Medieval and Renaissance: S. Maria del Popolo, one of Rome's finest art churches from Pinturicchio to Caravaggio, p.102

Baroqueorama: Trevi Fountain, one of the most lovable creations of the cynical, relaxed Rome of the papal twilight, p.113

Unexpected Rome: Rome's Wax Museum, woebegone but endearing, p.116

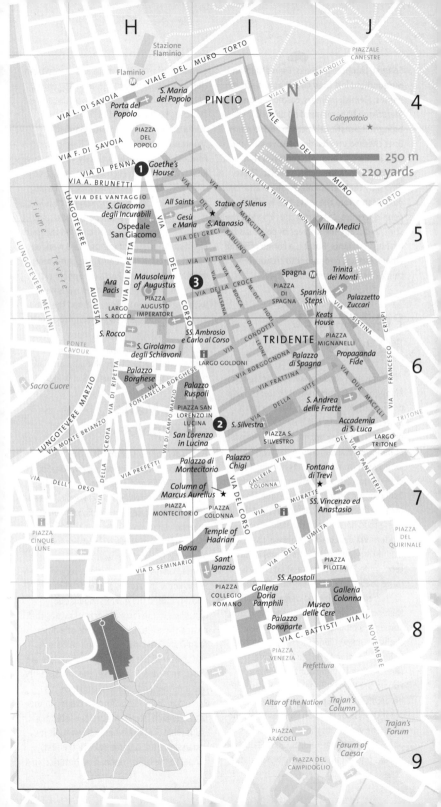

Spagna; Lombards, Greeks, Dalmatians and Burgundians left their churches and street names; Flemish painters, cosmopolitan *literati* and bohemians of all nationalities brought it artistic distinction; and so many Brits checked into its inexpensive inns and flats in the 18th and 19th centuries that it was nicknamed the English ghetto. These days only the czars of high fashion and '*buon gusto*' can afford the rents; this is where people-fanciers can watch the rich strut their stuff, and study the degrees of polite disdain in shop assistants. But it is a corner of Rome where Romans endeavour to create something – be it as ephemeral as style.

PIAZZA DEL POPOLO

This square is where travellers descending along the Via Flaminia would enter the city through the Aurelian walls. No city has a better introduction, but it only attained its present form, depicted in prints on the walls of half the pizza parlours in the world, after a long evolution. Its name has nothing to do with democracy, a Greek concept that never really caught on in Rome, but comes from the *popolus*, or hamlet, which in the Middle Ages stood here among the fields. The modern **Via del Corso** was always there, leading straight to the Capitol and Forum; Leo X added **Via di Ripetta** as an express route to the Vatican for pilgrims (presumably so they could buy his indulgences before their pockets were picked by too many other Romans); a bit later, for symmetry's sake and the 1525 Jubilee, Clement VII added **Via del Babuino**, leading to Piazza di Spagna. These three streets, fanning out from Piazza del Popolo, are Rome's 'Trident', and Sixtus V and his architect Domenico Fontana erected the great **Obelisk of Pharaoh Ramses II** to punctuate the view from the boulevards. This obelisk is 3,200 years old, but like all obelisks it looks mysteriously brand new; Augustus

carried it off from Heliopolis and planted it in the Circus Maximus. In the late 17th century Cardinal Gastaldi added the two little domed churches to emphasize the Trident, **Santa Maria dei Miracoli** and **Santa Maria in Montesanto** by Carlo Rainaldi, Bernini and Fontana; unless you look closely, you miss Rainaldi's main achievement – making two differently shaped churches look like twins. In 1814 Napoleon, reserving Rome for his last great triumph, had Valadier give the square its current oval shape; he also added the four **Egyptian lions**, spitting razor-sharp wedges of water around the obelisk. The three monumental arches of the **Porta del Popolo** were designed in the 16th century, in alignment with the Trident; Alexander VII had the internal façade adapted as a triumphal arch to welcome Queen Christina in 1655. In the old days Piazza del Popolo was the centre of Rome's crazy carnival (*see* 'Roman Carnival', p.103); the piazza now awaits a new identity.

Santa Maria del Popolo H4

Piazza del Popolo 12, t 06 361 0636; metro Flaminio, bus 117, 119. Open Mon–Sat 7–7, Sun 8–1.30 and 4.30–7.30.

On the far side of Piazza del Popolo, tucked in next to the gate, is one of Rome's finest art churches. Long ago its site was the tombs of the Domitia, where Nero's mistress furtively buried his unloved ashes. Walnut trees were planted on his grave, and soon everyone in Rome knew the stories of how the Emperor's ghost haunted the grove, sending out demons – in the form of flocks of ravens that nested there – to perform deeds of evil. In 1099 Pope Paschal II cut down the walnuts and scattered the ashes, and to complete the exorcism built a chapel over the top. Sixtus IV had it rebuilt and enlarged, and gave it a Renaissance façade by Andrea Bregno in the 1470s; Bernini later Baroqued the interior.

But what S. Maria is best known for is its Renaissance art, beginning with the first chapel to the right, frescoed by Pinturicchio

Roman Carnival

In a sense the Carnival mirrors the history of Rome itself – only in reverse. When Rome was full of pomp and power, Carnival evoked the Golden Age of Saturn, a time without arms or empires. Under the popes, it became a bawdy free-for-all. And in today's secular, sophisticated city, where anything would be tolerated, nothing happens.

Under the Caesars, in an age when nothing succeeded like excess, one Carnival just wasn't enough. At proper Carnival time, there was Lupercalia, a pastoral feast in honour of the old Latin shepherd god Lupercus; Roman men raced through the streets, naked except for goat skins, whipping the crowds with leather thongs for fertility and good luck (as in the first act of Shakespeare's *Julius Caesar*). A more direct ancestor was the Saturnalia, around Christmas time, a week of utter licence, with a mock kingship, gift-giving, continuous parties, and a symbolic inversion of society – the slaves ruled each household, waited upon at table by their masters (as in Shakespeare's *Twelfth Night*). The ancient origins of Saturnalia had a darker side: celebrations among the legionaries on the frontiers involved human sacrifices as late as the 4th century AD. Yet a third Carnival came at the spring equinox, the Hilaria, a Festival of Joy where no office or dignity was above the general buffoonery. Crowds of masqueraders thronged the streets all night, although the festival ended abruptly the following day with a solemn procession in honour of Cybele and Attis.

Carnival during the Middle Ages isn't very well documented, but we can guess there were plenty of casualties, and everybody else had a good time. In the Renaissance, in a city finally overawed by the clerical and noble elites, the affair seems to have suffered some sanitization; opulent, self-glorifying pageants dominated the festivities, provided by the leading families. But decadence won out, and during the papal twilight the Romans reclaimed their Carnival once more. By the 18th century, it was the most irresistibly folkloric attraction in Italy, a must for all Grand Tourists from the north. The best account of it may be read in Goethe's *Italian Journey*: the famous riderless horse races, the masques, and the clowning, all performed with a democratic abandon that proved fascinating to Europe on the eve of the Romantic Era. The races down the Corso from Piazza del Popolo to Piazza Venezia were typically Roman, with sharp barbs fixed to the horses' private parts to make them go faster, and inevitable accidents involving the trampling of spectators. Another, crueller, race featured elderly Jews, kidnapped from the Ghetto and forced at swordpoint to stuff themselves with cakes before they ran.

Carnival's downfall began with the revolutions of 1849. When Pius IX returned to power, he suspended it for a time to punish the Romans. Since 1879, and the modernization of Rome, the festival has been on a long downhill slide. Nowadays you'll see only children in costumes. Adults still have them (stylish and ridiculously expensive, of course), but they only wear them to private gatherings and to the nightclubs, where there are big New Year's Eve-style parties. Gags like hand-buzzers and exploding cigarettes seem to be popular.

in the 1480s, with a lovely pastel *Nativity* to complement its two Renaissance tombs, the one on the left by Mino da Fiesole and Andrea Bregno. The second chapel, Capella Cybo, is a colourful *pietra dura* work by Carlo Fontana (1687); the third, by Pinturicchio or his school, is frescoed with *scenes from the Virgin's life*. In the right transept, there's a fine tabernacle by Bregno, paid for by Alexander VI, framing a Sienese painting of the *Madonna*.

Walk behind the altar to see the **Tribune**, by Bramante and financed by Julius II (1509), which incorporates some of the architect's original plans for the choir in St Peter's, with its coffered barrel vault and shell niches. The elegant frescoes in the vault, of golden *Sibyls*, *Evangelists*, and *Doctors of the Church*, framed by grotesques, are by Pinturicchio; the stained glass is by the all-time master of that art, Guillaume de Marcillat (1509), and the two beautifully carved tombs of sleeping cardinals Ascanio Sforza (brother of Milanese boss Ludovico il Moro) and Girolamo Basso are early cinquecento works by Andrea Sansovino. On the high altar in front is a venerated 13th-century icon of the *Madonna*.

Cerasi Chapel

In the left transept, next to the choir, the Cerasi Chapel offers an opportunity to compare paintings by Rome's leading artistic rivals of the seicento, Annibale Carracci and Michelangelo Merisi da Caravaggio; this was the only project they worked on together. But Carracci's *Assumption of the Virgin*, even though the Virgin dramatically bursts from the tomb, seems hopelessly vacuous next to the psychological intensity of Caravaggio's two masterpieces, *The Crucifixion of St Peter* and *Paul on the Road to Damascus* – in both the figures are brought right up to the forefront of the canvas and lit by a highly artificial but extremely effective lighting that heightens the sense of inner illumination. Caravaggio had no use for conventional iconography; in the painting of St Paul there is no sign of supernatural agency, but sympathetic gazes from horse and attendant.

Chigi Chapel

In the left aisle the mood changes again with the Chigi Chapel, designed by Raphael for Renaissance banking tycoon Agostino Chigi. A good friend of Julius II, Chigi was described in a papal bull as hoping in his chapel 'to convert earthly things into heavenly', and to oblige him Raphael went back to eternal forms of the Eternal City; the Chigi Chapel is, if nothing else, a personal-sized Pantheon, with mosaics of God the Father in the *oculus* of the dome and figures of the planets, describing Chigi's horoscope. Planned to achieve an austere perfection in its decoration as well as its geometry, the project was brought to an abrupt halt by the deaths of both Raphael and Chigi in 1520, and

it was finished by Bernini and Lorenzetto, on the orders of the Chigi Pope Alexander VII. The pyramid tombs of Agostino and his brother were made to Raphael's design, as was the statue of *Jonah* emerging from the whale's mouth (left of the altar), executed by Lorenzetto; Bernini added *Habakkuk* on the right. The altarpiece, the *Birth of the Virgin*, is by Sebastiano del Piombo, while Salviati painted the frescoes of the *Creation* and *Fall*.

As you leave the church, don't miss the very different attempt at immortality erected in 1672 by a certain G. B. Chisleni, who wanted posterity to think of him as a praying skeleton (a bust of what he looked like with his skin on is on top); in between are bronze reliefs of a larva and moth, symbolizing the metamorphosis of the soul.

Via del Babuino H4–I5

***Metro** Flaminio and Spagna, **bus** 117, 119.*

Staid 'Baboon Street' was originally Via Clementina. One of its ornaments was a fountain-statue of Silenus by Giacomo della Porta, so ugly that the Romans named it the Baboon. Although the statue was long hidden through embarrassment, it has since resurfaced in all its mouldering, leprous glory, ludicrously topped with a new head and covered with loony graffiti, in front of the Greek Catholic church of Sant'Atanasio (at the corner of Via dei Greci). By 1581 the whole street was named after this ape, except for the section near Piazza del Popolo that went by the even more ignoble title of Borghetto Pidocchioso (Fleabag Alley). Although within the Aurelian wall, this corner of Rome was filled with ornamental gardens in antiquity and vegetable plots in the Middle Ages, and it remained rural until it caught the eye of the late Renaissance popes; Rubens and Poussin are only the most famous of the foreign artists who had studios with the fleas and the baboon. At no.153, the Anglican church of All Saints is a neo-Gothic building of 1882 by G.E. Street, with a bright white spire poking above the roofs like 'a summer hat worn out of season'.

Via Margutta I5

This lane, skirting the Pincio parallel to Via del Babuino, was long the refuge of Rome's artsy bohemians. Though the high cost of trendiness has forced the artists elsewhere, a few galleries remain. Large outdoor exhibits perk up the street in spring and autumn; the paintings are similar to street art worldwide.

Pincio Gardens I4–J5

Entrance from the Salita del Pincio (eastern edge of Piazza del Popolo) or Viale Trinità del Monte (at the top of the Spanish Steps); metro Flaminio or Spagna, bus 117, 119.

One of the uncanonical hills of Rome, the Pincio is best known as *the* place to watch the sun set over the city, with the sun-finger obelisk of the Piazza del Popolo in the foreground and the dome of St Peter's on the horizon melting in the twilight to the bells of the Angelus. The formal gardens of the Pincio were laid out by Valadier in 1814; throughout the 19th century Rome's fops and belles posed and postured here each evening.

In the early 1980s an atavistic vandal decapitated the scores of busts of famous Italians, lending the Pincio a weird, surreal touch in its hundreds of empty pedestals.

The equally unadorned **obelisk** (I4) in central Viale dell'Obelisco, to the right of Casina Valadier, was brought from the tomb of Hadrian's darling Antinous, who was drowned in the Nile while saving Hadrian's life and was deified by imperial decree.

Walk down Viale dell' Obelisco and turn left on Viale dell'Orologio for one of Rome's more quirky fountains, the rustic-romantic **Water Clock**, designed by a Dominican priest named Embriago for the Paris Exhibition of 1867. (Don't trust any of the different times the four sides of the clock display – but then, a public clock in Rome with the right time would be a rare find indeed.)

Muro Torto I4–J5

At the back of the Pincio Gardens, the Muro Torto – 'Crooked Wall' – was the only section

of the Aurelian Wall Belisarius didn't repair, for the Romans assured him that St Peter himself would defend it, and apparently they were right, for it was never assaulted. Later this area was the cemetery for prostitutes, thieves and actors, a tradition recalled by the merry whores in Fellini's *Nights of Cabiria* who waited for clients cruising the sunken highway, Viale del Muro Torto. On the other side of the road, to the right, is the circuit of the **Galoppatoio** (J4), where the sight of grazing horses and trotting Italians is a pleasant surprise in the middle of Rome.

PIAZZA DI SPAGNA AND THE SPANISH STEPS

Metro Spagna, bus 116, 117, 119.

Even the most experienced old Rome hand envies every visitor's virgin sighting of the Piazza di Spagna, with charms enough to disarm the most chaste Baroqueophobe. For a pretty square is like a melody; and what could be more lyrical than the ochre, pink, salmon, and russets of the 18th-century palaces along its butterfly-winged confines, crossed by the languid silhouettes of slender palms. Then, these part like a curtain to reveal the rippling Rococo theatrics of the Scalinata di Trinità dei Monti, better known in English as the **Spanish Steps** (J5), which must niggle the French, since they paid Francesco De Sanctis to build them in 1725. At once, Romans hoping to pick up jobs as artists' models came to pose on this unique stage dressed like Madonnas or Caesars; when tourists began bringing cameras they donned peasant costumes for a lira a shot.

In May the steps are frocked with banks of pink azaleas, but there are always flowers in the stand at the foot of the steps, by the leaking marble barge of the 1629 **Fontana della Barcaccia** (I6), believed to be the last work by Bernini's father, Pietro, whose ingenious solution to the problem of low water pressure of the Acqua Vergine was to sink the fountain below ground level. The inspiration may have been the stupendous Tiber flood of Christmas Day 1598, which stranded a similar barge on the Pincio Hill.

Keats-Shelley Memorial House I6

Piazza di Spagna 26, t 06 678 4235; metro Spagna, bus 116, 117, 119. Open Mon–Fri 9–6, Sat 11–6; adm €2.50.

When Spain and France were at war, Piazza di Spagna was divided to form a temporary 'Piazza di Francia' to keep belligerents apart. The English presence was less quarrelsome and more poetic. Byron, who could pen 'Oh Rome! my country! city of the soul!', then actually spend less than a month there, lodged at Piazza di Spagna no.66. John Keats stayed only a bit longer, but it is his ghost that wanly flits over the boisterous pageantry of the square, fondly remembered in this house just to the right of the Steps.

The flat was rented by the young artist Joseph Severn, who invited his friend John Keats to stay with him in September 1820. Keats was suffering from consumption and unkind literary criticism in the *Quarterly Review*. His doctor ordered a change of climate, but winter in Rome wasn't the answer, and he died anyway on 23 February 1821, aged 25, comforted to the last by the faithful Severn. Shelley composed *Adonais* in his memory; Byron's obituary was terser:

'Who killed John Keats?'
'I,' said the Quarterly,
'So savage and tartarly
'It was one of my feats.'

Since 1909 the house has been a library and memorial to Keats and Shelley, who also died young, drowned near Viareggio, with a volume by Keats in his pocket. Highlights include Byron's carnival mask, Shelley's charred jawbone in a jug, a lock of Keats' hair and his death mask, and what is touted as the 'most sacred relic of English literature', a silver scallop reliquary once owned by Pius V (who excommunicated Queen Elizabeth I),

containing strands of Milton's and Elizabeth Barrett Browning's hair, worn by Addison, Dr Johnson, Leigh Hunt and Robert Browning. Beyond these Romantic memories, the main interest lies in the books and numerous reprinted articles and essays on the poets liberally scattered through the rooms.

Trinità dei Monti J5

Piazza della Trinità dei Monti, t 06 679 4179; metro Spagna, bus 116, 117, 119. Open 9–8.

The Spanish Steps lend a graceful majesty to the simple French church at the summit, conventual church of the Minims, founded in 1493 by Louis XII, with a late 16th-century façade by Domenico Fontana (if you can't face the steps, take the metro escalator).

It contains two fine paintings by Daniele da Volterra, Michelangelo's star pupil: a faded *Assumption* in the right aisle, and in the left, a vigorous but damaged *Descent from the Cross*, which Poussin rated as one of the three greatest paintings of all time. Behind the grille in the transept are colourful frescoes by Raphael's best pupil, Giulio Romano, and Perin del Vaga.

The **obelisk** (J5) in front of the church is a 2nd-century Roman model from the Gardens of Sallust. Like a *meta* in the circus, it and the obelisk in the Pincio Gardens (*see* p.105) marked the length of the most fashionable *passeggiata* of the 18th and 19th centuries, where a pale John Keats met Napoleon's vampy sister Pauline in one of history's more awkward coincidences.

Palazzetto Zuccari J6

Via Sistina at Via Gregoriana.

Built in the 16th century by Federico Zuccari, its striking rounded loggia was added later by the quirky late-Baroque architect Juvarra. Federcio Zuccari, however, is responsible for the main façade on Via Gregoriana, with doors and windows framed by hideous genie faces with gawping hell-mouths – a sneak preview of Bomarzo's Monster Park, one of Rome's more intriguing historical day trips.

Villa Medici I–J5

*Viale della Trinità dei Monti 1, **t** 06 676 1305,
w www.villamedici.it; **metro** Spagna, **bus** 116,
117, 119. **Open** for guided tours of the gardens
1 Mar–31 May and 6–25 Oct, Sun every half-
hour 10–12.30. Frequent exhibitions.*

Built in 1540, the villa was remodelled to
Medici taste by Florentine Mannerist
Ammannati, who added a magnificent decorative collage of Roman antiquities to the
garden façade. Galileo, under the discreet
protection of the Medici Grand Dukes, stayed
here under house arrest by the Inquisition
(1630–3); Napoleon purchased it in 1801 and
made it the seat of the French Academy
(which it still is). In front of the villa the
round fountain has a Roman basin and a
spout made from a cannonball, shot here
from Castel Sant'Angelo by madcap Queen
Christina – her way of saying that she would
be a little late for an appointment.

Colonna dell'Immacolata J6

*Piazza Mignanelli; **metro** Spagna,
bus 116, 117, 119.*

Towering erect above Piazza Mignanelli is
the **Column of Mary Immaculate**, commemorating the proclamation by Pius IX in 1854 of
the Immaculate Conception of the Virgin
Mary, a dogma first mentioned in the Koran.
On 8 December, when the Pope comes to
pray by the column, Roman firemen climb
their ladders to place a wreath on the head
of the Madonna's statue.

Collegio di Propaganda Fide J6

*Via di Propaganda 1; **metro** Spagna,
bus 116, 117, 119.*

Promoting Catholic dogma is the job of the
ecclesiastical PR-men based in this building.
If the Spanish Steps are Baroque at its most
graceful, the College for the Propagation of
Faith sees it at its most claustrophobic. Its
principal façade, on Via di Propaganda, was

by Borromini (1664), and nowhere is he more
disconcerting; the looming Collegio seems
ready to pounce and crush passers-by.
Architectural psychologists, if there are such
people, can ponder the fact that Borromini
committed suicide after designing it.

Sant'Andrea delle Fratte J6

*Via Sant'Andrea delle Fratte 1, **t** 06 679 3191;
metro Spagna, **bus** 116, 117, 119. **Open**
6.30–12.30 and 4.30–7.30.*

Across the street from the Propaganda
Fide, Borromini was also responsible for the
fantastical tower (1653) atop Rome's pre-
Reformation Scottish church, of 12th-century
origins. Sadly the architect never had a
chance to finish more than the fantastical
tower, with its delicate cherub and spiky
crowned curly scroll ornament, meant to
offer a contrast to the heavy buttressed
dome. The interior, covered with plush frescoes, has two of Bernini's original 'Breezy
Maniacs' from the Ponte Sant'Angelo and the
tomb of Swiss painter Angelica Kauffmann.

NORTHWEST OF THE CORSO: VIA DI RIPETTA

Old prints of Rome often feature the Porto
di Ripetta, a lovely ensemble of churches and
stairs that was also a busy port, destroyed to
make way for the Tiber embankment in the
19th century (although you can see what it
looked like on a painting in the foyer at Via di
Ripetta no.73) Whatever life the neighbourhood retained afterwards was obliterated by
Mussolini's Piazza Augusto Imperatore, an
envelope of ponderous Fascist architecture
enclosing the Mausoleum of Augustus,
where it is rumoured that the Duce himself
intended to be interred. Two of its churches
survive on Via di Ripetta. **San Girolamo degli
Schiavoni** (H6), rebuilt by Martino Longhi in

the 1580s, was the church of the Slavic dock-workers ('Schiavoni'), who came to Rome as refugees after the Battle of Kosovo in 1389. **San Rocco** (H6), next to it, built by Alexander VI with a neoclassical façade tacked on later by Valadier, belonged to the Tiber boatmen and innkeepers.

Mausoleum of Augustus H5

Piazza Augusto Imperatore; **bus** *81, 204, 628, 926.* **Closed** *to the public.*

> Look round: You see a little supper room;
> But from my window, lo!
> great Caesar's tomb!
> And the great dead themselves,
> with jovial breath,
> Bid you be merry and remember death.
>
> Martial

There's no longer anything jovial about the pathetic cylinder of shabby brick, once covered in white marble and topped with diminishing arcaded cylinders, its summit crowned by a golden statue of Augustus and planted with cypresses, its entrance flanked by two obelisks. The ashes of all the Julian emperors except Nero were interred here, in the middle of what were Augustus' enormous gardens. After the centuries despoiled the tomb of its riches, the Colonnas turned the hulk into one of their fortresses. Further indignities were in store. Until 1823, when the Pope forbade them, bullfights were popular in Rome, and a Spanish entrepreneur found the circular enclosure perfect for the *toreros*. The tomb was later used as a concert hall, until Mussolini had it excavated and planted with cypresses. Beyond that, no one knows what to do with it; it sits locked up and forlorn, surrounded by weeds.

Ara Pacis or Altar of Peace H5

Via di Ripetta, **t** *06 6710 3819;* **bus** *81, 204, 590.* **Closed** *for restoration.*

Mussolini's attempts to link his regime symbolically to Imperial Rome scarred the city with bombastic fascist pomposity, but in the case of the celebrated Ara Pacis, next to the Mausoleum on the Tiber embankment, he returned to Rome a lost work of great historical importance and a proper memorial for Augustus, a beautiful evocation of the Romans at their most noble.

Now sheltered by a modern glass pavilion, the Ara Pacis was commissioned by the Senate for Augustus on 4 July 13 BC, on his return from Spain and Gaul; it was completed in 9 BC and dedicated to the peace of the Empire; so he wrote in his auto-biographical *Res Gestae Augusti*, part of which is engraved on the wall of the pavilion. After centuries of civil war and conquests, Peace must have seemed like the only god the Romans couldn't tempt over to their side – until Augustus willed it.

The altar was originally located where the Palazzo Fiano now stands in Piazza S. Lorenzo in Lucina. Fragments of superb reliefs were first discovered there in 1525, and snapped up by collectors like the Medici, though no one knew what monument they belonged to. In the 19th century, during restoration work on the palace's foundations, more slabs were discovered, and it dawned on archaeologists that they formed part of the celebrated Ara Pacis. But to remove any other sections would have endangered the palace, and nothing else was done until 1937, when Mussolini took the extraordinary measure of having the ground water frozen to support the palace while completing the excavation. Missing sections and casts were gathered from various museums of Europe, and the altar was reassembled here.

Currently under restoration, it is enclosed by a sanctuary decorated with some of the finest reliefs ever made by Roman artists, influenced by the lyrical lines of Hellenistic art. Acanthus-leaf patterns adorn the façade, along with two reliefs, of Aeneas sacrificing to the Penates (household gods) and a much-damaged scene of the Lupercalia, or feast of Pan (*see* 'Roman Carnival', p.103); on the back façade is a lovely allegory of the earth goddess Tellus, or perhaps Peace, with two toddlers, and a damaged portrait of the goddess Roma. Along the flanks we see the procession through the Campus Martius dedicating this very altar: leading the procession on the right side are the *lictors*, originally 12 in number, holding their *fasces*, the symbol of authority, followed by the tall, handsome, but half-ruined figure of Augustus and the *flamines*, priests in curious T-top bonnets who would light the sacrificial fires; then Augustus' son-in-law Agrippa, the Empress Livia, and Augustus' daughter, Julia, and her husband Tiberius, accompanied by the young Germanicus and Claudius, and followed by friends of the family. On the Tiber side the procession includes the priests, senators, magistrates, and the Pontifex Maximus (with his head covered), whose office would soon be assumed by the emperor himself.

Palazzo Borghese H6

Largo della Fontanella Borghese; **bus** *70, 86, 87, 116, 116T, 204, 492.*

A Mannerist *tour de force* by Vignola, nicknamed the 'harpsichord of Rome' after its quaint shape. It was purchased by Camillo Borghese, the future Pope Paul V. The palace became famous for the lavish entertainments held in its lovely courtyard and on the riverside terrace. It now houses the Circolo della Caccia, a men-only members' club; the harpsichord's keyboard houses a carpet warehouse, from which the perspective of the palace's curve is most striking. The piazza is the site of Rome's daily old print market.

San Lorenzo in Lucina H–I6

Via Lucina 16/a. **Open** *8–12 and 4–7.30;* **bus** *81, 117, 119.*

Founded in the garden of a Roman matron named Lucina in the 4th century, S. Lorenzo's portico and campanile date from a rebuilding in the 1100s, while the interior is all Baroque. The church's chief relic is a

portion of St Lawrence's gridiron, in the first chapel on the right, while a bit further on is its celebrity tomb, that of Nicolas Poussin, who died in Rome in 1665; the tomb, by Lemoyne, was commissioned by Chateaubriand and has a bust of the painter and a relief of his famous and mysterious painting *Et in Arcadia Ego*. The fourth chapel on the right contains the monument of Innocent X's goateed doctor Gabriele Fonseca, by Bernini, in the pious jack-in-the-box style, his head popping out of the wall to participate symbolically in the mass. The *Crucifixion* by Reni over the altar is one of the Divine Guido's few startling works, with a touch of Daliesque religious kitsch in the lone glowing figure of Christ in the foreground, against a dark and dingy world. As you leave, look into the Rococo chapel near the door, where the font is topped by what is believed to be the model for Bramante's original plan for St Peter's. Around the corner are two of the landmarks of the Corso: the vast **Palazzo Ruspoli** (H–I6), by Bartolomeo Ammannati, and Pietro da Cortona's 1668 **SS. Ambrosio e Carlo al Corso** (H6), one of Rome's big domes.

SOUTHWEST OF THE CORSO: PIAZZA COLONNA

Halfway down the Corso, this busy square is shared by shoppers and politicians. The Prime Minister lives here, and the parliament is just a block away, while the city's biggest shopping district begins just across the way.

Column of Marcus Aurelius I7

Piazza Colonna; **bus** *62, 63, 81, 85, 95, 116, 116T, 117, 160, 175, 204, 492.*

Rome's stoic philosopher-emperor would not have appreciated the expenditure of public funds on such a bauble, but his son

Commodus returned to conventional behaviour by commissioning this expensive monument to Marcus' relatively modest victories over the Germans and Sarmatians. Built in AD 180–93 in imitation of Trajan's Column, it has the same spiral bands of battle scenes – only more realistic ones, more concerned with the horrors of war than the serene, Olympian tableaux of Trajan's day (some casts can be seen up close in the Museum of Roman Civilization at EUR; see p.241). Originally capped by a statue of the emperor and his wife, a 1589 restoration saw them replaced with a figure of St Paul. Like Trajan's Column, this one has a spiral stair inside, leading 97ft to the top (rarely open).

Facing the column on Piazza Colonna, **Palazzo Chigi** is the most expensive hotel in Italy – it's the Prime Minister's residence, and on average it has known at least one new occupant a year since the founding of the Republic. Palazzo Wedekind, opposite, now the offices of the newspaper Il Tempo, was the home of two nasty robber bands: the Fascist Party during the Mussolini years, and the corrupt, defunct Socialist Party of Craxi.

Palazzo di Montecitorio H–I7

Piazza di Montecitorio, t 06 67601; bus 52, 53, 61, 71, 80, 85, 116, 116T, 160, 992. Open to the public late Sept–July first Sun of every month 10–6. For admission to parliamentary sessions or tours, apply at the rear, Piazza del Parlamento no.24. Visitors must be at least 14 years old and suitably dressed (jacket and tie for men); non-EU visitors must bring a letter from their country's embassy in Rome.

Just west of Piazza Colonna, in a broad square full of cars, with a weary obelisk, stands a large, nondescript palace with a clock on top. It could be a museum or library, or municipal offices or even the Ministry of Superfluous Paperwork, but in fact the Palazzo Montecitorio is nothing less than the seat of the Chamber of Deputies.

Few major nations would tolerate such a modest setting for their political holy-of-holies. Nonetheless, this is the centre stage of Italian politics, and something is nearly always happening in Montecitorio that will 'cause polemics', as the Italians say, in the newspapers tomorrow.

Bernini constructed this palace for a noble family in 1650. Confiscated from the pope and handed over to the politicians in 1870, it was expanded and given a new façade in 1918. Under Mussolini, it held a rubber-stamp parliament called the 'Chamber of the Fasces and Corporations'. Inside, the remodellings left some fine Art Nouveau details, including a great coloured glass skylight and the huge, remarkable frescoes (1908–12) by Giulio Aristide Sartorio, a circular frieze around the parliament chamber that represents Italian civilization in 5,000 square feet of allegorical ladies, horses and writhing youths. Sartorio, who later made one of Italy's first feature-length movies (Il Mistero di Galatea, 1920), is an artist who deserves to be better known; here he borrows a monumental approach to the human form and a liking for pale greens and purples from Michelangelo's Sistine Chapel ceiling.

The **obelisk** in front, a 4th-century BC work from Heliopolis, came to Rome in Augustus' time along with the one in Piazza del Popolo. Augustus took it to his spacious gardens (kept as a public park, although later emperors sold it off to building speculators); it was erected, not far from its present location, to form the *gnomon* of a gigantic sundial, with time and date markers all over the park. On Augustus' birthday, its shadow fell over the Ara Pacis, originally located nearby. Augustus' own personal Greek-Egyptian astronomers designed it for him – the same gentlemen who kept his calendar, and who ordained the census that made Mary and Joseph travel to Bethlehem.

Temple of Hadrian I7

Piazza di Pietra; bus 116, 116T.

No stock changes hands at the Borsa (the stock exchange) any more – they do that in Milan – but the back wall is one of the seldom-noticed, most complete relics of antiquity: an entire *cella* wall and colonnade of the huge Temple of Hadrian, a good example of the best 2nd-century style, dedicated in 145 by Hadrian's successor, Antoninus Pius.

Sant'Ignazio I7–8

Piazza di Sant'Ignazio; **bus** *62, 63, 81, 85, 95, 117, 175, 204, 492.* **Open** *7.30–12.30 and 4–7.15.*

Before entering this Jesuit church, take a look at Piazza di Sant'Ignazio, a delightful Rococo confection of oddly shaped and exotically decorated apartment blocks, created in 1728 and still, although a little dingy, one of the most successful architectural ensembles in Rome. Architect Filippo Raguzzini made it a treat for the eye by a subtle plan, playing three ellipses (incorporating the curving façades of the buildings) against the monumental, serious façade of the church.

That façade is not a bad one; it was designed by a Jesuit mathematician and dilettante architect named Padre Orazio Grassi; the church was begun in 1626 to celebrate the canonization of the Jesuits' founder (the military, somewhat disturbing character Ignatius of Loyola, buried in the nearby church of the Gesù). Once inside, gird your imagination and prepare for some of the Baroque's dizziest ceiling pyrotechnics. Another Jesuit, Padre Andrea Pozzo, conjured up this *Allegory of the Missionary Work of the Jesuits* (1694), full of charming detail; saved souls of every race and colour take flight and soar up to heaven, following in the train of a smiling Pied Piper Jesus. To the eye, this Jesus seems several times as high as the ceiling of the church; here Pozzo created the trickiest of all Baroque feats of *trompe l'oeil*, making another storey of heavy arches and columns – of nothing but paint – rise above the nave, with an open, limitless heaven beyond that.

Pozzo also contributed the dome – not a dome at all of course, but a flat disc of paint made to look like one (with all the Order's other projects, there wasn't money enough for a real cupola). The trick works perfectly when the light is on, and when you view it from the circle set into the floor near the centre of the nave. The political ramifications of all this should not be lost on us; the Jesuits did not indulge such fancies because they were incurable dreamers. To the bullied and overawed crowds of the Baroque city, paintings like these were an ingenious reminder that truth was what the Jesuits said it was.

Palazzo del Collegio Romano I8

Piazza del Collegio Romano; **bus** *40, 46, 62, 63, 64, 70, 81, 87.*

The Collegio Romano (north side of the square, built 1585) was the equivalent of the war ministry of the Jesuits, 'storm troopers of Christ', founded by third General St Francis Borgia. The Collegio was also a sort of university, and a Jesuit astronomer started a century-long delusion when he discovered the 'canals' of Mars here in 1858. After the unification of Italy, the building was used to store the priceless hoard of books and manuscripts garnered by the state from Italy's disestablished monastic institutions; there they rotted until the 1880s when a scholar found his butter wrapped in a letter signed by Columbus – the porter had sold manuscripts as scrap paper to buy wine.

Palazzo e Galleria Doria Pamphili I8

Piazza del Collegio Romano 2, **t** *06 679 7323,* **w** *www.doriapamphilj.it;* **bus** *40, 46, 62, 64, 70, 81, 186, 492.* **Open** *Fri–Wed 10–5;* **adm** *€7, includes audio guide in English.*

The sumptuous Palazzo Doria Pamphili contains one of Rome's best surviving private collections of art. The Doria half of this well-upholstered Roman family hails from Genoa, heirs of Admiral Andrea Doria; the Pamphili (or 'Pamphilj' as they like to affect) began their great fortune as perhaps the rawest money grubbers ever to win the papal sweepstakes. Their kinsman, the mean, prudish, and singularly unloved Innocent X (elected in 1644; see 'Worst Pope', p.217) was henpecked by his shrewish sister-in-law Olimpia Maidalchini, who visited the Pope on his deathbed to steal one last box of coins he had managed until then to hide from her. The family reputation improved with age – the popular, anti-Fascist Prince Filippo Doria Pamphili was named Mayor of Rome after the Liberation in 1944.

The Doria Pamphili palace is organic architecture, its ornate Rococo façade (by Gabriele Valvassori, 1734) hiding the building and rebuildings of centuries. Acquired in 1659, its main purpose was to show off the family's collection, for if Innocent X and Olimpia had no scruples, they at least had a taste for art. In the first arm of the gallery look for: exhibit **10.** Titian's dire-sounding *Spain Succouring Religion*; **20.** Correggio's sketch for *The Allegory of Virtue*; **23.** a sombre *Double Portrait of Two Venetians*, by Raphael; **29.** Titian's *Salome*, coyly cradling the Baptist's head on a dish; **40.** Caravaggio's *Maddalena*, with her vanities spilled on the floor, and **42.** *Rest on the Flight into Egypt*, one of his most tender paintings, where the Virgin and Child sleep while Joseph holds up the musical score for an angel playing a lullaby; **46.** Lo Spagnoletto's *St Jerome* in its own little chamber; and then **1.** Algardi's *Bust of Olimpia Maidalchini*, a portrait with all the charm of a stout, hooded cobra.

In the adjacent **Salone Aldobrandini** are 16th-century tapestries of the *Battle of Lepanto*, Guercino's violently *tenebroso Herminia Finds Wounded Tancred* and a good collection of pseudo- and classical sculpture: Odysseus hiding under the ram's belly, a merry centaur snapping his fingers at the world, and the relief labelled **II.** *Fighting Putti* by François Duquesnoy. Back in the main gallery: **117.** a 17th-century Rembrandt forgery, believed to be by Luca Giordano, who could paint in any style he chose but unfortunately usually chose his own.

The second gallery holds little allure, but **Room II** has **174.** and **176.** *The Birth and Marriage of the Virgin* with Islamic touches, by the 15th-century Sienese Giovanni di

Paolo; **185.** a copy of Bellini's *Circumcision of Christ*; **191.** Frangipane's *Christ and Veronica* in a modern zoom shot; **200.** Parmigianino's windblown *Nativity*, and **207.** his *Madonna*; **203.** a bleak *St Jerome* by Beccafumi; **216.** and **217.** by Lodovico Mazzolino (d.1530), whose primary colours stand out in the century of *sfumato*. **Room IV** is devoted to the Dutch and Flemish: **237.** Thomas de Keyser's *Portrait of a Woman*; **262.** *Aeneas Conducted by the Sibyl into Hell*, complete with flying lobster, by an imitator of Jan Breughel, who painted in person **278.** *The Creation of Man* and **280.** *Vision of St John on Patmos*; **317.** *Battle in the Bay of Naples* is a fine work by Pieter Breughel the Elder.

At the end of the 18th-century **Gallery of Mirrors** is a cabinet with the showpiece of the collection, Velazquez's *Portrait of Innocent X* (1650), so accurately portraying the Pope's weak and suspicious nature that Innocent himself remarked that it was 'Too true, too true'. Bernini's more flattering bust of the Pope, also in the cabinet, seems vacuous in comparison. The last arm of the gallery contains 17th-century landscapes, **342, 346, 348, 351,** and **352** by Claude Lorraine.

The guided tours of the palace's lavish **Private Apartments**, still used now and then by the family, include the **Winter Garden** with ancient busts, elegant board games and an 18th-century children's sledge and sedan chair; the **Smoking Room**, surely one of the cosiest rooms ever to find its way into any Italian palazzo (there isn't even a word for cosy in Italian; this was built for a homesick English bride); the Andrea Doria room with memorabilia and two portraits of the great admiral by Sebastiano del Piombo as well as Lorenzo Lotto's fine *Portrait of a Gentleman*. In the **Green Salone** are a huge 15th-century Tournai tapestry of the *Legend of Alexander the Great*, 40 years in the weaving, Filippo Lippi's *Annunciation*, with a beautiful Renaissance angel, a *Holy Family* by Beccafumi and *Deposition* by Hans Memling. The second set of rooms surrounds the delightful **Ballroom**; the **Chapel** has two bodies from the catacombs; in the **Yellow**

Room are tapestries of the months, made for Louis XIV, and two Ming vases; the charming Venetian-style **Green Room** and **Red Room**, with four allegories by Pieter Breughel the Elder, complete the tour.

From the entrance, a little street called Via Lata leads back to the Corso; along the way it passes a weathered fountain relief of a man holding a cask, known to the Romans as **Il Facchino**, the porter (18); one old Roman tradition claims he is Martin Luther (another says he was just a celebrated local drunk). Back on the Corso, you can see the church of S. Maria in Via Lata, with a heavy, solemnly classical façade by Pietro da Cortona.

EAST OF THE CORSO: TREVI FOUNTAIN

Trevi Fountain J7

Piazza di Trevi; **bus** *52, 53, 61, 63, 71, 80, 95, 116, 116T, 119.*

If you wanted to avoid the Trevi Fountain because of its corny connotations, we must politely disagree. Hollywood in the 1950s may have done its worst (*Roman Holiday* and *Three Coins in the Fountain*) to trash this quiet corner of Rome, and it may well be surrounded by gawking camera-bugs 12 months of the year. Nevertheless, this is one of the most lovable creations of the cynical, relaxed Rome of the papal twilight. Tucked unobtrusively among a nest of twisting alleys, it comes as one of Rome's nicest surprises when you finally find it. Scholars believe Pietro da Cortona first had the idea of combining a fountain with a palace façade (often falsely attributed to Bernini). Clement XII's architect, Nicola Salvi, oversaw its building from 1732 to his death in 1762; the time he spent among the mists killed him.

The water you see is the Acqua Vergine, with the reputation of being Rome's sweetest since Augustus built the aqueduct in 19 BC. Cut off during Totila's siege in the Greek-Gothic Wars, the aqueduct was not repaired until the 1400s; a Renaissance basin was enough to commemorate its conclusion until the reign of Benedict XII. Salvi's design, carried out by a number of sculptors, follows the popular marine mythology of the age: two tritons blowing conch shells conduct Neptune's chariot, flanked by figures representing Abundance and Health (ironically for poor old Salvi). The result is so much like a theatre set that later architects added rows of seats for people to sit and watch it.

The story about throwing a coin over your shoulder into the fountain to ensure your return to Rome seems to be true. Every day, hundreds of tourists do it, and they all seem to come back. The coins get raked out every week or so, and supposedly they go to charities. There doesn't seem to be any law against fishing them out yourself – but try telling that to a Roman cop. By day, the Trevi is too busy; come back at night when the hordes have gone, and the waters and sea gods are beautifully illuminated, as they were for Anita Ekberg and Marcello Mastroianni in *La Dolce Vita*.

Santi Vincenzo ed Anastasio J7

Piazza di Trevi, **t** *06 678 3098;* **bus** *52, 53, 61, 63, 71, 80, 95, 116, 116T, 119.* **Open** *7–9am.*

Across from the Trevi Fountain, the church of SS. Vincenzo ed Anastasio squats like a Baroque toad, mulling over the macabre secret within. In the days when the popes lived at the nearby Quirinale Palace, this was their parish church. Nobody knows exactly why, but from about 1600 to 1903, almost all the popes bequeathed their hearts and entrails to this church; they are kept in marble urns down in the crypt. A neighbourhood boy, the famous Cardinal Mazarin, built it. Calling his church a toad is entirely unfair to the architect, Martino Longhi; his façade, with its muscular ranks of columns, is one of the boldest statements of the High Baroque.

The Emperor who Invented Christmas

Piazza di San Silvestro is the home of Rome's main post office; a beautiful map in ceramic tiles in its lobby shows you nearly every important building in ancient Rome. The building and the piazza also conceal ancient secrets underneath. Archaeologists long disputed the location, but today the general consensus says that this was the location of the last great pagan temple built in Rome, Emperor Aurelian's AD 273 **Temple of the Invincible Sun**. No trace of it remains; no doubt the Christians were especially zealous about doing away with all traces of a very inconvenient relic.

Aurelian lived in an age when Rome was beset by enemies on every side. With remark-able effort and determination he beat them all, but to shore up flagging loyalty, and partially to celebrate his own triumphs, he magnified the well-established deification of emperors into the greatest of all Rome's abominations – full-blown worship of the state, personified by the Almighty Sun.

Combining philosophical monotheism with Syrian Greek solar mysticism (as in the famous temple of Baalbek), Aurelian created a new cult of Sol Invictus, and made it the official religion of the Roman Empire. When Christianity captured the Empire, it based some of its own practices on this cult, and recast its holidays to smooth the religious transition – 25 December, a date close to the winter solstice, had been for imperial believers the Birthday of the Sun.

Accademia di San Luca J7

Piazza dell'Accademia di San Luca, t 06 679 8850; bus 52, 53, 61, 62, 63, 80, 116, 116T, 119. Open Mon–Fri 9–1, Tues–Wed 3–6; adm free.

In business since 1577, Rome's art academy only moved here in the 1930s, when its old home was cleared to make way for Via dei Fori Imperiali. At the end of the Renaissance, academies were sprouting all over Italy. Partly because of the restrictive atmosphere of the Counter-Reformation, individualism was going out of fashion, and institutions like this one seemed, both to rulers and their favoured artists, the best way to train future generations in the rules of conformist art.

Nevertheless, the gallery contains a few choice works: portraits of serene, worldly-wise old Romans who would make jolly company at a dinner party, doubly welcome if they could bring all that delectable-looking seafood from the 18th-century still-lifes. In **Room 1** is a fresco fragment by Raphael, a lovely though perplexed *putto* that seems to be asking 'why am I here, under glass?' Works attributed to Titian include a *St Jerome* and two contemporary portraits. In **Room 2**, the Cavaliere d'Arpino, who has taken a lot of flak

in this book, answers critics with a delightful *Perseus and Andromeda*. An *Annunciation* from the school of Lorenzo di Credi illustrates Florence's early Renaissance style.

The next rooms and the main hall contain 18th–19th-century painting, foreigners, espe-cially Italianized Dutchmen – classical Roman landscapes of Gaspare Vanvitelli (Van Wittel); works by *grande dame* of late 18th-century Roman art, Angelica Kauffmann, including a *Self Portrait*. In **Room 5**, Salvator Rosa offers studies of the cat, in which you will recognize the arch expression of the Roman puss. Best of all, in the main hall, is the most sensuous and memorable *Venus* of all the Venuses in Rome, by Guercino. And finally, if you couldn't get into Palazzo Montecitorio to see the fres-coes of Aristide Sartorio, on the stair going out take some time to consider his luminous, colossal *Monte Circeo*, a vision from the enchanted, malarial wilds of southern Lazio.

Calcographia Nazionale J7

Via della Stamperia; bus 52, 53, 61, 62, 63, 80, 116, 116T, 119. Open for exhibitions.

Just across the street from the Accademia San Luca is perhaps the largest collection of prints and etchings in the world. Begun in 1738, it includes over 20,000 plates from copper engravings, and endless books of the actual prints. The most famous of course are the works of G.B. Piranesi: his mysterious and unsettling series of fantasy dungeons, the *Carceri*, and hundreds of views of ancient and contemporary Rome. The museum keeps only a small number of its treasures on display, in changing exhibitions on the ground floor, but all the rest can be seen in the library upstairs upon request (with ID). They will also make copies for you, some from the original plates, for around €50.

Palazzo e Galleria Colonna J8

Via della Pilotta 17, t 06 678 4350; wheelchair accessible from Piazza SS. Apostoli 66; bus 40, 60, 64, 70, 117, 170. Open Sept–July Sat 9–1; free guided tours in English at 11.45; group visits can be arranged at other times; adm €5.

In the Middle Ages, when the Colonna family was the most powerful feudal faction in Rome, they took the Ghibelline side in scuffles against the popes and their great enemies, the Orsini. But in 1424 they elected a pope of their own, Martin V (Oddone Colonna), and used the papal bonanza to begin a huge new family compound, **Palazzo Colonna**. Rebuilt in the 1700s, there is more size than art in the building itself, but by the 1700s the family that was once so martial and quarrelsome had also settled down to be quiet aristocratic collectors of art. The result is a hoard of late Renaissance and Baroque painting, displayed in the **Galleria Colonna**, the only part of the building open to the public. The paintings are not labelled, but a key to the works is available.

The first room, after the vestibule at the top of the stairs, features portraits of various Colonnas, along with polished, languishing Venuses by Florentine Mannerists Bronzino and Salviati, and Roman fantasies of the 1400s Florentine Bartolommeo di Giovanni; certainly the most arresting painting is a *Temptation of St Anthony* by an unknown

follower of Hieronymus Bosch, with ladies, monsters, mysterious fish and bagpipe-birds – the subconscious of the holy hermit.

Next comes the glorious, gilded **Great Hall**, with ceiling frescoes representing the apotheosis of Marcantonio Colonna, and scenes of the Battle of Lepanto, the great naval defeat of the Turks in 1571, where Colonna played a small role; paintings include a flaccid *Assumption* by Rubens, more Colonnas, and a *Madonna del Soccorso* by the Umbrian artist L'Alunno – a familiar subject in Umbrian art: the Devil trying to steal a baby, the Madonna ready to whack him with a big club.

The third room, the **Hall of the Desks**, takes its name from two serious pieces of furniture, one cabinet covered with intricately carved ivory panels, reproducing works of Michelangelo and Raphael, the other in *pietra dura* arabesques, with bronze statuettes of the muses. We owe the ceiling, a powdered fairyland of battles, *putti*, terrible Turks, voluptuous maidens, and dreamy pink and blue boats, to Sebastiano Ricci, a happy 18th-century virtuoso better known in Venice than his Roman birthplace. Underneath, Gaspard Dughet left a memorable series of enchanted Baroque landscapes.

The ceiling in the fourth room deals with the apotheosis of Martin V, the only Colonna to become a pope. Pier Francesco Mola contributes a solemn, almost Impressionist *Cain and Abel*, and Guido Reni an *Angel Gabriel*. Next comes the **Throne Room**, where a chair (turned to the wall) is kept ready just in case a pope should drop in for a visit. On the wall is a beautiful portolan map of Europe from the 1500s that belonged to Marcantonio Colonna (note how Britain is almost *terra incognita*).

The sixth and last room is named after Maria Mancini. Perhaps better known as a once-famous brand of cigars, the real Maria was the niece of Cardinal Mazarin, the fellow who ran France for much of the late 17th century. His father, who must have been a remarkable fellow himself, had been the Colonnas' butler. He somehow married into the family (and on the death of his wife, picked up another among the Colonnas' arch rivals, the Orsini); his granddaughter Maria married Prince Colonna himself. The paintings include an eloquent, shadowy *Moses* by Guercino, and a *Madonna* from the workshop of Botticelli; Maria herself appears in a portrait by Caspar Netscher.

From the museum, you can look across Via della Pilotta into the other half of the Colonna estate, a garden (no admittance) strewn with ruins of one of ancient Rome's most impressive exotic shrines, Caracalla's Temple of Serapis (65ft columns, all marble; one piece of marble from the roof weighs over 100 tons). Finding a private garden like this in the centre of a city is something that could only happen in Rome.

Santi Apostoli J8

Piazza dei SS. Apostoli, t 06 679 4085; bus 62, 85, 95, 117, 119. Open 7–12 and 4–7.

The church of Santi Apostoli is encased in the bulk of the Palazzo Colonna like a pearl in a Rococo oyster. Emperor Justinian's favourite eunuch – Narses; the general who whipped the Goths and reconquered Italy for the empire – built it in 560. After an unfortunate rebuilding in 1702 (destroying Renaissance frescoes) and a new façade by Napoleon's architect, Valadier, this building shows little of its origins. In the portico, added under Julius II, is an 1807 tomb by Canova, two Byzantine lions and a relief of a Roman imperial eagle, found in the Forum of Trajan.

SS. Apostoli belongs to the Franciscan Friars Minor, who look after it well – the cleanest statues and squeakiest floors in all Rome. Leopold II, the kind and liberal Duke of Tuscany who allowed himself to be overthrown in 1859, obligingly getting out of the way of the Risorgimento, is buried here, as is Clementina Sobieska, the wife of the pretender James III, and the famous Greek scholar Cardinal Bessarione; the cardinal gave the church a fine 15th-century Greek *Madonna*, which can be seen in the first chapel on the right aisle. Thoroughly Baroqued by Carlo Fontana, nothing inside would make you guess that parts of the church are almost 1,500 years old, although there are two lovely Renaissance tombs flanking the high altar. That on the right may have been designed by Michelangelo; the other is from the school of Andrea Bregno, who contributed another one himself, that of Raffaello della Rovere, Julius II's father. It's down in the crypt.

Across the narrow Piazza dei Santi Apostoli, the 1665 **Palazzo Odescalchi** sports a façade by Bernini. At the end of the piazza, **Palazzo Muti** was the Roman abode of the exiled James III, the Old Chevalier, a gift of the Pope in 1719. Bonnie Prince Charlie was born here and despite great expectations, died here.

Wax Museum J8

Piazza dei Santi Apostoli 67, t 06 679 6482; bus 40, 60, 64, 70, 117, 170. Open 9–8; adm €4.

Woebegone but endearing, Rome's Museo delle Cere is a family-run operation, in a corner of the old Palazzo Colonna block, where the young folks can be seen after school dusting off the statues and spraying around cans of room freshener. There's more than just wax: a genuine gas chamber and an electric chair, for example, and a fine display of ceramic dinosaurs. Among the figures represented, all with wonderfully big ears, are a Roman rock band, the Big Three at Yalta, the Seven Dwarfs, and the famous charlatan Cagliostro predicting to Marie Antoinette her fate – with a fishbowl for a crystal ball. The biggest tableau portrays the last meeting of the Grand Council of Fascism, on 25 July 1943, with dozens of nasty blackshirts who haven't yet mentioned to Mussolini that the king was about to have him arrested and packed off in an ambulance. A natty fellow in a 1920s suit, looking on in the background, is identified as 'Lord Byron, a famous English poet'.

Capitoline Hill and Tiber Banks

Capitoline Hill and Tiber Banks

The Capitol was the head of the world, where the consuls and senators abode to govern the Earth ... all adorned with gold and silver and brass and costly stones, to be a mirror to all nations. And it was therefore called Golden Capitol, because it excelled in wisdom and beauty before all the realms of the world.

The 12th-century guidebook
Mirabilia Urbis Romae

None of the above is really true, but by the time a monkish chronicler compiled the *Mirabilia Urbis*, the Capitoline Hill had completely passed into legend. Rome did not begin here, nor did the hill ever serve as a seat of government in ancient times. But so entangled is this smallest and steepest mount with Rome's state myths and its presiding deities, that for all the citizens of the empire it was indeed the *caput* of the world they knew.

According to the historian Dionysius of Halicarnassus, workers digging the foundations for King Tarquin Priscus' original Temple of Jupiter found the head of a freshly slain man, dripping blood. Unable to get an explanation from the local soothsayers, Tarquin turned to the Etruscan oracles, who assured him that the prodigy meant that Rome was ordained by fate to be 'head' of all Italy. Another story had the name coming from *Caput Tollii*, the head of a mythical hero Tollius; either way, the tale follows a recurring motif in myth – like the head of the ancient god Bran buried under the Tower of London, which keeps England from harm.

The archaeologists' story is that sometime in the 7th century, the hill became a joint religious sanctuary for the scattered communities on the other Roman hills. Tarquin's great Temple of Jupiter (traditionally 590 BC)

1 Lunch

Piperno, *Via Monte de' Cenci 9*, t 06 6880 6629; wheelchair accessible; *tram* 8, *bus* 23, 280. *Open* Sept–July Tues–Sat 12.45–2.30 and 8–10.30, Sun 12.30–3. *Expensive*. Hearty, filling Jewish-Roman cuisine and good wines; you'll need a good post-prandial stroll to work off the *crostata di ricotta*.

2 Coffee and Cakes

Caffè dei Musei Capitolini, *Piazza del Campidoglio*, t 06 678 2862; *bus* 46, 62, 64. *Open* Tues–Sat 9–6. Snacks and ice creams on a breezy *terrazza* – quiet, relaxing and just what you need to rest your feet and eyes after sightseeing.

3 Drinks

Da Bleve, *Via di S. Maria del Pianto 9/a–11*, t 06 686 5970; *tram* 8. *Open* Tues–Sat 12–6. A traditional *enoteca*, which also serves light meals to gastronomes (smoked fish, cheeses, cured meats and salads) at lunchtime.

became the chief shrine of the state religion, replaced several times in the following centuries. Like most of the other temples on the hill, it disappeared almost without a trace during the Dark Ages, when the former hub of the Roman world became known as Monte Caprino – Goat Hill. The Capitol's long-delayed reappearance in history came in the 1140s, during Arnold of Brescia's republican revolution, when the Romans refounded the Senate and built a fortified palace for its meetings. Throughout the Middle Ages, this new Capitol was the symbol of popular aspirations, and often of resistance against the popes.

Nowadays, you'll have to get around the looming hulk of the Vittoriano to even see it. In antiquity, the main approaches to the hill were on the south side, facing the Forum; since medieval times, when the centre of Roman life shifted to the Campus Martius, new ascents were created from the north.

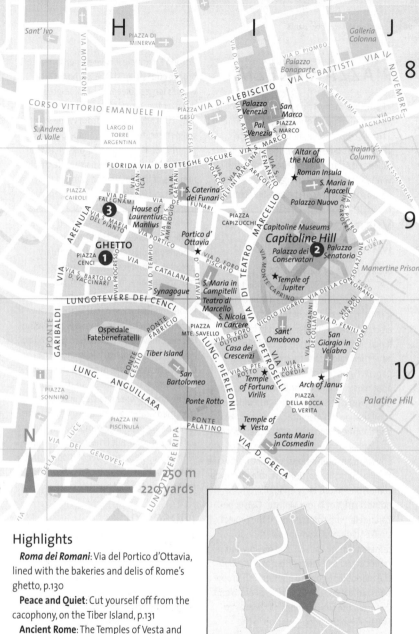

Highlights

Roma dei Romani: Via del Portico d'Ottavia,
lined with the bakeries and delis of Rome's
ghetto, p.130

Peace and Quiet: Cut yourself off from the
cacophony, on the Tiber Island, p.131

Ancient Rome: The Temples of Vesta and
Fortuna Virilis, p.128

Medieval and Renaissance: Michelangelo's
classic masterpiece of urban design, the
Piazza del Campidoglio, p.124

Baroqueorama: The complex façade of
Rainaldi's Santa Maria in Campitelli, p.130

Unexpected Rome: Dare to stick your hand
into the Bocca della Verità, p.127

PIAZZA VENEZIA

Rome has many a fine urban ornament, but Piazza Venezia isn't one of them; it's more of a traffic-crazed black sheep, reduced to playing vestibule to a man-made glacier called the Altar of the Nation. But Piazza Venezia is the closest thing modern Rome has to a centre, where the bus lines converge.

Vittorio Emanuele II Monument [9]

Bus 40, 46, 62, 63, 64, 70, 81, 87.

Risorgimento Italy's own self-inflicted satire, the Vittorio Emanuele II Monument (or Vittoriano, or Altar of the Nation) was erected between 1885 and 1911 in honour of Italian unity, an airy concept that the Italians have tried vainly to secure with this giant paperweight, one of the world's greatest apotheoses of kitsch, 500ft long and 200ft high. Giuseppe Sacconi's design, a unique combination of typewriter, wedding cake, and dentures which the architect envisioned as a 'public container', was chosen out of 95 entries in an international competition, while the glaring white *botticino* marble of Brescia comes, understandably enough, from the home district of Prime Minister Giuseppe Zanardelli, who commissioned the project. Unlike traditional Roman travertine, it refuses to 'drink the sun' and mellow, but rather bleaches ever brighter; like *The Blob* the monument grew to nightmarish proportions, until it hid the Capitol and Forum and distorted the surroundings all the way to St Peter's, so the pope, holed up in the Vatican, could look out over the city and feel its glacial chill. In one of history's most devastating backhanded compliments, Kaiser Wilhelm called the Vittoriano the 'maximum expression of Latin genius'.

Lately its guardians have been very peevish about letting people roam over its arctic wastes to enjoy the superb views from the top or inspect its complex sculptural allegory. In the centre of it all, the modest virtues of Vittorio Emanuele II have earned him a 40ft bronze equestrian statue, perhaps the world's largest, bleeding his blue-green guts out over the immaculate white. Underneath, Italy's Unknown Soldier from World War I sleeps peacefully with a round-the-clock guard. Even if there's no admission to the monument, you can see, on the left, the remains of the Republican tomb of tipsy-sounding C. Publicus Bibulus that once marked the beginning of the Via Flaminia.

Few living souls have penetrated the vast, mildewing bowels of the Vittoriano, where models and plaster casts of its statuary collect dust under some fine turn-of-the-century mosaics. Intrepid explorers have noted a long-forgotten museum of the Risorgimento tucked in one corner; a tiny museum-sanctuary of Marine Flags, on the left side, may be breached from 9.30 to 1.30.

Among the medieval alleys under the Capitol, cleared away to form a stage for the Vittoriano, was the home and studio of Michelangelo, where he died in 1564 (commemorated by a plaque on the phoney-Renaissance insurance company opposite Palazzo Venezia). But if he were still nearby, what would he, as founder of modern artistic egomania, have thought of the boondoggle that replaced his old home?

Museo di Palazzo Venezia [8]

Via del Plebiscito 118, t 06 679 8865; bus 40, 46, 62, 63, 64, 70, 81, 87. Open Tues–Sun 9–7.30, Sat until 11pm; adm €4.

The square is named after the Palazzo Venezia, the dark, fortress-like palace that occupies the entire west side of the square. A Florentine creation of fine proportions, attributed variously to Giuliano da Maiano or Alberti, it was Rome's first important secular building of the Renaissance (1455). The fun-loving Cardinal Pietro Barbo of Venice (later Paul II) enlarged it a few years later so he could watch the finish of his Carnival horse races from Rome's most famous balcony – the same one used by Mussolini to whip up the 'oceanic' crowds in the piazza (renamed the Forum of the Fascist Empire in those days) and declare war on the United States. In between, the palace was used as a residence for popes, Venetian ambassadors and cardinals, and the Austrian ambassador after the fall of the Venetian Republic.

The museum contains Rome's most important collection of decorative arts. At the time of writing the exhibits have been partially rearranged as part of a long-term but as yet unrealized plan for their display. Byzantine jewellery and finely carved ivory triptychs and coffers, especially an 11th-century one portraying the life of David; a valuable collection of Florentine *cassoni* (wooden marriage chests), one carved like a medieval cathedral; the 13th-century gilded bronze *Lunette della Mentorella* found near Palestrina; silver work from Abruzzi, paintings by early Renaissance artists Starnina, Bicci di Lorenzo and Giovanni da Modena and a golden quattrocento Venetian triptych studded with gems, are all in the collection. One long hall is devoted to small Renaissance bronzes, the favourite dust magnets of the 16th century, including a club-wielding Venetian *Hercules* who has a stride and swing uncannily reminiscent of Joe Di Maggio in Yankee Stadium. After home-run Hercules come plaster models and sketches by Jacopo Sansovino, Bernini and Algardi and later paintings: a double portrait attributed to Giorgione, works by Guercino, Pietro Novelli, and two small works by Gothic master Pisanello. Waiting to be arranged are the collections of armour, tapestries, and other paintings.

There's almost always a special exhibition – often the most interesting shows in town and well worth checking out – in the stately Venetian-opulent halls, including the vast mosaic-floored **Sala del Mappamondo**, with a frescoed map of the world of 1495. This was Mussolini's office, where he routinely rogered anything in a skirt and intimidated out-of-favour male visitors by making them walk 60ft in silence to his desk. Another of his tricks was to leave the lights burning all night so passing Romans would think he was working late. Luigi Barzini, in *The Italians*, remarked that in the '30s he 'stumbled on one of the darkest state secrets of the time', from a soldier to whom he had given a lift; apparently Mussolini spent most of his day in the palace courtyard, chatting with the drivers and doormen.

Palazzo Bonaparte 18

Vicolo Doria; **bus** *40, 46, 62, 63, 64, 70, 81, 87.*
Mussolini wasn't the only celebrity to spend time in Piazza Venezia. On the corner of the Corso, the Palazzo Bonaparte now houses a café, but between 1815 and 1836 its chief resident was Napoleon's mother, Letizia Bonaparte, who had her boy's eagle emblazoned on the façade. Pius VII, the very pope Napoleon had exiled, had welcomed her to Rome, perhaps partly because she offered to lend him money at an interest rate that undercut the city's banks. The big Rococo palace on the other side of the Corso is the Palazzo Doria Pamphili, with its notable collection of paintings (*see* p.111).

PIAZZA SAN MARCO

San Marco 18

Piazza San Marco 48, **t** *06 679 5205;* **bus** *40, 46, 62, 63, 64, 70, 81, 87.* **Open** *7.30–7.30.*
Adjacent to the Palazzo Venezia, in Piazza San Marco, the ancient church of San Marco is the most convenient place to see an example of one of Rome's glories – mosaics from the Dark Ages.

Founded in 336 by Pope Mark, San Marco is one of Rome's oldest titular churches, traditionally that of the cardinal from Venice. Popes have revamped it constantly since, but always preserved its ancient basilica form. The beautiful mosaic (833) in the apse shows one of these pontiffs, Gregory IV, holding a model of his version of the church while being introduced to Christ by Pope Mark; along the bottom caper white llama-horses.

When Cardinal Pietro Barbo built the Palazzo Venezia he incorporated San Marco into the palazzo, rebuilding it and adding the ornate gilded ceiling and the Cosmati pavement, still partially visible. Leon Battista Alberti and Giuliano da Maiano gave it an elegant new portico and loggia from which the pope gave his blessing. The rest was Baroqued over in the 18th century; the chapel just right of the high altar has a painting of Pope Mark by Melozzo da Forlì.

Palazzetto Venezia 18

Piazza San Marco; bus 40, 46, 62, 63, 64, 70, 81, 87.

On the west end of Piazza San Marco, the Palazzetto Venezia (mid-15th century) formerly stood in Piazza Venezia, and was moved to reveal the Vittoriano in all its blazing enormity. It has what many believe is the loveliest Renaissance courtyard in Rome, though to see it you have to make a special request next door, at no.49, to see it. Just to the right, rather forgotten now in its corner, is a large bust of the well-endowed 'Madama Lucrezia' (a recycled statue of Isis), who since the 15th century has been Rome's only female 'talking statue' in the style of Pasquino (*see p.84*).

CAPITOLINE HILL

Aracoeli Staircase 19

Bus 40, 46, 62, 63, 64, 70, 81, 87, then foot.

Two travertine staircases lead up to the Capitol from Via Teatro di Marcello, behind the Vittoriano, one (on the left) to Santa Maria in Aracoeli, the other to Michelangelo's Piazza del Campidoglio. The foot of these steep stairs is a fatal spot in Rome's history. In 121 BC a gang of senators and their clients and slaves murdered the great reformer Tiberius Gracchus here. In 1354 the scene was repeated when Cola di Rienzo, trying to escape Rome in disguise, was recognized by the rings on his fingers and torn to pieces by a mob of the citizens he had so grievously betrayed. Rienzo himself built the left-hand staircase, the Scalinata d'Aracoeli, and was the first to climb it; half-way up is a flattering statue of the *Last Tribune*, on a base of random antique fragments (like a view inside Rienzo's brain). While he ruled Rome, the church at the top was the meeting place of the reconstituted 'Senate'. As you ascend the steep flight of steps, be sure to swivel round for a wonderful view of Roman rooftops.

Roman *Insula* I9

To the left of this staircase is a jumble of ancient brick and masonry that most visitors never notice – the best surviving example of an *insula* in Rome. Originally six storeys tall, reconstructions of it in the Museo della Civiltà Romana in EUR (*see* p.241) show a building that would look perfectly at home on any modern street, with a row of shops on the ground floor (now under the street level) and large windows on the mezzanine that may have been a wealthy house or offices.

The incongruous little steeple and frescoed apse on the side belonged to the church of **San Biagio della Pagnotta**, built into the half-occupied ruin in the Middle Ages.

Santa Maria in Aracoeli I9
Scalinata d'Aracoeli, t 06 679 8155. Open 6.30–6.

Originally built in the 6th or 7th century, the 'altar of Heaven' commemorates the legend that the ancient Sibyl of Tivoli proph-esied the coming of Jesus and told Augustus to build a temple here to the 'first born of God'. Until quite recently, people believed this to have been the site of the Temple of Jupiter. Edward Gibbon thought so, and while 'musing over the ruins' here he resolved to write the story of Rome's fall. Marcantonio Colonna also thought Jupiter's temple was here, celebrating the last old-fashioned Triumph on the site after helping the Spaniards and Venetians beat the Turks at Lepanto in 1571. In fact, it was the site of the *Arx*, Rome's first citadel, where the honking of the geese, warning of a surprise night attack, saved the besieged Romans during the Gaulish sack of 390 BC. For centuries, the Romans commemorated the event each year by leading a goose on a triumphal parade in a chariot through the Forum (and crucifying a dog in memory of the sleeping watchdogs).

Later, the site held the temple of Juno Moneta. The title translates as 'warning' or 'admonishing' (in memory of the geese), but for us it means the origin of our words *mint* and *money*; the Roman state mint and treasury were part of the temple complex.

Some of Juno's columns found their way into the original church. Though it was rebuilt in the 1200s and again in 1575, no one was ever able to give it a façade; its stark brick wall with the tiny rose windows, looming over the stairs, is still somehow one of the landmarks of Rome. Beyond it, the gaudily decorated interior makes a striking contrast, hung with ballroom chandeliers under a gilt ceiling. On one of the columns on the left side of the nave, you can see the inscription *a cubiculo Augustorum* – it came from Augustus' apartments on the Palatine.

Near the entrance are three Renaissance tombs, including that of Giovanni Crivelli, by Donatello – not a very representative work of the greatest Renaissance sculptor, and badly worn down from too many centuries on the floor, but one of his only two works in Rome (the other is in St Peter's). Another tomb, that of the astronomer Lodovico Margani by Sansovino, stands opposite the main door.

In the first chapel of the right aisle is the series of frescoes by Pinturicchio on the *Life of St Bernard of Siena*; brilliantly coloured and drawn with a careful attention to detail (note the fantasy architecture and the charming band of angel musicians), they rank among the finest early Renaissance cycles in Rome. Beyond the grotesque giant figure of Pope Gregory XIII, the **Tomb of Luca Savelli** is probably by Arnolfo di Cambio, the great medieval sculptor-architect who designed Florence's Cathedral and Palazzo Vecchio. As was common in the Rome of the Middle Ages, Arnolfo built the tomb around an ancient sarcophagus.

Besides contributions of the Renaissance Tuscans, the Aracoeli has some fine embell-ishments by the medieval Cosmati family: the pavement and the lovely pair of pulpits (*ambones*), and in the right transept, the **Tomb of Matteo di Acquasparta**, with a painting by Pietro Cavallini.

The most celebrated miracle-working icon in Rome, and perhaps the only one that still makes house calls, used to reside in the second chapel of the right aisle: the **Santo Bambino** (Holy Child), carved by angels in olive wood from the Garden of Gethsemane, and encrusted with gold and jewels. Sadly, the original Holy Baby was stolen from the church and never retrieved; a copy was immediately made, however, blessed by the Pope, and set in its place. The Bambino is often taken out, as a last resort, to the sickbeds of the desperately ill (according to Dickens, who witnessed such an occasion, its sudden appearance often succeeded in scaring them to death), and it receives letters from troubled souls the world over. Every year at Christmas, Roman children pay their respects to the image, reciting the poems and songs they have composed in its honour.

In the left aisle, besides monuments to Popes Leo X and Paul III – neither of whom is buried here – is a *St Anthony* by another early Renaissance Florentine, Benozzo Gozzoli (second chapel), and an unusual 16th-century *Allegory of the Virgin*, drawn from the Book of Revelation (first chapel).

Piazza del Campidoglio I9

Bus *40, 46, 62, 63, 64, 70, 81, 87, then foot.*

Rome's civic centre, at the summit of the Capitoline Hill, was begun in 1534. It contains the city hall and the Capitoline Museums, in an ensemble of buildings around a piazza that is Michelangelo's great contribution to urban design. To reach it, take the right-hand stairway, the **Cordonata**, up to the Capitol from Via Teatro di Marcello. Also designed by Michelangelo, it's an effortless climb, up a ramp crossed with shallow ridges – stone versions of ropes traditionally laid across hilly paths to help animals climb up them (hence the name: *cordone*= rope). As you climb, the piazza slowly comes into view, a miniature open-air museum of Roman sculpture.

The two big fellows at the top of the stair are the **Dioscuri** (the heavenly twins, Castor and Pollux). The striking thing about them is their peculiar headgear: the odd caps (which they always sport in classical art) recall the eggshell from which they were born, after Zeus in the form of a swan ravished their

mother Leda. Keeping them company are stone images of triumphs, milestones from the Appian Way, and statues of Constantine and Constans. Their most famous neighbour, gilded bronze equestrian **Marcus Aurelius**, has now, after years of restoration, been placed behind a glass screen in the courtyard of the Palazzo Nuovo, so unless you buy a ticket you can only see the copy.

The modern replica of Marcus Aurelius stands on the original pedestal, designed by Michelangelo, who was also responsible for the lovely geometric pattern in the pavement around it. The pattern is best seen from atop the stairs in front of Palazzo Senatorio.

Palazzo Senatorio I–J9

Rome's city hall occupies the site of the medieval Senate House; its tower is almost a copy of its medieval predecessor, where a big bell hung to summon the citizens to war or to assemblies, imitating the practice of the free trading cities of Tuscany and northern Italy. Below Michelangelo's elegant double staircase, the goddess Roma herself gazes over the piazza; she was originally a statue of Minerva, transformed when the Empire evolved the artificial cult of the deified Rome. The building has seen more than its share of history: Mazzini and Garibaldi's Roman Republic was born here in the revolutions of 1848, and the present Italian Republic was declared here after the plebiscite in 1946; it was also the birthplace of the European Community, upon the signing of the Treaty of Rome here in 1957. The building is closed to visitors, but Rome's birthday, 21 April, is celebrated with free entrance to city museums, and the palazzo is sometimes one of them.

The palace rests on the massive foundations of the **Tabularium**, the Roman state archive; these can be seen better from the Forum. From the right-hand side of the Palazzo del Senatorio, Via di Monte Tarpeo runs downhill. From here there are stupendous views over the Roman Forum. The steep cliffs on the hill are generally believed to be the famous **Tarpeian Rock**, from which the Romans tossed condemned criminals.

Tarpeia, after whom it is named, was a Roman maiden who betrayed the Capitol to the Sabines; they smashed her to pulp with their shields by way of thanks; no one liked a traitor in those days.

Capitoline Museums |9

Piazza del Campidoglio; Palazzo Nuovo, t 06 678 2862; Palazzo dei Conservatori, t 06 6710 2071. Open Tues–Sat 9–7, Sun 9–6.45, holidays 9–1.45; adm free last Sun of every month.

Both of the other palaces on the piazza are part of the Capitoline Museums, the best-kept and richest collection of Roman art. The *palazzo* and the musuem displays were extensively restored for the Giubileo (millennium) and reopened in the spring of 2000. **Palazzo dei Conservatori** is now particularly attractive, with coffered ceilings and 16th-century frescoes. A corridor under the piazza now joins the two palaces and the *tabularium* under Palazzo Senatorio.

The **Palazzo Nuovo** (1655), on the north side of the square, houses the greatest sculptures, many donated by Sixtus IV in 1471, before there was a Vatican museum to contain the papal hoard. **Marcus Aurelius** is its newest captive; mottled with gold and verdigris, the benign and serious image of the philosopher-emperor represents Rome at its best. The statue survived destruction only because the Christians believed it was really Constantine, and they set it up for centuries in front of the pope's palace at the Lateran; Michelangelo moved it here when he redesigned the Campidoglio. An old Roman superstition holds that the world will end when the last bit of gold flakes off. Fortunately, thanks to the restorers and the new glass cage, that doesn't look too imminent. Marcus shares the courtyard with the huge, vaguely sinister form of *Marforio*, a 2nd-century AD river god. Before he was imprisoned in a fountain, Marforio sprawled at the foot of the Capitol, where, as one of Rome's 'talking statues', he exchanged witticisms with Pasquino. Next are two famous *sarcophagi*, one carved with a vigorous battle between the Romans and Gauls; the other,

an unusual double sarcophagus of the 3rd century AD, has scenes of the life of Achilles.

Other marble celebrities are gathered on the first floor; beginning with the *Dying Gaul*, a copy of a bronze made in Pergamon in the 3rd century BC, commemorating Attalos I's defeat of the Gauls – surely the most poignant and noble work a nation ever created in memory of a defeated foe. Next, the graceful *Young Satyr*, a copy of Praxiteles' original, which inspired Hawthorne's *The Marble Faun*, the book every traveller in the 19th century brought to read in Rome; a Hellenistic *Eros and Psyche* that inspired many later baubles; the red marble *Laughing Silenus*, a copy of a Hellenistic work; *Infant Hercules*, wrestling with a snake, said to be a portrait of Caracalla already ugly at the tender age of five. Two rooms are lined with busts of philosophers (Homer, Socrates, Pythagoras and other leading lights) and emperors, where the Roman fascination with realism is striking – unlike the idealizing Greeks, the Romans wanted to be remembered with all their flaws intact, creating unflattering marble 'photographs' in which Augustus comes out fairly august; Caracalla with his sideburns looks like a Victorian robber baron and Elagabalus like the child molester he probably was.

Among the emperors sits a fine statue of Helen, mother of Constantine, and on the walls are two exquisite bas-reliefs of Endymion and Perseus rescuing Andromeda. Two expressive statues of old women stand out – one terrified and one tipsy. The voluptuous *Capitoline Venus* is so steamy she gets a room to herself; an excellent Roman copy of Praxiteles' *Aphrodite of Cnidos*, which so aroused at least one ancient Greek that he sexually assaulted it; the statue was discovered in the 17th century where its owner, fearing prudish Christians, had walled it up for safekeeping. The *Room of Doves* is named after two charming works: a jewel-like mosaic from Hadrian's villa and a statue of a little girl sheltering a dove in her hands.

Save your ticket for the rest of the museum across in the **Palazzo dei Conservatori** the piazza, rebuilt in 1564 after a design by Michelangelo. Dominating the courtyard like lost props from a Fellini movie are the giant head, foot, and pointing hand from a colossal statue of Constantine found in the Basilica of Maxentius (the rest of him was apparently made of wood, dressed in sheets of bronze); here, too, is an inscription from the **Arch of Claudius** (AD 51) celebrating his conquest of Britain, and reliefs of other Roman conquests taken from the temple of Hadrian in Piazza di Pietra. Inside are more triumphal reliefs from the **Arch of Marcus Aurelius** – some of the finest ever done in Rome, including scenes of the emperor's clemency and piety, and his victorious receptions in Rome. Marcus always looks a little worried in these, perhaps considering his good-for-nothing son Commodus and the empire he would inherit, more than ever sunk into corruption and excess.

Among the bronzes is the famous *Capitoline Wolf*, an Etruscan work of the 6th century BC, to which Antonio Pollaiuolo added the suckling twins in 1510; the *Spinario*, a 1st-century BC bronze of a boy pulling a thorn from his foot; a beautiful but uncomfortable bronze bed, a litter, a reconstructed chariot (used to transport images of the gods to the Circus games), a hermaphrodite, a horse and half a bull. The late Empire works are often in a kitsch style recalling the 1964 New York World Fair, such as the swollen head, hand and globe of *Constans II*, and another ball from the top of the Vatican Obelisk, once believed to contain the ashes of Julius Caesar and used for target practice in the 1527 Sack of Rome.

One room holds statues, in the popular 'archaic' fashion of the 1st century AD; another has imported Attic vases of the 6th century BC, one with pictures of *Achilles playing dice with Ajax* and another with *Odysseus and the Cyclops*. More recent efforts include statues of *Charles of Anjou* by Arnolfo di Cambio, *Innocent X* by Algardi, and *Urban VIII* by Bernini. A passage leads past a musty tufa wall of the 6th-century BC Temple of Jupiter Best and Greatest (*see* p.127) to the

New Wing, with Republican art, including some of the earliest Roman frescoes ever discovered (3rd century BC), a relief of *Marcus Curtius* hurtling into the abyss, mosaics, friezes, and a 5th-century BC *Apollo the Archer*. The exhibits continue in the **Museo Nuovo** in Palazzo Caffarelli, off the tufa wall passage: look especially for the Hellenistic statue of the *Muse Polyhymnia*, one of the loveliest pieces in the museum; also more good Roman busts and reproductions of Greek art.

The **Pinacoteca** on the second floor has a small but diverse collection of paintings: from the 14th century, a series of panels on New Testament scenes; a beautiful but anonymous 16th-century *Madonna, Child, and Saints*; Guercino's *Burial of S. Petronilla* (1622), painted for St Peter's, with a gaping tomb in the foreground from which mysterious hands emerge to support the saint's body, while above she is welcomed into heaven. Another Baroque painting, even more influential in its day, was Pietro da Cortona's *Rape of the Sabines* (1629), with its romantic-antique detail and twisting, sculptural groups of figures. Caravaggio contributes two works: *The Fortune Teller*, predicting adventure to a young man (a self-portrait?), and the *Young St John*, in a never-before-seen pose – a painting lost in a long gallery of 18th-century china monkey musicians in powdered wigs.

There's also a giant gilt bronze *Hercules*, found in the Forum Boarium, and a medley of Venetian art: masculine portraits by Gentile and Giovanni Bellini; *Mary Magdalenes* by Veronese and Tintoretto; an *Adulteress* by Palma Vecchio, and Lorenzo Lotto's sly *Gentleman with a Crossbow*. There's a copy of Jacopino del Conte's *Portrait of Michelangelo*, perhaps the best-known likeness of the artist; some cocky *Dutchmen* from Van Dyck; an eerie *Witch* by proto-romantic Salvator Rosa; rosy-cheeked *Romulus and Remus* by Rubens; and, disdainful of his fellow paintings, Velazquez's *Portrait of a Gentleman*, thought by some to be Bernini.

Temple of Jupiter |9

Via del Tempio di Giove, **t** *06 3996 7800.*

The street leading down behind the Palazzo dei Conservatori from beside the Cordonata passes gardens where fragments of the **Temple of Jupiter Optimus Maximus**, centre of the Roman world, can be seen through a gate. Currently under excavation and closed to the public, it is to be made part of the Capitoline Museums.

Before the Etruscans dominated Rome, Mars was the city's chief deity; when victorious generals finished their triumphal parades at the foot of this temple, they had their faces painted red to 'imitate Mars'. When King Tarquin Priscus began the Temple of Jupiter 'Best and Greatest' around 590 BC, he was expressing in stone an unrecorded but important religious revolution. As in all Etruscan temples, this one took the classical Greek form, but with three chambers instead of one, perhaps originally dedicated to the triad of Jupiter, Juno and Minerva (Tinia, Uni and Menvra to the Etruscans). It was dedicated by Tarquin the Proud in 534 BC.

The fragments of the cornice are from the last Temple, rebuilt by Domitian after a fire in AD 80. Even under the Empire, rubber-stamp consuls and other magistrates of ancient fame would come here to receive their insignia of office. Every year the Senate held its first meeting in the Temple, making the appropriate sacrifices, and on certain occasions the images of the three gods were carried through Rome in solemn procession – just as Italians today parade their Madonnas and saints on holy days. The 'Golden' Capitol, so called for its gilded roof, was not the largest temple ever built in Rome (that of Venus and Rome surpassed it), but shining atop its hill it would have been the city's most conspicuous landmark. Emperor Honorius' general, the Vandal Stilicho, made off with the gilt bronze roof and the golden doors and statues to pay his army, but the records are silent as to how the temple came to disappear so completely. Christians were no doubt anxious to be rid of it, as chief symbol of the old religion.

PIAZZA BOCCA DELLA VERITÀ

Rome's first settlement may have existed here, in the marshy area south of the Capitol called the Velabrum, the legendary spot where Romulus and Remus' basket washed up and where the she-wolf found them. Like all of Rome south of the Capitol and Forum, this quiet, almost deserted area is full of old churches; all have something of interest but many are rarely open.

Santa Maria in Cosmedin |10

Piazza Bocca della Verità, **t** *06 678 1419;* **bus** *81, 160, 204.* **Open** *10–7, in winter until 5.*

In the 8th century, this was the centre of the Schola Graeca, the Greek neighbourhood of Rome, its ranks swelled by refugees from iconoclast persecutions in the East. They must have loved their holy images dearly; the church Pope Adrian I rebuilt for them in the 770s soon acquired the appellation 'in Cosmedin', meaning 'decorated', from the same Greek root as our word *cosmetics* – and also, oddly enough, *cosmos*.

The church's best-known ornament is a marble disc that probably began life as a lid for a well or cistern. Carved with the ghostly face of a man, it was built into the façade of the medieval church to become the **Bocca della Verità** – the mouth of truth, which gives the piazza its name. Romans would come here to swear oaths, test the chastity of their wives, and close business deals. If you tell a lie with your hand in the image's mouth, he will bite it off. Go ahead and try it.

A fortuitous restoration of the 1890s peeled off the Baroque façade imposed by a well-meaning cardinal in 1741, leaving the exterior much as it was in the Middle Ages, but without the mosaics or paintings that must originally have covered it.

Inside, decorations include some excellent Cosmati work: pavement, candlesticks, choir screen, and bishop's throne, all dating from the 12th-century rebuilding that gave the church its campanile. The Gothic baldaquin over the altar came later (c.1290) but it too was the work of a Cosmati descendant. Among the more ancient remains are the recycled columns in the nave, and columns from an altar of Hercules in the crypt (possibly to commemorate his slaying of the giant Cacus here).

The medieval mosaics in the apse are very faded, but there is a lovely 8th-century mosaic of the *Adoration of the Magi* (detached) in a room off the right aisle. Little else remains of the Greek church, excepting perhaps the odd bit of marble latticework on the west wall, and the ceiling painted with stars – almost too faded to see, but the Greek original must have glittered with a bright blue and gold firmament.

Like San Teodoro, and several other early Roman churches, this one had its beginnings as chapel of a *diaconicon* – one of the pope's combination supply centres, military stores and charity distribution points. Gregory the Great began the system, commandeering the old warehouses to reorganize the food supply for Rome's beleaguered populace in the 590s. This centre, a stone's throw from the Circus Maximus, had been the bread of the bread and circuses – the *Statio Annonae*, headquarters of the imperial dole. Around the walls of the church are embedded 17 impressive columns from the *Annonae*, and near the door you will see a pair of round stones – the market's standard weights.

Temples of Vesta and Fortuna Virilis 110

Piazza Bocca della Verità; **bus** *81, 160, 204.*

To see the two best-preserved pagan temples in Rome you wouldn't look in the Forum or on the Palatine, but in this unlikely spot (where few visitors ever do find them). Across Via Petroselli, on the other side of Piazza Bocca della Verità, stand the round **Temple of Vesta** and the rectangular **Temple**

of Fortuna Virilis. Or so they've been named – both attributions are in fact mistaken guesses by early archaeologists. Vesta's, so called because its round shape reminded them of the Vestal Virgins' shrine in the Forum, was probably dedicated to Hercules Victor (2nd century BC); one of the very first marble buildings in Rome, built by a Greek architect and connected to the altar under S. Maria in Cosmedin. Its cornice and domed roof are long gone.

The other, originally much older, was rebuilt about the same time. It seems to have honoured Portunus, a god of harbours; this stretch of river was Rome's first port (and perhaps there was a connection with the safe landing of Romulus and Remus). Both temples, like the Pantheon, only survived thanks to their reconsecration as Christian churches.

Cloaca Maxima 110

Lungotevere Pierleoni; **bus** *81, 160, 204.*

If you lean over the Tiber embankment near the temples, you can see the mouth of King Tarquin's famous sewer, the Cloaca Maxima, still efficiently draining the Forum area after 2,400 years. The present tunnel, wide enough to drive two carriages through, is from the 2nd century BC. The Etruscans may get too much credit for engineering here – their drain was an open ditch.

Ponte Rotto 110

Lungotevere Pierleoni; **bus** *81, 160, 204.*

Just beyond the Ponte Palatino stand the sorrowful remains of Rome's first stone bridge, the Pons Aemilius, built in 142 BC. Now better known as the Ponte Rotto – the broken bridge – it was already collapsing in the 16th century when the popes started raiding its stone, inexplicably leaving the lone arch in midstream. Originally there were seven, a good indicator of how much wider the Tiber was, with its shallow banks, before the building of the embankments.

Arch of Janus I10

Via del Velabro; **bus** *63, 81, 95, 170.*

This bulky arch was built in honour of Constantine, or perhaps Constans II; its form, and the woeful fragments of older monuments snatched off to decorate it, testify to the decadence of the age. Of the figures on the keystones of the four arches, the standing ones were Janus and the goddess Roma, the seated ones Ceres and Minerva.

San Giorgio in Velabro I–J10

Via del Velabro 19; **bus** *63, 81, 95, 170.*
Open *9–1 and 3–6.30;* **adm** *free.*

A bomb explosion in 1993 destroyed the portico of this 7th-century basilica and damaged the apse by Pietro Cavallini; they have been carefully restored. The interior is elegant and simple. Attached to the side, the **Arcus Argentarium** was built in AD 204 by the moneychangers of Rome in honour of Septimius Severus and his family – you can make out the figures of the emperor, his wife, Julia Domna, and his son Caracalla. The space next to Caracalla was occupied by his brother Geta, until Caracalla murdered him. Geta instantly became a non-person, and his portrait, like the inscription on the Arch of Septimius Severus, was effaced. On the outer wall, under the cornice, is a hale and hearty relief of Hercules in his lion's skin.

The moneychangers had plenty of business on this spot; it was the **Forum Boarium**, early Rome's cattle market, and though it's hard to imagine cows tramping through the Urbs in imperial times, plenty of market business was transacted in the arch's shade.

Casa dei Crescenzi I10

Via Luigi Petroselli; **bus** *81, 160, 204.*

Incorporating fragments scavenged from every sort of ancient building, this is one of the best examples of medieval Rome's magpie school of architecture. It was built around 1100 for the powerful Crescenzi clan, descendants of former Castel Sant'Angelo dwellers and pontiff-killers Theodora and Marozia. The younger generation was conscious enough of Rome's great past to attempt this imitation of a classical noble dwelling – also conscious of the need to make it a strong fortress for defence.

Sacred Area of Sant'Omobono I10

Via Luigi Petroselli, **t** *06 6710 3819;* **bus** *44, 63, 81, 160, 170.* **Open** *Tues–Fri 9–1 by appointment only.*

Continuing back towards the Capitol on Via Petroselli, the church of Sant'Omobono stands amid excavations in what may be the oldest inhabited corner of Rome. Over the fence, you can see the foundations of 5th-century BC 'twin temples' to Fortuna and to Mater Matuta (the former under the church). Some fragments of pottery here go back as far as 1100 BC.

San Nicola in Carcere I10

Via del Teatro di Marcello 46; **bus** *46, 715, 716.*
Open *Mon–Sat 7–12 and 4–7.*

Across the street from Sant'Omobono, the church of incarcerated St Nick was built over the ruins of temples to Janus, Juno, and Spes (Hope) and last remodelled by Della Porta in 1599; the columns of the temples are still in plain view, helping to hold up the walls. This area, full of temples in ancient times, continued the densely populated string of markets, warehouses and docks along the Tiber; it was the **Forum Holitorium**, the marketplace for fruit and vegetables.

Teatro di Marcello I9–10

Via del Teatro di Marcello; **bus** *23, 44, 46, 60, 63, 81, 84, 95, 160, 170; can be viewed well from the street.*

Julius Caesar, the sort of Roman who might have appreciated real theatre, began the work on this weathered hulk; he planned it big (15,000 seats) to upstage Pompey, whose own theatre was just being completed. Augustus finished it in 23 BC, dedicating it to son-in-law Marcellus, who had just died. Despite the poets of the Latin New Comedy, serious theatre never caught on in Rome, and degenerated into bloody spectacles differing little from shows at the Colosseum. By 235, the public had decided it liked them better in amphitheatres, and this pile was abandoned; by the age of Constantine, Romans were carting off the stones to repair bridges.

In the Dark Ages, noble families turned the ruin into a fortress; its location dominated the Tiber and southern approaches to the shrunken city. It changed hands often; Fabii, Caetani, Savelli, Pierlioni, and Orsini all controlled it at one time or another. The Savelli commissioned Baldassare Peruzzi to add Renaissance style to the upper storeys, now fashionable apartments. Mussolini's archaeologists cleared the surroundings to excavate; before that, the half-sunken ruin with little shops hiding under the arches was one of the picturesque sights of the city.

Walking around the north side of the theatre, you pass three elegant standing columns which belonged to the **Temple of Apollo**, a 5th-century original rebuilt in 33 BC.

Santa Maria in Campitelli I9

Piazza di Campitelli, t 06 6880 3978; bus 44, 63, 81, 95, 160, 170. Open 7.20–12 and 4–7.

This Baroque church of 1663–7 is the masterpiece of Carlo Rainaldi, introducing North Italian elements to the Roman Baroque in the complex façade (very like his earlier S. Andrea della Valle) and the striking interior, where carefully placed pairs of columns shape the main axis into an unusual perspectivist effect.

Portico d'Ottavia I9

Via del Portico d'Ottavia; bus 44, 63, 81, 95, 160, 170.

The well-preserved Portico of Octavia is only a part of the original (the columned *propylaeum*, or entrance), which built by Augustus and named after his sister; behind it stretched a great square colonnade of some 300 columns, enclosing twin temples to Jupiter and Juno. There was also a library, and some celebrated works of Greek sculpture for decoration. The unusual thing about such a complex is its setting, at the edge of the hurly-burly of the Roman markets. It would not have seemed strange to a Roman, accustomed to crowds and noise, with every facet of urban life jumbled together. The ancient fishmarket was here too, the Forum Piscarium, and even if there were no stands inside the complex itself, the fish and their aroma were certainly close enough to distract the priests in the temples and the scholars at their desks.

THE GHETTO

In the Middle Ages, though the fish markets remained, this neighbourhood acquired a different destiny, as the home of the city's Jewish community. Much reduced from ancient times, when some 30–50,000 Jews populated both sides of the Tiber in this district, the community has survived every sort of persecution and hard times.

Via del Portico d'Ottavia H9

Walk down the main street of the Ghetto and do not be surprised to find a faint resemblance to a street on New York's Lower East Side: Jewish restaurants, a famous bakery, a kosher butcher, clothing wholesalers and workshops on the back streets. The four broad city blocks south of the street, bordered by Piazza delle Cinque Scuole and the Tiber, were the area of the Jewish Ghetto.

It is something of a misconception that ghettos are a relic of the bad old Middle Ages. In Italy at least, systematic, carefully planned persecution is a relatively recent phenomenon. That Counter-Reformation charmer, Paul IV, the father of the Inquisition, decreed that Jews should be locked up in a ghetto only in 1555. He also forced them to wear distinctive clothing, and attend sermons for their conversion, and he limited their livelihood to the trade in used clothes and old iron. Within this four-block area as many as 5,000 people lived, in an anthill-like maze of tall tenements and narrow alleys. Behind the Ghetto walls, which were locked at dusk, few non-Jews ever penetrated, other than society ladies sneaking in incognito to visit the renowned Jewish fortune-tellers.

Though all sources agree on the degradation of the closely packed Ghetto, it had its advantages: a refuge, physical and psychological, from common bigotry, and fixed rents in perpetuity. In 1870, one of the first acts of the new Italian Kingdom after the liberation of Rome was to tear down the Ghetto walls. Since then the Jewish community has largely moved on to other neighbourhoods, and the land has been completely cleared for new streets and buildings.

House of Laurentius Manlius H9

Via del Portico d'Ottavia 1/d; bus 44, 63, 81, 95, 160, 170.

Via del Portico d'Ottavia is an ancient street, with Roman and medieval remains built into later structures. Laurentius' house is the most outlandish, with its richly decorated façade, carved with family portraits and patriotic inscriptions. Manlius is fooling us; he is not an ancient Roman, but a Renaissance Lorenzo Manilio who built the house in 1468 – or year 2221 of the founding of Rome, as the Latin inscriptions attest.

Synagogue H9

Lungotevere dei Cenci, t 06 6840 0661; bus 44, 63, 81, 95, 160, 170. Open Mon–Thurs 9–6.30, Fri 9–1.30, Sun 9–12.30; closed Jewish holidays; adm €5.

The imposing main synagogue was built over the ruins of the Ghetto in the 1870s. Pope John Paul II paid a historic visit here in April 1986, the first modern pope to make such an ecumenical gesture. A visit to the

small adjoining museum, the **Mostra Permanente**, includes a brief tour of the synagogue. The *mostra* displays historical and ritual objects. Across from the synagogue, facing the Tiber, is a lonely little church with a faded Christian fresco and Hebrew inscription above the door. **San Gregorio** was one of the places where Ghetto Jews were compelled to attend Mass; the inscription uses a quotation from Isaiah (65.1-2) to reproach them for not converting.

TIBER ISLAND

The Isola Tiberina, the little island with the tapering ends, suggests a ship anchored in the river, and the ancient Romans used the thought to create a fond landmark, building a big stone prow and stern for it (remains of which can still be seen on the downstream side), and an obelisk in the middle for a mast. Most of the island is covered by a hospital – now, as always, for the Tiber Island has been dedicated to medicine since 289 BC.

The graceful bridge with the two arches leading to the island from the Ghetto is the oldest surviving bridge in Rome, the **Ponte Fabricio** or *Pons Fabricius* (H10), begun in 62 BC. On the other side, the second oldest complete Roman bridge, the **Ponte Cestio** or *Pons Cestius*, begun in 30 BC and much restored since, leads to Trastevere.

Ospedale Fatebenefratelli H10

Piazza Fatebenefratelli; bus 23, 280.

Legend states that after a plague in 293, the Sibylline Books directed the Romans to seek aid from the famous Temple of Aesculapius in Epidauros. The Greek god of healing sent one of his snakes (the serpents that twine around the staff of Aesculapius, a medical symbol to this day) into the Romans' ship where it coiled around the mast. Amazed at the prodigy, the Romans sailed home, where the serpent slid off the ship and swam up-river to this spot. A temple to the god was founded here, connected to a famous hospital.

Classical medicine (at least until the time of Galen, the great Roman scientist and physician of the 2nd century) depended heavily on the psychological side of healing; it would drive a modern doctor crazy. There were dream cures, requiring physicians or priests to appear to drugged patients in the guise of Aesculapius, holy serpents to apply to wounds, hypnotism and water from the sacred well. No one knows if a hospital survived here through the Dark Ages, but there was something like one in medieval times. The present Ospedale Fatebenefratelli ('Do well, brothers') dates from 1538. Despite its venerable appearance, it is a thoroughly up-to-date institution today.

San Bartolomeo H10

*Piazza San Bartolomeo all'Isola; **t** 06 687 7973; **bus** 23, 280. **Open** 9–10.30 and 4–6.30.*

Built over the ruins of Aesculapius' temple, the church of San Bartolomeo was built by Emperor Otto III in the late 900s, in honour of his friend St Adelbert, patron of Bohemia. The high altar is recycled from one of the greatest status symbols an ancient Roman could own – a porphyry bathtub; in front of it, the covered medieval well is probably the fount of the ancient hospital's sacred spring, carved with images of Christ and St Adelbert. In the chapel to the right, the expressive fresco of the Madonna and Child (with two pet Byzantine lions) dates from the founding of the church. One of the monks here, Padre Martini, is a notable sculptor, and the church is well endowed with his elegantly ascetic semi-abstract works.

Forums, Colosseum and Palatine Hill

06

Forums, Colosseum and Palatine Hill

Thou stranger, which for Rome
in Rome here seekest,
And nought of Rome
in Rome perceiv'st at all,
These same olde walls, old arches,
which thou seest,
Olde palaces, is that which Rome men call.
Behold what wreake, what ruine,
and what wast,
And how that she,
which with her mightie powre
Tam'd all the world,
hath tam'd herselfe at last,
The prey of Time,
which all things doth devowre.
Rome, living, was the world's
sole ornament,
And dead, is now the world's
sole moniment.

> Spenser, *The Ruines of Rome*

Spenser never visited Rome, but like many Elizabethans he loved to indulge in the melancholy of wreake and ruine, nowhere more striking than in the fossil heart of the ancient Empire – the seat of government, with its temples, forums, imperial palaces and the brooding shell of the Colosseum. Much of what awed visitors 1,500 years ago is now the world's most glorified rubble, poignantly setting off the few columns and arches that have survived a cannibalizing citizenry too close to Rome's past to have any respect for the sanctity of its remains. The most famous buildings of the empire were enthusiastically consigned to the dustbin of history and their building stone to homes and churches, their marble to the maw of the lime kiln. The Roman Forum became the Campo Vaccino, or Cow Pasture; the Palatine, residence of emperors, was planted with gardens; the Via Sacra, route of golden triumphs, renamed Via Fabatosta, or Street of Roast Beans; and nature forgave the Colosseum its enormities by strewing it with wild flowers. History's dust was so deep that scholars once argued that the Roman Forum was actually located elsewhere.

For Rome's dreamy-eyed lovers, these romantic, ivy-wreathed ruins among the cowpats were far more evocative than the sterile archaeological pits that they have become. The tendency in recent years has been to step back again, plant trees, and let the grass grow between the stones, making this walk through the core of ancient Rome a treat for the eye as well as for your historical imagination. Bring plenty of the latter, along with a pair of comfortable shoes and a bottle of wine to tantalize the thirsty ghosts. Or better yet, plan a picnic (discreetly, as the guards may not approve) in the Palatine gardens, over the ruins of Caligula's dining-room. In summer, start as early as possible to avoid heat stroke; there's little shade in the Forum, although the groves of the Palatine are a fine refuge from the afternoon sun.

1 Lunch

Pasqualino, *Via dei SS. Quattro Coronati 66*, **t** *06 700 4576*; **metro** *Colosseo*, **bus** *60, 84, 85, 175; wheelchair accessible.* **Open** *Tues–Sun 12–4 and 7–11.* **Inexpensive**. A venerable old trat dishing up classic Roman fare such as *spaghetti alla carbonara* and *saltimbocca*.

2 Coffee and Cakes

Ristorante Ulpia, *Foro Traiano 1/b–2*, **t** *06 678 9980*; **bus** *60, 84, 85, 175; wheelchair accessible.* **Open** *Mon–Sat 12–11.* Rome's oldest restaurant. A beautiful location overlooking the Imperial Fora, but awful food, so come between 4 and 7, when it functions as a café.

3 Drinks

Cavour 313, *Via Cavour 313*, **t** *06 678 5496*; **metro** *Cavour*, **bus** *75, 84, 117; wheelchair accessible.* **Open** *Oct–June Mon–Sat 12.30–2.30 and 7.30–12.30, Sun 7.30–12.30; July and Sept daily 12.30–2.30.* A civilized wood-beamed bar which serves delicious snacks to accompany whichever of its 500 wines you care to drink.

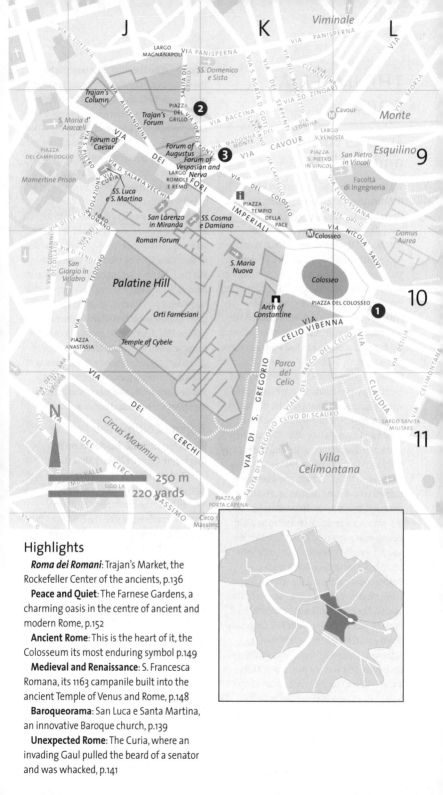

Highlights

Roma dei Romani: Trajan's Market, the Rockefeller Center of the ancients, p.136

Peace and Quiet: The Farnese Gardens, a charming oasis in the centre of ancient and modern Rome, p.152

Ancient Rome: This is the heart of it, the Colosseum its most enduring symbol p.149

Medieval and Renaissance: S. Francesca Romana, its 1163 campanile built into the ancient Temple of Venus and Rome, p.148

Baroqueorama: San Luca e Santa Martina, an innovative Baroque church, p.139

Unexpected Rome: The Curia, where an invading Gaul pulled the beard of a senator and was whacked, p.141

THE IMPERIAL FORA

Trajan's Forum and Markets J9

*Via dei Fori Imperiali, entrance on Via IV Novembre; **bus** 40, 60, 64, 70, 117, 170.* ***Open** Tues–Sun 9–6.30; **adm** €6.*

Begun in AD 107, Trajan's Forum, the grandest of the five imperial forums, was the Rockefeller Center of the Empire, a huge project of impeccable design by Apollodorus of Damascus. In building it, Trajan completed the twofold plan begun by that urban visionary, Julius Caesar, when he added the first imperial forum: to eliminate crowding in the Roman Forum and to link southern Rome to the Campus Martius by lopping off a spur of the Quirinale. This was no mean achievement in the pre-bulldozer era, especially when you consider that the base of Trajan's column marks the original ground level. The forum and marketplace he built in the new space awed contemporaries, and the nobility of its architecture inspired noble acts: here slaves were freed, Hadrian and Aurelian burned lists of state debtors and political prisoners, and Marcus Aurelius auctioned off the emperor's personal treasures to avoid raising new war taxes. When Constantine saw it he sadly conceded that nothing he could build in his new 'Rome' on the Bosphorus would equal the work of Trajan.

The modern entrance gives access to the second floor of the **market** hemicycle, built into the side of the Esquiline Hill. Originally it faced a matching hemicyclical wall, screening the forum, and now completely destroyed. This was the Harrods or Macy's of ancient times, lacking only escalators; 150 booths in all, now utterly bare, but 1,700 years ago stocking, it is thought, wine and oil on the ground and first floors; imports, pepper and spices on the second (even in the Middle Ages this floor remained the lane of pepper sellers, the flagstone-paved Via

Biberatica); on the third floor was the hall of the Congiaria, or welfare office, where food and money were distributed to the needy; and on the fourth, fresh fish were kept alive in two ponds, one filled with sea water piped in from Ostia, and the other fed with fresh water from an aqueduct; among them there might have been a mollusc or two from Colchester, delivered express by oyster-relay along the Roman roads.

The market owes its preservation to its conversion into a convent, while the south side was used as a castle. A mighty reminder of this is the knobby, medieval **Torre delle Milizie**, built on a Byzantine base over the hemicycle; according to one anachronistic tradition, it was from its splendid vantage point that Nero fiddled while Rome burned.

Steps lead down to the ground floor of the hemicycle and the once porticoed forum, of which lazy cats are the main feature today. From the corner, a tunnel (used for storing archaeological bits and pieces) cuts under the street to the second enclosure.

Trajan's Column J8–9

*Via dei Fori Imperiali; **bus** 64, 70, 117, 170.* ***Open** same hours as Trajan's Market.*

Built of marble drums, this 100 Roman feet-high column (perhaps designed by Trajan himself) was the centrepiece of Trajan's Forum. It commemorated the emperor's two victorious campaigns in Dacia (modern Romania, AD 101–2 and 105–6), the subject of the magnificent sculptural frieze, 650ft long and originally brightly painted, that winds around the column. The sculptors, anonymous but some of Rome's finest, expertly hid the drum joinings and the 43 windows that light the internal spiral stair leading to the viewing platform on top (closed). When Trajan died in Cilicia, his successor Hadrian brought his ashes back to Rome and buried them at the foot of the column. Never before had anyone been interred within the sacred limits of the *pomerium*; Hadrian explained that Trajan was no mere mortal, but a god.

The scrolling reliefs were designed to be read from the balconies of two libraries, one

Cats of Rome

Perhaps every country gets the cats it deserves.

H. V. Morton

The far left-wing parties in Venice once circulated petitions to have their town declared the 'World Capital of Stray Cats'. No Roman, feline or human, has spoken up to defend their own city's right to the title, confirmed by centuries of tradition – a sad reflection on the political lassitude of modern Rome. Well, forget Rome – what about Tàranto, on the Ionian Sea, where the first cats to discover Europe stepped ashore, some 2,500 years ago, carried on a Greek merchant ship from their Egyptian home? And what of Naples, with its precarious food chain involving some 30 rats per inhabitant, and in some areas a cat for each rat?

The oldest cat in Rome is the pampered stone pussy that sits looking over the city from a cornice on the Via della Gatta, just off the Corso – she used to be part of Emperor Domitian's Temple of Isis. Ever since, millions of cats have found a home in this city. When humans abandoned the Forum and the rest of the ancient centre, the cats made it their own; hordes of them still occupy Trajan's Market, the Imperial Fora and whatever city land hasn't yet been covered with unsightly blocks of flats. Wherever there are colonies of strays, some kind lady comes to feed them the classic Italian cat meal of leftover pasta and the boiled celery that flavoured the sauce. Not every Roman is so solicitous of their welfare. Small circuses are reputed to pay children per cat or dog, to feed them to the lions and tigers.

Take time to consider the Roman cat; commonly splotched in white and grey, or black, in most un-aesthetic patterns, he has a dirty face, and doesn't care who notices it. He is an artful thief, whose morals are beneath reproach. Try and talk to him, in English or Italian, and he will show you pure aristocratic disdain. Say 'kitty kitty kitty' or 'mici mici mici', but he won't even acknowledge your presence until you show him a slice of prosciutto. He's the little pussy heir of the Caesars, fleas and all.

Greek, one Roman, flanking the column. From ground level making sense of the reliefs is not easy (you can see eye-level casts in the Museum of Roman Civilization in EUR). Trajan's column survived centuries of rapacious Romans mainly as a profitable tourist attraction in the Middle Ages, connected to a pious tale; Gregory the Great, strolling one day through the forum, noticed the relief on the column showing Trajan dismounting to grant justice to a poor widow. The good Pope wept to think of a good man condemned to suffer eternal torment for merely being a pagan, and as he wept, a voice in St Peter's announced that his request for Trajan's salvation had been granted. The area around the column became sacred, and was used as a cemetery. Legend adds that when Trajan was exhumed there, his tongue was miraculously alive in his skull, to tell of his salvation from hell. In 1588 a statue of St Peter was placed on top of the column, as if to rubber-stamp as much of the tale as you care to believe.

After the pious emperor's death, Hadrian added a massive **Temple of Trajan**, located where the twin churches of Santa Maria di Loreto and SS. Nome di Maria now stand, although it was later quarried until only part of one great granite column survives. The broken columns and fragments of marble pavement you see in front of the column mark the **Basilica Ulpia** (named for Trajan's family), one of the largest basilicas in Rome, extending across the width of the forum.

Santa Maria di Loreto 18

Piazza Madonna di Loreto; bus 64, 70, 117, 170. Open 7.30–12 and 4–6.

One of the twin domed churches overlooking Trajan's Forum, a High Renaissance bauble begun by Antonio da Sangallo, and crowned by a pretty lantern by Giacomo del Duca in 1582. If it's open, pop in to see François Duquesnoy's statue of *S. Susanna*, a highly influential 1633 masterpiece that unites classical grace and beauty with a gentle naturalism, a Baroque alternative to Bernini's twists and shouts. The second church, **SS. Nome di Maria**, was added to balance the composition in the 18th century.

Forum of Augustus J9

Via dei Fori Imperiali; bus 84, 85, 87, 117, 175. ***Closed** to the public; view from the street.*

The Forum of Augustus was built soon after Octavian changed his name. The vast wall that begins in Piazza del Grillo and continues down the street once protected the forum from the teeming, fire-ridden slum of Subura.

The wide stair and a few columns survive from the **Temple of Mars Ultor** (Avenging Mars), which Caesar vowed to the god while driving Brutus and Cassius to suicide during the Battle of Philippi. The temple became a kind of imperial reliquary, containing Caesar's sword among its mementoes. Of the forum's two basilicas, only a few suggestive fragments remain.

The **Casa dei Cavalieri di Rodi** was built over another building in the forum in the 12th century. Now owned by the Knights of Rhodes, it preserves the Augustan atrium as its chapel, a portico, and three ancient shops housing the Antiquarium of the Forum of Augustus.

Forums of Vespasian and Nerva J9

Via dei Fori Imperiali; bus 84, 85, 87, 117, 175. Closed to the public; view from the street.

Vespasian's Forum was built in AD 70 with booty from the Jewish wars. Today, part of it is covered by the tremendous stump of the 12th-century **Torre de' Conti**, which Petrarch called the mightiest in Rome. Lightning and earthquakes have since lopped off most of the tower's storeys; its base is faced with black and white stripes, a common decoration in northern Italy but rare in Rome.

Nearly all the rest of the forum is under Via dei Fori Imperiali, the wide street built by

Mussolini in the 1930s so he could see the Colosseum from his window in Palazzo Venezia. Its fate is still debated in Rome; the Fascist government performed only a perfunctory excavation of the forums of Augustus, Nerva, and Vespasian before filling them in to construct the road, and archaeologists would love to tear it up and investigate, but the prospect of turning the entire city centre into a lifeless dig – and causing yet more gridlock – appals everyone else.

Some excavations have taken place in the **Forum of Nerva**, a narrow corridor with a temple of Minerva at one end. Two beautiful Corinthian columns survive from the temple, topped by reliefs of the goddess. The carved entablature has a frieze illustrating the myth of Arachne, who challenged the goddess' weaving art and was zapped into a spider; the ensemble, known as the Colonnacce, served for years as a bakery.

To atone for burying the forums, Mussolini placed statues of the emperors in front of their works along Via dei Fori Imperiali.

Forum of Caesar J9

Via dei Fori Imperiali; bus 84, 85, 87, 117, 175. ***Closed** to the public; view from the street.*

The first of the imperial forums was built by Julius Caesar after he redesigned the Roman Forum. Its temple, of which only the base and three re-erected columns remain, was dedicated to his ancestress, Venus Genetrix, the goddess of love, and contained statues of the famous lovers, Caesar and Cleopatra. Twelve columns survive of a later basilica added by the indefatigable Trajan.

Mamertine Prison J9

Via del Carcere Tulliano; bus 84, 85, 87, 117, 175. ***Open** 9–12 and 2.30–6; donation requested.*

Beneath the little church of **San Giuseppe dei Falegnami** (1598) lies the Mamertine Prison. This was actually the more pleasant upper floor of the hideous dark dungeon called the *Tullianum*, possibly part of a tomb of the legendary hero Tullius. The only entrance to the Tullianum was a hole in the floor (now there's a modern stairway) and the only exit was death, and a drain that led into the Cloaca Maxima (see p.128) for the convenient disposal of corpses.

Important captives, after being paraded in chains in their conqueror's triumph through the Forum, were taken here to be slain. Vercingetorix was strangled, but Jugurtha, the unrepentant North African, was tossed into the Tullianum to starve to death.

Famous political prisoners included the Catiline conspirators and, according to tradition, St Peter, although as a non-citizen he wasn't important enough to be slain here; the relief over the altar portrays him baptizing his gaoler.

San Luca e Santa Martina J9

*Clivo Argentario. **Closed** for restoration.*

Opposite the Mamertine stands one of Rome's most innovative Baroque churches, built in the 7th century on the site of the *Secretarium Senatus* (a tribunal to judge erring senators, built by the late emperors), and rebuilt by Pietro da Cortona in 1635–50.

St Luke is the patron of painters, and Pietro, in remodelling the ancient crypt to build his own tomb, was surprised to find the body of S. Martina lost among the dead artists.

The church was rededicated to San Luca e Santa Martina, and Pietro hired to rebuild it. To keep both saints happy, he created a double-decker façade, half for each saint, which curves in a rich play of Florentine Mannerist motifs, a theme continued in the Greek cross plan of the interior.

Unlike Bernini and the Roman school, Pietro disdained the use of colour to highlight the vigorous lines of the walls, which seem to ebb and flow with columns, mouldings, and decorative motifs. The drum and cupola, viewed either from within or without, continue the play of soft and rigid forms in a highly original manner that inaugurated the best and most subtle phase of Roman High Baroque.

ROMAN FORUM

*Largo Romolo e Remo, on Via dei Fori Imperiali, t 06 699 0110; **metro** Colosseo, **bus** 84, 85, 87, 117, 175. **Open** daily 9–one hour before sunset; **adm** free. For location of sites within the Forum, see plan, pp.144–5.*

For a place that was once the centre of the Mediterranean world and saw so much history, the Roman Forum is a strangely quiet, empty place. Cats keep it clear of the king-sized rats who rule subterranean Rome. Originally a sodden valley lying between the Capitoline and Palatine hills, the area was first used as a graveyard by the surrounding Iron Age hill dwellers, who called it the forum, a word that meant 'outside' the walls (like the Italian *fuori*). According to legend it became the tribes' common ground and shared marketplace when Romulus made peace with the Sabines near the *Lapis Niger*; and it has always been the sacred symbol of the founding of the united city of Rome.

During the seven centuries of the Republic the Forum was the Rome's heartbeat, its legal, political, religious and commercial centre; an Italian piazza, where an orator could address the city's representatives, senators, and people. By the 2nd century AD, it had lost most of its importance; the Sacred Way became the haunt of idlers, fortune-tellers, and tourists from Gaul or Egypt who gawked at Vestal Virgins or togaed senators ambling to the Curia. Power shifted to the imperial palace on the Palatine, commerce to Trajan's more up-to-date market. Temples (most of them used as art museums) and memorials enclosed the once spacious square, strewn with ranks of statues and monuments that gave it the appearance of a king-size modern Roman souvenir stand.

Temple of Antoninus Pius and Faustina J9–K10

From the ticket office the ramp descends to the Temple of Antoninus Pius and Faustina (AD 141) converted in the Middle Ages to the church of **San Lorenzo in Miranda** (J10), rarely opened, however, by its gloomy monks. The temple gives an idea of the height of the Forum's buildings; the front door added by medieval monks is surreally suspended, but marks the ground level of the old Campo Vaccino before excavations. Along the side is a fine, well-preserved frieze of griffins, although the mighty Corinthian columns at the front bear the marks of chains used by the Christians trying to pull them down.

Basilica Aemilia J9–K10

To the right of the ramp as you descend it was the Basilica Aemilia, headquarters of Rome's moneychangers, which Pliny the Younger classed as one of the three most beautiful buildings in the world. It was the Forum's first basilica, built by M. Aemilius Lepidus in 179 BC, but lavishly restored after later fires; fragments of its republican-era reliefs (of the Romans abducting the Sabine women and the Sabines preparing to kill Tarpeia) have been placed in the corner. Although nearly completely scavenged for its marbles during the Renaissance, the Basilica's decline (at least according to legend) began with Alaric in 410. Apparently some of the moneychangers waited in the basilica to do business with the Goths, but their exchange rates were unfair; you can see their bronze coins fused into the coloured marble pavement by the fire of Gothic fury.

Sacred Way J9–K10

The Basilica faces the **Via Sacra** or Sacred Way, Rome's most ancient road. It seems remarkably narrow for the splendid triumphs that once passed along it; try to imagine all of Rome gathered to watch the parade of victorious legions, the booty, the prisoners, and the *triumphator* himself, dressed in a purple toga, face painted red like the god Mars, his chariot drawn by four white horses, accompanied by a slave who constantly repeated in his ear: 'Remember that you are a man'. More often, though, the Sacred Way would see the likes of Horace, absent-mind-

edly strolling along with a slave; and even more often, Horace's Bore, the spiritual father of so many Romans down to this day, who glued himself to the poet, endlessly singing his own praises in the hopes of scaring up an introduction to the poet's wealthy patron Maecenas. Poor Horace feared he would be talked to death before he was suddenly rescued by a man who was suing the Bore in court that very morning and suspected him of trying to escape.

In front of the Basilica Aemilia a bare round foundation marks the site of the **Shrine of Venus Cloacina**, near the lid of the Cloaca Maxima (and who, you may ask, worshipped this Venus of the Drains? Plumbers?). Equally perverse in its own way is the tale of Virginia, said to have taken place here: the maiden was about to be seduced by the deceiver Appius Claudius Crassinus, when her father Virginus stabbed her to save her chastity. Like the story of the Rape of Lucrezia, it was piously repeated to drill Roman women in the virtue of chastity.

Closer to the Argiletum stood the now vanished **Temple of Janus**, the two doors of which stood open when Rome was at war and were closed in times of peace, which history declares happened only three times in a thousand years. Just east of the Basilica Aemilia, the Sacred Way met the thronging **Argiletum**, an important street once lined with bookshops.

Curia J9–K10

The open space between the Argiletum and the Curia was the **Comitium**, the centre of civic life during the republic. Here the representatives of the city's 30 neighbour-hoods (the Comitia Curiata) met to cast their votes. Scant remains of the **Republican Rostra** were found here, dating from 338 BC; the name *rostra*, for speaking platforms, came from the iron beaks of captured ships which were used to adorn them.

Here, too, is the austere, tawny brick **Curia** or Senate House itself, built by Julius Caesar, and rebuilt by Diocletian after a fire in AD 283

– by that time the emperors rarely visited Rome, and it was a mere sop to let the senators prattle away on whatever topic they chose. Gothic King Theodoric rebuilt it for the last time, and the senators were probably still prattling into the 600s.

The Curia, minus its marble facings and decorations, was found intact under the 7th-century church of Sant'Adriano. Sadly, owing to staff shortages, the Curia is rarely open, but if it is, it's well worth popping inside to see the original pavement, the steps where the senators sat in marble seats, and a set of reliefs called the *Plutei of Trajan*, found near the **Column of Phocas** and depicting lively scenes of the Forum itself. When the Gauls invaded Rome in 390 BC, they entered this building's predecessor, to find what looked like statues of senators, so still did they sit in their full senate regalia, ivory wands in hand. One of the Gauls summoned the courage to pull one of their beards, to see if it was real; the senator whacked him with his wand; he and all of his fellows were massacred.

At one end of the Curia is the base for the famous golden statue of Victory, the reigning deity of the Senate and the subject of another instructive anecdote. The statue was removed by the Christians, replaced by Julian the Apostate, and removed again by Gratian (380s) when it became the rallying point for die-hard pagans among the patricians, led by the aristocratic orator Symmachus. 'These rites have repelled Hannibal from the city and the Gauls from the Capitol', he wrote in his petition to the emperor, asking that the statue be returned in the name of freedom of religion. He was answered by the eloquent St Ambrose and by 394 Victory had disappeared for good. When Alaric sacked Rome 16 years later the pagans grumbled their inevitable I-told-you-so, only to be refuted by another saint, Augustine, in his *City of God*.

Lapis Niger J9–K10

In front of the Curia, in the ancient Comitium, is the Forum's most venerable relic, the **Lapis Niger**, named for the slab of fractured black marble that marked the **Tomb of Romulus**. It may have originally been a chthonic shrine to the forging god of fire, Vulcan. Under the slab a chamber was discovered (reached by a modern stair behind one of Rome's numerous eternally locked gates) containing an altar of tufa with the ashes of massive sacrifices, a broken column, and a stele inscribed with one of the most ancient Latin inscriptions ever discovered (6th century BC), written with alternate lines from left to right and right to left in a style called 'boustrophedic', warning against profaning the sacred site.

Arch of Septimius Severus J9–K10

'*Geta sit divus dum non sit vivus*' (Geta may be a god as long as he's a dead one), Caracalla grimly jested after slaying his brother the co-emperor, a murder recorded on the Arch of Septimius Severus, erected in AD 203 in honour of their father's tenth year in power. The marble reliefs relate some rather trivial victories over the Arabs and Parthians, and a notable artistic decline since the Arch of Titus; conservative Romans of the time must have strongly resented this upstart African, Severus, planting his monument in such an important spot, between the Comitium and the Capitol. The inscription on the arch also commemorated his sons, but after Geta's murder Caracalla had his name removed from the fourth line and replaced with an inscription glorifying himself. Time dislodged both sets of bronze letters, making it possible to read both the original and edited versions.

The area to the left, behind the rostra, is fenced off, and the best view of what lies behind is from Via di Monte Tarpeo on the Capitoline. To the left of the arch stood the **Umbilicus Romae**, the conical brick 'navel of Rome' (at 9ft-high, a definite 'outie') marking the centre of the city; to the left of this, under a shelter, is the **Vulcanal**, an altar carved in the living rock, and along with the Lapis

Niger, the most ancient monument in the Forum. A bit beyond the curved steps of the Imperial Rostra (*see* opposite) stood the **Golden Milestone**. This was actually a bronze column, erected by Augustus, from which all the roads of the empire symbolically began, and from which all distances in the empire were calculated.

Temples of Concord and Saturn J9–K10

Between Severus' arch and the Capitol stood the **Temple of Concord**, of which only the platform remains; this was reconstructed by Tiberius from a republican original celebrating the peace – now enforced by the emperors – between patricians and plebeians. Next to it are three elegant corner columns from the **Temple of Divine Vespasian** (AD 79) – a fitting memorial to the emperor who died laughing: 'My goodness, I think I am about to become a god'.

To the left of Vespasian's temple, on the other side of the Clivus Sacer (an extension of the Sacred Way), are the eight grey and red columns from the portico of the **Temple of Saturn**. This is one of the Forum's oldest temples (479 BC), dedicated to the ancient Etruscan god of purification against blight, although later Saturn was associated with agriculture and the 'Golden Age'. The cult statue in the temple was filled with olive oil, and from 17 to 23 December it was the centre of the Saturnalia, a holiday that combined many of the rituals Christmas and Carnival. A huge sum of gold was secretly stored here, with the provision that it only be used if the Gauls re-invaded Rome. Caesar, who always needed cash, purloined it with the excuse that thanks to him there would be no more Gallic troubles (though as spendthrifts go, he was a tiddler compared to Mark Antony, who spent billions in his lifetime, with much less to show for it). The columns date from the Senate's rebuilding of AD 284, done so clumsily that one was put in upside down.

Behind the Temple of Saturn and left of the Temple of Vespasian are 12 columns from the

Portico of the Dei Consentes, dedicated to the 12 Olympian gods; restored in AD 367, during the reign of Julian the Apostate, it was the last work on a pagan temple in Rome. Behind you stands the last monument erected in the Forum in ancient times, the **Column of Phocas**. In 608, the Exarch Smaragdus stole the column from an older building to honour the Byzantine usurper, Nikephorus Phocas, probably as a thank-you present for giving the Pantheon to Pope Boniface IV. As the silt of centuries covered its base, its identity was forgotten, which many, like Byron ('Thou nameless column with the buried base!'), found as evocative as its sharp-fluted beauty. The Duchess of Devonshire ruined their romance by having it excavated. The brick wall next to the column was the **Imperial Rostra**, moved here from the Comitium by Julius Caesar, to replace the Republican Rostra.

Basilica Julia J9–K10

Closing the south end of the Forum stood the vast **Basilica Julia**, begun by Julius Caesar in 54 BC as a pendant to the Basilica Aemilia. Augustus completed it, although what you see are the bare roots of a 305 rebuilding. The four tribunals of the Centumviri tried civil cases here and, as the Romans had one of history's worst cases of litigation fever, it was one of the noisiest places of the Forum, where lawyers struggled to outshout other lawyers presenting their cases elsewhere in the basilica. Idlers, or perhaps defendants waiting their turn at court, carved the game boards you can still see in the steps.

In front of the Basilica Julia, just beyond the Column of Phocas, are a fig tree, olive, and vine, symbols of Italian agriculture, replanted where they stood in ancient times. Lacking is the statue of Marsyas, the musician who challenged Apollo to a hoedown, and was flayed by the god, apparently as a warning against presumption.

Next to the trees is the irregular-shaped pavement of the **Lacus Curtius**. The Lacus was a pond before the Forum was drained,

Mere Words

In Rome's case, historical revisionism is all too easy. Like the archaeologists, delving courageously to find the bottom level of its endless tunnels and catacombs, historians have yet to plumb the lowest depths of the ancient city's gluttonous turpitude. Achievements once credited to Rome in the arts and sciences always turn out to have been the work of someone else, and Rome's original civic virtue and later piety have been exposed too many times, and convincingly, to be cynical frauds. Romans didn't invent concrete, or plumbing, or even gladiators – is there any one thing the Great Pretender has really contributed to our culture?

When you stand in the Forum, consider all the words that had their birth in the bit of land you see around you: forum itself, of course, along with committee, rostrum, republic, census, plebeian, plebiscite, civic, suffrage, censor, forensics, magistrate, classes, dictator and even pontificate. From the Capitoline Hill in front of you, we get capitol, mint, money and asylum, and to your left, the Palatine would later contribute prince and palace. A Latin scholar could probably find a few dozen more of these without too much effort. It is a reminder of just how much we owe to the Romans for our institutions and public life today. They may have failed badly in their visions of the republic and of the rule of law, but their centuries of anguished constitutional history prove how hard they tried. To us, their ideals are more important than their failures. For better or worse, all the figures on our political stage – the statesmen, legislators and philosophers, along with the tyrants, the crooks and the lawyers – all went to school in Rome.

and a place made holy in 445 BC, when lightning blasted a fissure in the pavement. But most famously, it marks the site of one of Rome's favourite legends. In 362 BC, Livy recounts, a bottomless abyss suddenly opened in the Forum, and nothing the Romans could do could fill it up again. The Sibyls were consulted, and gave the answer: it would never close until 'the thing the Romans held most precious' was thrown in. A young Consul, Marcus Curtius, took this to mean a Roman citizen and a soldier. Dressed in full armour, he mounted his horse, dedicated his death to the gods, and rode into the chasm, and the crack closed over him. A noble story, apparently the result of later Roman romancing over the human sacrifices that once took place on the spot.

Temple of Castor J9–K10

To the left of Basilica Julia, across the ancient Vicus Tuscus (Etruscan Lane, once the resort of Etruscan rent-boys), stand the three grand columns of the **Temple of Castor**, the mortal twin of the Dioscuri, the brothers of Helen of Troy and patrons of the cavalry. The Dioscuri were the first gods to be bribed away by the Romans from their enemies, in this case from the Latin tribes that they fought at the Battle of Lake Regillus in 496 BC. The odds were against the Romans, whose cavalry was woefully inadequate, but in the heat of the battle they offered Castor and Pollux, the chief gods of the Latins, a huge temple if they would change sides. The twins couldn't resist the offer, and were seen in the Forum soon after, battle-stained with sweating horses, which they watered in the fountain of Juturna near the Temple of Vesta. 'And like a blast, away they passed/And no man saw them more', as Macaulay put it. The Romans built their temple on the spot, and it became the meeting place of Rome's Equites (knights, but later the class of businessmen), who had their safe-deposit boxes in the basement, along with the standards and measures of the empire.

In the fenced-off area just to the east of the temple is a reconstructed shrine to the healing waters of the Lacus Juturnae. Behind this, the **Oratory of the 40 Martyrs** commemorates soldiers who were forced to wade into an icy lake in Armenia; it preserves some of its 8th-century frescoes. Far better preserved are the excellent 7th- and 8th-century

Roman Forum

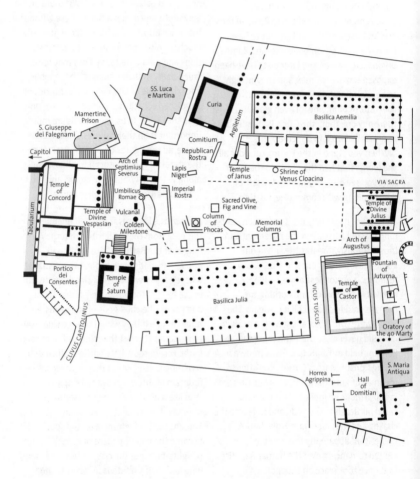

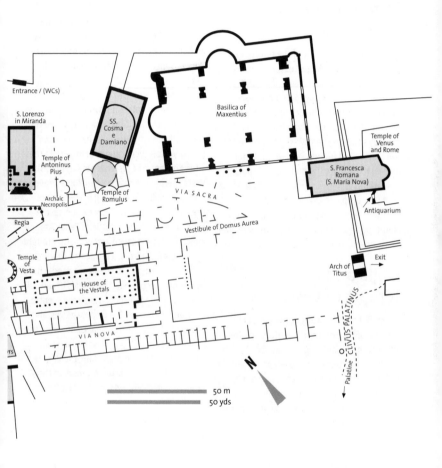

Byzantine frescoes in **Santa Maria Antiqua**, just south of the oratory, the oldest church in the Forum. It's rarely if ever open; though you could try asking at the Forum Antiquarium.

Temple of Julius Caesar J9–K10

Walk back to the front of the Temple of Castor; the **Arch of Augustus** once crossed over the street, symbolically linking the basilica with the **Temple of Julius Caesar**, marked by its large altar. Here Caesar's body was brought after his assassination in Pompey's theatre; here Mark Antony read his will and incited friends, Romans and countrymen to cremate the body on the spot, in spite of the religious prohibitions. Augustus built the temple to Divine Julius 15 years later, and decorated the altar with the prow of Antony and Cleopatra's ship. The bare altar has survived, marking where Caesar lay.

Regia and Temple of Vesta J9–K10

East of it stood the **Regia**, the oldest cult building of the Forum (7th century BC). The office of the Chief Priest or Pontifex Maximus, the Regia was closely identified with Mars, the chief god of the Romans before the Etruscans introduced Jupiter. Mars' shields and spears were kept here, and if the spears rattled on their own it was an ill omen indeed. To help prevent such calamities the Pontifex Maximus presided over the ancient rite of the October Horse, when a horse race would be held along the Sacred Way, although the prize for the winning pony was a real booby: immediate decapitation. Its blood, used for purification ceremonies, was given to the Vestal Virgins; its genitals were dedicated to Mars; its skeleton used for special juju to protect the city; and its head was fought over viciously by the residents of the Via Sacra and Subura for the honour of nailing it up in their quarter.

The Pontifex Maximus was the only male ever allowed to enter the **Temple of Vesta**, located just across the Via Nova. Votive offerings to the hearth goddess date the first temple back to 575 BC, and the pretty circular edifice (partially reconstructed in the 1930s) was designed to recall the original Latin hut, where the ancient kings' daughters had the task of keeping the tribe's fire alight. The rites of the Vestal Virgins were consciously archaic; they were, after all, the guardians of Rome's soul and sacred totems: the embers of the temple's sacred fire had been brought from Vesta's temple in Troy by Aeneas, and if a negligent Vestal let it go out, she would be flogged by the Pontifex Maximus, while the superstitious city awaited calamity (few sleepy Vestals were caught in imperial times – the Romans had just invented matches). Vesta's temple also contained Rome's seven holiest of holies, preserving in themselves the nation's safety and very existence: the Palladium (a wooden statue of Pallas Athene which fell from heaven and was also brought by Aeneas from Troy); a terracotta chariot from Veii; the ashes of Orestes; a needle used by the mother of gods; the shields of the Salii (the 12 Leaping Priests of Mars); the sceptre of Priam; and the veil of Ilione. The Vestals protected these for 1100 years, and when the imperial pervert Elagabalus tried to steal them for his Temple of the Sun, the Virgins outwitted him with fakes. Memory of their ultimate fate perished with the last Vestal.

House of the Vestals J9–K10

Adjacent is the **House of the Vestals**, now the rose garden of the Forum, with its three pools that once adorned the centre of its rectangular two-storey courtyard. The similarity between the Vestals and the sisters of the Church are probably no accident: their house was like a cloister, forbidden to all men except the Pontifex Maximus; their hair was cut when they entered the order, and they wore long robes and a veil, which you can see in the mostly decapitated 3rd-century AD statues in the court (the one statue with her head intact but name effaced is believed to be the Vestal Claudia, who became a Christian). There were only six Vestals at a time, all from patrician families and chosen between the ages of six and ten. They would spend the next 30 years of their lives in this large cloister; the first decade learning the austere and complex rites, the second decade practising them, and the third teaching novices, after which they were free to do as they liked. Most stayed on until they died.

For the Vestals enjoyed great honour and privileges, as women second only to the Empress herself: if they came across a condemned prisoner, they could stay his execution; they could ride about in chariots in the city, in daytime. They had front row seats in the Circus and Colosseum, and were in charge of all wills and treaties; the eldest Vestal could demand an audience with an emperor at will. They were, however, bound by the strictest vows of chastity; the punish-ment for breaking these was being buried alive (the penalty for incest under Roman law) in what is now Piazza dell'Indipendenza. Since it was sacrilege to starve a priestess, the poor sinners would be given a lamp, a loaf, and a pitcher of water before the door above was closed forever; some 20 are believed to have died cruelly in this way, and as far as anyone knows, they're still there under the piazza's heaving traffic.

Basilica of Maxentius J9–K10

Across from the House of the Vestals, up the Via Sacra, is a short row of rooms, sunk below the level of the Forum's other build-ings. It's believed to be a republican-era brothel. Alongside is the circular **Temple of Romulus**, a mysterious place, perhaps built in AD 309 by Maxentius in memory of his young son Romulus. Later used as the vestibule of SS. Cosma e Damiano, it is one of the Forum's best-preserved buildings, its original bronze doors on their original hinges, the ancient lock still opened by the original key.

Next to this loom the three immense vaults of the **Basilica of Maxentius**. Begun by Maxentius in 306, it was completed by his arch-rival Constantine, who installed the colossal statue of himself (naturally), now amputated in the Capitoline Museums. The Basilica was some 300ft long, with a nave and two aisles, of which only the north aisle still stands, as well as part of the apse and (just outside the 20th-century fence) a porphyry portico added by Constantine. The audacity of its soaring barrel vaults was studied by Bramante and Michelangelo for the design of St Peter's; the last of its mighty Corinthian columns now stands in front of S. Maria Maggiore.

Forum Antiquarium J9–K10

At the corner of the basilica is S. Francesca Romana (see p.148; entered from Via dei Fori Imperiali), built into the Temple of Venus and Rome.but next to its 1163 campanile (in the Romanesque party style, decorated with coloured circles) the convent contains the Forum Antiquarium. The old-fashioned displays include models and furniture of the various Iron Age necropolises excavated in the Forum's lowest levels, from the days when Rome was a cluster of hill villages, of which some cremated their dead, and others buried them. Upstairs are friezes, sculptures, inscriptions, and reliefs found in the Forum, and a fresco of the *Virgin with Saints* origi-nally in S. Maria Antiqua.

Arch of Titus J9–K10

Nearby, crowning the summit of the Sacred Way is the **Arch of Titus**. Erected by Domitian in AD 81, the arch commemorates the victo-ries of his father Vespasian and brother Titus over the rebellious Jews, one of the fiercest struggles Rome ever had to fight; the reliefs within the arch proper show a triumphal procession carrying off the treasure from the Holy of Holies in the Temple, including the seven-branch candlestick and the altar, which were deposited in Vespasian's Temple of Peace. Whatever eventually became of them is a subject of considerable dispute. Roman Jews believe they were thrown in the Tiber; another story has them hidden along with Alaric, who carried them off in 410 – when he died in Calabria, soon after the sack, his men buried him along with his loot in a secret place, then diverted the river Busento over it.

Santa Francesca Romana or Santa Maria Nuova K10

Piazza di Santa Francesca Romana (in the Forum). **Open** *daily 9.30–12 and 4–7.*

Once the titular church of Cardinal Cesare Borgia, Santa Francesca Romana was built into the portico of the Temple of Venus and Rome. It began in the 8th century as a shrine dedicated to SS. Peter and Paul, for its most holy relic: paving stones from the Via Sacra bearing the knee prints of the two saints: Peter and Paul had to do some very weighty praying to bag their rival Simon Magus. The sorcerer had challenged them to a magic duel to prove who had the most power. Simon at first seemed to get the better of them by soaring over the Forum, but the saints asked God to make him fall, and he crashed to his death nearby. Grope your way through the dim candlelit church to the right transept, where the alleged knee prints are incorporated into the wall.

In the same transept, there's a late Renaissance **Monument to Gregory XI**, the pope who returned to Rome from Avignon in 1377 and regretted every minute of it, but died before he could go back to France. The monument, showing a merry St Catherine of Siena leading the pope home, was paid for by the grateful people of Rome. In the crypt you could pay your respects to the shrouded skeleton of the only native Roman to found a religious order, S. Francesca Romana, who founded the Oblates for lady nuns in the 15th century, and who has been appointed patron saint of motorists; on 9 March, her feast day, the Piazzale del Colosseo is packed solid with Fiats come for her blessing.

S. Francesca Romana has three lovely Madonnas: a 12th-century mosaic of the *Madonna and Saints* in the apse; a painting

of the same century over the altar; and the *Madonna* that was discovered beneath it, a unique easel painting of the 6th century. The painting, of an eerie, strangely distorted Madonna with elongated nose and gigantic eyes, is now kept in the sacristy.

Temple of Venus and Rome K10

Behind S. Francesca Romana, rising up on the levelled mound of the Velian Hill, are the massive ruins of the **Temple of Venus and Rome**. This unusual double-feature was built and perhaps designed by the dilettante emperor Hadrian over the vestibule of Nero's Golden House – in the face of objections by his architect, Apollodorus, who dared to point out that if the statues seated in the niches stood up, they would bang their heads on the roof. It had two doors: facing the Forum was the side dedicated to Immortal Rome (now part of the church of S. Francesca Romana); facing the Colosseum was the entrance to the sanctuary of Venus. One of the last pagan temples to close, it survived until Pope Honorius I tore off its bronze roof for the original St Peter's. Some columns have been re-erected; its twin *cellae* still stand in the centre, back to back.

SS. Cosma e Damiano J9

Largo Romolo e Remo (in the Forum). **Open** *daily 9–1 and 3–6.30.*

Built over the library of Vespasian's forum, converted to a church in 527 and rebuilt in 1632, Santi Cosma e Damiano preserves the beautiful gold ground mosaics of the 6th century that influenced subsequent Roman artists. In the triumphal arch are the Lamb, angels and symbols of the Evangelists and, in the apse, SS. Peter and Paul introducing Cosmas and Damian (two doctors from the Middle East) to Christ, with twelve lambs symbolizing the Apostles, and four rivers, for the Gospels. Signs point the way to an elabo-rate 18th-century Neapolitan *presepio*, or Christmas crib (illuminate with coins).

COLOSSEUM

Arch of Constantine K10

Piazza del Colosseo; metro Colosseo, bus 75, 85, 87, 117, 175, 86.

From the Forum's exit, turn right and follow Via dei Fori Imperiali to the Colosseum. Turn right again into Via S. Gregorio, the ancient Triumphal Way of Rome's generalissimos, who would turn into the Forum's Sacred Way near the Arch of Constantine, erected in AD 315 in honour of Constantine's victory over rival Maxentius at the Milvian Bridge. According to Christian tradition, it was before this battle that Constantine had his vision of the cross and was instructed to fight under its sign. Much is made out of the seemingly fence-sitting inscription crediting 'the inspiration of the Deity' for his victory, although by that point all emperors were divine and he was surely referring to himself rather than either Christ or Jove.

The Arch is attractive, covered with fine bas-reliefs and medallions, but Constantine, however divine he might have been, had nothing to do with them – nearly all were stolen from other structures, in an attempt to link his regime with the past glories of divine Rome. The medallions on the arch's flanks, of the sinking moon in her chariot and the rising sun, are believed to be late works, though the Romans rarely mustered such charm and grace in their decline.

Colosseum K10–11

Piazza del Colosseo; metro Colosseo, bus 75, 85, 87, 117, 175, 86. Open daily 9–one hour before sunset; adm €7, audioguide €4.

Only the memory remains of the gilt Colossus of Nero, at 120ft the largest bronze statue ever made, transported here by 24 elephants from the vestibule of the Golden House after Nero's death. It was renamed after the sun god, and its head frequently changed to match that of the reigning emperor, but what eventually became of this glowering golden giant is a Roman mystery.

It did, however, lend its name to the neighbouring amphitheatre, which has come down to posterity as the **Colosseum**.

Earthquakes and pillage, subsidence, pollution and the vibrations of traffic and the metro line that runs below it have taken their toll on the fabric of the Colosseum, although from 1992 to 2000 a restoration programme took place to tackle the problem of subsidence. Via dei Fori Imperiali has also been closed to traffic, reducing the dual evils of vibration and pollution but the arena still lacks a floor – it was removed during 19th-century excavations.

The ruin to beat all ruins, the Colosseum is perhaps Rome's greatest marvel, breathtaking and beautifully built – for the pure delight in watching the cruellest torture and slaughter of men and animals. As vast as it is, what you see is less than half of the original structure, the bare skeleton of a travertine oval once a third of a mile in circumference.

The Colosseum was called the Flavian Amphitheatre after the family of emperors who built it, beginning with Vespasian in AD 72. Vespasian, the first post-Julian emperor to reign for more than a minute, was a self-made man who had to build popular support for his dynasty. One of his more successful public relations efforts was to return Nero's pleasure gardens to public use, then to out-do his predecessors by erecting the world's largest amphitheatre in the middle of Nero's lake – an astounding engineering feat that required what must be the Sistine Chapel of drains, as well as foundations that go down several tiers of arches beneath the surface.

Yet Vespasian and his son Titus were, if nothing else, practical men. The massive amount of labour required to build the Colosseum was performed by Jewish slaves, brought here for the purpose after the suppression of their revolt. The lake was selected as its location, not for the mere sake of showing off, but because it was the perfect site – accessible from the Forum and Esquiline, Palatine, and Caelian hills, yet still isolated enough to maintain crowd control.

Some 50,000 thumbs could go down at once inside, and Vespasian's engineers provided 76 numbered entrances with free-flowing corridors to the seats, enabling all ticket-holders to be in position for the first round of death in only ten minutes. All modern stadiums have copied its general plan, and all have envied the unique adjustable awning that once covered the stands, protecting the crowds from the baking sun. Manipulated with poles (the sockets of which still remain) the awning was manned by a detachment of sailors from Cape Misenum (the Roman naval headquarters, near Naples); they also crewed the miniature galleys in the frequent mock sea battles, easily enough staged in the Colosseum by closing off its drains.

In the year 80, Titus opened the amphitheatre with a gala massacre of 5,000 animals, roughly one every 10 seconds; the Romans' appetite for such sport led to the extinction of the native elephant and lion of North Africa and Arabia. Although it appears unlikely that Christians were ever thrown to the lions here (the Colosseum, after all, was built after Nero, the arch martyr-maker), there were plenty of other games to make it the most sadistic and best-organized perversity in all history.

Nearly every primitive society indulged in human sacrifice in its darkest days, but the Romans were the only ones to make a sport of it once it had lost its religious purpose. The earliest gladiatorial contests were first noted among the Samnites around 400 BC; the Etruscans are said to have held prototypical combats; and tradition has it they were introduced to Rome during the First Punic War 'to boost morale' and make Romans better soldiers by rendering them indifferent to the sight of death. It worked. Indifferent and brutalized, the Roman crowds' chief interest in the show was their wagers.

Later emperors introduced new displays to make the odds more interesting – men versus animals, lions versus elephants, women versus dwarfs, sea battles, and even genuine athletics, a Greek import the Romans never much cared for. The emperor

and other important people had front-row seats in marble, while the rest of the concrete seats (now all eroded away) were divided by wealth and social class; women were confined to the uppermost reaches. An exception were the Vestals, who sat near the emperor, a privilege the younger, more sensitive girls didn't always appreciate; occasionally they had to be escorted further back, along one of the 160 vertical passages between the seats, appropriately called *vomitoria*. If it's open, the view from the top ranks is unforgettable, both looking across the Roman Forum towards the city and gazing down what seems to be the corrugated cone of a man-made volcano.

In the 8th century, the Venerable Bede recorded a favourite Latin proverb of Rome's Saxon pilgrims, best known in Byron's translation from *Childe Harold*:

> While stands the Coliseum, Rome
> shall stand;
> When falls the Coliseum, Rome shall fall;
> And when Rome falls – the world.

Which, however, didn't prevent the Romans from trying to tear it apart. Although it was quickly repaired after several fires caused by lightning, earthquakes in the Dark Ages turned the outer ring of arches, once filled with statues and embellished with bronze shields, into a quarry that Renaissance popes used to build the Palazzo Venezia, Palazzo Barberini, a few other palaces and bridges and part of St Peter's. Their job had been made easier by Constans II, who in 664 looted the metal clamps that held the travertine skeleton together, leaving the holes that pockmark the exterior today. The plunder stopped only in 1744, when Benedict XIV consecrated the Colosseum to its supposed Christian martyrs and set up the Stations of the Cross in the arena; later Popes, especially Leo XII in 1825, prevented further crumbling of the outer walls with the familiar sloping smooth buttresses. The confusing labyrinth of walls and passages in the arena contained cages for the wild beasts and mechanisms for the more elaborate spectacles; in ancient times these were covered with a wooden floor and sand (arena), which kept the gladiators from slipping and soaked up the blood.

The excavation of the arena in the 19th century gravely offended romantics who loved to contemplate the mighty ruin by moonlight; strange humours were said to rise from the uncovered marshy depths, the 'Roman fever' that killed Henry James's poor susceptible Daisy Miller. Although the surrounding haze of electric light has cooled the old romance, the Colosseum is specially floodlit so that the shadows in its arches become endless tunnels of dark and mystery, sinister enough to be haunted by the fiery demons that arose when sculptor Benvenuto Cellini and a renegade priest conjured them in a seance one midnight in 1534. Cellini, in his *Autobiography*, is full of bluff, but he wasn't the only one who believed in the fiends; in 1522, a bull was sacrificed to them during a plague that the saints couldn't end.

Right across from the Colosseum, on the eastern side, you can see ruins of the Ludus Magnus, an imposing quadrangle with a smaller amphitheatre inside. The gladiators trained here, and some of the emperors used it to put on private shows.

PALATINE HILL

Entrance through the Roman Forum or from Via di San Gregorio; **metro** *Colosseo,* **bus** *84, 85, 87, 117, 175.* **Open** *daily 9–one hour before sunset;* **adm** *€6.*

A road leads up from the Arch of Titus in the Roman Forum to the Palatine Hill (J10–K11), the site of the imperial residences that went on to give the word 'palace' to nearly every European language. But the stones of these palaces keep their secrets well; the ruins of the Forum seem elementary in comparison. Look at it as 'the *malaise de pierre* of a number of extremely odd and ill-adjusted Caesars', as H. V. Morton says, or as a landscape of picturesque ruins, the kind beloved in the 18th century, planted with parasol pines, cypresses, ilexes, and wild

flowers. At any given time a third of the Palatine will be obscured by the archaeologist's net and fence; some of this crazy quilt of vaults, arches, walls, and columns is simply unsafe to walk around in. What you really want to see will probably be closed.

Both myth and archaeology confirm that Rome began on the Palatine, perhaps in the 9th century BC; the city's birthday on 21 April was originally the feast day of the hill's namesake, the shepherd god Pales. One of Pales' followers discovered the foundling sons of Mars, Romulus and Remus, suckling wolf-flavoured milk on the hill, and brought them up as his own. But it hardly ended their wolfish behaviour. Remus, when he grew up, established himself on the Aventine, and argued with his twin over the name of the new city they meant to found. 'Roma!' 'No, Rema!' they shouted back and forth, until Romulus saw the 12 vultures fly over the Palatine while Remus only saw six fly over his hill. Romulus declared his extra vultures indicated the gods' favour, and began to build Rome's first walls on the Palatine, later known as '*Roma Quadrata*'. To show his disdain for their puny height, Remus leapt the walls; and his twin, goaded beyond control, slew him, baptizing the newborn city with his own brother's blood.

The cool breezes enjoyed by the Palatine made it an elite residence in later years: Cicero, Catullus, and Antony called it home; Augustus was born on the hill and lived here simply all his life, modestly pretending he didn't rule the world. His less worthy successors, almost in proportion to their inability, had no qualms about building themselves magnificent palaces, and when they ran out of hill they added huge substructures (the main feature of the Palatine today) to support even more rooms. The biggest builders were: Tiberius, whose palace is now mostly covered by the Farnese Gardens; crazy Caligula, who extended it and built a catwalk over the Forum to the Capitol, so he'd never have to rub elbows with the masses; Nero, who built a new palace, the Domus

Transitoria, which burned in the fire of AD 64, whereupon he used the bits that survived as mere outbuildings for his even grander Domus Aurea, extending over the Esquiline. Domitian, however, is responsible for much of what you see today: official and residential palaces and the stadium.

Although abandoned by the emperors after Diocletian, Rome kept the palaces in repair in case they ever changed their minds. Odoacer and Theodoric made short stays, as did Byzantine Emperors Phocas and Constans II, the latter here on his ten-day pillaging spree. Several medieval popes called it home before the ensemble became a building inspector's nightmare; the last genuine emperors to visit were German Ottos, in the 900s.

Farnese Gardens J10–11

At the top of the lane leading up from the Forum are the shady Orti Farnesiani and garden pavilion. In the 1550s, Pope Paul III's grandson, Alessandro Farnese, purchased the palace of Tiberius, dug for statues, then filled the ruins with rubble and hired Vignola to lay out a classical garden that extended down the Palatine slope to the House of the Vestal Virgins.

After centuries of weeds and neglect, the great archaeologist of the Forum, Giacomo Boni (1859–1925), replanted the trees and hedges, creating a charming oasis in the centre of ancient and modern Rome. At the highest point stands the casino, added by Rainaldi in the 17th century. There are excellent views over the Forum from the belvedere terrace built on top of great arches of the substructures; these were added in the 3rd century AD as guard rooms for the Praetorians. At some point in strolling through the gardens you may pass over the spot where they stabbed Caligula, or where they found his uncle Claudius hiding behind a curtain, expecting to be slain instead of proclaimed the new emperor. It set a catastrophic precedent; from then on, arms and not the decision of the Senate would choose the master of the world.

Nymphaeum and Cryptoporticus J10–11

Steps by the side of the casino descend to the creeper-dripping fountains of the **Nymphaeum** and, around the corner, Nero's remarkable **Cryptoporticus**. This half-submerged vaulted passageway, partially decorated with stuccoes, was built to connect the Palatine with the Domus Aurea. Stretching 425ft, it may well have served the imperial household as a cool promenade in the summer; it extends past **Tiberius' fish-pond** (all that remains of his palace above ground) back to the House of Livia. In the middle of the gardens box hedges have been planted, following the shape of the *impluvium* in the *Domus Augustana*.

Temple of Cybele J10

South of the Farnese Gardens are the romantic, ilex-shaded ruins of the podium and sanctuary of the **Temple of Cybele** (Magna Mater), dedicated in 191 BC according to the instructions in the Sibylline Books. Earlier, one of the Sibyls had warned the Romans that they could never hope to defeat Hannibal without the lumpy black image (perhaps a meteorite) that represented Cybele, the Phrygian Mother of the Gods, in her principal temple at Pessinus. What the Phrygians had to say about this is unrecorded, but the Romans somehow obtained the image, won the Second Punic War, and built this temple; in April games called the *Ludi Megalenses* were dedicated in honour of the goddess. Her cult, one of the first oriental religions to reach Rome, was as popular with the masses as it was offensive to conservative Romans, who disapproved of its orgies and the self-castration of its priests, in imitation of Cybele's consort Attis. The temple is last mentioned in the 4th century, when Serena, the wife of the Vandal General Stilicho, visited it in the company of one of the last Vestal Virgins, and removed the beautiful necklace from Cybele's image (perhaps the same one you see today) and placed it on her own neck. The Vestal put a curse on Serena for her sacrilege, and not long after she was strangled by the Senate for collusion with the Goths.

Roma Quadrata J10–11

South of the temple, protected by corrugated iron roofs, are traces of the tufa walls of **Roma Quadrata** and the 9th-century BC village, including the holes used to plant the roof poles of the huts and channels dug in the rock to carry the rain. The traditional **Casa di Romulus** was maintained here for centuries as a kind of museum piece, and in the same area of the slope, two famous cave-dens. One, the **Lupercal** (which no one has actually found yet), was in the sacred grove of the god Lupercus, where the she-wolf suckled the twins. It is best known for a kinky festival, the Lupercalia (15 February), in which priests clad in goat skins pranced around the hill whipping everyone they encountered, purifying them; and bestowing fertility, a rite that attracted many women.

The second cave belonged to the flame-belching giant Cacus, who decorated it with human skulls (another reminder of early Rome's human sacrifices); a sharply declining path before one of the gates in the tufa walls of Roma Quadrata was named Scalae Caci after him. Cacus lived in the time of legendary King Evander, an exile from Arcadia who came to Rome 60 years before the Trojan War and brought the Latins their alphabet. He welcomed Hercules to Rome as the hero was driving Geryon's cattle home from Spain; but when Hercules left the herd overnight in the Forum Boarium, Cacus slipped down and carried some of them off. When Hercules found him, a terrible wrestling match ensued (a favourite subject of Renaissance sculptors) in which Cacus scorched Hercules' bare behind and Hercules smashed Cacus' face to pulp. The Greek hero (afterwards known as 'great black bottom') is also said to have freed Evander from a tribute owed the Etruscans, and to have halted the practice of tossing men into the

Tiber each May, forcing the Romans to substitute dummies made from bulrushes.

Houses of Augustus and Livia J10–11

East of the Scalae Caci are the ruined rooms of the **House of Augustus**, painted with bright frescoes though not open to the public. But just beyond in the rooms of the **House of Livia** (currently closed for restoration) you can sometimes see delicately painted scenes of the same period: Hermes, Io, and Argus; a street scene; and a faded Polyphemus pursuing Galatea. Lead pipes found within (and now hung along the wall) labelled 'Iulia Augusta' identified the house with Augustus' wife, but now it is believed the rooms formed part of Augustus' house. Later emperors left it intact in honour of his memory. Less remains of Augustus' famous **Temple of Apollo**, vowed to the god just before the Battle of Actium, and in its day celebrated for its rare marbles and beautiful carvings; it burned in 363, and according to some, the Sibylline Books then lodged inside burned with it.

Palaces of Domitian J10–11

One of the more ill-adjusted Caesars was Domitian, who built the Domus Flavia, the Domus Augustana, and the Stadium on the east end of the Palatine, housing himself in splendid paranoia. Domitian was obsessed with death, especially his own, and had the walls of the courtyard of the **Domus Flavia**, the emperor's official residence, lined with slabs of shiny mica from Cappadocia, in which he would be able to see assassins trying to sneak up from behind, bearing the dagger that was to kill him in the end. The rooms of the palace are located around this large peristyle with an octagonal maze-shaped *impluvium* in the centre: the **Aula Regia**, or emperor's throne room; the **Basilica**, in the north corner, perhaps used as an auditorium, linked by an extension to the **Cryptoporticus**; and the so-called **Lararium**, which is more likely to have been home to the Praetorian Guard than household gods (Lares). More interesting than the meagre decoration remaining in these, however, are the rooms from the republican era found below: the **Aula of Isis**, under the Basilica, and the **House of the Griffins**, under the Lararium, with wall paintings and stuccoes of griffins. On the opposite side of the peristyle is the large dining room, the **Triclinium**, paved with coloured marbles, which have unfortunately been covered with a protective layer of gravel. The room is so-named because the diners reclined three to a couch, although the emperor dined apart, on the podium. Domitian held the most bizarre banquet on record here, when he draped the hall in black and for place cards used tombstones; funeral cakes, usually offered to the dead, were served, while for entertainment Domitian told tales of violent death, which the guests themselves expected at any moment. But it was all just Domitian's little joke, and instead of the sword they were given presents. Elagabalus liked the odd prank in the Triclinium as well; if the dinner threatened to fall flat, he would set panthers and tigers upon his guests to liven things up.

By the time Domitian wanted to build on the Palatine, there was virtually no room left, so in order to create space for a new palace his architect, Rabirius, cut a step out of the side of the hill and used the excavated soil to fill in the cleft between the two peaks. In the process, earlier buildings were buried; some day you may be able to visit them.

Beyond, to the east, is Domitian's **Domus Augustana**, the private residence of the emperors, built on the two levels of Rabirius' 'step'. From the sunken courtyard (closed to the public) a passage led to the imperial box overlooking the Circus Maximus. Two other peristyles, one open and one surrounded by rooms (one converted into a chapel in the 4th century), are on the upper level. A former convent building in between houses the **Palatine Antiquarium**. It contains detached frescoes, fragments of pavement, statues, and the infamous 3rd-century *Graffito of Alexamenos*, discovered in the **Paedagogium**, in which a boy is shown with a crucified figure with a donkey's head and the caption: 'Alexamenos worships his god'. The Paedagogium, or pages' school, was located to the south, overlooking the great hollow of the Circus Maximus. Until recently, the **Altar to the Unknown God** stood near the Paedagogium; even though the Romans worshipped every god they could find, they feared to inadvertently offend one they may have neglected to invite to the party, like the bad fairy in Sleeping Beauty.

For more intimate sports, Domitian built a small **Stadium** east of the Domus Augustana, with a two-storey portico scooped into the side, from which the imperial family could watch in comfort. In latter years the emperors may have converted the stadium into a garden; the stubby stone oval enclosure at the far end was built by Theodoric, for reasons unknown. Around the back of the stadium's *exedra* are the remains of the **Baths of Severus**, supported by the great substructures visible from the Circus Maximus; the water came by way of Domitian's aqueduct.

From the Stadium a path, the **Clivus Palatinus**, descends back to the Arch of Titus and the path to the Forum's back entrance on Via di S. Gregorio.

Caelian Hill
and the Aventine

07

Caelian Hill and the Aventine

In late imperial days, Monte Celio had a population of several hundred thousand, and contained some of the most fashionable quarters of the city. Today, the western half of the hill is almost entirely empty. When the besieging Goths cut the aqueducts in the Greek-Gothic wars of the 530s, property values dropped a bit for the wealthy villas and apartment blocks on Rome's southern hills. As the population gradually moved down to the Campus Martius, the area became abandoned, leaving behind monumental ruins and some of the most important early Christian churches, sitting among vineyards and cow pastures.

Somehow, much of this area escaped the post-1870 speculative building boom that ruined so much of Rome. The western half of the Caelian Hill particularly remains one of the most tranquil and beautiful sections of the city, a Roman fantasy of cypresses and parasol pines. For more than a decade now, there have been plans to turn the entire area into a park, along with the equally empty lands to the south, around the Baths of Caracalla – but in Rome, these things happen slowly.

West of the Caelian Hill, the little Aventine is a peaceful residential neighbourhood now, though in early Roman days it was the stronghold of the plebeians, where they made 'Aventine secessions' – strikes, in fact – against the greedy Senate bosses. Now it is one of the more obscure corners of the city, home to some lovely ancient churches and the capital of the Sovereign Order of the Knights of Malta. South of the Aventine is the smallest and strangest of Rome's hills, Monte Testaccio, made entirely of broken ancient pots.

1 Lunch

Checchino dal 1887, *Via di Monte Testaccio 30*, **t** *06 574 3816*; **metro** *Piramide*, **bus** *95*. **Open** *Sept–July Tues–Sat 12–3 and 8–11.30*; *reserve*. **Expensive**. In a cool Testaccio wine cave, dine on some of Rome's most authentic specialities – a match for one of the city's best wine cellars. Try the *menu degustazione*.

2 Coffee and Cakes

Caffè du Parc, *Piazza della Resistenza dell'8 Settembre*, **t** *06 574 3363*. **Open** *5am–10pm*. Famous for its *cremolato* – fresh fruit sorbet – served at a kiosk in the park behind the post office in Testaccio.

3 Drinks

Il Seme e la Foglia, *Via Galvani 18*, **t** *06 574 3008*. **Open** *Sept–July Mon–Sat 8am–2am, Sun 6pm–2am*. The best place for a coffee or a drink before heading for a Testaccio club.

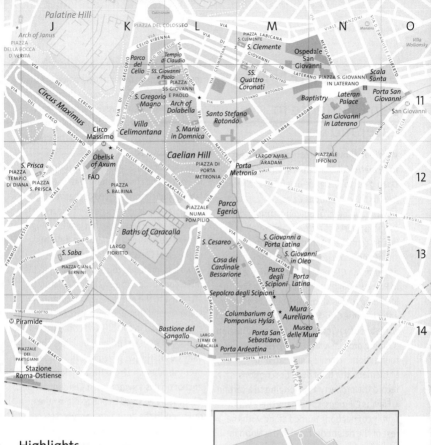

Highlights

Roma dei Romani: Monte Testaccio, once the venue for the Testaccio games – a wild urban rodeo with live pig-slicing – now a trendy clubbing district, p.171

Peace and Quiet: Villa Celimontana, a beautiful park, where the summer peace is broken by jazz concerts, p.161

Ancient Rome: The Baths of Caracalla, a grand symbol of Roman opulence, which could service 2,000 bathers at a time, p.162

Medieval and Renaissance: Santi Quattro Coronati, destroyed in the 1084 Norman sack and rebuilt as an abbey fortress, p.160

Baroqueorama: San Gregorio Magno, one of the first landmarks of the emerging Baroque, p.162

Unexpected Rome: Four levels of building and shrines of two religions can be found in San Clemente, p.158

SAN CLEMENTE

San Clemente in Laterano M10

Via di San Giovanni in Laterano, t 06 7045 1018; metro Colosseo, tram 3, bus 85, 117, 175. Open 9–12.30 and 3.30–6; adm to the church free, to the excavations €2.50.

With four levels of building, shrines of two religions, works of art from almost all of the last 20 centuries, along with a subterranean street and some good old solid Roman engineering, San Clemente offers a unique lesson in Rome's many-layered history. The site, including many 1st-century buildings, apparently became Christian property in the early 300s; about 375, one of the first big Christian building projects was begun over the older foundations, a basilica dedicated to St Clement, the third pope (inscriptions record the property as belonging to a certain T. Flavius Clemens, so perhaps there was a family connection). Burned along with the rest of the neighbourhood in the Norman sack of 1084, the church was soon after rebuilt over the remains of the original,

which was filled in with soil and rubble. It remained unknown until 1857, when the prior, Father Joseph Mulhooly, started excavations on his own initiative. Some 40 years and scores of wagon-loads of debris later, the ancient basilica was cleared, and the lower levels discovered.

Usually only the side entrance is open, but in front of the church, along with the plain late Baroque façade added in the 1700s, is a medieval *quadroporticus*, one of the few left in Rome – a survival of an ancient building style more common in southern Italy; most of the early Christian basilicas had one, a square, colonnaded courtyard leading to the main door. Inside, the eye is immediately attracted to the exquisite *schola cantorum* (choir screen) that fills the centre of the church, carved in the 6th and 7th centuries and saved from the original building. The early Cosmatesque pavement and baldaquin over the altar date from the rebuilding. The anchor on it is a symbol of St Clement, who supposedly was tied to one to make sure he drowned. In the apse, 12th-century frescoes detail the *Triumph of the Cross* – note the 12 doves, representing the Apostles, and the four rivers of Paradise springing from the

Rise and Fall of a God

As Mitra, he is mentioned in the Hindu Vedas as early as 1400 BC. In Persia he was one of the important gods of the old pantheon, pushed into the background but never entirely supplanted by Zoroastrianism, and his cult came into the west with the returning soldiers of Alexander the Great, just as it was dying out at home. The Greeks never cared much for Mithras; he was after all the god of their arch-enemies. But the Persian cult, along with the other gods and mysteries of the east, found a home in various places around the Mediterranean, and made a spectacular upsurge in the 2nd and 3rd centuries AD. Historians can't explain it, but it seems imperial patronage had a lot to do with the new Mithraism. Emperors such as Commodus, Caracalla and Albano's founder Septimius Severus were initiates.

Mithras was a god of light, but also associated with friendship, bonds and contracts of all kinds, the patron of loyalty to one's sovereign and brotherhood on the battlefield. Altogether a perfect deity for the imperial service and the army, and that is where Mithraism was the strongest. Its practice seems a kind of freemasonry. Only men took part, and there were seven levels of achievement, corresponding to the seven planetary spheres, each with its initiation. Like its competitor, Christianity, and in contrast to all the other cults of the day, Mithraism carried with it a big dose of morality and ethics; the Seven Deadly Sins were originally a Mithraic concept (one for each planetary sphere).

Imperial Romans saw nothing amiss with combining religion with pleasure, and their *mithraeums* were often parts of bath complexes like Albano's, or the famous one foot of the cross. Below it are fine frescoes of saints from the 1300s, and a tabernacle from the same period by Arnolfo di Cambio.

In the left aisle, near the side entrance, there is a chapel with a beautiful series of frescoes on the *Life of St Catherine* by Masolino (1420s; perhaps assisted by his precocious pupil Masaccio), one of your few chances in Rome to experience the vivid, revolutionary painting of the Florentine early Renaissance. Along with St Catherine (on the left wall) there is a Crucifixion and portraits of the Apostles, Evangelists, and Doctors of the Church. In the sacristy, just before the stair down to the Lower Church, there is a souvenir stand with posters and slides of the paintings below, rare works of the 9th–11th centuries. Take a look at them, for the actual frescoes are not in nearly as good a shape – every year sees them a little more faded. The stairway, lined with a jumble of fragments from the different ages of the church, leads down to the narthex, with 11th-century frescoes of the *Life of St Clement*.

The **Lower Church** itself was somewhat larger than its medieval successor, although the space is broken up by piers and walls added to support what is above. Frescoes on the wall facing the narthex include scenes of the *Life of Jesus* and the *Ascension* (9th century); in a niche on the right-hand wall is a portrait that may be, intriguingly, either the Virgin Mary or the notorious Byzantine Empress Theodora. On the opposite wall, more 9th-century frescoes tell the typically ingenuous saint story of *Sisinius* – but are remarkable for the inscriptions below, perhaps the oldest in the Italian language.

On one of the supporting walls is a little plaque erected by, of all people, Mr Todor Zhivkov, former Chairman of the Bulgarian Communist Party. And not without reason. From this church, in the 10th century, SS. Cyril and Methodius were sent out to convert the Slavs. They made a good job of it, and also invented the Cyrillic alphabet to translate the Bible into Old Slavonic, creating the first written works in any Slavic language. San Clemente has a history of missionary work to exotic places: the first two bishops of New York came from the Irish college next door.

Climb down another level (the steps are near the right wall) for the 1st-century AD block housing the **mithraeum**. Of at least a dozen temples of Mithras discovered in Rome, this is by far the most accessible and

discovered under the Baths of Caracalla in Rome. Often they were taken over by the Christians, as at Sutri or at San Clemente. Mithraeums are always underground, and the major feature is always a fresco or relief of Mithras sacrificing the sacred white bull. He didn't want to do it, and the sorrow on his face is often skilfully portrayed in the cult images. But Mithras was literally born with the knife in his hand. It was his destiny, and his father the sun god ordered him to make the sacrifice – it meant the creation of our world. The bull's blood poured out and formed all the plants and trees, while its sperm created men and animals. Its body was transformed into the moon, while Mithras' cloak became the firmament of stars. Usually the icons in *mithraeums* show a serpent, or scorpion, or both underneath the bull. They are the origin of evil, attracted

up from the primeval depths by the sacrifice to lick up the bull's spilled blood.

In the 3rd century, Mithraism probably had more adherents than Christianity, and it came very close to becoming Rome's state religion. In 307, Diocletian founded a new temple to Mithras for the armies on the Danube, near Vienna, and declared the god 'Patron of the Empire'.

But only six years later Diocletian was dead, and Emperor Constantine had already taken the first fateful steps toward converting the Empire to Christianity. The rapid demise of Mithraism demonstrates how artificial a religion it always was. With little attraction for intellectuals, or women, or the majority of people for whom the Roman state meant oppression, there was little chance of its survival once the Empire shifted its favour elswhere.

best preserved. Mithraism was a mystery religion, imported from Persia, which as late as the 300s could probably claim more adherents in Rome than Christianity (*see* box).

This *mithraeum* was one of the larger complexes, built into the block in the 2nd or 3rd century. After an antechamber with an ornamental stucco ceiling, there is the *triclinium*, with an altar portraying – as always on Mithraic altars – Mithras dispatching a white bull with a knife. The room gets its name because the form, and the benches lining the walls, suggest it was used for ritual suppers. Originally the ceiling was decorated with stucco reliefs representing the constellations, with narrow shafts of light through the roof for the stars. Adjacent to this is another chamber with a better-preserved ceiling, believed to be a school where boys were instructed in the religion before their initiations.

And still there is one more level below, foundations of **Republican-era buildings** that burned in Nero's great fire. These have never been excavated, but from the *mithraeum* you can walk out into a 1,900-year-old Roman alley, now some 30ft below street level. At the end of it (where the excavations stopped), you will hear water rushing below. No one knows if this outlet of the eerie sub-Roma of underground lakes, caves and buildings is an ancient sewer or an underground stream, but according to one story a child fell into it during a school outing a hundred years ago; they found him, barely alive, in open country miles from the city.

Santi Quattro Coronati M11

Via dei SS. Quattro Coronati 20, t 06 704 7547; tram 3, bus 85, 117. Church open 9–12 and 4–6; Capella di San Silvestro open 9–11 only.

Like San Clemente, the original version of this church was destroyed in the 1084 Norman sack. When Paschal II rebuilt it, around 1111, he made the church and its abbey into a veritable fortress, with some of the thickest walls in Rome. The entrance,

under a campanile that is really a defence tower, leads to another *quadroporticus*, and then a second court, once occupied by the nave of the original church. The interior, restored over centuries, has a *matroneum*, one of the last to be built in Rome, and some fragmentary medieval frescoes. The large apse, with Florentine Baroque frescoes by Giovanni di San Giovanni, gives an idea how much larger the original building was.

Ring the bell near the door in the left aisle, and a nun will admit you to the peaceful medieval **cloister**, its walls lined with fascinating bits of the pre-1084 decoration: neo-Celtic reliefs and other such barbaric stuff; one little plaque may be Rome's oldest surviving stick-no-bills sign – *applicar non licet*. Off the cloister, the small **Chapel of Santa Barbara** has more remains of medieval frescoes, and lovely ancient capitals recycled to support the brick vaulting.

Much better preserved frescoes can be seen in the **Chapel of San Silvestro**, off the second courtyard in front of the church (ask the nun to let you in). These scenes (*c.*1246) chronicle a very important part of Church mythology, the story of the sainted Pope Sylvester, how he cured Emperor Constantine of leprosy, and how in return the Emperor bestowed temporal authority over the West on the papacy – the *Donation of Constantine*, all a fairy tale, but the basis of the popes' claim to absolute authority over the centuries.

CAELIAN HILL

Santa Maria in Domnica L11

Piazza della Navicella 12, t 06 700 1519; bus 81. Open 8.30–12 and 4–7, in winter until 6.

This early 9th-century church was restored by Pope Leo X. In the simple interior, bathed in a golden light and lined with ancient granite columns, the climax is the lovely, Ravenna-style **mosaic** in the apse, added around 820 under Pope Paschal I – he is the fellow you see kneeling at the foot of the enthroned Madonna, wearing a square nimbus instead of a halo, this, according to the artistic conventions of the time, because he was still alive.

Vanity or not, Paschal was canonized later. This pope was a special friend of the English in Rome. When the wooden Anglo-Saxon Borgo caught fire in the 820s, he ran out barefoot at midnight from the Vatican to help put it out, then contributed the money for its rebuilding.

Above Mary, on the triumphal arch, Jesus is flanked by the Apostles, arranged like a chorus line among the mosaic flowers; the figures below represent Moses and Elijah.

No one ever mentions this church's very singular ceiling. Ferdinand de' Medici, Grand Duke of Tuscany and part-time alchemist, added it in honour of his kinsman Leo X. It is replete with cryptic inscriptions about the 'mystic rose' and 'tower of David', along with plenty of arcane symbolism, in which the Navicella from which the square takes its name is a recurring theme (sometimes as Noah's Ark).

The **Navicella** in question is an ancient stone boat, probably an ex-voto offering by sailors to the goddess Isis. It was discovered in the time of Pope Leo X, who had it incorporated into the fountain in the square.

Santo Stefano Rotondo L11

*Piazza della Navicella, at Via di Santo Stefano Rotondo, t 06 7049 3717; bus 81. **Open** Tues–Sat 9–1 and 3.30–6, Mon 3.30–6 only.*

The huge round church of Santo Stefano was built in 470. The round shape has made many scholars think it was built over a meat market – the *Macellum Magnum* of Nero (round market buildings were common, as at Pompeii and Pozzuoli near Naples).

Remains of a *mithraeum* have been found underneath. Another opinion has it designed after the round Church of the Holy Sepulchre Constantine erected in Jerusalem. Perhaps the biggest of all early Christian churches

(before the outer ring of columns was pulled down in the 1400s, it was over 200ft in diameter), it's a peaceful, harmonious church, whose serenity is spoiled by the perverse frescoes of martyrdoms, added in the 1580s, which now cover its walls. Stretching behind S. Stefano, you see impressive remains of the **Acqua Claudia**, its tall arcades designed to bring water to the highest points of the city.

Arch of Dolabella L11

*Via di San Paolo della Croce; **metro** Colosseo, **bus** 75, 85, 86, 87, 117, 175.*

Built on the site of an old gate, the arch dates from AD 10 (Dolabella was Consul in that year); it was later used to carry the Acqua Claudia over the road.

San Tommaso in Formis

*Via di San Paolo della Croce (behind a locked gate in the wall), t 06 3542 0529; **metro** Colosseo, **bus** 75, 85, 86, 87, 117, 175. **Open** for Mass on Sunday mornings.*

To the left of Dolabella's arch, S. Tommaso has a mosaic of 1218 above the door of *Christ Between Two Christian Slaves*.

Villa Celimontana K–L11

*Entrances from Piazza della Navicella and in Piazza SS. Giovanni e Paolo; **metro** Colosseo, Circo Massimo, **tram** 3, **bus** 62, 63, 81, 85, 95, 117, 160, 175. **Open** daily 7am–sunset.*

The most beautiful and agreeable park in this part of Rome. The southern end has a small obelisk dedicated to Isis, twin to the one in front of the Pantheon. A nobleman named Ciriaco Mattei moved it here in 1582, as part of an odd plan to build a classical Circus on what was his family villa gardens.

Santi Giovanni e Paolo K11

*Piazza SS. Giovanni e Paolo 13, **metro** Colosseo and Circo Massimo, **bus** 62, 63, 81, 85, 95, 117, 160, 175. **Open** 8.30–12 and 3–6.30.*

Although there was a Christian centre here as early as 400, incorporating older apartment buildings, the present building is from the 11th–12th centuries, rebuilt after the Norman sack. One of the few medieval buildings to escape the attentions of the Baroque spoilers, it remains largely as it was built, with a tall and graceful detached campanile, an Ionic portico (later partially enclosed) and an arcaded Romanesque apse. The exterior was restored in 1950 under the direction of its titular cardinal, the Archbishop of *Neoboracum* – New York in Latin, as you'll see it written on the plaque in the portico.

The Baroque had its way with the interior, but the real treasures are underneath. Some 70 years ago, one of the Passionist fathers in the adjacent monastery, digging just on instinct, discovered the Roman apartments now called the **House of SS. John and Paul**, after the two 4th-century martyrs honoured in the church above. Cardinal Spellman also oversaw the rest of the excavations, uncovering a lavish abode with its own baths, a library and a wine cellar. Many of the rooms are painted, some later ones with Christian subjects, and one exceptional mythological scene of the 3rd century, most likely representing Persephone (or perhaps Achilles' mother Thetis) and another divinity, reclining on a couch while little cupids sail by.

San Gregorio Magno K11

Piazza di San Gregorio, t 06 5526 1617; metro Circo Massimo, tram 3, bus 75, 85, 86, 87, 117, 175. Open 8–12.30 and 4–6.30.

One of the last of the wealthy Romans to keep up a villa on the Caelian was Pope Gregory the Great. Upon his election in 590, in the prostrate, devastated Rome that followed the wars and the Lombard invasion, Gregory donated a third of his wealth to the Church and its relief efforts. He turned his mansion into a monastery and continued to live there. From here he reorganized Rome and its Church, and sent St Augustine out to convert the heathen Angles and Saxons.

This villa-monastery – one of the sites in Rome most worth excavating – still lies below the surface; all that remains now is

the church of San Gregorio Magno, completely rebuilt in the 1620s, with a fine façade by Giovan Battista Soria that is one of the first landmarks of the emerging Baroque. Three small chapels stand to the left of it on **Clivo di Scauro**, dedicated to S. Silvia (S. Gregory's mother), S. Andrea and S. Barbara. Built over parts of Gregory's monastery, they are full of Baroque frescoes – notably *S. Silvia with an Angel Choir*, which could make even a sceptic appreciate the work of Guido Reni.

CARACALLA

Obelisk of Axum K12

Viale delle Terme di Caracalla; metro Circo Massimo, tram 3, bus 75, 85, 86, 87, 117, 175.

The newest and oddest of Rome's obelisks was stolen by Mussolini from the Ethiopian holy city of Axum and put up along the new Triumphal Way as a symbol of Italy's new imperial pretensions. It is probably really a funeral monument from the 4th century. Successive Italian governments now debate its return to Ethiopia. The clean, modern building behind was intended to be Mussolini's Ministry of Africa. Still unfinished at the end of the war, it has found a better use as the Food and Agriculture Organization of the United Nations, **FAO**.

Baths of Caracalla K12–L13

Viale delle Terme di Caracalla 52, t 06 3996 7700; metro Circo Massimo, tram 3, bus 160, 760. Baths open Tues–Sun 9am–one hour before sunset, Mon 9–2; Mithraeum open, by reservation for guided tours in Italian on the 2nd Saturday of each month at 10.30; adm €4.

Alexander Severus finished the baths that Caracalla started, but somehow it is fitting that this grand symbol of Roman opulence should be associated with this most decadent of emperors. The sprawling complex, covering some 27¼ acres, could service over 2,000 bathers at a time, although tens of thousands more could have disported themselves in the gardens, exercise yards and libraries. Its marble basins were salvaged to hold fountains all over Rome, and its works of art (like the famous *Farnese Hercules*, now in Naples) take pride of place in many Italian museums. Closed after the aqueducts were cut during the Gothic siege of 546, the baths were gradually abandoned, leaving for us only the giant arches of the central halls, and weirdly eroded brick and concrete forms that give a faint clue to the original layout. Large mosaics have been restored and displayed around the central building, and beneath the outer wall near the entrance is the largest *mithraeum* yet discovered in Rome.

This is not the most enlightening of Roman ruins to visit, but it is one of the best known, thanks largely to the summer opera season begun here in Mussolini's time (sporadically suspended due to damaging vibrations caused by the singing). A large tunnel, built to bring in tons of firewood to heat the baths, runs from here to the Palazzo Venezia; Mussolini liked to drive his Alfa roadster through it, popping up magically on stage, car and all, for the opera's opening festivities.

San Cesareo L13

*Via di Porta San Sebastiano; **bus** 218, 360, 628.* **Open** *Sun 10–1.*

The discovery of a great black and white 2nd-century mosaic of sea monsters suggests that this ancient church was built over a Roman bath. In the late 16th century it was given a façade by Giacomo della Porta and an exquisite wooden ceiling of gold and blue, which colourfully complements the Cosmatesque choir, ambo and altar.

Casa del Cardinale Bessarione M13

*Via di Porta San Sebastiano, **t** 06 6710 3833; **bus** 218, 360, 628.* **Open** *by arrangement only.*

Just beyond San Cesareo is this peaceful little garden and 15th-century villa. Its owner (d.1472) was the great Greek cardinal and

scholar who came to Rome during the luckless ecumenical council called by Pope Eugenius IV to reconcile the Eastern and Western churches. It's charmingly preserved inside, with frescoes and Renaissance furniture, but can only be seen on special tours.

Sepolcro degli Scipioni M14

*Via di Porta San Sebastiano 9; **bus** 218, 360, 628.* **Closed** *for restoration.*

Discovered in 1780 under a 3rd-century house, the tomb of the Scipios is one of the oldest on the Via Appia, built around 290 BC. It was melancholy enough to ignite Byron's romantic imagination in *Childe Harold*:

> Niobe of nations! there she stands
> Childless and crownless, in her voiceless woe,
> An empty urn within her withered hands,
> Whose sacred dust was scattered long ago;
> The Scipios' tomb contains no ashes now;
> The very sepulchres lie tenantless
> Of their heroic dwellers.

In truth it never did contain ashes; the Scipios claimed descent from the gods, and instead of cremation they were entombed in marble *sarcophagi*. The best one (replaced by a cast) is of the tomb's builder, Consul L. Cornelius Scipio Barbatus, conqueror of the Samnites, whose grandsons were Rome's generals in Spain during the 2nd Punic War, and whose great-grandson, Scipio Africanus, defeated Hannibal at Zama, bringing that war to a close. A brilliant, charismatic, and humane individualist when the rest of the Romans were stolid conformists, Scipio Africanus was the first Roman leader to stand out, a kind of proto-Caesar. His remarkable family (including his brother, Scipio Asiaticus, who introduced eastern luxuries and dancing girls to Rome, and Cornelia, his daughter and Rome's first liberated woman, mother of the revolutionary Gracchi) were round pegs in a square empire. The ultra-conservative Cato (one of the most nauseatingly cruel figures in Rome's cruel history) forced Scipio Africanus into retirement, and he died in 183 BC near Naples, shunned by an ungrateful Rome. Hence he was not buried here, although many of his kin are; like the mausoleums of the Caesars, it exudes *tristesse*.

A small Christian **catacomb** branches off from the gloomy halls of the Scipios' tomb; in front, steps lead down to a wonderful mossy, fern-festooned *columbarium*, its dovecote niches still holding a few urns.

Columbarium of Pomponius Hylas M14

Via di Porta Latina 10, t 06 6710 3819; bus 218, 360, 628. Open by arrangement, Tues–Fri 9–1.

The 1st-century AD Columbarium of Pomponius Hylas is nothing less than the most luxurious *columbarium* ever discovered, embellished with wonderfully preserved mosaics, stucco, and frescoes. Pomponius Hylas himself is believed by archaeologists to have been a kind of Roman cemetery plot salesman, and you can just imagine him in a checked toga, intoning: 'Hurry, hurry, hurry, the best niches are going fast...'.

San Giovanni in Oleo M13

Via di Porta Latina; bus 218, 360. Open daily 7–12.30 and 3.30–6.

Just before Porta Latina is the little octagonal chapel of San Giovanni in Oleo, 'St John in Oil', built in the 16th century and attributed to Bramante. It marks the site of an attempt by the authorities to deep fry the saint, from which he emerged 'refreshed'. The disappointed Romans let him go. The chapel has a pretty frieze added by Borromini.

San Giovanni a Porta Latina M13

Via di Porta Latina; bus 160, 628. Open daily 7–12 and 3.30–7.30.

In a little cul-de-sac, San Giovanni a Porta Latina is a delightful country church often in demand for weddings. Built in the 5th century by St Gelasius I, and fiddled with often since, what you see today is essentially

12th century, with a fine husky campanile, a Romanesque portico, and a charming, richly carved marble well; within, it has three apses in the Greek style, and some curiously diaphanous 12th-century frescoes, lit by three lacy selenite windows.

THE AURELIAN WALL

Museo delle Mura M4

Via di Porta San Sebastiano; t 06 7047 5284; bus 118, 218. Open Tues–Sun 9–7, in winter until 5.30; adm €2.50.

At the end of Via di Porta San Sebastiano stands the mightiest gate in the Aurelian Wall, originally the Porta Appia. Honorius, Belisarius, and Narses fortified it, and now **Porta San Sebastiano**'s twin canister towers contain the Walls Museum; among the more interesting exhibits is an ancient country calendar called the *Menologium Rusticum Colutianum*. This is your chance to play Roman patrol along the wall, as far as the powerful **Bastione del Sangallo**, built by Antonio da Sangallo the Younger; this section of walls offers the illusion of defending Rome from its greatest enemy: the endless traffic spewing along the boulevards just outside.

SAN GIOVANNI

San Giovanni in Laterano N11

Piazza San Giovanni in Laterano, t 06 6988 6433; metro San Giovanni, tram 3, bus 117, 650. Open 7–7.30.

This Patriarchal Basilica of St John Lateran is nothing less than the 'Mother and Head Church of Rome and the World', the first church founded by Constantine, and still the city's cathedral. Lying just within the Aurelian Wall, the site originally belonged to a patrician named Plautinius Lateranus, executed by Nero for plotting against him; the property, however, retained the family name (*Domus Faustae in Laterano*) even when it passed to Fausta, the wife of Constantine. After 19 years of marriage, Constantine had Fausta smothered in a hot bath, but in the meantime he used her palace (the site of the present baptistry) for a church council with Pope Miltiades in 313. It became a cult centre for the new religion, and all the surrounding land was donated by Constantine to Rome's Christians; St John's itself was built over the barracks of the emperor's personal guard. When building it, the Christians chose one of the forms they knew best – a basilica – which with its five naves was designed to stand up to the architecture of the pagans. As it contained the *cathedra*, or chair of Rome's bishop, it became the city's cathedral. And although nothing remains of the original structure (sacks by Vandals and Normans, two earthquakes and several fires have seen to that) it has maintained the same basilican form that inspired countless later churches.

The Lateran was the chief papal residence before the papacy relocated to Avignon, and throughout the Middle Ages was regarded as the Vatican is today. Popes were crowned here until the 19th century. Charlemagne came here to be baptized in 774. Five Councils of the Church were held here in the Middle Ages. But there have been other moments that the Church would rather forget, such as the 897 posthumous trial of Pope Formosus. The Romans were notorious for mocking dead popes, but this was an extreme case, especially since the sick charade was acted out in the basilica by Formosus' successor and arch-enemy, Stephen VII, who had the grinning corpse exhumed and dressed in full pontifical regalia. The papal lawyer drilled the mummy with questions. Formosus, though given time to respond, failed to defend himself. Declaring him an usurper, Stephen cut three fingers from his benedicting hand, and tossed the rest in the Tiber.

The church building itself has suffered its ups and downs, too. When Boniface VIII declared the first Jubilee in 1300 it was the wonder of the age, and the priests with their long rakes couldn't scrape in the pilgrims' donations fast enough. By 1350, when papal finances demanded another Jubilee year, Petrarch mourned that 'the mother of all churches stands without a roof, exposed to wind and rain'. It was collapsing again just before the 1650 Jubilee, when Innocent X ordered Borromini to repair the interior; the façade needed to be replaced in the 1730s, and was the subject of a competition, in which Alessandro Galilei triumphed over his 22 competitors with a stretched-out version of Maderno's façade for St Peter's, striking for the deep *chiaroscuro* in its arches. Along the roof a giant Baroque Christ and saints model the latest in marble draperies. The central bronze door came from the Senate House in the Forum; to the right is the **Porta Santa**, opened in Holy Years; and to the left stands a whopping great statue of Constantine, carted here from his baths on the Quirinale.

Borromini's solution to reinforcing the basilica's structure was to fill in the spaces between the pillars, creating massive piers with alcoves for more overgrown 18th-century Apostles, glaring down at puny humanity like Roman emperors of old. The intricate, geometric Cosmati floor is matched by the rich ceiling by Daniele da Volterra. Although sheer size is the main effect, there are occasional details worth looking for: Giotto's fresco of *Boniface VIII's Jubilee*, just behind the first pier on the right, and on the next pier a Hungarian-made 1909 memorial to Pope Sylvester II (*see* 'Santa Croce', p.236), who crowned St Stephen, founder and first king of Hungary, in 1001. The memorial incorporates part of his original tombstone, said to sweat and rattle when a pope is about to die. Other chapels contain carefree Baroque, with some Jesuit-style cut-out saints.

The **Papal Altar**, with its silver reliquaries said to contain the heads of SS. Paul and Peter, is sheltered by a festive Gothic *baldaquin*. In the Confessio is the fine bronze tomb slab of Pope Martin V, on whom the Romans drop flowers and coins for good luck. The apse had to be reconstructed in 1885, and the mosaics you see now are a copy of a 13th-century copy by two Iacopos, Torriti and da Camerino, from a much older original; the scene shows a dove descending on the Cross, worshipped by a reindeer, while the four Gospels flow like rivers and the Virgin and saints stand by.

In the left transept is the **Altar of the Holy Sacrament** (1600), sheltering half St Peter's communion table, from S. Pudenziana; the bronze columns and lintel are said to have been melted down from the ships' prows that decorated the Forum's Imperial Rostra.

The right transept holds the tomb of the most powerful medieval pope, Innocent III (d.1216), who was poisoned in Perugia (some suspect through his slippers. He was found in the cathedral stark naked). His remains were brought here in 1891; frescoes tell the story of his life. The 14th-century Cosmatesque tomb of Boniface IX is in the chapel to the right.

Cloister of San Giovanni

Cloister and museum open 9–6, in winter until 5; adm €2.

The most beautiful thing in the cathedral, however, is its **cloister** (off the left aisle), built by the Vassalletti (father and son) between 1215 and 1223. Once Rome was full of such individualistic medieval jewels, well outside the mainstream of Gothic and reviving classicism; this cloister, with its pairs of spiral columns and glittering 13th-century Cosmatesque mosaics, is the most striking survival of this lost chapter in art. All around the cloister walls, fragments from the earlier incarnations of St John's have been assembled, a wistful collection of broken pretty things that includes an interesting tomb of a 13th-century bishop by Arnolfo di Cambio.

A small Lateran **museum** is stuffed with ecclesiastical finery – golden vestments, golden reliquaries, and so on; the best piece is a 14th-century gilded silver cross called the Constantiniana, depicting Adam and Eve.

Baptistry of San Giovanni N11

Baptistry open 8–12.30 and 3.30–7; adm free.

In the piazza's southwest corner is the Baptistry of St John, nothing less than the first in Christendom, built by Constantine in the 320s in an octagonal form copied by baptistries throughout Italy. It was in this holy place that Cola di Rienzo went over the top, even by Roman standards; after a bath in the baptismal font, he spent the night in vigil and emerged in the morning dressed like a Liberace in golden spurs, self-christened as 'Knight Nicolas, Friend of the World'. The green basalt basin, where Rienzo took his presumptuous bath, is surrounded by eight porphyry columns, and there are two famous **bronze doors** on either side.

One set of doors, from 1196, etched with scenes of how the Lateran basilica appeared at the time, opens into the **Chapel of St John the Evangelist**, with alabaster columns by the altar and an exquisite 5th-century mosaic with birds and flowers in the vault. The other doors, traditionally from the Baths of Caracalla, although they may be original to the Baptistry, 'sing' with a low, harmonic sound when slowly opened.

The baptistry has two other chapels, the **Chapel of SS. Secunda and Rufina**, with another exquisite 5th-century mosaic, of vines on a blue ground, and the **Chapel of S. Venanzio** with mosaics of Dalmatian saints from the 640s, a time when artistic *rigor mortis* had already set in.

Lateran Palace N11

Piazza San Giovanni in Laterano, t 06 6988 6452; metro San Giovanni, tram 3, bus 117, 650. Open Mon–Sat 8–1; adm €3.

Opposite the Baptistry, adjoining the Basilica, is the Lateran Palace, address of the popes before they became voluntary 'Babylonian Captives' in Avignon in 1309. After the massive fire of 1309, which destroyed church and palace, it remained a ruin until 1586 when Sixtus V had it rebuilt by Domenico Fontana.

Piazza San Giovanni N11

The Lateran's north front has an impressive 1586 façade by Domenico Fontana, incorporating two earlier bell towers in its design. It looks over Piazza San Giovanni, base for the tallest obelisk in the world, just over 100ft of red granite from the Temple of Ammon at Thebes, erected by Thothmes IV in the 15th century BC and stolen by Constantius II in 357 for the Circus Maximus. Across the grass is **Porta Asinara**, one of Rome's best-preserved ancient gates, and **Porta di San Giovanni**, rebuilt in 1564 and now leading to a huge clothes market.

Scala Santa and Sancta Sactorum N11

Piazza San Giovanni in Laterano, t 06 772 6641; metro San Giovanni, bus 117, 650. Open 6.15–12 and 3–6.30, in winter until 6.

On the east of the piazza are two holy relics that survived flames. The **Scala Santa** is the legendary stair from Pontius Pilate's palace in Jerusalem, descended by Christ after his judgement and brought to Rome by Constantine's mother, St Helen. Serious pilgrims ascend them on their knees – the only way permitted, ever since 1510, when Martin Luther crawled halfway up and heard a little voice saying 'The just shall live by faith, not by pilgrimage, not by penance', whereupon he did the unthinkable; he stood up and walked back down.

At the top of the stairs is the Holy of Holies, the **Sancta Sanctorum**, or Chapel of St Lawrence, built in 1278 as the Pope's private chapel. Through the locked gate you can see a miraculous 'handless' portrait of Jesus painted by angels, frescoes attributed to Pietro Cavallini, and a mosaic of Christ, perhaps by the Cosmati. East of the Scala Santa is a **Tribune** erected by Fuga in 1743 to house copies of mosaics from the dining hall, or *triclinium*, of the medieval palace.

AVENTINE HILL

In Republican times, the depression of the *Vallis Murcia* and its Circus Maximus formed the boundary between the high-rollers on the Palatine and what Juvenal called 'the

mob of Remus', the solidly plebeian quarter on the Aventine Hill. The psychological distance, however, was so great as to make even the Circus Maximus seem like a penny sideshow, beginning in the days of those nasty twins, Romulus and Remus, whose Aventine cause ended on the point of Romulus' Palatine dagger. In the eyes of later Palatine residents, the Aventine was a hotbed of dangerous democratic ideas imported by Greek merchants, who lived just below the hill along the Tiber. In 494 BC, when the double standards of the Palatine patricians were finally written down for all to see on the Twelve Tables, the plebeians were so appalled by their blatant unfairness that they invented that venerable Italian phenomenon, the general strike; they retreated to the Aventine, refused to work, and vowed one another mutual help – the first 'Aventine Secession', a phrase Italian journalists still use when a left-wing party walks out of a government coalition.

The Greeks, when not eroding the Roman class system, kept themselves busy subverting Roman piety. In the hidden caves on the slopes of the Aventine they introduced the midnight rituals of Dionysus and Bacchus. Though secret, their wild, often bloody orgies came to the attention of the Senate and in 186 BC thousands of men and women were executed for participating in the rites. From then on, men were banned from taking part. In the imperial age, the old plebeian hill was usurped by patricians, and rents have remained high ever since. But you could say that in the end the Aventine won the battle of the hills – while the Palatine lies in ruins, it is a genteel residential neighbourhood today.

Circus Maximus J11

Via del Circo Massimo; metro Circo Massimo, tram 3, bus 81, 160, 175, 204.

For fans of Ben Hur this must be the most disappointing ruin in all Rome: it was too convenient a quarry, and all that has survived is a banked, horseshoe-shaped depression, where Romans come to walk their dogs. But in its day archaeologists estimate that as many as 300,000 people squeezed into its 2,000ft by 650ft expanse and placed bets on their favourite charioteers. They did so with a vehemence, according to Juvenal's famous passage: 'Now that no one buys our votes, the public has long since cast off its cares; the people that once bestowed commands, consulships, legions and all else, now meddles no more and longs eagerly for just two things – bread and circuses.' The Caesars had to provide for an estimated 150,000 idlers; this was their insurance against revolt. But in the time of the first kings the horse races held between the Palatine and Aventine had a religious significance; the pounding hooves awoke the powers of the underworld, promoted fertility and appeased the spirits of the dead; the competitive aspect brought out the courage of warriors, who worshipped the war god Mars. The Etruscan king Tarquinius Superbus built the first stands around the old course, and a temple dedicated to the fertility goddess Ceres on the Palatine, overlooking the Circus.

Early piety soon went by the boards. Jérôme Carcopino writes how the Roman crowd found 'in the circus itself a miniature projection of the universe and, as it were, an epitome of its destiny'. In the astrological symbolism of the race, the obelisk on the central *spina* ('backbone') symbolized the sun; the 12 starting stalls of the chariots, or *carceres*, became the 12 symbols of the zodiac; the seven laps, measured by seven wooden eggs, and later seven bronze dolphins, evoked the planets or days of the week. Augustus added the imperial box (*pulvinar*) linked to his house on the Palatine, the prototype of the famous *kathisma* of the Byzantine emperors in Constantinople's Hippodrome. Beneath this, in the massive *cavea*, the first tier of seats was of marble (for Senators), the second of wood, and the third was standing room only, although unlike the Colosseum the sexes were not separated; Ovid recommends a day at the races to pick up girls or husbands.

There would have been plenty of time for making passes as well as bets; from the time of Caligula, it was usual to have 24 races spread through the day, some with two-horsed chariots (*bigae*), or with acrobatic jockeys leaping from one horse to another, although it was always the four-horsed chariots, the *quadrigae*, that were the most exciting – and costly. To finance the men and horses, there grew up four factions, each represented by a colour: the Whites and Greens, and Reds and Blues (often the favourites of the Emperors), who had their stables and headquarters around Campo de' Fiori. The emperors also had to deal with the unhappiness of punters who lost, placating them with gimmicks like 'the hail of eatables' and free raffle tickets.

Santa Sabina I12

Piazza Pietro d'Illiria; metro Circo Massimo, bus 23, 44, 95, 280, 716. Open daily 7–11.30 and 3.30–7.

On the north edge of the Aventine, take in the fine views over the Circus Maximus and Tiber from the orange trees and parasol pines of the Giardino degli Aranci of **Parco Savello** in Via di S. Sabina (sometimes closed off during the day time in summer). A door in the corner of the park leads to Piazza Pietro d'Illiria, with a glowering mask fountain in the wall and what many people consider the loveliest church in Rome, the early Christian basilica of **Santa Sabina**.

In ancient times this was the site of the Temple of Juno Regina, the patroness of Rome's Etruscan arch-rival Veii, who was seduced into changing sides in 392 BC. Some 600 years later, a Roman matron named Sabina who lived in the neighbourhood was converted to Christianity by her Greek slave Seriphia. They were martyred together, and in 425 a Dalmatian priest named Pietro d'Illiria built this basilica. In 1219 Pope Honorius III gave it to St Dominic, and the Dominicans have held on to it ever since, restoring it to its original appearance in 1936. The 15th-century portico houses ancient *sarcophagi* (the waving lines symbolize eternal life) and what may be the oldest wooden church doors in the world, carved from cypress wood in the 5th century with parallel reliefs of Old and New Testament scenes, made with consummate devotion and a creeping forgetfulness of the proportions of the human body.

The beauty within S. Sabina is that of a pure, contemplative simplicity, so rare in Rome that it takes a moment to adjust; one, instinctively by this point, expects at least a little Baroque curlicue or eyeball-rolling saint somewhere. The ceiling is of simple wood, supported by 24 beautiful Corinthian columns, probably from the temple of Juno, linked by arches decorated with discreet marble inlay. The delicate windows, illuminating the nave with a soft, magical light, were reconstructed from 9th-century fragments; their glass, as in the originals, is really a mineral called selenite. A portion of the 5th-century mosaic inscription remains over the door, referring to the founder, with allegories of the churches of the Jews and Gentiles who have converted to the new faith. In the floor of the nave is Rome's only mosaic tomb (c.1300), and the painting in the apse by Taddeo Zuccari, the only jarring note, is believed to represent the same subject as the original mosaics. A chapel in the left aisle contains Sassoferrato's almost anti-Baroque 1643 *Madonna del Rosario*, painted with pre-Raphaelite clearness. By the door, on a pedestal, sits the black 'martyr's stone' that the devil hurled at St Dominic, although his aim was off. If there are any Dominicans around, you can ask them about it, or better yet, ask to see S. Sabina's beautiful cloister (1225).

Santi Bonifacio e Alessio H12

Piazza di Sant'Alessio; metro Circo Massimo, bus 23, 44, 95, 170, 716. Open daily 8.30–8.

Grimy Sant'Alessio is almost as old as Santa Sabina, but was completely remodelled in the 18th century, preserving only its intricately worked bell tower outside and sections of fine Cosmatesque pavement in its pastel interior. To the left of the door is one of Rome's more curious chapels, hung with the stair down which St Alexis was pushed (not one of the more exciting martyrdoms!).

Piazza dei Cavalieri di Malta H12

Metro Circo Massimo, bus 28, 44, 95, 170, 781, 716, 280.

Giambattista Piranesi's delightfully quirky piazza is lined with baby obelisks and classical trophies, and surrounded by a dark wall of cypresses. Peep through the bronze-lined keyhole, at the monumental entrance of the Priory of the Sovereign Order of Malta for the famous **view of St Peter's**, framed at the end of a tree-lined path.

Santa Maria del Priorato H12

Piazza dei Cavalieri di Malta, t 06 675 811. Open for guided tours Sat 10–11, by special arrangement.

You'll have to get permission from the Order of Malta's headquarters to see the priory church, a fanciful, winsome Rococo ornament emblazoned with knightly motifs, also by Piranesi. Feel privileged if they let you in. This corner of the city has been off limits since the roaring 900s, when Rome's big boss, Alberic, watched over his fief from this commanding spot over the Tiber. In the 1100s his fort was bought by the Templars, and when they were suppressed for heresy in 1312, it was inherited by the Knights Hospitallers of St John, now the Knights of Malta. The Knights no longer wait for the popes to unleash them against Saracen and Turk; since they left Malta, this social club for old nobles bestirs itself to assist hospitals, its original job during the Crusades.

The **Priory**, with its lovely gardens, is the residence of the Grand Master (currently a kinsman of Winston Churchill), and of the Order's ambassadors to Italy and the Vatican City – which seems like an enormous state in comparison. The Knights, however, get their own car number plates (S.M.O.M.), and the Aventine is a good place to see their modern-day squires, the chauffeurs, awaiting them double-parked.

Sant'Anselmo H12

Piazza Sant'Anselmo, t 06 57911.
Open *during Mass.*

In the southeast corner of Piranesi's square, the neo-Lombard Sant'Anselmo is the Benedictines' seminary church and one of the best places in Rome to hear Gregorian chant (Sunday mornings); it also has a 3rd-century black and white mosaic of Orpheus in the cloister.

Mithraeum of Santa Prisca J12

Via di Santa Prisca, t 06 3996 7700; metro Circo Massimo, bus 23, 44, 95, 170, 716.
Open *Mon–Fri 9–1; adm €2.*

Not a trace remains of the famous Temple of Diana that Servius Tullius built here in 540 BC to steal Nemi's thunder as a cult centre for the Latin people (*see* 'Lake Nemi', p.279). The worship of Diana, in her turn, was upstaged by the more personal religions practised at Santa Prisca.

The church occupies the site where Prisca and Aquila, a married couple mentioned in a letter by St Paul, entertained St Peter. In the 2nd century a sanctuary was built next to their house – not dedicated to the saints but to their most obdurate pagan rival, the Persian god Mithras (*see* 'Rise and Fall of a God', p.158). In the year 400, with Christianity the victorious cult, the *mithraeum* was vandalized, covered up by the new church, and only rediscovered in 1958.

The early Christians would be appalled to learn that the *mithraeum* is now S. Prisca's claim to fame. The stucco statues of Mithras slaying the bull and a reclining Saturn (made from an *amphora*) that they hacked to bits have been carefully put back together, and the rare frescoes they axed have been restored. On the right wall is a scene of the

highest Roman sacrifice, that of a bull, ram, and pig, called the *suovetaurilia*; on the left wall, a procession of initiates and a sacrificial feast. One room, believed to have been a *nymphaeum*, contains pieces of glass, stucco reliefs, and ceramics.

San Saba J13

Via di S. Saba; metro Piramide, bus 175.
Open *7–12 and 4–7.*

When the Arabs invaded Syria and Jordan in the 7th century, as many monks as could fled to Italy; in Rome they built a monastery and S. Saba, in the Greek style, with three apses. Much has been added since, including the delightful quattrocento loggia, which shelters a relief of a knight and falcon, perhaps made by the first monks, and the door, from the early 1200s by Master Jacopo, the head of the Cosmati tribe, who also worked on the superb mosaic floor. The centre apse has a lovely baldaquin, and in the triumphal arch, a Renaissance painting of the *Annunciation*; in the truncated fourth aisle are frescoes on the life of St Nicolas, from the 1200s; detached 7th-century frescoes from the original church are in the corridor leading to the sacristy.

PORTA OSTIENSE

One of the best-preserved gates in the Aurelian Wall, the Porta Ostiense (I14) was renamed **Porta San Paolo** long after St Paul walked through it on his way to execution. While the inner side of the gate is Roman, the outside face was reconstructed by Belisarius in the 6th century.

Pyramid of Gaius Cestius I14

Piazzale Ostiense; metro Piramide, tram 3, bus 23, 75, 280, 702, 715, 719.

Looming beyond Porta San Paolo is this Roman oddity, the **Piramide di Caio Cestio** built in 12 BC by a wealthy praetor and tribune of the people. Gaius Cestius spent time in Egypt when the Romans were in the midst of their post-Cleopatra craze, carrying off obelisks and immersing themselves in the cult of Isis. Cestius went one step further and, in terms of terrestrial immortality, he made a sound choice, for while the tombs of the emperors themselves have suffered countless indignities, his pyramid survives intact, even if it was built, as the inscription claims, in a manner that any self-respecting pharaoh would have disdained. The pile is made of brick, covered with white marble from Luni, and was completed in 330 days.

Protestant Cemetery H14

Via Caio Cestio 6, t 06 574 1900; metro Piramide, tram 3, bus 23, 75, 280, 702, 715, 719. Open Tues–Sun 9–6, in winter until 5; ring the bell at the gate; donation expected.

Aurelian incorporated the pyramid in his wall, and the English and German communities incorporated his wall in turn into their cemetery, the **Cimitero Accatolico**. The Romans have become rather sentimental about this most romantic of graveyards, and often quote Shelley's preface to *Adonais*:

The Cemetery is an open space among the ruins, covered in winter with violets and daisies. It might make one in love with death to know that one should be buried in so sweet a place.

But throughout the 19th century, burials had to made at night, by torchlight, for fear that the mourners would be harmed by the intolerant populace; and until 1870 neither crosses nor inscriptions referring to heaven were permitted, on the grounds that no salvation was possible outside the Church.

Only a handful of people came to watch Keats' (1796–1821) burial in the lovely lawn of the Old Cemetery, to the left as you enter. 'Here lies one whose name was writ in water' is the epitaph he composed for himself in his sad and bitter last days, believing his poetry a failure; entombed with him are the letters from his sweetheart Fanny, which, once he knew he was dying, he could no longer bear

to open. Buried next to him is his friend Severn, who survived him by 65 years. Shelley, whose description of the cemetery was prophetic, drowned the year after Keats died; his ashes lie next to the grave of his friend Trelawny, with the inscription '*Cor cordium*' (heart of hearts) and the appropriate verse about having 'suffered a sea change' from *The Tempest*.

A map given by the caretaker will help you locate the other 'Acatholics' buried here: Goethe's only son, Julius; the Renaissance historian J. Addington Symonds; philosopher and founder of the Italian Communist party Antonio Gramsci; and the American sculptor William Story, who sculpted the '*Angel of Grief*' despairing over his wife's tomb.

British War Cemetery H14

Entrance on Via N. Zabaglia. Open daily 8–12 and 1–4.

Near the Protestant Cemetery, the **Cimitero Inglese di Guerra** is a touching memorial to 429 British troops killed fighting for the liberation of Rome.

TESTACCIO

To the right of the British War Cemetery rises the uncanny weed-tonsured bulge of Rome's youngest and most peculiar hill, **Monte Testaccio** (G–H14). Norfolk, Virginia's Mount Trashmore may be the biggest mountain made of rubbish, but Monte Testaccio, or the Monte dei Cocci was the first.

Testae means 'potsherds' in Latin, and that is what Testaccio is made of; nothing but broken *amphorae* (mostly used to bring cheap wine from Spain) which Tiber longshoremen mysteriously but systematically piled here, behind the ancient warehouse district of Marmorata.

If nothing else, Monte Testaccio is the world's biggest monument to the butterfingered: over the centuries enough *amphorae* were broken to build a mound 115ft high and 3300ft round, covering seven city blocks.

Its strangeness has attracted both extremes of the human condition: the pious would come here to perform the Stations of the Cross, while the not-so-pious came for low-life fun and the Testaccio games, a wild urban rodeo with live pig-slicing and other sports. Rome's communal wine cellars were dug into Monte Testaccio's flanks, for the densely packed potsherds were found to maintain an even temperature year round.

Nowadays Testaccio has as many car-repair grottoes as wine cellars, and nearly as many lively clubs and theatres. The Tiber side of Via di Monte Testaccio is blocked by the massive buildings of the former city abattoir, the Ex-Mattatoio, entered by way of an impressive 1889 gate crowned by a bronco-busting angel. The city now uses it as a cosmopolitan Centro Sociale aimed at the young, a Villaggio Globale for exhibitions, various performances, political and other meetings, and the occasional rave or rock gig. It's also the place in Rome to sample *trippa alla romana* and other classic, heavy-duty Roman dishes (*see* 'Eating Out', p.311 and 'Nightlife', p.319).

Quirinale, Viminale and Esquiline Hill

Quirinale, Viminale and Esquiline Hill

These three hills, parallel ridges stretching eastwards from the Campo Marzio and the Forums, became depopulated after the fall of the empire, and stayed that way a long time. The Quirinale was redeveloped to be the home of the popes in the 16th and 17th centuries; the other two had to wait until the 19th to be rebuilt in the worst way.

In a part of town rather lacking in Roman charm, there are some surprising attractions. In the 1600s the Quirinale gained two of the defining works of the Baroque; these point the way to one of the great patrician art collections, in the Palazzo Barberini, and the ancient works in the Museo Nazionale Romano. The Esquiline begins right across from the Colosseum, with the recently-restored remains of Nero's Golden House, the *Domus Aurea*, and extends to S. Pietro in Vincoli, with Michelangelo's famous tomb of Julius II, and the ancient Patriarchal basilica of S. Maria Maggiore.

1 Lunch

Monte Caruso (Cicilardone), *Via Farini 12*, *t 06 483 549*; **bus** *105, 360, 649*. **Open** *Sept–July Tues–Sat 1–4 and 7–11, Mon 7–11; reserve*. **Expensive**. Excellent home-made *maltagliati* with ricotta and tomato. Lively atmosphere aided by a good wine list.

2 Coffee and Cakes

Antico Caffè del Brasile, *Via dei Serpenti 23*, *t 06 488 2319*; **metro** *Cavour*. **Open** *Mon–Sat 7am–8pm; closed 2 weeks Aug*. The Monti neighbourhood's café and *torrefazione*.

3 Drinks

Trimani, *Via Goito 20*, *t 06 446 9661*; **metro** *Termini*, **bus** *60, 61, 62, 75, 84, 90, 116T, 175, 492*. **Open** *Mon–Sat 11.30–3 and 5.30–12.30*. Well known for its fine wine selection, with a casual atmosphere nonetheless.

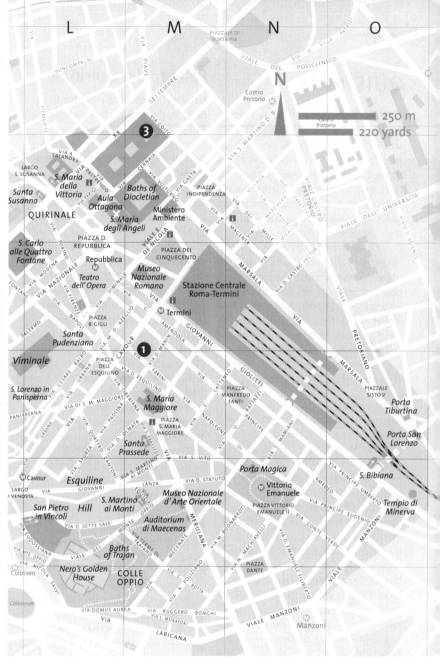

Highlights

Roma dei Romani: Palazzo del Quirinale, where the Roman Republic was reborn in 1848, p.176

Peace and Quiet: The cool incense-scented darkness of Santa Prassede, p.187

Ancient Rome: The repository of antiquities in the Museo Nazionale Romano, p.181

Medieval and Renaissance: Santa Maria Maggiore, most medieval of the seven Patriarchal basilicas, p.186

Baroqueorama: Sant'Andrea al Quirinale and San Carlino, masterpieces of the Baroque by rivals Bernini and Borromini, pp.176–7

Unexpected Rome: The joyous celebration of Death in the Capuchin Cemetery, p.180

QUIRINALE

The Quirinale is the highest of the Roman hills. According to Roman mythology it was occupied by the Sabines in the time of Titus Tatius, when the rape of the Sabine women occurred. Its name may come either from *Cures*, the name of the Sabine settlement, or from *Quirinus*, a title of Romulus; Romans as late as the Middle Ages liked to refer to themselves romantically as the 'Quirites'. In Classical Rome, the hill was always a quiet residential neighbourhood, with a number of odd religious sanctuaries – to personified Hope and Fortune, to Venus Erigena from Sicily, to Mithras and the Egyptian god Serapis. None of them, as far as is known, ever did anything to depress property values or attract the attentions of the police.

Piazza del Quirinale J7

Bus 40, 60, 64, 70, 117, 170.

So great was the abandonment of the hill in the Middle Ages that even its name was forgotten. 'Monte Cavallo', the farmers and shepherds of medieval Rome called it, from the half-buried **horses' heads** projecting above the ground in what is now Piazza del Quirinale. These were dug up in the 1500s, along with broken remains of the **Dioscuri**, imperial-era copies of a Greek sculptural ensemble of Castor and Pollux. Renaissance wags reassembled them and carved upon them the lying inscriptions claiming to be a 'work of Phidias' and a 'work of Praxiteles'. Pius VI added the **obelisk** to complete the new monument, along with a basin that, appropriately enough, formerly served as a horse trough in the Forum.

Behind them is the **Palazzo della Consultà** (1739), a stately Rococo work by Ferdinando Fuga that not even an Enlightenment Frenchman of the time would have sneered at; it now witnesses the pettifoggery of the Corte Costituzionale, Italy's Supreme Court, as it debates the intricacies and refinements of the Italian constitution.

Palazzo del Quirinale J7

Piazza del Quirinale, t 06 46991; bus 40, 60, 64, 70, 117, 170. Open late Sept–early July Sun 8.30–12.30; adm €5.

The dreary palace with the interminable façade is the Palazzo del Quirinale, residence of most of the popes after it was built in 1574, of the kings of Italy after 1870, and of the presidents of Italy since 1947. Bejewelled Carabinieri (all chosen to be well over 6ft tall) guard the entrances. Kings and popes used to appear to their people on the balcony overlooking the piazza, but the palace has also seen real action in its history. The Roman Republic was reborn here in November 1848, when a mob attacked and captured the pope. Radical nationalist Mazzini lived here, and the Republican council met here until the French drove it out.

The Quirinale is, however, a treasure house of art, from the **Roman frescoes** in the cellars to those of Melozzo da Forlì and Pietro da Cortona above ground. On the south side of the palace is the *manica lunga* – the 'long sleeve' – designed by Bernini, a wing of the palace extending down Via del Quirinale that is a sixth of a mile long, and two rooms deep.

Sant'Andrea al Quirinale K7

Via del Quirinale 29, t 06 4890 3187; bus 40, 60, 64, 70, 71, 116T, 170. Open Wed–Mon 8–12 and 4–7.

Across from the *manica lunga* stand two provocative masterpieces of the Baroque, built by the two great rivals Bernini and Borromini. The first, **Sant'Andrea**, is Bernini's most renowned church (1658–70), a building that can compel an objective look even from sworn enemies of the Baroque. This *tour de force* involves architectural forms hardly seen before or since, ideas never fully understood by his contemporaries. There is no façade at all, only an elegant classical portal embraced by a semi-elliptical wall; inside is an elliptical building that reverses the entrance scheme; a unique oval space surrounded by eight side chapels, still emphasizing the main altar; the interior design is unified by a bold elliptical cornice and a decorative scheme including maritime motifs that remind us of the fisherman St Andrew. A shaft of light falls on the high altar from a cleverly placed window.

Sant'Andrea is a small, aristocratic building, full of family symbols of the wealthy Roman clerics who paid for it; remove the altar and it could just as easily be a ballroom as a church. Its rich columns of red *cottanello* marble from Sicily, and trim in almost every other variety of expensive stone, commemorate the Jesuits who commissioned it, with their philosophy that the glory of heaven could best be imparted to the faithful by the glory of worldly opulence. The best of the decoration is the stucco putti and angels by Antonio Raggi around the dome; not really angels at all, they seem, but stray mythological creatures caught in a very Catholic century, looking for a lost mythology.

San Carlo alle Quattro Fontane (San Carlino) K7

*Via del Quirinale 23, t 06 488 3261; **bus** 40, 60, 64, 70, 71, 116T, 170. **Open** Mon–Fri 9–1 and 3–4, Sat 9–12.30, Sun 10.30–1.*

Borromini had his say here in 1646. At first, this may seem to be a High Baroque showpiece much like Sant'Andrea, but despite the classical pediments and Corinthian columns inside, these two creations have surprisingly little in common. Bernini, though perhaps inspired by his rival's work to a greater freedom of form, chose to stick closer to the book, planning his church by the proportions of the classical Orders and carefully maintaining the distinction between architectural elements and sculptural decoration. On the other hand Borromini never used the Orders, preferring to revive the constructive geometry of the medieval cathedral builders. Tiny San Carlino, with its undulating shapes and ellipses, may be the most complex building in Rome – but if you were as clever as Borromini, you could prove every point in its design with a compass and straight-edge.

To the eye, however, this tiny church seems more a sculptural fantasy than a bundle of mathematics. And this blurring of boundaries between sculpture and architecture is a purpose of Borromini's art. This is true of the interior as a whole, a continuous space where it is difficult to rest the eye on any particular part, and also in the details: the unusual geometrical coffering on the dome, and on the façade, where a pair of angel wings forms an arch to frame the statue of San Carlo (St Charles Borromeo, bishop of Milan and one of the protagonists of the Counter-Reformation). This façade, completed only in 1668, was Borromini's last work, just as the interior was his first; together they sum up his achievement as the most creative master of the Roman Baroque.

There are some other virtues to point out: an unusual crypt, with curves echoing the church, and a small cloister, designed by Borromini too. The entire complex is a lesson in economy, how to get the best use out of a small and irregular plot of land. There is a story, probably apocryphal, that Borromini planned San Carlino to be the same size as one of the four great piers of St Peter's; the dimensions are in fact very close.

One of the constraints on Borromini's façade was to make it fit in with the **Quattro Fontane** (1593), four fountains built into the street corner that represent the Tiber and the Aniene, Strength and Fidelity. Via delle Quattro Fontane was one of the grand boulevards of Sixtus V's planning scheme. At one end you can see the obelisk of Trinità dei Monti; at the other, S. Maria Maggiore's.

Palazzo Barberini K6–7

*Viale Barberini 18, t 06 481 4591; **w** www. galleriaborghese.it; **metro** Barberini, **bus** 52, 53, 56, 58, 60, 61, 95, 116, 175, 42, 590. **Open** Tues–Fri 9–7, Sat and Sun 9–8; **adm** €6.*

Here you can see what became of the profits of the papacy during the 1620s and 1630s. Urban VIII was pope then, and Rome's artists were kept busy building and embellishing his family preserve. Now owned by the state, the palazzo houses the **Galleria Nazionale d'Arte Antica**, an odd name for a few medieval pictures alongside plenty from the late Renaissance and later, sometimes upstaged by the effusive original decoration.

The unusual design, primarily by Carlo Maderno, resembles an outsize country villa with three storeys of arcades; the windows of the upper floor are a famous innovation, made to match the size of those of the *piano nobile* by a perspectivist illusion. After Maderno's death the palace was finished by Bernini (who added the theatrical square staircase on the left) and the more imaginative Borromini (the oval spiral staircase to the right, and the windows on the upper floor of the façade).

Once up Bernini's stair, the gallery starts sedately with a 13th-century Tuscan *Crucifixion* and a few choice quattrocento works – an old-fashioned *Madonna* by Neri di Bicci; two paintings by Filippo Lippi: an *Annunciation* with a lovely Renaissance angel, and a *Madonna* with an ugly *Bambino*; a triptych by Fra Angelico; an unusually studious *Maddalena* by Piero di Cosimo; *Madonna and Saints* by Umbrian artist L'Alunno – one of his better works, especially St Jerome with his specs and pussycat lion, asking to be stroked; and a sombre *S. Nicola da Tolentino* by Perugino.

After these works, Andrea del Sarto's *Holy Family* and Beccafumi's *Madonna, Child, and St John* startle with their more-lifelike-than-life Mannerist colours and life. Here, too, is the gallery's most famous painting, Raphael's portrait of a courtesan, which experts like to think is his beloved baker's girl, *La Fornarina*. It was painted in the year of his death which, according to popular rumour, resulted from a fever caused by her demanding passion. In the same room is a *Rape of the Sabines* by the perversely nicknamed Il Sodoma; also a *Portrait of Stefano Colonna* by Bronzino.

Note the ceiling of Room VII, with its fresco by Andrea Sacchi called *The Triumph of Divine Knowledge* (1633), from which the enthroned Virgin looks down on the round earth in a Baroque attempt to create a new astronomy. There are paintings by Titian (*Venus and Adonis*, a copy of the painting in the Prado), Tintoretto, two small but busy El Grecos (more Mannerist than any Italian Mannerist could dream) and Garofalo's fantastical *Picus Transformed into a Woodpecker*.

The inevitable Counter-Reformation blast of the mindless and mawkish is shut up in the next rooms. Only the bizarre really stand out in the crowd – works like Jacopino del Conte's *Deposition*; Il Mastelletta's dark and elongated forms in *Christ by a Lake*; and most of all Caravaggio (*Narcissus* and *Judith and Holofernes*) and his numerous followers. Press on for more seicento treats: playful Poussin's *Bacchanale* of putti; Guido Reni's famous *Portrait of a Girl*, which has always been presumed to be the ill-fated Beatrice Cenci, although apparently Reni never saw her; Guercino's *Et in Arcadia Ego*, a must for Merovingian conspiracy addicts and French occultists; Holbein's *Henry VIII* (1540, painted on the day of his marriage to Anne of Cleves); Quentin Metsys' *Erasmus*; and the 'curious perspectives' of Jean François Niceron (1613–46), who took the Renaissance science of artificial perspective to a mad extreme, painting portraits that seem to have been stretched around the rim of a goldfish bowl.

The beautifully restored **Gran Salone** (often used for temporary exhibitions) comes as a grand finale, its ceiling embellished by Pietro da Cortona's overwhelming *Triumph of Divine Providence* (1633–9), a Baroque masterpiece of Rome, set in an illusionistic architectural framework – only to then explode beyond its limits. The depth and complexity of the imagery were intended to apotheosize that big spender, Urban VIII; the three bees flying in formation from Divine Providence towards the tiara and laurel wreath are from the Barberini coat of arms, much in evidence elsewhere in the palace.

The upper floor offers no relief for the foot-sore, but instead works from the 1700s (good views of Rome by Pannini and Van Wittel, and other works by Fragonard, Boucher, Guardi, and Canaletto). It was a delightful period for interior decoration, as seen in the frescoed Barberini apartments, period furnishings, Meissen china, costumes, Chinese porcelain, and the Barberini toddlers' carriage.

Piazza Barberini K6

Metro *Barberini,* **bus** *52, 3, 56, 58, 60, 61, 95, 116, 175, 42, 590.*

If it's possible to feel sorry for any marble child of Bernini, it would have to be the marine god in his **Fontana del Tritone** (1637), gamely blowing his shell through the buzz of traffic. This busy crossroads is named after the Florentine family that gave Rome Urban VIII, whose coat of arms and papal tiara are entwined in the tails of the sea-creatures supporting the triton. He's honoured too in the piazza's second fountain, the **Fontana delle Api** (1644), from which three huge Barberini bees slake their thirst. Most of the piazza is really the roof of the Barberini's underground stables, now a forgotten grotto supposedly inhabited by the biggest and fiercest rats in Rome.

Via Veneto K5–6

Metro *Barberini,* **bus** *52, 3, 56, 58, 60, 61, 95, 116, 175, 42, 590.*

The shady, curving Via Vittorio Veneto has been the stage background for Roman society since it was first laid out. But few parts of Rome have become as grievously mangled in the last two centuries as this one. In papal Rome, this area was the edge of the city, and everything to the east was villas and gardens. First came Via del Tritone, in the 19th century, opening the area to development, and the villas and gardens soon disappeared, victims of the post-1870 speculative boom. Perhaps the greatest casualty was the Villa Ludovisi, an extensive wooded preserve that was one of the beauty spots of Rome. Romans loved the poetic justice that overtook the family that sold it to the speculators. They built a mammoth palace on Via Veneto with the proceeds – now the US

Embassy – but soon found they had created a neighbourhood too dear even for them; the tax man ruined them and snatched away their palace not long after. This neighbourhood, known since 1885 as the aristocratic 'Ludovisi District', with the Via Veneto as its centre, was just in time to claim the ornate Grand Hotels, mansions and cafés of the *belle époque.* The last century added Via Barberini, lined with Mussolini-style airline offices and banks, perhaps the most gruesome street in Rome.

Via Veneto really caught the world's attention in the 1950s, thanks to a fortunate convergence of Italy's new-found talent for making movies and the post-war tourist boom. With Roberto Rossellini and Ingrid Bergman likely to turn up at the next table of the Café de Paris, and the first hordes of paparazzi combing the street to see who among the international film set was flirting with whom, the life epitomized by Fellini's *La Dolce Vita* was in full swing. One step behind the paparazzi came the Americans. Just as Piazza di Spagna was the English quarter on the Grand Tour, so Via Veneto became the American Rome in the days of bulky Kodaks and Hawaiian shirts. Even now, perhaps owing to the presence of the gargantuan, well-fortified US Embassy (gained after 1945 in a trade-off for some tons of war surplus), the street has an American air about it, as if any minute fleets of '59 Cadillacs with lofty tailfins could come gliding around the bend.

Unfortunately, the *dolce vita* in Rome faded away long ago, and today's Via Veneto is as fashionable as gas-guzzling cars. First-time visitors often do not know this, and the street still does a grandstand business vacuuming out the pockets of package tourists.

Santa Maria della Concezione K6
Via Veneto 27, **t** *06 487 1185.* **Church open** *Mon–Sat 7–12 and 3–6, Sun 7–6;* **crypt open** *Fri–Wed 9–12 and 3–6; compulsory 'donation'.*

Cardinal Antonio Barberini must have been a strange bird. While Baroque was blooming, and his relatives were rolling in the loot from Urban VIII's papacy, he devoted himself to building the Convento dei Cappuccini and its austere church, S. Maria della Concezione; here you can see his tomb, with the inscription 'Here lies dust, ashes, nothing'.

The real treat, however, lies downstairs: the **Capuchin Cemetery**, a joyous celebration of Death unequalled this side of Palermo (where there are some even better Capuchin catacombs). A French Capuchin, back in 1528, came up with the idea; his brethren kept at it until 1870, turning the church crypt into five glorious chapels decorated in Baroque frippery – entirely made of human bones and skulls, with a few whole Capuchin skeletons wired up to the walls in period dress. Some 4,000 monks contributed their remains for the work, which is not without artistic merit. Somehow mouldering bones and Baroque go well together; shoulder-blades and vertebrae especially make some attractive patterns. All this rests on a floor of dirt brought specially from Jerusalem. Visit on the first Sunday of October, and by the grace of Pope Paul VI you'll earn a special indulgence.

Santa Maria della Vittoria L6

Via XX Septembre, t 06 482 6190; metro Repubblica, bus 16, 36, 60, 61, 62, 64. Open 7–12 and 4.30–7.

The victory this church commemorates is a sad one, the 1620 Battle of White Mountain, during the Thirty Years' War, at which the religious and political freedom of the Czechs was snuffed out by the Catholic armies, an enslavement that was to last 298 years.

Such a feat deserved the finest foolishness Baroque had to offer, and this is one of the most decorated churches in Rome. Giovan Battista Soria added the façade. Most of the interior is by Bernini and his pupils, the highlight being the ornate **Cornaro Chapel**, a kind of stage set squeezed into a shallow space; Bernini had once worked as a stage designer, and here he carries the conceit so far as to include members of the Venetian Cornaro family sitting in theatre boxes at the sides. The show in this case is Bernini's remark-

able sculpture of the **Ecstasy of St Teresa**, with a smirking angel about to drive a burning arrow into the soulfully agitated girl's heart (this is the vision Teresa had in Avila, Spain, in 1537, that started her on her career as a contemplative mystic and monastic reformer). You may take this as advertised, an illustration of 'divine love and mystic ecstasy', but nothing could be more cynically Baroque than taking an ostensibly religious subject and tossing in a dose of refined titillation. Not for nothing is Rome called the Eternal City; poor Teresa has been five seconds away from climax for 300 years.

Another bit of premature Baroque stands next to the church: the fountain of the **Acqua Felice**, built in 1587 for the reopening of the ancient aqueduct by Pope Sixtus V. The big gruesome fellow in the middle is Moses, by a sculptor named Prospero Antichi who was sure he could upstage Michelangelo's Moses, and do it even bigger.

Across Largo di Santa Susanna from Santa Maria is the church of **Santa Susanna** (L6), with a façade by Maderno. A prototypical work of the Baroque (1603), it is now the American national church. In 1992, Roman ruins were unearthed beneath the sacristy. **San Bernardo** (L6), on the other side of Via XX Septembre, was built into one of the circular halls, probably used as temples, that stood at the corners of Diocletian's Baths.

Baths of Diocletian M6

Via del Museo delle Terme, t 06 481 5576; metro Repubblica, bus 60, 61, 62, 75, 84, 90, 116T, 175, 492. Open Tues–Fri 9–7.45, Sun 9am–11pm; adm free.

On any map, you can see the outline of the Baths of Diocletian preserved in surrounding streets. Though largely demolished over the centuries, the complex has left relics over 20 blocks of Rome between the Quirinale and Viminale: from Via XX Settembre to Piazza dei Cinquecento, between Piazza della Repubblica and Via Volturno. It is one part of the Museo Nazionale Romano (*see* below).

The biggest and one of the last of Rome's baths, it cost the dour Illyrian emperor enormous sums to build in 298, at a time when the empire was nearly bankrupt and his price-fixing, debased coinage and high taxes were crushing the life out of Europe.

With **Piazza della Repubblica**, Rome's post-1870 planners came up with one of their very rare good ideas; the semicircular piazza is still often called Piazza dell'Esedra, and its curve follows the *exedra* of the baths, where ancient Romans could exercise and pursue their favourite ball games.

The baths' main entrance was where Via Nazionale enters the piazza, aligned directly with the vast central hall, later converted into the church of **Santa Maria degli Angeli** (L–M6). Michelangelo designed the interior, one of his weaker attempts at architecture, and considerable tinkering by later architects such as Vanvitelli did nothing to improve it. Nevertheless, the original form of the hall stands out clearly; Michelangelo's respect for the ancients kept him from making any great changes to the form of the building. It remains the best example we have of the architecture of the late empire: short on aesthetics but long on engineering, with soaring concrete vaulting and gabled roofs.

Much of the rest of the baths survives: the Aula Ottagona, across Via Cernaia, and the other ruins stretching up that street. The baths were well-preserved enough until modern times; the popes used their rambling spaces for centuries to house monasteries, granaries and even prisons. After about 1600 they began quarrying the stone, and huge parts of the original buildings disappeared.

Museo Nazionale Romano M7

The museum is split between four sites: **Palazzo Massimo alle Terme (M7):** *Piazza del Cinquecento (by Stazione Termini), t 06 4890 3500;* **metro** *Repubblica and Termini,* **bus** *16, 36, 60, 61, 62, 64, 90, 116, 175, 492.* **Open** *Tues–Sun 9–7.45;* **adm** *€6.* **Palazzo Altemps**

(near Piazza Navona; G7): **t** *06 683 3759.* **Open** *Tues–Fri 9–7.45, Sun 9am–11pm;* **adm** *€5.* **Terme di Diocleziano** *(M6):* **t** *06 481 5576;* **metro** *Repubblica,* **bus** *60, 61, 62, 75, 84, 90, 116T, 175, 492.* **Open** *Tues–Fri 9–7.45, Sun 9am–11pm;* **adm** *free.* **Aula Ottagona** *(L6): Via Romita,* **t** *06 487 0690;* **metro** *Repubblica,* **bus** *16, 36, 60, 61, 62, 64, 90, 116, 175, 492.* **Open** *Tues–Sat 9–2, Sun 9–1;* **adm** *free.*

Besides the church of Santa Maria degli Angeli, Michelangelo built a pair of cloisters for the adjacent Carthusian monastery. With some adjoining rooms of the baths, these have been incorporated into the Museo Nazionale Romano, perhaps the greatest collection of Roman art and relics anywhere. It was closed for decades, awaiting restoration, but has now reopened on four sites.

You can't miss the **Palazzo Massimo alle Terme** here, the big building opposite the baths, recently painted a nauseous shade of peach. It now houses busts and frescoes from the Villa di Livia, as well as an interesting display on the ground floor of objects from everyday life (coins, tools, and so on).

The **Baths of Diocletian** are described above. The **Aula Ottagona**, originally part of Diocletian's Baths, was once used a planetarium, and now serves as a display space for classical bronze statues. **Palazzo Altemps** houses classical statuary, including the famous Ludovisi throne, named for the family in whose garden it was unearthed.

VIMINALE

If the Seven Hills were Snow White's Seven Dwarves, the Viminale would be Sleepy. Only in Rome, perhaps, would the heart of the modern city be of only peripheral interest. Via Nazionale, the main drag of this area, is a dull shopping thoroughfare linking Termini Station with Piazza Venezia, cutting its tiresome way between the Quirinale and the Viminale hills – although recently somewhat enlivened by the Palazzo delle Esposizioni (*see* p.182).

Santi Domenico e Sisto K8

Largo Magnanapoli, t 06 483 667; bus 117. Open by appointment only.

An unheralded Baroque gem, Santi Domenico e Sisto is finely positioned at the top of Rome's first grand Baroque stair (1654). If it happens to be open, you can ponder Domenico Maria Canuti's ceiling fresco of the *Apotheosis of St Dominic* (1674), in which one of the sternest members of the heavenly hierarchy rockets to grace in a curlicue stage set.

San Lorenzo in Panisperna L8

Via Panisperna, t 06 483 667; bus 81. Open Sat 8.30–11.30 and 4.30–7, Sun 9–1 and 4.30–7.

Behind the vast Ministry of the Interior, the prettily situated church of San Lorenzo in Panisperna marks the site of Lawrence's martyrdom, and contains an oversize fresco of the saint on the grill within.

Palazzo delle Esposizioni K7

Via Nazionale 194 (main entrance), Via Milano 9/a (entrance via café-bar; wheelchair accessible), t 06 474 5903; bus 46, 62, 64. Open Wed–Mon 10–9; adm varies for temporary exhibitions; free to café-bar and shops.

Dating from the 1870s, the grand, recently renovated Palazzo delle Esposizioni hosts contemporary art and photography exhibitions, and screens interesting programmes of films in its arts cinema. It also houses a design shop, an arts bookshop and a pleasant café-bar and rooftop restaurant.

The palazzo's neighbour on Via Nazionale, the church of **San Vitale**, hides timidly below street level, evidence of just how much the valleys between Rome's hills have been filled in. Although some parts of the church date back to the original of 416, little of interest actually remains inside.

Galleria Pallavicini K8

Via Nazionale, t 06 475 1224; bus 46, 62, 64. Princess Pallavicino opens her gallery on the first day of each month, 10–12 and 3–5. Group visits by special arrangement.

Further down Via Nazionale is the **Palazzo Pallavicini Rospigliosi**, built by Cardinal Scipione Borghese over part of the **Baths of Constantine**, and later the Roman residence of Cardinal Mazarin. On the first floor (entrance on Via XXIV Maggio 43), the Galleria Pallavicini has a collection of paintings from the 15th–18th centuries. Adjacent **Casino dell'Aurora Pallavicini**, frescoed by Guido Reni with a famous scene of Aurora and the sun, was near the top of the list of sights for any 19th century traveller.

Termini Station M7–N8

Piazza dei Cinquecento; metro Termini, bus 16, 36, 60, 61, 62, 64, 90, 116, 175, 492.

At the southern end of the biggest square in Rome, Stazione Termini (named after the baths) was begun by Mussolini, although not finished until after the Second World War. Perhaps the busiest station in Europe, the building itself is one of modern Rome's very few architectural triumphs. The post-war architects threw out Mussolini's planned façade of tired neoclassical colonnades, replacing it with a bold cantilevered roof projecting over the ticket hall and taxi area. The result is well planned and functional in every respect – if only there were anywhere to sit. To the left of the main entrance is a surviving corner of the **Servian Wall**.

The square outside is named not after Rome's Renaissance century, but in memory of the 500 soldiers who died at Dogali, Ethiopia, in 1887, a battle so embarrassing to the nation that it decided it had to conquer the country to save face; this led to an even bigger disaster at Adowa nine years later before they finally gave up. it's now a chaotic bus terminus, with a sample of Rome's low life on permanent display, sprawled around the northern fringes of the piazza.

ESQUILINE HILL

The Esquiline Hill (Esquilino), along with its western spur, Colle Oppio, runs from the Colosseum to Termini Station. It was first home to Rome's knights; later, the earliest Christian communities lived here. By the Middle Ages their churches stood remote in open countryside. No longer. In the 19th and 20th centuries, the presence of Termini Station made this a favourite zone for building, and the Esquiline was swallowed by the city once more, leaving holy islands in the doldrums of speculative sprawl. Today much of this backside of Rome is infected with the terminal ugliness of everything within a mile of the station, a cocktail brewed by Beelzebub himself. Pilgrims here deserve whatever indulgence the Church has decreed. Yet for all that, its rewards are of this world as well as the next. Step inside the cool incense-scented darkness of the ancient churches, and as your eyes adjust to the light, you'll find some of the most beautiful things in Rome: richly-coloured golden mosaics, shimmering and magical as fairy-tale illustrations, their saints living in a fresh, springtime never-never Rome that makes the newness and cacophony only a few steps away seem shabby, tiresome and a hurly-burly waste of everything good and fair.

Colle Oppio L9–M10

Nero's Golden House L9–M10

Colle Oppio, **t** *06 3996 7700 (Mon–Sat 8–8);* **metro** *Colosseo,* **tram** *3,* **bus** *85, 87, 117, 186, 204.* **Open** *daily 9–8; advance booking essential;* **adm** *€6.*

Nero may not have started Rome's great fire of AD 64, but he knew how to take advantage of it, buying or expropriating huge tracts of burned properties for a palace to end all palaces. 'At last I am lodged like a man!' he is reported to have said when he moved in. Covering nearly a quarter of central Rome, stretching over most of the Esquiline, Palatine and Caelian Hills, the complex included extensive gardens and an artificial lake (where the Colosseum is now), as well as baths, menageries, and an avenue with triple colonnades a mile long. At the entrance, near the eastern approaches to the Forum, stood a 120ft gilded statue of (who else?) Nero himself, the largest ever made in antiquity; from this 'colossus', surpassing even the more famous one at Rhodes, the nearby Colosseum took its name. All the greatest painters and sculptors available were kept working full time to decorate the Golden House, until work stopped abruptly upon Nero's death in 68.

To the honest emperors that followed, this sprawling symbol of vulgar tyranny was not the best possible advertisement for imperial government. Vespasian and Titus cleared much of the ground for the Colosseum and other buildings, Hadrian built the Temple of Venus and Rome in its vestibule, and Trajan demolished most of the palace itself for his baths on the Esquiline. The very location of the fabled Golden House was forgotten by the Middle Ages, but in the 1490s one wing was accidentally discovered, a section that Trajan had saved to use as a foundation for the baths. Renaissance artists flocked to see the delicate, fanciful paintings on its walls, the same sort of purely decorative faces, twining foliage and fantasy pavilions common in the villas of Pompeii. In one of the long corridors there is an arch, inscribed with the names of many visiting artists including Raphael's assistant, Giovanni da Udine. Raphael and his circle were impressed enough with this style of decoration (subsequently called *grottesche,* or grotesques, from this 'grotto' in which they were first seen) to copy it in such places as the Vatican Loggie.

Another work of art found here, just as influential in the Renaissance as the paintings, was the famous Laocoön (dug up in 1506), mentioned by Pliny and other ancient authors. Although probably only a Roman copy of an older Greek work, its discovery became an artistic event of the first magnitude. Michelangelo praised it, Julius II snapped it up for the Vatican Palace (where it can be seen today), and as it was carried through the streets, the Romans showered it with flowers. The contorted, suffering forms of the Trojan priest and his sons, with Apollo's serpents coiling around them, were for centuries considered one of the greatest works of all time – and were influential on artists contemporary to its rediscovery.

Baths of Trajan L9

*Colle Oppio; **metro** Colosseo, **tram** 3, **bus** 75, 85, 87, 117, 175, 186.*

Above the Domus Aurea, the large park of Colle Oppio is littered everywhere with remains of the Baths of Trajan. Built in 109 by Apollodorus of Damascus, the master architect who also laid out Trajan's Forum, this was the first of the truly monumental bath complexes, its plan copied in all those that followed. The baths have never been excavated, and nowadays the city's homeless sleep beneath their brick vaults and old men while away their afternoons playing cards, after lunching in the local soup kitchen.

The **Sette Sale**, an enormous vaulted structure built as the reservoir for the baths, are behind the high walls of **Palazzo Brancaccio**. You can often wander into the palace's opulent gardens from the entrance on Viale del Monte Oppio.

San Pietro in Vincoli L9

*Piazza di San Pietro in Vincoli, **t** 06 488 2865; **metro** Cavour, Colosseo, **bus** 75, 84. **Open** daily 7–12.30 and 3.30–6.*

This was long one of the main pilgrimage churches in Rome. Restoration of the nave has recently been completed, giving way to restoration of the **Mausoleum of Julius II** – what everyone comes to see because it features a Michelangelo *Moses*.

The name 'St Peter in Chains' is derived from the manacles used by King Agrippa I in Jerusalem to bind Peter, which miraculously separated to free him (Acts 12, 1–13). In 440 the relics were given to Empress Eudoxia, wife of Valentinian III, who founded this church. It was practically rebuilt in 1475 by Sixtus IV, who added the fine portico; and its titular cardinal Giuliano della Rovere touched it up as well, not knowing that one day he would be Pope Julius II and his tomb by Michelangelo – what was to be the 'greatest monument in the world' – would end up here and not in St Peter's. The 'tragedy of a tomb', as the artist bitterly called it, was to have 40 figures in a massive tabernacle, but disputes with the strong-willed Julius, the distraction of the Sistine Chapel frescoes, and commissions from subsequent popes prevented Michelangelo from ever completing more than the highly individualistic and powerful figure of **Moses**, perhaps the closest anyone has ever come to capturing prophetic vision in stone – even if the end result bears an uncanny resemblance to Charlton Heston. The director of *The Ten Commandments*, Cecil B. DeMille, was struck by this likeness. 'If it's good enough for Michelangelo, it's good enough for me,' he decided, after scribbling a beard on a photograph of the actor.

Under Moses' arm are the tablets inscribed with the Ten Commandments; his glance is furious because the Israelites are worshipping the golden calf; his 'horns' come from the sculptor's reading of the Vulgate translated into Latin by St Jerome, in which the saint made Moses *cornutum* ('horned') instead of 'radiant' as in the original Hebrew. Michelangelo signed this work, not with his name, but with his profile, formed by the upper part of the beard. Michelangelo also had a hand in the figures of Rachel and Leah on either side of Moses, but the rest of the tomb is by his students, not all of them so gifted; if Moses resembles Heston, the effigy of Julius II reclining could pass for the caterpillar in *Alice in Wonderland*.

The famous chains, enclosed in a gilt and glass casket, may be seen in the chapel of the Confessio; in the Dark Ages pilgrims would queue for filings, one of the most potent holy relics to be had in Rome; for the virtuous the filings came right off, but the chains refused to yield a splinter for real sinners. The Confessio holds a 4th-century sarcophagus too, believed to have held the remains of the seven Maccabees, whose gruesome martyrdoms prefigured those of the Christians (II Maccabees 7). A 7th-century mosaic of St Sebastian (a rare portrayal as an old man with a beard) is well preserved in the left aisle, next to the macabre Hallowe'en tomb of Cardinal Aldobrandino.

San Martino ai Monti M9

Viale del Monte Oppio 28, t 06 487 3126; ***metro*** *Cavour, Vittorio Emanuele,* ***bus*** *75, 84.* ***Open*** *8–12 and 3–6.*

San Martino's 17th-century appearance evolved from one of Rome's most ancient titular churches, the 3rd-century *Titulus Equitius*. In the next century it was rededicated to St Martin of Tours by Pope Sylvester, whose life was so uneventful that a more exciting one was invented for him: this fantasy life included curing Constantine of leprosy and slaying a dragon that slid out of a crack in the Forum. The church's wide, spacious interior is decorated with faded frescoes of Roman landscapes and scenes from the life of Elijah, painted in the 1640s by Poussin's brother-in-law Gaspar Dughet. In the left aisle, near the altar, note the rare fresco of the interior of old St Peter's, complete with its giant pine cone, while towards the door another scene portrays the interior of St John Lateran in pre-Borromini days. The priest, who is usually around in the morning, can let you into the grey netherworld of the ancient Titulus Equitius, under the crypt (beware the treacherous steps); it contains a badly restored mosaic with the face of Pope Sylvester surrounded by what looks like mouldy ricotta, also patches of fresco, tomb slabs, and pretty sculpted fragments. Outside, from Via Equizia you can see the ancient stone walls of the *titulus*, and in Piazza di S. Martino, two medieval towers restored to look spanking new.

Museo Nazionale d'Arte Orientale M9

Via Merulana 248, t 06 487 4415; ***metro*** *Vittorio Emanuele,* ***bus*** *16, 714.* ***Open*** *daily 9–2,* *on Tues, Thurs and Sun until 7pm, except the first and third Mon of each month;* ***adm*** *€4.*

This museum in the **Palazzo Brancaccio** is one of the few places in the world that tries to answer the question posed by Edward Lear in one of his greatest poems: 'Who, or why, or which, or what, Is the Akond of SWAT?' The finds from SWAT, in northeast Pakistan, are fascinating. Hellenistic, Buddhist and Hindu influences combined to create sensuous and graceful reliefs from the 1st–5th centuries AD, of dashing fellows with big moustaches and Carmen Miranda costumes, and women with hourglass figures outlined in delicate draperies. There are strange and colourful hundred-armed gods from Tibet; 14th-century Last Judgement scenes, armour and helmets from Japan; Chinese porcelains, bronzes, and funeral statues; 9th–16th-century Islamic ceramics; ancient gold and silver art from Parthia, showing the Hellenizing influence of Alexander the Great; bronze idols from Luristan (1500–700 BC); and 3rd-millennium BC pots with Paul Klee-esque animals, from Tepe Siyalk in Iran.

Auditorium of Maecenas M9

Largo Leopardi, t 06 487 3262; ***metro*** *Vittorio Emanuele,* ***bus*** *16, 714.* ***Open*** *Tues–Sun 9–5;* ***adm*** *€2;* ***loggia open*** *9–1 and 3–6, 15-minute guided tour in English;* ***adm*** *€2.50.*

Everything in the immediate environs of the Palazzo Brancaccio was once a part of the gardens of Maecenas, Augustus' fabulously wealthy minister and patron of the arts. During the republic this land was haunted by witches, and was used to bury paupers and crucify slaves, whose skeletons were left rattling on their crosses; Maecenas and other plutocrats built their villas over the troubled grounds to exorcize the spooks.

Across Via Merulana (immortalized in Carlo Emilia Gadda's postmodern crime classic, written in Roman dialect, *Quer Pasticiaccio Brutto de Via Merulana*) from the palace is the only bit of the gardens to survive: the newly roofed **Auditorium of Maecenas**.

It could also have been his *nymphaeum*, with an apse and tiered seats, where Virgil, Horace, and other great poets may have recited their latest works to their patron.

Santa Maria Maggiore M8

Piazza di Santa Maria Maggiore, t 06 483 195; ***metro*** *Termini, Cavour,* ***tram*** *14, 516,* ***bus*** *105, 157.* ***Open*** *7–7.*

In ancient times a temple of the mother goddess Juno Lucina stood here, and when the 431 Council of Ephesus proclaimed Mary 'the Mother of God' it seemed like the logical place to build her a church, too – the greatest of all Rome's Mary churches – Santa Maria Maggiore. The ancient basilica is concealed behind an elegant 18th-century shadow-filled façade by Ferdinando Fuga and its incongruous campanile, Rome's tallest and fairest, a brightly decorated relic from the 1380s. The mighty column in front, in Piazza di Santa Maria Maggiore, is a sole survivor from the Forum's Basilica of Maxentius.

Of the four Patriarchal basilicas, S. Maria Maggiore has best preserved its medieval appearance. Try to pass by at least once after nightfall, when the upper floor of Fuga's loggia is illuminated, and you can see the 12th-century mosaics from the medieval façade, telling the legend of the church's founding: on 4 August 352, the Virgin Mary appeared to a wealthy Christian and to Pope Liberius, directing them to build a church on the Esquiline. The two found the exact spot Mary wanted by a miraculous snowfall that outlined the shape required. This porch was long the favourite place to burn heretical books, as the Church decided such literary sacrifices were pleasing to the Virgin.

S. Maria Maggiore's elegant basilican nave is almost unchanged since its construction by Pope Sixtus III in the 5th century, except for a coffered ceiling by Renaissance architect Giuliano da Sangallo, gilded with the first gold brought back from the New World by Columbus – a gift to Alexander VI from King Ferdinand. Above the columns runs a remarkable cycle of 5th-century mosaic panels of Old Testament scenes – 36 of them in all – while the triumphal arch shows mostly apocryphal scenes of the youth of Christ. They are a bit hard to see, unless you have binoculars; try to arrive at noon, when the light is brightest. The fine Cosmatesque floor dates from the 12th century.

Two enormous chapels were fixed to the basilica by popes who feared that if they left it to posterity to build them the memorials they deserved, they wouldn't get any. The first, in the right aisle, is the sumptuous **Sistine Chapel** of Sixtus V, designed by Domenico Fontana in 1585 and built of the coloured marbles of the ancient Septizonium (a mysterious three-storeyed, columned building with seven zones), which the pope cannibalized into oblivion as part of his policy to convert pagan Rome into Christian Rome. But in his eagerness to build himself a really special chapel, the pope inadvertently destroyed one of Christian Rome's most venerated treasures as well: S.Maria Maggiore's *presepio*, or Christmas crib, which had stood outside the basilica since the 6th or 7th century, in a grotto simulating Bethlehem's stable. Lined with precious mosaics and containing 13th-century crib figures by the great Arnolfo di Cambio, it was the place where the pope traditionally said Christmas Eve Mass (as Hildebrand was doing in 1075 when armed thugs suddenly burst in and dragged him off by the hair to the tower of their Ghibelline boss Cencius. When the people learned next morning where their pope had been taken, they stoned the tower until he was released – whereupon he returned to finish the Mass). But Sixtus V ordered Domenico Fontana to move the presepio into his chapel, and despite all the architect's careful prepara-tions (after all, this was the man who moved the Vatican obelisk) it collapsed and broke into bits. Only Arnolfo's charming figures of Joseph, the Magi and animals survive (Mary and Jesus are 16th-century replacements), locked away in the crypt beneath a wooden canopy shaped like an ideal Renaissance temple and supported by four angels. The sacristan may open the gate to let you in.

The Borghese Pope Paul V bears the onus for the hyper-decorated **Pauline Chapel**, across the nave from Sixtus' pile, although to his credit nothing was destroyed to build his precious inanity. An altar of semi-precious stone holds an ancient and highly venerated icon of the Madonna and Child known as the Salus Populi Romani, painted by angels. This is the place to come on 5 August, when during mass white petals fall like snow from the dome in memory of the basilica's legendary founding.

Fuga designed the porphyry-pillared baldaquin over the altar; in the Confessio below a colossal, ungainly statue of Pius IX kneels in prayer before the basilica's chief relic, five pieces of wood bound with iron said to be nothing less than the genuine manger from Bethlehem. Shimmering above the altar is the magnificent apse mosaic of the *Coronation of the Virgin*, tessellated in 1295 by Iacopo Torriti, who is believed to have reproduced the subject of Sixtus III's original, honouring Mary's new divine status. To the right of the apse is the most beautiful tomb in the church, of 13th-century Cardinal Consalvo Rodriguez, by Giovanni Cosmati.

You can't walk up the magnificent ripple of steps leading to the rear façade of the basilica, even though the restoration of this side of the church has been finished, but you can get a good look at it anyway. The **obelisk** at the bottom, in Piazza dell'Esquilino, came from the Mausoleum of Augustus.

Santa Prassede M8

Via S. Prassede 9/a, t 06 488 2456; metro Vittorio Emanuele, bus 16, 70, 71, 75, 204. Open 7–12 and 4–6.30.

A modest pink doorway hides the masterpiece of Rome's Carolingian Renaissance, Santa Prassede (make sure you have change for the lights). When Pope Paschal I built it in 822, two decades after Charlemagne's visit to the city, his desire was to create an edifice that would be compared to the magnificent ruins that lay on every side – from which he borrowed some beautiful columns (near the sanctuary) and pieces of architrave. But Paschal was not your typical Roman magpie: to embellish his churches he imported artists from Byzantium who brought with them the latest advances in mosaic work and painting. By this time the last lingering naturalism of the late classical period had vanished – not because Byzantine artists had forgotten how, but because they now preferred to work in a less realistic, more spiritual vocabulary.

In the triumphal arch these 9th-century mosaics portray New Jerusalem, Christ and the saints; in the apse SS. Peter and Paul introduce the sisters SS. Prassede and Pudenziana to Christ. The stylized figures evoke a certain tenderness; note the way the Apostles lay their hands on the shoulders of the two women.

Save another coin to illuminate the jewel of Santa Prassede, the **Chapel of San Zeno**, or 'Garden of Paradise' in the right aisle, built as a mausoleum for Pope Paschal's mother, Theodora. Gold-ground mosaics completely cover this little square-vaulted chamber. These ones represent Christ Pantocrator, saints, Theodora (the lady with the square halo), and some very dignified, classical angels who look as if they never heard about the fall of Rome. Tradition holds that the piece of jasper in the corner shrine, bedecked with plastic flowers, is a fragment of the column where Christ was scourged. On a pillar outside the chapel is the bust and memorial of Santoni, carved by a 19-year-old Bernini.

The **Confessio** contains the relics of the sisters Prassede and Pudenziana, who, according to legend, hosted St Peter when he first came to Rome, and were especially known for giving refuge to Christians. The Church has now decided that they never existed, although the remains of some 30 massacred bodies were discovered in a well (marked by the slab of porphyry in the Cosmatesque pavement). The corpse of Prassede was buried with the sponge she used to mop up their blood.

Santa Pudenziana L8

Via Urbana 160, t 06 481 4622; metro Cavour, bus 71, 75, 204. Open 7–7.

The church of Prassede's imaginary sister is on the other side of S. Maria Maggiore. The ground level has risen 23 steps since it was built over a room of a Roman bath sometime in the 4th century. Here, according to tradition, stood the house where the sisters entertained St Peter; its chief relic is half of the table where he would celebrate Mass. The present façade with faded frescoes is 19th-century, but incorporates two ancient columns and a medieval relief of the holy sisters over the door. Rather disappointingly the interior has been restored often, at one point cutting off a section of S. Pudenziana's beautiful claim to fame, its apse adorned with the earliest Christian mosaic in Rome (390). Artists had yet to decide on the familiar iconography of the saints; here all have become honorary Romans – reminiscent of S.Prassede's angels, especially the Apostles in their senatorial togas.
SS. Pudenziana and Prassede stand with laurel wreaths, ready to crown SS. Peter and Paul, while Christ, enthroned in the centre, sits in what looks like Jupiter's throne, before a classical city.

Piazza Vittorio Emanuele N9

For a bit of Roman funkiness, take a look at what used to be the city's smelliest market square. The market has now been moved to the nearby Caserma Pepe (Via Ricasoli) and Via Turati. The move is the result of a years-long battle by city hall and local residents to move the market in order to restore beautiful Piazza Vittorio and its 19th-century porticoes

to their original looks, while the market traders did all they could not to be moved. The garden in the centre has long been a favourite siesta flop for the down and out, but they too may now be moved on. It has a ruined fountain from the time of Alexander Severus, in ancient Baroque; nearby stands a fenced-in brick mass that on ce held the marble Trophies of Marius (later moved to the Campidoglio).

Directly behind this, in the northernmost corner, is one of Rome's oddities: the **Porta Magica** (N9), all that survives of the Villa Palombara. The story goes that an alchemist once found hospitality with the marchese who owned it, and in return left a small lump of gold and a page of magic formulas. In 1653, after years of trying to decipher this recipe for the 'Great Work', the marchese had the magic page carved on to a door of his villa, putting it at the disposal of all. Now broken, you can barely discern the symbols of the planets and the mysterious inscriptions in Latin and Hebrew. A typical one, over Mars, reads: 'He who burns with water and washes with fire makes a heaven of earth and of heaven a precious land.'

Santa Bibiana O9

Via Giovanni Giolitti 154, t 06 446 5235; metro Vittorio Emanuele, bus 71. Open 7.30–11 and 5–6.30.

This church of 1625 was the proving ground for two of Rome's Baroque trinity. Bernini's Palladio-inspired façade was his first architectural work, and the pious, rapt statue of S. Bibiana above the altar his first religious commission. To the left, above the arches, are Pietro da Cortona's vibrant frescoes of the saint's life, his first important work in Rome, especially the one showing Bibiana refusing to sacrifice to idols.

Trastevere and the Janiculum

Trastevere and the Janiculum

In every city that has ever had a river flowing through it, it's the same story. The Left Bank, Shakespeare's Southwark, Buda and Pest, Brooklyn: once over the bridge everything is different. Often, as in Brooklyn, the odd bit across the river conserves the old ways and look of the city better than any other. The people of Trastevere hold Rome's best try at a real neighbourhood festival each July, the Festa de' Noantri (roughly 'we ourselves' in dialect); in a city full of recent migrants they claim to be the only real Romans left. Indeed, neighbourhood historians like to trace the origins of the community to the imperial sailors kept in Rome to work the great canvas awning at the Colosseum and man the ships for the mock sea battles.

Trastevere ('across the Tiber') has become a very trendy spot these days; in the evenings it fills up with Roman tourists from the other side, come to dine at its many restaurants and take a stroll around the romantic envi-rons of Piazza S. Maria in Trastevere. But being fashionable hasn't changed the place too much; Italian rent control, as much as the strong attachment of the old-time residents, keeps Trastevere sane and serene.

Divided by its Viale, Trastevere has a split personality. Everything to the west, old as it is, seems well kept and occasionally elegant; the other side, a little ragged, is full of the warehouses and workshops that indicate that this has always been a proletarian, seafaring neighbourhood, with pockets of alleys that have changed little in 500 years.

1 Lunch

Augusto, *Piazza de' Renzi 15, t 06 580 3798; bus 23, 280. Open Sept–July Mon–Fri 12.30–3 and 8–11, Sat 12.30–3 only. Inexpensive.* A classic Trastevere trattoria. *Habitués* squeeze past the tightly packed tables, exchange insults with Augusto, lay their own table and usually end up collecting their own wine and food from the kitchen hatch.

2 Coffee and Cakes

Renella, *Via del Moro 15 and Via del Politeama 29; tram 8, bus 23, 280. Open daily 7–8.30.* This bakery is too good to miss. Among the sweet pastries, the *pian giallo romano* – made with dried figs and nuts – and the *brutti ma buoni* ('ugly but good' hazelnut macaroons) stand out.

3 Drinks

San Calisto, *Piazza San Calisto 3–5, t 06 583 5869. Open Mon–Sat 6am–1.30am.* The most authentic, unpretentious bar of Trastevere; low prices and no frills. Laid back, scruffy and open all day, with a small terrace that spills out into the piazza on summer nights.

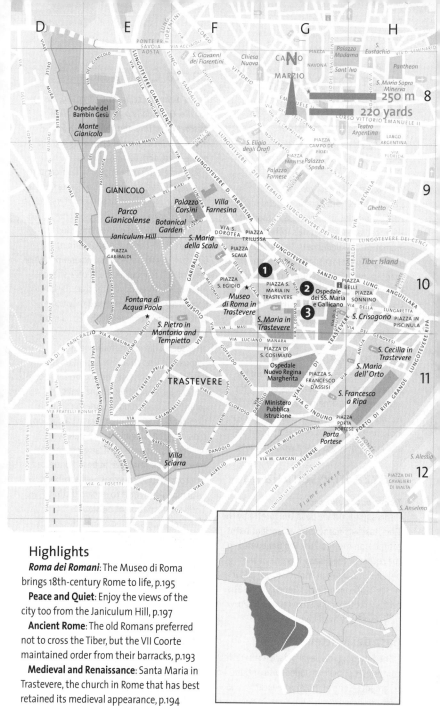

Highlights

Roma dei Romani: The Museo di Roma brings 18th-century Rome to life, p.195

Peace and Quiet: Enjoy the views of the city too from the Janiculum Hill, p.197

Ancient Rome: The old Romans preferred not to cross the Tiber, but the VII Coorte maintained order from their barracks, p.193

Medieval and Renaissance: Santa Maria in Trastevere, the church in Rome that has best retained its medieval appearance, p.194

Baroqueorama: Palazzo Corsini, to see Salvator Rosa's gory Prometheus, p.195

Unexpected Rome: Monks still run a pharmacy at Santa Maria della Scala, as they have done for centuries, p.195

EAST OF VIALE TRASTEVERE

Piazza Gioacchino Belli H10

Tram 8, bus H, 23, 280, 780.

Trastevere's front door, at the end of the Ponte Garibaldi, this square is named after the most famous of Rome's 19th-century 'Romanesco' dialect poets. That's Signor Belli looking dapper in his top hat, atop the monument in the piazza's centre; a relief on the back of its pedestal portrays an old Roman scene, a group of citizens gathered to read some political satire pinned on to the 'talking statue' Pasquino.

Palazzo Anguillara

With its medieval defence tower on the corner, Palazzo Anguillara was built in the 13th century; an ambitious modern restoration did its best to make the palace look the part. Today it houses an institute and library devoted to the work of Dante.

Piazza in Piscinula H10

Tram 3, bus 23, 280, 630.

This square, off Via della Lungaretta by the Tiber, takes its name from an ancient baths complex on the site. Tiny **San Benedetto**, in the corner of the piazza, has one of the oldest campaniles in Rome (*c*.1090) and a fresco inside picturing St Benedict, the 6th-century father of Christian monasticism, who may once have lived here.

Casa dei Mattei

The frowning medieval palace (13th–14th centuries) opposite, studded with antique fragments – one of the most evocative and best-preserved of such buildings in Rome – is the **Casa dei Mattei**, original home of one of Rome's most notoriously quarrelsome noble families.

Santa Cecilia H11

Piazza di Santa Cecilia, **t** *06 589 9289;* **bus** *23, 44, 280.* **Open** *daily 9.30–6.30;* **Cavallini frescoes open** *Tues and Thurs 10–12, Sun 11.30–12;* **adm** *€1.5;* **crypt open** *daily 9.30–12 and 4–6.30;* **adm** *€2.*

Standing behind an imposing 12th-century *quadroporticus* is the church of Santa Cecilia. One of the most popular early martyrs, the wealthy Cecilia is said to have had her house on this site. The bad old Romans tried to pressure-cook her in the *caldarium* of her own baths, without success, whereupon they determined to chop her head off – she still hung on for three days after that. (By law, Roman axemen were allowed only three strikes; the one charged with Cecilia must have been sent back to the minor leagues after such a dismal performance.)

Apparently no church was built on the site until the 820s; almost nothing from the original can be seen, although the walls and columns remain, hidden under a complete 18th-century rebuilding. It wasn't a bad job, replacing the old gallery with clerestory windows to create a light, airy interior; the frescoes are inoffensive, at best. Connected to a convent, the church is well-scrubbed, with piped-in hymns to remind us that Cecilia is the patron of music.

The rebuilders spared a fine 9th-century apse mosaic, a bit archaic in the Ravenna style; Pope Paschal, who built the church, appears in the square halo, offering the building to Christ. The two cities on the ends of the mosaic possibly represent Jerusalem and Bethlehem.

Below the mosaic, the high altar is graced with a glorious Gothic baldaquin by Arnolfo di Cambio. The saint, moved here from the catacombs by Pope Paschal when he built the church, was dug up again in 1599, for reasons not entirely clear; the pose of her uncorrupted body is captured exactly in the lovely statue by Stefano Maderno, under the high altar.

Other survivals include some medieval frescoes of St Cecilia's martyrdom, in the first chapel on the right, and the Renaissance tomb of Cardinal Forteguerri by Mino da Fiesole near the door; on the opposite tomb, that of an English titular cardinal called Adam Easton, who died in 1398, can be seen the coat of arms of the Plantagenets.

Down in the crypt, besides some flashy neo-Byzantine decoration of the 1900s, you can see the tombs of Cecilia and other saints, along with rooms from what may have been the saint's home (some with mosaics).

The Rococo restorers may have done one very serious disservice to Roman art when they bulldozed their way through this church with their gilding. Much of the church was originally covered by frescoes by Pietro Cavallini, perhaps his finest work. You can see fragments of his *Last Judgement*, later recovered and detached from the walls.

No one else, in Italy or anywhere in Europe, was capable of anything like this work in the year 1293. The careful, naturalistic draughtsmanship and intensely spiritual expression (especially in the figure of Christ himself) make the greatest evidence for considering Cavallini, along with Giotto, as one of the precocious antecedents of the Renaissance.

Santa Maria dell'Orto H11

Via Anicia; bus 23, 280. **Closed** *to the public.*

Not too interesting to look at in this city of 901 churches, but a landmark of a strange interlude in the progress of the expiring Renaissance. Vignola, that restless and underrated architect from Modena, built it in 1566; its façade, spare and strange with its little obelisks, but correct according to the architectural canons of the age, records a modest reaction against the busy and overdecorated work of the High Renaissance.

This tendency was even more pronounced in Spain, where Juan de Herrera had inaugurated the *estilo desornamentado* three years earlier with his design for El Escorial. Herrera too was notoriously fond of obelisks.

San Francesco a Ripa G11

Piazza San Francesco d'Assisi, **t** *06 588 1331;* **tram 3, bus 23, 280. Open** *daily 7.30–11 and 4–6.30.*

One of the first Franciscan churches in Rome, San Francesco a Ripa has two treasures: the squirming, erotic statue of the Beata Ludovica Albertoni by Bernini, in the last chapel on the left, expressing divine ecstasy with the same Hollywood spirituality as his famous Santa Teresa in S. Maria della Vittoria; and the cell in the adjacent cloister where St Francis stayed in 1219, while trying to persuade the pope to reform the Church. The thoroughly Baroqued cell includes a 13th-century painting believed to be a likeness of Francis himself. Ripa, incidentally, was the old name for Trastevere's *rione*.

WEST OF VIALE TRASTEVERE

San Crisogono G10

Piazza Sonnino, **t** *06 581 8225;* **tram 8, bus H, 23, 280, 780. Open** *Mon–Sat 7am–7.30pm, Sun 8–1 and 4.15–7.30;* **crypt open** *Mon–Sat 8–11.30 and 4–7, Sun 8–1 and 4–7.*

San Crisogono has a rather sober Baroque façade (by G.B. Soria, 1623) and a typical Roman portico (Fontana, 1702) covering a largely medieval church. The 13th-century campanile survives, along with the pavement inside and mosaics in the apse by followers of Pietro Cavallini. Down in the crypt, the body of the original church of AD 499, fragments of medieval frescoes remain.

Caserma dei Vigili della Settima Coorte H10

Via della VII Coorte 9, **t** *06 671 0381 (Mon–Fri 9–1).* **Open** *by special arrangement only, call ahead;* **adm** *€2.*

The small, currently empty building with the papal arms down a little street opposite

San Crisogono is the Caserma dei Vigili della VII Coorte, the world's oldest police station. t was built in the 19th century, but imagine the surprise of the papal gendarmes when archaeologists in 1866 discovered beneath it the *excubitorium* of the 7th cohort of ancient Rome's police – like the modern Carabinieri, the Roman *vigili* were technically part of the army, and organized in cohorts and centuries. Conscripts probably often wished they had been sent to the German frontier; besides doing the night watch on pitch-dark streets full of desperadoes, they had to double as firemen, and pull down collapsed buildings.

Just behind San Crisogono, on Via di S. Gallicano, you can see a delightful Rococo building by Rome's most imaginative 18th-century architect, Filippo Raguzzini's **Ospedale di San Gallicano** (G10).

Santa Maria in Trastevere G10

Piazza di S. Maria in Trastevere, t 06 589 7332; tram 3, 8, bus 23, 280, 630. **Open** *7.30–7.*

Piazza di S. Maria in Trastevere is the peaceful, completely lovable heart of the district – no traffic, no Baroque, no obelisks, only a few cafés and children playing ball. Behind Fontana's fountain, with an ancient Roman basin, you'll see the only church in all Rome that has retained its medieval appearance, Santa Maria in Trastevere.

It may be the oldest church in Rome, and the first dedicated to the Virgin Mary. An old legend had it that on the day of Christ's birth, a spring of olive oil – an Italian housewife's dream – miraculously gushed up from this spot, flowing down to the Tiber.

There may have been a Christian building here as early as 220, but the building you see now was begun by Pope Julius I in 337, and rebuilt in the 1140s. Carlo Fontana built the portico, probably replacing an earlier, simpler one. Above it, the beautiful 12th-century gold-ground mosaic on the façade shows how most important medieval Roman churches were decorated; this is the only one

to survive time and the Baroque rebuilders. Mary in the centre is flanked by 10 maidens with lamps who probably represent the *Wise and Foolish Virgins* (from Jesus' parable, Matthew 25, 1–14); the exquisite palm trees below were a symbolic 'tree of life' in some early Christian art, and quite common in some Islamic work. Palms weren't grown in Rome in the Middle Ages, part of the case for ascribing this mosaic to artists from the Greek East.

The portico, full of inscriptions and early Christian decorative panels, leads to an interior with a Cosmati pavement (restored), accented with deep red porphyry and green *verde antico*. Many of the massive nave columns came from the Baths of Caracalla, and some of the capitals atop them are especially fine. Like the pavement, the pretty Cosmatesque spiral candlestick, choir screen, tabernacle and throne owe more to the 19th century than to their medieval originals – by that time the pendulum of Roman taste had swung completely back, and instead of covering churches in Baroque plaster, the pope and cardinals were trying their best to imaginatively recreate the Middle Ages.

The **apse mosaics** are among Rome's best, done at the same time as those on the exterior. The *enthroned Virgin* sits among *Jesus and the saints*, with *Isaiah*, *Jeremiah*, and the *symbols of the Evangelists* on the surrounding triumphal arch.

Note the caged birds underneath them – a charming conceit, reminding the faithful how Jesus imprisoned his own spirit in an earthly body to redeem the sins of the world. The rich colouring, and nervous yet controlled line of these mosaics reflect the classical revival in Byzantium, an influence to which the Italians (however much they hate to admit it) owe many of their own advances in late medieval and Renaissance art. How well they learned their lessons can be seen in the mosaic scenes from the *life of Mary* below, another masterpiece by Pietro Cavallini (1290), which complement his paintings a few blocks away at Santa Cecilia.

To the left of the altar, the pleasant, airy **Altemps Chapel** has frescoes of 1588 portraying the Council of Trent. In the left aisle, the **Chapel of S. Girolamo** is an elaborate late Baroque fancy (Antonio Gherardi, 1680s), a little theatre lit by its own small cupola. At the entrance to the sacristy are two small ancient mosaics.

Museo di Roma in Trastevere F10

Piazza di Sant'Egidio; **bus** *23, 280.* **Open** *Tues–Sun 10–8;* **adm** *€2.50.*

An unassuming former convent just behind S. Maria in Trastevere has been converted into this interesting but little-known tribute to the Eternal City's not so distant past. You can read all you like about Rome in the last centuries of papal rule, the timeless, retrograde city that captivated northerners on the Grand Tour, but this is the only place to see it come to life, with a unique collection of prints and paintings from the 18th century. The British artist Paul Sandby starts the fun with a series of Hogarthian prints of the old Roman Carnival, with colour and incident unthinkable in the staid Rome of today. Others include scenes from the fish market at the Portico d'Ottavia, public scribes scratching out *billets doux* and government forms for the illiterate, housewives doing the wash in the Acqua Vergine fountain, and picturesque *ciociari*, peasants from southern Lazio (so called for their wooden clogs, or *ciocie*), posed around a half-buried Porta San Lorenzo – until the archaeologists got seriously to work in the 1800s, most of the ancient monuments projected from the centuries' accumulation of soil like so many marble and travertine spring posies.

Some amazing pictures record the fireworks and illuminations of old Rome, the greatest shows any 19th-century Italian city had to offer. For papal festivals, papal roofers would clamber over Castel Sant'Angelo and St Peter's dome, placing strings of oil lamps to light the outlines of the buildings against the night sky, while their fellows below set off giant Catherine wheels and, of course, Roman candles by the hundred.

Beyond these, there are casts of Pasquino and the Bocca della Verità, and every other old Roman landmark, a series of life-sized **tableaux** with waxwork figures, portraying Roman shops, taverns and homes from long ago, and – quite inexplicably to the foreign visitor – the reconstructed quarters of one of the last and most beloved of Roman dialect poets, Trilussa (Carlo Salustri, d.1950). Trilussa's works can be found in any good Roman bookstore; although not the sort of stuff likely to be found in anthologies or poetry courses, they comment blithely on the passing Roman scene, with some pointed satire reserved for Mussolini and the Fascists (and not at all hard to read if you know some Italian). Trilussa seems to have been interested in everything, and on a slow day the curators will be glad to point out his funny mythological paintings, bug collections, and other clutter. Keep an eye open for exhibitions, often held on the lower floor.

Santa Maria della Scala F10

Via della Scala, **t** *06 580 6233;* **bus** *23, 280.* **Open** *for Mass only, Mon–Sat 7.30 and 5.30, Sun 7.30, 11.30 and 5.30.*

Santa Maria della Scala serves the adjacent Carmelite monastery, and has had a reputation in the practice of medicine for centuries. The monks run a completely modern and up-to-date **pharmacy**, facing the square, but if you ask, they'll be glad to take you up for a look at the old one, a genuine 18th-century Roman pharmacy with pretty majolica jars full of exotic herbal cures.

Palazzo Corsini F9

Via della Lungara 10, **t** *06 6880 2323;* **bus** *23, 280.* **Open** *Tues–Sat 9–7, Sun 9–1;* **adm** *€4.*

Sharing the collection of the Galleria Nazionale d'Arte Antica with the Palazzo Barberini is this small, attractive museum hardly ever troubled with visitors. The *palazzo*, one of the more ambitious creations of 18th-century Rome, turns its back on Via della Lungara, waiting for a grander façade facing the Janiculum Hill, which was never built. The Corsini were bankers, and relatives of more than one 17th-century pope, one of the last families to make it big off the centuries-old papal banking racket.

Queen Christina lived here for a while, as did Napoleon's mother, Letizia Bonaparte. The back of the palace suffered considerable damage during the French attacks against the Roman Republic in 1849; after Napoleon III's armies breached the Janiculum walls, this part of Trastevere found itself in the front line of French reprisals.

You enter through a quiet courtyard, then up a stairway decorated with miscellaneous ancient sculptures and neoclassical works of the Napoleonic era. In the first room, there is a little model of how the palace was meant to look; it would have been the grandest in Rome, or at least the biggest.

The paintings are typical Roman museum fare, largely Italian artists, with a few Flemish, ranging from the late 1500s through the Baroque. Murillo's *Madonna and Child* stands out, one of the pious Spaniard's less saccharine attempts.

The second room is devoted to the northerners, with two Breughel winter scenes and some overripe Rubens: a *Madonna* and a *St Sebastian*. Followers of Caravaggio occupy rooms three and four, including one fine painting of *St John the Baptist*, a copy made by the master himself of the work in the Capitoline Pinacoteca.

Room five was Queen Christina's bedroom; she died here in 1689. This and the last two rooms contain works of painters Mattia Preti, which include a striking *Martyrdom of St Bartholomew*; Pier Francesco Mola; Guido Reni; Carlo Dolci; Guercino (one of the *Et in Arcadia Ego* paintings); Luca Giordano; and Salvator Rosa, who wins the prize for fright and gore with his *Prometheus*, complete with hungry eagle.

Botanical Gardens F9

Via Corsini 24, t 06 686 4193; bus 23, 280.
Open *Mon–Sat 9–6, winter until 5; adm €2.*

Behind the palace, the Corsini grounds have become Rome's Botanical Gardens, or Orto Botanico. They are your best chance in this part of the city for some rest and shade under the tall palms. *See* also 'Sport and Green Spaces', p.337

Villa Farnesina F9

Via della Lungara 230; bus 23, 280.
Open *Mon–Sat 9–1; adm €3.*

The Chigi family came originally from Siena. Banker Agostino Chigi hit the jackpot in the early 1500s, at the beginning of the great Renaissance orgy of Roman acquisitiveness, by winning the papal account. Other families, most notably the Medici of Florence, had already made their fortunes in this way; the Chigi never became Grand Dukes like the Medici, but for conspicuous consumption nobody could beat them. In the gilded reign of Leo X, nouveau riche Agostino's Trastevere villa was the cynosure of Rome, with cardinals, poets, princes, tremendous courtesans and fashionable artists for dinner almost every night. The best story about Agostino has him hosting banquets on the riverbank, with the servants tossing the gold and silver plates into the Tiber after each course to show off. Of course there was a net at the bottom, to retrieve the loot afterwards.

Baldassare Peruzzi, another Sienese, designed the villa in 1508 and helped decorate it with his paintings, along with Raphael and Sebastiano del Piombo. After decades of the high life, the Chigi found themselves overdrawn, and sold the property to the Farnese family. The Bourbons of Naples held it for a while, and since the 1920s it has served as home for the Accademia dei Lincei, a scientific circle founded in the early 1600s (Galileo was an early member).

For visitors, the main attraction is Raphael's famous fresco on the ground floor, of Galatea daintily riding the waves like a marine Venus; Cupids aiming rather dangerous-looking arrows float above. Raphael's elegant mytho-logical fantasy, just what Renaissance bankers and cardinals preferred, sets the tone for the rest of the villa. The architect, Peruzzi, added the ceiling frescoes of astro-nomical constellations, and the semicircular paintings below are vignettes from Ovid's *Metamorphoses* by Sebastiano del Piombo.

In the other room on the ground floor, the **Loggia of Cupid and Psyche**, Raphael's pupils, including Giulio Romano, contributed a series of paintings from Apuleius' *Golden Ass*. Upstairs, the main hall of the villa is an eccentric masterpiece of Peruzzi, the **Salone delle Prospettive**; *trompe l'oeil* archways enclose mock window views of Roman vistas, a rare chance to see what Trastevere and the Vatican Borgo looked like in the 16th century. Nearby is Agostino Chigi's own bedroom. Il Sodoma did this room, the Sienese painter whose name reflects contemporary opinion crediting him with every sort of vice; really he was a good family man, devoted entirely to his pet badger and the rest of his sizeable menagerie. He was also one of the greatest artists of his time, who never got over the shock when his frescoes in the Vatican were destroyed by Julius II, to be replaced by the sweeter, more fashionable art of Raphael. His major work here is a large scene of the *Marriage of Alexander the Great and Roxana*.

Via della Lungara continues northwards towards the Vatican from here, passing the Regina Coeli Prison, Rome's main lockup for centuries, and the scene of some memorable Nazi atrocities in 1943–4; the prisoners murdered in the Fosse Ardeatine, in reprisal for partisan activities, were taken from here.

JANICULUM HILL

The trans-Tiberine Janiculum Hill (E8–10), or Gianicolo has always been the odd man out among Rome's hills – the biggest, but not even one of the canonical Seven, and not included within the city walls (a branch of the fortifications, following the crest of the Janiculum, was built strictly out of defensive

necessity). In latter days most of the hill has been preserved as parks. It's worth a climb for the views over Rome, and for one very special building – the Tempietto of Bramante, the most characteristic work of the Roman High Renaissance.

San Pietro in Montorio F10

Piazza San Pietro in Montorio, t 06 581 3940; bus 870. Open 9–12 and 4–6; if closed, ring bell at door to right of church.

This ancient church was rebuilt at the behest of Ferdinand and Isabella of Spain in the 1480s. And a good choice it was for the Spaniards. Today's students at the adjacent Spanish Academy enjoy one of the most peaceful corners of Rome, with the best views over the city. One of the Academy's more recent students was King Juan Carlos, who still remembers his days on the Janiculum with affection, and drops in for a visit every now and then. In the church, the most noteworthy painting is a *Flagellation of Christ* by Sebastiano del Piombo, in the first chapel on the right. The next chapel's ceiling has a *Coronation of the Virgin* by Peruzzi; two chapels further on, Florentine Mannerism makes one of its rare appearances in Rome, with sculptural work by Ammannati and a fresco of St Paul by Giorgio Vasari. Under the high altar are buried two troublesome Irish earls, Hugh O'Neill and Roderick O'Donnell, unsuccessful Catholic rebels against King James I.

Tempietto del Bramante F10
Piazza San Pietro in Montorio, t 06 581 3940; bus 870. Open 9–12 and 4–6.

Bramante's Tempietto can be seen in the little courtyard to the right of the church. Do not think that this ambitious attempt at perfect architecture was intentionally tucked away in an obscure spot; at the time (about 1501) this was believed to be the exact loca-tion of St Peter's upside-down crucifixion, making it one of the most important pilgrimage sites in Rome. But at the climax of the Renaissance, somehow this holy ground acquired a monument steeped in pagan antiquity. Bramante was the first modern architect to recapture entirely the Doric order from Vitruvius' ancient textbook. His tiny temple, only large enough for a few worshippers at a time, stands as a unique monument to the Renaissance ideal of expressing the inexpressible in architecture.

Everything is sliced down to basic principles, without a trace of Gothic bravura or the free-spirited experimentation of the early Renaissance. The perfect symmetry of the 16-columned, radial temple proclaims abject submission to a simple ideal. Bramante wished to build as the ancients did, and he sacrificed all the experience of the medieval centuries to erect his impeccable little cylinder. The clumsy hulk of St Peter's only emphasizes the impotence of an architecture that sought to translate its perfection to larger sizes. Michelangelo and his successors could never have built this, but only mock its form into shapeless gigantism.

Across the road from this exhilarating, perhaps disturbing building is the brazenly fascist **Monument to the Fallen of 1849–70**, a chill travertine pavilion (1941) with battle scenes of the Risorgimento wars, and imbecilic patriotic inscriptions from Gabriele D'Annunzio. There was some talk of moving Garibaldi's remains here from his last home, in Sardinia, before the war intervened.

Fontana dell'Acqua Paola F10

Via Garibaldi; **bus** *870.*

This fine miniature Trevi Fountain built under Paul V is part of the papal works which used the remains of Trajan's aqueduct to bring the waters of Lake Bracciano into Rome. In ancient times, near this spot, water from the aqueduct powered ranks of mills that ground Rome's flour. The columns of Paul's fountain come from the façade of the original St Peter's, and other parts came from the forum. For the first three decades of the 20th century, the waters of the fountain powered a hydroelectric generator.

Piazzale Garibaldi E8

Bus *870.*

This is a fine viewpoint, adorned with tourist clutter (including a miniature puppet show). There's a huge bronze equestrian **Garibaldi** in the piazza, but even better is the equally massive bronze equestrian **Mrs Garibaldi** a little further on.

The remarkable Anita, who is buried underneath, certainly did her part through all the battles of 1849 – even though she was pregnant; the statue shows her galloping towards destiny with a pistol in one hand, and cradling her baby in the other. The Brazilians erected it to honour their brave daughter; Garibaldi had brought her home to Italy after fighting in the South American wars of independence.

Vatican City
and St Peter's

Vatican City and St Peter's

The popes do nothing on a small scale; by a mystery of the faith, the world's smallest country contains the world's largest museum, piazza and church. It is next to impossible to see the Vatican Museums, St Peter's and the Castel Sant'Angelo all in one day, but a good day to see the museums and basilica is a Monday (when all the state museums are closed anyway). If you've had the foresight to book an afternoon tour of the ancient necropolis under St Peter's you can even, with some fancy footwork, fit that in too. If you happen to be in Rome on the last Sunday of any month, take advantage of papal charity – the Vatican Museums are free. The one attraction that even the saints in heaven couldn't squeeze into a single-day itinerary is the tour of the Vatican Gardens, although from the dome you get a bird's eye view of the little state and its gardens.

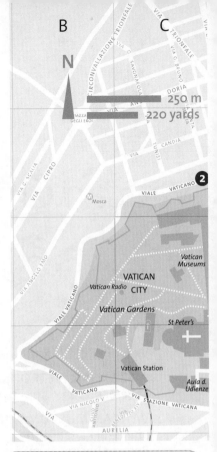

1 Lunch

Taverna Angelica, *Piazza delle Vaschette 14/a*, **t** *06 687 4514; wheelchair accessible.* **Open** *Sept–July Tues–Sat 12–2.30 and 7.30–12, Mon 7.30–12 only.* **Expensive**. A cosy restaurant near Castel Sant'Angelo, with good roast pork. Vintage wine by the glass and one of the world's best cheeses: Castelmagno.

2 Coffee and Cakes

Gelateria Old Bridge, *Viale Vaticano;* **metro** *Ottaviano,* **tram** *19,* **bus** *32, 81.* You might notice this hole-in-the-wall ice-cream stand *en route* to the Vatican Museums. *Pinolata* (vanilla and pine nuts) and *fragola* (strawberry) are particularly good.

3 Drinks

Il Simposio di Costantini, *Piazza Cavour 16,* **t** *06 321 1502;* **bus** *34, 490, 590, 913.* **Open** *Sept–July Mon–Fri 11.30–3 and 6.30–1am and Sat 6.30–1am.* Gorgeous wine bar serving snacks for gastronomes.

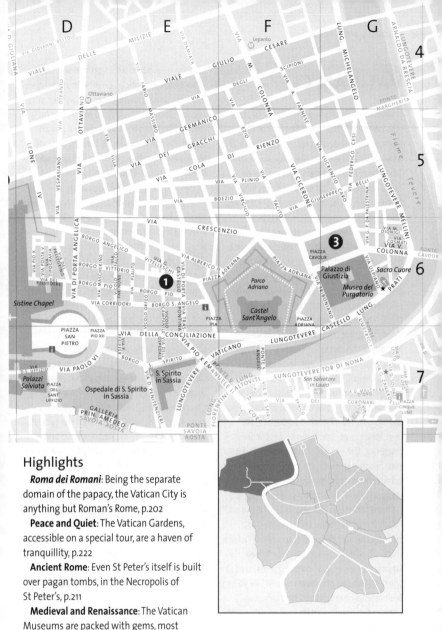

Highlights

Roma dei Romani: Being the separate domain of the papacy, the Vatican City is anything but Roman's Rome, p.202

Peace and Quiet: The Vatican Gardens, accessible on a special tour, are a haven of tranquillity, p.222

Ancient Rome: Even St Peter's itself is built over pagan tombs, in the Necropolis of St Peter's, p.211

Medieval and Renaissance: The Vatican Museums are packed with gems, most famously, of course, the Sistine Chapel, p.218, Borgia Apartment, p.218, and Stanze di Raffaello, p.215

Baroqueorama: Bernini's little joke on antiquity: the size and dimensions of Piazza San Pietro almost exactly match the Colosseum, p.203

Unexpected Rome: Castel Sant'Angelo, where Tosca leaped to her death, p.223

VATICAN CITY

Vatican, curiously, means 'prophecy', for it was on this eighth hill of Rome that King Numa received tips on religion from the Sibyls. But as it was on the wrong side of the Tiber land was cheap, and Caligula used it to build his personal circus, later known as Nero's; here St Peter was crucified – upside down, at his own request, so that his martyrdom would not resemble Christ's. He was buried in a nearby cemetery, on a spot that has been hallowed ever since. It has been the chief residence of Peter's successors most of the time since the late 14th century.

'The Papacy is not other than the Ghost of the Deceased Roman Empire, sitting crowned upon the grave thereof,' said Thomas Hobbes, although since Hobbes this imperial ectoplasm has been confined like an afrit in a magic lamp. Better known as the Vatican City, an independent state (pop. 1,000), it was the papacy's consolation prize negotiated in the 1929 Lateran Concordat. But popes' temporal power had been in decline for centuries; the old Papal States were by the 18th century the worst run in Europe, kept 'alive only because the earth refuses to swallow them', as Goethe so neatly put it.

Thanks to Mussolini, the power of the Papal States has been concentrated in a country the size of a golf course – one where the duffers don't always count all their strokes. For instead of creating a realm of the spirit, as Vatican brochures would like you to believe, members of the Curia who run Vatican City have used its sovereignty (read unaccountability) to create the Corporate Papacy, the world's last real autocracy, with a tiny tax haven all its own. The scandal of Vatican finances, Mafia connections, the laundering of drug money through the Vatican Bank, and the circumstances surrounding the sudden death of John Paul I have been so unsavoury that the government across the Tiber has responded by steadily decreasing the Church's role in the state, legalizing divorce and abortion, making religious instruction optional in schools, taxing Vatican profits from the stock markets, and removing Roman Catholicism's special status as the official religion of Italy. Ask any Roman about it, and you'll get an earful. It's one reason why the city has one of the lowest percentages of church attendance in Italy – 'Faith is made here and believed elsewhere', is an old Roman saying.

Yet as you stroll among the merry crowds of pilgrims and tourists chattering in every known language, remember Boccaccio's story in the *Decameron*, of two friends who live in Paris, one Christian and one Jewish, the former constantly pestering the latter to convert. Finally the Jew agrees, on the condition that he first visits Rome, to see if the life and habits of the pope and his cardinals are evidence of the superiority of their faith. The Christian naturally despairs, but off the Jew goes to Rome, returning with the expected tales of a thousand abominations, declaring that the pontiff and the rest were 'doing their level best to reduce the Christian religion to nought and drive it from the face of the earth'. That the faith can survive and prosper with such sharks in charge is enough to convince him that it must indeed be holy and genuine – so he converts immediately.

Vatican City (B–c6) is surrounded by a high wall, designed by Michelangelo; its only public entrances are through St Peter's Square and the Vatican Museums. Swiss Guards (still recruited from the four Catholic cantons of Switzerland), dressed in a scaled-down version of the striped suits designed by either Michelangelo or Raphael, stand ready to smite you with their halberds if you try to push your way in elsewhere. The Vatican has its own stamps and postal service – like every postal system in the galaxy, far more efficient than the Posta Italiana. The official language in Vatican City is Latin, although its own semi-official daily newspaper, *L'Osservatore Romano*, is in Italian (with a weekly digest in English) and its Vatican Radio broadcasts in 26 languages; lately the neighbours have been complaining about the microwave levels from its transmitters.

Vatican Gardens

Open for 2hr tours in English Mon–Fri at 10am; call **t** 06 6988 4466 (Mon–Sat 9–5) to reserve, or ask at the tourist office in Piazza San Pietro; **adm** €8.50.

A tour of the Vatican Gardens also gives intriguing glimpses of some of the City's working areas. After a bus ride through the Arco delle Campane, past the 8th-century German cemetery and a plaque marking the original site of the obelisk now in Piazza San Pietro, you'll see the Vatican railway station, used for bringing in goods to be sold tax free in the Vatican supermarket. It was used only once by a pope, when John XXIII went to Assisi (John Paul II prefers the heliport) and is said to be fitted with a choir loft and organ. Laugh you may, but popes long forbade railways in the Papal States for fear that passengers would snog in the tunnels.

Next are various office *palazzi*, the mosaic workshop, and the Ethiopian Seminary, where the Pope sheltered students during Mussolini's imperial adventures. The well-manicured grounds are planted with fine specimens of exotic trees and roses, with beds arranged in 16th-century Italian garden geometry. The most beautiful building is Pirro Ligorio and Peruzzi's **Casino of Pius IV** (1558–62), a jewel-like summer pavilion where popes and cardinals engaged in elegant conversation.

PIAZZA SAN PIETRO

Not even all the photographs you've seen can quite prepare you for Piazza San Pietro (D6–7), where 'small is beautiful' is dashed as heresy. The gigantic proportions force you to suspend your normal visual belief; all is so superscale that only by constant reference to the measurements of man, a mere tiddly-wink next to St Peter's 350ft-long façade, can you begin to digest its outrageous size.

Someone has calculated that there is room for about 300,000 people in the piazza, with no crowding. Few, however, have ever noticed Bernini's little joke on antiquity; the open space almost exactly matches the size and dimensions of the Colosseum. And as Norwood Young wrote, in the 1901 *Story of Rome*, the intention of the architects is not dissimilar – to overawe and crush the individual. 'But now I feel the cold scrutiny of Bernini's self-complacent columns,' writes Mr Young. 'Their long octopus arms ready to encircle me, while the body of the monster waits eyeing me from the distance. I cannot escape.' Bernini would prefer us to see his **Colonnade**, with its 284 massive columns and statues of 140 saints, as 'the arms of the Church embracing the world'. Stand on either of the two dark stones at the foci of

Sixtus and the Obelisk

Sixtus V was no stuck-in-the-sedia-gestatoria pope, but a man of action, the only one, Queen Elizabeth I claimed, jokingly, who was worthy of her hand. One of his pet projects was to humble the ancient pagans of Rome, whose monuments, even in ruins, still threatened to overshadow the grandeur of the Church. In 1586, he ordered Domenico Fontana to move the obelisk to the piazza, to show how puny this heathen ornament was in comparison to the Biggest Church in the World. The problem was, no one could remember how to move an obelisk. Fontana made elaborate plans (Sixtus hinted that failure would mean the chopping block), and on 18 September 900 men, 150 horses and 47 cranes creaked into action. A vast crowd had gathered to watch, but the Pope insisted on perfect silence (underlined by the presence of a gallows) so the workmen could hear Fontana's orders. Slowly they hauled the obelisk upright by the ropes, then hesitated, the ropes too taut with the strain to finish the task. Suddenly the silence was broken by a Ligurian sailor's cry, 'Water on the ropes!' saving the obelisk and Fontana's neck. Sixtus showed his gratitude by giving the sailor's home town of Bordighera the monopoly of palm fronds for the Vatican on Palm Sunday.

the elliptical piazza, and you will see the forest of columns resolve into neat rows, a subtly impressive optical effect like the hole in the dome of the Pantheon. Bernini designed the colonnade so that the nobility could drive their carriages underneath to St Peter's, sheltered from sun or rain.

Flanked by two lovely fountains, luxuriantly spraying water all over the pavement – the one on the right by Carlo Maderno (1614) and the other copied from it in 1667 – the **Vatican Obelisk**, though only average size for an obelisk, is one of the most fantastical relics in all Rome. It comes from Heliopolis, the Egyptian city founded as a capital and cult centre by Ikhnaton, the semi-legendary Pharaoh and religious reformer who, according to Sigmund Freud and others, founded the first monotheistic religion, influencing Moses and all who came after. It arrived here apparently by divine coinci- dence; originally in the *spina* of Nero's Circus Vaticanus, it may have overlooked the martyrdom of St Peter. For a millennium and a half it remained in place, just to the left of the present basilica, until Sixtus V had it moved, accompanied by one of the city's favourite, and probably fabricated, anecdotes (*see* below). Originally the obelisk was topped by a golden ball, long believed to contain the ashes of Julius Caesar (it proved empty when cracked open); now it holds a sliver of the True Cross inside an iron cross.

Off to the right of the square, as you look at St Peter's, is a cluster of Vatican palaces, built over the years to satisfy some of the bigger papal egos. Modern popes take up less room; since 1903, when the newly elected Pius X refused to move from the servants' quarters of the **Apostolic Palace** (the tallest building), where he stayed during the conclave, the popes have lived there, behind the last two windows on the right on the top floor.

The stories of Pius' simplicity do much to counter the tons of travertine bombast: one story goes that a nun prone to leg cramps asked to borrow Pius' old woollen stockings, and came back declaring a miracle, for the stockings had completely cured her pains.

'How extraordinary!' the Pope replied. 'They never did anything for me.' On Sunday at noon the current pope appears at the window and blesses the crowd in the piazza.

The gallery along the right, the **Corridore del Bernini**, leads to the great **Bronze Door**, the ceremonial entrance to the Vatican for visiting dignitaries, which leads to the **Scala Regia**. At the end is the **Arco delle Campane**, under St Peter's bells, guarded by the Swiss; if you're booking to see the necropolis, just tell them 'Ufficio degli Scavi'. On the left of the square are the Vatican information office (*t 06 6988 1662*), post office and first aiders.

St Peter's C6–7

*Piazza San Pietro; **metro** Ottaviano, **tram** 19, **bus** 32, 39, 40, 62, 81, 492. **Basilica open** daily 8–7. **Grottoes open** same hours as the basilica, except when the pope is present; **adm** free. **Dome open** 9–5.45; **adm** €4. **Treasury open** 9–6.15; **adm** €4.*

Looming over all is the massive façade of the Basilica of St Peter, scrubbed up nicely for the Holy Year. Mr Young compares it to the great Gothic Cathedrals: '"Come," say Milan, Amiens, Cologne, York, "come and worship God with me. See how comely it is to do so." But Rome says, "See how grand and powerful I am, and how contemptible you are."'

Old St Peter's was much cosier. Begun by Constantine over the Apostle's tomb in 324, it was a richly decorated basilica, in form much like San Paolo fuori le Mura, full of gold and mosaics, with a vast porch of marble and bronze in front, and a lofty campanile topped by the famous golden cockerel that everyone believed would some day crow to announce the end of the world. This St Peter's, where Charlemagne and Frederick II received their imperial crowns, was falling to pieces by the 15th century, conveniently in time for the popes and artists of the Renaissance to plan a replacement. The first to do so was Nicholas V, who, in about 1450, conceived an almost Neronian building programme for the Vatican, ten times as large as anything his ancestors could have contemplated – a complex that would have stretched all the way to Castel Sant'Angelo. It was not until Julius II realized that there was not enough room in the basilica for his planned tomb that he commissioned Bramante to demolish the old church and begin the new. His original plan called for a great dome over a central Greek cross. Michelangelo, who took over the work in 1546, basically agreed, and if he had had his way St Peter's might indeed have become the crowning achievement of Renaissance art everyone hoped it would be.

Unfortunately, despite nearly 200 years of construction and a massive expenditure, too many popes and too many architects created instead of a masterpiece a monster of compromise. Raphael, who took over as architect after Bramante's death (nick-naming his former mentor 'Ruinante' for his summary demolition of much that was sacred and could have been preserved in the old basilica), opted for a Latin cross. A number of architects succeeded him: Peruzzi returning to the Greek cross of Bramante, followed by Antonio da Sangallo the Younger, another advocate of the Latin cross. Paul III then summoned Michelangelo, aged 72, who reluctantly took over the mess, on the condition that the Pope gave him a free hand (in return, he worked for free, too), whereupon he demolished everything Da Sangallo had built and started afresh on Bramante's lines, although changing his plans for a Pantheon-type dome to a higher cupola modelled on Brunelleschi's dome over Florence Cathedral. But even this was reshaped by one of his successors, Giacomo della Porta, who completed it in 1590.

The most substantial tinkering came in 1605, when Paul V and his committee of cardinals decided on a Latin cross after all. Carlo Maderno was given the task of demol-ishing the portico of the old basilica to extend the nave, which had the unforeseen effect of blocking out the view of the dome, and he designed the façade (1612) with Paul V's name blazoned on top. But Maderno shouldn't be blamed for its disproportionate width: Bernini had the idea of adding twin campaniles to the flanks which were such a dismal failure that they were levelled to the same height as Maderno's façade. On 18 November 1626, the supposed 1,300th anniversary of the original basilica, Urban VIII consecrated the new St Peter's. In the centre is the balcony from which popes give the Christmas and Easter Urbi et Orbi blessing.

Portico

Some of the best art in St Peter's is in the portico, beginning with the oldest and hardest to see, Giotto's 1298 mosaic of Christ walking on water, called the *Navicella*, located in the tympanum over the central door; it has been so often restored that almost nothing remains of the original. At the far right of the portico is Bernini's eques-trian statue of *Constantine*, showing the emperor staring at the vision of the cross.

There are five sets of **bronze doors** leading into the basilica, the work of some of Italy's leading modern sculptors. They start on the right with the **Holy Door**, opened only in Holy Years (1950, by Vico Consorti). The next set is by Venanzio Crocetti (1968). The central doors, from Old St Peter's, are by Antonio Filarete (1439–45), with scenes from the life of Pope Eugenius IV; he held an ecumenical council in Florence in 1441, an attempt to reconcile differences between the Eastern and Western Churches in face of the mutual Turkish threat; you can recognize Emperor John Palaeologos by his pointy hat, while Ethiopian monks pay homage to Eugenius. Crudely carved on the other side of the right door, at the bottom, Filarete and his workmen dance with their tools below an inscription in pidgin Latin. The next set of doors are by Giacomo Manzù (1963), with harrowing scenes of death, martyrdoms and victims torn like paper bags. On the back of these Manzù cast a scene from the Vatican Second Ecumenical Council: Pope John XXIII conversing with a cardinal from Tanzania – a reference to Filarete's doors. The last set, by Luciano Minguzzi (1977), shows a hedgehog.

The plodding equestrian statue at the left end is of *Charlemagne*, by Cornacchini, giving

St Peter's

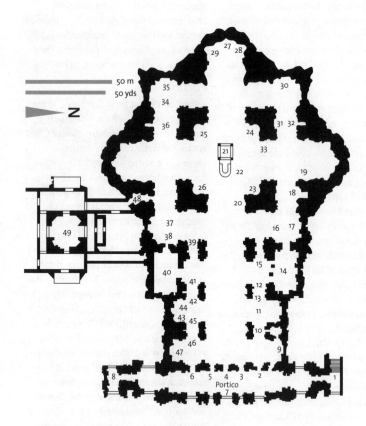

50 m
50 yds

N

the portico two knights in case any of the giant marble saints ever want to play chess. The floor of the portico is by the indefatigable Bernini, embedded with the giant coat of arms of John XXIII by Manzù to commemorate the Second Vatican Council of 1962.

First Impressions of the Interior

Most people find the interior disappointing, again partly because your eyes are confused by its scale; its proportions, as everyone said a hundred years ago, are so harmonious you don't notice how large it is, but probably no architect who ever lived could have found a solution to making such a vast barn visually stimulating.

Bernini, in charge of decorating the interior, made it into a holy Grand Central Station, full of stone saints and angels, keeping an eye on the big clocks overhead as they wait for trains to Paradise. Up the middle of the nave, bronze markers showing the length of other proud cathedrals prove how each fails miserably to measure up – the fact that they aren't accurate, and make Milan Cathedral 65ft too small, proves (at least to the Milanese) that Roman duplicity knows no bounds.

The round porphyry stone in the pavement near the central door marks the place by the altar of the old basilica where emperors would kneel to be crowned.

The *Pietà*

The best work of art is right in front, in the first chapel on the right: Michelangelo's famous *Pietà*, now restored and hard to see behind the glass that has protected it from future madmen, since a past madman attacked it with a hammer in 1972.

Finished in 1499, when he was only 25, the statue helped make Michelangelo's reputation. Its smooth and elegant figures, with the realities of death and grief sublimated on some ethereal plane known only to saints and artists, marked a turning point in religious art – from here, the beautiful, unreal art of the religious Baroque was the logical next step. The *Pietà* is the only work Michelangelo ever signed (on the band of the Virgin's garment); he added his signature

after overhearing a group of tourists from Milan who thought the *Pietà* was the work of a fellow Milanese.

Michelangelo sculpted the *Pietà* for the French ambassador; significantly, none of the art made to order for St Peter's can match it. By the time the basilica was finished, the great artists of the Renaissance were dead, and whatever glories they may have contributed have been replaced by huge Counter-Reformation paintings and assembly-line Baroque statues, in turn replaced by 'more eternal' mosaic copies.

The cold feeling is made more oppressive by the ranks of papal funerary monuments with ghoulish Baroque effigies, like Babylonian potentates in their beehive tiaras, their fat fingers laden with rings while voluptuous female allegories pose dutifully below.

The Right Aisle

Two of the few memorials to real women may be seen in the right aisle: in the arch after the Pietà is a *Monument to Queen Christina of Sweden*, topped by a large, flattering portrait of the frowzy monarch, who at one point embarrassed her papal sponsors by falling in love with a nun; and in the next chapel, the **Cappella di San Sebastiano**, Bernini's *Monument to Countess Matilda of Tuscany*, the great benefactress of the temporal papacy who died in 1115, and whose remains were brought here from Mantua in 1635. The pride of the next chapel, the **Cappella del Santissimo Sacramento**, is its iron grille by Borromini; on the altar the ciborium by Bernini is a miniature copy of Bramante's Tempietto of S. Pietro in Montorio. In the next arch an allegorical figure of Courage lifts the cover of the sarcophagus of the *Monument of Gregory XIII* by Camillo Rusconi (1723), to reveal an allegory of Gregory's calendar reforms and, underneath, a hobgoblin of a dragon. Beyond, the **Cappella Gregoriana** defines the original, pre-Maderno limits of St Peter's; it was designed by Michelangelo. The altar painting of the *Madonna del Soccorso* is an

11th-century relic from the old basilica. In the next arch is the lift up to the roof.

The right transept contains three altars, the one on the right dedicated to good King Wenceslas (of Bohemia), the same who 'looked out on the Feast of Stephen'. Around the enormous pier sits the famous bronze *Statue of St Peter*, its extended foot worn away by the kisses of the faithful (a 50-day indulgence per smack, according to Pius IX). Its date is a mystery: long believed to belong to the 5th century, made from the bronze of the statue of Capitoline Jove, it was later assumed to be a 13th-century work by Arnolfo di Cambio, although the latest scholarship has reverted to the original date; it may have been part of the tomb of Emperor Honorius, which later became the French monastery of St Martin, just to the left of St Peter's: early Christians, like ancient Romans, often added statues of a personal divine intercessor to help them through the beyond. On 29 June, the feast day of SS. Peter and Paul, the statue is dressed up in full pontifical garb.

The High Altar and the Dome

The **High Altar**, where only the Pope may celebrate mass, is sheltered by Bernini's celebrated **Baldacchino** (1633), cast from bronze looted from the Pantheon roof by his Barberini patron, Urban VIII. The canopy is as tall as the Palazzo Farnese, to give a hint of its scale, and in form it resembles the *baldacchino* of old St Peter's, with its twisted columns and hangings (although now made of bronze). Barberini bees swarm over it as if it were real barley sugar, and on the pedestals supporting the columns, incorporated into coats of arms, are seven female faces expressing labour pains, and lastly a happy baby's face; Urban VIII commissioned the *baldacchino* as an ex-voto for the safe deliverance of a favourite niece from a dangerous pregnancy.

But even the world's biggest canopy shrinks under the world's biggest **Dome** (the Pantheon's shallow dome is about 6ft wider, and there are two even bigger ones in Malta,

but if inverted this one could hold the most soup). Decorated with a *minestrone* of religious mosaics spooned on by the tedious Cavaliere d'Arpino, it is a dizzy 352ft to the top. By Michelangelo's death it was completed only so far as the drum, where 7ft-high letters spell out the words of Christ to Peter: '*Tu es Petrus* ...'

The horseshoe-shaped **Confessio**, designed by Maderno and perpetually lit by 95 lamps, contains, behind the grille, a shaft leading down to the tomb of St Peter through which the woollen palliums (the long strips of cloth that bishops wear around their necks) are lowered to be sanctified. It was when workmen were lowering the floor in the crypt below the Confessio in 1939 that the ancient cemetery was discovered, along with the presumed relics of St Peter.

The four massive **Piers** supporting the dome are graced by mastodontic statues of saints associated with St Peter's most treasured relics. These relics used to be publicly displayed during Holy Week from the piers' upper balconies, each of these adorned with a pair of columns from old St Peter's – six of which were brought from Byzantium by Constantine, while the others are copies made shortly after. Nearest the bronze statue of St Peter is *St Longinus* (statue by Bernini) whose relic is the lance that Longinus, a Roman soldier, used to pierce the side of Christ; underneath is the entrance to the Vatican Grottoes. Also on the right is *St Helen* (whose relic is a piece of the True Cross); across from her is *St Veronica*, whose handkerchief (now missing) preserved an imprint of Christ's features; and last of all is *St Andrew*, by Duquesnoy, whose relic was his head – recently returned to the church in Patras, Greece, from which the Despot of Morea grabbed it in the 15th century.

The Tribune

Meant to be seen under the *baldacchino* from the moment you enter is Bernini's Tribune, a gaudy 1665 work encasing St Peter's cathedra, the chair from which the Apostle was said to have delivered his first sermon to the Romans. Bernini's training was in the theatre, and this is one of his smash hits, with a multi-media cast of gilt bronze, coloured marbles and stucco, illuminated by a glowing window with a dove emblem that forms an integral part of the composition.

This part of the basilica is usually roped off, but if you have binoculars and are prepared to engage in various bodily contortions, you may just be able to see Bernini's *Monument of Urban VIII* (begun in 1628) to the right of Bernini's throne. Here again the sculptor effectively uses different materials and colours: the *Pope*, jauntily waving from the afterlife, and *Death*, penning his epitaph, are in dark bronze, while the more worldly figures of *Charity* and *Justice* are of white marble. To the left is Guglielmo della Porta's notorious 1575 *Monument of Paul III*, flanked by figures of *Prudence* (modelled on the Pope's mother) and *Justice*, a portrait of his sister, the lovely Giulia Farnese, who as mistress of Alexander VI did her part to advance Paul's career. Originally the statue was nude; the story goes that its beauty drove a Spanish student to distraction, until one night he hid in the basilica to make love to it. In the morning he was found dead at its side; ever since it has worn metal draperies.

To the right of the tribune, around the Pier of St Helena, is the **Cappella San Michele**, with a mosaic of Guercino's *St Petronilla* (original in the Capitoline museum); behind, on the pier itself, is the *Altar of the Navicella* by Lanfranco, inspired by Giotto's mosaic in the portico; directly across from it is Canova's neoclassical *Monument of Clement XIII*. Continue around the pier for Michelangelo Slodtz's 1744 *St Bruno*; the bald, effeminate saint is gracefully refusing a bishop's mitre.

The Left Aisle

Backtrack across Bernini's Tribune to the left aisle; behind the Pier of St Veronica is the **Cappella della Colonna**, named after a column from the old basilica, painted with a much venerated picture of the Virgin. The chapel contains the *Tomb of Leo the Great*, with Algardi's relief of St Leo halting the

advance of Attila the Hun (the pope is said to have threatened Attila with a fatal nosebleed if he should enter Rome, but since Attila couldn't understand Latin, we see SS. Peter and Paul translating). In the next arch is Bernini's *Monument of Alexander VII*, a late work that juxtaposes the serenely praying pope with Death, popping out of the curtains below, waving a warning hourglass. Across the left transept is the **Cappella Clementina**, decorated by Giacomo della Porta and containing the *Monument of Pius VII* (1823) by Thorvaldsen, the only Protestant to contribute to St Peter's, and probably also the only Icelander.

Beyond, in the arch, is Algardi's *Monument of Leo XI*, whose pontificate lasted only 27 days; the relief shows him as a cardinal watching Henry IV abjure Protestantism. In the next arch, beyond the ornate **Cappella del Coro** is Antonio Pollaiuolo's bronze *Monument to Innocent VIII* (1492), the only survivor from the old basilica, with its good-humoured papal effigy of Innocent blessing with a smile and holding the blade of Longinus' spear, a gift of Sultan Beyazit II, while below another effigy represents Innocent in death. Across is the *Monument of St Pius X*, whose tomb is in the next chapel, the **Cappella della Presentazione**. Next on the right is Emilio Greco's *Monument of John XXIII*. The following arch is dedicated to the last Stuarts: up on the right, the *Monument of Clementina Sobieska*, wife of the Old Pretender and granddaughter of the saviour of Vienna, and here called 'Queen of Great Britain, France, and Ireland,' while on the left, Canova's pyramid-shaped *Monument of the Old and Young Pretenders and Henry, Cardinal of York* was paid for by George IV. The **Baptistry** contains an ancient font made of Emperor Otto II's sarcophagus lid turned upside-down, with a metal cover made specially by Carlo Fontana.

Treasury

St Peter's treasury contains a choice selection of the bits that the Saracens, Normans, Spaniards and Napoleon didn't steal. Near the entrance are two famous relics from the old basilica: the golden cockerel that Leo IV set atop the campanile, whose cock-a-doodle will announce the end of the world, and the beautiful twisted *Colonna Santa*, of Parian marble, traditionally the column on which Christ leaned while disputing with the doctors in the Temple – in the Middle Ages exorcists would place their patients against it to chase out the devil. The bejewelled *Vatican Cross* was given to St Peter's by Justin II in 578, and has portraits of the emperor and empress on the back, who raise their arms as if to say 'Surprise!'; in the same room is the so-called *Dalmatic of Charlemagne*, which tradition claims he wore during his coronation, although it dates from the 11th century (even then, a rare enough example of Byzantine ceremonial dress). Equally intriguing is a 1974 copy of *St Peter's Chair*, the original of the one enclosed in Bernini's Baroque confection, though chances are slim that Peter ever sat in it, as it was donated to the basilica in 875 by Charles the Bald. The upper part is Carolingian, while the lower half, from the 3rd century, is surprisingly decorated with fine ivory reliefs of the *Labours of Hercules*.

Beyond is a lovely marble *tabernacle* (1435) by Donatello, saved from the old basilica; it frames a much revered painting of the *Madonna della Febbre*, invoked against malaria. The *Tomb of Sixtus IV* by Antonio Pollaiuolo (1493) is a masterpiece of bronze casting, with its fine effigy of the sleeping *Pope* and the allegories of the *Seven Virtues* and *Ten Sciences* that adorn its sides; it can be viewed from the platform above. This is followed by a 14th-century Giottesque fresco of *SS. Peter and Paul*, found in the crypt; a 13th-century bust reliquary of *St Luke*; a key of St Peter's tomb (one of many copies made; after a time in the sacred keyhole it would become one of the most prized relics a pilgrim could obtain); Sixtus IV's ring; choir antiphonies embellished with beautiful grotesques; the gilded bronze *SS. Peter and Paul* by Torrigiano (most famous for having broken Michelangelo's nose in a fight); a pair

of enormous candelabra attributed to Cellini; the jewelled tiara that crowns the ancient statue of St Peter, followed by chalices and other Church paraphernalia studded with precious stones, much of it given to the popes since Napoleon; and last, the remarkable *Sarcophagus of Junius Bassus*, prefect of Rome in 359; the reliefs portray Old and New Testament scenes and baby Bacchuses.

Sacred Grottoes

The entrance to the crypt of St Peter's is usually by way of the stair by the Pier of St Longinus. The Grottoes, on the floor level of the old basilica, follow the floor plan of the basilica above, and are lined with tombs: a full house, with a pair of queens, 20 popes, and an emperor. The horseshoe-shaped **Grotte Nuove**, built in 1534–46 under the area of St Peter's altar, are 'new' because their decoration is more recent. Most beautiful here is the Renaissance *Tomb of Paul II*, on which Mino da Fiesole and Giovanni Dalmata laboured for ten years without finishing. Further along, placed in the wall, are lovely marble reliefs from the *baldacchino* made for Sixtus IV. In the centre of the horseshoe, directly under the High Altar and over the *Trophy of Gaius* (the 3rd-century shrine built around St Peter's tomb), is the **Cappella Clementina** (1605); if the lights are on in the necropolis below, you can see a section of it in a gap to the left of the altar.

The adjoining **Grotte Vecchie** were built at the same time that Maderno extended the nave. The central altar has another exquisite Renaissance work, a relief of *Christ in Majesty* from the tomb of Nicholas V, by Giovanni Dalmata (1450s). In the area under St Peter's right aisle are the simple tombs of John XXIII (always covered with flowers), John Paul I, and Paul VI, while those of Christina of Sweden and Charlotte of Cyprus face each other. Canova's large statue of praying *Pius VI*, formerly in the Confessio, was moved to the end of the Grottoes in 1980. The Old Pretender, Bonny Prince Charlie, and Henry, Cardinal of York are in the left aisle, as is the English pope, Adrian IV, in a 3rd-century sarcophagus (no one brings him pretty flowers – the Romans remember him best for burning Arnold of Brescia). Off the left aisle are a few rooms used to house fragments of the old basilica.

Dome

To ascend the dome, one of Rome's biggest thrills and chills (especially if you suffer from vertigo), leave the basilica and join the queue on the far right-hand side of the square. You can take a lift – it's another 200 steps from the roof to the top of the dome.

The lift leaves you on the roof, a strange world of domes on wavy pavement, where you can measure yourself against the saintly titans who will look over Piazza San Pietro until kingdom come; here, too, is a souvenir shop, post office, soft drinks machine, WCs, and buildings of the workmen who maintain the basilica. In the old days they not only worked on the roof, but lived here with their families, producing sons who scoffed at heights and would later inherit their jobs.

Stairs within the dome lead up to the **First Gallery**, for a death-defying view 173ft above the floor of St Peter's that brings home the basilica's scale. A narrower stair, tilted for the curve in the dome, continues up to the **Second Gallery**, 240ft up, but this is closed to the public. An even narrower spiral stair continues the rest of the way up to the terrace under the lantern, from where, on a clear day, all Rome, much of the *campagna*, and the Tyrrhenian coast lie spread out at your feet. The golden ball, which looks like a marble from below, is actually big enough to hold 16 people.

Ancient Necropolis of St Peter's

Open by reservation only for 1½-hour guided visits (in English); **adm** *€8. Call the Ufficio degli Scavi, t 06 6988 5318, for information; then fax them, f 06 6988 5518, with your name, nationality, the language you want a tour in, the dates you are in Rome, an email address and a contact number in Rome – they will then confirm a date and time for the tour.*

In 1939, when Pius XII ordered the workmen to lower the floor of the Sacred Grottoes and prepare a tomb for Pius XI, they discovered not only the floor of the Constantinian basilica, but below this, signs of an ancient tomb. Although its existence has been documented since Bramante's day, Pius XII was the first pope to consent to an exploration of the area (previous popes had superstitiously feared to disturb the bones, or worse yet, to learn that the Saracens in 846 had stolen St Peter's relics after all). During the war, the secret excavations continued, uncovering one of the most remarkable sights in all Rome: the Ancient Necropolis of St Peter's, a pristine street of pagan and early Christian tombs built around that of the Apostle.

Apparently the pagan tombs originally overlooked the Vatican Circus, so the dead could enjoy the games even in the afterlife. The guides know their subject well and take you past the delightful, brightly painted tombs lined with niches for urns, described by H.V. Morton as 'little sitting-rooms for the soul'. The burials date from AD 150–300; the Christians, naturally, are near St Peter; one tomb has what is believed to be the earliest Christian mosaic ever found – *Christ depicted as the sun god Helios*.

Deep under the High Altar the excavations revealed the red walls of a shrine, or *aedicula*, believed to be the so-called *Trophy of Gaius* (built around AD 160, and described by the priest Gaius around the year 200). When constructing St Peter's basilica, Constantine enclosed the trophy in marble and porphyry, filled in the tombs, and laboriously excavated a section of the Vatican hill to ensure that this spot would be under the altar. Physical evidence was found of the Saracens' raid, and a hole which probably contained St Peter's bronze casket. But outside the *aedicula* were found the headless bones of a strong old man; graffiti on the wall above invoke the aid of St Peter. After years of consideration, Paul VI announced that these bones were indeed the relics of St Peter. Jammed around are the tombs of Christians anxious to be buried near the Apostle. No one is quite sure how far the pagan tombs extend – but it could be as far as Castel Sant'Angelo.

VATICAN MUSEUMS

*Viale Vaticano, t 06 6988 1662 (Mon–Sat 8.30–7); **metro** Ottaviano, **tram** 19, **bus** 23, 32, 34, 40, 46, 49, 62, 64, 81, 492; wheelchair accessible. **Open** Mar–Oct Mon–Fri 8.30–3.30, Sat 8.30–12.30; Nov–Feb Mon–Sat 8–12.30; **adm** €9. **Also open** last Sun of the month 8.30–12.30; **adm** free (packed with Romans).*

It's a half-mile hike around Michelangelo's forbidding walls to the museums' entrance on Viale Vatican (C5–D6) and the entrance fee is twice that of any other sight in Rome, but the popes give value for money: 12 museums, two miles of galleries, the Sistine Chapel, Stanze di Raffaello and Borgia Apartment – and there isn't much dull museum clutter to pass over lightly. Seeing all 7km of exhibits would take a lifetime but, on the bright side, the museum is managed more thoughtfully than any run by the Italian state. It has won an EU award for welcoming people with disabilities; there are two routes for people in wheelchairs – ask the guards at the entrance.

To control the crowds, the Vatican imposes a shorter (2hr) and a longer (4hr) itinerary. In practice, the guards don't mind if you change your itinerary, but they will enforce the one-way rule if the galleries are full.

Don't be discouraged as you squeeze down the dangerously narrow pavement to the entrance. Within the museums all is tidy and almost rational. An impressive double spiral ramp of steps (1932, by Giuseppe Momo) takes you up to the gallery level and the museums' main crossroads, the **Atrio dei Quattro Cancelli**; from here a door leads into the most striking feature, the **Cortile del Belvedere**, enclosed by twin half-mile long galleries. Designed by Bramante for Julius II as a great outdoor auditorium, the courtyard has since been subdivided.

The section you can now see is the **Cortile della Pigna** (named for the monstrous bronze pine cone, once part of a fountain by the Temple of Isis, and later a landmark on the Portico of Old St Peter's) leading to the **Braccio Nuovo**. If you want to see the fabulous collection of antique sculpture you must first pass through the Egyptian Museum.

Egyptian Museum

Founded by Gregory XVI in the 1830s and housed in earnest, phoney Egyptian rooms, this has the usual mummies, *sarcophagi*, figurines, monumental statues of gods and pharaohs (a sandstone *bust of Mentuhotep II* is one of the finest and also the oldest in the museum, *c.*2040 BC). Keeping him company are bizarre deities – baboonish Thot with chin on knees and a cooky grin, and the pot-bellied moon-faced Bes.

Most people walk right through **Room III** without realizing that its contents are Roman imitations of Egyptian art, nearly all made for Hadrian's Villa at Tivoli; so pop back and have a look: the presence of little wolf-headed gods in togas and a marble Egyptianized statue of his beloved Antinous gives it away, if nothing else.

Chiaramonti Sculpture Gallery

This long, dead-end gallery jam-packed with busts, reliefs, and statues – Greek originals, Roman copies, and Roman originals – was founded by Pius VII and arranged by Canova. It occupies half of Bramante's east gallery and probably should be skipped if you're pressed for time or not a serious student of ancient art. Otherwise, it's worth a stroll for the nightmarish hypnosis of being watched by a 1,000ft double row of blank eyeballs. A 5th-century BC Greek *bust of Athena* in section XVI, startles with her keen gaze of ivory and semi-precious stones; she at least can see you, she knows you're really looking for *Apollo Belvedere* (*see* below).

Braccio Nuovo

Built in 1822 as an extension of the Chiaramonti Gallery, this was graced with a number of celebrated works: a fine copy of the *Wounded Amazon*, Polycletus' prize winner in a 5th-century competition in Ephesus; a copy of a famous 3rd-century statue of the orator *Demosthenes*, whose marble mouth betrays his stutter; a Hellenistic statue of *The Nile*, who reclines like Goliath near a little sphinx, with 16 lilliputian children (the 16 cubits the Nile rises when flooded); and nearby, a noble bust of the young *Marcus Aurelius* (no.94), and a not-so-noble one of *Mark Antony* (89). Beyond is the central hall with the *Giustiniani Athena*, an excellent copy of a famous 4th-century BC work; a fine portrait bust of *Philip the Arab* (Emperor in 121); the *Doryphoros*, or spear thrower, a copy of a Greek original by Polycletus, a work famous for its study of human proportions; the lovely *Modesty*, actually the Greek mother of the Muses, Mnemosyne (Memory); and the handsome *Augustus of Prima Porta*, found at the Villa di Livia at Prima Porta, and considered the finest portrait of the emperor. He wears a beautifully carved cuirass, showing the king of Parthia returning to Tiberius the Roman military insignia captured from Crassus in 53 BC; the Cupid on the dolphin refers to the Julian family's Venusian ancestry. The only detail lacking is his platform sandals (usually hidden by a toga; Augustus was only 5ft 7in).

Museo Pio Clementino

This contains the Vatican's most celebrated classical sculpture, and its most irritating plaster fig leaves. The first prize is the 3rd-century BC Etruscan-influenced *Sarcophagus of L. Cornelius Scipio*, taken from the Tomb of the Scipios; the second, in Room X, is an excellent Roman copy of Lysippus' 4th-century bronze *Apoxyomenos* (the 'Scraper'), the weary athlete scraping oil from his body after his game.

Beyond is the **Octagonal Court of the Belvedere**, which lent the marble *Apollo Belvedere* his name; this is a 2nd-century copy of Leochares' bronze statue that once stood in the Athenian Agora, and shows the young god, long held as the paragon of male beauty, looking after an arrow he has just shot. Clockwise, he is followed by an original relief from Augustus' Ara Pacis, and beyond, the famous *Laocoön*, discovered near Nero's Golden House in 1506 and immediately recognized as the famous group described by Pliny the Elder. Sculpted *c.*50 BC by the Rhodian sculptors Agesander and his sons Polydoros and Athenodoros, this most violent and contorted of all Hellenistic sculpture portrays the Trojan priest of Apollo, Laocoön, with his two young sons struggling desperately in the constricting coils of the sea serpents sent by Apollo as punishment for telling the truth about Greeks bearing gifts. A photo of a plaster cast shows how the group appeared for centuries, according to Michelangelo's idea; the present reconstruction came about when Laocoön's original arm was found in a pawn shop. Next, guarding the exit, are two Hellenistic hounds from Pergamon, and beyond them a Roman copy of Praxiteles' beautiful *Hermes* and a *Perseus*, carrying the head of Medusa, by the neoclassical sculptor Canova, who made it to compensate for some of the ancient pieces carted off by Napoleon.

A door between the hounds fittingly leads into a delightful bronze and marble zoo. Some of the animals are antique (the sow, the camel head, *Meleager*, a young marble god who wouldn't look out of place pestering females on the Spanish Steps, with his dog and boar's head, and *Mithras* slaying a bull while a scorpion goes for its testicles) but the rest were made in the 18th century for Pius VI, by sculptor Francesco Antonio Franzoni. The colourful mosaics of animals are from Hadrian's Villa in Tivoli.

The **Gallery of Statues** (Room V) has two fine copies of Praxiteles' work: *Apollo Sauroktonos* (the god about to kill a lizard) and the *Resting Satyr*; the so-called *Eros of Centocelle* (no.250), copy of a 4th-century BC Greek statue, a charming work said to represent Thanatos, or Death; the *Sleeping Ariadne*, a copy of a Hellenistic original, with the famous 2nd-century AD Barberini

Candelabra on either side, found in Hadrian's Villa, where they were used to support flaming lamps.

At the end of the Gallery of Statues is the **Gallery of Busts** (often closed), featuring portraits of *Caracalla*, the ugly brute (no.292), *Julius Caesar*, *Augustus* as a youth (273), the fair *Antinous* (357) and the seated *Jupiter Verospi*. Backtracking through the Gallery of Statues you might find the **Gabinetto delle Maschere** open, named after the brightly coloured theatrical mask mosaics from Hadrian's Villa; it contains one of the best copies of Praxiteles' *Venus of Cnidus* (4th-century BC), the famous nude commissioned by the people of Kos and rejected for its voluptuous nudity, a prudery not shared by the Cnidians, who set it up in a seaside temple as a tourist attraction.

Backtrack further, through the animal room, to the great octagonal **Sala delle Muse**, where Roman copies of 4th-century BC Greek muses, *Apollo*, Greek philosophers and writers (*Homer*, *Socrates*, *Plato*, *Euripides*, etc.) gaze upon the taut, muscled *Torso del Belvedere* in the centre, signed by Apollonius of Athens (1st century BC), found in the Campo de' Fiori, snapped up by Julius II, and much studied by Michelangelo.

The next room, the **Sala Rotonda,** is a neoclassical copy of the Pantheon, built around an enormous porphyry basin from Nero's Golden House; the floor is paved with the *Mosaic of Otricoli*, representing a battle of Greeks and centaurs, and a sea fight between the mermen. Among the busts of the emperors is the magnificent head of *Jupiter of Otricoli* (no.539) next to a serenely beautiful *Antinous* dressed as Bacchus, much studied by Bernini and other sculptors in Rome; beside him stands *Demeter*, or Ceres, a fine copy of a 5th-century BC original, and next to her towers a gilded bronze *Hercules* with a tiny ET-like head, originally in Pompey's Theatre.

Room I, the **Hall of the Greek Cross**, has two remarkable porphyry *sarcophagi*, of *St Helen* (with nary a Christian symbol in sight among the Roman soldiers, war-captives and phallic missiles) and the less warlike tomb (with palaeo-Christian symbols of peacocks, grapes, etc.) of *Constantia*, the nasty daughter or granddaughter of Constantine, brought here from the church of S. Costanza.

Museo Gregoriano Etrusco

Founded in 1837 by Gregory XVI, this museum is too good to skip. Recently reorganized, the Etruscan collection was mostly unearthed in Southern Etruria, the land of the old Papal States, and features the 7th century BC **Regolini-Galassi Tomb**, discovered near Caere and reconstructed here, with its fine golden ornaments and tomb furniture for two, a warrior and a priest of considerable standing. Elsewhere you can see fine bronzes, especially the 4th-century *Mars of Todi*, influenced by the Greeks; along with beautifully engraved mirrors and boxes (*cistae*) for toiletries, some charming examples of the Etruscan knack for portraiture.

The Greeks never cared for it, although they would probably have approved of Bramante's elegant stair, which can be seen from one of the next rooms; each column is of a slightly different length (a kind of *entasis*, as used by the Greeks in building the Parthenon), here creating the illusion of a perfect spiral.

Room XII, of the **Greek Originals**, houses superb works from the 5th century BC: a *head of Athena*, fragments from the Parthenon friezes, and loveliest of all, the *funeral stele of a young athlete with his servant*.

The two floors of the **Hemicycle**, embracing the pine cone in the court, are home to a collection of vases imported by the Etruscans from Greece in the 7th–5th centuries BC: the black-figured *amphora* of Achilles and Ajax playing dice, signed by Exekias; the famous *kylix* by Duris, of *Oedipus solving the riddle of the Sphinx*; and upstairs, a *hydria* of Apollo of Delphi on a tripod and a jug with a *Scene of a cockfight*. Other vases in these rooms, from Magna Grecia and Etruria, make interesting comparisons.

The Long Galleries and the Upper Floor

The popes decorated these interlinking galleries, which lead to the papal apartments and the Sistine Chapel, in various styles. They begin with the **Gallery of the Candelabra**, named for the ancient marble pairs of candelabra that stand sentry among its sculpture, with especially good sarcophagus reliefs. The next section, the **Gallery of the Tapestries**, is hung with 16th-century tapestries woven to designs by the 'New School' of Raphael – by his pupils after his death, based on his drawings. Next comes the equally long **Gallery of Maps**, with colourful 16th-century frescoes of Italy's regions and cities and papal territories by a Dominican monk and cartographer, Ignazio Danti, painted for Gregory XIII, best known for reforming Caesar's calendar. The last bit of corridor is the **Gallery of Pius V**, with 15th-century tapestries from Tournai, including a *Last Supper* represented as a Renaissance dinner party; the **Sobieski Room**, with a painting of the Polish king who came to the relief of Turk-besieged Vienna in 1683; and the **Hall of the Immaculate Conception**.

Stanze di Raffaello

These small rooms were built by Nicholas V as his private apartments and were originally frescoed by Piero della Francesca, Andrea del Castagno and Benedetto Bonfigli; when Julius II was elected, he hired Signorelli, Il Sodoma, Lorenzo Lotto, Perugino, and Peruzzi to finish the decoration. Yet this unique trove of Renaissance art was utterly destroyed when Julius was smitten by the 26-year-old Raphael – as if there wasn't enough empty wall space left to fresco! But the Pope wanted nothing less than the most up-to-date interior decoration, and the sweetheart of the Renaissance obliged by painting some of his greatest masterpieces. Though a mind-boggling egomaniac, Julius II had whatever mixture of bullying, kindness, and coaxing it took to get the very best from his artists.

Raphael began the Stanze in 1509 and left them unfinished at his death in 1520. Yet in these four little rooms you can trace his progress over his years in Rome, if at least you're prepared to skip back and forth to see them in the order in which they were painted. The official route begins with the Stanza di Costantino, and runs through the Stanza di Eliodoro and Stanza della Segnatura to the Stanza dell'Incendio, but we recommend starting with the Stanza della Segnatura.

Stanza della Segnatura

The room where the pope signed his bulls contains the very quintessence of the High Renaissance in its celebrated frescoes. These were Raphael's first works for Julius II (1508–11), and done entirely by his hand. On the long wall, his first fresco, the *Disputation on the Holy Sacrament,* glorifies the triumph of religious truth, and masterfully portrays two zones; the heavenly one shows God the Father, Christ, the Virgin, John the Baptist, and an intermingling of figures from the Old and New Testaments (the latter with haloes). On the terrestrial sphere, grouped around the altar with a monstrance of the Host, are the Doctors of the Church, popes, bishops, and the faithful, including, on the far left, Fra Angelico, and Dante (with a laurel crown) on the right, and Savonarola, made to play the bad guy in the black hat.

Opposite is the great *School of Athens* or the triumph of philosophical truth, a painting that has become a symbol for the Renaissance itself. Set in an imaginary temple, suggested by Raphael's mentor Bramante and by the Baths of Diocletian, the fresco depicts the greatest philosophers and scholars, separated into two camps on either side of the central figures of Plato, holding a copy of *Timaeus* (perhaps with Leonardo da Vinci's features, although Leonardo's interest in nature would make him more of an Aristotelian), and Aristotle, holding his *Ethics*. On Plato's side it's easy to find the snub-nosed Socrates making a point with Alcibiades, dressed in armour, next to the

The Worst Pope

It would be no easy job to decide which popes made the greatest contributions to religion and culture. Many fine papal art commissions are described elsewhere, and the best of the popes, no doubt, are written up in heaven in St Peter's book; just for fun we have tried to find the worst for ours. This too has its difficulties; out of the myriad scoundrels, drunkards, thieves, children, idiots, poison artists, political tools, gluttons and perverts who have decorated St Peter's throne over two millennia, we have found some candidates, based on a minimum of scholarship and a good dose of spleen.

We cannot agree with the obvious choice: **Alexander VI**, the notorious Borgia pope. Although a reasonably effective looter of Church money, a sex-crazed hedonist, and possibly a closet pagan, his greatest sins seem to have been first, not spreading the grease widely enough, and second, not having been born an Italian. The constant vilification he received from his contemporaries convinces us he wasn't such a bad fellow after all, and didn't poison nearly as many people as he is given credit for.

Sifting through the evidence, here are some of the top contenders for the prize: **Benedict IX** (1033–46), heir of Marozia, the third pope in succession to come from the family of the Counts of Tusculum. Elected at the age of ten, this 'Nero of the papacy' took to rapine and homicide at an early age. Twice he was deposed, and once put the papacy up for auction in order to marry an unwilling sweetheart. **Boniface VIII** (1294–1303), the most arrogant and unlovable of popes, who wrecked the powerful medieval papacy with his impostures. He got his job by tricking his predecessor, the saintly but not too clever hermit Celestine V, into abdicating. During a council at the Castel Nuovo in Naples, Boniface whispered through a hidden tube into the pope's cell, pretending to be the voice of God commanding him to quit. **John XII** (955–63). Another of the house of Tusculum, and another teenager, best known for the harem he maintained at the Vatican. **Leo X**, the Medici pope (1513–22). 'Let us enjoy the papacy, since God has given it to us,' said Leo. In fact it wasn't God, but Leo's father, Lorenzo de' Medici, whose money purchased the office. Enjoy it he did – and almost

---

shorter figure of Xenophon. On the far left, in bearded profile, is Zeno, near Epicurus crowned with vine leaves; in the forefront sits Pythagoras, writing down his harmonic scale with Averroes in a turban and bald Empedocles looking on. Julius had Raphael add his young hostage, Federigo Gonzaga, seated behind Averroes, and his nephew, Francesco Maria della Rovere, the fair youth in white. No one is quite sure of the identity of the prominent figure with one foot on a block of marble; but the seated figure to the right is Heraclitus, the great pessimist, who did not appear in the original cartoon and was added by Raphael after half of the scaffolding was taken down from the Sistine Chapel ceiling. Like everyone else in Rome he was astonished, and he paid Michelangelo the sincerest of compliments by painting the philosopher in his style.

On Aristotle's side, Diogenes the cynic sprawls on the steps, while in the foreground is Euclid, with Bramante's features, teaching his students; to the right, wearing a crown (a confusion with the Hellenistic dynasty in Egypt) and holding a terrestrial sphere, is the back of Ptolemy, facing Zoroaster, holding a celestial sphere. To his right stand Raphael himself and Sodoma, the older man in a cap.

Above the window is *Parnassus*, representing Beauty, with Apollo playing his violin for the Muses and the poets, including on the left Homer, Dante, Virgil, and Sappho, and on the right Ovid and Boccaccio, and seated, Horace and Pindar. Across are the Virtues of Fortitude, Temperance, and Prudence, by Raphael, and below, symbolic of Law, Justinian delivering the Pandects by Perin del Vaga, who also had a hand in Gregory IX handing the Decretals to Raymond de Penafort (the Pope is a portrait of Julius II).

bankrupted it, while his attempts to make up the deficit by selling indulgences and bishoprics were an immediate cause of the Reformation. **Stephen VII** (896–7), an agent of the Dukes of Spoleto who was so rotten, he exhumed the corpse of his predecessor, Pope Formosus, and put it on trial (see p.165).

No one could dispute the credentials of **Paul IV** (1555–9), one nasty piece of work. Giovanni Carafa was the real father of the Inquisition, and his reign of terror in his native Naples caused a revolution there. As pope, he presided over the height of the Counter-Reformation, burning more books and more Christians than any other pope, all the while milking the Church to enrich his family. Paul's hobby was persecuting Jews, and one of the proudest acts of his reign was the creation of the Roman Ghetto.

But there is a sentimental favourite. Not as vicious as many, and living in a quiet and decorous age, he nevertheless could claim the award for his pure grasping, grubby mediocrity – **Innocent X** (1644–55).

Felix I didn't have a very happy papacy, and **Urban VI** was really a country boy from Campania, but it is this Innocent who can claim the honour of the most misnamed pope. A tremendous grafter, Innocent devoted his undistinguished papacy entirely to the enrichment of his vile family, the Pamphili. A fair judge of art, he oversaw the development of Piazza Navona (meant to increase property values around his new family palace) and prudishly installed all the metal fig leaves and dresses on the Vatican's nude statues.

Innocent met a memorable end – dragging out his last hours while his relatives looted everything around him, even his clothes. Finally there was nothing left but the brass candlestick on his night table – until a servant came back and stole that too. No one could be found to pay for a funeral, and for a while the body lay in a tool shed in the Vatican crypt, in a plain coffin so small that the pope's feet stuck out the end.

Francis Marion Crawford, who tells the tale (in *Ave Roma Immortalis*), remarks that eventually the corpse was taken to Sant'Agnese in Piazza Navona, where, 'in the changing course of human and domestic events, it ultimately got an expensive monument in the worst possible taste'.

Stanza di Eliodoro

This room was painted by Raphael in 1512–14 with subjects chosen by Julius II. The compositions are more dramatic and more richly coloured: the marvellous *Deliverance of St Peter*, with its striking night lighting, shows the angel entering the prison, unchaining St Peter and leading him in the escape. On the main wall is the *Expulsion of Heliodorus from the Temple*, which gave the room its name; the incident portrayed (of King Seleucus' treasurer Heliodorus trying to seize the treasure of the Temple, and chased out by a horseman and angels) is from the Apocrypha (Maccabees II, 3), and refers to Julius II's battles to expel foreign powers from the Papal States; Julius may be seen, watching the scene from his litter. The *Mass of Bolsena*, over the window, represents the miracle of 1263, when a priest who doubted the truth of transubstantiation celebrated mass and found the Host bleeding; Julius II, in a fine portrait, is seen kneeling on the right. The fourth fresco, the *Meeting of St Leo and Attila*, lacks the verve of the others; it is mostly by Raphael's assistants, who had to change St Leo's face from a portrait of Julius II to Leo X when the latter pope was elected. Leo X had already been portrayed among the cardinals, so the same fat face appears twice, enough to spoil any painting.

Stanza dell'Incendio

By this time (1514–17) Leo X was pope, and the subject he chose for the papal dining room was the great fire in the Borgo, in 847, which stopped when the saintly Leo IV made the sign of the cross. This was designed by Raphael and painted by his pupils, and shows his tendency towards Mannerism: grand gestures, greater emphasis on the human body as a means of expression, often in difficult poses, and the use of more violent colours. Leo IV has Leo X's fat features (*see above*); the fresco refers to his efforts to end the flames of war in Italy. The other frescoes in the room, with more pupil than Raphael in them, show Leo X playing Leo III at the *Coronation of Charlemagne* and Leo IV in the *Victory over the Saracens*, both alluding to related events in the life of Leo X. The ceiling, by Raphael's master Perugino, is the only original fresco to survive.

Stanza di Costantino

The last room was painted after Raphael's death by Giulio Romano and pupils; only the *Victory of Constantine over Maxentius* was done after the master's sketches. Beyond this are the **Loggie di Raffaello** (open to scholars with special permission), which Raphael built after Bramante's death, also contributing designs for half of the scenes from the Old Testament (hence the 'Bible of Raphael' in contrast with the Sistine Chapel, the 'Bible of Michelangelo'). Executed by his students, especially Giovanni da Udine, the *loggie* are most interesting for their grotesque borders, inspired by a visit to Nero's Golden House.

Also off the Stanza di Costantino is the **Sala dei Palafrenieri** (better known as the **Sala dei Chiaroscuri** for its monochrome Raphael-school frescoes) with a beautiful carved ceiling glorifying the Medici, and beyond that, a memory of a simpler and more pious age, the small **Chapel of Nicholas V**. This was closed off and forgotten until someone, counting the windows of the Vatican palace, noted that there was an extra one; inside are rarefied, pastel frescoes by Fra Angelico, on the *lives of SS. Stephen and Lawrence*.

Borgia Apartment

Although the words 'Borgia Apartment' in the popular mind may conjure up a Chamber of Horrors, it is actually one of the most delightful corners of the Vatican, intimate and embellished with all the colours of spring. The rooms were frescoed in 1492–5 for Alexander VI by Pinturicchio (whose name means 'rich painter' for his use of gold

and expensive colours), a Renaissance reactionary who rejected the innovations in colour and composition of contemporaries like Leonardo and Piero della Francesca. Sprinkled throughout are Borgia family symbols of the bull, twin crowns of Aragon, and flaming pennant.

A sample of Pope Paul VI's modern art displayed in the little rooms could not be more incongruous; Pinturicchio's room of Sibyls is next to a room full of copes designed by Matisse. **Rooms III** and **IV** are by Pinturicchio's pupils; Room IV, by Antonio da Viterbo, was Alexander's study, where his daughter Lucrezia would help him with his correspondence, and where his hidden treasure was discovered after his death. The next room (often roped off), with scenes of the saints, is Pinturicchio's masterpiece. According to tradition, the large fresco of the *Disputation of St Catherine of Alexandria and Emperor Maximian* portrays the fair and much calumnied Lucrezia Borgia as St Catherine and Prince Djem, ambitious brother of Sultan Beyazit II, as the oriental soldier on the right; the Sultan paid Alexander to keep him as a 'guest' until, wearied of his company, the pope had him poisoned. Above the far door is a portrait of Alexander VI's mistress, Giulia Farnese. In the next room, of the **Mysteries of the Faith**, Alexander VI's richly robed, unflattered self appears in the scene of the *Resurrection*, with a young Roman bearing the features of his eldest son, the Duke of Gandia, and a soldier believed to be the awful Cesare. The ceiling of the last room collapsed on Alexander's head and almost killed him; Leo X ordered the new beautiful, frescoed and stuccoed ceiling from Perin del Vaga and Giovanni da Udine.

Gallery of Modern Religious Art

Between the Appartamento Borgia and the Cappella Sistina it's a long march through the Vatican's game attempt to prove that modern religious art exists (more by sheer acreage than anything else). But there are a few pearls hidden in the gaudy sea of kitsch, among them some curious works by Chagall, Picasso, Kokoschka, Feininger, Munch, Bacon, Siqueiros and many, many more – and some genuinely beautiful paintings – American Charles Burchfield's *Eye of God in the Woods* and the fairy-tale paintings of Yugoslavs Ivan Lackovic and Ivan Vecenaj.

Sistine Chapel

The Sistine Chapel has been one of Rome's chief tourist attractions ever since the day in 1512 when the weary, paint-spattered Michelangelo finally unlocked the door. (Of course the one time not to come is during a conclave, when the cardinals are sealed inside until they elect a new pope.)

What some people would claim as the greatest achievement in art, ever, by a single artist, a work of consummate vision and genius, may have been the result of petty jealousy and intrigue. According to Vasari's *Lives of the Artists*, Bramante talked Pope Julius into sending his rival Michelangelo up to the ceiling of the ungainly barn of a chapel built by his Della Rovere kinsman, Sixtus IV. Some of the finest painters of the Renaissance had already decorated the walls with a beautiful series on the Old Testament, but the vast ceiling had only a simple pattern of stars. Bramante hoped Michelangelo would refuse the commission and anger the pig-headed pope, or else fritter away the time he needed to work on the tomb.

Michelangelo hated the idea, but Julius was adamant, and in 1508, he reluctantly agreed to get out his brushes. The pope, like most Renaissance patrons, required only some virtuoso interior decoration: until then, ceiling frescoes had been simple small-scale patterns. Julius envisaged something similar, only somewhat bigger (131ft by 42ft, equal to the wall surface of 4½ average suburban bungalows). No one can say what drove Michelangelo to create a masterpiece instead: the fear of wasting his time, the challenge of an impossible task, or maybe

just to spite Bramante and Julius – he exasperated the Pope by making him wait four long years, and refused all demands that he hire some assistants. 'When will you finish?' railed Julius. 'When I can,' the equally stubborn Michelangelo invariably replied. The Pope was ready to hurl him off the scaffolding when Michelangelo finally agreed to forego the highlights in gold and blue and let Julius show Rome and the world what he had got for his 3,000 ducats: no mere illustrations from the Scriptures, but the way the Old Testament looked in the deepest recesses of his imagination.

Centuries of candle smoke slowly darkened Michelangelo's masterpiece, as well as incidents like that which occurred at the conclave that elected John Paul I, when clouds of black smoke meant to issue from the chimney backed up into the chapel, nearly suffocating the 111 cardinals. Now that the restorers (financed by a Japanese TV network) have finished their controversial cleaning of the ceiling, it is more startling than ever. Michelangelo's true colours have been revealed – bright yellows, sea-green and purple, with dramatic shadows – colours no interior decorator would ever dream of using. He totally eschewed stage props; one of the tenets of his art was that complex ideas could be expressed by the portrayal of the human body alone. Perhaps the inspiration that kept Michelangelo suffering on the ceiling (and the physical hardship, in the heat and cold, was extreme; it is said that after painting it he could only read letters by holding them over his head) was the chance of distilling from the book of Genesis and his own genius an entirely new vocabulary of images, Christian and intellectual. His most original innovation, the famous nude youths, or *Ignudi*, may well represent forms he despaired of ever having the time to sculpt; they also serve as a unique perspective device, and like the rest of the ceiling's programme, probably have a deeper, secret meaning that would take years of inspired wondering to decipher. Michelangelo's style became more daring and confident as he painted; compare *The Intoxication of Noah*, where he began, with the impressionistic *Separation of Light and Darkness* by the altar. Most rubberneckers (and after looking up for a while, you'll wish your neck really was made of rubber) direct their attention to the all too famous scene of the *Creation of Man*, perhaps the only representation of God the Father ever painted that escapes being merely ridiculous. Here, one might suspect that the figure is really some ageing Florentine artist, and that Michelangelo only forgot to paint the brush in his hand. Along the sides are six-toed prophets and powerful Russian masseuse Sibyls (Michelangelo never had much use for women, even as models); in the lunettes over the windows are figures of the forerunners of Christ.

The magnificent, supremely confident spirit of the High Renaissance in first bloom, when man was the measure of all things and man was a giant, never recovered from the shock of the Sack of Rome. Seven years after that brutal event, in 1534 (22 years after the ceiling), Paul III commissioned Michelangelo to paint the harrowing *Last Judgement* on the altar wall; its utter disenchantment with the world is in violent contrast with the ceiling. The saints swarming around the beardless, implacable Christ demand vengeance on humanity for their martyr-doms, while angels come hurtling over, bearing the Cross, the crown of thorns, the pillar from Pilate's palace as if to remind Christ of his own passion. Only the Virgin shows any sign of pity, but she shrinks back against her son, unable to intervene (curiously, Michelangelo's preliminary sketches show her actively imploring mercy). Just below and to the right of Christ gestures a furious St Bartholomew (a portrait of Pietro Aretino, Renaissance satirist and one of Michelangelo's bitter critics. He clutches a skin with the features of the artist he had 'flayed'). To the right below him, isolated from the angels sounding the trumpets of doom, and from another group beating the condemned down to hell, is perhaps the most famous vision of despair in art, the damned soul, hugging himself, one eye uncovered and open wide in a horror beyond words; he is made doubly effective by being the only figure in the whole composition to gaze out at the viewer.

Nippon TV also financed the restoration of the *Last Judgement*, leaving a square on the top right to show the pre-1994 candle-darkened hues. The delicate question of whether or not to remove the 'breeches' from the nude figures added by Daniele da Volterra (on orders from Pius IV, in 1564, the year of Michelangelo's death) became a moot point when the restorers found nothing under them but bare plaster. Presumably da Volterra scraped off the painted genitalia. Just as well for him that the maestro was dead – the prudish Biagio da Cesena, Paul III's secretary, dared to criticize the nudity while the artist was alive and ended up being painted in hell as Midas (entwined in a serpent's coils, with asses' ears). When he complained to the Pope, he received the famous reply, that had Michelangelo placed him in Purgatory he could have helped, but over Hell he had no influence.

Pull your eyes away from Michelangelo to take in the lovely Cosmatesque-like floor, the marble screen by Mino da Fiesole, Giovanni Dalmata and Andrea Bregno, and the frescoes of the lives of Moses and Christ along the walls. Among the finest are Botticelli's *The Burning Bush*, *Moses Driving the Midianites from the Well*, the *Daughters of Jethro*, with maidens full of Botticellian grace, and the *Punishment of Korah, Dathan, and Abiram*, set in Rome, before the Arch of Constantine and the ruined Septizonium. On the other side is Ghirlandaio's *Calling of Peter and Andrew* and Perugino's *Christ Donating the Keys to St Peter*, set before an ideal Renaissance temple.

Library Gallery

The lower floor of Bramante's long corridor is lined with cupboards holding some of the Vatican Library's million books, and tens of thousands of manuscripts and *incunabula*.

The core of the collection dates back to the humanist Pope Nicholas V. The most precious and secret were removed in 1983 to a bunker 40ft underground, but many unique possessions are on display, such as the 16th-century maps in the **Gallery of Urban VIII**, Bramante's wooden machine for stamping the papal seal, or *bollo*, on documents (hence 'bull') and a fresco showing the erection of the obelisk in Piazza S. Pietro in 1586.

Pinacoteca

Rome's finest collection of paintings is arranged in chronological order, beginning with Byzantines and medieval Italians, including 'Big Daisy' Margaritone d'Arezzo's *St Francis of Assisi*, a near-contemporary portrait, and the elegant Bernardo Daddi's paintings on *The Life of St Stephen*, and the light-bulb shaped *Universal Judgement* (11th century) signed by Giovanni and Nicolò of Rome, who invented much of their own iconography.

In **Room II** centre stage is given to the *Stefaneschi Triptych*, by Giotto and assistants, taken from the Confessio of Old St Peter's, portraying the martyrdoms of SS. Peter and Paul on either side of the enthroned Christ (note the donor, Cardinal Stefaneschi, kneeling to the left). Sharing the same room are beauiful works by early Tuscan masters Daddi, Simone Martini, Pietro Lorenzetti, Lorenzo Monaco, and Gentile da Fabriano.

In **Room III** are Fra Angelico's brightly coloured *Scenes from the Life of St Nicholas of Bari* and a triptych by the more worldly monk, Filippo Lippi; Room IV is dedicated to Melozzo da Forlì's charming frescoes of angel musicians from SS. Apostoli, and the famous Sixtus IV conferring the Vatican librarianship on the humanist Platina, with the Pope's nephew, the future Julius II, standing between Platina and the Pope.

Rooms V and **VI** house 15th-century paintings and polyptychs, including a fine *Pietà* by Carlo Crivelli. **Room VII** is devoted to the Umbrians: Perugino's *Madonna Enthroned with Saints* and a work by Raphael's father,

Giovanni Santi, which hardly prepares you for **Room VIII**, dedicated to the works of his son.

The *Coronation of the Virgin*, painted by Raffaello Sanzio at age 20; the *Madonna di Foligno*, painted for Sigismondo Conti of Foligno as an ex-voto, after he survived a cannon ball hitting his house; and Raphael's last painting, the *Transfiguration*, unfinished at his death and placed on his bier; the bottom half, showing the healing of a mad boy, was completed by his students, Giulio Romano and Francesco Penni. Also in this room are tapestries woven in Brussels after Raphael's cartoons and originally hung in the Sistine Chapel.

Room IX contains Rome's only work by Leonardo da Vinci, an unfinished monochrome *St Jerome*, and a lovely *Pietà* by Giovanni Bellini. In the next rooms are later works, of which Caravaggio's *Deposition* is the most striking, where again the viewer is drawn uncannily into the scene by the gaze of a figure.

Also look for one of the finest of Domenichino's paintings, the *Communion of S. Girolamo*; Poussin's surgical *Martyrdom of S. Erasmo*; Titian's *Madonna dei Frari* (where the artist placed his name between the saints and the Madonna), and his *Portrait of Doge Nicolò Marcello* in the last room.

Lateran Museums

These three museums were relocated by John XXIII when the Lateran Palace became the offices of the Vicariate of Rome. The ultramodern building (opened in 1970) is located near the cafeteria, but is currently closed for restoration.

Museo Gregoriano Profano

The first of the museums houses Roman and Greek sculpture and mosaics, much of it in the eclectic, academic neo-Attic style. Founded by Gregory XVI to house Vatican overflow, the Gregoriano Profano has a copy of Myron's 5th-century *Marsyas*; a handsome statue of *Sophocles*, a copy of a 4th-century work, and the *Heraclitus Mosaic*, found on the Aventine and depicting the remains of what must have been a pretty wild banquet.

One of the loveliest ladies in the whole Vatican is the headless *Chiaramonti Niobid*, a Roman copy of a 4th-century Greek original; she is followed by Roman portrait busts and statues, and two snoozing Sileni.

The intriguing *Tomb of the Haterii* is thought to show the funeral of a member of a family of construction workers. They had no qualms about using the sad occasion to advertise their business – the tomb is covered with reliefs of the buildings (including the Colosseum) which they worked on, and a natty Roman crane.

The next section contains a fascinating collection of pagan *sarcophagi*, decorated with reliefs ranging from the *Triumph of Bacchus* to the *Myth of Orestes*. As you go upstairs, be sure to look down on the *Mosaic of Athletes* found in the Baths of Caracalla, a black marble stag, and several fine Roman bas-reliefs.

Museo Pio Cristiano

This has *sarcophagi*, inscriptions, and statues found in the catacombs, of prime importance to the study of the evolution of Christianity in Rome. Among the statues is the famous 3rd-century *Good Shepherd*, showing a young, beardless Christ, inspired by the *Hermes Kriophorus* in the Museo Barracco, and a statue of the martyred doctor *St Hippolytus*, with the dates of Easter for the years 222–334 carved on the side.

On the balcony is part of the tombstone of Abericus, bishop of Hierapolis, who lived in the 2nd century, describing his journeys to Rome and through the Middle East.

Museo Missionario Etnologico

Founded in 1927 by Pius XI, this museum features displays on local cultures, religions and arts from around the world. Among the most curious are native adaptations of Christian iconography; others illustrate missionary activities, along with beautiful wood carvings brought back by priests from South America and Polynesia.

THE BORGO

Another set of walls, originally built by Leo IV after the Saracen raid in 846, surrounds the Borgo, the small neighbourhood in the shadow of St Peter's. The word comes from the Anglo-Saxon burgh, or town, founded in the early 8th century by Anglo-Saxon kings and pilgrims. They were soon followed by the Franks and Frisians, who each built their own *schola* as a school and a hostel to protect their pilgrims from the wiles of Roman innkeepers. Today the Borgo, numbed by the predominance of its self-contained institutions, retains few memories of its English origins beyond its street names. But it, too, has a mastodontic landmark of its own – the Castel Sant'Angelo.

Via della Conciliazione E–F7

Bus *32, 39, 40, 62, 81, 492.*

This ugly boulevard is one of the Borgo's blights. As you leave Piazza San Pietro, note the building to the left of Bernini's colonnade: this is the **Palazzo del Sant'Uffizio** (D7), or Holy Office, or Inquisition. The same kind of perversely reasoned force that it used to stamp out heresy was employed in 1936–50 to bulldoze two pleasant old lanes of the Borgo and create Via della Conciliazione, planned as a triumphal way to St Peter's, and an opportunity to view the famous dome. Critics have always complained that it ruined one of the best surprises in Rome, that of suddenly stumbling upon Bernini's grand piazza. Worst of all, its bossy airs make Via della Conciliazione a sterile no man's land, a runway for squadrons of tourist buses descending on St Peter's, souvenir shops with 3D winking Jesuses – and three Renaissance *palazzi* salvaged by Mussolini's new 'Ruinantes': the **Palazzo dei Convertendi**, on the left at no.34, where Raphael died of love and exhaustion and an ill-advised bleeding by his surgeons, reassembled here in the 1930s from its site in Via Scossacavalli; in the next block, no.30, **Palazzo Torlonia**, a 1504 mini-Cancelleria palace by Andrea Bregno, headquarters of Rome's richest banking family; and opposite, at no.33, the **Palazzo dei Penitenzieri**, built in the 1470s (now a hotel).

Ospedale di Santo Spirito in Sassia E7

Borgo Santo Spirito 2, t 06 687 9310; bus 23, 46, 98, 280, 870, 881, 982. Chapel open daily 7.30–12 and 3–7.30.

This hospital, successor to the Schola Anglorum, was founded by King Ina of Wessex in 717, and was the largest and best run of the Borgo's national school-hospices. Unfortunately, it was made of wood, and went up like a torch in the great fire of 847 (depicted in the Stanze di Raffaello in the Vatican). Seven years later, King Ethelwolf came with his son, the future Alfred the Great, and rebuilt the Schola, funding it and the pope by a voluntary contribution of his subjects known as Peter's Pence – which soon became a mandatory hearth tax until Henry VIII abolished it (curiously, a fortune in Plantagenet silver pennies was discovered in 1883, hidden in the House of the Vestal Virgins). Among the most famous pilgrims to have stayed in the Borgo were Macbeth, who came in 1050 with a guilty conscience, and the semi-legendary Tannhauser, who came in the 13th century and was refused absolution for his love of Venus. But by the time he arrived (walking the whole way with his eyes shut, to deny himself the beauty of Italy), the English had let their Schola decline to such a state that Innocent III converted it into a hospital (1204). It was rebuilt in 1473 as Rome's main home for foundlings – an improvement on the old practice of leaving unwanted children on the banks of the Tiber. You can still see the wooden revolving table in the façade where infants could be anonymously dropped until the mid-19th century. Next to it is the church of **Santo Spirito in Sassia** (E7) – as in Saxony. Although rebuilt after the Sack of Rome, with a façade by Antonio da Sangallo the Younger, it was

founded in the 9th century to serve the Borgo's Anglo-Saxon community.

Castel Sant'Angelo F6

Lungotevere Castello 50; bus 23, 34, 40, 280. Open Tues–Sun 9–7; adm €5, audioguide €3.50. Guided visits by reservation: of the castle in English Tues–Fri 10.30am, Sat–Sun 10.30, 12.15 and 4.30, adm €3.50; of the prisons in English Tues–Fri 3pm, adm €3.50.

Before going into the ancient Mausoleum of Hadrian, note the unusual wall that links the fortress with the Vatican like a stone umbilical cord. Rome is full of aqueducts but this is a pope-a-duct, the famous Covered Passageway used by St Peter's successors since 1277 to escape to the castle when things became too hot to handle. You can see the windows along the top; try to imagine glimpses of the pale Clement VII fleeing down the passage during the Sack of Rome, his robes flying and prelates racing desperately behind to the safety of the fortress-like Castel Sant'Angelo.

Hadrian thought he could not go wrong when he designed this new tomb for the emperors in 138, three years before his own death. He placed it on the uninhabited bank of the pestilential Tiber, where the imperial megalomania would cause no resentment, and he built it solidly to defend his memory against Time itself. Instead, his last resting place has seen more blood, treachery, and turmoil than any in Rome; his ashes were still warm in the urn when Aurelian made it a bulwark in his walls, inaugurating its history as Rome's chief citadel and dungeon.

Hadrian's original design harked back to Augustus' Mausoleum, although on a pharaonic scale, consisting of a massive 292ft solid square base topped by a cylinder 210ft in diameter and 65ft high, made of travertine with a white Parian marble veneer. Like a giant planter, cypresses grew out of its top, while at the very summit of the tower stood a gilded *quadriga* driven by a colossal statue of Hadrian (now replaced by the bronze angel). The emperor was a great art collector, and beautiful statues adorned the sides; these, whether made by Praxiteles or Roman assembly-line chisels, were used as ammunition in 537, when Belisarius' besieged troops were holed up inside the mausoleum: a rain of marble gods that persuaded the Goths to give up the attack. Some 50 years later, when the even deadlier plague besieged Rome, Pope Gregory the Great was leading a procession through the city, praying for divine mercy, when he had a vision of St Michael on top of the mausoleum, sheathing his sword to announce the end of the pestilence. Henceforth it was known as Castel Sant'Angelo.

For a thousand years the master of Castel Sant'Angelo was the master of Rome. There would be no papacy, perhaps, without it, at least not in its present form. With rebellions of some sort occurring on average every two years before 1400, the popes often had recourse to this place of safety. It last saw action in the Sack of 1527, when according to Cellini's *Autobiography* he personally saved the castle and Clement VII from the crazed Lutherans, while back at the Vatican the valiant Swiss Guard were slain to a man. For several months the Pope and his followers watched helplessly as Rome burned; Clement eventually escaped, disguised as a servant. Subsequent popes, fearing similar long stays, had the castle's interiors fashionably decorated, but mostly they found it a convenient prison and torture chamber for the likes of Cellini, Beatrice Cenci and Giordano Bruno. Opera-goers will recognize it from the last act of Puccini's *Tosca*, when Cavaradossi's foul murder makes Tosca literally go over the top (in a memorable performance in New York, the soprano leaped from the stage-set Castel Sant'Angelo onto an over-taut trampoline, and bounced back on stage to wild applause). In 1992 a TV production of the opera was shot on location in Rome at precisely the times specified in Puccini's score and broadcast live to 107 countries. At 5am Rome time, millions watched as the TV Tosca leapt to her death. Actually her fall was a mere 6ft to a pile of cushions.

Nothing very humorous ever happened for real in the castle; from 1849 to 1870 it was occupied by French troops, and until 1901 by the Italians. It then underwent a 30-year restoration and was opened as a museum.

Still, there is something uncanny about Castel Sant'Angelo. It exhales the musty air of one of evolution's mistakes, a muscle-bound dinosaur or ungainly iron-clad ship run aground behind a frilly Baroque bridge. For all the torture and death that stain its bowels it tells no ghost stories. But come back at twilight, when it becomes a malignant vortex for swarms of sparrows that blacken the sky; the parasol pines in its moat-cum-garden vibrate with their wings; their twittering thunder drowns even Rome's traffic. (Their other evening rendezvous is in front of Termini Station.)

Interior

At the entrance of Castel Sant'Angelo, steps descend to the **vestibule**, with four models of the mausoleum's previous incarnations. Straight on is the shaft of fat and lazy Leo X's man-powered lift, which no longer works, so turn right, and walk up Hadrian's sombrely impressive **spiral ramp**, which still preserves patches of its original floor mosaic.

Four ventilation shafts rose up through the earthen tumulus; the third one was converted into a dread prison in the Middle Ages. The ramp leads to a bridge that passes over the gloomy, stripped bare **sepulchral chamber**, where the ashes of the emperor were kept. This bridge was built in 1822 to replace a drawbridge, which could be pulled up to isolate the papal apartments in case of siege. The **Stair of Alexander VI** continues up to the left, to the **Court of the Angel**, named for Raffaello da Montelupo's marble angel, whose position atop the castle was usurped by Van Verschaffelt's bronze Michael in 1753. The court is decorated with piles of cannon balls, and Michelangelo's façade of the **Chapel of Leo X**, perhaps Il Divino's most obscure work (directly across the court, by the stair of Urban VIII). To the right is a row of old guard rooms, housing a **Museum of**

Weapons and Armour featuring Stone Age arrowheads, fancy Renaissance metal suits, and overstretched 18th-century rifles. A door on the left leads into the two **Rooms of Clement VIII**, with an ornate stucco chimney-piece; the **Hall of Justice**, reached through a second doorway near the Chapel of Leo X, is directly over the tomb chamber and was used as the seat of Rome's tribunal in the 16th–17th centuries; it contains a fresco of the Angel of Justice by Perin del Vaga.

Giving on to this room is the **Sala dell'Apollo**, painted with grotesques for Paul III. Beyond this are the two small **Rooms of Clement VII**, where he lived during the Sack of Rome, the first decorated with a frieze by Giulio Romano. They are now used as an art gallery, with a triptych by Giotto's best pupil, Taddeo Gaddi, Montagna's *Madonna and Child* and Signorelli's *Madonna and Saints*.

A passageway leads into the **Courtyard of Alexander VI**, with a pretty Renaissance well-head bearing the Borgia arms and a large catapult ready to fire in case the Goths want to make another go of it. In Alexander's time the courtyard was used for theatrical performances. A small stair leads up to the **Bathroom of Clement VII**, the most charming corner of the castle with its colourful frescoes and stuccoes by Giulio Romano, where the miserable Pope could forget his troubles in a hot bath. The semicircular two-storey building enclosing this was formerly used as prisons, which seem luxurious compared to the cramped and dreadful **Historic Prisons**, down the steps from the courtyard. Skeletons unearthed beneath the floor confirmed the stories of prisoners tortured to death or murdered in their cells. Also down at this level are the vast **Oil Stores**, holding over 20,000 litres for frying meals or pouring on the heads of assailants. The adjacent rooms were grain stores, but the popes used them to store excess political prisoners.

Walk back up to Alexander VI's courtyard, and from there up to the **Loggia of Paul III**, designed by Antonio da Sangallo the Younger. There are excellent views from here and the other galleries that encircle the castle, a restored cell of a political prisoner of the 1830s, and a panoramic bar.

A few steps lead up from the Loggia of Paul III to the main **Papal Apartments**, decorated for Paul III, beginning with the lavishly stuccoed **Sala Paolina**, painted by Perin del Vaga and Pellegrino Tibaldi. Note the *trompe l'oeil* fresco of a doorway, through which a black-robed courtier appears to be entering. The next room, the **Camera del Perseo**, is decorated with a frieze on the myth of Perseus by Perin del Vaga and furnished in 16th-century style; the **Camera di Amore e Psyche**, also painted by Perin del Vaga, is arranged as a bedroom of the same period.

Return to the Sala Paolina, from which a curved corridor painted with grotesques leads to the ornate **Library**; beyond this are two more rooms, the **Camera dell'Adriano** with frescoes of the Mausoleum of Hadrian, and **Camera dei Festoni**, with paintings by Dosso Dossi (*Bacchanal*) and Lorenzo Lotto (*St Jerome* and *Madonna and Saints*). From the Library a stair leads up to three little rooms with more paintings, the **Cagliostra**, so named for the greatest con man of the 18th century, the Count of Cagliostro. Also from the Library, a small passage leads into the circular core of the castle, the **Room of the Secret Archives**, lined with walnut cupboards where the popes stored their treasure until 1870, when it was moved to the Vatican.

From here, a Roman-era stairway built in the thickness of the wall leads up to another circular room, with military memorabilia. Above this is the **Terrace** under the great bronze angel, the scene of the last act of *Tosca*, with a famous view of St Peter's and the rest of Rome. The large bell here, the **Campana della Misericordia**, was only rung when a prisoner was executed in the castle.

Ponte Sant'Angelo F7

Dark, too, is the history of Castel Sant'Angelo's bridge (pedestrian only), Hadrian's *Pons Aelius*, built in 134 to link his Mausoleum to the city (the three central arches are Hadrian's, the other two were added with the Tiber Embankments).

While a solid stillness hangs over the rest of Rome, the famous angels of Ponte Sant'Angelo battle a perpetual Baroque hurricane to display the symbols of Christ's passion; **Bernini's Breezy Maniacs** they were dubbed almost immediately after they appeared in 1688, sculpted to Bernini's design by students. They replace the rows of gallows erected for the Jubilee of 1500, when 18 swinging corpses formed a memorable welcome to Rome, although the death toll was worse in the 1450 Jubilee, when 200 pilgrims were crushed to death in a panic on the bridge. Previously the right bank of the bridge was occupied by the horrible Tor di Nona, a prison tower favoured for night-time executions; both this and Castel Sant'Angelo had permanent nooses on display and they were rarely vacant.

Museum of Purgatory, or Souls of the Dead G6

Lungotevere Prati 12, t 06 6880 6517; bus 70, 81, 87, 186, 492, 628, 913, 926. Open 7.30–11 and 4.30–7; adm free.

Doubting Thomases unconvinced by St Peter's and the rest should continue up the Tiber from Castel Sant'Angelo to this museum in the sacristy of the **Sacro Cuore del Suffragio** (you may have to ask the sacristan to unlock it). Its one dingy display case contains bits of cloth and faded prayer books singed by the burning hands of souls from Purgatory. A handout explains the story of each suffering soul; some dead people do the darndest things!

Outside the Centre

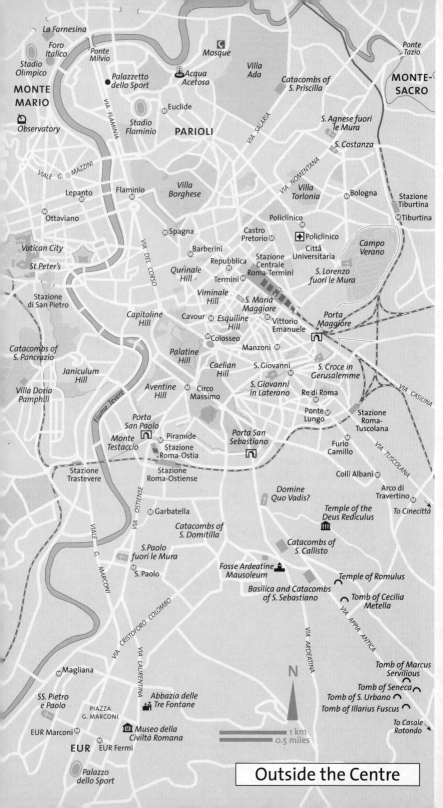

La Farnesina
Foro Italico
Ponte Milvio
Stadio Olimpico
Observatory
MONTE MARIO
Palazzetto dello Sport
Acqua Acetosa
Mosque
Villa Ada
VIA FLAMINIA
Euclide
Stadio Flaminio
PARIOLI
Catacombs of S. Priscilla
Ponte Tazio
MONTE-SACRO
S. Agnese fuori le Mura
S. Costanza
VIA SALARIA
VIALE G. MAZZINI
Lepanto
Ottaviano
Flaminio
Villa Borghese
VIA DEL CORSO
Spagna
VIA NOMENTANA
Villa Torlonia
Bologna
Policlinico
Stazione Tiburtina
Tiburtina
Vatican City
St Peter's
Stazione di San Pietro
Barberini
Repubblica
Quirinale Hill
Termini
Castro Pretorio
Policlinico
Città Universitaria
Stazione Centrale Roma-Termini
S. Lorenzo fuori le Mura
Campo Verano
Catacombs of S. Pancrazio
Capitoline Hill
Cavour
Viminale Hill
Esquiline Hill
Colosseo
S. Maria Maggiore
Vittorio Emanuele
Manzoni
Porta Maggiore
Janiculum Hill
Villa Doria Pamphili
Palatine Hill
Caelian Hill
S. Giovanni
S. Giovanni in Laterano
Re di Roma
S. Croce in Gerusalemme
VIA CASILINA
Aventine Hill
Circo Massimo
Ponte Lungo
Stazione Roma-Tuscolana
Porta San Paolo
Monte Testaccio
Piramide
Stazione Roma-Ostia
Porta San Sebastiano
Furio Camillo
VIA TUSCOLANA
Fiume Tevere
Stazione Trastevere
Stazione Roma-Ostiense
Colli Albani
Arco di Travertino
To Cinecittà
VIA OSTIENSE
Garbatella
Domine Quo Vadis?
Temple of the Deus Rediculus
VIALE G. MARCONI
Catacombs of S. Domitilla
S.Paolo fuori le Mura
S. Paolo
Catacombs of S. Callisto
Temple of Romulus
VIA CRISTOFORO COLOMBO
VIA LAURENTINA
Fosse Ardeatine Mausoleum
Basilica and Catacombs of S. Sebastiano
Tomb of Cecilia Metella
VIA APPIA ANTICA
Magliana
SS. Pietro e Paolo
PIAZZA G. MARCONI
Abbazia delle Tre Fontane
VIA ARDEATINA
Tomb of Marcus Servilious
Tomb of Seneca
Tomb of S. Urbano
Tomb of Illarius Fuscus
To Casale Rotondo
EUR Marconi
Museo della Civiltà Romana
EUR Fermi
EUR
N
1 km
0.5 miles
Palazzo dello Sport

Outside the Centre

NORTH OF THE CENTRE

Foro Italico Outside the Centre map

Lungotevere Marasciallo Diaz; **bus** *32, 48, 53, 186, 200.*

Its original name was Foro Mussolini, but in the late 1940s the city decided to change it. Il Duce had planned to snare the Olympics like his friend Hitler, and began a huge sports complex along the Tiber to celebrate the games with proper Fascist solemnity. The result rivals the best of Roman Baroque for pure kitsch entertainment. We can only regret that Mussolini never got to finish it. The final plan called for, among other ornaments, a 250ft statue of the dictator himself, dressed as Hercules.

At the entrance, a 55ft obelisk proclaims MUSSOLINI DUX, in letters too big to ever be effaced. The 'Forum' behind it, now used as a roller-skating track by children, is paved with black and white mosaics of heroic athletes in various sports, interspersed with scenes of Italian soldiers bayonetting Ethiopians. More mosaics and inscriptions celebrate the mystic creative force of Fascism, set among borders with the endlessly repeated words 'Duce' and 'Balilla' (the Fascist youth group, whose members did most of the work here). To the right of the Forum, the sunken **Marble Stadium** was to be the site of the games. Knowing Mussolini, it's not surprising that this monstrosity is really built of travertine; the 60 colossal stone athletes around the top of the oval are still impressive. Rome finally got the Olympics, in 1960, and built the huge geometric steel spider to the left of the Foro, the **Stadio Olimpico,** for them.

The travertine-trimmed raspberry **Piscina** (swimming pool) and **Palazzo di Scherma** (fencing hall) are modest examples of the sunnier side of Mussolini architecture.

Just upstream from the Foro Italico stands the famous **Milvian Bridge**, or Ponte Milvio, better known to Romans as *Ponte Molle*. Built about 109 BC, it holds a place in history from the battle of AD 312, when Constantine defeated rival Emperor Maxentius; the night before, Constantine had had his famous dream of the cross, hearing the words 'In this sign you shall conquer'. The battle took place a mile upstream, but Maxentius drowned in the Tiber here while trying to flee.

Villa Borghese H3–K4

Open *dawn–sunset.*

The beautiful gardens of Villa Borghese, where the pines of Rome are most pinishly Roman, can be either a perfect antidote to Baroque fever or a day's sightseeing in itself. Etruscan, Baroque and modern art are on show here, along with Rome's Zoo.

The heights around the Muro Torto have been planted with gardens since the days of the Republic, when Monte Pincio was known as the 'hill of gardens' or *Collis Hortulorum*. The most famous gardens belonged to the Villa of Lucullus, the 1st-century BC general and epicure, who conquered Mithridates of Pontus in Northern Anatolia and brought back the first cherries to Europe among his trophies. Claudius' third wife, Messalina, later retreated here, murdering the owner and publicly 'marrying' her lover; she in turn was murdered here by the troops of her husband.

In 1605, Scipione Borghese, the first of Rome's princely cardinal-nephews (nephew of Paul V), set a new standard in nepotism with the acquisition of vast estates outside Porta Pinciana, creating a Lucullian retreat to entertain his friends and house his art collection. Scipione's heir, Prince Marcantonio Borghese, had the formal Italian gardens redesigned *all'inglese* by Scotsman Jacob Moore in 1773. Camillo Borghese, brother-in-law of Napoleon, added neoclassical touches. In 1901 the state purchased the garden and Borghese *palazzina*, and linked them with the Pincio and Villa Giulia to create Rome's most popular public park (*see* p.338).

The neoclassical **Temple of Aesculapius** (13; Tempio di Esculapio) stands on the shores of a romantic lakelet, where you can do as the Romans do and hire a rowboat.

Villa Borghese

Galleria Nazionale d'Arte Moderna I2–3

*Viale delle Belle Arti 131, **t** 06 322 981; **tram** 3, 19. **Open** Tues–Sun 8.30–7.30; **adm** €6; guided tour in English by reservation, Sun 11, €4 extra.*

The elephantine hulk of the 1911 Galleria Nazionale d'Arte Moderna contains one of Italy's most important hoards of modern art. Paintings and sculptures of the 20th century fill the ground floor. Start with the four colourful Art Nouveau panels by Galileo Chini (1914), designer of opera sets for Puccini and the throne room of the King of Siam. Compare these oriental-influenced panels with Gustav Klimt's more Byzantine *Three Ages of Woman*. Paintings follow by Cézanne and Modigliani, and a shimmering pointillist view of the Villa Borghese by Giacomo Balla, a father of contemporary Italian art. His style changed after he became a signatory of the 1910 Futurist Manifesto, which propounded a new Italy, dynamic, technological and speedy (Balla's 1913 *Ponte della Velocità*; also his menacing 1915 *Insidie di Guerra* and Ferruccio Ferrazzi's swirling *Carrosello*). The talented Umberto Boccioni combined the tenets of Futurism and Cubism in *Cavallo + Cavaliere + Caseggiato* (1914) and in sculpture (the grinning/grimacing *Ritratto Antigrazioso*).

The post-war reaction of the 1920s is represented by Mondrian, Duchamp, Schwitters, and in Italy by the Metaphysical School of Ferrara, questioning perceptions of reality with haunting scenes populated with the lifeless but human forms of mannequins by Giorgio de Chirico (*Ettore e Andromaca*) and Carlo Carrà (*Ovale delle Apparizioni*). In a similar vein is Italian sculpture of the 1920s and '30s on the first veranda, its phalanx of famous and unknown portrait busts gazing back *en masse* at the spectator. From the '30s too are paintings by Kandinsky, Miró, Utrillo, some dull abstract Italians, weird Fascists (*Bacchus at the Inn*) and most interestingly, the Magic Realism of Filippo de Pisis, Antonio Donghi (*Il Tevere*) and Mario Broglio (*La Rusticana* and *La Sorgente*), who create uncanniness in simple, everyday objects and scenes. Just off the second veranda, don't miss the prints from the 1920s and '30s by

Bruno da Osino (1888–1962) and Disertori Benevenuto (1887–1969). There are also works by Van Gogh, Monet, Degas, Casorati, Klee, Arp and Ernst.

Highlights of the 19th-century collection include Tuscan Impressionists ('Macchiaioli'), led by Giovanni Fattori, Silvestro Lega, and Telemaco Signorini; the *Bois de Boulogne* by Giuseppe de Nittis; two melodramas by Aristide Sartorio, with the *Gorgon* and *Diana of Ephesus* in the lead roles; and sculptures by Medardo Rosso. Among the non-Italians, look for Dante Gabriele Rossetti's *Portrait of Mrs William Morris* (1874) and prints and drawings by Goya, Blake, Hogarth, Renoir, Toulouse-Lautrec, Géricault, Delacroix, Millet, Corot, Munch, Whistler, Burne-Jones, Rodin, Manet, Beardsley, and William Morris.

Museo Etrusco Nazionale di Villa Giulia I2

Piazzale di Villa Giulia 9, t 06 321 7224; tram 3, 19. Open Tues–Sun 9–7.30; adm €4.

Villa Giulia was the pleasure dome of Julius III (1550–5), a pope fond of antique statues, young boys, large Gaeta onions and parties. It now houses Italy's top Etruscan museum.

To entertain like a true Roman, Julius III hired Ammannati, Vignola and Vasari, with Michelangelo as consultant, to create a villa and garden, fountains and statuary – as graceful a Mannerist conceit as could ever be. Although stripped of its ornaments and 300 ancient and Renaissance statues by more prudish popes, the villa is still a delight, heavily rusticated on the outside like an oyster, secreting a pearl of a semicircular portico, with ceiling frescoes of trellises, vines and birds. The most charming innovation, the **Nymphaeum**, was designed by Vignola, sunk into the garden to hold the clear waters of the Acqua Vergine and provide a cool refuge from the summer heat.

The villa in 1889 became the Museo Nazionale Etrusco – the place to learn about the Romans' shadowy predecessors, their mentors and later rivals. Enter their realm just beyond the left portico, where you are greeted by two rare archaic Etruscan sculp-

tures, of a centaur and a youth riding a sea monster, from the 6th century BC. These, like nearly all the other exhibits in the museum, were found in tombs, but are not morbid. Few have ever smiled at the Grim Reaper like the Etruscans, who chose to face eternity reclining on a banquet couch, like the couple on the terracotta **Sarcofago degli Sposi** from Cervéteri (6th century BC).

From the Temple of Portonaccio at Veio come their cousins, giant terracotta statues of *Apollo* and *Hercules*, believed to be by Vulca, the Etruscan sculptor famed for his work in the Temple of Capitoline Jupiter for Tarquin the Proud. The Etruscans bridge the centuries with their talent for portraiture in terracotta ex-votos (some of children), for honed minimalism (the tall and thin 'blade' figures) and for the risqué, in vase paintings by the 'Pittore di Micali' of Vulci.

The Etruscans were superb metalworkers, casting bronze incense burners in the form of overcrowded chariots, hut-shaped crema-tion urns and, most magnificently of all, the **Chigi Vase** (7th century BC), embellished with hunting scenes and a *Judgement of Paris*. Their gold jewellery has rarely been matched in its intricate filigree and miniaturism (50 golden rams in a square inch of brooch); compare it with the lovely baubles in the **Castellani Collection** of gold from Minoan (1400 BC) to pre-Columbian civilizations. Etruscan warriors were buried with their armour and in one case with a chariot and two horses, whose tiny skeletons are no larger than Great Danes.

Other rooms display Greek *kraters* and *amphorae* with mythological scenes, and Etruscan imitations. Some of the best are in **Rooms 23–27**, from the *Ager Faliscus* area between Lake Bracciano and the Tiber, inhab-ited by the Falisci, Latin cousins influenced by the Etruscans, famous for their ceramics. Don't miss the plate with a war elephant and her baby, painted in the 3rd century, inspired by Pyrrhus' Pyrrhic victories in South Italy.

In the grounds is a life-sized reproduction of the colourful and ornate **Temple of Alatri**, built in 1891 but now closed owing to its fragile condition. Near the entrance is a room of artefacts from Pyrgi, the port of Cervéteri. It includes a beautiful high relief of *The Seven Against Thebes* and laminated gold inscriptions in Etruscan and Phoenician from the 5th century BC, when Etruria and Carthage were allies against the Greeks.

Zoo J2–K3

Piazzale del Giardino Zoologico, t 06 360 821, w www.bioparco.it; tram 19, 30. Open daily Mar–Oct 9.30–6, Oct–Mar 9.30–5; adm €7.

Rome's zoo, founded in 1911 but recently rebranded a 'Bioparco', is trying hard to shed its dingy image of old. All of its 900-odd residents (197 species, of which 58 mammals, 84 birds and 55 reptiles) are being given more space and natural green habitats with vegetation and hiding places. The bears have a bear valley with a river and waterfall all of their own; the chimps and gorillas have a hill-top ecosystem; and the flamingoes have been given a new aviary with an African savannah pond. There is also a reptile house and a children's farm with activities for kids. At the time of writing the zoo's newest residents are a moufflon and a pigmy hippo, both born in captivity.

Museo Civico di Zoologia J–K2

Via Ulisse Aldrovandi 18, t 06 322 1031; metro Flaminio, Spagna, tram 3, 19, 30, bus 52, 53, 95, 490, 495, 910. Open Tues–Sun 9–5; adm €4.

On the north side of the zoo, the Museo Civico di Zoologia has existed since the 18th century, although it only moved here in 1932. It too is shedding its old image – as home of stuffed critters – with innovative biodiversity and research projects.

Museo e Galleria Borghese K3

Piazzale del Museo Borghese, t 06 32810; bus 52, 53, 217. Open Tues–Sun 9–7; adm €6; advance booking (€1 fee) recommended.

The Palazzina Borghese of Cardinal Scipione Borghese was built between 1608 and 1615 by Flaminio Ponzio and Giovanni Vasanzio (Jan van Zanten). Like the Villa Giulia, it was not built as a residence, but in the mode of an ancient *villa suburbana*, for

entertaining. The plump Scipione was famed for his lavish banquets; in its original form his *palazzina* was covered with an equally lavish feast of Mannerist reliefs, statues and baubles, all whisked away in the early 19th century. An inkling of his taste remains in the 'secret' gardens, with Borghese dragons, grotesque masks, floral reliefs and so on.

The *palazzina* contains one of Rome's greatest patrician collections, the **Galleria Borghese**. Despite the name, Borghese taste was anything but bourgeois. The exquisitely cultivated Scipione not only advised his uncle Paul V on artistic matters, but with papal riches amassed one of the world's greatest private collections of sculpture and paintings. Borghese descendants added to the collection, much of which ended up in the Louvre, thanks to Prince Camillo Borghese, who donated or sold a large portion of it to his brother-in-law Napoleon. The Italian state purchased what remained in 1902.

The **Ground Floor** stars the Borghese's marble men and women. Scipione was the first to discover the precocious talent of Gianlorenzo Bernini; the sculptor produced many of his earliest works for the cardinal. Several statuary groups of mythological subjects date from the early 1620s, before Bernini got religion. They break new ground, for better or worse, in the contrived drama of their virtuoso *figura serpentinata* poses. Each scene is portrayed in the most intense, climactic moment of its story. Looking at them you may think, as many have before you, that Bernini was the Michelangelo of his day, although, as F. Marion Crawford drily put it, 'no one has yet been bold enough, or foolish enough, to call Michelangelo the Bernini of the sixteenth century'.

The statuary in each room lent its theme to the grand 18th-century décor of Prince Marcantonio, who had a weakness for brightly coloured, mildly *trompe-l'oeil* ceiling frescoes. Begin with Room I, where Canova's notorious sculpture of *Pauline Bonaparte Borghese* reclines half-nude as Venus under a ceiling portraying the *Judgement of Paris*. When asked by an acquaintance how she could have posed nearly naked, Pauline replied that it wasn't so hard because 'the artist had a furnace in his studio'. Although serenely neoclassical, Napoleon's sister is one of Rome's spicier tomatoes (she had the statue made shortly after marrying Prince Camillo Borghese, to please him); but as saucy as she was, she was minute – the statue is life-sized; connoisseurs may want to compare her breasts with the cast in the Napoleon Museum. In Room II Bernini's *David* (bearing the modest 25-year-old sculptor's own features) is about to discharge his loaded sling, although his set look of determination is mocked by the playful *putti* of the ceiling frescoes. Sharing the room are fine sarcophagus panels illustrating the *Labours of Hercules*.

Room III is designed around another hot piece of marble, Bernini's *Daphne and Apollo*, the former in the act of turning into a laurel tree to avoid the embraces of the god. Also watch out for mysterious *Maga Circe* by Dosso Dossi, contemplating her next spell. Room IV, the large **Sala degli Imperatori**, is a chilly cynosure of 18th-century design, the 17th-century alabaster and porphyry busts of the emperors in perfect chromatic accord with the precious marbles of the floor, pillars, and ceiling, all looking icily at Bernini's *Rape of Proserpina*, the goddess struggling in Pluto's arms, although perhaps not as desperately as she might have done.

Room V contains a replica of the famous Hellenistic *Hermaphrodite*, the inspiration of the **Hermaphrodite Room**; Room VI features *Aeneas and Anchises*, carved by young Bernini with his father Pietro; Aeneas is carrying his father out of burning Troy, while the older man clutches the Palladium. The **Egyptian Room**, Room VII, is actually built around an archaic Greek statue of a young girl. Room VIII contains the gallery's finest ancient sculpture, the *Dancing Faun*, restored by Thorvaldsen, as well as two of Caravaggio's best, the *Boy with a Fruit Basket* and *David with Goliath's Head*. Beyond this is the **Salone**, crowned by a fresco of Marcus Furius Camillus breaking the treaty with the Gauls

and a relief of Marco Curzio leaping into the abyss. Set into the floor are rather grisly 3rd-century AD mosaics of gladiatorial scenes from Torrenuova.

Upstairs, Room IX features Raphael's Manneristic *Deposition* (1507), inspired by Leonardo and Michelangelo and filched with papal aid from a church in Perugia; and his *Lady and the Unicorn*, believed to a portrait of his fiancée, Maddalena Strozzi. The two greats in Room X are Correggio's melting, erotic *Danae* and Algardi's statue of *Sleep* – a slumbering boy with a sleepy dormouse. Colourful paintings by L. Mazzolino and Ortolano in Room XI contrast with the grim *Pity* by Il Sodoma in Room XII. Room XIII contains Florentine and Bolognese works.

Room XIV is devoted mainly to Bernini paintings and sculptures; don't miss his portrait busts of *Cardinal Scipione Borghese* (mouth partly open as he inhales his next asthmatic breath) and *Paul V*, and his model for the curly flowing equestrian statue of *Louis XIV* (now known as Quintus Curtius Rufus, at Versailles). Note also the beautiful set of *Four Seasons* by F. Albani. Room XV has many works by Dosso Dossi, as well as Bassano's *Last Supper*, in which Christ looks appalled by the noise his apostles seem to be making. In Room XVI notice Zucchi's *Allegory of the Discovery of America*, where everybody is having a great time on cloud-like islands or swimming in the clear water. Room XVII contains a *Madonna* by Sassoferrato and one by Pompeo Batoni, and Room XVIII displays scenes of *Christ* after his death. Room XIX features the *Hunt of Diana* by Domenichino, whose amazing control of colours is best displayed in this painting. Some of the best is saved for last. In Room XX check out Titian's *Sacred and Profane Love*, the beautifully coloured, ambiguous masterpiece of his youth, in which the two women have the same face. There is also a good *Madonna* by Giovanni Bellini and one by Lorenzo Lotto. Finally, there is Antonello da Messina's *Italian Gentlemen*, a 1475 prototype of the portrait genre.

EAST OF THE CENTRE

Catacombs of Priscilla Outside the Centre map

Via Salaria 430, t 06 8620 6272; bus 63, 86, 92, 310. Open Sept–July Tues–Sun 8.30–12 and 2.30–5, for guided tours, available in English; reserve; adm €4.

There are at least a dozen catacombs in the east of the city. The only one open to visitors is the largest and oldest, the Catacombs of Priscilla, on the eastern side of Villa Ada.

Priscilla, the founder of the cemetery, belonged to a wealthy senatorial family of the 1st century AD, the Acilii. Their estate occupied most of the neighbourhood, and their villa may have been directly connected to the catacombs. Greatly expanded in the 3rd and 4th centuries, the place became a sort of society catacomb after 300. Several popes are buried here. As such, it has some good paintings – scenes like the *Drowning of Jonah*, and *Jesus as the Good Shepherd*, along with a 3rd-century fresco of a mother and baby, long thought to be the earliest surviving image of the Madonna and Child. It is actually now thought to be simply a portrait of two of the catacomb's occupants. The 'Greek Chapel', where funeral services were held, may have been a *cryptoporticus* from the Acilii villa. Besides stucco decoration it has well-preserved frescoes, including one behind the altar that may represent an early Christian *agape*, or ritual banquet.

Sant'Agnese fuori le Mura Outside the Centre map

Via Sant'Agnese, just off Via Nomentana, t 06 820 5456; bus 36, 60, 62, 84, 90. Church open daily 7–12 and 4–8; catacombs open 9–12 and 4–6, except Sun am and Mon pm; adm €5.

Via Nomentana is one of Rome's flashier suburban boulevards, lined with trees and boutiques. Several old villas survive, some of them converted into hotels. One of the largest, the Villa Torlonia, was Mussolini's residence for most of his dictatorship.

About a mile beyond **Porta Pia**, a gate in the Aurelian Wall rebuilt in 1561 by Michelangelo, the lovely early Christian complex of Sant'Agnese fuori le Mura sits inconspicuously on the left.

St Agnes met her end on Piazza Navona when, having rejected a noble suitor, she was exposed in public; her hair miraculously grew to cover her nakedness. An attempt to burn her at the stake failed when the flames did not burn her, so Diocletian beheaded her. She was buried here, in the Via Nomentana catacombs, in about 350. As one of the most popular early martyrs, representing Christian chastity despite the fact that she never bathed, her tomb became a pilgrimage site for Roman women. The first church was built soon after Constantine's reign. Completely rebuilt in 625, it has suffered every sort of tinkering in the last 1400 years. Much of it was necessary: S. Agnese witnessed one of the last great papal miracles in 1855, when the floor collapsed under Pius IX. Divine Providence, humourless as ever, scotched this perfect opportunity for a pontifical pratfall; while everyone else tumbled into the basement, Pius floated in the air for a bit, then settled gently down to earth. Small wonder that Pius later declared himself Infallible.

All around the narthex and the rear of the church, early Christian reliefs and inscriptions have been arranged as in a museum. The columns and capitals were recycled from ancient buildings; above them, the Greek-style *matroneum* (women's gallery) survives from the 625 rebuilding. Above the Cosmatesque altar, holding the remains of St Agnes, the apse has one of the simplest, most beautiful ancient mosaics in Rome. The serene figure of Agnes, in rich Byzantine court dress, is flanked by the church's two builders, Popes Symmachus and Honorius I. You can visit the 3rd–6th-century **catacombs** below – no paintings, but one of the more peaceful catacombs in Rome; it's also one of the smaller ones – a mere 7km of tunnels.

Santa
Costanza Outside the Centre map
Via Santa Costanza; **bus** *36, 60, 62, 84, 90.*
Open *daily 7–12 and 4–7.30.*

An exceptional jewel of late Roman art is tucked away behind Sant'Agnese in a park where the neighbourhood kids play football. Circular **Santa Costanza** isn't very impressive from the outside – its portico and marble decoration disappeared centuries ago – but its vaults are graced with exquisite mosaics, geometric and floral designs combining both Christian and pagan motifs. According to Church history, Emperor Constantine was persuaded to build S. Agnese by his pious daughter Constantia, who retired here as a nun and built S. Costanza as her mausoleum. This fairy tale is really a comment on Church history. The sainted Constantia, Christian or not, seems to have been as naturally vicious as the rest of Constantine's family. Never a nun, but the scheming wife of a tyrannous provincial governor, she is recorded by the reliable contemporary historian Ammianus Marcellinus as 'insatiable as [her husband, Gallus] in her thirst for human blood'.

A nice story was needed to convert the mausoleum to a baptistry in the 4th century. The mosaic, with a variety of images, has more of Bacchus in it than Jesus: vines and vintage scenes, Cupids, birds and creatures of the sea, a mirror, and *amphorae*. Originally the dome had even better Bacchic mosaics; these were destroyed by Paul V in 1622.

San Lorenzo fuori
le Mura Q7

Piazzale del Verano, **t** *06 491 511;* **metro** *Policlinico, Castro Pretorio,* **tram** *3, 19,* **bus** *C, 71, 204, 492.* **Open** *7.30–12 and 3–7.30, in winter 6.30;* **catacombs open** *3–5.30.*

Lawrence was a 3rd-century deacon with spunk: when commanded by the Roman authorities to hand over the treasures of the Church, he produced all the sick and destitute people he could round up. 'Grill this wise guy,' the Roman police sergeant must have growled, and his minions obeyed – literally.

But as they toasted him on the gridiron, Lawrence kept his sense of humour. 'You can turn me over now,' he told his tormentors. 'I'm done on this side.' Even the worst Romans had to admire the courage of such martyrs, which, in no little way, led to their own acceptance of the new religion.

Lawrence's tormented body was interred in the catacombs here, and in the 4th century Constantine dedicated a basilica to him. A second church, dedicated to the Madonna, was built nearby in 440. In 1216, in response to the increased number of pilgrims visiting the basilica (one of the canonical seven churches), Pope Honorius III stuck the two churches together by chopping off their apses, which gives the basilica its odd form. None of this is apparent from the façade, with its medieval portico rebuilt after the war (S. Lorenzo was the only church bombed in Rome), decorated with 13th-century frescoes on the life of St Lawrence, and Manzù's tomb of Italy's post-war leader, De Gasperi.

The nave, formerly the church of the Madonna, has a Cosmatesque pavement, pulpit, paschal candlestick, episcopal throne, and other 12th-century furnishings, although a mosaic on the inside of the triumphal arch dates back to the 6th century and shows Pope Pelagius II offering the basilica to Christ. The long chancel that begins here was once the nave of Pelagius' older, more important basilica of 579, with its Corinthian columns and embroidered marble windows. SS. Lawrence, Stephen, and Justin are buried in the crypt under the altar, while in the chancel is the 'medieval' tomb of Pio Nono (Pius IX, d.1878). He spent his last eight years a self-made prisoner in the Vatican and was probably glad to get out, even as a corpse. The cloister, beyond the sacristy of Pelagius' basilica, is lined with a hotchpotch of ancient columns and sarcophagus fragments.

From the basilica you can visit the **Catacombs of Santa Cyriaca**, where Lawrence originally lay, although they offer little unless you're a true catacomb fiend. All Rome's Catholics eventually end up in the nearby **Campo Verano Cemetery** (R5–S8).

Around Porta Maggiore P10

Santa Croce in Gerusalemme P10

Piazza di Santa Croce in Gerusalemme, t 06 701 4769; tram 3, bus 649. Open 7–7.

According to tradition, Constantine's mother Helen not only found Pilate's stair in Jerusalem, but the True Cross as well, and brought a piece of it back to her palace, which was later converted into Santa Croce in Gerusalemme, another of the seven churches of Rome. In Roman legend, it is linked to Gerbert (Sylvester II), the pope of the first millennium, which everyone believed would be the end of the world. The election of the Frankish Gerbert, educated in the Muslim schools of Toledo, was a fearful portent; one of the few real scholars of the day and inventor of a hydraulic organ, he was believed to be a wizard. He reputedly owned a prophetic bronze head (like the Templars three centuries later) which told him, among other things, that he would die in 'Jerusalem'. And so it happened, in 1003, while saying Mass in this church, he dropped dead.

S. Croce was rebuilt in 1144 (the date of the campanile) and in 1744, when Domenico Gregorini and Pietro Passalacqua added the bold convex rococo façade and oval vestibule. The Cosmati pavement dates from the first rebuilding; the gaudy quattrocento fresco in the apse, of *St Helen Finding the Cross*, is by Antoniazzo Romano; the tomb below, of Charles V's confessor Cardinal Quiñones, is by Jacopo Sansovino; the delicate baldaquin is from the 1600s. Steps from the right aisle lead down into the **Chapel of St Helen** (built over St Helen's bedroom), S. Croce's jewel, with a gorgeous Renaissance vault mosaic of an avuncular *Christ* designed by Melozzo da Forlì in 1494. The statue of *St Helen* was converted from a Juno found in Ostia. Off the left aisle is the **Cappella della Croce**, built in 1930 to shelter pieces of the True Cross, a larger chunk from the Cross of the Good Thief, and the genuine finger St Thomas stuck in Christ's side.

Museum of Musical Instruments P10

Piazza di Santa Croce in Gerusalemme, t 06 701 4796; tram 3, bus 649. Open Tues–Sun 9–7; adm €2.

This houses musical instruments that once belonged to tenor Evan Gorga (d.1957), famous as the first Rodolfo of *La Bohème*. But an obsession for collecting took over his operatic career, and these instruments (only one of his 30 collections, purchased by the state when he declared bankruptcy) have ended up here: trumpets, lutes, viols, and lap organs that look as if they have been lifted from Renaissance paintings, the golden 16th-century Barberini harp, and one of the three surviving pianofortes by Bartolomeo Cristofori, signed and dated 1722, just 12 years after he invented the instrument. There are folk instruments from around the world, made of armadillo shells and jawbones, hurdy-gurdies, ocarinas, music boxes and early record players. Recordings are provided, although the speakers aren't always turned on; ask if they're not.

Porta Maggiore P10

Piazza di Porta Maggiore; tram 3, 4, 5, 19, bus 105, 157.

From S. Croce in Gerusalemme, wander down Via Eleniana, lined with the arches of the **Acqua Claudia**, an aqueduct begun by Caligula and completed by Claudius in AD 52, carrying spring water from Subiaco 68km away to slake Rome's thirst. This aqueduct, and the even longer Anio Novus, were incorporated, one on top of the other, into Aurelius' Porta Prenestina, now known as **Porta Maggiore**, arching over a section of the ancient Via Prenestina for Palestrina.

Even more peculiar is the great block of travertine, carved with circles to symbolize bread pans. This is the **Baker's Tomb** (30 BC), built for a certain Marcus Virgilius Eurysaces, who earned his fortune by supplying to the state the more nutritious half of the daily bread-and-circus. In the frieze you can see the deceased in his toga, directing his slaves in their work.

Underground Basilica of Porta Maggiore P9

Piazzale Labicano; tram 3, 5, 14, 19. Open by special permission from the Comune di Roma, t 06 6710 3819.

On the far side of Piazza di Porta Maggiore, directly below the railway line, is the entrance to one of Rome's most remarkable sights. Discovered in 1916 while work was being done on the main line into Termini Station, the basilica, unlike Rome's other buried ruins, was not covered with the debris of centuries – it was built underground for a secret religious sect in the 1st century AD and closed up not long after. Its elegant stucco reliefs are fascinating; scholars, unable to decipher the sect's beliefs from the décor, call them 'neo-Pythagorean'. Its form, intriguingly, is that adapted by later churches, with a nave, two aisles, an apse and a porch.

SOUTH OF THE CENTRE

Appian Way

The further reaches of the 'queen of roads' are described in the Appian Way walk, p.247; map p.248. Those below are at its start.

Domine Quo Vadis?

Via Appia Antica 51, t 06 512 0441; bus 118, 218. Open 7.30am–6.45pm.

The first reason to get off the bus is 1km outside the Aurelian Wall, where there's a triple fork in the road and the little church of **Domine Quo Vadis?** (1637). The tale goes that Peter, fleeing from the dangers of Rome, met Christ here coming the other way. 'Whither goest thou, Lord?' Peter asked. 'I am going to Rome to be crucified once more,' was the reply. As the vision departed the shamed Apostle turned back to face his crucifixion in Nero's Circus. The curious footprints inside, said to be Christ's, are a cast of a pagan ex-voto from the Catacombs of S. Sebastiano (for the real thing, *see* p.249).

Temple of the Deus Rediculus

Via Appia Antica; bus 118, 218.

To see one of Rome's more obscure sights, the 2nd-century AD **Temple of the Deus Rediculus**, turn left at Via della Caffarella, continuing on an unmade track, to a farm with a pretty terracotta and jonquil-hued temple (no access). Neither dedicated to the gods of ridicule, as it sounds, or even, as once believed, to the gods who turned back Hannibal, this was really the tomb of Annia Regilla, the wife of perhaps the wealthiest man in antiquity, Herodes Atticus, whose villa estate occupied the next two miles or so just beyond the Via Appia. Herodes made his fortune Arabian Nights-style – his father found a buried treasure under the Acropolis in Athens and he married a wealthy heiress. Cultured and educated, he was Marcus Aurelius' professor of rhetoric and the great benefactor of Athens, erecting a number of public buildings. When his wife Annia died in childbirth, his grief was proverbial; and he built in his gardens this rich tomb of contrasting colours of brick and stucco decoration that has survived remarkably intact.

Catacombs of San Calisto

Via Appia Antica 126; bus 660. Open for guided tours only, summer Thurs–Tues 8.30–12 and 2.30–5.30, winter 8.30–12 and 2.30–5; adm €4.

The first official Christian cemetery in Rome, and burial place of the first bishop of Rome, St Calixtus, this is the most visited of the catacombs. It becomes surreal at peak efficiency, when seven different language groups are conducted on a synchronized dance through the labyrinth, the Germans padding past one way, the French arguing beyond the next wall, while echoes of Polish drift down from above. Although all the catacombs have their unique points of interest, the truth is, if you've seen one, you've seen them all, and you'll find a more appropriately dead atmosphere in the equally interesting Catacombs of S. Domitilla (*see* below).

But why did the early Christians create these enormous termitaries? Few other

Mediterranean cities have catacombs (Naples, Syracuse, Malta, and the Greek island of Milos are among those that do), and all exist thanks to tufa or some other easily excavated rock. Everyone wanted to be near a martyr in the hopes of preferential treatment at the pearly gates. When the galleries became too long – some go on for kilometres – they added another floor below, and another, and another. San Calisto, the largest, has five levels, yet to be completely explored. Most of the burials were in simple shelves carved in the walls, called *locali*, or in the floors, where the shrouded bodies were laid, and sealed with a marble or terracotta slab. It's a sad comment on the infant mortality of the day to see row upon row of tiny *locali*. The *arcosolia* are a bit fancier, topped by an arch and decorated with bits of painting or stucco that constitute the catacombs' chief interest, representing the earliest stages of official Christian iconography. Artistic standards were not high, a reflection more on the dire state of the late Roman imagination than on the Christians. Most elaborate of all are the *cubicula*, or family vaults.

St Calixtus was appointed caretaker of this cemetery by Pope Zephyrinus before he himself became pope, and it was used into the 4th century. The main attraction is the **Crypt of the Popes**, where the first bishops of Rome were interred after their martyrdoms: SS. Pontianus, Anterus, Fabian, Lucius, and Eutychianus, whose names are preserved in Greek inscriptions. It is assumed, on the basis of an inscription placed here in their memory by Pope St Damasus, that other martyred popes were buried here too – SS. Stephen I, Dionysius, and Felix I, and Sixtus II, who was killed in this very cemetery in the persecution of Valerian. Next to it is the **Crypt of Santa Cecilia**, where her body originally lay before Pope Paschal I moved it to the church of S. Cecilia in 821; it contains a copy of Stefano Maderno's famous statue of the saint. The tour takes in other highlights of the second floor – including the fascinating 3rd-century **Crypts of the Sacraments** and two mummies in glass cases.

Fosse Ardeatine
Via Ardeatina 174, t 06 513 6742; bus 218. **Open** *Mon–Fri 8.15–6.45, Sat–Sun 8.15–3.30.*

A road west of S. Calisto leads to the most harrowing funerary memorial outside Rome's wall, the stark **Mausoleum delle Fosse Ardeatine**. On 23 March 1944 the Italian Resistance killed 32 German soldiers in Rome, and the next day, in reprisal, the Nazis rounded up 335 innocents, and shot and buried them here in a sand pit under a tall tufa cliff. When the Germans retreated, the bodies were recovered, identified and re-buried together; the chapels carved in the tufa have been compared to the catacombs.

San Paolo fuori le Mura Outside the Centre map

Catacombs of Santa Domitilla
Via delle Sette Chiese 283, t 06 511 0342; bus 218, 716. **Open** *Feb–Dec for guided tours only, Wed–Mon 8.30–12 and 2.30–5; adm €5.*

The old pilgrimage route to San Paolo fuori le Mura (now noted for its speeding traffic) leads to the Catacombs of Santa Domitilla. These are nearly as large as S. Calisto, and are even older. Santa Domitilla was the Christian niece of Domitian's sister. She and her two servants Nereus and Achilleus were buried here in a pagan *hypogeum*, which included the imperial Flavian family's cemetery. Over the tombs of SS. Nereus and Achilleus a basilica was built in the 4th century, with a rare bas-relief showing the martyrdom of St Achilleus. The **Chapel of St Petronilla** adjoins it, with a fresco of the saint who was the adopted daughter of St Peter. There are hundreds of inscriptions and paintings, one of a beardless young Jesus teaching his apostles, all wearing togas; underneath is a scene of a warehouse; also an early scene of the *Epiphany*, the *Raising of Lazarus*, and in the *cubiculum* of Diogenes, a *Portrait of St Paul*.

The **Catacombs of San Sebastiano** (*see* p.249), are also open to the public. The **Jewish Catacombs** and **Catacombs of Pretestato** are only open to scholars.

San Paolo Outside the Centre map

Via Ostiense 186, t 06 541 0341; metro San Paolo; bus 23, 128, 702. Church open 7–7, in winter until 6.30; cloister open 9–1 and 3–6; adm free.

In the Dark Ages this stretch of the ancient Via Ostiense was one of the marvels of Rome, sheltered by a 1½km-long portico supported by 800 marble columns, built by Pope John VIII in the 870s to shelter pilgrims between Porta San Paolo and the basilica. A separate walled suburb, 'Giovannipoli', grew up around St Paul's.

The colossal portico may as well have been constructed of breadcrumbs for all that has survived; Giovannipoli, pummelled by the Normans in 1084 and every other roughneck coming up the Tiber, was given its *coup de grâce* in an 1823 fire that began when two roofers, horsing around on top of St Paul's, spilled a bucket of hot coals. One fell in a gutter, where it smouldered until the night, when the most beautiful of the four Patriarchal basilicas and its suburb went up like a torch. The church was rebuilt, and today it is surrounded by industrial sprawl.

When condemned, St Paul, as a Roman citizen, merited the relatively painless death of decapitation along the road to Ostia. According to an embarrassing tradition, his head bounced three times, bringing forth three springs, now occupied by the Abbazia delle Tre Fontane. Paul's head ended up in the Lateran, while over the grave of his trunk Constantine built the first shrine. Theodosius and his children, Honorius and Galla Placidia, erected a basilica over the site, and over the years it was as frequently restored and embellished as it was pillaged. It became the special church of the kings of England, who were honorary canons here until the Reformation; the abbots of St Paul's were automatically made Knights of the Garter.

The nearly total reconstruction in the early 19th century followed the outline of the original basilica, making it the second largest church in Rome. The entrance faces the Tiber, through a massive but pointless courtyard called the **Quadriporticus**, relieved by four tall palms and the gold of the 19th-century mosaic on the façade that blazes in the setting sun; in the middle a giant marble St Paul, sword in hand, seems ready to thump any would-be art critics. On the right, one of the few things to survive the fire, is the original bronze **Holy Door** with panels inlaid in silver, brought from Constantinople in the 11th century. The long, long nave, lined with a double forest of granite columns, glossy marbles, and polished stones, has the cool, solemn majesty of an ice palace, although there are critics who say its shiny newness better evokes the feel of an original basilica than any other. The famous frieze along the nave and aisles has mosaic portraits of all 265 popes, from St Peter on; the first 40 are survivors from the fire. According to Roman tradition, the world will end when there is no room for a new pope's portrait; there are only eight spaces left.

The **Triumphal Arch**, adorned with mosaics paid for by Galla Placidia in the 5th century, survived the fire. Art Deco is not what you would expect from those times, but these bear an uncanny resemblance to Roosevelt's public works murals of the early 1930s: a severe-looking *Christ* in the centre circle, worshipped by winged symbols of the *Evangelists*, two angels with pointers, and the *Elders of the Apocalypse* bearing crowns, all posed as if for the last number of a Hollywood musical. Underneath, porphyry columns support another relic of the original church, the ornate 1285 baldaquin by Arnolfo di Cambio, built over the confessio housing the tomb of St Paul. Whether or not Paul's remains are still there is a matter of debate; his bronze sarcophagus was looted by the Saracens in 846, when they picked up some five tons of gold and silver treasure from St Paul's and St Peter's, all of which went down to Davy Jones' locker off Sicily's coast. If the confessio is open, you can see the inscription PAULO APOSTOLO MART, carved in a stone slab pierced by two holes for inserting cloth to be made sacred by the proximity of his relics. Just to the right of the altar is a massive, fantastically medieval **Paschal**

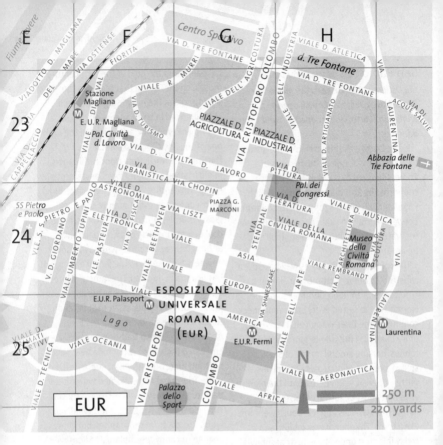

Candlestick from the 12th century. The mosaics in the apse with a giant Byzantine *Christ* and smaller saints were made by Venetian artisans in 1220.

The short transepts, covered with precious marbles, are closed by altars of malachite and lapis lazuli donated by Czar Nicholas I, one of many heads of state who contributed to the rebuilding – even Mohammed Ali of Egypt sent a column or two. Of the chapels, only the one to the left of the apse survived the flames; designed by Carlo Maderno, it houses a fine 13th-century **Crucifix** and the altar where St Ignatius and his followers took the formal vows that made the Jesuits a religious order. Off the right transept are the lovely **Cloisters**, finished in 1208 and similar to those of San Giovanni in Laterano, with their glittering mosaics and columns that delightfully shun symmetry. The basilica's little **museum** contains a copy of the stone slab over St Paul's tomb along with a souvenir stand and some highly missable art.

EUR E23–G25

Metro EUR Palasport, EUR Fermi.

By the late 1930s, Mussolini was proud enough of his accomplishments to plan a world's fair to show humanity the fruits of Fascism. Its theme was to be the 'Progress of Civilization', measured from the invention of the wheel up to the invention of the 'Corporate State'. A vast area south of Rome was cleared and transformed into a grid of wide boulevards broken by parks and a long artificial lagoon. Huge pavilions and colonnades were begun, and a design was accepted for a tremendous aluminium arch – like the famous one in St Louis, but many times bigger – that would overspread the entire fairground, a fake rainbow, a Fascist symbol of hope. War intervened, the arch never appeared, and the Esposizione Universale di Roma never came off. After 1945 the Italians tried to make the best of it, turning EUR into a model satellite city and trade centre on the lines of La Défense in Paris. The result will derange your senses as much as it does most Romans', a chilly nightmare of modernism with Fascist names like the Boulevard of Humanism, Boulevard of Electronics and Boulevard of Social Security. These can be as haunted and void of life as a De Chirico painting, or wide speedways where the few foolish pedestrians are mowed down like ducks in a shooting gallery. The post-war glass skyscrapers looming over them make the crumbling old Mussolini buildings look positively cosy and cheerful.

Still, for those who can appreciate the well-landscaped macabre, EUR can be fun. Some of the older corners reveal giant Fascist mosaics of heroic miners, soldiers, assembly-line workers, and mothers, and at the end of Viale della Civiltà del Lavoro, you can have a look at the modest masterpiece of Mussolini architecture and EUR's most striking landmark, the elegant **Palazzo della Civiltà del Lavoro**, also known as the Quadrato della Concordia. Liberal, post-war Italy has rarely, if ever, been able to conceive anything with such a sure sense of design and a feeling for history. Of course some Roman malcontents call it the 'Square Colosseum'.

The fun reason to come to EUR is to take a spin on the old-fashioned rides in Rome's fun fair, **LUNEUR Park**; the serious reason is to see its museums, especially the Museo della Civiltà Romana (H24). Other sights in EUR are the massive church and dome of **Santi Pietro e Paolo** (E24), best seen from a distance and the park around the **Lago Artificiale** (F–G25), with its Japanese cherry trees and bridges leading to the **Palasport** (E–G25), designed by Pier Luigi Nervi and Marcello Piacentini for the 1960 Olympics and crowned by a striking rib-vaulted dome 100m in diameter.

Museo della Civiltà Romana H24
*Piazza Giovanni Agnelli, t 06 592 6041; **metro** Laurentina, **bus** 761. **Open** Tues–Sat 9–7, Sun 9–1; **adm** €4.*

Born from the 1911 archaeological show, the museum was housed in this exposition building (Fascist-Art Deco Temple of Karnak)

to celebrate Emperor Augustus' 2,000 years in 1937. Models of ancient buildings help to evoke the Rome of the Caesars, especially the **Plastico di Roma**, a 1:250 scale model of 4th-century Rome, with every building present within the Aurelian Walls, a great place to seed your imagination with 'the grandeur that was Rome'. Scholarship of the last 50 years would quibble on a few of the details: the *insulae*, or apartment buildings, should be taller than shown, the Circus Flaminius is missing, and Aurelian's Temple of the Sun is in the wrong place.

Other exhibits include models of Roman furniture, musical instruments, sundials, surgical tools, reliefs of various shops, and – prize exhibit – a series of casts made from Trajan's Column in 1861. This is your chance to examine its magnificent reliefs up close. The last room charts the history of the museum itself, including some interesting old photos of Rome. Check before you go that the sections you want to see are open.

Abbazia delle Tre Fontane I23
*Via Acque Salvie 1, t 06 540 1655. **Open** daily 6–12.30 and 3–8.*

A kilometre east of LUNEUR Park and predating EUR by 1,300 years is this abbey, founded by refugee monks from Syria on the traditional site of St Paul's martyrdom. The three fountains of its name supposedly sprang forth on the three places where the saintly head rebounded. A miracle, although not the long-distance record for holy noggins; that belongs to a 3rd-century Florentine saint named Minias, whose severed head bounced nearly a kilometre – uphill – from the chopper's block.

St Bernard lodged here while visiting Rome in 1138–40, and wrote of the inhabitants: 'Who is ignorant of the vanity and arrogance of the Romans? Dexterous in mischief, they have never learnt the science of doing good. Odious to earth and heaven, impious to God, seditious among themselves... Adulation and calumny, perfidy and treason, are the familiar arts of their policy...'. Some things never change, although Bernard's vision may have been coloured by the fact that the Tre Fontane was a famous malarial swamp. Rahere, King Henry II's jester, came down with the sickness during a stay here, and vowed to build a church in London if he were cured; thus the origins of St Bartholomew the Great, and its hospital, named after San Bartolomeo on the Tiber Island.

In the 19th century, Trappists came to live in the dismal place and sucked the swamps dry with groves of eucalyptus, from which they distil a humdinger of a liqueur. Now one of the more serene garden corners of Rome, there are three churches to visit: **Santi Vincenzo ed Anastasio** (*open 6–12.30 and 3–8*), founded by Honorius I in 625, rebuilt in 1221 by Honorius III, and preserving its original appearance. To the right, the octagonal **S. Maria Scala Coeli**, the 'Stairway to Heaven', (*open 8–6*) was so named for a vision of St Bernard. While he was praying for a departed friend, the soul suddenly appeared before him, ascending from purgatory to paradise thanks to his good offices. The crypt preserves the Cosmatesque altar on which the vision appeared. The third church, **San Paolo alle Tre Fontane** (*open 8–6*), dates from the 5th century, but was rebuilt by Giacomo della Porta in 1599; St Paul was supposed to have been bound to the column on the right. The prettiest things inside are two mosaic pavements from Ostia Antica.

Walks

12

A SPANISH STEPS WALK

Under the joyfully cascading Spanish Steps, you'll find Rome's swishest designer boutiques and its favourite streets for a stroll. Cars have been banished from most of them, to be replaced by green carpets and elegant trees in boxes. Unlike other corners of Rome, with their mighty monuments of history, Church and State, the concentration here is on the Romans of the here and now, the Rococo stair providing a perfect stage backdrop for the rich and the flakey enjoying their favourite pastime – showing off (or *fare il fico* – 'making the fig' – as the Romans say). To see the show at its flamboyant best, come on a weekday afternoon (except Monday).

Note: Along the way you will pass kerbside public fountains made up of a standpipe column with a curving pipe ('*nasone*'), from which fresh drinking water pours.

Start at the irresistible **Spanish Steps** (*see* p.105), descending to their sunken boat of a fountain, the Barcaccia. People have been posing here as artists' models ever since the steps were built, and today, on occasion, fashion models replay the custom in nationally broadcast extravaganzas. Although there are now signs at the top and bottom of the steps prohibiting sitting, dancing and playing music, as often as not you'll still have to zigzag your way around clumps of young people participating in another time-honoured Roman pastime – *far niente*. Any

attractive young woman, if blonde and possibly Swedish, will probably have to contend with the 'parrots' – *pappagalli* – slick young Romans equipped with a few words of English participating in yet another favourite pastime – *caccia alla svedese*. This, and the Trevi Fountain, are their favourite haunts.

Walk up the steps (or take the metro escalator if you're feeling lazy) for the view from the **Trinità dei Monti** church (*see* p.106). To the left you can make a leg of the classic *passeggiata* to the **Villa Medici** (*see* p.107), where Galileo was held under rather benign house arrest by the Inquisition in 1630–3, since 1803 the seat of the French Academy. You may linger over a coffee or ice cream in the villa gardens at **Ciampini al Café du Jardin**, taking in a view once enjoyed every day by the likes of Ingres, Fragonard, Berlioz and Debussy.

Retracing your steps to the top of the Spanish Steps, pass the Trinità dei Monti and continue to the corner of Via Sistina and Via Gregoriana. In the triangle formed by the two roads is the **Palazzetto Zuccari**, built in the 16th century as an art academy by Mannerist painter Federico Zuccari. Its striking rounded loggia was added in 1711 by Filippo Juvarra when the palace became the residence of Queen Maria Casimira of Poland. Zuccari, however, was responsible for the main façade on Via Gregoriana, with doors and windows framed by hideous ogre faces with gawping hell-mouths – a sneak preview of the Monster Park at Bomarzo (*see* p.266). Back when this part of Rome was the 'English ghetto', painter Sir Joshua Reynolds lodged here (1752–3). Another famous 18th-century resident was German archaeologist Johann Winckelmann, the first critic to study classical art as art. On a Sunday morning, stop for an elegant brunch at the nearby **Hotel de la Ville**, Via Sistina 69 (*see* p.288).

Take the first stair down in front of the Palazzetto to **Piazza Mignanelli**, where the secretive J.M.W. Turner had his Roman studio at no.12. If you've skipped brunch and it's time for a snack, **Caffè Leonardo** at no.21 will provide you with *bruschettoni* and salads.

Start: Metro Spagna.
Finish: Piazza di Spagna.
Walking time: 1½ hours.
Lunch and drink stops: Il Re degli Amici, *see* p.305; Fiaschetteria, *see* p.305; Babington's Tea Rooms, *see* p.306; Caffè Greco, *see* p.306; Caffè Leonardo, *see* p.306; Canova, *see* p.306; Ciampini al Café du Jardin, *see* p.306; Enoteca Antica, *see* p.305; Fratelli Roffi Isabelli, *see* p.306; Rosati, *see* p.306.
Suggested start time: 4pm, if you want to mingle with the cruising crowds.

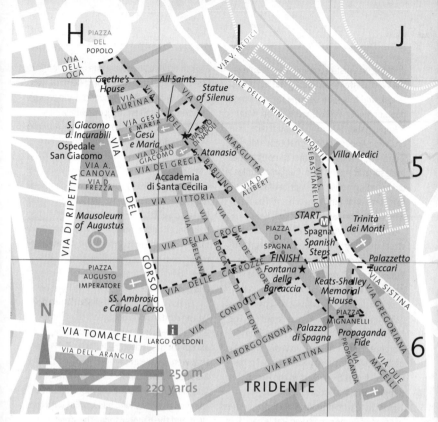

From Piazza Mignanelli, turn left past Borromini's anxiety attack of a building, the **Propaganda Fide** (*see* p.107), passing a discreet McDonald's. Anyone who was in Italy in the late 1980s will recall the volcanic controversy that erupted when the company announced the opening of their first outlet in Rome here. The city took the position that it had enough arches of its own and didn't want any golden ones lowering the tone. The compromise is a burger stand with marble Roman décor, plashing fountains and private vigilantes to pick up any McLitter; the place seats 700 and is always full – of Romans.

Turning right from Piazza Mignanelli is the **Keats–Shelley House** (*see* p.106) and, on the far side of the steps, another English institution, since 1896 – **Babington's Tea Rooms**, where you can have a good if rather pricey cup of the leafy stuff with a scone and order a Christmas pudding for the holidays.

But it was the Spanish who gave their name to the square, and they're still here: at no.57, directly opposite Piazza Mignanelli, is the **Palazzo di Spagna**, the Spanish embassy

to the Holy See since 1622. This stands at the head of the gilt and glam grid of Rome's most celebrated shopping district, a woof and warp of immaculate consumption.

From the piazza, turn down **Via Condotti** (straight ahead from the steps), which, in spite of its humble name, referring to its underground pipes that carry the Acqua Vergine, is now the most glamorous street of them all; if the temperature is less than 25 degrees, you'll see more fur coats here than in the zoo. As you walk along, you can inspect the windows of **Gucci** at no.8, **Bulgari** (Rome's legendary jewellers, their windows aglow with fabulous creations in sapphires, emeralds and 'pigeon blood' rubies) at no.10, **Valentino** at no. 13, **Battistoni** (Rome's greatest name in tailoring, with a very posh boutique in a courtyard of the Palazzo Caffarelli) at no.60, **Ferragamo** at no.72–74, **Armani** at no.76–77 and **Prada** at no.93. Look back for the dramatic view of the Spanish Steps framed at the top of the street.

The **Caffè Greco**, opposite Bulgari, was founded in 1760 by a Greek when coffee-drinking was just becoming fashionable in the West. Caffeine proved a great incentive to talk, and this soon become the city's most popular *rendez-vous:* Goethe, Byron, Wagner, Schopenhauer, D'Annunzio, Baudelaire, Hans Christian Andersen, Stendhal, Leopardi, Gogol and a thousand other famous names have sat and sipped here. Bulgari occupies an old boarding house, a favourite of British visitors– among them Tennyson and Thackeray, who wrote *The Rose and the Ring* here.

Turn right up **Via Bocca di Leone**, another street dripping with designers – **Versace** at no.26–27, **Roccobarocco** at no.65, **Mariella Burani** at no.28, **Yves Saint Laurent rive gauche** at no.35 and four or five jewellery shops, including **Corradini** at no.35, which sells copies of ancient Roman jewellery. The Brownings, when they came down from Florence, lived at **no.43**. *Quo Vadis?* was based on the novel written by Polish Nobel prize-winner Henryk Sienkiwicz in the **Hotel d'Inghilterra**, Via Bocca di Leone 14.

From here turn into **Via della Croce**, address of some of Rome's more venerable bars, food shops and restaurants. **Il Re degli Amici**, at no.33/b, goes back to 1939, while a few doors down the **Fiaschetteria** has been in place since 1889. Pick up a prize bottle of wine, olive oil or grappa to take home at the **Fratelli Roffi Isabelli** at no.76, an atmospheric 19th-century wine shop and wine bar. **Enoteca Antica** at no.76 has a good wine selection by the glass or by the bottle.

At the east end of Via della Croce, turn left into **Via del Babuino**. Although within the Aurelian Wall, this corner of Rome was covered with ornamental gardens in antiquity and vegetable plots in the Middle Ages. It remained rural until it caught the eye of the late Renaissance popes. In 1717, on a last open space at the corner of Via Alibert, Count Antonio d'Alibert built the **Teatro delle Dame**, once famous for its operas and *castrati* singers, who fascinated the Grand Tourists. Occasionally they mistakenly fell in love with the ones who resembled women and dressed the part 'as pretty and tempting as may be', according to one 18th-century

English tourist. They were one attraction, but the main one for theatre-going Romans was chatting with friends throughout the entire performance and eating ice cream, which was all the rage in Rome at the time. All, rich or poor, indulged in it at every opportunity, even during Mass.

Staid 'Baboon Street' was originally Via Clementina. One of its ornaments was a **fountain-statue of Silenus** by Giacomo della Porta, so ugly that the Romans named it the baboon. Although the statue was long hidden through embarrassment, it has since resurfaced in all its mouldering, leprous glory, ludicrously topped with a new head and covered with loony graffiti, in front of the Greek Catholic church of **Sant'Atanasio** (at the corner of Via dei Greci). By 1581 the whole street was named after this ape, except for the section near Piazza del Popolo that went by the even more ignoble title of **Borghetto Pidocchioso** – 'Fleabag Alley'. Rubens and Poussin are the most famous of the foreign artists who had studios with the fleas and the baboon; today the street is lined with fancy shops selling antiques and objets d'art.

After pondering the baboon, you may want to take a brief detour down **Via dei Greci**, seat of the **Accademia Nazionale di Santa Cecilia**, Rome's music academy (*see* p.324). It often hosts small recitals by professors and students; the main entrance is actually round the corner at Via Vittoria 6. Rome's anglophones know Via dei Greci for the **Lion Bookshop** at no.36, with perhaps the largest selection of English books in the city.

Back on Via del Babuino, at no.153, Rome's Anglican church of **All Saints** is a pretty neo-Gothic building of 1882 by G. E. Street, with a bright white spire poking above the roofs like 'a summer hat worn out of season' (open mornings except Saturday and during services). From here take little **Via Orto di Napoli** to **Via Margutta**, a straight narrow lane, skirting the Pincio and long the refuge of Rome's artsy bohemians. Although the high cost of trendiness has forced them most elsewhere, a few galleries remain; large outdoor exhibits perk up the street in spring and autumn. Peek in any open gateway or door into the picturesque courtyards of the houses here, often with a bit of old sculpture in the middle, and refreshingly cool air even during the stifling Roman summer. As the street is pedestrianized, it makes a pleasant escape from cars and mopeds. There are still some *botteghe* where artisans repair furniture; one strange little shop, at no.53/a, sells marble slabs engraved with Latin and Roman sayings. Also look out for the building where Gregory Peck lived in *Roman Holiday*, at **no.51**.

At the end of Via Margutta, turn left back into Via del Babuino, then continue right, to **Piazza del Popolo** (*see* p. 102), the traditional gateway to Rome. Most of the Ferraris you see here belong to the patrons of the piazza's two rival cafés, favourites of film stars: **Canova** at no.16, of *dolce vita* vintage (1952), and the older **Rosati**, with an upstairs tea room once much frequented by metaphysical painter Giorgio de Chirico and that popular raconteur of Roman post-war mores, Alberto Moravia.

Turn down the **Via del Corso**, which begins its long straight cut between Piazza del Popolo's twin churches; a few steps will take you to no.18, Goethe's Roman residence from 1786–88 and now a museum to the great man, who once wrote that he never really had a happy day after leaving Rome (**open** Wed–Mon 10–6). The letters and diaries he wrote here became part of his travel classic, *Italian Journey*. A bit further along, on the right, stands **San Giacomo degli Incurabili** (**open** for Mass), with a façade by Maderno and a large oval interior; its name refers to the syphilis patients admitted to the adjacent hospital before the invention of penicillin. Across the street, yet another church, **Gesù e Maria** (*also* **open** for Mass only), was used to take the idea of Bernini's jack-in-the-box bust of Fonseca in S. Lorenzo in Lucina (*see* p.109) one step further, into the nave itself; animated statues of the Bolognetti family chat and worship from their tombs atop the confessionals in a fine colour-coordinated High Baroque interior.

A WALK DOWN THE APPIAN WAY

The 'queen of roads' has, like many a queen, a public and a private personality. The public one that most people see is the two-mile stretch near Rome, a shooting gallery with pedestrians for targets, where tour buses drop trippers at the catacombs. The second, the more personal, carries on past the last catacomb, cutting straight and true across the Roman campagna into the horizon. This is the Appian Way that her lovers remember, beautiful and haunting, where parasol pines, acanthus, and wild flowers create an ideal romantic background for ancient tombs and villas, their bricks blasted by time into hollow shells and forlorn stumps, to say nothing of the four-wheeled love-nests parked along its verges. Where marching legions, ox carts, and imperial pony-express riders once created the world's first traffic jams, the silence is now only broken by a distant cicada, the droning of a lazy fly – or groans emerging from a steamy-windowed Fiat.

The Via Appia Antica was built in 312 BC by Consul Appius Claudius the Blind, in those distant days when a wealthy citizen thought it his civic duty to contribute to the good of the state. It linked Rome to Capua, and was later extended to the port of Brindisi, making it Rome's chief route to conquest in the East. By 4th-century BC standards it was a super-highway, 4m wide, with two wide pavements on either side and, although built primarily to move armies as quickly as possible, it was soon lined with inns,

Start: Largo dei Martiri Fosse Ardeatine, reached on bus 218 from Piazza di Porta San Giovanni in Laterano.

Finish: Via Erode Attico, where you can catch bus 765 back to metro Arco di Travertino, or Casale Rotondo, just beyond the sixth milestone.

Lunch and drinks stops: L'Archeologia, *see* p.316; Cecilia Metella, *see* p.316.

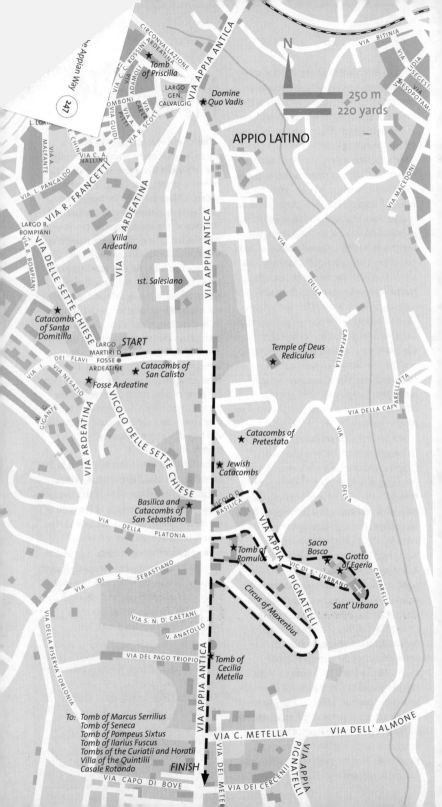

workshops, farms, villas, tombs, catacombs, and on one unhappy occasion, by 4,000 crosses bearing the followers of Spartacus. When Hadrian had it repaved, it cost him 190,000 *sestercii* a Roman mile – and that was non-union labour. Yet after 1,750 years large sections of flagstone paving still remain, a record our modern road builders may have trouble matching.

The Appian Way these days is best known for its catacombs and tombs. According to Roman law, inherited from the Etruscans, all burials had to be outside the *pomerium*, the sacred ground of the city itself, and like all consular roads the Appian Way was soon crowded with cemeteries and elaborate mausoleums. Later the early Christians built some of the most extensive catacombs here – the word itself is believed to come from the cemetery of San Sebastiano near a dip – *ad catacumbas* – in the road.

A main pilgrimage destination in the Dark Ages, the catacombs were first pillaged by the Goths and the Lombards, and then by relic hunters. After the Saracen raid of 847, the whole Appian Way declined, and became infested with cut-throats and malaria. The catacombs were largely abandoned and forgotten. Honest traffic on the road was reduced even further by the toll gate erected in 1300 by the Caetani family in the Tomb of Cecilia Metella. To get around the gate, the Via Appia Nuova was constructed, and the Via Appia Antica was left to push up weeds until the 19th century. The great archaeologist Giambattista De Rossi rediscovered the lost Catacombs of San Calisto (*see* p. 237) in 1850, while the sculptor Antonio Canova deserves the credit for the idea of leaving the tombs where they were found instead of carting them off to rot in a museum.

In recent years, the Rome administration dusted off old plans to make all of this area, along with the Caelian Hill, into a park. Since 1997 the Appian Way has been closed to traffic on *giorni festivi* and is now known as the **Parco Appia Antica**.

Get off the bus at Largo dei Martiri Fosse Ardeatine and follow a short path east to the

---

Parco Appia Antica Information

There are two Parco Appia Antica information points, which can inform you about guided tours down the road on foot or bike, and rent you a bike. One is at *Via Appia Antica 58–60, t (freephone) 8000 2 8000.* **Open** *Sun and hols.* The other is based at **Bar Caffè dell'Appia Antica**, *Via Appia Antica 175.* English tours available for groups of 20 or more. Bike rental €2.50 an hour or €10 a day.

Basilica and Catacombs of San Sebastiano (*Via Appia Antica 136, t 06 788 735; Basilica open 8.30–12 and 2–5.30; catacombs open* for guided tours only, Fri–Wed 8.30–12 and 2.30–5.30). In the 3rd century, during the persecution of Valerian, the Christians feared even for the safety of their dead martyrs, and brought the relics of SS. Paul and Peter from their original tombs to be temporarily interred here. Under Diocletian's persecutions, a young officer in the imperial household named Sebastian was tied to a tree and pumped full of arrows. He recovered, only to be martyred again and laid out in these same catacombs. Thus rendered twice holy, a basilica was built over their tombs in the 4th century, and was called SS. Apostoli, one of the pilgrims' must-see seven churches of Rome. But 500 years later – after the bones of Peter and Paul had been removed to their respective basilicas – the Romans renamed it for Sebastian. Always depicted as the most handsome and dashing of saints in art, Sebastian's charms were potent against the plague, but not much good when it came to keeping rot and rain out of his basilica. In 1612 Cardinal Scipio Borghese paid Flaminio Ponzio and Giovanni Vasanzio to raze and rebuild it. Aesthetically exciting it is not, but in the chapel on the right are the original set of **Domine Quo Vadis?** footprints (*see* p. 237) and a marble *San Sebastiano* by Antonio Giorgetti after a design by Bernini, full of such languid pathos that he seems in love with his own death.

A door to the left of the basilica leads down into the catacombs of Saint Sebastian. As the only ones to have remained open through the centuries, these galleries have suffered the most from relic pirates, but they are still among the most interesting. The burial ground was originally pagan, from the time of Trajan, but once the remains of the two Apostles were brought here the Christians began to bury their dead nearby. They also held funerary banquets here to honour Peter and Paul and benefit the poor, a meal known as a *refrigerium*. These banquets took place in the *triclinium* under the basilica, which the Christians built over the mausoleums of the pagans around the year 250. Inscriptions on the walls refer to the Apostles, confirming the tradition that their relics were here, for at least 40 years. Paintings in the *arcosolia* include a unique manger scene. There are some charming frescoes in one of the pagan tombs, the **Hypogeum of Clodius Hermes**. The ambulatory of the 4th-century basilica is a museum, with a model of the complex and some fascinating early Christian *sarcophagi*, especially one belonging to a certain Lot.

From S. Sebastiano, continue 100 metres or so along the Appia Antica to the narrow **Vicolo della Basilica**. Turn right and continue to busy Via Appia Pignatelli, which links Via Appia Antica to Via Appia Nuova. Turn right and walk some 200 metres to **Vicolo Sant'Urbano** (on the left), a little lane that ends at the gate of a villa much favoured by wealthy Romans for wedding ceremonies. Beyond is the charming little church of **Sant'Urbano**. Sadly you will not be able to see inside it unless you gatecrash a wedding. In ancient times, much of the land to the east of the Appian Way belonged to Herodes Atticus. Another relic of the plutocrat's vast estates, S. Urbano was once a garden temple. Its conversion took place relatively late, in the 10th century, and the columns are perfectly preserved in the walls of the church. Inside are rare frescoes from 1011, depicting New Testament scenes and the lives of contemporaries Santa Cecilia and Pope St Urban, who reputedly hid out in this area during the Christian persecutions.

Take the narrow path to the right around the villa walls, and tramp along it through a field that soon reveals a slice of the old Roman *campagna*. The three trees on the ridge to the right are all that remains of the **Sacro Bosco**, or Sacred Wood, where tradition has it that King Numa Pompilius had his encounters with the nymph Egeria. The path continues down and around to her secret home, the so-called **Grotto of Egeria**. Cool and dark, mossy and mouldering, watered by a trickling stream and hung with draperies of ivy, this artificial grotto with crumbling niches and a headless statue of a reclining nymph was one of the favourite excursions of Romantic tourists of the 18th and 19th centuries. The few people who come here these days are the more actively romantic.

Retrace your steps to the Appian Way, and turn left down to the **Circus of Maxentius** (*Via Appia Antica 153, t 06 780 1324. Open April–Sept Tues–Sat 9–7 and Sun 9–1; Oct–March Tues–Sat 9–5, Sun 9–1; adm €2.50*), the last of the great Roman race tracks and the best preserved. Almost a quarter of a mile long and with a capacity of 18,000 spectators, it was part of a villa complex built by Emperor Maxentius in 309. Its late date meant it saw little action, although the builders incorporated all the latest circus technology: starting stalls for chariots arranged at an angle to make the race as fair as possible and vaults over the stands lightened by inserting *amphorae* as skylights in the masonry. Its distant reaches, down the vast lawn, must be the quietest corner in Rome now. Even the obelisk that once stood in its *spina* (Maxentius stole it from Domitian's Temple of Isis) has gone off to become a celebrity in Piazza Navona.

Next to the Circus, surrounded by looming high walls, is the round **Tomb of Romulus**, Maxentius' young son, with an old farmhouse built over the top. In its vestibule are remains of frescoes, one of which seems to be of a joust. Below, the hollow doughnut of a tomb is shadowy, dank, and empty as all the rest of them.

On a low hill, dominating this stretch of road, is the Appian Way's most famous monument, the **Tomb of Cecilia Metella**

(*Via Appia Antica 161*, *t 06 780 2465*. **Open** *Tues–Sun 9–7*; *adm* €2). Cecilia was the daughter-in-law of the wealthy *triumvir* Crassus, who made a mountain of *sestercii* by following the fire brigades through Rome to buy up the land of burnt-out properties for speculation. Of Cecilia herself little is known but that her family must have loved her dearly to build a tomb nearly as big as those of some emperors. Its ox-head frieze gave the name Capo di Bove to the neighbourhood, which in the 14th century came under the control of the Caetani, the family of Boniface VIII. The Caetani added the crenellations to Cecilia's tomb, making it the castle keep of their fortified toll booth; ruins of their castle and Gothic church moulder across the road. You can walk down into the steep core of the empty tomb; a courtyard contains fragments of other tombs found along the road.

After the Tomb of Cecilia Metella, most of the traffic veers off for Via Appia Nuova. The half mile of Via Appia Antica, shaded with plane trees, has a number of ancient memorials. On the right is the so-called **Heroic Relief** of a naked man with a cape thrown over his shoulder. Just beyond, on the left, is the **Tomb of Marcus Servilius**, a 3D jigsaw puzzled together by Canova, who embedded fragments of rosettes, stylized vegetation and an inscription in a brick cube.

A little further on, also on the left, is the supposed **Tomb of Seneca**, with a lion's head peeking through a curtain of ivy. Condemned to die by his old pupil, Nero, he slit his wrists in a nearby villa and calmly continued to dictate to his weeping secretary, while his equally stoic wife quietly bled her life away in the next room. The cast of the tomb shows a *Relief of the Dying Atys*.

Also on the left is the **Tomb of Pompeus Sixtus**, featuring a *Relief of a Mother and Child*. Beyond, a right turn along Via dei Lugari leads to the scant ruins of a villa, passing the **Tomb of St Urban** (virtually invisible behind a high wall and screen of cypresses). Back on the Appian Way, you soon come to the **Tomb of Ilarius Fuscus** on the right, with five portrait busts.

Beyond the crossing with Via Erode Attico/Tor di Carbone, the Appian Way comes into its own – peaceful, sun-drenched, dotted with cypresses and parasol pines, voluptuous with wild flowers in the spring, surrounded by some of the last unspoilt fields and hills of the classic Roman *campagna*; any moment you expect a chariot to come racing up from Brindisi with news of the legionaries' latest conquest. Large sections of the Appian Way's original pavement have been uncovered, enormous stones softened and smoothed by time and ancient travellers. It is now one of the most attractive places in all Rome, especially the spot just ahead where the engineers made a bend in the road to avoid the ancient tower-crowned **Tomb of the Curiatii**. Further on are two mounds called the **Tombs of the Horatii**.

If your feet are telling you it's time to quit, you can continue south to the corner of Via Erode Attico and catch a bus back to the city. If you're still game, one of the highlights awaits another five minutes down the road: the splendid ruins of the **Villa of the Quintilii** (**open** *Tues–Sun 9–6*; *adm* €4). Dating from the early 2nd century AD, this vast villa belonged to the soldiers and agricultural writers Condianus and Maximus Quintilius, who ran it as a magnificent model farm – so magnificent that it was coveted by the awful Emperor Commodus. To get his hands on their property he had them killed. At the villa's main entrance on the Appian Way are the ruins of a *nymphaeum*, later converted into a fortress. Beyond, in a sheep pasture, are remains of an aqueduct, a hippodrome, and a *cryptoporticus*; further east, near Via Appia Nuova, are even more impressive walls and arcades, and a small amphitheatre.

Another mile or so beyond, just before the sixth milestone is the largest tomb on the entire road, the **Casale Rotondo**, a massive round republican tomb, later enlarged, and now topped by a house and garden. Beyond this the Appian Way, still dotted with scattered tombs and towers, is travelled largely by men heading out to the prostitutes who sit huddled over braziers at the roadside.

A RIDE ON TRAM 3 AND 19

Why walk when you can take the tram? And if you want a look at the real Roma dei Romani, nothing could be finer than ATAC tram routes no.3 and no.19, which take you on a rewarding but somewhat eccentric ramble through half the city's neighbourhoods, with plenty to see along the way. These lines, which overlap along their route, are two of the city's few surviving trolley lines (although there are plans to expand the tram system once more, including a tourist 'Archeotram' to run from Santa Maria Maggiore to the Via Appia Antica).

Some of the trams on the 3 and 19 routes are almost new, others date back to the 1940s. They are all narrow orange carriages, made in Italy, with the city's SPQR arms proudly displayed on the side. But, unlike the city buses, they offer a gentle, smooth and entirely convivial ride. The drivers and even the passengers seem to know they are enjoying something just a little bit special.

Most city transit lines at least pretend to have a destination in mind, but with these two lines this is not the case. The no.3 starts from Trastevere Station, meanders through Trastevere, veering away from the Campo Marzio to cross the Tiber at Porta Portese, pass the Piramide and skirt the Aventine and Circus Maximus. Next it passes the Colosseum, and makes for Termini Station. It never quite gets there, but along its merry way it passes three of the pilgrims' seven churches of Rome: San Giovanni in Laterano, Santa Croce in Gerusalemme and San Lorenzo fuori le Mura, and hidden treasures at Porta Maggiore. After that it tours some modern districts of Rome's east side and around the edges of the Villa Borghese, finishing up outside the Museo Etrusco Nazionale di Villa Giulia. The no.19, which joins the route at Porta Maggiore, carries on beyond. You can ride it back, almost full circle, across the river to the Vatican.

From Trastevere Station, the no.3 begins uneventfully, up shady Viale di Trastevere. Get off just before it turns at Via Induno if you want to see **Santa Maria in Trastevere** (see p.194) and the lovely old quarter around it. Otherwise, your tram carries on through **Porta Portese** on the Tiber, home to Rome's great Sunday morning flea market. Once over the Ponte Sublicio, you're on Via Marmorata, under the southern slope of the **Aventine Hill** (see p.169); the big complex on the left is the **Priory of the Knights of Malta**. A bit further, on the right, you may catch a glimpse of **Monte Testaccio** (see p.171), a hill made entirely of discarded ancient pottery – a relic from the time when this was Rome's port and warehouse district.

Via Marmorata ends in a memorable corner of the city, Piazza San Paolo, decorated with the mighty **Porta San Paolo** in the Aurelian Wall, and just behind it, Rome's own Pyramid – the **Pyramid of Gaius Cestius** (see p.170). Considering how many obelisks the Romans borrowed from Egypt, it wouldn't be surprising if they nicked a pyramid too, but this marble one was built as a tomb by a rich politician named Gaius Cestius in 12 BC. Just behind it is the **Protestant Cemetery** or

---

Start: Trastevere Station.

Finish: Piazza del Risorgimento, near the Vatican.

Lunch and drink stops: Relais le Jardin, see p.316; Caffè delle Arti, see p.316; Al Ceppo, see p.315; Fauro, see p.316; Semidivino, see p.316; La Soffitta, see p.316; Pommidoro, see p.316; Tram Tram, see p.316; Il Dito e la Luna, see p.316.

Tram ticket information: The public transport authority, ATAC, sells a daily pass called a Biglietto Integrato Giornaliero, for €3. It is valid for all metro lines and buses, as well as the trams. The BIG pass can be bought at the Trastevere Station tram terminus (where this route begins), at any bus terminus or metro stop, or at tabacchi, news-stands and kiosks. It must be stamped when you first get on the tram and is valid until midnight on the day of travel.

Cimitero Acattolico (*see* p.171), where Keats is buried. As the tram turns onto Viale della Piramide Cestia, you'll get a brief glimpse on the right of one of Mussolini's bigger planning schemes: **Stazione Ostiense** and the piazza around it. It's a slightly uncanny, very Roman Fascist sort of travertine ensemble. When it was built, this was called Piazzale Adolf Hitler – now they call it Piazzale dei Partigiani.

After the tram skirts the Aventine, along Viale Aventino, it passes the open site that was once the **Circus Maximus** (*see* p.167) to the left and, to the right, the UN's food and agriculture organization, the **FAO**. Its building, left unfinished during the war, was intended as Mussolini's Ministry of Africa – an integral part of Il Duce's grandiose imperial project. His invading army stole the **Obelisk of Axum** (*see* p.162) from Ethiopia's holy city to decorate the piazza in front; only now is Italy thinking of giving it back.

Once Roman emperors and generals celebrating triumphs rode in delirious processions up Via di San Gregorio. Now you can do it on the streetcar. To the left is the **Palatine Hill** (*see* p.151), where Romulus founded his city and emperors built their palaces. After **S. Gregorio Magno** (*see* p.162), with its landmark early baroque façade, a pretty street on the right called **Clivo di Scauro** invites you to hop off for a tour of the quiet delights and ancient churches of the Caelian Hill (*see* p.160).

At the end of the ancient Roman Triumphal Way stands the **Arch of Constantine** (*see* p.149). The entrances to the **Forum** (*see* p.139) are just down to the left, and you can already see the **Colosseum** (*see* p.149). If you stop for a look around here, don't miss the recently restored and reopened remnant of Nero's famous **Golden House** (see p.183). From the Colosseum, it's down Via Labicana, skirting on the left the **Colle Oppio** and the **Esquiline Hill** (*see* p.184). After a right turn, you might notice another obelisk lurking on the right – the tallest ever made, marking Piazza San Giovanni and the great basilica of **San Giovanni in Laterano** (*see* p.164), with its

medieval cloister and the adjacent palace that was home to the popes for over a thousand years.

When medieval pilgrims did their tour of the seven churches, S. Giovanni and the others in this part of Rome stood among open fields. Now the tram passes through a busy neighbourhood around Piazza di Porta San Giovanni and down Viale Carlo Felice, just inside the Aurelian Wall, to the next of the seven churches, **Santa Croce in Gerusalemme** (*see* p.236). Last rebuilt in 1744, this church was founded by Constantine's mother Helen to keep a relic of the True Cross. After Piazza di Santa Croce, the route follows Via Eliena, passing the arches of the **Acqua Claudia**, an aqueduct begun under Caligula and completed by Claudius in AD 52, carrying Acqua Vergine spring water from Subiaco, 68km away.

The next stop, **Porta Maggiore** (*see* p.236), offers a look at two more ancient relics. First is the **Baker's Tomb** (30 BC), carved with circles to symbolize bread pans; on reliefs you can still make out the master baker, Marcus Vergilius Eurysaces, in his toga, directing his slaves at their work. For the other, look left down Via Giolitti as the tram leaves the piazza to see the **Temple of Minerva Medica**. This unusual geometrical fancy, built on the plan of a double pentagon, was really a nymphaeum in the gardens of a 4th-century nabob named Licinius; before its dome caved in it was an inspiration to many of the artists and architects of the Renaissance. Crossing the tracks behind Termini Station, you'll pass a third relic, one of the strangest sights in Rome, the mysterious, 1st-century AD **Underground Basilica**, (see p.237).

Once over the tracks, Viale dello Scalo di San Lorenzo takes you to the last big church, **San Lorenzo fuori le Mura** (*see* p.235), wedged between the Campo Verano Cemetery, Rome's biggest, and the unremittingly dull Mussolinian Città Universitaria. From here on, it's into modern Rome, up the long, straight Viale Regina Margherita (like pizza Margherita, this was named for the gracious wife of King Umberto I).

As the tram passes Via Nomentana, look left and you'll see the **Porta Pia**, designed by Michelangelo; near it is the famous **Breccia**, the breach blown in the Aurelian Wall by Italian troops in 1870 when they seized Rome to complete the unification of Italy.

The second tram stop after Via Nomentana is Piazza Buenos Aires, where you can stop to tour the marvellously overripe villas of the **Coppedé** neighbourhood. Built after World War I, when Art Nouveau was going out of fashion everywhere else, these blocks of architectural madness take the style to its wildest extremes: fairy-tale castle apartment blocks on Via Dora, just east of Viale Regina Margherita, and mock-medieval villas on Via Brenta that Dante might have imagined in Paradise.

After crossing into the wealthy bourgeois suburb of the **Parioli** neighbourhood, the tram makes a left on Via Bellini, heading towards the **Villa Borghese** park (see p.229), where you can stop for a picnic or a tour of the excellent collection of art in the **Museo e Galleria Borghese** (see p.232). The park has its other attractions; after the entrance at the end of Via Bellini the tram skirts the outer wall of the **Zoo**.

After that, at Piazza Thorvaldsen it meets Rome's 19th-century museum district. The massive embarassment on the right is the **Galleria Nazionale d'Arte Moderna** (see p.230), an incongruous setting for the hoard of modern Italian painting inside.

Tram no.3 does not care to go any further than this, so you'll have to switch over to the no.19 here if you have not done so already. It's a good place for a stop anyhow, with one of Rome's genuine seldom-seen delights, the **Villa Giulia**. Pope Julius III called on the great Giacomo da Vignola, with Michelangelo as a consultant, to build this garden villa and nymphaeum; now it holds the **Museo Etrusco Nazionale di Villa Giulia** (see p.231), with a collection of art from one of antiquity's most fascinating peoples.

No.19's route is a little anti-climactic after all this art and greenery. The tram finds its way from the museums down to Via Flaminia, the old imperial route north to Gaul, then turns on Via Azuni and passes the imposing building of the Navy Ministry before crossing the Tiber again on the Ponte Matteotti. Through the 19th-century Prati district it passes down Via delle Milizie and Via Ottaviano to the end of the line at Piazza del Risorgimento. Did we say anti-climactic? Here is the entrance to the **Vatican Museums** (see p.210), and **Piazza San Pietro** (see p.203) is only a short walk to the south down Via di Porta Angelica.

Day Trips

'... I am convinced that no inhabited site among the peoples of old was as badly placed as Rome,' wrote Goethe in 1768. 'In the end, when they had swallowed up everything, in order to live and enjoy life, the Romans had to move out again and build their country villas on the sites of the cities they had destroyed.' They are still doing it. A *scampagnata*, the Romans call it – an escape into the countryside, the celebrated Campagna Romana, beloved of landscape artists in the 18th and 19th centuries. Since Goethe's day it has become an urban-suburban-rural grab-bag, blasted by the curse of car lots and uncontrolled speculation, though some corners have managed to keep a modicum of pristine delight. When Rome begins to wear you down, such places

are worth seeking out. Some suggestions: the countryside and gardens around Tivoli and the Castelli Romani, being perhaps the most easily accessible; Lake Nemi and the botanical paradise of Ninfa the most enchanting; Viterbo the most medieval; Cervéteri and Tarquinia the most Etruscan; the Monster Park of Bomarzo the most bizarre. But there are times when it's best not to do as the Romans do, especially at weekends, when planning a jaunt into the country – unless conga-lines of cars inching along the autostrade is your cup of tea.

The day trips proceed clockwise from Ostia Antica. Most will occupy the better part of a day, though with a car you can combine two, like Caprarola and the Bomarzo Monster Park or Palestrina and Subiaco.

OSTIA

After Pompeii and Herculaneum, Ostia Antica is the best-preserved Roman town in Italy, a fascinating lesson on everyday life in ancient Rome itself. Set amid parasol pines and wild flowers, it is as lovely as it is interesting, its brick walls festooned with garlands of ivy, its ruined temples home to scores of sunning lizards and tiny blue butterflies.

Ostia Antica

*t 06 5635 8099. **Open** Tues–Sun 9–one hour before sunset; **adm** €4.*

According to legend, Ostia was founded in the 6th century BC by the fourth king of Rome, Ancus Martius, although archaeological evidence prefers a 4th-century date. Its name derives from Ostium, or river mouth, for it was here 'that the waters of the Mediterranean mingled with the Tiber', as the Romans used to joke. Originally built as a walled *castrum* – perhaps the prototype for all subsequent 'camps' that in the next four centuries would stretch from Britain to the Near East – Ostia both guarded the main entrance to Rome and produced salt from the surrounding marshes. Rome's growing sea trade soon made it a thriving port; the First Punic War made it of necessity a naval base as well. Its major setback came from its own mother's hands, when the Romans under Marius sacked it; Sulla immediately rebuilt it, with the wall that still bears his name (the Cinta Sillana).

By the 1st century AD, the port of Ostia could no longer handle Rome's insatiable demand for more and more goods, and Claudius began a new port at Portus. But still Ostia grew. After Rome's great fire of AD 64, Nero sent tons of debris down the Tiber to reclaim the surrounding swamplands. Hadrian poured money into the town, rebuilding it as a 2nd-century garden suburb for middle and working-class families. Although many businesses had relocated to Portus, Ostia's warehouses, *horreae*, managed Rome's huge dole, the Annona.

Ostia's worst enemy proved to be Constantine, who conferred all of its ancient rights as a city on Portus, perhaps because the residents had little use for his new religion – 18 *mithraeums* have been uncovered

Getting There

By Metro

Overland Metropolitana trains run to Ostia Antica from Porta San Paolo or EUR-Magliana **metro** stops, every 30 minutes throughout the day. The excavations are a 5-minute walk from the Ostia Antica station.

By Car

From Porta San Paolo drive 23 km along Via del Mare, parallel to the ancient Via Ostiense.

Tourist Information

Ostia Antica: *t 06 5635 8099.*
Ostia Lido: *t 06 562 7892.*

Eating Out

Ostia Antica

One option is to buy supplies in the village of Ostia, and picnic amid the ruins. Other options are unashamedly touristy.

Allo Sbarco di Enea, *Viale dei Romagnoli 675, t 06 565 0034; wheelchair accessible.* **Open** *Tues–Sun, except 3 weeks in Jan.* **Moderate**. 'Aeneas's Landing', between excavations and station, has a Ben Hur chariot in the yard. Dining under the trellis in summer.

Lido di Ostia

In Lido di Ostia there are plenty of pizzerias and fish restaurants, but don't expect to find any bargains. Those below are worth a try.

Sporting Beach, *Lungomare A. Vespucci 8, Ostia Lido, t 06 5647 0256; parking.* **Open** *daily.* **Moderate**. You can dine on the beach at this reasonably-priced fish restaurant, which also offers a few meat dishes.

Il Segreto di Pulcinella, *Via Rutilio Namaziano 31, t 06 567 2194; parking.* **Open** *Oct–May Tues–Sun, June–Sept daily. No credit cards.* **Inexpensive**. Genuine Neapolitan pizza 'al fresco'.

so far, in contrast to only a handful of Christian buildings. Still, the city survived as a residential backwater; new, more splendid *domus*-style homes were built, until the 5th century brought total decadence, and even worse, malaria. Ostia was neglected, looted, and covered with sand; the silt of the Tiber moved the coastline a few miles west, and in 1575 a flood altered the course of the Tiber.

The excavations, begun in the 19th century, have so far uncovered two thirds of the city. Earlier shovels and chisels were at work along the **Via delle Tombe**, at the entrance to the site; fortune hunters have left only a few *columbaria* and *sarcophagi* undamaged. The road from Rome, **Via Ostiense**, its flagstones deeply grooved by ancient cart wheels, leads up to the Republican-era **Porta Romana**, Ostia's main gate. Emperor Domitian added two winged Minerva Victories to flank the gate, one of which survives in the **Piazza della Vittoria**, a weird creature that would not look out of place in the science-fiction palace of Ming the Merciless.

Once through the gate, Via Ostiense becomes the main street, the **Decumanus Maximus**; on the right it passes a series of **Horrea**, or warehouses, one of which was converted in the 1st century AD by the ancient equivalent of the bus drivers' union into a bath complex, known as the **Baths of the Cisiarii**; a mosaic in the *frigidarium* shows the guild members at work, carting passengers about in wagons. The fancier **Baths of Neptune**, still on the right side of the Decumanus, were built by Hadrian and decorated with elaborate mosaics of frolicking sea gods and a *palaestra* for gymnastics.

Just before the baths, Via dei Vigili leads back to a fine *Mosaic of the Winds*; on the left Hadrian built the **Police and Firemen's Barracks**, marked by a curious, steeply inclined ramp (an early version of a firemen's pole?). The mosaic in the centre, of men leading a bull to sacrifice, was part of the barracks' shrine to the deified emperors, or Augusteum. On the narrow lane behind the barracks is a well-preserved row of *insulae*,

with their shops on the ground floor and stairs leading up to the flats (the average *insula* at Ostia had four floors). The shop at the end of the lane, facing the Decumanus, was the **Tavern of Fortunatus**, with a mosaic advertisement from the halcyon days before Madison Avenue: 'Fortunatus says: if you're thirsty, drink a bowl of wine.'

Beyond stands the much-restored **Theatre**, built by Agrippa, who included shops in the arcades under the seats, one now selling souvenirs, another is a bar, and a third the WC. Three marble masks, once part of the stage decoration, have been set up on tufa columns. In front of the theatre is the fascinating **Forum of the Corporations**, a quadrangle where 61 of Ostia's various maritime concerns had their offices around a quadrangle. The temple in the centre was dedicated either to Ceres or 'Annona Augusta', the Divinity of Imperial Provisions, to which each firm was devoted, heart and soul. Black and white mosaics indicate the special business of each (most depict cargo ships; those with elephants and reindeer dealt in land transport), its trademark, and the nationality of its merchants and fitters. Ponder them. As Jérôme Carcopino wrote, 'And suddenly you see the throngs of people, strangers to each other, born in far distant lands, rowing to meet each other here in answer to the needs of Rome, and you feel that there gravitates forever round this unforgettable enclosure not only the mass of goods which Rome appropriated for herself in every corner of the earth, but the cortège of docile nations whom she had consecrated to her service'. Or picture Rome as a queen termite, too bloated to move, with scores of tiny servants whose sole job is to bring food to drop in her insatiable maw.

Next to the Forum is the **House of Apuleius**, a domus with a peristyle, like the houses of Pompeii; adjacent, along the Decumanus, is the well-preserved **Mithraeum of the Seven Spheres**, named for the seven semicircles shown on the mosaic floor, symbolizing the seven stages of initiation and/or the seven planets. Its neighbour, the **Great Horrea**, the largest warehouse in Ostia, has a porticoed court surrounded by some 60 small rooms for storing corn. Across the Decumanus, the **Seat of the Augustales** was the headquarters of the priests in charge of the official emperor-worship.

Via dei Molini and Via Semita dei Cippi mark the eastern limits of the original *castrum*. Via dei Molini is named for the Apartment of the Millstones (still containing mills and olive presses). The adjacent **Casa di Diana**, one of the more posh *insulae*, was originally four storeys, with taverns and shops on the ground floor and spacious flats above, with its own latrine, balconies, cistern and pool in the court, and its own private *mithraeum*. Across Via di Diana, don't miss the **Thermopolium**, or snack bar, which wouldn't look out of place in Rome today with its shiny marble bar and shelf to display the various snacks, these illustrated by a surviving fresco; it has a small wine cellar, vessels set in the floor for storing oil, and an area for sitting outside in good weather, complete with a little fountain. Next to the Casa di Diana, the **Casa dei Dipinti** was equally large, and the most luxurious *insula* ever found, once entirely covered on the outside with festoons and paintings; through the gate you can see a colourfully frescoed room. Climb the stairs to the top floor for a view of the excavations.

Museo Ostiense

Open Tues–Sun 9–one hour before sunset; adm included in the excavations ticket.

Just to the north, a converted 15th-century salt deposit now contains the **Museo Ostiense**. Among the most interesting items are the bas-reliefs in the first room, portraying daily life in ancient Ostia (including a birth scene) and beyond, a 1st-century BC round relief of the 12 gods, statues of Mithras stabbing the bull, Trajan in a cuirass (looking very uncomfortable with a slice of his abdomen missing), also Perseus with Medusa's head, Julia Domna (Septimius Severus' wife), dressed as Ceres; the headless but very virile Hero in Repose; Maxentius as

Pontifex Maximus; a beautifully carved sarcophagus of a boy from Pontus' necropolis at Isola Sacra, and what is believed to be a portrait of Christ, a beautiful polychrome *opus sectile* pavement. Strangest of all are the marble footprints, facing in opposite directions. Found in the temple of the war goddess Bellona, they were probably a soldier's votive offering of thanks for returning safely from war.

From the museum, Via Tecta leads past the **Piccolo Mercato**, a well-preserved grain ware-house, and continues into the **Forum**, with its two temples facing each other across the square: nearest, with the broad stairway, is the **Capitolium**, a temple dedicated to the Etruscan/Roman trinity of Jupiter, Juno, and Minerva, rebuilt by Hadrian. Throughout the centuries its high walls have always been visible, and were used by local farmers as a sheep pen. Across the Forum stands the older **Temple of Rome and Augustus**; marble frag-ments of both temples that escaped the busy medieval lime kilns lie near each. Much less has survived of the other Forum build-ings: the **Curia**, seat of Ostia's Senate, the **Basilica**, and the **Round Temple**, probably dedicated to emperor worship; its ruined spiral staircase once led up to the dome.

Next to the Temple of Rome and Augustus the **Casa Triclini** is named for the dining couches found in the rooms along the right; built into this *insula*'s right-hand corner is the public lavatory, or **forica**, a 20-holer once equipped with a revolving door and a constant flow of water. The only thing lacking was paper; the Romans used swabs on the end of sticks (hence the expression 'to get the wrong end of the stick'). Across from the loo were the **Forum Baths**, Ostia's largest (2nd century AD, but remodelled many times). You can make out the furnaces used for heating the steam baths and *caldarium*, and the ornate *frigidarium* for cooling off. Just to the south is another bath complex contributed by Hadrian, the **Terme del Faro**, named for its mosaic of Ostia's lighthouse surrounded by sea creatures; it also has a fresco of a bull-riding *nereid*.

Across the Cardo Maximus is the **Casa di Giove Fulminatore**, decorated with a relief of a foot-long phallus, like an arrow pointing to the door (as at Pompeii, these are good luck charms). The **Domus delle Colonne**, named for the white marble columns in the courtyard, is the next building south; in the adjacent lane, the 3rd-century AD **Caupona del Pavone** was one of Ostia's nicer inns, perhaps even the one St Augustine mentions in his Confessions, where he had his famous conversation with his mother St Monica before their departure for Africa – though as Monica fell ill and died before they set sail, the inn may not have been so nice after all. Near the Porta Laurentina is the triangular sacred precinct of the **Campo della Magna Mater**, most of which was strictly off-limits for women. Against the gate is the **Temple of Bellona** and its college of adepts, the **Schola of the Hastiferii**; here, too, flanked by two telamones of Pan, is the **Sanctuary of Attis**, part of the **Temple of Cybele**, the Great Mother. A slight detour from the gate up Via Semita dei Cippi will take you to the **Domus of the Vestibule**, with a fine polychrome mosaic, and the **Domus of Fortuna Annonaria**, with a mosaic of the she-wolf, a nymphaeum, and a one-hole *forica*.

Returning to the Forum, walk beyond the Curia to Via Epagathiana, a street marking the western limits of the *castrum* – a puny place compared to Ostia's later size. On the right is **Horrea Epagathiana**, a private warehouse, with the two owners' names still inscribed over the door and a large swastika in the floor mosaic (one of the most ancient sun symbols, though once its religious meaning was forgotten, it became a lucky charm if the arms bent to the right, and bad luck if they went to the left). Across the lane stands the **House of Cupid and Psyche**, an attractive 4th-century *domus* named for the statue group discovered within; it has a lavish *opus sectile* pavement, and is believed to have been owned by a wealthy merchant who preferred Ostia in its decline to dense and noisy Portus. The adjacent **Baths of Buticosus** is named after a bath attendant

whose portrait in mosaic was discovered here, along with another rollicking mosaic of sea monsters.

South of here the Decumanus Maximus forks; the branch called Via della Foce continues towards the Tiber. On the right are the **Baths of Mithras**, this one especially good for exploring its subterranean plumbing if it's not flooded by ground water; note the marks left by the water wheel, which filled the lead pipes running into the boiler. Next door is the **Hall of the Wheat Measurers**, with a fine mosaic illustrating their tasks.

Heading back along Via delle Foce, note the high-walled group of buildings on the right, nearly all built by Hadrian in what may have been a kind of ancient self-sufficient estate complex, with condominiums, baths, a *mithraeum*, and shops. First on the right is the **House of Bacchus** and the **House of Serapis**, a pair of *insulae* with one of Ostia's finest mosaics, of Bacchus and Ariadne. Next are Hadrian's **Baths of Trinacria**, with more fine mosaics and plumbing fixtures underground. Then come the **Baths of the Sette Sapienti**, or Seven Sages, though here you'd call them the seven wise guys: each is frescoed with a caption with advice on how to wash your rude parts. Don't miss the beautiful mosaic of a hunting scene in the circular hall. Adjacent to the baths is the **Insula Aurigi**, or House of the Charioteers, named for its fresco of two jockeys; its high, upper level of arches gives a fair idea of what the insulae looked like.

The last section of Ostia lies along the extension of the Decumanus Maximus to the Porta Marina. Head back to the fork; wedged between the two streets is a presumed **Christian Basilica**, while across the Decumanus is the **Macellum**, or meat market, complete with mosaics and marble counters and basins that once held live fish. The **Schola di Traiano**, headquarters of a corporation (of shipbuilders?), was a monumental complex with a long niched pool, named for the statue of Trajan discovered on the site. Further down and across the Decumanus stands the **Insula of the Painted**

Vaults (usually closed, but you could try asking for access at the museum), an apartment house built by Hadrian and later converted into a *lupanare*, or bordello, as the traces of fresco and graffiti bear witness. Evidence suggests that the ancient sex business was fairly specialized; a mosaic nearby that the tour groups never get to see depicts the services offered by male dwarfs. This is right next to Ostia's high rent district, another complex of *insulae* built by Hadrian, luxurious and most innovative in style, the perfect home for an upper-crust Roman. First, there's the **Casa delle Muse**, with a restored roof and wall paintings of Apollo and the Muses (though again only visible through a gate); the **Casa dei Giardini**, the Garden Homes, which looked onto their private garden like a Bloomsbury square; and the **Domus of the Dioscuri**, embellished with beautiful polychrome 4th-century mosaics.

The Decumanus leaves Ostia by the **Marine Gate**, which by the time of Hadrian had been built over by citizens who felt no threat from a sea they called their own. One of the old towers was converted into an inn, the Caupona of Alexander Helix, whose name may be read on the floor mosaic; other mosaics in the tavern show Egyptian contortionist-dancers, Venus, and two wrestlers. Beyond the gate, towards the ancient beach, stood funerary monuments, including the imposing travertine **Monument of C. Cartilius Poplicola**, along with some seaside villas and the **Baths of Marciana**, with mosaics of athletes warming up in the dressing room. Four tall columns with composite capitals are all that remains of the **Synagogue** (1st century AD), which stood right on the beach; some of the mosaic floor remains, as well as the apse that once held the ark of the Torah, and an adjacent oven probably used to bake unleavened bread.

Ostia

From the excavations it's a 10-minute walk to the sleepy hamlet of Ostia, founded in 831 as 'Gregopolis' by Pope Gregory IV, to defend Rome after the Saracens captured Sicily. Pope Julius II, while he was still Ostia's cardinal, built the huge brick **Castello**, Ostia's 1483 landmark sample of Renaissance fortifications. It frightened Turks and marauders up the Tiber until the river itself moved; now it holds a humble historical collection.

Within the walls of Ostia are Renaissance-era attached houses built for workers in the papal salt pans, and the small Renaissance church of **Sant' Aurea**, built over the 5th-century basilica of Ostia's first martyr. Ask if the **Episcopio**, or bishop's palace is open, to see the unusual decorations by Baldassare Peruzzi, 1511–13, recently discovered under layers of whitewash. Julius at the time was trying to kick the French out of Italy, and the 15 *grisaille* frescoes, adaptations of scenes from Trajan's Column, painted to look like reliefs, are pure Renaissance flattery, comparing wars of the pope to conquests of the emperor.

Portus

Remains of Emperor Claudius' new port were found during the construction of Fiumicino airport. In ancient times its most spectacular feature was its lighthouse, the Pharos of Portus, built on an artificial island, created by sinking the massive ship that transported the Vatican obelisk from Egypt. Trajan later added a canal linking the port to the Tiber, creating an island known as the **Isola Sacra**. Isola Sacra was the necropolis of ancient Portus until the 4th century, discovered excellently preserved under layers of sand. The inhabitants of Portus, unlike many Romans, had to work for a living and couldn't afford big fancy monuments. Instead the dead were laid out in simple barrel-vaulted tombs or 'trunk tombs' shaped like 19th-century travelling trunks, or had their ashes deposited in columbaria. Many opted for fine terracotta, stucco, or mosaic decoration, often depicting the deceased's trade; one Egyptophile lies under a baby brick pyramid.

Of Portus itself, only a small village remains (Porto), though there are plans to excavate the ancient ports of Claudius and Trajan. The latter's hexagonal docks have survived as an inland lake, **Lago Traiano**, on Via Portuensis; you may see it when flying into Fiumicino.

Museo delle Navi Romane

t 06 652 9192. **Open** *Tues–Sun 9–1.30, Tues and Thurs also 2.30–4.30;* **adm** *€2.*

Near the airport, the museum contains seven ships uncovered during the construction of the airport in 1961.

Lido di Ostia

Rome's own beach used to be the city's summer seaside resort. Half the city still comes down here to cool off, despite the fetid brew of pollution just beyond the sands, but Lido di Ostia has grown into a huge and densely-packed suburb. It's a likeable enough place, with two remarkable Mussolini-era buildings: the **Post Office** on Via del Mare and the **Fire Station** two streets south. A monument at **Idroscalo**, near the mouth of the Tiber, marks the spot where film director Pier Paolo Pasolini was murdered in 1975.

Though the water isn't so nice, the beaches are broad and fine. If you mean to do any swimming, try further south, away from the Tiber; better, less crowded beaches stretch past the pine forests of Castelfusano and for miles down the Lazio coast (*see* p.282).

ETRUSCAN TOWNS

It is hard to believe, but this empty quarter of northern Lazio, once used by Cinecittà for spaghetti western settings, was the richest and most heavily populated part of ancient Etruria and includes the only two sites worth visiting for those not enchanted with archaeology: the museums and necropolises at Cervéteri and Tarquinia.

Of the cities themselves, little remains. Living Etruscans preferred ephemeral homes and temples of wood and clay, but when it came to the afterlife they built for eternity.

Their cities of the dead, of stone tombs carved in the rock, contained their luxuries and favourite things, 'a pleasant continuance of life, with jewels and wine and flutes playing for the dance,' as D. H. Lawrence wrote after visiting the region.

Cervéteri

Locally famous for its artichokes, Cervéteri is named for the abandoned medieval citadel of Caere Vetere ('Old Caere') in memory of Caere, the Etruscans' richest city.

Caere also had the closest cultural ties to Greece; according to Herodotus, it was the only non-Greek city with a sanctuary at Delphi. It had three seaports (for a population of 25,000) and mined the Tolfa mountains for the metals it exchanged for Attic vases and other luxury goods.

Decline began when the Greek cities in southern Italy defeated the Etruscan fleet in 474 BC, ending their naval supremacy. Caere then turned to agriculture and became a close ally of Rome.

A falling out came in the 3rd century BC, when Caere rebelled and was put in its place, minus the rights of full Roman citizenship. In the early Middle Ages the city was abandoned, then had a brief renaissance in the 13th century; the Orsini later added a small castle in the piazza, which now serves as the **Museo Nazionale di Cervéteri** (*t 06 994 1354.* **Open** *Tues–Sun 9–one hour before sunset;* **adm** *free*), with a well-arranged display of tomb finds from the 8th–1st centuries BC, including a magnificent collection of Greek and Greek-style vases.

Banditaccia Necropolis

A 2km drive or walk from the museum in the village; turn right from the piazza, and then right again on the narrow branch lane; t 06 994 1354. **Open** *Tues–Sun 9–one hour before sunset;* **adm** *€4.*

This is only one of Cervéteri's four cemeteries (which cover three times the area of the city for the living!), but it's the most interesting, in a park setting of cypresses and

Getting There

By Bus

COTRAL buses leave from metro Lepanto to Cervéteri (46 km), Tarquinia (96 km) and Tuscania (130 km) several times a day; for information call *(freephone)* **t** *800 431 784 (Mon–Fri 8–6)*.

By Train

Tarquinia can also be reached by train from Termini. Tarquinia station is 2km from central Piazza Cavour, connected by a bus every 40 minutes; from there you can catch a bus to the necropolis (Mon–Sat, two departures every morning) or walk (25 minutes).

By Car

Follow Via Aurelia (SS1).

Tourist Information

Cervéteri: **t** *06 994 2348*.
Civitavecchia: **t** *0766 22727*.
Tarquinia: **t** *0766 856 384*.
Tuscania: **t** *0761 436 371*.

Eating Out

The Etruscans certainly won't mind if you bring a picnic to any of their necropolises.

Otherwise the Etruscan towns offer a hearty mixture of mountain meat and fish from the coast nearby.

Cervéteri

Antica Locanda Le Ginestre, *Piazza S. Maria 2*, **t** *06 994 0672*. **Open** *Feb–Dec Tues–Sun; Aug eves only*. **Expensive**. An atmospheric, refined old inn, serving a memorable tagliatelle with truffles, and well-made fish dishes. Outside seating.

Tarquinia

Restaurants in Tarquinia tend to be of the cheap, touristy kind, with the odd exception. **Le Due Orfanelle**, *Vicolo Breve 4 (off Via di Porta Tarquinia)*, **t** *0766 856 307*. **Open** *Wed–Mon*. **Inexpensive**. Better than most, with a large dining room and a fireplace in winter. The speciality here is grilled meat.

Civitavecchia

La Bomboniera, *Corso Marconi 50*, **t** *0766 25744; parking*. **Open** *Tues–Sun; closed 3 weeks Aug–Sept*. **Moderate**. Great fish dishes in the Sardinian style. The must here is a dessert: *seadas* – light ravioli-like fritters with a ricotta filling served with warm honey.

---

parasol pines. The tombs were laid out in the form of a town, with streets and squares, an Etruscan model tumulus show where you can see every style available, from the early grave trenches carved in the tufa to 'cube' tombs resembling houses, to the round mounds with *hypogeums* carved into the rock below – heavy stone domes, set low to the ground, that look more like defence bunkers than tombs. The largest measure over 130ft in diameter, and in them you can see the forerunners of the Mausoleums of Augustus and Hadrian. The tombs of men are marked at the entrance with a phallic symbol, while women get a little house.

Not all of the tombs are lit; the site is quite large, and you may want to buy the map on sale at the entrance to find your way (€0.50). For serious exploration, ask a guide to unlock and light the more distant tombs for you, although in winter and early spring these

may well be flooded. Don't miss the **Tomb of the Capitals** near the entrance, carved from tufa to resemble Etruscan houses, or the **Tomb of the Shields and Chairs**, with unusual military decoration. Another tomb, the even stranger **Tomb of the Stuccoes**, is covered with painted stone reliefs of cooking utensils and other household objects.

Civitavecchia and Tarquinia

Between Cervéteri and Tarquinia, you'll pass the not-so-old-looking city of **Civitavecchia**, a port for Rome and the gateway for ferries to Sardinia. The big fortress overlooking the harbour was designed by Michelangelo for the popes, but there's little else to detain you.

Further up the coast, **Tarquinia** is a large, modern town of interest in its own right, with a 12th-century Cosmatesque church and a Roman aqueduct, rebuilt in the Middle Ages and still in use. In the 15th-century Palazzo Vitelleschi, many of the finest discoveries from the Etruscan city and its necropolis have been assembled.

Museo Nazionale Tarquinia

Piazza Cavour, t 0766 856 036. **Open** *Tues–Sun 8.30–7; adm €4, or €6 combined ticket for museum and necropolis.*

The stars of the collection are the famous **Winged Horses** from the 'Altar of the Queen' temple on the acropolis; beautiful beasts, but made of terracotta like most Etruscan temple decorations, which explains why so few have survived. Well-carved *sarcophagi* are present in abundance, and there is a collection of Greek vases by some of the greatest 6th–5th century Attic painters. The Etruscans were talented at ceramics, too, as seen in fine samples of *bucchero* ware, black pottery incised or painted with puzzling Etruscan images. Some of the paintings from the tombs have been relocated here for their protection, including scenes of chariot-riding and athletics – almost any subject is likely to turn up on Etruscan tomb walls; the **Tomb of the Triclinium** with its dancers is one of the most beautiful.

Monterozzi Necropolis

A 15-minute walk (signposted) from the museum, t 0766 856 308. **Open** *Tues–Sun 8.30–one hour before sunset; adm €4, or €6 combined ticket for necropolis and museum.*

There aren't enough staff to keep open the hundreds of tombs at Tarquinia's necropolis, all that remains standing of the city of 100,000 strong (in legend, anyhow) that dominated southern Etruria for centuries and enforced on Rome its early dynasty of Etruscan kings . The few you can see on any given day, however, rank among the finest examples of Etruscan painting. Tombs like that of the Augurs and the Lionesses with their beautiful 'Ionic' style paintings, seem remarkably close to the art of ancient Crete. These began to appear in the 6th century BC

in the tombs of the richest Etruscans; more typical of the rest is the **Tomb of the Warrior**, carved simply out of the tufa and hung with arms and trophies. The **Tomb of the Leopards** is decorated with fascinating scenes of an Etruscan feast. Don't overlook the separate part of the necropolis, opposite and just down the road from the main entrance; here the **Tomba degli Anina** has uncanny funeral scenes featuring the Vanth and Carontes, the conductors of souls in the underworld.

Tuscania

Northeast of Tarquinia, Tuscania stands alone in one of the emptiest, eeriest corners of Italy, a region of low green hills where you will find Etruscan ruins, old castles, and religious shrines but no people. Tuscania was a leading city after the 4th century BC, and regained its importance for a short while in the early Middle Ages. Today the city is still recovering from a bad earthquake in 1971. Etruscan *sarcophagi* from several nearby necropolises are on display in the **Museo Archeologico** in the former S. Maria del Riposo (*t 0761 436 209.* **Open** *Tues–Sun 9–7; adm free*); best among them are the complacent bonvivants of the Curunas family reclining lazily on their urns, and a mysterious Etruscan rebus from the 6th-century BC Tomb of the Dado in Pescheria.

Tuscania itself is a sombre, elegant town, with a wonderful ensemble of medieval buildings around Piazza Basile, centred on a fountain that has flowed since Etruscan days. Best of all are two unique churches east of town. **San Pietro** and **Santa Maria Maggiore** were both begun in the 700s, with additions in the 11th and 12th centuries. Besides their carved altars, pulpits, and bits of painting from the 8th to 14th centuries, both churches feature unusual sculpted façades – San Pietro especially, with colourful Cosmati work, fragments of ancient sculpture, and carved grotesques. Perhaps some of the churches in Rome looked like this before their Renaissance and Baroque rebuilding.

VEII AND LAKE BRACCIANO

From the 8th to the 6th centuries BC Veio, or *Veii*, was the largest city in the Etruscan Federation and Rome's most bitter rival. From the ruins of Veii you can get to the **Lago di Bracciano**, a favourite weekend resort of the Romans, who often use its storybook castle for film sets. Don't go on a Monday; everything's closed.

Veii

The sparse, scattered remains of ancient Veii, once enclosed in walls 11 km around, make it the most difficult Etruscan site to visit, with more of the country ramble to it than archaeological thrill. Compensating for the meagre ruins, however, is Veii's striking position, on a sheer tufa plateau over a moat formed by two streams. But these natural

defences were not enough for the ancient Veians; they wanted a port, and managed to muscle in a fortified trading post on the Tiber – defying the claims of both Cervéteri and the Latins of Alba Longa. In 753 BC the Latins, under the leadership of Romulus, united with Cervéteri to oust Veii from its Tiber port, founding in its place *Rumon*, which as any Etruscan will tell you means 'city on the river'.

Veii, minus a port and the precious salt pans of Ostia, held a mighty grudge against the new town of Rome. When Rome's Fabii clan took it upon themselves to patrol and harass Veii, the Veians ambushed and massacred all but one (475 BC). Some 25 years later, neither city could tolerate the other, and a fight to the finish became inevitable; of all Rome's wars, this was the most crucial, for its very existence was at stake. Veii called upon its fellow Etruscan cities for aid (none came) and the Romans under M. Furius Camillus began a siege that ended only when the Romans unblocked one of Veii's marvellous irrigation tunnels leading under the walls.

Getting There

By Bus

ATAC bus 201 from Piazza Mancini (across the Tiber from the Foro Italico) will take you to La Giustiniana, where you can pick up **bus 032** to Isola Farnese and Veio. Otherwise, there's a **COTRAL bus** from metro Lepanto.

By Train

From Termini to Stazione Lago di Bracciano.

By Car

If you're driving to Veio, take Via Cassia (N2) to La Storta; after another kilometre you'll see a sign for Isola Farnese and excavations. From here Via Braccianese Claudia carries on to the lake.

Eating Out

There are innumerable places to eat along Bracciano's shores; all are designed to exploit the massive weekend exodus of Romans and several are delightful places to while away a summer's day near the water. You may pay above the odds for an average meal, but you

can eat good lake fish. Otherwise buy a picnic in Bracciano or Anguillara Sabazia.

Vino e Camino, *Piazza Mazzini 11, t 06 9980 3433.* **Open** *Tues–Sun; closed 3rd week of Aug.* **Moderate**. Dine with a romantic view of the Castello Odescalchi at this stylish restaurant with antique cutlery and crystal glasses on Bracciano's central piazza. The menu offers traditional dishes such as tonnarelli *cacio e pepe* (square spaghetti with strong ewes' milk cheese and freshly ground black pepper), roasted leg of baby lamb stuffed with artichokes, and vegetarian soups. Outside seating, and live jazz on Thursdays.

Al Fresco a Bracciano, *Via Fioravanti 22, t 06 9980 4536; parking; wheelchair accessible.* **Open** *Wed–Mon.* **Moderate**. A terrace facing the lake. Chef Silverio Morbidelli uses vegetables and poultry from the family farm to prepare simple and tasty dishes like pasta with zucchini and *pesce persico* (local fish), stuffed pigeon, and turkey with mozzarella and truffles. Non-smoking room.

Veii was thus surprised, captured and destroyed; its chief deity, Juno, was carted off to a new temple on the Aventine. Julius Caesar and Augustus tried to plant a colony on the site, but it never prospered.

Excavations of Veio

Open *Tues–Sun 9–one hour before sunset.*

Among the remains to be seen are the **Temple of Portonaccio**, dedicated to Apollo (where the Villa Giulia's beautiful *Apollo of Veio* was found), cisterns, a tunnel in the rock (where Camillus led the Romans?), and best of all, the 7th-century BC **Tomba Campana**, containing some of the oldest Etruscan paintings ever discovered, of strange animals and Mercury escorting the dead to the underworld. Further up the path is the **Ponte Sodo**, an Etruscan bridge and picnic spot.

Lake Bracciano

This broad sheet of water, sloshing about in the round volcanic crater of Monte Sabatini, is best known for its eels, whose babies sometimes get sucked in to the fountains in St Peter's Square and clog the pipes. A scenic road (especially between Bracciano and Trevignano on the north shore) encircles it.

Bracciano

From June to Sept you can take boat tours from the town of Bracciano, but the best view of it is from the ramparts of the grim, five-towered **Castello degli Orsini** (*t 06 9980 4348. **Open** Oct–Mar Tues–Sun 10–12 and 3–5, April–Sept Tues–Sun 10–12 and 3–6.30; guided tours only, in English by appointment; adm €6*), stronghold of the bearish clan from 1470 to 1696, when they ceded castle and town of Bracciano to the more civilized Odescalchi.

Although the Orsini tended to support the papacy against their nemesis, the Colonna, they knew the Roman pot could boil over at any time, and built this castle as a private bunker close to Rome – not exactly in the style of the day, but when did the Orsini ever care to be progressive? It served them in good stead, fending off the attack of the entire papal army of Alexander VI when the

Orsini were caught fraternizing with the French invader, Charles VIII. Frescoes and painted ceilings by Antoniazzo Romano in the 1490s, later frescoes by the two Zuccari, busts of the Orsini by Bernini, and suits of armour decorate the interior.

Vigna di Valle

During the First World War, Lake Bracciano was Italy's dirigible and seaplane testing area. Two old hangars in Vigna di Valle, 6km east of Bracciano, were converted in the 1970s to hold the **Aeronautica Militare Museo Storico di Vigna di Valle** (*w www. edl.it/museo vigna di valle.* **Open** *Tues–Sun 9.30–6*). Exhibits include a model of Leonardo da Vinci's wing-flapping machine, fighter planes, racing planes, sea planes, planes that went to the North Pole and the plane that D'Annunzio flew over Vienna in 1918. Most curious of all is a hot air balloon launched from Paris in 1804 in honour of Napoleon's coronation, bearing instead of a basket a large glass replica of the little emperor's crown. Water being always Napoleon's nemesis, from his island exiles to Waterloo and Wellington, it was no small omen that the glass crown fell into Lake Bracciano before reaching Rome.

Trevignano Romano

Only ruins remain of the Orsini castle in this pretty village; make the walk up to see the church of the **Assunta**, for its views over the lake and a beautiful fresco of the Assumption by the school of Raphael.

THE MONSTER PARK OF BOMARZO

Bomarzo, t 0761 924 029. **Open** *daily 8.30 to one hour before sunset; adm €7.50.*

Bomarzo is one of the most woebegone little *comuni* in this part of Italy, a setting that adds to the uncanny charm of its late Renaissance **Parco dei Mostri**, located just

Getting There

By Train and Bus

Bomarzo can be reached by train from Termini to Orte (Rome–Florence line), then bus (30 minutes), or by bus from Viterbo (also 30 minutes).

By Car

By car, Bomarzo combines well with a trip to Viterbo, or Lake Vico and Caprarola.

Eating Out

For lunch, you can make use of the picnic tables and bar at the Monster Park, or try one of Bomarzo's humdrum trats. For a proper meal, you'll have to go further afield, to Orte or Viterbo (*see* p.268).

Orte

Taverna Roberteschi, *Via Vittorio Emanuele 7, t 0761 402 968.* **Open** *Tues–Sun.* **Moderate**. An attractive inn housed inside a historic building, where you can sample good local fare including wild boar (*cinghiale*) and goose (*oca*), as well as some fish dishes such as gnocchi with shrimp and *arugula*. Delicious Sicilian desserts from the chef's *paese*. Outside seating.

below the town. So does the habit of the present owners of running it like an Alabama roadside attraction, complete with tame deer for the children to pet, an albino peacock, miniature goats and plenty of souvenirs.

Curiously, a few of the same sculptors who worked on St Peter's in Rome made this shabby little nightmare, hidden away in the Lazio hills. Somehow the two works do seem related, opposite sides of the coin that may help in explaining the tragic, neurotic atmosphere of late 16th-century Italy. One of the Orsini commissioned this collection of strange, oversized sculptures; he called it his *Sacro Bosco* – Sacred Wood – and in its present state it's impossible to tell whether it was the complex allegory it pretends to be, or just a joke.

Near the entrance stands the impressive though dilapidated **Tempietto**, a domed temple of uncertain purpose attributed to Vignola. From here, wander the ill-kept grounds, encountering at every turn colossal monuments and eroded, illegible inscriptions: there's a screaming face, with a mouth big enough to hold several people, a dining table and benches, beneath a warning that reads 'every thought flees'; a life-sized elephant, perhaps one of Hannibal's, crushing a terrified Roman soldier in its trunk; a giant wrestler, in the act of ripping a defeated opponent in two from the legs up; and a leaning tower, just for fun. Under every glade decayed Madonnas, mermaids, sphinxes, nymphs, and harpies wait to spook you. All are done in a distorted, almost primitive style. It would be almost too easy to read too much into these images; a cry of pain from the degraded, humiliated Italy of the 1560s, half-pretending madness as the only way to be safe from the Spanish and the Inquisition – or perhaps merely a symbol for the loss of mental balance that followed too many centuries of high culture and over-stimulation. Whatever, the Monster Park will make you feel like an archaeologist, discovering some peculiar lost civilization. Perhaps the Italians understand it too well; it may be the only major monument of the 16th century that neither government nor anyone else shows much interest in preserving.

VITERBO

Viterbo ought to be visited. It has the kind of medieval spirit that the popes baroqued over in Rome; and where else can you drink in a café on Death Square, or stroll over to the Piazza of the Fallen to pay your respects to Our Lady of the Plague? Surrounded by grey, forbidding walls and ghastly modern districts, Viterbo's heart is actually a living medieval town, with well-preserved 13th-century streets brightened with flowers and fountains. The population seems evenly divided between teenagers on scooters and blasé soldiers from Italy's biggest army base.

Like the rest of Lazio, Viterbo has seen more than its share of troubles, most of them

Getting There

By Bus

Viterbo can be reached by **COTRAL bus**, *(freephone)* **t** *800 431 784*, from metro Saxa Rubra, every 30 minutes. Buses to Tarquinia, Bolsena, Civitavecchia and other provinical towns leave from Piazza Martiri d'Ungheria, next to Piazza dei Caduti in central Viterbo.

Eating Out

Porta Romana, *Via della Bontà 12*, **t** *0761 307 118*; *parking*. **Open** *Mon–Sat except 3 weeks in Aug*. **Inexpensive**. Large portions of country food – homemade pasta and warming vegetarian soups – are dished up with a smile at this family-run *trattoria*. The house speciality is *pignattaccia*, a tasty stew made with different kinds of meat. No-smoking room.

Richiastro, *Via della Marrocca 18 (next to the Palazzo Mazzatosta)*, **t** *0761 228 009*; *parking*. **Open** *Sept–June Thurs–Sat and Sun lunch*. **Inexpensive**. Excellently prepared traditional dishes, which have little to do with Roman cuisine.

---

traceable to the proximity of Rome. But that same geographical fact also gave the town its greatest period of glory. For much of the 13th century, Viterbo, and not Rome, was the seat of the popes. In this most confusing period of Italian history, over a dozen popes were crowned, died, or at least spent some time here, in short stays on their way to or from France, Tivoli – and sometimes even Rome. In 1309, when the 'Babylonian Captivity' began, Viterbo could only decline, and when the popes returned from Avignon, the city that once was Rome's strongest rival found itself a mere provincial town in the Papal States.

In Viterbo's centre, two not-so-fierce lions, the city's ancient symbols, gaze out over the 13th-century **Palazzo del Podestà** with its clock tower, and the **Palazzo Comunale** of the 1460s, the typical pair of buildings representing the often conflicting imperial and local powers. The politicians won't mind if you look around the Palazzo Comunale and its fine Renaissance courtyard; if you ask, they'll let you see the Council Chamber, the **Sala Regia**, done in fanciful Mannerist frescoes on the history of Viterbo from Etruscan times. Across the square, the Roman *sarcophagus* built into the façade of **Sant'Angelo** contains the body of a medieval lady of incomparable virtue named Galiena; accounts of her fatal charm and sad demise vary from one Viterban to another.

From here, Via Ascenzi leads under the arch to the Piazza dei Caduti and the **Madonna delle Peste**, an octagonal Renaissance church next to the tourist office. Beyond, at the walls, stands the **Rocca** built by Cardinal Albornoz in 1354 to keep watch on the Viterbans when the pope returned to Rome. This squat palace-fortress has been restored to hold the **Museo Archeologico**'s small collection (**t** *0761 325 929*. **Open** *9–7*; *adm* €2).

Two of Viterbo's 13th-century popes are buried in the 13th-century **San Francesco** church, near Porta Murata at the northern end of the walls. Nearby, off Piazza Verdi, stands the late 19th-century church of **Santa Rosa**. Santa Rosa enshrines the considerable remains of Viterbo's 13th-century patroness, too holy to decompose and usually on display for all to see. Rosa's preaching helped the Viterbans defeat a siege by the heretical Emperor Frederick II in 1243, and to commemorate her, each year on 3 September the local men carry a 100ft wooden steeple called the *macchina* through the streets, surmounted by an image of the saint. Local artists create a new *macchina* every four years; the best are works of art.

East of Piazza del Plebiscito, Via Cavour takes you to the **Casa Poscia**, an interesting 13th-century house on a stairway to the left, and then to the **Fontana Grande**, the best of Viterbo's many fountains. Via Garibaldi leads east to the Roman Gate and **San Sisto**, a church in parts as old as the 800s, with an altar made of sculptural fragments. Outside the walls and across Viale Capocci, the 13th-century **Santa Maria della Verità** suffered terrible vandalism at the hands of the 18th-century redecorators. The frills and plaster frosting are gone now, but only a few bits of the Renaissance frescoes by Melozzo da Forlì survived. The **Cappella Mazzatosta**, behind an iron grille, has the best painting Viterbo can offer, frescoes of the *Marriage of the Virgin* (1469) by a local Renaissance artist named Lorenzo of Viterbo. In the adjacent cloister, a fine work from the 1300s, Viterbo keeps its **Museo Civico** (*t 0761 325 462. Open Tues–Sun 9–7, until 6 in winter; adm €3*), with an archaeological section and picture gallery.

From Piazza del Plebiscito, Via S. Lorenzo leads into the heart of Viterbo's oldest quarter. Three blocks down and off to the left, **Santa Maria Nuova** is the best-preserved of the city's medieval churches. On the façade there is an ancient image of Jupiter set into the portal and a small outdoor pulpit where St Thomas Aquinas once preached. On the other side of Via S. Lorenzo, Viterbo's old market square faces the **Gesù Church** (11th century), a medieval tower-fortress, one of several left in the city, and a palazzo that long ago was the town hall. To the south, trailing down from the aforementioned **Piazza di Morte** – ironically one of the lovelier squares in Viterbo – the **San Pellegrino** quarter hangs its web of alleys, arches, and stairs along Via S. Pellegrino with a romantic and thoroughly medieval air, although in fact few of the buildings are quite that old.

In the opposite direction from San Pellegrino, a bridge on Roman and Etruscan foundations called the **Ponte del Duomo** carries over to Piazza San Lorenzo and the **Papal Palace**, begun in the 1260s by Alexander IV. Moving the papacy to Viterbo (then pop. 60,000) from Rome (then pop. 18,000, of mostly bullies and layabouts) seemed like a good idea at the time, and this squarish, battlemented palace, very much in the style of a medieval city hall, is a finer building than the pope's present address in Rome, though admittedly much smaller. On its handsome open Gothic loggia, you will see in the decoration lions (for Viterbo) interspersed with the striped coat-of-arms of the French pope Clement V, who completed the work on the building.

But fate conspired against the move from the start: Alexander IV died 17 days after settling into the palace. Five popes were afterwards elected in conclaves held in the Great Hall, among them, Urban IV, who was chased out by the Imperial army of Manfred, and then Clement IV, who died two weeks after his coronation. In selecting his successor, arguments between the French and Italian factions led to a two-year deadlock among the cardinals. The exasperated Viterbans tried to speed up the conclave, first by locking the cardinals in the palace, and then by tearing off the roof; somehow, according to the story, the churchmen got around this by making tents in the Great Hall. Finally the people decided to starve them out, and before long the Church was blessed with the rather undistinguished compromise of Gregory X. He had the roof fixed, but maybe skimped on the materials, for the whole thing came down six years later on the head of his successor, John XXI, who was quickly entombed next door in the plain Romanesque **Cathedral**. That was the last straw; the cardinals high-tailed it back to Rome before Viterbo ruined the Church.

East of Viterbo, the road for Orte enters the old suburb of La Quercia, passing in front of a landmark of Renaissance architecture: **Santa Maria della Quercia**, built in the late 1470s. Its distinctive 1509 façade has a carved oak tree (*quercia*), lions and lunettes by Andrea della Robbia over the doors. Inside, the beautiful marble tabernacle contains a miracle-working painting of the Virgin, and there is also a fine Gothic cloister. Ask someone to let you into the **Museo degli Ex-Voto**, a collection of some 200 devotional plaques brought to this shrine over the centuries, painted with endearing scenes of miracles attributed to the Madonna.

Six kilometres further east is **Bagnaia**, an old hill village expanded by wealthy Viterban bishops into a residential town. In the 1570s they commissioned Vignola to create the **Villa Lante** (*t 0761 288 008. Gardens open Tues–Sun 9–one hour before sunset, guided tours every 30 minutes; adm €2*). Besides the villa, there is one of the most striking of all Italian Renaissance gardens, geometrically arranged and full of groves and statuary; water from the fountains cascades down decorative stairs and terraces, culminating in the Grand Fountain at the bottom, navigated by stone boats and giant Moors – an impressive sight, especially when they feel up to turning it on.

LAKE VICO AND CAPRAROLA

The smallest and perhaps loveliest of the lakes north of Rome, **Lago di Vico** is ringed by rugged hills; parts of the shore are unspoiled marshes, a favourite stop for migratory birds, now protected as a wildlife preserve. At the northern edge, this ancient crater has a younger volcano (also extinct) poking up inside it: **Monte Venere**. Pristine and unpolluted, it is Lazio's best swimming hole.

Villa Farnese

Caprarola, t 0761 646 052. Open daily 8.30–6.30 (5.30 in winter), guided tours of the villa and gardens every 30 minutes; adm €2.

When Alessandro Farnese, member of an obscure noble family of Lazio, set his sister Giulia up as mistress of Pope Alexander VI, his fortune was made; Alessandro later became Paul III, a great pope who called the Council of Trent, rebuilt Rome, and kept Michelangelo busy – but also a rotten pope,

who oppressed his people, refounded the Inquisition and became the most successful grafter in papal history. Before long the Farnese family ruled Parma, Piacenza, and most of northern Lazio. With the fantastic wealth Alessandro accumulated, his grandson, also named Alessandro, built this family headquarters; Vignola, the family architect, turned the entire town of Caprarola into a setting for the palace, ploughing a new avenue through the centre as an axis that led to a grand stairway, then a set of gardens (now disappeared), then another stairway up to the huge pentagonal villa, built over the massive foundations of an earlier, uncompleted fortress. The villa today is empty; the Farnese lost everything in later papal intrigues, and someone, sometime, had to sell the furniture.

Nevertheless, it is still an impressive if not very cosy home; some of the highlights of the tour include Vignola's elegant central courtyard, a room with uncanny acoustical tricks that the guides love to demonstrate, a room frescoed with the *Labours of Hercules*, another with a wonderful ceiling painted with figures of the constellations, and Vignola's incredible **spiral staircase** of stone columns and neoclassical frescoes.

The best part, however, is behind the extensive park of azaleas and rhododendrons: a '**Secret Garden**' populated with grotesques and fantastical telamones that recall the Monster Park (there's a connection; one of the Orsinis of Bomarzo was Alessandro Farnese's secretary), and a delightful summer house called the **Little Palace of Pleasure**.

Getting There

By Bus

COTRAL buses make the journey from metro Saxa Rubra (1 hour). Call *(freephone)* **t 800 431 784** for times.

Eating Out

There are tables and shady spots for a picnic around the lake, or try this restaurant.

L'Altra Bottiglia, *Via delle Palme 18, Città Castellana (23 km east of Lake Vico)*, **t 0761 517** 403. **Open** *Sept–July Thurs–Sat and Mon–Tues eves, and Sun lunchtime.* **Expensive.** If you are up for a short drive, you should treat yourself to one of the region's best restaurants. Warm and friendly, with three *menu degustazione* and an excellent wine list. 'The Other Bottle' focuses on traditional fare prepared with flair. The chick pea ravioli with fresh tomato, garlic and rosemary and the roasted kid with artichokes are just divine.

TIVOLI

The most popular day trip from Rome, Tivoli offers both natural beauty and some of the more unbridled efforts of the human imagination – the unique gardens of the Villa d'Este; the ruins of Hadrian's country retreat – the size of a small city; and the plunging artificial waterfall of the Villa Gregoriana.

Ancient *Tibur*, set in a cliff with a beautiful view over the Roman *campagna*, became a sort of garden retreat for the senatorial class in the early days of the empire. But a town with a view is also usually easily defensible, and by the early Middle Ages, despite all the dirty work of Goths and Huns, Tibur had changed its name to Tivoli and managed a successful transition from posh resort to gutsy, independent hill town. Once, in its struggles with Rome, it even defeated its bossy neighbour and captured a pope. But pachydermic Rome never forgets a grudge, and in the 1460s Pope Pius II built a castle, the **Rocca Pia**, at the town's door to keep Tivoli in line.

Villa d'Este

t 0774 312 070. Open Tues–Sun 8.30–two hours before sunset; adm €6. From May to early Oct the gardens are illuminated nightly Tues–Sun 9pm–midnight.

Wealth returned to Tivoli in the late Renaissance in the form of moneybags cardinals; one in particular, Ippolito d'Este, son of Lucrezia Borgia and Duke Ercole I of Ferrara, created in 1550 perhaps the most fantastically worldly villa and gardens Italy had seen since antiquity, the Villa d'Este. The musty villa itself, designed by Pirro Ligorio and heavily coated with Mannerist frescoes, was rented by Franz Liszt from 1865 until his death in 1886 (it was the inspiration for his *Fountains of the Villa d'Este*).

The residence is entirely upstaged by the **gardens**, set on a descending series of terraces. Among the palms and cypresses water shoots and cascades from an incred-ible hydraulic fantasyland, weaving intricate patterns of water: the **Fountain of Glass** by Bernini, the stuccoed Grotto of Diana, the Fountain of Dragons, the Fountain of the Owl and Birds, a favourite water trick that no longer warbles or moves; nor has the cardinal's Water Organ worked for donkey's years. One of the most curious features is Little Rome, a pint-sized replica of the Tiber Island, with models of ancient buildings.

Tivoli has an interesting Romanesque church with early medieval frescoes, **San Silvestro**, located on steep and narrow Via del Colle (just north of the Villa d'Este); at the bottom, just beyond the gate, are the remains of the vast **Sanctuary of Hercules** (2nd century BC), once the office of the Sibyl of Tivoli. Like Cumae near Naples, Tibur had a college of Sibyls (pictured so memorably on the Sistine Chapel ceiling and elsewhere, for the sake of the story that they prophesied the birth of Christ). The presence of these oracular ladies, cousins to the oracle at Delphi, shows the influence of Greek thought and religion in Latium from the earliest times. The stiff climb up Via del Colle leads eventually to Tivoli's gaudy 17th-century **Cathedral** at the corner of Via del Duomo, containing a moving, 13th-century wooden sculpture of the *Deposition*.

From here, Via del Colle becomes Via Valerio and crosses the Aniene on its way to the nearly vertical gardens of the **Villa Gregoriana** (*closed for restoration*). The gardens were named in honour of Pope Gregory XVI, who in 1831 put an end to the regular flooding of the Aniene with the construction of a vast double tunnel through Mt Catillo. The river then emerges with dramatic flair high up in a natural chasm, forming a 400ft pluming mist of rainbows called the **Grande Cascata**. Shady paths wind down past viewpoints over the waterfall; if you can trick yourself into forgetting about the awful climb back up, descend past the rather scanty remains of a Roman villa to the artificial **Cascata Bernini** and the limestone cavern called the **Grotta della Sirena**, where the waters are squeezed into an abyss.

Getting There

By Bus

Tivoli (31km) and the Villa d'Este are most easily reached by **COTRAL bus** from metro Ponte Mammolo; buses leave every 20 minutes and take 30 minutes. For Villa Adriana the bus drops you a 20-minute walk away on the Via Prenestina at the Bivio Villa Adriana; **local buses** from Tivoli will take you much nearer the entrance.

By Car

Take the Via Tiburtina.

Tourist Information

Tivoli: *t 0774 312 070.*

Eating Out

Hadrian's Villa is a great place for a picnic lunch, and Tivoli has no lack of restaurants:
Sibilla, *next to the Temple of the Sibyl on Via della Sibilla, t 0774 335 281.* **Open** *Tues–Sat.* **Moderate**. The Sibilla is admittedly touristy, but it's also fun, in a great setting, moderately-priced, and serves good grilled trout.
Antica Hostaria de' Carrettieri, *Via Giuliani 55, t 0774 83243; parking.* **Open** *Thurs–Tues.* **Moderate**. In the centre of Tivoli, this is your best bet. It's run by two sisters, who'll guide you through the day's specials as there is no menu. You might find onion soup, gnocchi in a hot cheese sauce, or beef with balsamic vinegar. Save room for homemade dessert.

From the bottom a path leads up the other lip of the chasm, the acropolis of *Tibur*, where stand two remarkably well-preserved Roman temples, the famous circular **Temple of Vesta** and the rectangular **Temple of the Sibyl**, as fancy has named them (if you don't care to climb, they can also be reached from above, on Via della Sibilla). Both temples date from the Republican era; the Temple of Vesta, in particular, with its beautiful frieze and Corinthian columns, was a favourite of romantic tourists, and has been reproduced in many a Hyperborean's park.

Along the Via Tiburtina towards Rome are the strange, sheer-sided travertine quarries that have helped Tivoli make a living since ancient times. Almost all of Rome is built of it; one solemn grey variety went into the Colosseum, the city gates, and most of the other ruins. The other, streaked with beige and black, is the material Mussolini used for scores of railway stations all over Italy. Nowadays demand is still great, and Tivoli ships travertine all over the world.

Hadrian's Villa

t 0774 382 733; **Open** *daily 9–90 minutes before sunset; adm €6.*

Just outside Tivoli, signs direct you to the quiet residential neighbourhood that has grown up around Villa Adriana, a 180-acre spread that was nothing less than one man's personal World's Fair and the largest villa ever built in the entire Roman Empire; the Villa d'Este is a mere anthill in comparison.

To get some idea of the scale on which a 2nd-century AD emperor could build, stop first at the room-sized model of the villa near the entrance. Made entirely of marble and travertine, and about the same size as the monumental centre of Rome – the Imperial Fora included – Hadrian's dream 'house' clearly shows the excess that even the most intelligent and useful of emperors was capable of. Archaeologists have found features that would surprise even a Californian – a heated beach with steam pipes under the sand, and a network of subterranean service passages for horses and carts (a private metro!). Other emperors used the villa until Constantine, unable to create anything as fine, plundered it to embellish Constantinople; invaders, builders, and lime burners gnawed at it until Pope Alexander VI began the first excavations. Yet despite the depredations many of the finest Roman statues in Europe's museums were discovered here.

Hadrian fancied himself as an architect, contributing to the Pantheon, the Temple of Venus and Rome, and the urban redevelopment of Ostia Antica; but unlike most dilettantes, he had the resources of the

Roman Empire at its peak at his disposal. Hadrian especially wanted to remember famous buildings he had seen on his travels, and helped design reproductions: the **Stoa Poikile** of Athens, near the entrance, a rectangular peristyle with a massive fish pond in the centre; the **Canopus**, or Temple of Serapis near Alexandria, complete with a canal reproducing the Nile and decorated with Egyptian statues (now mostly restored; a nearby museum contains finds from the most recent excavations); the **Platonic Academy** in an ancient olive grove, with an Odeion, a round Temple of Apollo, and beyond this, the entrance to an underground rectilinear hell, or Hades.

Baths, libraries, an imperial palace, *nymphaeums*, temples, Praetorian barracks, and a reproduction of the Valle di Tempe with a Greek theatre are among the other buildings discovered in the ongoing excavations. But the most charming corner of the complex is the so-called **Naval Theatre**, actually a little circular palace on an island in an artificial lagoon, attainable only by a retractable bridge on rollers; it may have been Hadrian's private retreat, where he could escape the cares of empire to write poetry and paint.

UP THE ANIENE VALLEY TO SUBIACO

The scenery on this trip is especially pretty, varied and wooded and dotted with unspoiled hill towns. It ends at the ancient monasteries of Subiaco, where St Benedict became the father of Christian monasticism.

One of the first stops in the valley is **Vicovaro** (46km east of Rome), noted for its little octagonal Renaissance **Tempietto di San Giacomo** (1450), a work by two Dalmatian architects, Domenico da Capodistria and Giovanni Dalmata, who designed the charming porch.

Just beyond Vicovaro, a road turns left up a lovely valley towards Licenza for **Horace's Sabine Farm and Antiquarium** (*t 0774 46031; bus travellers should ask the driver to stop at the unpaved lane leading to the Villa d'Orazio. Open Tues–Sun 9–one hour before sunset; adm free*). No farm has ever enjoyed as many poetic musings as the country estate Maecenas gave to Horace in 33 BC, which was all the poet asked for in the world: 'a portion of land, not so big, a garden and near the house a spring of never-failing water, and a little wood beyond. The gods have done more and better. It is well. I ask no more.' The spring still flows; the lovely mosaics, pavements, garden swimming pool, and some of the lead pipes and the pretty surroundings survive to complete Horace's picture of an idyllic retreat. The custodian of the site has a roomful of small finds from the excavations; the more interesting items are in the little Antiquarium (*open 9–6*) 8km up the road in the castle of **Licenza**, one of Lazio's handsomest hilltowns.

Most of the hilltowns in the Aniene valley have escaped the worst of modern tourism, like lovely **Antícoli Corrado** on its steep cliff, famous for producing the most beautiful artists' models in Rome. The town has had an

Getting There

The Aniene Valley is most easily reached by **car**, but **COTRAL buses** from metro Ponte Mammolo go to Vicovaro, Licenza and Subiaco (1 hour). Call *(freephone) t 800 431 784* for times.

Tourist Information

Subiaco: *t 0774 822 013*.

Eating Out

The quiet groves and fields along the route beg for a picnic, your best option for lunch.

La Botte di Bacco, *Contrada Varole 4, t 0774 8323; parking; wheelchair accessible. Open Dec–Oct Wed–Mon, Aug daily.* In a lovely little hotel not far from the centre, 'Bacco's Barrel' is a little pricey, but has a good view and interesting, creative Italian cuisine.

art colony of its own for almost 200 years, whose works fill the town museum. Recently discovered frescoes by their predecessors in the 1100s may be seen in the well-preserved church of San Pietro, in the piazza with a fountain of Noah's Ark. Another striking town, **Saracinesco**, was founded on a crag by Saracen raiders in the 9th century; the present townspeople are their descendants.

Subiaco

Few towns can claim as glorious a past as Subiaco, 74km from Rome at the head of the Aniene Valley, where in the troubled late 5th century St Benedict retired, wrote his *Rule* and set Christian monasticism on its way. All through the dark centuries his monasteries provided a haven for learning and piety, and retained so much standing in the 1460s that the first printing press in Italy was brought here by two monks from Germany.

Originally Subiaco had 12 monasteries; those not destroyed by the Lombards fell to earthquakes and the worldly ambition of the monks. Today there are but two, 2.5km above town, reached by road or footpath, both passing by way of the dismal remains of Nero's once grand Sublaqueum villa and his dried-out artificial lake.

Convento di Santa Scholastica

t 0774 85525. Open daily 9–12.30 and 3.30–7.

A feudal abbey in the Middle Ages, and later ruled by princely abbots of Rome's noblest families, S. Scholastica (she was Benedict's twin sister) remains a holy bulwark of the faith, guarded by a stout Romanesque campanile. It has three **cloisters**, the first that you come to built in 1580, incorporating columns from Nero's villa; the second, an early Gothic cloister of 1052; the third, beautifully decorated in the 13th century by the Cosmatis. The **library** contains the first two books printed in Italy. Apparently the Germans and their new-fangled contraption upset the monastery's scribes, and after printing these two tomes they went off in a huff to Rome.

Convento di San Benedetto

t 0774 85039. Open daily 9–12.30 and 3–6.

Partly natural, and partly built into the mountain side, the monastery (also known as Sacro Speco, after the cavern to which St Benedict retired as a hermit and attracted his first disciples) includes a 14th-century **Upper Church** with fine Sienese frescoes and a 13th-century **Lower Church**, built on several levels to incorporate St Benedict's Holy Grotto, now lined with marble from Nero's villa. The frescoes illustrating the saint's life are by a Master Consulus, a 13th-century painter. In 1210, an anonymous monk painted the *Portrait of St Francis* upstairs in the Chapel of St Gregory, believed to be the first live portrait done in Italy since Roman times. Don't miss the 15th-century frescoes of deathly Death along the Scala Santa leading to the Shepherd's Grotto, which contains a rare fresco from the 700s. From here you can see what was an ancient bramble where Benedict had lain to mortify his flesh, but which turned into a rose tree at the gentler touch of St Francis.

Nearby, at the bottom of the gorge of the Aniene, there's a beautiful little lake with a waterfall; it may have been one of the three mentioned by Tacitus in connection with Nero's villa. Just outside Subiaco town, the **church of San Francesco** contains frescoes attributed to Pinturicchio, Sodoma, and Sebastiano del Piombo, and on the altar a triptych undoubtedly by Antoniazzo Romano, who knew enough to sign his work.

PALESTRINA

Take the bus so you can doze through the gruesome eastern suburbs that go on endlessly along Via Casilina. One advantage of driving, however, is that you can detour south 9km to Labico for lunch in one of Lazio's top restaurants: the **Antonello Colonna** (*see* box).

This is the birthplace of the composer Giovanni Pierluigi da Palestrina (1524–94),

Getting There

COTRAL buses depart frequently from metro Anagnina (1 hour). Call *(freephone)* **t** *800 431 784* for times.

Tourist Information

Palestrina pro-loco: **t** *06 957 3176*.

Eating Out

In Palestrina lunch can be anything from a slice of pizza or a picnic in the city park, to a plate of homemade fettuccine.

Stella, *Piazza della Liberazione 3*, **t** *06 953 8172; wheelchair accessible*. **Open** *daily*.

Inexpensive. An old fettucine favourite. If you pay a little more you can eat fish.

Antonello Colonna, *Via Roma 89, Labico*, **t** *06 951 0032; wheelchair accessible*. **Open** *Sept–July Tues–Sun lunchtime*. **Expensive**. *Make sure to reserve*. One of Lazio's top restaurants, presided over by the eponymous top chef; worth visiting the region for.

Taverna degli Anici, *Via Anicia 39*, **t** *06 9531 0061*. **Open** *Tues–Sun*. **Inexpensive.** If you don't have time to drive to Labico, you can sample cuisine in the style of Antonello Colonna, thanks to skilful young chef Fabiana who trained at his restaurant.

who invented the polyphonic Mass in the nick of time, just when the Council of Trent was about to ban church music altogether, with its melodies straight from popular love songs and the tavern. But ancient Praeneste was on the map long before there was such a thing as a church.

One of the oldest Latin towns, traditionally founded by Telegonus, son of Odysseus and Circe, it predates Rome and long battled the upstart on the Tiber before making an alliance, rebelling, submitting, etc. But it had something even Rome couldn't match – the greatest Hellenistic temple in Italy, dedicated to Fortune, the mother of gods: the **Sanctuary of Fortuna Primigenia**. When Palestrina was bombed in the war, it revealed that the sanctuary was as large as the entire modern town. Like many ancient temples, it was built into the side of a hill, neatly combining nature with architecture – although here on a scale previously unheard of. No one is sure when it was built, but in 80 BC it was partially burned during the Social Wars, and rebuilt by Sulla; it was revolutionary in its use of the Romans' special high-silica concrete that would later top the Pantheon and vault a hundred baths.

Remains of the ancient sanctuary stretch from the bottom to the top of Palestrina in a series of wide, artificial terraces. Along Via degli Arconi, you can see the first level of arches that supported the town core; from the COTRAL bus stop, near the top of Via degli Arconi, a road curves up to the 17th-century **Porta del Sole** and the remains of Praeneste's cyclopean polygonal walls.

Continue up to Via Anicia and turn left for Piazza Regina Margherita, on the terrace of the ancient Forum. Like squares in Rome, it has a certain spontaneous cubism, embellished with a pizza shop, a statue of Giovanni Pierluigi, a section of the ancient road and steps, and the unique, brick collage façade of the **Cathedral**, built in the 5th century on the foundations of an ancient temple, perhaps dedicated to Jupiter. The nave is lined with a frieze of portraits of Palestrina's cardinals; in the left aisle is a copy of the Palestrina *Pietà*, sometimes attributed to Michelangelo (the original was carted off to Florence).

Adjacent to the cathedral are Corinthian columns embedded like fossils in the side of the former Seminary. This was built around Praeneste's sacred area and is not always open to the public; try ringing the Seminario bell, and if they want to let you in, they will. Or you can try asking at the tourist office. Within is the so-called **Apsidal Hall** (perhaps a temple of Isis) where the famous Barberini mosaic was discovered (*see below*); the **Aerarium**, or treasury, containing the remains of an obelisk, busts, and votive offerings; and the **Antro delle Sorti**, formerly believed to be the home of the oracle, and now thought to be the temple of Serapis, decorated with a beautiful mosaic of Alexandria.

Above rise the great steps of terraces leading to the main sanctuary of Fortune. To get there, continue up the steep streets and stairways to the top of Palestrina – if you're driving, begin with Via delle Monache from Piazza S. Maria degli Angeli and zig-zag up to Piazza della Cortina. This, the highest terrace, was once the courtyard of the sanctuary's theatre; the *cavea* of seats was restored in 1640 to form the steps of the Palazzo Colonna-Barberini, built around the highest temple in the sanctuary.

Museo Nazionale Archeologico Prenestino

*t 06 953 8100. **Open** daily 9 to one hour before sunset; adm €2, including excavations.*

The palazzo now houses the archaeological museum, which contains a model of the sanctuary, a fine bas-relief of a triumph with a slave whispering in the triumphator's ear, pine cone-shaped tombstones, eroded busts, the cistae, or bronze vanity cases with etched pictures (a local speciality), and most splendiferous of all, on the top floor, the exquisite **Barberini mosaic of the Nile**, a brilliantly coloured Hellenistic masterpiece of the 2nd century BC, showing the Nile in flood, with all of Egypt's flora and fauna on islands in the stream, a lovers' banquet, a religious procession, the Canopus of Alexandria, obelisks, a towered city, etc.

Opposite the museum is the excavated area of the sanctuary; from the large rectangular courtyard steps descend to a colonnaded terrace, and then down again to the **Terrazza degli Emicicli**, or hemicycles, lined with Doric columns high up on a huge wall and the famous oracle of Fortune in the centre. This was the heart of the sanctuary, where the Sibyl of Palestrina responded to queries with sorti, or small wooden lots with letters carved in them, some of which were discovered in a well. From here there is a splendid view reaching to the sea, and it is said that in ancient times – until the temple was disbanded in the 4th century – two fires would be lit every night as beacons for sailors to get home.

To the left of the museum is the pretty little church of **Santa Rosalia** (1660), and beyond it, 3.5 km up the road to Palestrina's citadel, the ruined **Castel San Pietro**, once the property of the Colonna. Pietro da Cortona made the altarpiece in its little church, but the magnificent view steals the show.

Anagni

East of Palestrina and the Castelli Romani, towards Frosinone, is the humble corner of Lazio known as the **Ciociaria**, after the *ciocie*, or bark sandals, worn by the countrymen not so long ago when this was one of the backwaters of Italy. As they were the first outsiders to come to the new capital of Italy seeking work, Romans tend to call all new arrivals Ciociari – rarely in a flattering way.

From Palestrina Via Casilina leads out to Anagni, which held centre stage in European politics on several occasions during the Middle Ages. Four 14th-century popes were born here, and several others made it their summer home. Greatest among them was Boniface VIII, a nasty intriguer who had the poor timing to loudly proclaim the temporal supremacy of the popes long before anyone took the idea seriously. Captured in Anagni by the Colonna family and the king of France, Boniface received a resounding slap across the face from Sciarra Colonna – the famous 'slap of Anagni', putting a temporary end to papal dreams of world domination.

Parts of Boniface's palace may still be seen, along with the stout and squarish **Cathedral**, sharing a little of the genius of Tuscan and Apulian churches of the period. Outside, it is 11th-century Romanesque; a rebuilding in the 1300s left it tentatively Gothic within. There is a Cosmatesque pavement and a wonderful 13th-century stone baldaquin over the altar. Be sure to see the crypt, with blue and gold Byzantine frescoes from the 1200s that are among the best of their kind in Italy.

Take time for a walk around Anagni, a medieval time-capsule with its walls, towers, and palaces like the **Casa Barnekow** that have changed little in 600 years.

CASTELLI ROMANI

'Extinction' may be one of the dirtiest words of the 20th century, but with volcanoes it usually translates into lovely scenery, romantic lakes, and fertile soil for vines. Such are the charms of the Colli Albani, the ruins of a horseshoe-shaped crater, 60km round, just south of Rome. But Rome was still a twinkle in Mars's eye when the ancient Latins found these hills a convivial place to settle, and their villages, the foundations of the small towns called the Castelli Romani, grew to become some of the strongest members of the Latin League. Since being pounded into submission 2,200 years ago, their role has been reduced to that of providing the capital with wine, flowers, and a pleasant place to spend summer weekends. Heavy bombing in 1944 during the battle for Rome wrecked many fine old churches, villas, and artworks in the Castelli, and though the damage has been repaired, much is new; some of the nearer Castelli are becoming strangled in Rome's suburban tentacles. Still, the countryside, especially around Lake Nemi, is beautiful.

Another attraction is the numerous old-fashioned wine cellars; so old that one in Marino, along the lake road, was formerly used as an underground *mithraeum*, and has a fine fresco of the god inside. Further afield are the ruins and gardens of Ninfa, one of the most enchanting places near Rome.

Frascati

Frascati, the nearest of the Castelli (21km, on Via Tuscolana) and one of the most visited, was a medieval replacement for the ancient Etruscan and Latin city of Tusculum, which whipped the Romans in 1167 and was destroyed in a vendetta in 1191. Ancient Tusculum was famous for its magnificent villas, most famously Cicero's, and Frascati inherited the tradition on its refreshing hillside. Unfortunately Field Marshal Kesselring made it his headquarters, and 80 per cent of

the town was destroyed in the bombing to squeeze him out. Still famous for its white wine, Frascati is mostly visited for its two parks: the magnificent 17th-century **Villa Aldobrandini** (*open Mon–Fri 9–1 and 3–6, in winter until 5*), known for its views of Rome, and the shady **Villa Torlonia** (*open dawn to dusk*), once part of a 16th-century estate, notable for its grand derelict fountain by Carlo Maderno called the Theatre of Waters.

In the centre of Frascati, Piazza San Pietro has a pretty fountain and cathedral, much restored after bombing; and beyond the fountain, the church of the **Gesù** designed by Pietro da Cortona, decorated with frescoed 'perspectives' by Antonio Colli.

Tusculum, Frascati's predecessor and fief of Senatrix Theodora, whose family ran Rome for two centuries, lies 5km east, on a minor road from Villa Aldobrandini. Its brutal 1197 sack by the Romans was the medieval equivalent of saturation bombing, but you can still pick out the ruins of the Villa of Cicero and have a picnic in the well-preserved theatre. Climb up to the former citadel (2,500ft) for one of the finest views over the Colli Albani.

Grottaferrata and Marino

Grottaferrata, another Castelli town only 3km south of Frascati, was built around an 11th-century abbey, the well-fortified Basilian **Abbazia di Grottaferrata** (*t 06 945 9309. Open Tues–Sun 8.30–12 and 4.30–6; adm free, guided tour by a monk*), founded by SS. Nilus and Bartholomew and still home to a congregation of Greek Catholic monks. The monastery's museum contains some classical sculpture, as well as frescoes, vestments, and icons, all with a Greek touch. The abbey church of **Santa Maria**, consecrated in 1025, has a colourful 12th-century campanile and a wonderfully carved marble portal of the same period, topped by a Byzantine mosaic. In the **Chapel of St Nilus**, Domenichino painted what fans claim are his best frescoes, on the lives of the abbey's founders. Another 6km will take you to **Marino**, like Frascati a

Getting There

All the Castelli, and Cori, can be reached by **COTRAL bus** from metro Anagnina but links between them are slow. Call (freephone) **t** 800 431 784 for times. **Trains** go to Frascati and Albano from Termini. By **car** you can easily see the highlights in a day (traffic can be ferocious at the pre-*pranzo* rush hour).

Tourist Information

Frascati: *t 06 942 0331.*
Albano Laziale: *t 06 932 4081.*

Eating Out

Frascati

Cacciani, *Via A.D. Diaz 13*, *t 06 92 0378; parking.* **Open** *Feb–July and Sept–Dec Tues–Sun.* **Moderate**. A dependable address for good traditional food, prepared with the freshest ingredients. You can see the chefs at work, or sit outside on the breezy terrace.

Grottaferrata

La Briciola di Adriana, *Via Gabriele D'Annunzio 12*, *t 06 945 9338; wheelchair accessible.* **Open** *Sept–July Tues–Sun lunchtime.* **Moderate**. A varied choice of local dishes such as chestnut and chickpea soup in autumn or the *vignarola*, made with artichokes, *fava* (broad) beans and fresh peas in spring. Also more meaty specialities, like roast beef with balsamic vinegar and 'truffled' birds. Outside seating.

Marino

Cantina Colonna, *Via Carissimi 32*, *t 06 9366 0386; parking.* **Open** *Thurs–Tues, eves only in the week.* **Moderate**. A bastion of hearty (and heavy) Roman cuisine. Among the lighter options are beans tossed in wild fennel, *bucatini cacio e pepe* (with ewes' milk cheese and black pepper) and delicious *capretto scottadito* (chargrilled kid).

Albano

Antica Abazia, *Via San Filippo Neri 19*, *t 06 932 3187; parking.* **Open** *Tues–Sun.* **Moderate**. Step inside even if you haven't worked up a real appetite – a glance at the menu is enough to make you hungry. Dishes such as *tonnarelli* with *mozzarella di bufala*, zucchini and aubergine, and pork with caramelized baby onions are irresistible.

Velletri

Benito al Bosco, *Contrada Morice 20*, *t 06 964 1414; parking.* **Open** *Wed–Mon.* **Expensive**. One of Velletri's most pleasant restaurants, out of town at the foot of Monte Artemisio. You'll find lamb and game, but also seafood and excellent fish dishes. Outside parking.

famous wine town that suffered seriously during the war. Marino's topers are devoted to the local stuff; on any sleepy afternoon the wine shops will be the only establishments open. The liveliest time to visit is the first Sunday in October, when the town's fountains flow with last year's vintage in its merry Sagra dell'Uva. One of these, the **Fountain of the Four Moors** in Piazza Lepanto, commemorates the many natives who fought in the Battle of Lepanto – a Turkish shield taken as a trophy still hangs in the church of San Barnaba.

Lake Albano and Monte Cavo

From Marino you can continue along the panoramic **Via dei Laghi** (SS217) which overlooks the elliptical **Lago di Albano**. Romans, whose taste for vicarious battles followed them even on holiday, used to come to watch mock sea fights from their lakeside villas; now they prefer trout fishing. Beyond the lake there's a turn-off for **Rocca di Papa**, a dramatically sited town, with a picturesque medieval citadel named the Quartiere dei Bavaresi after the Bavarian troops of Emperor Ludwig stationed here in the 1320s. A private toll road leads up from Rocca di Papa to the second highest of the Alban Hills, Monte Cavo (3,100ft; you can also walk up from town).

Monte Cavo, the ancient Mons Albanus, was the sacred mountain of the Latin tribes. Aeneas' son Anchises founded Alba Longa, their most ancient city and political centre, nearby at Castel Gandolfo (*see* below), while at the summit was the sanctuary of Latian Jupiter, the cult centre of all Latium. Sir James Frazer writes how one of the ancient kings of Alba Longa considered himself the equal of Jupiter, inventing machines that mimicked thunder and lightning, banging and sparking to drown out the real storm. Jupiter did not take kindly to the competition and blasted the impudent king with a tremendous thunderbolt, followed by a cloudburst that drowned his very palace under the waters of Lake Albano, traces of which, legend says, are visible when the water is low.

Despite this setback, Mons Albanus remained the political and religious centre of the Latin League until the Romans did steal Jupiter's thunder by building him a superior temple on the Capitol. But the importance of his first sanctuary was never forgotten, and it became the practice for any conquering hero whose victories weren't momentous enough for the Forum to be given a second-class triumph here, along Monte Cavo's **Via Triumphalis**. The footpath from the upper reaches of Rocca di Papa follows its route beyond the **Campi d'Annibale**, the hollow of an ancient crater, where Hannibal and his elephants are said to have camped, to the top where there are fabulous views in all directions.

No trace of the temple of Jupiter Latiaris has ever been discovered here; as god of sky, thunder, and oaks he was apparently worshipped outdoors in a sacred grove. Tarquin the Proud built a wall to define the sacred precinct, and when Cardinal Henry, Duke of York, built a Passionist monastery here (now a hotel) he reused some of its blocks. Where the ancient pagans and not so ancient Passionist fathers worshipped, there is now a television transmitter.

Lake Nemi

Next along the Via dei Laghi is **Nemi**, a picturesque little village wrapped around its 9th-century castle, famous for its June wild strawberry festival. From here (or from Genzano, see below), you can go down to the magical 'Mirror of Diana', the round, deep, blue **Lago di Nemi**, its still waters encompassed by dripping forests and plastic-coated strawberry farms. As it descends, the road passes the meagre ruins of the **Temple of Diana Nemorensis**, the celebrated sanctuary of Diana of the woodlands, in whose forest, known as the grove of Aricia, were held the barbaric rites that inspired Sir James Frazer's monumental *The Golden Bough*, the foundation of modern anthropology. Within this sanctuary grew an oak forest, guarded by a priest known as King of the Wood, a former runaway slave who had become Diana's priest by plucking a sprig of mistletoe from the trees, which gave him the right to fight and slay the former king. And so, even into the days of Hadrian, the next king would be made by slaying the former. Ancient authorities linked the mistletoe to the golden bough plucked by Aeneas before his descent into the underworld.

Caligula took a special interest in the cult, so much so that when he tired of one king he purposefully set a runaway slave to kill him. He had two magnificent ships constructed to ferry visitors across the lake to the temple (and entertain with his notorious perversities on the way). These ships were sunk during the reign of Claudius, and although they were discovered in 1446 by Leon Battista Alberti, they remained in a remarkable state of preservation at the bottom of the lake until 1932, when Mussolini had them brought up. It's a shame that they didn't stay there a little longer, for as a last act of gratuitous chagrin the retreating Germans set fire to the lakeshore **Nemi Museum of Roman Ships** (*t 06 939 8040. Open May–Sept daily 9–6, Oct–April 9–2; adm €2*) and burned them to cinders. The museum has since been reconstructed, with bronze figurines, bits salvaged from the fire and models.

Across the lake from Nemi is the larger town of **Genzano di Roma**, overlooking the Via Appia; it is best known for the Infiorata on the Sunday after Corpus Christi, when the streets are covered with patterns made from over 8,000lb of flower petals.

Viaducts Up the Via Appia

From here the Via Appia crosses a series of viaducts on its way to Rome, passing by way of **Aríccia**, a pretty village immersed in trees, with summer villas. It boasts several minor works by Bernini, who was employed by the Chigi to beautify the village, beginning with the unexciting S. Maria di Galloro on the edge of the town. Within Aríccia, he restored the medievalesque Palazzo Chigi, set in a gorgeous park, while his round, domed S. Maria dell'Assunzione resembles the nipple of a baby's bottle with porticoes and not one but two bell towers.

The biggest viaduct of all, the three-tiered Ponte di Aríccia, leads to Albano Laziale, where it passes on the left the striking truncated cones of the so-called **Tomb of the Horatii and Curiatii**, built in the Etruscan style. Roman legend has it that three Roman Horatii and three Latin Curatii fought in single combat to end the war between Alba Longa and Rome during the reign of Tullus Hostilius; but Alba Longa's tyrant proved deceitful, resulting in destruction by Rome.

Alba Longa's name lingers on in **Albano Laziale**, but spoilsport historians insist the town wasn't founded until Septimius Severus created a large permanent camp for the 2nd Legion here, called Castra Albano, ostensibly to defend the Via Appia but perhaps more to impress travellers and get the troops out of Rome. The modern town, shaped like a wedge on the slope of Monte Cavo's crater, just about fills the space of the legion's huge camp. Along the main Corso Matteotti, the church of **San Pietro** was built over the camp's baths in the 6th century and has a fine Romanesque campanile. On the next street up, Via Don Minzoni, you can see the mighty ruins of the **Porta Praetoria**, the camp's principal gate, rediscovered after a bomb fell on the surrounding buildings.

From here, a left on Via Saffi takes you to **S. Maria della Rotonda**, an unusual circular medieval church built over a *nymphaeum* of Domitian; inside there's a pulpit of Cosmati work, which shares the space with ancient mosaics and a relief of Mithras in the vestibule. At Via Saffi 100 is a perfectly preserved underground reservoir, or *cisternone*, carved into the living rock to supply the troops, and still used today to hold Albano's water. Ruins of the **amphitheatre** lie behind the church in genteelly dilapidated Piazza San Paolo. From the very top of the hill, you can see Lake Albano shimmering far below.

Castel Gandolfo

The prettiest route from Albano to Castel Gandolfo is the upper of Urban VIII's two roads, called the **Galleria di Sopra**, or upper tunnel, for its roof of interwoven ilex branches – the lower 'tunnel', the **Galleria di Sotto**, is the busy main road. The Upper Road begins above Albano's Piazza San Paolo and follows the rim of Monte Cavo's crater, with views of the lake and surrounding country.

Castel Gandolfo itself is a happy little village, perched 1,400ft above Lake Albano, and famous as the Vatican enclave where the pope spends the dog days of summer. The discovery of an Iron Age necropolis used in the 9th–7th centuries BC strengthens Castel Gandolfo's claim that it was the site of Alba Longa. Interestingly, the graves were found coated with a thin layer of lava, supporting the old, discredited legend that volcanic eruptions forced the early inhabitants down from these hills to Rome. Finds from the cemetery are in a Museo Preistorico in EUR.

Castel Gandolfo is named after the Gandolfi family of Genoa, who built a castle here in the 12th century. The **Papal Palace** was constructed on its ruins by Carlo Maderno in 1624, and was much remodelled by Pius IX. To attend the pope's general audience on summer Wednesdays at 11am you need tickets from the Vatican (*see* 'Vatican', p.204), though on Sundays in the summer, John Paul II appears at noon to give a homily to the crowd in the palace courtyard.

The other thing to do in Castel Gandolfo is walk down the track below the rail station to the cave entrance of the **emissarium**, a tunnel nearly 1½km long, carved in the living rock by the Romans in 397 BC. At the time the war with Veii seemed endless, and they asked an oracle what it took to win. 'Drain the lake,' came the reply, and so they did in their literal Roman way. They did the job well; the *emissarium* is still used to control the lake's level.

Velletri and Ninfa

If you really want to escape Rome and its bedroom townlets, continue south instead of north along the Via Appia from Genzano to **Velletri**, an ancient Volscian town that has grown to become the largest of the Castelli. Although bombed to smithereens in the war, its landmark **Torre del Trivio**, a leaning 150ft needle-like campanile from 1353, has been restored and its museum contains Volscian *sarcophagi*, while the crazy quilt of a **Cathedral**, built over a Roman basilica, has artworks from the Cosmati to the hapless 1950s, with nearly every style in between. Under the portico is the entrance to a small museum, with *Madonnas* by Gentile da Fabriano and Antoniazzo Romano and a fairy-tale 12th-century Byzantine reliquary.

With a car you can press on further, into the Monti Lepini and charming old hill towns well off the beaten track. **Cori**, like Rome, likes to trace its founding to Trojan refugees. It may well be 3,000 years old; that, at least, is the date archaeologists assign to its 'cyclopean' walls, built of huge, neatly fitted polygonal chunks of rock. There are also Roman ruins, including an intact bridge and at the summit of the town, the **Temple of Hercules** (really a temple of Jupiter), a small Doric building complete except for its roof.

Three interesting towns beginning with 'N' lie 10km further south, especially **Ninfa**, a 'Medieval Pompeii' abandoned in the 17th century because of malaria. Many buildings survive in a romantic setting of streams and lakes, overgrown with wildflowers and trees that form the **Caetani Botanical Gardens** (*t 0773 695 404. Open some summer weekends; call for dates and reservations; adm €6*). **Norma**, built on the edges of a steep, curving

cliff, seems almost like a city hanging in the air. Nearby are more cyclopean walls around the ruins of **Norba**, once capital of Rome's bitter enemies, the Volscians. It was besieged and destroyed by the legions in the Social Wars in 89 BC, never to be rebuilt.

PONTINE MARSHES, ANZIO AND NETTUNO

... nowhere else has the creative power of Fascism left a deeper mark. The immense works can be summed up in the lapidary phrase of Il Duce: 'You redeem the land, you found some cities.'

From a 1939 Italian guidebook

From the Castelli Romani, the Via Appia continues south into a region you wouldn't have travelled in before the 1930s, when the broad plain of the **Pontine Marshes**, or Agro Pontino, was the biggest no-man's land in Italy, wracked by malaria and healthy only for water buffalo. Julius Caesar was the first to plan its drainage, but the design died with him. Augustus later dug a ditch along the Via Appia to reclaim the swamps, and canal barges helped to make the soles on many a traveller's *caligae* last longer. In the Dark Ages the canals became blocked, but once again, during the 13th century, some of the marshes were drained. A few centuries of papal rule had the area back to its pristine emptiness when Mussolini decided to make it a showpiece of his regime. Today, except for the small corner preserved as a park and wildlife refuge, the marshes no longer exist, and brand-new towns like Aprilia, Pomezia, Pontinia, and Sabaudia sit amid miles of prosperous farms as curious monuments to the brighter side of fascism.

Along N148, Pomezia is just east of the site of ancient **Lavinium**, which readers of Virgil will recognize as the town founded by Aeneas and named for Lavinia, daughter of the local king Latinus, who becomes the

Getting There

Frequent **trains** from Termini to Anzio and Nettuno (1 hour).

Tourist Information

Anzio/Nettuno: *t 06 984 5147*.

Eating Out

Anzio

Da Alceste al Buon Gusto, *Piazzale Sant'Antonio 6, t 06 984 6744; parking.* **Open** *Wed–Mon.* **Expensive.** Excellent seafood, served on a terrace in summer.

Pierino, *Piazza C. Battisti 3, t 06 984 5682; parking; wheelchair accessible.* **Open** *Tues–Sun, in summer eves only except Sat and Sun lunchtime.* **Expensive.** More excellent seafood here, with a refreshing sea breeze.

Nettuno

Gambero Secondo, *Via della Liberazione 50, t 06 985 2459; wheelchair accessible.* **Open** *Tues–Sun.* **Moderate.** Fish dishes on a terrace.

hero's wife at the end of the Aeneid. It was the custom of elected officials in Rome to make a sacrifice in Lavinium. Beyond that, nothing was known until the 1950s, when archaeologists studying aerial photos taken during the war noticed that the flora near the village of Prática di Mare had a different shade from its surroundings, a tell-tale sign of ancient ruins. Excavations have revealed a row of 13 stone altars from the 6th–4th centuries BC and an earlier, monumental tomb that may have been worshipped as Aeneas'. In 1977 some 100 life-size terracotta votive statues from the 5th–4th centuries BC were discovered under the wall of a temple of Minerva, apparently deposited in a pit in the 2nd century BC when a new temple was constructed. Many of the statues are of children carrying toys and pets, left with the goddess when the real child passed to adulthood. Others are of Minerva, and one that has especially interested scholars is a 4th-century BC terracotta copy of the wooden Palladium, the statue of Athena that Aeneas brought from Troy; it ended up as one of the Vestal Virgins' holiest of holies; its discovery in Lavinium suggests not only an early link between Greek and Latin cultures, but a mythic tradition older than Virgil.

Between Pomezia and Aprília is **Ardea**, the capital of King Turnus, Aeneas' rival for the hand of Lavinia. It is also a destination for admirers of one of Italy's best contemporary sculptors, Giacomo Manzù, long a local resident; the **Raccolta Amici di Manzù** (*t 06 913 5022.* **Open** *Tues–Sun 9–7; adm €5*) in the village displays over 400 of his works.

If you drive along the coast you'll find many boring beaches and **Anzio**, the Antium of the ancient Volscians. One of the more uppity cities from Rome's point of view – Coriolanus took refuge here when banished from Rome in 491 BC – Antium was captured, rebelled again, and in 338 BC was recaptured and humiliated by having all of its ships stripped of their beaks, or *rostra*, which were carted off to the Roman Forum. Caligula and Nero are believed to have been born here, and the latter built a large seaside villa, traces of which may still be seen at the promontory of Arco Muto (where the Apollo Belvedere was discovered in 1510).

After that the town fell out of history until January 1944, when British, American, and Polish troops found its beaches an ideal spot for a landing, the bloody but successful end run that forced the Germans to abandon their Gustav Line and opened the way for the liberation of Rome. Much of Anzio had to be rebuilt after the war, and British and Polish military cemeteries stretch from Anzio to an ominously named crossroads called Campo di Carne (Field of Flesh). The largest American military cemetery in Italy is near **Nettuno**, with 7,862 graves near the beach head. A nearly solid 3km of beach umbrellas and pizzerias link Anzio to Nettuno, although above the beacharama Nettuno has retained its moated castello, built for Alexander VI, and a pretty medieval quarter, the Borgo. Anzio does it one better with summer hydrofoils to the beautiful crescent island of **Ponza**, Lazio's Capri, offering the possibility of a long day trip from Rome.

Where to Stay

For a city that has been entertaining crowds of visitors for the last 2,000 years, Rome does not seem to have acquired any special flair for accommodating them. Hotels here are neither better nor worse than anywhere else in Italy. From *belle époque* palaces on Via Veneto to grimy hovels on the wrong side of Termini Station, little is truly distinctive; places with a history, a famous view, or quiet gardens to shut out the noise are few and far between (and so well known that you can never book too far in advance). Rome has been rated the noisiest capital city in Europe – a score of decibels higher than EU standards reckon good for your health. If you can, avoid main streets, avoid the station area, and aim for something on a medieval lane in central Rome – it will probably be quieter than a hotel in the suburbs. If you're staying for a week or more, Rome's Hotel-Residences – flats to let for a minimum of a week or a month – may be good value. At the other end of the scale are the numerous hostels for pilgrims and students, many run by religious orders. Because of puny lifts and stairs in old buildings, accommodation accessible to wheelchair users is almost entirely limited to Rome's four and five star hotels; those that do not follow this rule are so designated.

The price categories used below were appropriate at the time of writing. As a rule, rates rise by a maximum of 10 per cent every year at Easter. Single rooms are roughly two-thirds the price of a double. Adding an extra bed to a room will add 35 per cent, or less, to the bill. If you show up asking for a single, and all that's left is a double, by law the hotel should let you have it for two-thirds the rate, but hoteliers may try to charge 100 per cent. Taxes and service charges are included in the given rates, although some hotels charge extra for air conditioning (from €5–15 per day) and breakfast (from €4–40 per person).

Breakfast can be anything from a rich buffet with an ample choice of fresh fruit, cereals, yoghurt, honey, jam, eggs, cheese, ham and cakes to a stale *cornetto* to be dunked in a not-so-frothy cappuccino. If breakfast is not included in the rates, walk to the nearest bar, where a cappuccino and a fresh pastry will cost you less than €2.

Rooms without bath share a toilet and shower across the hall. In cheaper establishments you may have to pay an extra €1–2 to have a shower. Prices are by law listed on the door of each room or inside the wardrobe, and discrepancies in your disfavour can be reported to the tourist office (but don't expect much). Rome's high season is from April–May or June and September–October. In July–August rates can drop by 20 per cent or more. The rest of the year you may get discounts of around 10 per cent. Try haggling, but a few hotels charge fixed rates all year, so don't get huffy if it gets you nowhere.

Price Categories

Price categories for a double room with a private bathroom in high season are as follows:

luxury	over €250
expensive	€150–250
moderate	€100–150
inexpensive	€50–100
cheap	under €50

Booking

The best thing to do when booking is to telephone, fax or email and find out if a room is available. Be ready to give your credit card details as a warranty for reservation. You'll find that hotel clerks in Rome often speak English. Ascertain as many details as possible of your room – is it quiet? does it have a view? is the bathroom en suite? etc. – bearing in mind that rooms vary even in the best hotels. Overbooking is common, so ask for a written confirmation specifying dates, number of nights and costs.

If you turn up without a reservation, or don't fancy any of the hotels listed below, try one of the following agents:

Countrywide Inphonline, *t 02 2630 6076, f 02 256 4030, or freephone in Italy t 800 008 777, e info@initalia.it, w www.initalia. it. Open Mon–Fri 9am–7pm.* A free reservation service for hotels belonging to this association across Italy. All ranges covered.

Hotel Reservation, *t 06 699 1000. Open daily 8am–10.45pm.* Rome's free reservation service.

venere.com, *e sales@venere.it, w www.venere.it.* An internet booking service representing 400 one- to five-star hotels in Rome.

Campo Marzio

Anyone serious about seeing Rome at its best should try to stay in its oldest and most convivial neighbourhoods, where there is quite a wide choice of hotels. The most atmospheric is the Raphael, near Piazza Navona. The most modern is the new Holiday Inn near the Pantheon. A few steps away the Santa Chiara also offers apartments with balconies. Book well in advance of your departure.

Luxury

Holiday Inn Crowne Plaza Minerva***** H8
Piazza della Minerva 69, 00186, t 06 695 201, f 06 679 4165, e minerva@pronet.it, w www. crowneplaza.com; bus 46, 62, 64; wheelchair accessible.
A 17th-century *palazzo* for visiting ecclesiastics, stunningly revamped by postmodern architect Paolo Portoghesi. Large bedrooms (in which under-19-year-olds sharing with parents stay for free) and wittily kitted out public rooms. Brilliant views from the rooftop terrace. TV, bar, restaurant, garage, business facilities and air conditioning. Breakfast extra.

Raphael**** G7
Largo di Febo 2, 00186, t 06 682 831, f 687 8993, e info@raphael

hotel.com, *w* www.raphael
hotel.com; *bus* 30, 70, 81, 87, 116,
116T, 204, 492.
Very near Piazza Navona, a vine-
covered old charmer, decorated
with antiques. Try to get a top-
floor room for the views. TV, bar,
restaurant, air conditioning and
business facilities. Breakfast extra.

Sole al Pantheon**** H8
*Via del Pantheon 63, 00186, t 06
678 0441, f 06 6994 0689,
e hotsole@flashnet.it; bus 46, 62,
64, 116.*
A small, charming hotel a block
from the Pantheon, mentioned as
an inn in the 15th century –
Ariosto slept here. TV, bar and air
conditioning. Breakfast extra.

Expensive

Due Torri*** H7
*Vicolo del Leonetto 23, 00186, t 06
6880 6956, f 06 686 5442, e hotel
duetorri@interfree.it, w www.hotel
duetorri.roma.it; bus 70, 86, 87, 116.*
On a tiny street, with comfortable
rooms. TV, bar, air conditioning.

Portoghesi*** H7
*Via dei Portoghesi 1, 00186, t 06
686 4231, f 06 687 6976, e info@
hotelportoghesi.roma.com,
w www.hotelportoghesi.roma.
com; bus 116, 116T.*
A small, well-kept hotel on a quiet
but central street north of Piazza
Navona, with optional air conditioning. The suite with a private
balcony on the roof is worth
splashing out on.

Rinascimento** G8
*Via del Pellegrino 122, 00186, t 06
687 4813, f 06 683 3518, e htl
rinascimento@iol.it, w www.hotel
rinascimento.com; bus 116.*
Just west of Campo de' Fiori.
Thirteen very pleasant rooms with
bathroom (don't worry, 13 isn't
unlucky in Italy – it's 17 you have
to watch out for). TV, bar and air
conditioning.

Santa Chiara*** H8
*Via di S. Chiara 21, 00186, t 06 687
2979, f 06 687 3144, e info@
albergosantachiara.com, w www.
albergosantachiara.com; bus 46,
62, 64, 116.*

A comfortable apartment hotel.
TV, bar and air conditioning.

Del Senato*** H8
*Piazza della Rotonda 73, 00186,
t 06 679 3231, f 06 6994 0297,
e delsenato@italyhotel.com,
w www.albergodelsenato.it;
bus 116, 116T.*
Fairly charmless, but comfortable,
with some rooms facing the
Pantheon. TV, bar, business facilities and air conditioning.

Teatro di Pompeo*** G8
*Largo del Pallaro 8, 00186, t 06
6830 0170, f 06 6880 5531; e hotel.
teatrodipompeo@tiscalinet.it.*
The most upmarket hotel around
Campo de' Fiori. Twelve beamed
bedrooms, and a breakfast room
in the vaults of Pompey's Theatre.

Moderate

Campo de' Fiori** G8
*Via del Biscione 6, 00186, t 06
6880 6865, f 06 687 6003,
e campofiori@inwind.it,
w www.campodefiori.com;
bus 46, 62, 64, 116.*
A revamped hotel with hall-of-
mirrors corridor, and theme-park
bedrooms (the kitschest of which
boasts a bathroom roofed with
hewn logs). Vertiginous views
from the roof garden. Bar and air
conditioning. Some much cheaper
rooms are available without bathroom. Breakfast extra.

Della Lunetta** G8
*Piazza del Paradiso 68, 00186, t 06
686 1080, f 06 689 2028; bus 46,
62, 64, 116.*
Near Campo de' Fiori, fairly large,
and nice, quiet rooms. Cheaper
rooms available without bathroom. No breakfast.

Pensione Primavera** G8
*Piazza San Pantaleo 3, 00186, t 06
6880 3109, f 06 6880 3109; bus 46,
62, 64.*
A little-known *pensione* with eight
simple rooms, two minutes' walk
from both Campo de' Fiori and
Piazza Navona.

Sole** G8
*Via del Biscione 76, 00186, t 06 687
9446, f 06 689 3787, e info@sole
albiscione.it; bus 46, 62, 64, 116.*

Near Campo de' Fiori, on the
foundations of Pompey's Theatre,
rises the not very sunny but
endearing 'Sun', a family-run
favourite of backpackers, grand-
parents and everyone else under
the sun. Book in advance and
request a room facing the upstairs
courtyard. TV room and garage.
Cheaper rooms without bath
available. No breakfast.

Inexpensive

Abruzzi** H7
*Piazza della Rotonda 69, 00186,
t 06 679 2021; bus 116.*
Directly across the square from
the Pantheon. The rooms in the
back without the view aren't so
great, but at least they're quiet. A
bit ragged, but amenable.
Showers in the hall. TV, bar, air
conditioning.

Mimosa* H8
*Via di S. Chiara 61, 00186, t 06
6880 1753, f 06 683 3557, e hotel
mimosa@tin.it; bus 116.*
Near the Pantheon. Eleven rooms
on a quiet street overlooking a
Carabinieri barracks. Cheaper
rooms available without bathroom. Breakfast extra.

Navona* H8
*Via dei Sediari 8, 00186, t 06 686
4203, f 06 6880 3802, e navona@
posta2000.com, w www.hotel
navona.com; bus 30, 70, 86, 87, 116.*
Worth it for the location rather
than the intrinsic quality of its 18
rooms. Friendly owners from
Down Under. Slightly cheaper
rooms are available without bathroom. Restaurant. Breakfast and
air conditioning extra.

Piccolo** G8
*Via dei Chiavari 32, 00186, t 06
6880 2560; tram 8, bus 116.*
A charming little hotel on a quiet
street near Campo de' Fiori.
Cheaper rooms available without
bathroom. Breakfast and air
conditioning extra.

Pomezia** G8
*Via dei Chiavari 12, 00186, t 06 686
1371, f 06 686 1371; tram 8, bus 116.*
Immaculate rooms in a pleasant,
friendly little hotel.

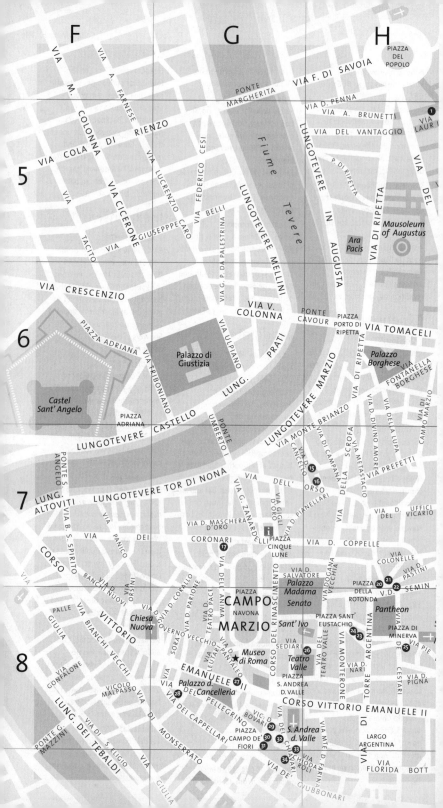

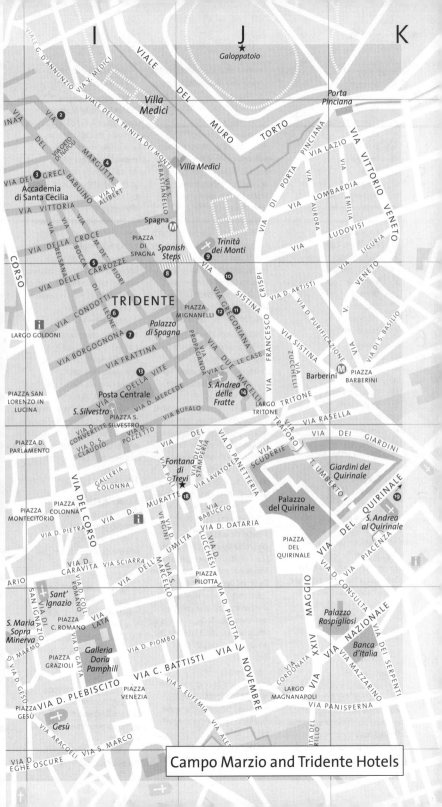

Campo Marzio and Tridente Hotels

Map Key

Tridente

This has been a favourite lodging place for foreigners for the past 300 years, and it still is fashionable today. It's expensive, though, and if you don't book early you won't find a room anywhere in the neighbourhood. It's central and transport is good.

Luxury

Carriage*** I6
Via delle Carrozze 36, 00187, t 06 699 0124, f 06 678 8279, e carriage@hotelcarriage.net, w www.hotelcarriage.net; metro Spagna, bus 117, 119.
A small hotel with 1600s décor, ideally placed for bouts of designer retail therapy in the Via Condotti boutiques. Ask for a room at the top so you can have access to the roof terrace. Bar, air conditioning and TV.

Hassler Villa Medici***** J5
Piazza Trinità dei Monti 6, 00187, t 06 699 340, f 06 678 9991, e hasslerroma@mclink.it, w www.hotelhasslerroma.com; metro Spagna, bus 117, 119; wheelchair accessible.
This is Rome's swankiest and best-appointed hotel, perfectly located on top of the Spanish Steps; every luxury, and a famous roof-top restaurant with a view. In fair weather the garden courtyard becomes the breakfast room; air conditioning, private garage, business facilities etc. Breakfast extra.

Hotel d'Inghilterra**** I6
Via Bocca di Leone 14, 00187, t 06 69981, f 06 6992 2243, e info@charminghotels.it, w www.charminghotels.it/inghilterra; metro Spagna, bus 117, 119.
The Hotel d'Inghilterra opened its doors in 1850 but has been much smartened up since. Henry James, Felix Mendelssohn, the King of Portugal and Ernest Hemingway checked in here before it had air conditioning, TV and business facilities, although they may have enjoyed the bar and restaurant. Breakfast extra.

Hotel de la Ville**** J6
Via Sistina 69, 00187, t 06 67331, f 06 678 4213, e rome@interconti.com, w www.interconti.com; metro Barberini, bus 52, 53, 61, 62, 63.
The Hassler's larger neighbour, it also has a great view from the roof and upper floors, as well as a restaurant, business facilities, TV, garage and air conditioning. Breakfast extra.

Manfredi I5
Via Margutta 61, 00187, t 06 320 7676, f 06 320 7736, e hotel manfredi@tiscalinet.it, w www.hmanfredi.com; metro Spagna, bus 117, 119.
Pretty rooms with fabric-covered walls and tastefully decorated public areas. Small, friendly and run by a charming family.

Scalinata di Spagna*** J5
Piazza Trinità dei Monti 17, 00187, t 06 6994 0896, f 06 6994 0598, e info@hotelscalinata.com, w www.hotelscalinata.com; metro Spagna, bus 117, 119.
A small, friendly family-run hotel at the top of the Spanish Steps, patronized by the occasional discerning film or soap star. Pleasant bedrooms (some with coffered ceilings and a couple with private roof terraces) and a homely dining room where guests breakfast together at a polished wooden table in the company of a parrot. Book months in advance. TV, bar, air conditioning.

Valadier**** H5
Via della Fontanella 15, 00187, t 06 361 1998, f 06 320 1558, e info@hotelvaldier.com, w www.hotelvaladier.com; metro Flaminio, bus 117, 119.
Smarmy nightclub-style décor for would-be seducers; bedrooms with mirrored ceilings and padded walls for those who succeed. Bar and restaurant to oil the process, business facilities to pay for it.

Expensive

Croce di Malta** I6
Via Borgognona 28, 00187, t 06 679 5482, f 06 678 0675, e info@crocedimalta.com, w www.crocedimalta.com; metro Spagna, bus 117, 119; wheelchair accessible.
In a good location on a designer shopping street. Smart bedrooms, some with opulent carved furniture and voluptuous candelabra. TV. Air conditioning and breakfast extra, or plenty of cafés nearby.

Fontana*** J7
Piazza di Trevi 96, 00187, t 06 678 6113, f 06 679 0024, e info@fontanahotel.com, w www.fontanahotel.com; metro Barberini, bus 52, 53, 61, 62, 63, 71, 80.
Nice rooms, some at slightly higer prices with views of the Trevi

Fountain. Restaurant, bar and TV. Air conditioning extra..

Gregoriana*** J6
Via Gregoriana 18, 00187, t 06 679 4269, f 06 678 4258; metro Spagna, bus 117, 119.
A former convent with 19 rooms, some with private balconies facing one of Rome's quietest streets, and corridors papered in unconventional leopard-skin print. Friendly staff. TV, air conditioning.

Homs*** I6
Via della Vite 71, 00187, t 06 679 2976, f 06 678 0482; metro Spagna, bus 117, 119; wheelchair accessible.
In a large renovated old building on one of the area's smaller, quieter shopping streets.

Keats–Shelley House I6
Piazza di Spagna 26, owned by Britain's Landmark Trust, t (01628) 825 925 (in the UK), e bookings@ landmarktrust.co.uk, w www. landmarktrust.co.uk; metro Spagna, bus 117, 119.
For something different, there is one self-catering flat in the Keats–Shelley House next to the Spanish Steps. It sleeps four. Reserve well ahead, by the week.

Mozart*** I5
Via dei Greci 23, 00187, t 06 3600 1915, f 06 3600 1735, e info@hotel mozart.com, w www.hotelmozart. com; metro Spagna, bus 117, 119; wheelchair accessible.
A lovely little place on a quiet cobbled street. Stone-flagged hall, small flowery rooms with parquet floors, and a pleasant café next door for breakfast or lunch. Bar, TV and air conditioning.

Moderate

Erdarelli** J6
Via due Macelli 28, 00187, t 06 679 1265, f 06 679 0705, e erdarelli@ italyhotel.com, www.italyhotel. com/roma/erdarelli; metro Spagna, bus 117, 119.
Basic rooms on a noisy street, a short stroll from the Spanish Steps. There are three prettier

rooms on the top floor with private balconies. Cheaper rooms available without bath. Air conditioning extra.

Suisse** J6
Via Gregoriana 56, 00187, t 06 678 3649, f 06 678 1258; metro Spagna, bus 52, 53, 61, 62, 63, 71, 117, 119.
A fine old *pensione*, with large rooms clean enough to satisfy even the Swiss. Ask for one at the back. Breakfast extra.

Inexpensive

Forte*** I5
Via Margutta 61, 00187, t 06 320 7625, f 06 320 2707, e forte@italy hotel.com; metro Spagna, bus 117, 119.
Hidden away in a pretty and quiet street leading to the Spanish Steps, the Forte was completely restored in 2000. Bar, TV and air conditioning.

Capitoline Hill and Tiber Banks

Casa Kolbe** J10
Via di San Teodoro 44, 00186, t 06 679 4974, f 06 6994 1550; metro Colosseo, bus 84, 85, 87, 117, 175; wheelchair accessible. Inexpensive.
Large rooms in a former monastery in one of Rome's most central but remote corners, with a garden, bar, and restaurant to retreat from the rigours of Rome. Business facilities.

Forums, Colosseum and Palatine Hill

The area can be a bit noisy on weekdays, but it's very convenient for the sights and public transport. At night it quietens down considerably – there are very few fun restaurants or bars nearby.

Forum**** J9
Via Tor de' Conti 25, 00184, t 06 679 2446, f 06 678 6479, e info@hotel forum.com, w www.hotelforum.

com; *metro Cavour, Colosseo, bus 84, 85, 87, 117, 175. Luxury.*
The only really luxury establishment near the centre of ancient Rome, dignified and somewhat old-fashioned, with a unique view over the ruins from the rooftop bar and restaurant. Also air conditioning, TV and business facilities.

Nerva*** K9
Via Tor de' Conti 3, 00184, t 06 678 1835, f 06 699 2204, e hotel nerva@libero.it, w www.hotel nerva.com; metro Colosseo, Cavour, bus 84, 85, 87, 117, 175. Expensive.
A view onto Augustus' Subura Wall for lovers of ancient masonry. A small hotel with friendly owners. Air conditioning, bar, TV.

Romano** J9
Largo Corrado Ricci 32, 00184, t 06 679 5851, f 06 678 6840, e hotel romano@iol.it, w www.venere.it/ it/roma/romano; metro Cavour and Colosseo, bus 84, 85, 87, 117, 175. Moderate.
Relatively simple accommodation across from the Forum; some rooms have views of the ancient ruins. Air conditioning, TV and bar.

Perugia* K9
Via del Colosseo 7, 00184, t 06 679 7200, f 06 678 4635, e htlperugia@ iol.it; metro Cavour, Colosseo, bus 84, 85, 87, 117, 175. Inexpensive.
Small, fairly quiet, fairly basic hotel near the Colosseum and the Colle Oppio. Cheaper rooms available without bathroom.

Quirinale, Viminale and Esquiline Hill

The 'American Ghetto' around the Quirinale, Viminale and Via Veneto, Tourist Rome's vortex, remains a choice area for hotels, although lacking the tone and sparkle it had in the *dolce vita* era of the 1950s. Nowadays the marble-frosted turn-of-the-20th century façades conceal packs of businessmen on expenses and well-heeled package tourists.

In the 1890s, when the Esquiline Hill area was the newest, choicest district in Rome, the streets near the Termini Station spawned hundreds of hotels, some quite elegant. Sadly, it has gone the way of all such 19th-century toadstool neighbourhoods: overbuilt, dingy, noisy and down at heel – not the place to savour the 'real' Rome – and it's inconvenient for most of the sights. But there is a choice of cheap hotels, from the respectable and cosy to the bizarre.

As a last resort, this area will do. But it isn't conducive to an enjoyable holiday. If you're looking for the tolerable and cheap, a general rule is to keep to the side streets, like Via Principe Amedeo; the east side of Termini is nicer, although there are fewer choices.

Luxury

Ambasciatori Palace** K6
Via Veneto 62, 00187, t 06 47 493, f 06 474 3601, e ambasciatori rome@diginet.it, w www.hotel ambasciatori.com; metro Barberini, bus 52, 53, 63, 80, 95, 116, 116T; wheelchair accessible.
A lovely palace from the Roaring Twenties, complete with sporty frescoes of Italian Gatsbys. All the luxuries at your fingertips, including restaurant, bar, TV, air conditioning and business facilities. Breakfast extra.

Artemide** L7
Via Nazionale 22, 00184, t 06 489 911, f 06 4899 1700, e hotel. artemide@tiscalinet.it, w www. travel.it/roma/artemide; metro Repubblica, bus H, 40, 60, 64, 70, 71, 116T, 170; wheelchair accessible.
Opened in 1994, and one of the only 19th-century *palazzetti* that offers disabled access, satellite TV, a stained-glass dome in a lobby full of antiques and paintings and jacuzzis in some of the marble bathrooms – as well as a bar and air conditioning.

Bernini Bristol*** K7
Piazza Barberini 23, 00187, t 06 488 3051, f 06 482 4266, e bbsina@tin.
it, w www.sinahotels.com; metro Barberini, bus 52, 53, 63, 80, 95, 116, 116T, 175, 492.
A luxurious hotel in an ugly brick building at the bottom of Via Veneto; it may win first prize in the most tons of marble category. Ask for a room on the upper floor for the fine views over the city, or lounge around in the roof garden. Restaurant, bar, business facilities, air conditioning. Breakfast extra.

Excelsior*** K5
Via Veneto 125, 00187, t 06 4708, f 06 482 6205, w www.westin.com; metro Barberini, bus 52, 53, 63, 80, 95, 116, 116T.
The hotel with Via Veneto's landmark tower opened its doors in 1911, setting a standard in hotel architecture that Rome has yet to achieve again. The reception areas have thicker carpets, bigger chandeliers, and more gilded plaster than any others in Italy. There are saunas, boutiques, a famous bar, restaurant and everything else, with as much personal attention as you could desire, as well as all the basics like air conditioning and TV. Breakfast extra.

Flora** K5
Via Veneto 191, 00187, t 06 489 929, f 06 482 0359, w www. marriothotels.com; metro Barberini, bus 52, 53, 63, 80, 95, 116, 116T.
Just a step from Villa Borghese, this confection from the 1900s, with its slightly faded elegance and magnificent rooms, is a favourite of romantics in Rome. It also serves the pragmatics with a bar, restaurant, garage, business facilities and air conditioning. Breakfast extra.

La Residenza** K5
Via Emilia 22, 00187, t 06 488 0789, f 06 485 721, e hotel.laresidenza@ venere.it, w www.venere.it/roma/ laresidenza; metro Barberini, bus 52, 53, 3, 80, 95, 116, 116T.
A pleasant base, just off Via Veneto, with beautifully appointed rooms in an old town house and the luxuries common in the most expensive hotels,
including air conditioning, parking, TV, a bar and, more unusually, a garden.

St Regis Grand*** L6
Via Vittorio Emanuele Orlando 3, 00185, t 06 47091, f 06 474 7307, e mailtorome.bu@stregisgrand. com, w www.stregis.com; metro Repubblica, bus 36, 60, 61, 62, 84, 175, 492; wheelchair accessible.
A sumptuous old hotel in a dreary location just off Piazza della Repubblica. Magnificent décor in the public rooms, although we recommend they jettison the lurid green tiles which grace some of the bathrooms. Restaurant, bar, garage, air conditioning, business facilities including a 3,842ft meeting room (one of three) and TV. Breakfast extra.

Expensive

Alexandra* K6
Via Veneto 18, 00187, t 06 488 1943, f 06 487 1804, e alexandra@ venere.it, w www.venere.it/roma /alexandra; metro Barberini, bus 52, 53, 63, 80, 95, 116, 116T.
A fine, old-fashioned moderate-sized hotel, with air conditioning, TV and garage.

Britannia* L7
Via Napoli 64, 00184, t 06 488 3153, f 06 488 2343, e britannia@ venere.it, w www.italyhotel.com/ roma/britannia; metro Repubblica, bus 36, 60, 61, 62, 84, 175, 492.
Not too inconvenient, small and up-to-date, with TV, optional air conditioning, bar and parking.

Massimo D'Azeglio** M7
Via Cavour 18, 00184, t 06 462 0561, f 06 482 7386, e dazeglio@ bettojahotels.it, w www.bettoja hotels.it; metro Cavour, Termini, bus 16, 75, 84, 195, 157, 204, 360, 590, 649, 714.
A grand hotel vintage 1875, which has been run by the same family for five generations. Spacious and traditional, but with telephones, TV and air conditioning in its newly refurbished, comfortable rooms. Its noted restaurant started life in 1575 as a hostelry for

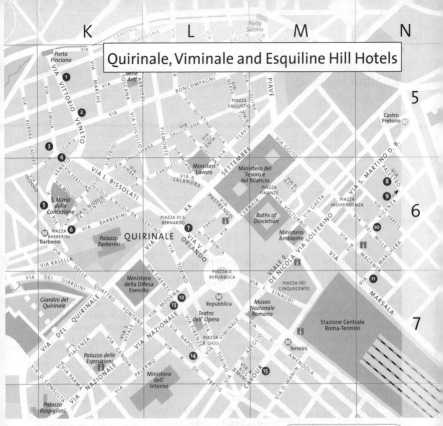

jubilee pilgrims to Santa Maria Maggiore and continues to serve regional Italian cuisine. The well stocked cellar offers the chance to taste exceptionally fine wines. Bar and business facilities too.

Villa delle Rose* N6**
Via Vicenza 5, 00185, **t** *06 445 1788,* **f** *06 445 1639,* **e** *villadellerose@ flashnet.it,* **w** *www.villadellerose.it;* **metro** *Castro Pretorio,* **bus** *204, 310, 492.*
Surely the most restful place to stay near Termini, in a former villa, offering 38 well-kept rooms with a fine little garden. Bar, business facilities and TV. Air conditioning extra.

Canada* N6**
Via Vicenza 58, 00185, **t** *06 445 7770,* **f** *06 445 0749,* **e** *info@hotel canada.com,* **w** *www.hotelcanada. roma.com;* **metro** *Castro Pretorio,* **bus** *204, 310, 492.*
A pleasant hotel, often used by British tour operators, with comfortable, thoughtfully designed rooms (and radio

speakers in the bathrooms!). Bar, air conditioning and TV too. Breakfast extra.

Moderate

Rimini N7**
Via Marghera 17, 00185, **t** *06 446 1991,* **f** *06 491 289,* **e** *rimini@travel. it,* **w** *www.hotelrimini.it;* **metro** *Termini,* **bus** *C, H, 36, 38, 40, 64, 86, 90, 92, 105, 170 and many others.*
Only a hop from the station, but the clean, comfortable rooms are high enough above the street level to miss most of the noise. TV. Air conditioning extra.

Inexpensive

Elide L7**
Via Firenze 50, 00184, **t** *06 474 1367,* **f** *06 4890 4318;* **metro** *Repubblica,* **bus** *H, 40, 60, 64, 70, 71, 116T, 170.*
A small, friendly, family-run place in a fairly quiet street off Piazza della Repubblica, with a few frescoes from the old days – a reminder that this area existed before 1900.

Map Key

5	Alexandra
4	Ambasciatori Palace
13	Artemide
6	Bernini Bristol
14	Britannia
9	Canada
12	Elide
	Excelsior
1	Flora
3	La Residenza
15	Massimo D'Azeglio
8	Restivo
11	Rimini
7	St Regis Grand
10	Villa delle Rose

Restivo* N6
Via Palestro 55, 00185, **t** *06 446 2172,* **f** *06 445 2629;* **metro** *Castro Pretorio,* **bus** *204, 310, 492.*
Immaculate *pensione* run by a sweet old lady, whose hall is cluttered with gifts from affectionate visitors. If it's full try **Mari** (**t** *06 446 2137,* **f** *06 6482 8313*) or **Cervia** (**t** *491 057,* **f** *06 491 056,* **e** *hotel cervia@wnt.it*), two other *pensioni* in the same *palazzo.*

Caelian Hill and the Aventine

One of the prettiest, coolest, and quietest corners in Rome, with safe street parking. It's connected by bus and metro to the centre, in walking distance of ancient Rome and has a direct link to Fiumicino airport from Stazione Ostiense nearby. The bars, restaurants and clubs of Testaccio are close too.

Expensive

Domus Aventina*** J12
Via S. Prisca 11B, 00153, t 06 574 6135, f 06 5730 0044, e info@domus-aventina.com, w www.domus-aventina.com; metro Circo Massimo, bus 175, 715.
A neat hotel in a former convent, very quiet and right next to the church of Santa Prisca. Bar, air conditioning and TV.

Sant'Anselmo*** H12
Piazza Sant'Anselmo 2, 00153, t 06 574 3547, f 06 578 3604, e info@aventinohotels.com, w www.aventinohotels.com; metro Circo Massimo, bus 23, 75, 280, 716; wheelchair accessible.
A former villa with exquisite décor, a bar and a garden to sit outside. TV and business facilities.

Villa San Pio*** I12
Via Santa Melania 19, 00153, t 06 578 3214, f 06 578 3604, e info@aventinohotels.com, w www.aventinohotels.com; metro Piramide, bus 23, 75, 280, 716; wheelchair accessible.
Another glorious Aventine villa with a gorgeous, secluded statue-studded garden. Bar and TV.

Moderate

Aventino** I12
Via S. Domenico 10, 00153, t 06 578 3214, f 06 578 3604, e info@aventinohotels.com, w www.aventinohotels.com; metro Piramide, bus 23, 75, 280, 716; wheelchair accessible.
Yet another Aventine villa, this one an annex of the S. Anselmo.

It's not as stylish as its elder sisters, but rooms are adequate and the garden is lovely.

Santa Prisca** I13
Largo M. Gelsomini 25, 00153, t 06 574 1917, f 06 574 6658; metro Circo Massimo, Piramide, bus 23, 75, 280, 716.
Owned and run by friendly, worldly nuns (no lock-out time). Quiet rooms on the inner court. Restaurant, bar, parking and business facilities. Breakfast and air conditioning extra.

Trastevere and the Janiculum

Carmel* F11
Via Goffredo Mameli 11, 00153, t 06 580 9921, f 06 581 8853; tram 8, bus 44, 75. Inexpensive.
One of the few places to sleep in Trastevere, in a quiet street, with a small garden. Nine rooms. Air conditioning and breakfast extra.

Esty* F12
Viale di Trastevere 108, 00153, t 06 588 1201; tram 8. Cheap.
Near the river. Comfortable modern rooms, all without en suite bathrooms. No breakfast.

Ripa Residence**** G12
Via Luigi Gianniti 21, 00153, t 06 58611, f 06 581 4550, e ripa@uni.net, w www.ripahotel.com; tram 8; wheelchair accessible. Luxury.
Once a residential hotel, the Ripa is now a rather fancy hotel – one of the few smart places to stay in Trastevere – with junior and senior suites. Restaurant, bar, parking and air conditioning.

Vatican City and St Peter's

The area around Vatican City, with the exception of the Borgo, is one of the dullest in central Rome but it's genteel and hassle-free. It's a good place to sleep but not to play, although Trastevere is a short bus ride away, and Piazza del Popolo is just across the Tiber. Off the main streets noise is not a

problem. The main drag is Via Cola di Rienzo, lined with department stores and shops, including two of Rome's best *alimentari* (see p.330).

Luxury

Atlante Star**** E6
Via G. Vitelleschi 34, 00193, t 06 687 3233, f 06 687 2300, e atlante.star@atlantehotels.com, w www.atlantehotels.com; bus 23, 34, 40.
Modern, cramped rooms with TV are compensated for by a beautiful roof garden restaurant with stunning views. Bar, air conditioning and business facilities.

Columbus**** E7
Via della Conciliazione 33, 00193, t 06 686 5435, f 06 686 4874, e hotelcolumbus@hotelcolumbus.net, w www.hotelcolumbus.net; bus 62; wheelchair accessible.
A somewhat staid but reliable place in the Renaissance Palazzo Penitenzieri, it's a favourite of visiting cardinals; a few frescoes and a courtyard survive from the good old days. Restaurant, bar, business facilities, TV and air conditioning.

Expensive

Farnese**** F4
Via Alessandro Farnese 30, 00192, t 06 321 2553, f 06 321 5129, w www.travel.it/roma/hotelfarnese.
Housed in a late 19th-century villa in walking distance of St Peter's, the Farnese has an intimate atmosphere. Sparkling new baths and attractive, well-maintained guest rooms decorated with wood panelling and rich fabrics. Air conditioning, bar, parking and TV. Breakfast extra.

Sant' Anna*** D6
Borgo Pio 134, 00193, t 06 6880 1620, f 06 6830 8717, e santanna@travel.it, w www.hotelsantanna.com; bus 23, 34.
A quiet, smartly refurbished hotel with well-designed rooms and a pretty garden courtyard at the back. Business facilities, air conditioning, TV and garage.

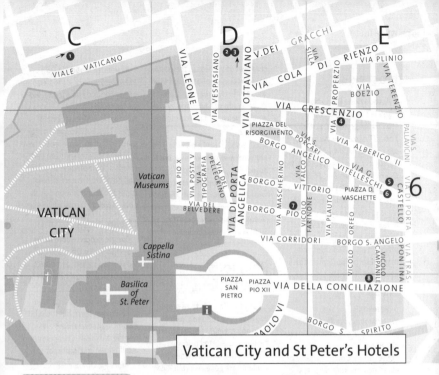

Vatican City and St Peter's Hotels

Map Key

6	Adriatic
1	Alimandi
5	Atlante Star
8	Columbus
3	Farnese
2	Forti's Guest House
4	Prati
7	Sant' Anna

Moderate

Adriatic** E6

*Via G. Vitelleschi 25, 00193, **t** 06 6880 8080, **f** 06 689 3552, **e** adriatic@ats.it, **w** www.adriatic hotel.com; **metro** Ottaviano, **tram** 19, **bus** 23, 32, 34, 40, 49, 62, 81, 492.*

A clean, simple *pensione* in the Borgo, but no bargain. Garden, air conditioning and TV. Cheaper rooms available without bath. Breakfast extra.

Alimandi*** C5

*Via Tunisi 8, 00193, **t** 06 3972 3941, **f** 06 3972 3943, **e** alimandi@tin.it, **w** www.alimandi.org; **metro** Ottaviano, **tram** 19, **bus** 490, 492.*

Next to the Vatican Museums entrance, in atmosphere a cut above its class, although the most winning feature is a large roof garden. Popular with young travellers. Restaurant, bar, TV and parking. Breakfast extra.

Inexpensive

Forti's Guest House* F4

*Via Fornovo 7, 00192, **t** 06 321 2256, **f** 06 321 2222; **metro** Lepanto, **tram** 19, **bus** 70, 88, 490, 913. **Open** Sept–July.*

A friendly, popular, and tranquil place to sleep in Prati – a civilized if slightly dull neighbourhood very close to the Vatican – well-run by its American owner. Near metro Lepanto, making it a good start for day trips on the numerous buses that leave the city for interesting out of town destinations from there. Cheaper rooms without bath. Good breakfast. Book early.

Prati** E6

*Via Crescenzio 87, 00193, **t** 06 687 5357, **f** 06 6880 6938, **e** prati@italy hotel.com, **w** www.hotelpratiroma. com; **bus** 23, 34, 49, 492.*

Pleasant, reasonably priced rooms. Slightly cheaper rooms available without bath.

Outside the Centre

Luxury

Lord Byron***** I2

*Via G. de Notaris 5, 00197, **t** 06 322 0404, **f** 06 322 0405, **e** info@lord-byronhotel.com, **w** www.lordbyron hotel.com; **tram** 3, 19, **bus** 52, 926.*

This plush hotel just beyond Villa Borghese offers everything you might need except wheelchair access – garden, bar, garage, business facilities, air conditioning and TV. it also hosts the famous Relais le Jardin restaurant (*see* p.316).

Students, Pilgrims and Campers

You can save money in Rome, but at a cost – nearly every hostel or religious institution locks its doors before midnight. Some are so hard to get to that a fleabag by Termini Station looks good in comparison. And do book early, especially if you come in spring and summer.

Hostels

Associazione Italiana Alberghi per la Gioventù (AIG) K9

Via Cavour 44, 00194, t 06 487 1152, f 06 488 0492, w www.hostels-aig.org; metro Cavour, bus 16, 75, 84, 105, 157, 204, 360, 590, 649, 714. Open Mon–Thurs 8–5, Fri 8–3.

To stay at Rome's youth hostel (*see* below), or any other, reserve at least 30 days in advance by letter or fax or go in person to any office to make a booking. There are AIG offices in all Italian cities and major resorts. The Rome office is near Termini Station.

Cheap

Marello L9

Via Urbana 50, 00184, t 06 482 5361, f 06 481, 9743; metro Cavour, bus 75, 84.

In the summer, male students or older men can stay in Rome's university dormitories, which are more civilized and more centrally located than the youth hostel. All rooms are doubles, most without bath. No breakfast. Reservations accepted for Jul–Sept.

Ostello per la Gioventù Aldo Franco Pessina Off maps

Viale delle Olimpiadi 61, t 06 323 6267, f 06 324 2613; metro Ottaviano, then bus 32 to Stadio Olimpico. Reception open 7am–11pm.

Rome's youth hostel (IYHF cards required) is inconveniently far out in one of Mussolini's dreamlands. Low-grade hospital atmosphere, stays of no more than three consecutive nights, plastic breakfast, and midnight curfew.

Sandy* L8

Via Cavour 136, 00184, t 06 488 4585; metro Cavour, bus 75, 84. Via Ottaviano 6, 00192, t 06 3973 7253; metro Ottaviano, tram 19, bus 32, 81, e gi.costantini@agora.stm.it, w www.pensioneottaviano.com.

Two laid-back *pensioni* run by the same family, offering some of the cheapest dorm beds in the centre. Rated as one-star hotels, but quite cheap anyway. American staff. Reservations can be made by email at least 30 days in advance.

YWCA L7

Via C. Balbo 4, t 06 488 0460, f 06 487 1028; metro Repubblica, bus H, 40, 60, 64, 70, 71, 116T, 170.

Pleasant staff and a quiet location with a street market outside. Book at least 2 weeks in advance. Midnight curfew. No breakfast on Sunday and holidays. Single rooms more expensive.

Religious Institutions

Early to bed, early to rise – and you may have to supply your own soap and towel. Many institutions besides those listed below have places in the summer, when their students are gone. Ask your local priest or a friend in Orders if they know of any hospitality in Rome .

Inexpensive

Madre Maria Eugenia L1

Viale Romania 32, 00197, t 06 8448 2300, f 06 8448 2302, e recasa feriea@atsap.net; tram 3, 19, bus 52, 53, 360; wheelchair accessible.

A quiet place surrounded by a small park. All rooms have private bathroom. Bed and breakfast, half or full board possible with advance booking. The kitchen only caters for large groups, but if there's a group booked in single visitors are welcome to join for a cheap meal. Single, double, triple and four-bed rooms available, as well as one five-bed room.

Nostra Signora di Lourdes J6

Via Sistina 113, 00187, t 06 474 5324, f 06 474 1422; metro Barberini, bus 52, 53, 63, 80, 95, 116, 116T, 175, 492.

Twenty-four single and double rooms for women a stone's throw from the Spanish Steps. Cheaper rooms available without bathroom. There's a 10.30pm curfew, so you'll have to enjoy the evening *passeggiata* from your room.

Residenza Madri Pie D8

Via A. De Gasperi 4, 00165, t 06 631 967 or 633 441, f 06 631 989; bus 34, 64, 98, 881, 916.

No, the Pious Mothers do not supply pies, but beds, and a little garden to sit in. Some rooms have a view of St Peter's. Private bathrooms and air conditioning. Bed and breakfast treatment. Single, triple and four-bed rooms available as well as the usual doubles.

Cheap

Congregazione Suore dello Spirito Santo Off maps

Via Pineta Sacchetti 227, 00168, t 06 305 3101; metro Valle Aurelia, then bus 446 or 994.

A relaxing place and a bargain once you get there, but it is a bit distant. Call several days ahead to reserve. No meals. Cheaper rooms available without bathroom.

Suore Pie Operaie H8

Via di Torre Argentina 76, 00186, t 06 686 1254; tram 8, bus 46, 62, 64, 70, 71, 87, 492.

Beds for women in five double and triple rooms, all without bath, a couple of minutes' walk from the Pantheon. 10.30pm curfew.

Residential Hotels

There are at least a score of these self-catering flatlets but nearly all are out in the suburbs or EUR, and who wants to commute in traffic-ridden Rome? The following are nearest the centre.

Inexpensive

Aldrovandi J2

Via Aldrovandi 11, 00197, t 06 322 1430, f 06 322 2181, e aldro@iol.it, w www. aldrovandiresidence.it; tram 3, 19, bus 231.

One of the more comfortable, conveniently located residences, just north of Villa Borghese. One, two or three-room flats with TV, telephone, parking and air conditioning. Minimum stay one week.

Aurelia Antica A10–D11
*Via Aurelia Antica 425, 00165, t 06
663 8808, f 06 6601 5516; bus 98,
881, 889, 892.*
A bit out of the way but quiet and
good value. One, two and three-
room flats with swimming pool
and garden, tennis nearby, maid
service, parking, TV and air conditioning. Minimum stay one night,
deposit required.

Palazzo al Velabro I10
*Via del Velabro 16, 00186; t 06 679
2758, f 06 679 3790, e velabro@
venere.it, w www.venere.it/rome/
velabro; bus 81, 160,. 204, 628.*
One, two and three-room
furnished flats centrally located
near the Capitoline Hill. Minimum
stay one week, with daily maid
service, air conditioning and TV.

Di Ripetta H5
*Via di Ripetta 231, 00186, t 06 323
1144, f 06 320 3959, e info@ripetta.
it, w www.ripetta.it; bus 81,
204, 628.*
One, two and three-room flats,
conveniently located between the
Tiber and the Spanish Steps, with
a garage, air conditioning and TV.
Minimum stay one week.

Campsites

Rome might not be the most
obvious place to go on a camping
holiday, but there are several
campsites within a reasonable
distance from the centre. All boast
a full range of mod cons, many
including a swimming pool, which
could make them a good base for
daily sightseeing excursions if
travelling with a family.

Cheap
Castelfusano Country Club
Off maps
*Piazza di Castelfusano 1, Lido di
Ostia, t 06 5618 5490, f 06 5618
5227; metro Ostia Antica, Lido
Stella Polare, bus 014, 018; wheel-
chair accessible. Open for camping
all year, bungalows available
March–Oct.*
A mile and a half from the ruins of
Ostia and near the beach.
Restaurant, bar, shop, launderette,
parking, boat dock, disco, chil-
dren's playground, beach volley
ball, tennis, table tennis, bowls
and swimming pool.

Flaminio Off maps
*Via Flaminia Nuova, km 8.2, t 06
333 2604, f 06 333 0653; metro
Mancini then bus 200, 232, or
metro Flaminio then train to
Due Ponti; wheelchair accessible.
Open Mar–Dec.*
The closest and perhaps the best.
Restaurant, bar, shop, launderette,
parking, playground and swim-
ming pool.

Nomentano Off maps
*Via della Cesarina 11, t 06 610
0296; bus 60 from Termini. Open
Easter–Sept.*
At the corner of Via Nomentana,
km 11.5; get off the bus at Via Ugo
Ojetii. Restaurant, bar, shop, laun-
derette, parking.

Roma Camping Off maps
*Via Aurelia 831, km 8.2, t 06 662
3018, f 06 6641 8147; e guideuro@
guideuro.it, w www.guideuro.it.
Bus 46 from Piazza Venezia, or
metro Aurelia-Cornelia then bus
246. Open all year.*
Restaurant, bar, shop and launderette as well as open space
away from the city's heat and
pollution in summer.

Eating Out

In many ways Rome is one of the best cities in Italy for dining out, not only for the variety of its restaurants, but also for the local custom of making dinner the main event of the evening. Most of Rome's nightlife is around its dining tables, especially in the warmer months, when everyone sits out in the delightful coolness of the piazza after a long hot day – one of the city's greatest charms. While Roman cuisine itself hasn't been the same since the ban on nightingales' tongues, the capital city has attracted chefs from every region in the country, offering a regional range unique in Italy; and as people from all over the world settle here, there are, unusually for Italy, a fair number of non-Italian restaurants – including 300 Chinese – although the quality of ethnic cuisine may disappoint visitors from cosmopolitan centres. Vegetarian menus are the exception and not the rule in traditional Italian restaurants, but most places in Rome offer a good choice of salads, vegetables and pasta dishes without meat.

Roman Habits

To eat like a Roman means a stop at a bar for a quick stand-up breakfast of coffee (usually a cappuccino) and a warm *cornetto* ('horn', like a croissant, plain, or filled with custard, raisins or jam) or a *brioche* (a flaky pastry, sometimes with chocolate inside). You can stop for refills as often as necessary, although around noon it's time to move on to an *aperitivo* of some sort: a Campari, some kind of vermouth (Italians prefer something bitter, to whet the appetite) or perhaps a fruit juice.

Between 1 and 2 is time for lunch (*pranzo*; most restaurants open at 12 and stop serving at around 2.30 or 3). This is traditionally the biggest meal of the day in Italy, although in practice many Romans prefer to grab a quick meal in a cafeteria-buffet or *tavola calda* (a selection of hot, prepared foods), or eat a *panino*

(roll, often flattened and toasted to melt the mozzarella in the middle) or a *tramezzino* (a white sliced-bread sandwich with no crusts, better than it looks), rather than commute home. But most will have some form of pasta (rather than in the evening, when it tends to sit on the delicate Italian stomach), a main meat or fish course (being wary not to strain the *fegato*, or liver), a salad or vegetable, wine or water, and fruit, followed by a coffee in a nearby bar. You may have a *digestivo* to aid gastric action, perhaps an anise-flavoured *sambuca*, with *tre mosche* ('three flies' or coffee beans), a Strega (made from saffron), a Fernet-Branca (made from mysterious herbs), an *amaretto* (sweet almond liqueur), or a Cynar (artichoke liqueur). Late afternoon snacks (at 5 or 6pm) would be an ice cream in the summer, or a *supplì* (a deep-fried rice croquette, usually with mozzarella inside), a slice of pizza (*al taglio*), or one of a hundred varieties of *tramezzino* washed down with a glass of beer or wine.

Romans eat dinner (*cena*) any time after 8 or 9pm, always caught between the desire to go late and that of finding a table at their favourite restaurant in Trastevere or near Piazza Navona. A plate of *antipasti* and a pizza is a popular (and economical) supper, as is having a light meal in one of the burgeoning number of *enoteche*, or wine bars; but there are always plenty of Romans ordering three- and four-course dinners. Flasks of the house wine, usually from the Castelli Romani, help fill out the evening. Last stop: another bar, another coffee (to help you sleep!), perhaps *corretto* (corrected) with a shot of *grappa* or Vecchia Romagna brandy.

Rome's restaurants are child-friendly: high chairs are common, or attentive waiters will prop your child on cushions. For a child-sized serving ask for a *mezza porzione*. You will also be able to order plain rice or pasta (*see* p.340).

Roman Tastes

Traditional Roman specialities tend to be simple, almost rustic, making use of inexpensive ingredients that are produced locally; pickled swan hearts and imported fish gut sauce went out with the Caesars. Now the most famous Roman first course, or *primo*, is spaghetti or *bucatini* (thin tubes) *all'amatriciana*, with a sauce of salt pork, tomatoes, chilli peppers, topped with grated *pecorino* (sharp ewes' cheese). *Spaghetti alla carbonara*, another popular dish, features bacon, eggs, pepper and parmesan (one tradition says it was invented by American GIs, who topped spaghetti with their breakfast rations). Other local specialities include *fettuccine al burro* (cholesterol heaven: ribbon egg noodles, with a double dose of butter, cream, and parmesan cheese); *penne all'arrabbiata* ('angry quills', with tomato sauce and lots of chilli pepper); *gnocchi di patate* (potato dumplings with butter or meat sauce, a favourite on Thursdays), or the much harder to find *gnocchi alla romana*, made of semolina and baked in the oven; *stracciatella* (broth with eggs, semolina, parmesan cheese); *spaghetti aglio e olio* (with garlic, olive oil, chilli pepper and parsley).

Typical Roman meat courses (*secondi*) are led by the famous 'jump-in-the-mouth' *saltimbocca alla romana* (veal scallops with ham and sage, cooked in butter and white wine). For heartier fare, try *trippa alla romana* (tripe stewed with onions, carrots, mint, meat sauce and parmesan), *coda alla vaccinara* (stewed ox tail), or *involtini al sugo* (rolled veal cutlets filled with ham, celery and cheese and cooked in tomato sauce). *Pajata*, for intrepid diners only, is veal intestine with its mother's milk clotted inside, dressed up with garlic, chilli peppers, tomatoes and white wine. Popular, but often expensive, is *abbacchio alla scottadito*, lamb chops 'burn the finger' grilled over a flame. *Tordi matti* are a kind of grilled *involtini*. Seafood is expensive; local dishes are *anguillette in umido* (stewed baby eels from Lake Bracciano), *filetti di baccalà* (dried cod fried in batter), and *seppiette con i carciofi* (cuttlefish with artichokes).

The Roman *campagna* produces tender, purple 'Roman' artichokes, used in *carciofi alla giudea* (deep-fried artichokes), the famous side dish or *contorno* adopted from Jewish cuisine. A *misticanza* is a green salad composed of wild and domestic greens. In the winter try Roman cauliflower, which grows in pale green Mandelbrot set spirals (but tastes pretty much like regular cauliflower). A typical dessert (also Jewish in origin) is *crostata di ricotta*, a tart filled with cream, ricotta, cinnamon and bits of chocolate; or *zuppa inglese alla romana*, the local version of trifle. The classic Roman cheese is *pecorino*, made from ewes' milk; *caciotta romana* comes from a mixture of cows' and ewes' milk.

Wine

Wine in Rome usually means a white Castelli Romani, most famously Frascati, which inspired the Trastevere's dialect poet Trilussa to rhapsodize: '*Dentro 'sta boccia trovi er bonumore/che canta l'inni e t'imbandiera er còre*' (something like: 'in a mouthful there's such good humour/that sings hymns and decks your heart with banners'). Straw-coloured, dry, and clear, Frascati, like all the Castelli wines, is a perfect accompaniment to Roman cooking.

Other white wines worth trying from the region are Marino, like Frascati a DOC wine; also Colli Albani, from near Castel Gandolfo, a pale gold in colour, soft and fruity; Colli Lanuvini, from south of Lake Nemi, good for fish and antipasti; and Velletri, both a white and a dry tannic ruby red, a friend to roast and grilled meats. The other regions around Rome produce a fair complement of *vini*: a full-bodied red wine and a slightly bitter, dry and aromatic white from Cervéteri; Zagarolo, a soft, harmonic white wine famous during the Renaissance; Monte Compatri Colonna, from the Zagarolo-Colonna area, another white that should be served quite cool with dishes like *fettuccine al burro*. Harder to find are Torre Ercolana, Fiorano (red or white), and the red Castel San Giorgio. If none of these please, Rome is a great place to find wines from all other corners of Italy, some as inexpensive. On the whole, the *vino della casa* is cheap and drinkable, although it's advisable, if you're quaffing cheap wine, to do as some Romans do and dilute it with water or lemonade to avoid a morning-after headache.

Prices

'The more you spend the worse you eat,' is an old Roman saying, although the city's restaurants are doing their utmost to keep prices rising above the Italian average. The humble, inexpensive *vini e cucina*, a mainstay of working-class Rome, are an endangered species. Watch out for tourist traps – those places near a major sight with a 'tourist menu' almost always mean mediocrity. Rome also has some quite expensive joints that could best be described as parodies of old, famous establishments; they advertise heavily, and aren't hard to smell out. The Romans have another pessimistic saying – that in a lovely setting you'll eat like a dog; it's true that many places with pretty outside terraces lose their ambition in the kitchen. Hotel restaurants, especially those in the deluxe class, can be very, very good but fiendishly expensive, places where you can easily drop €150. The distinctions between 'ristorante', 'trattoria' and 'osteria' have become confused – some of Rome's swankiest eating places are trattorias or osterias.

Sadly the old habit of posting prices in the window has fallen out of fashion, so it is difficult to judge prices. Generally, the fancier the fittings, the fancier the *conto* at the end, although neither price nor décor have anything to do with the quality of the food. When you eat out, mentally add to the bill the bread and cover charge (*pane e coperto*, usually €1.50, but can be a lot more in swanky restaurants) and a 15 per cent service charge. This is usually included in the bill (*servizio compreso*); if it says *servizio non compreso* you'll have to do your own arithmetic. An additional small tip is expected for good service, around €2 per person at a moderately priced restaurant.

Note that when a restaurant advertises a fixed-price menu, you won't see a trace of it inside – memorize what you want before you go in. Secondly, many of the places that take food seriously offer a *menu degustazione* – a set-price gourmet meal that allows you to taste whatever seasonal delicacies the chef has whipped up. Both are cheaper than if you had ordered *à la carte*. When you leave a restaurant you should be given a receipt (if not, the owners are tax-dodging), which by law you must hold on to until you are 60 metres from the door or risk an ambush from the tax police.

The same holds true in bars and cafés. These have a hierarchy of prices: the very same drink will have three prices, in ascending order, depending on whether you drink standing at the bar, sitting inside, or sitting outside.

Price Categories

The restaurant prices listed below are for an average meal – any three courses out of *antipasto*, *primo, secondo* and dessert – per person, and do not include wine. If you order seafood or truffles, the price will be considerably higher. With some discretion (drinking the house wine only) it could be considerably less.

expensive	over €35
moderate	€20–35
inexpensive	under €20

Campo Marzio

Restaurants

Expensive

Antica Enoteca Capranica H7
Piazza Capranica 97, **t** *06 6994 0992;* **bus** *116, 116T; wheelchair accessible.* **Open** *Mon–Fri 12.30–3 and 7.30–10.30, Sat 7.30–10.30 only.*
A favourite with the political crowd from nearby Montecitorio; excellent seafood and all the best Italian wines. Air conditioning.

Camponeschi G9
Piazza Farnese 50, **t** *06 687 4927;* **bus** *116, 116T.* **Open** *Sept–July Mon–Sat 8pm–12.30am. Reserve.*
Specializes in fish but serves many traditional Roman dishes alongside its extensive wine list. Interior air-conditioned; outside tables in front of the Palazzo Farnese.

Il Convivio G7
Vicolo dei Soldati 31, **t** *06 686 9432;* **bus** *30, 81, 116, 116T, 204.* **Open** *Tues–Sat 1–2.30 and 8–10.30, Mon 8–10.30 only, except 1 week in Aug.*
Some of the most innovative cuisine in Rome, prepared with a knowing touch – unbeatable chilled fruit soups, baked *zucchini* flowers and, for dessert, exquisite pastries. Air conditioning.

Il Drappo F8
Vicolo del Malpasso, **t** *06 687 7365;* **bus** *46, 62, 64, 116.* **Open** *Sept–July Mon–Sat 8pm–midnight. Reserve.*
Both traditional and innovative dishes from Sardinia in a pretty candle-lit, air-conditioned setting.

L'Eau Vive H8
Via Monterone 85, **t** *06 6880 1095;* **bus** *30, 81, 116, 116T, 204, 628.* **Open** *Sept–July Mon–Sat 12.30–3 and 7.30–10.30.*
In a 16th-century *palazzo*, run by the Christian Virgins of Catholic Missionary Action through Work, whose work is waitressing in national costume for the movers and shakers from the Vatican. Daily specials from around the world are served with solemn music and French wines. Set menu costs around half *à la carte.*

Evangelista G9
Via delle Zoccolette 11, **t** *06 687 5810;* **tram** *8,* **bus** *23, 280.* **Open** *Sept–July Mon–Sat 8pm–midnight. Reserve.*
Artichokes, prepared in a variety of ways, but most famously beaten flat and fried. The *primi* and *secondi* change daily, but tend to be unusual, making subtle use of game and offal. Sicilian sweets.

Papà Giovanni H8
Via dei Sediari 4, **t** *06 686 5308;* **bus** *30, 81, 204, 116, 116T.* **Open** *Mon–Sat 1–4 and 8–12, except 2 weeks in Aug. Reserve.*
Brick walls, bottles and postcards provide the intimate setting for some of the most heavenly food in Rome, entirely based on availability in the market. This is your chance to dine like Caesar; the chef specializes in reviving old Roman recipes. Air conditioning.

La Rosetta H7
Via della Rosetta 8, **t** *06 686 1002;* **bus** *30, 81, 116, 116T, 204, 628.* **Open** *Sept–July Mon–Sat 7.45–11.45pm and Thurs–Fri 1–3pm.*
A very upmarket classic, which specializes in fish with a Sicilian touch. Air conditioning.

Taverna Antonina I7
Via della Colonna Antonina 48, **t** *06 678 3717;* **bus** *116, 116T; veranda wheelchair accessible.* **Open** *Mon–Sat 12–4 and 7–11.*
Elegant and quiet, with candles and potted plants on the tables and an intimate veranda. This upscale restaurant makes the most of its proximity to the Italian parliament at Montecitorio, boasting a faithful clientèle of politicians. Here you can sample the Pugliese *burrata*, a mozzarella-like cheese with a creamy heart.

Moderate

Albistrò F8
Via dei Banchi Vecchi 140, **t** *06 686 5274;* **bus** *46, 62, 64.* **Open** *late Aug–early July Thurs–Tues 7.30–11, Sun 12.30–3 and 7.30–11.*
Sample lamb with honey sauce or chicken with leeks in this family-run restaurant. Try to find a table in the inner courtyard.

Roma dei Romani

Your best bet for authentic Roman cuisine is the neighbourhoods of Trastevere and Testaccio. If you'd rather eat as the contemporary does, try San Lorenzo.

Augusto (bus 23, 280; *see* p.312), **Checchino dal 1887** (bus 95; *see* p.311), **Checco er Carettiere** (bus 23, 280; *see* p.312), **Il Dito e la Luna** (bus 71, 204, 492; *see* p.316), **Da Felice** (bus 23, 30, 75, 280; *see* p.311), **Grappolo d'Oro** (bus 46, 62, 64, 116, 116T; *see* p.303), **Lo Scopettaro** (bus 23, 95, 280; *see* p.311), **Tram Tram** (bus 71, 204, 492; *see* p.316).

Armando al Pantheon H8
Salita dei Crescenzi 31, **t** *06 6880 3034;* **bus** *116, 116T.* **Open** *Mon–Fri 12.30–3 and 7–11, Sat 12.30–3 only.*
Exotic traditional dishes, prepared by Claudio, son of Armando.

Il Buco I8
Via S. Ignazio 8, **t** *06 679 3298;* **bus** *116, 116T.* **Open** *Sept–July Tues–Sat 12.30–4 and 7–12.*
Tuscan trat. *Pappardelle con la lepre* (pasta with hare sauce), *porcini* mushrooms and truffles in season. Outside seating.

Costanza G8
Piazza del Paradiso 5, **t** *06 686 1717;* **bus** *46, 62, 64, 116, 116T; wheelchair accessible.* **Open** *Sept–July Mon–Sat 12–4 and 7–12.*
A romantic place in the ruins of Pompey's Theatre – where Julius Caesar was assassinated – with a courtyard. Serves the best of the Italian regions, including *tagliolini ai porcini* scented with truffles and a famous *crème brûlée.*

Enoteca e Taverna Capranica H7
Piazza Capranica 104, **t** *06 679 0860;* **bus** *116, 116T.* **Open** *12–2.30 and 8–10.30.*
A restaurant – and pizzeria too – a stone's throw from the Pantheon. Creative Italian cuisine: dishes like *vellutata di peperoni e cipolla con pecorino e mentuccia* (pepper and onion soup with ewes' cheese and wild mint) and *carré di agnello con carciofi* (new lamb with artichokes). There is a €62 fish *menu degustazione.* Air conditioning.

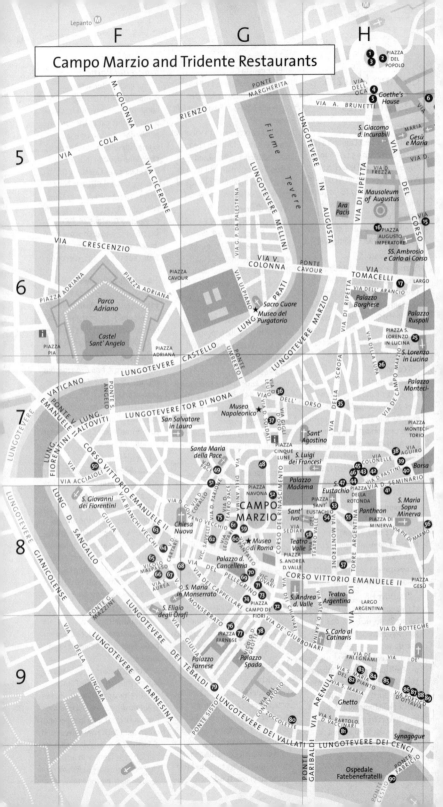

Campo Marzio and Tridente Restaurants

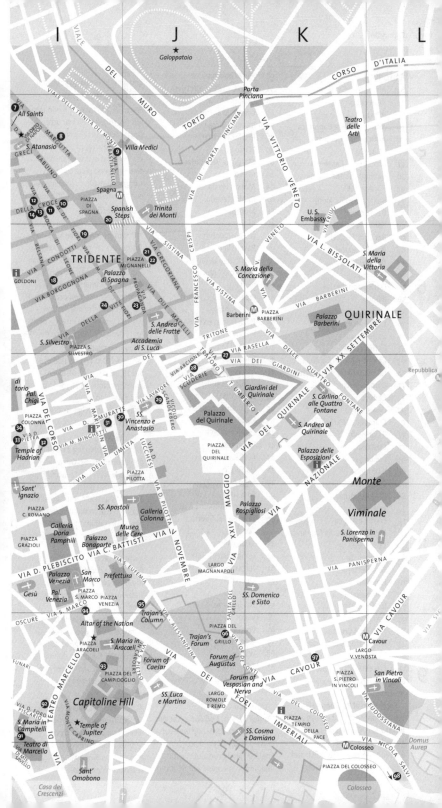

Map Key

64	Albistrò
27	Albrecht
16	Alfredo
39	Antica Enoteca Capranica
92	Antico Caffè del Teatro Marcello
47	Armando al Pantheon
20	Babington's Tea Rooms
94	Bar Ara Coeli
73	Bar (Campo de' Fiori)
25	Bar Europeo
49	Bar della Pace
53	Bar Sant'Eustachio
63	Bar Tramezzini
48	Bevitoria Navona
82	Da Bleve
3	Dal Bolognese
56	Il Buco
52	Caffè di Colombia
76	Caffè Farnese
19	Caffè Greco
22	Caffè Leonardo
93	Caffè dei Musei Capitolini
54	Camilloni a Sant'Eustachio
77	Camponeschi
2	Canova
97	Cavour 313
9	Ciampini al Café du Jardin
37	Il Convivio
72	Costanza
60	Cul de Sac
65	Il Drappo
70	Ditirambo
88	La Dolceroma
7	Edy
15	Enoteca Antica
38	Enoteca e Taverna Capranica
57	L'Eau Vive
80	Evangelista
14	Fiaschetteria
11	Fior Fiori
71	Il Fornaio
74	Il Forno
30	Forno
84	Forno del Ghetto
43	Fortunato al Pantheon
51	Da Francesco
12	Fratelli Roffi Isabelli
89	Da Giggetto
58	Papà Giovanni
33	Gran Caffè La Caffettiera
28	Golden Crown
69	Grappolo d'Oro
59	Insalata Ricca I
75	Insalata Ricca II
80	L'Orso 80
6	Margutta Vegetariano
24	Mario
96	Mario's Hostaria
62	La Montecarlo
66	Moretta
31	Al Moro
17	Le Pain Quotidien
98	Pasqualino
10	Pasticceria D'Angelo
29	Al Piccolo Arancio
67	Pierluigi
81	Piperno
32	Pizza Fantasy
85	Pizza Franco e Cristina
5	Pizzare
40	Pizza al Taglio
4	Pollarolo
21	Alla Rampa
13	Il Re degli Amici
44	Di Rienzo
95	Ristorante Ulpia
1	Rosati
46	La Rosetta
41	La Sagrestia
87	Al 16 (Sedici)
78	Da Sergio
23	Sogo Asahi
90	Sora Lella
34	Taverna Antonina
86	Taverna del Ghetto
50	Taverna Giulia
45	Tazza d'Oro
42	Tempio Bar
61	Terra di Siena
79	Thien Kim
26	El Toulà
55	Dai Tre Amici
18	Vanni
91	Vecchia Roma
35	Volpetti alla Scrofa
68	Walter
83	Zi' Fenizia

antipasti, pasta, and meat dishes – and what more could you want?

Pierluigi F8

Piazza de' Ricci 144, t 06 686 1302; **bus** *116, 116T;* **wheelchair accessible.** **Open** *Tues–Sun 12–4 and 7–12.*
A tempting array of *antipasti*, seafood and delicious pasta dishes. A good place to eat in summer, outside on a mellow old piazza. Interior air-conditioned.

La Sagrestia H8

Via del Seminario 89, t 06 679 7581; **bus** *116, 116T.* **Open** *Sept–July Thurs–Tues 12–3 and 7–11.* Reserve. Christmas lights around the door and air conditioning downstairs. Traditional Roman cuisine in modern décor: *saltimbocca, trippa,* etc. Try the *filetto alla Restovin* – with oil, lemon and rocket – or the roast fresh fish. Also a pizzeria.

Taverna Giulia F7

Vicolo dell'Oro 23, t 06 686 9768; **bus** *28, 46, 64, 116, 116T.* **Open** *July–Sept Mon–Sat 12.30–3.30 and 7.30–11.30.*
Tasty Ligurian dishes in an air-conditioned 15th-century house.

Walter G8

Via del Pellegrino 107, t 06 686 9361; **bus** *46, 62, 64.* **Open** *Sept–July Tues–Sun 12–4 and 8–12.*
In summer sit outside in picturesque Via del Pellegrino. Excellent seafood, in *antipasti* dishes and on pasta. Air conditiong inside.

Inexpensive

Cul de Sac G8

Piazza Pasquino 73, t 06 6880 1094; **bus** *46, 62, 64.* **Open** *Tues–Sun 12.30–3.30 and 7–12.30, Mon 7–12.30 only.*
A long-established wine bar with a choice of over 1,400 labels, serving simple but good dishes to accompany the prima donnas in the bottle. Air-conditioned interior, or outside seating.

Ditirambo G8

Piazza della Cancelleria 74, t 06 687 1626; **bus** *46, 62, 64, 116, 116T;* **wheelchair accessible.** **Open** *Sept–July Tues–Sun 1–3.30 and 8–11.30, Mon 8–11.30 only.* *Reservations essential.*

Fortunato al Pantheon H7

Via del Pantheon 75, t 06 679 2788; **bus** *116, 116T.* **Open** *Sept–July Mon–Sat 12–3 and 8–12.*
Eat with the locals, fresh fish and good service. Outside seating.

L'Orso 80 G7

Via dell'Orso 33, t 06 686 4904; **bus** *116, 116T.* **Open** *Sept–July Tues–Sat 12.30–3.30 and 7.30–11.30.*
Popular, family-run, not the most imaginative perhaps, but delicious

A favourite with young Romans; you'll have to take the noise along with the good food. Home-made pasta and vegetarian dishes such as ravioli with ricotta and almond filling, cabbage leaves stuffed with mozzarella, and potato and mushroom flan with a melted cheese and truffle sauce.

Da Francesco G7–8
Via della Fossa 29, no phone; **bus** *46, 62, 64.* **Open** *Sept–July Wed–Mon 12–3.30 and 7.30–12.30.*
A good array of *antipasti*, pasta, pizzas (with smoked salmon or *porcini* mushrooms and rughetta) and a fast turnover. Pizzas cost around half trattoria prices. Outside seating on Piazza del Fico.

Grappolo d'Oro G8
Piazza della Cancelleria 80, t 06 689 7080; **bus** *46, 62, 64, 116, 116T; wheelchair accessible.* **Open** *Sept–July Mon–Sat 12–3 and 8–11.*
One of the best places to sit outside at night and feast on Roman homecooking. Try the *linguine al pesto* or the *bucatini all'amatriciana.* Friendly service.

Insalata Ricca I G8
Largo dei Chiavari 85, t 06 6880 3656; **bus** *64, 492.* **Open** *daily 12–3.30 and 7–1 except 1 week Aug.*
Deluxe salads and light, healthy pasta dishes in a frenzied flurry of speedy waiters. Outside seating.

Insalata Ricca II G8
Piazza Pasquino 72; **bus** *46, 62, 64.*
The slightly less frenzied sister of Insalata Ricca I.

Moretta F8
Vicolo della Moretta, t 06 686 1900; **bus** *46, 62, 64, 116, 116T.* **Open** *Mon–Sat 12.30–3 and 7.30–11.*
Old neighbourhood favourite; traditional Italian fare reasonably prepared. Tables outside.

Da Sergio G9
Vicolo delle Grotte 27, t 06 686 4293; **bus** *46, 62, 64, 116, 116T; wheelchair accessible.* **Open** *Sept–July Mon–Sat 12.30–3 and 6.30–11.*
Located on a narrow alley off Campo de' Fiori, this family-run

trattoria brings to the table only the freshest ingredients from the nearby market. Roman cuisine at its simple best: pasta *carbonara, amatriciana* or *arrabbiata; abbacchio scottadito* or *vitello alla fornara.* Outside seating.

Terra di Siena G8
Piazza Pasquino 77, t 06 6830 7704; **bus** *46, 62, 64.* **Open** *Sept–July Mon–Sat 12–3 and 8–11.*
Refined south Tuscan cooking at a good price. Air-conditioned interior, or tables on the piazza.

Thien Kim G9
Via Giulia 201, t 06 6830 7832; **bus** *23, 204.* **Open** *Sept–July Mon–Sat 7pm–midnight.*
A charming, civilized Vietnamese restaurant, with duck dishes. Air conditioning.

Dai Tre Amici H8
Via Rotonda 7–9, t 06 687 5239; **bus** *30, 40, 46, 62, 64, 70, 81, 87.* **Open** *Thurs–Tues 1–4 and 8–12.*
Nice family-run restaurant that has its own wine specially bottled at Rocca Priora. Try the chef's specials on Sunday; any other day try the *orecchiette con i broccoli* or the *fusilli alla sorrentina.*

Pizzerias and Snack Bars

Bar Tramezzini F8
Corso Vittorio Emanuele; **bus** *46, 62, 64; wheelchair accessible.* **Open** *Tues–Sat 7am–7pm.*
A good address on this chaotic artery for a quick snack between sights. Well-prepared *tramezzini,* toasted sandwiches filled with vegetables and mozzarella, and *pomodori al riso* (baked stuffed tomatoes). Tables outside on quieter Piazza Sforza Cesarini.

Il Fornaio G8
Via dei Baullari 5; **bus** *116, 116T.* **Open** *Mon–Sat 8–2 and 4–8.*
Superior bakery selling excellent *pizza al taglio.*

Il Forno G8
Campo de' Fiori 22, **bus** *116, 116T.* **Open** *May–Sept Mon–Fri 7–1.30*

Peace and Quiet

Peace and quiet in Rome comes at a price. So if you want to eat in a refined hush, away from the hullabaloo of feasting Romans, be prepared to pay for it.

Dal Bolognese (bus 116, 116T; *see* p.304), **El Toulà** (bus 117, 119; *see* p.304), **Les Étoiles dell'Atlante Star** (bus 34, 49, 492, 990; *see* p.314), **George's** (bus 52, 53, 63, 80; *see* p.309), **Jaya Sai Ma** (tram 8; *see* p.312), **Relais le Jardin** (tram 3, 19, bus 52, 926; *see* p.316), **Taverna Antonina** (bus 116, 116T; *see* p.299).

and 5.30–8, Sat 7–1.30, Oct–April Fri–Sat and Mon–Wed 7–1.30 and 5.30–8, Thurs 7–1.30.
The source of most of the slices of *pizza bianca* you'll see being munched in the streets around.

La Montecarlo G8
Vicolo Savelli 12, t 06 686 1877; **bus** *46, 62, 64.* **Open** *May–Oct daily 12–3 and 6.30–1, except 2 weeks in Aug; Nov–April Tues–Sun only.*
Sit elbow to elbow with your neighbours and duck as pizzas, chairs and tables are whipped over your head. The pizzas are brilliant (€3–7) and there's plenty of time while you're queuing to peruse the menu board. Tables outside in summer.

Pizza Fantasy I7
Via di Pietra 79; **bus** *62, 63, 81, 85, 95.* **Open** *Mon–Sat 8.30–2.30 and 4.30–8.30.*
Large choice of good *pizza al taglio,* along with a *tavola calda.* Sit inside or out.

Pizza al Taglio H7
Via dei Pastini; **bus** *62, 63, 81, 85, 95.* **Open** *Mon–Sat 8–2 and 4–8.*
Stop for a slice after making your fortune at the Borsa; run by the same couple who first opened it in the early 1970s, with plenty of vegetarian toppings.

Volpetti alla Scrofa H7
Via della Scrofa 31, t 06 686 1940; **bus** *116.* **Open** *Mon–Sat 10–8.*
An old-fashioned *tavola calda* near the Pantheon (unrelated to

Ancient Rome

Pickled swan hearts and fish gut sauce may have gone out with the Caesars, but **Papà Giovanni** (bus 30, 81, 116, 116T, 204; *see* p.299) still offers you the chance to dine as an emperor; the chef specializes in reviving old Roman recipes. Otherwise the best taste you'll get of ancient Rome is in the setting. **L'Archeologia** (bus 218, 660; *see* p.316), **Cecilia Metella** (bus 218, 660; *see* p.316), **Costanza** (bus 46, 62, 64, 116, 116T; *see* p.299), **Pizza Forum** (metro Colosseo, bus 85, 87, 117, 850; *see* p.312), **Da Giggetto** (tram 8, bus 23, 280; *see* p.306); **Ristorante Ulpia** (bus 60, 84, 85, 175; *see* p.307).

the Volpetti of Testaccio). *Supplì* and other fried snacks, lasagne, roast chicken, vegetables dishes – and gnocchi on Thursdays.

Cafés

Bar (Campo de' Fiori) G8
Campo de' Fiori; bus 116, 116T. Open Mon–Sat from 6am (market opening) until the early hours.
OK sandwiches and great *frullati* (fruit smoothies) at this bar without a name; seats outside for watching the life of the piazza.

Bar Farnese G7
Via dei Baullari 106; bus 116, 116T. Open Mon–Sat 7am–2am.
Civilized café popular with businessmen and beautiful people. Scrumptious *cornetti alla crema* and *pizza romana*.

Bar della Pace G7
Via della Pace 5; bus 46, 62, 64. Open Tues–Sun 10am–2am.
Snooty fin-de-siècle bar; elitist in the evenings, but a pleasant retreat during the day. Tables in front of Santa Maria della Pace.

Bar Sant'Eustachio H8
Piazza Sant'Eustachio 82. Open Tues–Sun 8.30am–1am.
Known as the best place for coffee in the capital – and it takes its reputation very seriously. Ask for a *gran'caffè*. It also sells a selection of coffees to take home. It's a businesslike place and very central.

Bevitoria Navona H8
Piazza Navona 72; bus 30, 70, 81, 87. Open Mon–Sat 11am–1 am.
Well worth a visit on a cold evening for a glass of mulled wine (*vin brûlé*); sit outside in summer.

Caffè di Colombia G8
Piazza Navona; bus 30, 70, 81, 87. Open June–Sept daily, Oct–May Fri–Wed 9am–1am.
Fancy sit-down café, with a close-up view of Bernini's *Four Rivers* fountain. Tables on the piazza.

Camilloni a Sant'Eustachio H8
Piazza S. Eustachio; bus 30, 70, 81, 87, 116. Open Tues–Sun 8.30am–midnight.
Shiny bar with cooling fans and a large array of snacks. Arguably one of the best places to stop for a caffeine injection – rival Bar Sant'Eustachio (*see above*) would certainly argue. Outside seating.

Gran Caffè La Caffettiera I7
Piazza di Pietra 65; bus 46, 62, 64, 116, 116T; also Via Margutta 61/a, bus 117, 119. Open Sept–July Mon–Sat 7am–9pm.
An attractive café with a tempting array of Neapolitan snacks, *salati* as well as *dolci*, which can easily substitute for a full meal. Try the *timballo* of the day (baked pasta) or the *sartù di riso* (tiny meatballs, mozzarella, hard-boiled eggs and vegetables baked in a rice shell). The Neapolitan *sfogliatelle* (a heavy Italian version of *millefeuille* with lots of creamy custard filling) are a must, washed down with a very short, strong espresso – as drunk in Naples.

Di Rienzo H8
Piazza della Rotonda; bus 116, 116T; wheelchair accessible. Open 9am–1am
A nice café to sit outside and contemplate the Pantheon, but you pay for the view.

Tazza d'Oro H7
Via degli Orfani, just off Piazza della Rotonda; bus 116, 116T; wheelchair accessible. Open Mon–Sat 7am–8pm.
Not much to look at, but the latest contender for Rome's best cup of java (and coffee granita topped with cream), with many loyal supporters and fans.

Tempio Bar H7
Piazza della Rotonda; bus 116, 116T. Open 10am–2am
Tables in front of the Pantheon and good coffee, but as with Di Rienzo, you pay for the view.

Tridente

Restaurants

Expensive

Alfredo H6
Piazza Augusto Imperatore 30, t 06 687 8734; bus 81, 204, 590, 628. Open Mon–Sat 1–4 and 8–10.30.
One of several heirs of the creator of *fettuccine alfredo* with triple butter, now a slightly smug relic of the *dolce vita* days. Outdoor dining in summer.

Dal Bolognese H4
Piazza del Popolo 1, t 06 361 1426; bus 117, 119. Open Sept–June Tues–Sat 12.45–3 and 8.15–11, July–Aug Tues–Fri only.
Upmarket Emilia-Romagnan restaurant, popular with wealthy tourists and Roman carnivores. Excellent *bollito misto*. Air conditioned interior, or outside seating.

Margutta Vegetariano I5
Via Margutta 119, t 06 3600 1805; bus 117, 119. Open Mon–Sat 12.30–3 and 7.30–11.30.
One of Rome's few vegetarian restaurants. Rather chic and somewhat overpriced by international vegetarian standards. Air conditioning.

Al Moro I7
Vicolo delle Bollette 13, t 06 678 3495; bus 62, 63, 81; wheelchair accesible. Open Sept–July Mon–Sat 12–4 and 7–11. Reserve.
Popular with politicians and businessmen who come for super fresh food and daily specials that depend on market availability, prepared with an authentic Roman touch. Great pasta dishes and wonderful *baccalà* (salt cod).

El Toulà H7
Via della Lupa 29/b, t 06 687 3750; bus 116, 116T. Open Sept–July

Mon–Fri 12–3 and 8–11.30, Sat 8–11.30 only. Reserve.
Chic, and serving some of the finest risottos, lamb dishes and desserts in Rome, with plenty of swank; the high bills include a pay-to-see-and-be-seen surtax. Air conditioning.

Moderate

Al Piccolo Arancio J7
Via Scanderbeg 112, t 06 678 6139; bus 71, 117, 119. Open Sept–July Tues–Sat 1–4 and 8–12.
A find, if you can find it (follow signs for the Museo delle Paste Alimentari). This is an old *osteria*, done up brightly and featuring imaginative dishes: try *zucchini* flower, mozzarella and artichoke fritters, ricotta ravioli in a cream and orange sauce, or *orecchiette ai broccoletti*. Air conditioning.

Alla Rampa J6
Piazza Mignanelli 18, t 06 678 2621; metro Spagna, bus 117, 119; wheelchair accessible. Open Mon–Sat 12–4.30 and 8–12.30.
Italian, simple and good, and amazingly quiet for its proximity to the Spanish Steps. Service can be a bit rushed. Lots of tables on the piazza. Air-conditioned inside.

Il Re degli Amici I5
Via della Croce 33/b, t 06 679 5380; metro Spagna, bus 117, 119. Open Tues–Sun 12–4 and 8–12.
Dates back to 1939. Good grilled meat daily and fish on Tuesday and Friday. Air-conditioned interior, or outside seating.

Sogo Asahi J6
Via di Propaganda 16, t 06 679 8782; metro Spagna, bus 117, 119. Open Mon–Sat 12–2.30 and 7–10.30.
Wonderful Japanese restaurant seldom frequented by Westerners. Excellent-value lunch menu, but dinners can be expensive.

Inexpensive

Albrecht J7
Via Rasella 52, t 06 488 0457, bus 52, 53, 62, 71, 117, 119. Open 12–3 and 7–11.
Traditional Austrian fare: beer, sausages, goulash and *sauerkraut*.

Edy I5
Vicolo del Babuino 4, t 06 3600 1738; bus 117, 119. Open Sept–mid-Aug, Mon–Fri 12–3.30 and 7–12, Sat 7pm–midnight only.
A lovely family-run trattoria, lit by candles in the evening, serving memorable *fettuccine* with ricotta and artichokes.

Enoteca Antica I5
Via della Croce 76, t 06 679 0896. Wine bar open daily 11.15am–1am; restaurant open 12.30–3 and 7–11.
A fine wine selection, with bottles on sale too. The best option is to sit around the *bancone* (bar) and have a plate of sundried tomatoes and cheese with sour wine, which makes a lovely light meal.

Fiaschetteria I5
Via della Croce 39, no phone; metro Spagna, bus 117, 119. Open Mon–Sat 12–3.30 and 8–11. No reservations, no credit cards.
Jovial, studiously unaffected trattoria, which has been here since 1889. The new cook continues to prepare the traditional Roman dishes this place is famous for.

Fratelli Roffi Isabelli
Via della Croce 76; metro Spagna, bus 117, 119. Open Mon–Sat 12–10.
A beautiful 19th-century-style wine shop , where you can buy by the bottle or by the glass.

Golden Crown J7
Via in Arcione 85, t 06 678 9831; bus 71, 117, 119. Open Tues–Sat 1–3 and 7–11, except 2 weeks in Aug. Reservations suggested.
Authentic Hong Kong cuisine in a typical Roman-Chinese interior.

Mario I6
Via della Vite 55, t 06 678 3818; metro Spagna, bus 117, 119. Open Sept–July Mon–Sat 12.30–3 and 7–11.
Tuscan homecooking. *Crostini* (liver canapés), *ribollita* (thick, mostly cabbage soup), *bistecca alla fiorentina*, Chianti, and all the old favourites from the land of the bean-eaters. Tables outside.

Pollarolo H4
Via di Ripetta 5, t 06 361 0276; bus 81, 117, 119, 204. Open Fri–Wed 12–4 and 7–11, except 2 weeks in Aug.

> ## Medieval and Renaissance Rome
> One of the most enjoyable ways to enjoy the medieval and Renaissance layers of Rome is to sit outside over a delicious dinner in one of the city's fine piazzas. The following are just a few suggestions.
> **Camponeschi** (bus 116, 116T; *see* p.299), **Ditirambo** (bus 46, 62, 64, 116, 116T; *see* p.303), **Grappolo d'Oro** (bus 46, 62, 64, 116, 116T; *see* p.303), **Hostaria La Canonica** (bus 23, 280; *see* p.312), **Taverna Giulia** (bus 28, 46, 64,116, 116T; *see* p.302), **Vecchia Roma** (bus H, 30, 44, 63, 95, 160; *see* p.306).

Inexpensive, and popular among Roman TV and theatre people for excellent family-style Roman cooking. Air-conditioned interior, or outside seating.

Pizzerias and Snack Bars

Fior Fiori I5
Via della Croce 16; metro Spagna, bus 117, 119. Open Mon–Sat.
Excellent *pizza al taglio*.

Forno I7
Via delle Muratte 8; bus 52, 53, 61, 62, 63, 71. Open daily 8–8.
Deli-bakery on the corner of Piazza di Trevi selling delicious, reasonably priced sandwiches and *pizza al taglio*.

Pizzare H5
Via di Ripetta 14; bus 81, 117, 119, 204. Open all year except 2 weeks in Aug daily 12.45–3.30 and 7.30–12.30.
A properly Neapolitan pizza – including a '*pizza sostanziosa*' with everything on it. Also good sandwiches. Air conditioning.

Cafés

Babington's Tea Rooms I5
Piazza di Spagna 23; metro Spagna, bus 117, 119. Open Wed–Mon 9am–8.30pm.
Opened in 1896 by an English spinster who thought what Romans needed most was a cup

of tea like mum makes. Scones, crumpets and English breakfast in an uncosy English setting. Prices may make you do a double-take.

Bar Europeo H6
Piazza S. Lorenzo in Lucina 33;
bus 117. **Open** *7am–9pm.*
Treats for the sweet-toothed. Sicilian specialities like *cannoli* filled with sweetened ricotta. Tables on the piazza.

Caffè Greco I6
Via Condotti 86, **t** *06 678 5474;*
metro Spagna, **bus** *117, 119.* **Open** *Sept–July Mon–Sat 8am–9pm.*
A charming period piece opened in 1742 and last redecorated in 1860. It's the oldest café in the city and merits a visit for its décor, although service is appalling, and the food scarcely better. Sit where Casanova flirted, Ludwig of Bavaria raved and Keats coughed – and prepare to choke at the prices.

Caffè Leonardo J6
Piazza Mignanelli 21; **metro** *Spagna,* **bus** *117, 119.* **Open** *daily noon–11pm.*
Fancy snacks and ice cream, pastries and *tavola calda* dishes at lunchtime. Tables on the piazza.

Canova H4
Piazza del Popolo; **metro** *Flaminio,* **bus** *117, 119; wheelchair accessible.* **Open** *daily 8am–1am.*
Tea room, restaurant and piano bar. Quite nice but quite expensive. Tables on the piazza.

Ciampini al Café du Jardin I5
Viale Trinità dei Monti; **metro** *Spagna.* **Open** *May–Sept Thurs–Tues 8am–1am.*
Outdoor tables only – under the trees on the Pincio, with lovely views over Rome, truffle ice cream.

Le Pain Quotidien H6
Via Tomacelli 24, **t** *06 6880 7727;* **bus** *81, 117, 119, 590, 28.* **Open** *Tues–Sun 8am–10pm.*
This Belgian franchise fills a hole in the Roman eating scene. The rustic décor hints at its organic produce. Rye bread and French-style pastries made with butter for breakfast or afternoon tea, plus a small selection of vegetable soups, quiches and salads. It's

good place for Sunday brunch. All food is eaten around large communal tables.

Pasticceria D'Angelo I5
Via della Croce 30; **metro** *Spagna,* **bus** *117, 119.* **Open** *Mon–Sat 8–8.*
Bright and noisy, but that's how Romans like it. A bar, an ice cream counter and light lunches.

Rosati H4
Piazza del Popolo 4; **metro** *Flaminio,* **bus** *117, 119.* **Open** *Wed–Mon 7.30am–11.30pm.*
One of the prettiest Liberty-style cafés in Rome, with tasty and original cocktails, celebrated home-made sweets, pastries and cakes, and fine views over the square. There's an expensive restaurant upstairs.

Vanni I6
Via Frattina 94; **metro** *Spagna,* **bus** *117, 119.* **Open** *Tues–Sun 12–10.30.*
Good sandwiches, great cakes and delicious salads, consumed at the tables outside for maximum entertainment as you watch the beautiful people floating by.

Capitoline Hill and Tiber Banks

Restaurants

Expensive

Da Giggetto I9
Via del Portico d'Ottavia 21/a, **t** *06 686 1105;* **tram** *8,* **bus** *23, 280; wheelchair accessible.* **Open** *mid-Aug–late July Tues–Sun 12–3.30 and 7.30–12.*
Roman-Jewish dishes, served outside in summer by the Portico d'Ottavia. Wonderful *carciofi alla giudea* (crisp, golden deep-fried artichokes), and standards like *spaghetti alla carbonara* and *penne all'arrabbiata.* Air-conditioned interior, or outside seating.

Piperno H9
Via Monte de' Cenci 9, **t** *06 6880 6629; wheelchair accessible;* **tram** *8,* **bus** *23, 280.* **Open** *Sept–July Tues–Sat 12.45–2.30 and 8–10.30, Sun 12.30–3pm.*
Hearty, very filling Jewish-Roman cuisine and good wines; you'll

Baroqueorama
Baroque Rome offers some fine backdrops for dining. At **L'Eau Vive** you can get right into the spirit of the Counter-Reformation with the Christian Virgins of Catholic Missionary Action through Work (bus 30, 81, 116, 116T, 204, 628; *see* p.299). Other options are more prosaic, but one setting is Piazza di Spagna, with charms to disarm the most chaste Baroqueophobe.
Caffè Leonardo (bus 117, 119; *see* p.306), **Edy** (bus 117, 119; *see* p.305), **Fiaschetteria** (bus 117, 119; *see* p.305), **Mario** (bus 117, 119; *see* p.305), **Alla Rampa** (bus 117, 119; *see* p.305), **Il Re degli Amici** (bus 117, 119; *see* p.305).

need a good post-prandial stroll to work off the *crostata di ricotta.* Air conditioning.

Sora Lella H10
Via di Ponte Quattro Capi 16, **t** *06 686 1601;* **bus** *23, 280.* **Open** *Sept–July Mon–Sat 1–2.30 and 8–11.*
Hidden away deep in the wall of an old tower, 'Sister Lella' offers some of the best traditional Roman cuisine and a view of the Tiber Island on which it sits through the one window. Be sure to try the chef's speciality, *tonnarelli alla cuccagna.*

Taverna del Ghetto H9
Via del Portico d'Ottavia 7/b, **t** *06 6880 9771;* **tram** *8,* **bus** *23, 280.* **Open** *Sun–Fri 1–4 except Jewish holidays.*
Founded in the the year 2000 in a 14th-century building, this is Rome's only kosher restaurant, and you pay above average for it. Dishes from the Jewish-Roman tradition include *tortino di aliciotti e indivia* (baked anchovies and lettuce), *concia di zucchini e pâté di fegato* (marinated courgettes with liver paste) and *stracotto di manzo* (salt beef or brisket).

Vecchia Roma I9
Piazza di Campitelli 18, **t** *06 686 4604;* **bus** *H, 30, 44, 63, 95, 160; wheelchair accessible.* **Open** *Sept–July Thurs–Tues 1–3.30 and 8–11. Reserve.*

A serene place to sit out in the evening and try *bruschetta* with artichokes and capers, gnocchi with borlotti beans, bacon and tomatoes, *maltagliati* ('badly cut' pasta) with broccoli, garlic, chilli pepper and parmesan, or beef fillet in brandy sauce with foie gras and radicchio. Desserts are excellent too.

Moderate

Al 16 H–I9
Via del Portico d'Ottavia 16, t 06 687 4722; tram 8, bus 23, 280. Open Wed–Mon 12–3 and 7–10.30 except 1 week in Aug and 3 weeks in Jan.
Italianized Jewish food in this restaurant decorated with painted panoramas of Rome. Try the *fritti* – there is a chef whose only job is to make these fried mixed platters. Tables outside or air conditioning.

Pizzerias and Snack Bars

Pizza Franco e Cristina H–I9
Via del Portico d'Ottavia 5; tram 8, bus 23, 280; wheelchair accessible. Open Mon–Sat 10–2.30 and 4–8.
A good place to grab a quick slice on your way to the Forum.

Zi' Fenizia H9
Via S. Maria del Pianto 65; tram 8; wheelchair accessible. Open Sun–Thurs 8–8, Fri 8–3pm, except Jewish holidays.
Kosher sandwiches and pizza.

Cafés

Antico Caffè del Teatro Marcello i9
Via del Teatro di Marcello 42; bus H, 30, 44, 63, 95, 160. Open daily 8–8.
Standard sandwiches and *tavola calda* fare with outside tables for Fiat-watchers. It's the only spot to rest on this side of the Capitoline Hill and Velabrum.

Bar Ara Coeli I8
Piazza Venezia; bus 46, 62, 64. Open daily, 24 hours.
A few steps away from one of Rome's most visible landmarks, the Vittoriano 'wedding cake', and open 24 hours a day, every day,

this bar is a beacon for lost tourists and night people. All-night tobacconist inside.

Da Bleve H9
Via di S. Maria del Pianto 9/a–11, t 06 686 5970; tram 8; bus H, 63, 630, 780. Open Tues–Sat 12–6.
A traditional *enoteca* (wine shop) which serves light meals to gastronomes (smoked fish, cured meats, cheeses, salads and the like) at lunchtime.

Caffè dei Musei Capitolini I9
Piazza del Campidoglio, t 06 678 2862; bus 46, 62, 64. Open Tues–Sat 9–6.
Snacks and ice creams on a breezy *terrazza* – quiet, relaxing and just what you need to rest your feet and eyes after sightseeing. The museum reception can direct you to the café's separate back entrance if you don't have a ticket for the museum.

La Dolceroma I9
Via del Portico d'Ottavia 20/b; tram 8, bus 23, 280. Open Tues–Sun 9–1 and 4–7.30.
Run by an Austro-Italian couple, the 'Sweetrome' bakes very un-Roman cakes, all prepared with top-quality ingredients and rather pricey. American brownies and pecan pies share space with Austrian Sachertorte and Imperialtorte (crisp layers of nougat and chocolate mousse topped with marzipan).

Forno del Ghetto H9
Via del Portico d'Ottavia 2; tram 8, bus 23, 280. Open Sun–Fri 8–8 except Jewish holidays.
Kosher pastry shop in the heart of the Jewish ghetto, specializing in almond cakes and delicious pies filled with ricotta and *visciole* (sour cherries cherries) whole or by the slice.

Forums, Colosseum and Palatine Hill

The archaeological zone is full of dire eateries, cashing in on the droves of famished, foot-weary

tourists. However, if you are in the area of the Colosseum at lunchtime, there are some very pleasant retreats nearby.

Restaurants

Moderate

Mario's Hostaria J9
Piazza del Grillo 9, t 06 679 3725; bus H, 40, 60, 64, 70, 170. Open Mon–Sat 1–3 and 8–11.
A wide variety of dishes served at outdoor tables in a nice quiet location behind the Imperial Fora.

Ristorante Ulpia J8
Foro Traiano 1/b–2, t 06 678 9980; bus 60, 84, 85, 175; wheelchair accessible. Open Mon–Sat 12–11.
Ulpia claims to be Rome's oldest restaurant. It's in a beautiful location overlooking the Imperial Fora, but it serves awful food. Instead of eating a full tourist meal here, come between 4 and 7, when it functions as a café-bar. Sit outside to enjoy the view, or inside to cool down by air conditioning.

Inexpensive

Pasqualino
Via dei SS. Quattro Coronati 66, t 06 700 4576; metro Colosseo, bus 60, 84, 85, 175; wheelchair accessible. Open Tues–Sun 12–4 and 7–11.
A venerable old trat dishing up classic Roman fare such as *spaghetti alla carbonara*, *abbacchio al forno*, *saltimbocca* and *trippa alla romana*. Air-conditioned interior, or outside seating.

> ### Unexpected Rome
> Rome, almost uniquely among Italian cities, offers a fair selection of cuisine from outside Italy. If you've had enough Italian food for one stay, try a Chinese, India or Japanese meal.
> **Ci-Lin** (bus 23, 280; see p.312) **Court Delicati** (bus 23, 30, 75, 280; see p.311), **Golden Crown** (bus 71, 117, 119; see p.305), **India House** (bus 23, 280; see p.314), **Jaya Sai Ma** (tram 8; see p.312), **Sogo Asahi** (bus 117, 119; see p.305), **Surya Mahal** (bus 23, 280; see p.313).

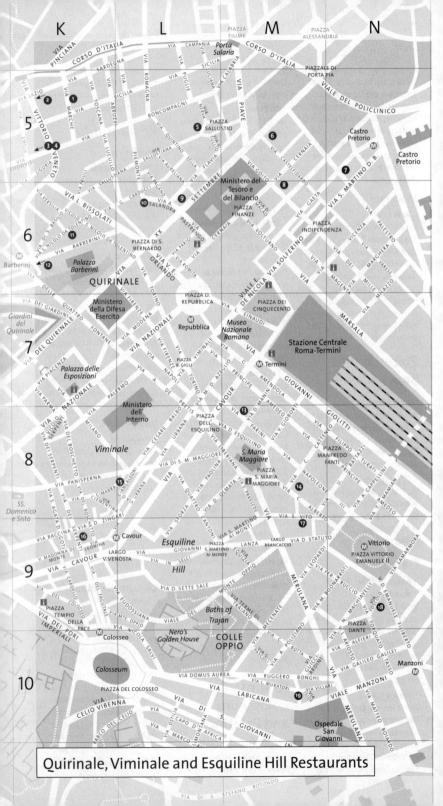

Quirinale, Viminale and Esquiline Hill Restaurants

Pizzerias and Snack Bars

Cavour 313 K3
*Via Cavour 313, t 06 678 5496;
metro Cavour, bus 75, 84, 117;
wheelchair accessible.* **Open**
*Oct–June Mon–Sat 12.30–2.30 and
7.30–12.30, Sun 7.30–12.30 only;
July and Sept daily.*
A civilized wood-beamed bar
which serves delicious, high-
quality snacks and light meals,
lunchtimes and evenings, to
accompany whichever of its 500
wines you care to drink.
Air conditioning.

Quirinale, Viminale and Esquiline Hill

There are not many choices in
the Quirinale/Viminale area; head
for Via Nazionale if you need a
quick hit of espresso or a limp
pizza. Don't expect to find
anything good near Termini
Station either, although there are
restaurants and bars in profusion;
there are, however, some excellent
choices for eating out on the
Esquiline Hill. The Italian regions
are well represented here.

Map Key

7	Africa
14	Agata e Romeo
16	Antico Caffè del Brasile
5	Cantina Cantarini
12	Colline Emiliane
4	Enoteca Nibbi
1	George's
10	Da Giovanni
18	Da Lisa
13	Monte Caruso (Cicilardone)
17	Monti
3	Peppone
2	Pino Il Sommelier
9	Taverna Flavia
15	Taverna Sottovento
19	Il Tempio di Iside
8	Trimani
11	Da Tullio
6	Da Vincenzo

Restaurants

Expensive

Agata e Romeo M8
*Via Carlo Alberto 45, t 06 446 6115;
metro Vittorio Emanuele, bus 71,
590; wheelchair accessible.* **Open**
*Mon–Fri 1–3 and 8–11 except 2
weeks in Aug.*
Creative cuisine and extensive
wine list in an elegant setting,
with plenty of nutritious dishes
on the menu. Air conditioning.

Colline Emiliane K6
*Via degli Avignonesi 22, t 06 481
7538; metro Barberini, bus 52, 53, 61.*
Open *Sept–July Sat–Thurs 12–3
and 8–11.30.*
Classic dishes from the Emilia-
Romagna, including *tortelloni di
zucca* (pumpkin), *lasagne verdi*
and, for offal-lovers, an impressive
bollito misto (beef tongue, calves'
cheek and pigs' trotters) and, in
autumn, dishes laced with truffles
– although obviously these bump
the price up. Air conditioning.

George's J5
*Via Marche 7, t 06 4208 4575; bus
52, 53, 63, 80.* **Open** *Sept–July
Mon–Sat 12.30–3 and 7.30–11.30
(piano bar until 2am). Reserve.*
An untarnished *dolce vita*-era
classic that remains posh and
elegant, with a gorgeous garden
terrace, refined service, tinkling
piano, and extensive wine list. Air-
conditioned interior.

Monte Caruso (Cicilardone) M8
*Via Farini 12, t 06 483 549; bus 105,
360, 649.* **Open** *Sept–July Tues–Sat
1–4 and 7–11, Mon 7–11. Reserve.*
Excellent home-made pasta
dishes, such as *spaghettoni con
cacio e pepe* (big spaghetti with
Roman ewes' milk cheese and
freshly ground black pepper) or
maltagliati ('badly cut' pasta) with
ricotta and tomato. The *secondi*
are less good, although the *pezze
pazze*, mad pieces (literally) of
beef in a piquant sauce, is interesting. Lively atmosphere, aided
by a good wine selection. Air
conditioning.

Taverna Flavia L6
*Via Flavia 9, t 06 481 7787; bus 16,
36, 60, 62, 63; wheelchair accessible.* **Open** *Mon–Fri 12–3 and 8–10,
Sat and Sun 12–3.*
An old favourite of the Cinecittà
set. Specialities include *penne alla
Flavia* (with mushrooms and
peas), a salad spiked with truffles
and gruyère, and *osso buco* with
risotto. Air conditioning.

Moderate

Da Lisa N9
*Via Foscolo 16, t 06 7049 5456;
metro Vittorio Emanuele, bus 360,
590.* **Open** *Sun–Thurs 12–3 and
7–11, Fri 12–3 only.*
Libyan and Israeli food: vegetable
soup, meat or fish couscous,
hummus, kebabs and wonderful
desserts. You can phone ahead
and order food to take away and
eat in your hotel room if you really
want to. Air conditioning.

Monti M8–9
*Via S. Vito 13/a, t 06 446 6573;
metro Vittorio Emanuele, bus 71,
590.* **Open** *Sept–July Tues–Sat
12.30–3.30 and 7.30–11.30.*
A small, friendly, genuine Roman
trattoria where you dine with the
TV for company. *Olive ascolane*,
home-made pasta and excellent
grilled meats.

Peppone K5
*Via Emilia 60, t 06 483 976; bus 52,
53, 63, 95, 116, 116T, 204; wheelchair
accessible.* **Open** *Sept–July
Mon–Sat 12–4 and 7–11, except
first week of Jan.*
Serious, old-fashioned restaurant
popular with business people. Air
conditioning.

Pino il Sommelier J5
*Via Aurora 10, t 06 474 2779; bus 52,
53, 80, 95; wheelchair accessible.*
Open *Sept–mid-Aug Tues–Sun
12–4 and 8–12.*
Especially nice for seafood; big
wine list. Air conditioning.

Taverna Sottovento L8
*Via dei Ciancaleoni 31, t 06 4742
2765; metro Cavour, bus 36, 60, 62,
84, 90.* **Open** *Mon–Sat 12–2.30 and
7.30–12 except 1 week in Aug.*
A pleasant new trattoria serving
typical Calabrian fare nicely spiced

Gelaterie

Rome is renowned for its *gelaterie* and in recent years some new contenders have sprung up alongside the old favourites – San Crispino (*see below*) first among them. There's no more Roman way of rounding off an evening than strolling the streets of the centre or one of the parks with an ice cream. A *cono* or *coppetta* (cone or little tub) will set you back €1–3, for two or three *gusti* (flavours).

Bar San Filippo (Off maps), *Via di Villa San Filippo 8–10*; *bus 53, 168, 217, 360.* **Open** *Tues–Sat 7am–12am (Parioli).* The Parioli quarter holds two of the city's best *gelaterie.* This serves delectable zabaglione, marron glacé and chocolate ices.

Caffè du Parc (113), *Piazza della Resistenza dell'8 Settembre*; *metro Piramide, tram 3, bus 23, 60, 75 118,* 280, 673,715, 716, 719. **Open** *daily 5am–10pm (Caelian Hill and the Aventine).* Famous for its *cremolato* – creamy fresh fruit sorbet, served at a little kiosk in the park, with tables around it behind the post office in Testaccio. It's a good place to go for a walk in summer.

La Casina dei Laghi, *Viale Oceania 90*, *metro EUR Palasport, EUR Fermi.* **Open** *8am–midnight (EUR).* The gardens of the EUR lake surround this *gelateria*, a beacon amid the Fascist architecture, with good ice cream. Tables to sit at.

Cecere (G11), *Via di San Francesco a Ripa 20*; *tram 8, bus 23, 280.* **Open** *Fri–Wed 6am–2am (Trastevere and Janiculum Hill).* Famed for its hedonistic zabaglione ices. Good *cornetti* for breakfast, too.

Duse (Off maps), *Via Eleonora Duse 1/e*; *bus 53, 168, 217, 360.* **Open**
Mon–Sat 8am–midnight (Parioli). Parioli's other hot option. Includes bitter chocolate in its repertoire.

Gelateria (C3), *Via Trionfale*; *bus 23, 30, 31, 69, 70, 81.* **Open** *8am–1am (Vatican).* All flavours are made from scratch here, as testified by the stacks of fruit crates from the nearby market piled up on the kerb. Favourite *gusti* are *fragola*, cappuccino, *pinolata* (made with pine nuts and honey), *zabaglione, stracciatella* (cream with bitter-chocolate drops) – just a few of the many.

Gelateria A. Cecere (17), *Via del Lavatore 84*; *bus 52, 53, 71, 80, 117, 119.* **Open** *8am–2am (Tridente).* Another Cecere, with good homemade ice cream. The speciality is a soft, decadently rich, zabaglione.

Gelateria Blue Ice (J6), *Via Due Macelli*; *bus 117, 119.* **Open** *daily*

up with the region's famous *peperoncino* (chilli pepper). Pasta rarities like *fileja* sautéed with broccoli, clams and beans or *tonnarelli con ricotta affumicata* (square spaghetti with smoked ricotta). Fish and pork baked in olive oil and herbs.

Il Tempio di Iside M10
Via Verri 11, t 06 700 4741; *tram 3, bus 85, 87, 186, 204, 810, 850; wheelchair accessible.* **Open** *Mon–Fri 12.30–3.30 and 7.30–11.30, Sat 12.20–3.30 only.*
The 'Temple of Isis' is named after the nearby piazza, and not for its Egyptian cuisine. Instead it offers a surprisingly affordable (Italian) fish menu that includes *linguine all'imperiale* (flat spaghetti with prawns, clams, mussels and a little tomato) or *gnocchettini alla pescatora* (fisher-style little potato dumplings) followed by baked fish with cherry tomatoes, potatoes and olives. Tables outside.

Trimani M5–6
Via Cernaia 37/b, t 06 446 9630; *bus 16, 36, 60, 61, 62, 84.* **Open** *Mon–Fri 12–12, Sat 8–12, except 2 weeks in Aug.*
A haven of sanity in the Termini Station area, where business types and intellectuals with demanding

tastebuds flock at lunchtime. It's great in the evening, too. Borlotti bean, tuna and onion salad, quiches, smoked fish, wild boar salami, a selection of regional cheeses and an unforgettable *caprese* (*mozzarella di bufala* with tomato and basil) served with dark rustic bread and a saucer of green nectar-like olive oil. Desserts include chestnut mousse. There's a mind-boggling range of wines.

Da Tullio K6
Via S. Nicola da Tolentino 26, t 06 474 5560; *metro Barberini, bus 61, 62, 116, 175.* **Open** *Sept–July Mon–Sat 12.30–3 and 7.30–11.*
A dependable restaurant, which specializes in traditional Tuscan fare. Try *pappardelle* (wide, flat noodles) *ai porcini* or *zuppa di verdura e fagioli* (vegetable and bean soup). *Secondi* include grilled meat and fish. Home-made desserts and a good choice of vintage red wines.

Da Vincenzo M5
Via Castelfidardo 4, t 06 484 596; *bus 13, 36, 60, 61, 62; wheelchair accessible.* **Open** *Sept–July Mon–Sat 1–4 and 8–11.*
Wonderful *antipasti* and fish specialities with *simpatico* service and air conditioning.

Inexpensive

Africa N5
Via Gaeta 26, t 06 494 1077; *metro Termini, bus 36, 38, 40, 64, 75.* **Open** *Tues–Sun 12–3.30 and 7.30–11.*
Wide-awake Eritrean specialities along with Italo-Eritrean combos like spaghetti with spicy sauce.

Cantina Cantarini L5
Piazza Sallustio 12, t 06 485 528; *bus 52, 53, 630, 910; wheelchair accessible.* **Open** *Mon–Sat except 2 weeks in Aug. Reserve.*
A century-old trattoria serving good honest fare with nuances from the Marches. Meat dishes Mon–Thurs, seafood Fri–Sat.

Da Giovanni L6
Via Salandra 1, t 06 485 950; *bus 16, 36, 60, 61, 910.* **Open** *Sept–July Sun–Thurs 12.30–3 and 7.30–11, Fri 12.30–3 only.*
Honest old trattoria serving a wide choice of favourites. Air conditioning.

Enoteca Nibbi K5
Via Emilia 44, t 06 488 2989; *bus 52, 53, 63, 95, 116, 116T, 204.* **Open** *Mon–Sat 10am–9pm.*
Upmarket stand-up bar where business men and women flock at lunchtime for a glass of wine and fresh sandwiches made to order.

8am–2am *(Tridente)*. Blue Ice *gelaterie* are scattered throughout the centre of Rome. Quality varies from branch to branch as ice cream is made on the premises by different *gelatai*. This one on Via Due Macelli is one of the best. Mango, often stored in the back room and not on display, is a favourite. There's also a small selection of non-dairy flavours.

Gelateria Old Bridge (B7), *Viale Vaticano; metro Ottaviano, tram 19, bus 32, 81 (Vatican City and St Peter's)*. You might notice this hole-in-the-wall ice-cream stand while waiting in line at the Vatican Museums. *Pinolato* (vanilla and pine nuts) and *fragola* (strawberry) are particularly good.

Gelateria della Palma (H7), *Piazza della Maddalena, bus 116, 116T. Open daily 10am–2am*

(Campo Marzio). Deluxe ice cream parlour, which scoops wacky flavours like fig and mascarpone.

Il Gelato di San Crispino (J7), *Via della Panetteria 42; bus 52, 53, 71, 80, 117, 119. Open Wed–Sun 12–12 (Tridente)*. Opened in 1992, the San Crispino is a cut above most Italian gelaterie and a pilgrimage site for Romans. €2 will buy you a smaller than average cup or cone, but after tasting their ice cream it's hard to go anywhere else. House specialities are the San Crispino (honey and vanilla), zabaglione, meringue and hazelnut, coffee, chocolate or whatever fruit is in season – try *lampone* (raspberry) – all made on the spot from fresh ingredients.

Fassi Palazzo del Ghiaccio (N9), *Via Principe Eugenio 65–67; metro Vittorio Emanuele, tram 5, 14, bus

105, 157 (Quirinale, Viminale and Esquiline Hill)*. Old-style *gelateria* with delicious flavours.

Giolitti (H7), *Via Uffici del Vicario 40; bus 116, 116T. Open Tues–Sun 7am–2am (Campo Marzio)*. Rome's historic ice cream family. Divine ice creams topped with cream (as if they are not rich enough). Eat out or indulge in a sundae in the fading splendour of its parlour.

Pellacchia (F5), *Via Cola di Rienzo 103–7; bus 81. Open 10am–1am (Vatican)*. High-quality ices, and the best hot chocolate in winter.

I Tre Scalini (G8), *Piazza Navona; bus 116, 116T. Open Thurs–Tues 8am–1.30am (Campo Marzio)*. Justifiably renowned for its *tartufo* (truffle) ice cream – served in slabs with a smear of cream. Prices are high if you choose to sit on the piazza.

Cafés

Antico Caffè del Brasile K9
Via dei Serpenti 23, t 06 488 2319; metro Cavour. Open Mon–Sat 7am–8pm, except 2 weeks in Aug. The 'Monti' neighbourhood's traditional café and *torrefazione*.

Caelian Hill and the Aventine

Restaurants

Expensive
Checchino dal 1887 G14
Via di Monte Testaccio 30, t 06 574 3816; metro Piramide, bus 95. Open Sept–July Tues–Sat 12–3 and 8–11.30. Reserve.
In a traditional, naturally cooled Testaccio wine cave, you can dine on Rome's most authentic and best-prepared local specialities, a perfect match for one of the city's best wine cellars. Order the *menu degustazione* for a memorable repast.

Moderate
Cannavota N11
*Piazza S. Giovanni in Laterano 20, t 06 7720 5007; metro S. Giovanni, tram 3, bus 16, 81, 85, 87, 650. Open

Thurs–Tues 12.30–3 and 7.45–11 except 3 weeks in Aug.*
Specializes in fish and seafood. The chef has a way with fresh scampi, clams and other fruits of the sea, in *antipasti* and generous pasta dishes. Charming service, good value and air conditionong.

Nel Regno di Re Ferdinando H14
Via di Monte Testaccio 39, t 06 578 3725; metro Piramide, bus 23, 95, 280. Open Tue–Sat 12–2.30 and 8–11.45, Mon 8–11.45 only.
Neapolitan cuisine in a small kingdom. Wide selection of *antipasti*, fresh pasta, *pesce all'acqua pazza* ('mad water' – fish poached in herbs and tomatoes) and *pizza alla napoletana*. Air conditioning.

Lo Scopettaro H12
Lungotevere Testaccio 7, t 06 574 2408; bus 23, 95, 280.
Wood veneer walls adorned with racing photos and the occasional lipstick-smeared wine-glass notwithstanding, this is one of the most popular of Testaccio's offal temples, attracting besuited business types as well as proletarian locals. There's no menu – dishes are reeled off by the waiter at top speed. The speciality is *riga-

toni con pajata* (pasta with veal intestine) but if this doesn't really appeal, try the perfectly cooked *bucatini alla carbonara* or all' *amatriciana*. Air conditioning.

Inexpensive
Augustarello G13
Via G. Branca 98, t 06 574 6585; wheelchair accessible; bus 23, 30, 75, 280. Open mid-Sept–mid–Aug Mon–Sat 12–3.30 and 7.30–11.30.
Augustarello's sons, Gianni, Alessandro and Massimo, now run the restaurant and prepare the same basic old-fashioned Roman dishes as their dad: *coda alla vaccinara, trippa alla romana, rigatoni con pajata* and *animelle e muscoletti con funghi* (sweetbreads with mushrooms). Nice outside garden to sit in on summer evenings.

Court Delicati J12
Viale Aventino 41, t 06 574 6108; bus 23, 30, 75, 280. Open Tues–Sun. Chinese and Thai dishes including Thai fish soup, satay chicken and *nasi goreng*, washed down with Chinese beer or jasmine tea.

Da Felice H13
Via Mastro Giorgio 29, t 06 574 6800; bus 23, 30, 75, 280. Open Sept–July Mon–Sat 12.30–2.45 and 8–10.30.

Since 1935, despite the lack of a sign on the door, the few tables at Felice's have been full of admirers of the home-style Roman cuisine: gnocchi, tripe, *pajata*, each served on its appointed day. Arrive before 1 for lunch and 8 for dinner to get a table, and don't be surprised at brusque service.

Luna Piena H13

Via Luca della Robbia 15, t 06 575 0279; bus 23, 30, 75, 280. **Open** *Aug–June Thurs–Tues 1–3 and 8–12.* Come here for home-made ravioli and gnocchi, but also try the traditionally Roman *secondi*.

Messico e Nuvole H15

Via dei Magazzini Generali 8, t 06 574 1413; metro Piramide, bus 23, 280, 716, 719. **Open** *Tues–Sun 7–12.* Rome's calmest Mexican restaurant, with a plant-filled terrace. Tacos, tortillas and enchiladas. In summer you can stay and have margaritas after midnight.

La Volpe Rossa N10

Via Alfieri 4, t 06 7045 3517; metro San Giovanni, tram 3, bus 16, 81, 85, 7, 650; wheelchair accessible. **Open** *Tues–Sun 12–3 and 7–11, Mon 7–11.* In the shadow of the basilica of San Giovanni in Laterano, the 'Red Fox' serves wonders for the price (lunch menu €12). The menu, based on healthy Mediterranean cuisine, changes daily; expect lots of fish and vegetables.

Pizzerias and Snack Bars

Via and Piazza San Giovanni in Laterano are studded with *pizza al taglio* joints and snack bars, all reasonable and fairly similar. Below are some classier joints.

Gennargentù I14

Via Ostiense 21–23, t 06 575 9817; metro Piramide, bus 23, 769. **Open** *Tues–Sun 7pm–1am.* Sardinian pizzeria known for its *pizza al Gennargentù* (tomato, mozzarella and spicy sausage), which you can wash down with Sardinian wine. Desserts are Sardinian, too: try *seada*, a sweet cheese fritter served with honey.

Pizza Forum L10

Via di San Giovanni in Laterano 34, t 06 700 2515; metro Colosseo, bus 85, 87, 117. **Open** *Tues–Sun 10–8.* A place you'd assume to be best avoided, kitted out as a theme-park version of an ancient forum, with fish-tank lighting to boot. Forget aesthetics for half an hour, and go in for a good Neapolitan style pizza (thicker bases than their Roman cousins).

Volpetti Più H13

Via Volta 8; bus 23, 30, 75, 280. **Open** *Mon–Sat 10am–10pm except two weeks in Aug.* Testaccio *tavola calda* run by the Gastronomia Volpetti around the corner (*see* p.331). De luxe *pizza al taglio* with *mozzarella di bufala* and *funghi porcini*, rice and pasta salads, roast beef, a good selection of vegetables and fresh fruit.

Trastevere and the Janiculum

Restaurants

Expensive

Alberto Ciarla G11

Piazza S. Cosimato 40, t 06 581 8668; tram 8, bus H, 44 75. **Open** *Mon–Sat 7.30–midnight except 2 weeks in Jan. Reserve.* This flash candlelit fairyland of seafood is unique in Rome not only for its variety of sea creatures, but for the variety of methods of preparation. Expect a bill hovering in the €60 zone. Tables outside, air conditioning inside.

Da Paris G10

Piazza S. Calisto 7/a, t 06 581 5378; tram 8, bus H. **Open** *Sept–July Tues–Sat 12–3 and 8–11, Sun 12–3.* Come here for *tagliolini con scampi e fiori di zucca* ('little cut' pasta with prawns and pumpkin flowers), *stracotto di manzo con crocchette di patate* ('extra-cooked' beef stew with potato croquettes), *zuppa di arzilla* (anglefish soup – unusual but delicious) and *gnocchetti al ragù di pesce* (potato dumplings with fish sauce). Air conditioning.

Peccati di Gola H10

Piazza dei Ponziani 7/a, t 06 581 4529; bus 23, 280; wheelchair accessible. **Open** *Oct–May Tues–Sun 1–4 and 7–12, June–Sept Tues–Sat 7–12, Sun 1–4 and 7–12.* Fish is the speciality, but there's some of everything else too, including old Calabrian recipes. A good place to eat outside.

Moderate

Checco er Carettiere G10

Via Benedetta 10, t 06 581 7018; bus 23, 280. **Open** *Mon–Sun 12–3 and 7–12, Sun 12–4.30.* One of Trastevere's oldest inns, with well-prepared versions of popular Roman specialities like *coda alla vaccinara* and seafood. Famous for making even tripe taste good. The fish is just right.

Il Ciak F10

Vicolo del Cinque 21, t 06 589 4774; bus 23, 280. **Open** *Tues–Sun 7–12, except 3 weeks Aug–Sept. Reserve.* Il Ciak's flaming fiery furnace makes it an ideal place to go on a cold winter's night. Hearty Tuscan fare like *ribollita* (a thick soup), polenta with hare or wild boar sauce, and thick Florentine and wild boar steaks grilled over the fire. Lighter dishes in summer.

Hostaria La Canonica G10

Vicolo del Piede 13/a; t 06 580 3845; bus 23, 280. **Open** *Wed–Sun 12–4 and 7–11, Tues 7–11 only.* A touristy restaurant with a cluttered mock-rustic dining room. The fresh seafood is good, however, and prices are reasonable. Some interesting dishes, too – smoked swordfish with *rughetta* (rocket), and, among the *contorni*, *puntarelle con salsa di acciughe*. Lovely, peaceful outside tables.

Jaya Sai Ma F13

Via A. Bargoni 11–18, t 06 581 2840; tram 8; wheelchair accessible. **Open** *daily 6.30pm–10.30pm.* 'Victory of Mother Earth' in Sanskrit. No meat, no alcohol, no cigarettes in this healthy haven, where you can linger after dinner and chat over a cup of herbal tea. Tables outside; air conditioning.

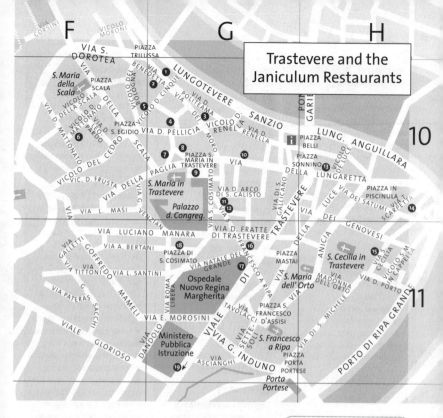

Map labels

F
G
H

VICOLO MORONI

VIA CORSINI

VIA S. DOROTEA

PIAZZA TRILUSSA

S. Maria della Scala

PIAZZA SCALA

VICOLO DELLA SCALA

VIA DELLA SCALA

LUNGOTEVERE

LUNGOTEVERE D. SANZIO

VICOLO D. CINQUE

VIA D. PELLICIA

VIA D. POLITEAMA

VIA DELLA RENELLA

VICOLO DELLA RENELLA

Trastevere and the Janiculum Restaurants

PONTE GARIBALDI

VIA DEL MATTONATO

VICOLO DEL MATTONATO

VIA D. S. EGIDIO

VIA D. MORO

PIAZZA BELLI

LUNG. ANGUILLARA

10

VICOLO DEL CEDRO

SCALA

VIA DELLA PAGLIA

PIAZZA S. MARIA IN TRASTEVERE

VIA D. CISTERNA

PIAZZA SONNINO

DELLA LUNGARETTA

VIA DI LUCE

VIA DEI SATURNI

PIAZZA IN PISCINULA

VICOLO DE' LUCE

S. Maria in Trastevere

Palazzo d. Congreg.

VIA D. ARCO DI S. CALISTO

VIA S. COSIMATO

VIA S. CALISTO

VIA S. GALLICANO

DELLA SCARSELLA

GENOVESI

VIC. D. FRUSTA

VIA L. MASI

VIA VENZIAN

VIA D. FRATTE DI TRASTEVERE

S. TRASTEVERE

VIA DEI

VIA LUCIANO MANARA

VIA GALLETTI

VIA GOFFREDO

VIA TITTONI

VIA A. BERTANI

VIA L. SANTINI

PIAZZA DI S. COSIMATO

VIA NATALE DEL GRANDE

VIA FRANCESCO A RIPA

PIAZZA MASTAI

PIAZZA MADONNA DELL'ORTO

S. Maria dell'Orto

S. Cecilia in Trastevere

VIA S. CECILIA

VIA D. PORTO

VICOLO S. M. IN CAPPELLA

VIA PATERAS

VIA C. MAMELI

VIA SACCHI

VIA ROMA LIBERA

Ospedale Nuovo Regina Margherita

VIA TAVOLACCI

VIA ANICIA

PIAZZA S. FRANCESCO D'ASSISI

VIA D. MADONNA DELL'ORTO

11

VIALE GLORIOSO

VIA E. MOROSINI

VIA DANDOLO

VIALE

Ministero Pubblica Istruzione

VIA G. INDUNO

VIA SETTE SOLI

S. Francesco a Ripa

VIA DI S. MICHELE

PORTO DI RIPA GRANDE

VIA ASCIANGHI

PIAZZA PORTA PORTESE

Porta Portese

Body text

Surya Mahal G10

Piazza Trilussa 50, t 06 589 4554; bus 23, 280. Open Mon–Sat 7pm–11.30pm.

Rome's best Indian restaurant. With excellent service, a pretty garden for summer eating and an entire vegetarian menu, even die-hard *aficionados* of Brick Lane and Rusholme should not be disappointed. Vegetarian dishes include dahl, spiced cauliflower or a pea and mushroom curry; fish-lovers and carnivores can savour lemon chicken, prawn korma and sword-fish tandoori, alongside all the usual poppadums, pakoras and samosas, lassi and a small, carefully chosen wine selection. Tables outside. Air conditioning.

Inexpensive

Augusto G10

Piazza de' Renzi 15, t 06 580 3798; bus 23, 280. Open Sept–July Mon–Fri 12.30–3 and 8–11, Sat 12.30–3 only.

A classic Trastevere trattoria, now in danger of becoming a parody of

itself. Habitués squeeze past the tightly packed tables, exchange insults with the boss Augusto – almost a caricature of a cheeky, grouchy Trasteverino – grab a paper tablecloth from the shelf at the back, lay their own table, place their order and usually end up collecting their own wine and food from the kitchen hatch. The food's not bad, prices are low and you can dine outside.

Ci-Lin G10

Via Fonte d'Olio 6, t 06 581 3930; bus 23, 280. Open Thurs–Tues 12–4 and 7–12.

One of the only Chinese restaurants where you can eat outside. The food is pretty good, too.

Da Gino G10

Via della Lungaretta 85, t 06 580 3403; terrace wheelchair accessible; tram 8, bus H, 23, 280. Open Thurs–Tues 12.30–3 and 7.30–11 except 2 weeks in Aug.

Simple trattoria-cum-pizzeria where you can sit down for just a bowl of pasta and a salad.

Map Key

18	Alberto Ciarla
4	Augusto
11	Bar San Calisto
9	Caffè di Marzio
2	Checco er Carettiere
5	Il Ciak
8	Ci-Lin
17	Frontoni
10	Da Gino
7	Hostaria La Canonica
15	India House
19	Jaya Sai Ma
6	Da Lucia
13	Papa Re
12	Da Paris
14	Peccati di Gola
3	Renella
16	Supplì e Pizza al Taglio
1	Surya Mahal

India House H11

Via S. Cecilia 8, t 06 581 8508; bus 23, 280. Open Tues–Sun, eves only.
Fixed price menu that changes daily, featuring Indian dishes from different regions. Special menu for vegetarians. Air conditioning.

Da Lucia F10

Vicolo del Mattonato 2/b, t 06 580 3601; bus 23, 280; wheelchair accessible. Open Tues–Sun 12–3 and 7.30–11 except last 2 weeks of Aug.

Hidden on a back street, but worth seeking out for some of the best real Roman cooking this side of the Tiber. Menu changes daily. Try *spaghetti alla gricia* (with cheese, pepper and bacon) and, on Fridays, *baccalà con zibibbo e pinoli* (salt cod with raisins and pine nuts). Outside seating.

Papa Re H10

Via della Lungaretta 149, t 06 581 2069; bus 23, 280; wheelchair accessible. Open daily 12.30–4 and 7.30–11. Reserve.

Pierluigi and wife Concetta prepare typical Roman dishes, including tasty *gnocchi ai broccoli* and *trote alle mandorle* (trout with almonds). Outside seating.

Pizzerias and Snack Bars

Frontoni G11

Viale Trastevere 52, t 06 3630 7865; tram 8, bus H, 23, 280, 780. Open Mon–Thurs 11am–1am, Fri and Sat 11am–2am.

Pizza bianca ripiena. Choose what to put in your pizza sandwich from a large selection of fillings.

Renella G10

Via del Moro 15 and Via del Politeama 29; tram 8, bus 23, 280. Open daily 7am–8.30pm.

This wonderful bakery with its *forno a legna* (wood oven) is too good to miss. Distinctive *pizza al taglio* with top-quality ingredients, which you can eat perched on a stool. Of the sweet pastries, the *pian giallo romano* (made with dried figs and nuts) and the *brutti ma buoni* ('ugly but good' hazelnut macaroons) stand out.

Supplì e Pizza al Taglio G11

Via San Francesco a Ripa; tram 8, bus 23, 280. Open noon–midnight.

Besides slices of pizza and roasted chicken to take away, here you can get the famous supplì – deep-fried rice balls with melted mozzarella in the middle.

Cafés

Bar San Calisto G10

Piazza San Calisto 3–5, t 06 583 5869; tram 8, bus 23, 280. Open Mon–Sat 6am–1.30am.

A good, cheap place to lunch – bring your own from one of the *pizza al taglio* outlets on Via di San Francesco a Ripa and sit outside for as long as you want.

Caffè di Marzio G10

Piazza di Santa Maria in Trastevere 14/b; tram 8, bus 23, 280. Open Tues–Sun 8am–midnight.

Outside tables which look directly onto the façade of Santa Maria in Trastevere. Good for a sandwich lunch or lingering drink.

Vatican City and St Peter's

Restaurants

Expensive

Les Étoiles dell'Atlante Star E6

Via Vitelleschi 34, t 06 687 3233; bus 34, 49, 492, 990; wheelchair accessible. Open daily 12–3.30 and 7.30–12.

Enjoy the amazing 360° panorama of Rome from the roof while chef Paolo Preo adds his own touch to many Mediterranean dishes, the menu depending on market availability. Extensive and well selected wine list. Air conditioning.

Taverna Angelica E6

Piazza delle Vaschette 14/a, t 06 687 4514; wheelchair accessible. Open Sept–July Tues–Sat 12–2.30 and 7.30–12, Mon 7.30–12 only.

A tiny, cosy restaurant near Castel Sant'Angelo, with good pasta dishes and roast pork. Vintage wine by the glass and one of the world's most expensive (and wonderful) cheeses: Castelmagno.

Moderate

Arlù D6

Borgo Pio 135, t 06 686 8936; tram 19, bus 32, 81. Open Sept–July Mon–Fri 1–3 and 7–11, Sat 1–3 only.

Good traditional fish-focused cuisine. Cheaper lunch menus.

Grotte di Castello E6

Borgo Vittorio 92, t 06 686 5143; bus 32, 34, 49, 81, 492. Open Tues–Sat 12.30–4 and 7.30–11.

Try any of the fresh fish and home-made pasta in this gracious restaurant, run by a mother and daughter team; vegetarian dishes too. Air conditioning.

Il Toscano D5

Via Germanico 58, t 06 3972 5717; metro Ottaviano, tram 19, bus 32, 81; wheelchair accessible. Open Sept–July Tues–Sat 12.30–3 and 8–11 except last week of Dec.

Conveniently located near the Vatican museums, this family-run Tuscan trattoria serves classic dishes such as *ribollita* (bread and vegetable soup) and *pici* (thick spaghetti with a wild hare sauce). The house speciality is the prized *bistecca alla fiorentina*, a thick, succulent steak grilled on charcoal but rare in the middle, accompanied by a strong Chianti or a *mezzo* of the Tuscan house wine. In winter home-made desserts such as cream tart, apple strudel and *castagnaccio* (a chestnut and pine nut delicacy) round off the hearty fare. In summer, enjoy the outside seating.

Inexpensive

Candido D1

Viale Angelico 275, t 06 3751 7704; wheelchair accessible; bus 32, 69, 628. Open Sept–July Wed–Mon 12–4 and 7–1.

It never seems large enough to accommodate all the hungry locals, but speedy service keeps the turnover rapid. The best pizzas in Prati (€6–9), along with modest Italian dishes.

La Cantina Tirolese E6

Via Vitelleschi 23, t 06 686 9994; bus 30, 62, 64, 70, 81. Open Tues–Sun 12–4 and 8–1, except 2 weeks in Aug.

A cheerful cellar in the Tyrolese style, with wooden benches, ironwork chandeliers and more than 30 Tyrolese fabric calendars on the walls – one for each year since the restaurant opened in 1971. Hearty, delicious food from the Alpine

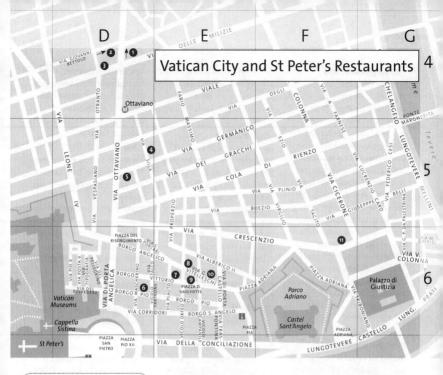

Map Key

6   Arlù
1   Candido
10 La Cantina Tirolese
3   La Casa del Dragone
8   Les Étoiles dell'Atlante Star
7   Grotte di Castello
2   Osteria dell'Angelo
4   Il Ragno d'Oro
11 Il Simposio di Costantini
9   Taverna Angelica
5   Il Toscano

region, best-enjoyed in winter: meat or cheese fondue, *ca.nederli* (dumplings), goulash soup flavoured with cumin, spiced meatballs and *stinco di maiale* – whole roast shin of pork (there are several vegetarian options too) – all washed down with draught beer and topped off by a slice of home-made apple strudel. The lunch buffet is very good value, and dinner is served until 1am.

La Casa del Dragone D4
Viale delle Milizie 116, **t** *06 372 4088;* **bus** *70, 490, 590.* **Open** *Sept–July daily 12–2.30 and 7–11.30.* Shanghai specialities. Fresh seafood dishes on Tues and Fri.

Osteria dell'Angelo D4
Via G. Bettolo 24, **t** *06 372 9470;* **metro** *Lepanto,* **tram** *19,* **bus** *70, 490, 590.* **Open** *July–Sept Mon–Sat 8pm–11.15pm, Tues and Fri also 12.45pm–2.30pm.*
Highly rated trattoria run by a former rugby player. Authentic Roman dishes.

Il Ragno d'Oro D5
Via Silla 26, **t** *06 321 2362;* **metro** *Ottaviano,* **bus** *32;* **wheelchair accessible.** **Open** *Mon–Sat 12–3 and 8–12 except 2 weeks in Aug.*
Good Italian home-cooking. Outside seating. Air conditioning.

Il Simposio di Costantini F6
Piazza Cavour 16, **t** *06 321 1502;* **bus** *34, 490, 590, 913.* **Open** *Sept–July Mon–Fri 11.30–3 and 6.30–1, Sat 6.30–1 only.*
Gorgeous wine bar serving snacks for gastronomes in a paradise of ironwork vines. Wines by the glass upstairs, or more bottles of wine than you could hope to try in a lifetime in the cellar. There's an expensive restaurant too, on the ground floor.

North and West of the Centre

Restaurants

Some of Rome's top restaurants are in the snooty neighbourhoods north of the centre – Parioli, north of Villa Borghese, and Monte Mario, across the Tiber by the Foro Italico, both house temples of haute cuisine. You'll find pleasant neighbourhood trattorias and pizzerias if you stray up here too.

Al Ceppo L1
Via Panama 2/a, **t** *06 841 9696;* **tram** *3, 19,* **bus** *53, 168;* **wheelchair accessible.** **Open** *Tues–Sun 1–3 and 8–11 except 2 weeks in Sept. Reserve for Sun lunch.* **Expensive.**
In the heart of the Parioli neighbourhood, with an open grill and warm, comfortable, elegant décor reminiscent of a bourgeois drawing room. Traditional Italian cuisine with specialities from the Marches, such as *linguine Monte Cònero* (with a clam sauce). Save space for the desserts. Tables outside in summer.

La Pergola dell'Hotel Hilton Off maps
Via Cadlolo 101, t 06 35091; shuttle bus runs to and from Piazza Barberini once an hour; wheelchair accessible. **Open** *Feb–Dec Tues–Sat 7.30–1145pm. Reserve.* **Expensive.**
One of the city's top restaurants, impeccably run by German chef Heinz Beck. A classy break from 'old Rome', in Monte Mario, where you can sample creative Italian cuisine at its best, followed by an impressive cheese cart and divine desserts such as the *tazza di cioccolato con gelato al caffè* (a cup made out of chocolate filled with coffee ice cream) or fresh chocs on a bed of ice. Meals can be enjoyed on the roof terrace. Around €110 a head before wine.

Relais le Jardin I2
Hotel Lord Byron, Via G. de Notaris 5, t 06 322 0404; tram 3, 19, bus 52, 926. **Open** *daily 12.30–2.30 and 8–10.30. Reserve.* **Expensive.**
The ultimate gastronomic experience in Rome, just north of Villa Borghese. Exquisite *haute cuisine* that makes this an extra-special occasion for most mortals.

Fauro Off maps
Via R. Fauro 44, t 06 808 3301; bus 53, 168, 217; parking; wheelchair accessible. **Open** *Mon–Sat except 2 weeks in Aug. Reserve.* **Moderate.**
An ever-popular trattoria, made even more famous in 2001 by the supporters of Berlusconi who, for the duration of their (successful) electoral campaign, turned it into convivial headquarters. The menu is based on fish, bought daily fresh from the sea at Fiumicino market by savvy owner Franco Zambelli, and on specialities from Mantua prepared by Franco's mother. Her *crostini con guanciale e gamberetti* (cured pork cheek and prawns on toast) are a revelation.

L'Insalatiera 2 C2
Via Trionfale 92, t 06 3974 2975; bus 70; wheelchair accessible. **Open** *July–Sept Mon–Fri 1–4 and 8–12, Sat 8–12.* **Inexpensive.**
It's worth the trip to Monte Mario for this tasty vegetarian menu. Pumpkin lasagne in the autumn,

barley and artichoke soup, *pizza di scarola* (filled with lettuce and olives and deep fried) and salads; leave some room for home-made desserts. No-smoking room.

Semidivino N4
Via Alessandria 230, t 06 4425 0795; wheelchair accessible; tram 3, 19, bus 36, 60, 62, 84, 90. **Open** *Sept–July Mon–Fri 12.30–2 and 7.30–11.30, Sat 7.30–11.30. Reserve.*
An attractive neighbourhood *enoteca* run by an Iranian expatriate who loves wine and Italian food. The choice is limited to two or three hot dishes, which usually include a hearty vegetarian soup or pasta, salads, cheese and cured pork, but it's all well prepared. The owner speaks fluent English.

La Soffitta N4
Via dei Villini 1/e, t 06 440 4642; bus 36, 60, 62, 84, 90. **Open** *Sept–July Mon–Fri 12–2.30 and 7.30–12, Sat and Sun 6.30–12.*
A bastion of thick Neapolitan pizza served on wooden trays. Pricey as pizza goes, but worth the extra. Desserts are imported from the best Neapolitan pastry shops.

Cafés

Caffè delle Arti I2–3
Viale Belle Arti, t 06 3265 1236. **Open** *Tues–Sun 7.30am–midnight, Mon 7.30am–6pm.*
An elegant place for Sunday brunch, the café of the Galleria Nazionale di Belle Arti has a lovely terrace with tables in the sun. Popular with families and couples.

East of the Centre

Restaurants

Once a gritty area on the wrong side of the tracks, San Lorenzo is now firmly established as a trendy bohemian and student quarter.

Pommidoro P8
Piazza dei Sanniti 44, t 06 445 2692. **Open** *Sept–July Thurs–Tues 12–3 and 7.30–12.* **Moderate.**
A classic San Lorenzo trattoria, popular with the neighbourhood's intellectuals and artists, serving

Roman dishes cooked by the talented wife of the owner. Good pasta dishes (like *spaghetti alla verdura* or *all'amatriciana*) and equally good meat and fish grilled *alla brace*. Tables outside.

Tram Tram Q8
Via dei Reti 44, t 06 490 416; bus 71, 204, 492. **Open** *Tues–Sun 12–3 and 7.30–12 except 1 week in Aug.* **Moderate.**
The best of San Lorenzo's trendy new restaurants. Seafood lasagne, scrumptious *involtini*, and a good range of main course salads. There's also a bar for pre- and post-dinner drinks.

Il Dito e la Luna P8
Via dei Sabelli 49–51, t 06 494 0726. **Open** *Mon–Sat 7.30–11pm.* **Inexpensive.**
Another of the newer breed of restaurants, frequented by a young crowd for its relaxed ambience and Sicilian cooking.

Appian Way

Restaurants

L'Archeologia Off maps
Via Appia Antica 139, t 06 788 0494; bus 218, 660; wheelchair accessible. **Open** *Wed–Mon 12–3 and 7.30–10.30.* **Moderate.**
Housed in an attractive farmhouse with a garden five minutes form the catacombs. Simple fowl and fish at reasonable prices, with tables outside.

Cecilia Metella Off maps
Via Appia Antica 125 (opposite the catacomb entrance), t 06 513 6743; bus 218, 660; parking. **Open** *Tues–Sat 12.45–4 and 7.30–11.*
Don't be turned off by a place that looks so obviously geared to large parties. They are not all package tours; in fact the Cecilia Metella caters especially for wedding banquets and family feasts, which shouldn't prevent you from enjoying a traditional Roman meal under the vines.

Preghiera a Santa Monica

Signore, Padre Santo,
misericordia di quanti sperano in te,
Tu hai concesso alla tua serva Monica
il dono inestimabile di saper riconciliare
le anime con Te e fra di loro;
con la vita, le preghiere e le lacrime,
portò a te il marito Patrizio
ed il figlio Agostino:
lodiamo in lei i tuoi doni.
Per sua intercessione concedici
le grazie a noi necessarie.

Tu, cara Santa Monica,
che nutristi spiritualmente i tuoi figli
generandoli tante volte
quante li vedevi allontanarsi da Lui,
prega per le nostre famiglie,
per i nostri giovani e per quanti
non trovano la via della fede.
Ottienici di rimanere fedeli a Dio,
di perseverare nel desiderio del Cielo
e di condurre al Signore quanti Lui ci affida.
Amen.

Gloria al Padre...

Estasi di Ostia (Basilica di Sant'Agostino - Roma)

3027112   B.N. Marconi - Genova - Tel. 010 6515914

Prayer to St. Monica

God, Holy Father,
mercy for those who trust in Your,
You granted Your servant Monica
the invaluable gift for reconciling
the souls with You and one another.
With her life, her prayers and her tears
she took her husband Patrick
and her son Augustine to You.
In her we praise Your gifts;
by her intercession
give us Your Grace.

O Saint Monica,
who spiritually nourished your children
giving them birth so many times
as you saw them becoming estranged from God,
pray for our families, for young people
and for those who can't find the path of sanctity.
Obtain for us he fidelity to God,
the perseverance in longing for Heaven
and the capacity to lead to the Lord
those He puts under our care. Amen.

Glory...

Ecstasy at Ostia (St. Augustine's Basilica - Rome)

2970411   B.N. Marconi - Genova - Tel. 010 6515914

Prayer to St. Monica

God, Holy Father,
mercy for those who trust in Your,
You granted Your servant Monica
the invaluable gift for reconciling
the souls with You and one another.
With her life, her prayers and her tears
she took her husband Patrick
and her son Augustine to You.
In her we praise Your gifts;
by her intercession
give us Your Grace.

O Saint Monica,
who spiritually nourished your children
giving them birth so many times
as you saw them becoming estranged from God,
pray for our families, for young people
and for those who can't find the path of sanctity.
Obtain for us he fidelity to God,
the perseverance in longing for Heaven
and the capacity to lead to the Lord
those He puts under our care. Amen.

Glory...

Ecstasy at Ostia (St. Augustine's Basilica - Rome)

2970411   B.N. Marconi - Genova - Tel. 010 6515914

Nightlife

Rome's club scene is hardly the most dynamic in Europe, yet this is a great city to be in at night. For a start, its beautiful façades and fountains are softly illuminated and through the open shutters of grand *palazzi* there are glimpses of sumptuously frescoed and stuccoed ceilings. Perhaps the loveliness of their city has made most Romans complacent: most are content to simply wander the *centro storico*, pausing perhaps to buy an ice cream or to sit on a café terrace sipping a tisane (Romans are modest boozers). It's as if they are spoiled by beauty and feel they don't need more than fabulous sunsets from Ponte Sisto or the gleaming cobbles of the Roman streets at night after rain.

Which is not to say the city is dull at night. You just have to know where to go to find the action. There are wine bars where you can hob-nob with the yuppies and intellectuals; smart bars which act as a backdrop for the preening and posturing of the designer set; trendy bars where the city's young hedonists congregate before moving on to a disco; gay and lesbian clubs and bars (*see* p.344) and, liveliest of all, the hangouts of Rome's vaguely alternative crowd, an eclectic bunch of young expats, bikers, ageing hippies and cultural gurus: the only people in Rome to take alcohol seriously.

As soon as spring starts, in April, every night is a night for going out until November: every Roman from 20 to 35, single or not, goes out every night in summer, meeting in piazzas and on street corners around 7pm and maybe going to the Vineria in Campo de' Fiori for an *aperitivo*. After a couple of hours of what, to an outsider, looks like loitering, groups move off to pizzerias and trattorias for a cheap dinner. Romans can spend hours trying to decide where to eat. After dinner, the streets teem once more with wandering Romans, maybe stopping off for an ice cream or a

coffee. In the few m... winter, nights out ma... to Fridays, Saturdays ...

Trovaroma and *Rom...* p.323) will let you know ... going on each night in t... clubs and discos, but it's als... worth calling in at the tren... bars, where you can usually p... up fliers that give discounted entrance into certain establish- ments or, if you're lucky, meet someone who'll get you in free. Most Romans head for the clubs some time after midnight; the worst time to arrive at a club is 1am, when you may have to wait to get in. Bouncers can be very selective about who they let in, according to Roman ideals of chic and beauty impenetrable to a visitor. There's generally no point in arguing if you're turned away, but you may be able to avoid the humiliation by phoning to reserve a table and a bottle, and arriving early (around midnight).

Every area has its own style. San Lorenzo, the area near the univer- sity, is where students rent their flats and has a lively 18–25 scene, casual and noisy, based around vegetarian restaurants, pubs and live music venues. Everything is cheap and crowded. Testaccio, at the foot of the Monte dei Cocci, is the biggest club district of the city; far from sleeping families, you'll find a wide selection of nightlife here. Ostiense, another student quarter, is also a night- time hotspot. Its Via di Libetta boasts a 100-metre strip of clubs, although it's a difficult place to reach on foot, and tricky to find. Campo de' Fiori, right in the centre, is much more accessible for visitors. It's where all ages meet for a drink at sunset, beloved by winos, expats and the trendy crowd alike. Alternatively, just off Piazza Navona, not more than five minutes' walk away, you will be plunged into the most glamorous corner of town, historically at least the meeting point for film and TV actors and fashion designers. Put on your walking shoes if you plan

...ight out in Trastevere. You can ...lore the *vicoli* – the alleyways – ... an ice cream, or check out ...ars and pubs in the area.

... the 18th century, when the ...rists hung out in the ...Caffè Greco, ...xpatriates have had their ...watering holes, where they can drink like Anglo-Saxons without shocking the locals. All are lively, most attract a fairly young crowd, and in all of them you should have no problem meeting people. They can be easily spotted by their names: you can be fairly sure you are not heading for an authentic Roman experience in a place called the Fox and Hounds.

For details of live music venues, *see* 'Entertainment', p.322.

Bars

Barflies can drink until around 1am on some of the loveliest piazzas in Rome, flit to a trendy little bar or late-night drinking den, and see the dawn in at one of Piazza Venezia's raffish all- nighters, the resort of carabinieri, hippies, buskers, whores and East European pimps.

Campo Marzio

Bar della Pace G7
Via della Pace 4–5, **t** 06 686 1216; **bus 116, 116T. Open** Tues–Sun 10am–2am.
This is the place for the *vitelloni*, Rome's loafers, wannabe TV stars and the fashion bunch. Drinks are expensive, but it's a great location on a corner a stone's throw from Piazza Navona; its terrace is an ideal location for watching young, glamorous Romans at play.

Bar del Fico G7
Piazza del Fico 26, **t** 06 686 5205; **bus 116, 116T. Open** daily 10am–2am.
Another trendy bar, with tables outside summer and winter under the ancient fig tree that gives its name. It's right in the heart of the Piazza Navona zone, one of Rome's most famous nightspots, and is

popular with a good Italian and international mix.

Jazz Café G7
Via Zanardelli 12, **t** *06 686 1990;* **bus** *70, 86, 87, 116, 116T, 204, 492.* **Open** *Tues–Sun noon–2am.*
Although it has changed hands and style frequently in the last five years, in its most recent incarnation the Jazz Café is a fun place to spend the evening, Roman-style, over a drink. There is a piano bar in the basement and, when no pianist is available, loud music is played – the style changes with each change of management.

Jonathan's Angel G8
Via della Fossa 16, **t** *06 689 3426;* **bus** *116, 116T.* **Open** *daily 1pm–2am.*
A kitsch alternative if you are browsing around the Piazza Navona area.

Il Piccolo G8
Via del Governo Vecchio 74–5; **bus** *40, 46, 62, 64.* **Open** *Mon–Sat 5pm–1am.*
Seductive little wine bar. Try the fruits of the forest sangria.

Sottosopra G8–9
Via dei Chiavari 4–5, **t** *06 6889 2857;* **tram** *8,* **bus** *63, 630, 780.* **Open** *Tues–Sun 6pm–3am.*
Rome's first art bar, the 'topsy-turvy' stages a new exhibition every week. The cocktail bar and restaurant also has disco nights on Friday, Saturday and Sunday.

Taverna del Campo G8
Campo de' Fiori 16, **t** *06 687 4402;* **bus** *116, 116T.* **Open** *Tues–Sat 8am–2am.*
A good selection of *aperitivi*, pizzas and *tartine* make a perfect light dinner for the taverna's trendy clientele. Pistachio shells on the floor is the rule.

Trinity College I8
Via Collegio Romano 6; **bus** *62, 63, 81, 85, 95, 117, 119, 492.* **Open** *daily 7am–5am.*
Popular two-storey pub. College-style décor. Guinness, Harp, Kilkenny and food are available.

Vineria Reggio G8
Campo de' Fiori 15; **bus** *116, 116T.* **Open** *Mon–Sat 9.30am–2pm and 6pm–1am; until 2am on Saturday.*

A peaceful place for a sandwich and glass of wine at lunchtime, the Vineria – as it is commonly called for short by its regulars – is anything but quiet in the evening, when it, the piazza and every Vespa seat and car bonnet around host an animated crowd of bikers, ageing hippies, intellectuals, art students, scruffs and the more alternative expats.

Tridente

Gusto Wine Bar H5
Via della Frezza 23, **t** *06 322 6273;* **bus** *81, 117, 119, 204, 590, 628, 926.* **Open** *daily 10am–midnight.*
A stylish 'cigar bar' with a tea room, which also serves cocktails and hosts live music sessions in the evenings. Next door there is a very good pizzeria (brunch on Sundays) and restaurant, as well as a shop selling all you need for an authentic Italian kitchen.

Victoria House H5
Via di Gesù e Maria 18; **bus** *117, 119.* **Open** *daily 6pm–1am.*
The most Anglo-Saxon of Rome's expat pubs, as you'll realize when you step in and have to duck to avoid a flying dart (the board is right by the door). All the furniture is imported from Sheffield.

Capitoline and Tiber Banks

Bartaruga H9
Piazza Mattei 8, **t** *06 689 2299;* **bus** *30, 40, 46, 62, 63, 64, 70, 87, 492.* **Open** *Tues–Sun 10am–2am.*
A good example of kitsch *barocco napoletano* – contemporary Rococo – on the piazza that houses the famous *tartaruga* (tortoise) fountain. It serves beers and cocktails, and is a very lively meeting place after dinner.

Caelian Hill and the Aventine

Il Seme e la Foglia H13
Via Galvani 18, **t** *06 574 3008;* **bus** *673, 719.* **Open** *Sept–July Mon–Sat 8am–2am, Sun 6pm–2am.*

The perfect place to stop for a coffee before heading for a club in Testaccio. Very lively at night.

Quirinale, Viminale and Esquiline Hill

Druid's Den M9
Via San Martino ai Monti 28; **metro** *Cavour;* **bus** *75, 84, 204.* **Open** *daily 6pm–12.30am.*
Animated – occasionally rowdy – Irish pub, popular with the pint-swillers from the FAO. Atmosphere resembles a students' union bar. Occasional live Celtic music.

Fiddler's Elbow L–M8
Via dell'Olmata 43, **t** *06 487 2110;* **metro** *Cavour;* **bus** *75, 84, 204.* **Open** *5pm–1.30am.*
Irish pub popular with Romans. Young and lively, although the presence of modestly drinking Italians makes it a little more subdued than Druid's Den; bring an instrument if you have one.

Trimani M6
Via Goito 20, **t** *06 446 9661;* **metro** *Termini;* **bus** *60, 61, 62, 75, 84, 90, 116T, 175, 492.* **Open** *Mon–Sat 11.30–3 and 5.30–12.30.*
Well known for its fine wine selection, with a relaxed atmosphere nonetheless.

Trastevere and the Janiculum

Bar Gianicolo E11
Piazzale Aurelio 5, **t** *06 580 6232;* **bus** *870.* **Open** *Tues–Sun 6am–3am.*
A good place either for breakfast or for an aperitivo at sunset. A meeting point for the crowd from Monteverde, the pleasant modern residential area just beyond it.

Bar della Malva F9
Piazza San Giovanni Malva 14, **t** *06 5882 0317;* **bus** *23, 280.* **Open** *Wed–Mon 6am–midnight.*
This bar in the centre of Trastevere is very lively during the daytime with 'Trasteverini'; in the evening you will find a vivacious international crowd, music and drinks.

Dog and Duck H10
Via della Luce 70; tram 8, bus H, 23, 280, 780. **Open** *8.30pm–4am.*
One of Rome's first Irish pubs, where no one speaks Italian. Darts and backgammon are played in a small room downstairs.

Friends G10
Piazza Trilussa 34, **t** *06 581 6111; bus 23, 280.* **Open** *6.30am–2am.*
A trendy design bar with very good *aperitivi*. Lively at night, when videos and art are shown.

Ombre Rosse G10
Piazza San Egidio 12–13, **t** *06 588 4155; bus 23, 280.* **Open** *Mon–Sat 7am–2am, Sun 5pm–2am.*
Right next to Rome's main English-language cinema, this bar attracts an international crowd for beers and cocktails. It's a good place to stop off in Trastevere.

San Calisto G10
Piazza San Calisto 3–5, **t** *06 583 5869; bus 23, 280.* **Open** *Mon–Sat 6am–1.30am.*
The most authentic, unpretentious Italian bar of Trastevere, low prices and no frills. Laid back, scruffy and open all day, with a small terrace that spills out into the piazza on summer nights.

Outside the Centre

Caffè Parnaso Off maps
Piazza delle Muse 22, **t** *06 807 9741; bus 360.* **Open** *7.30am–1.30am.*
It's not quite Parnassus, but Monte Parioli does offer fine views over Rome. The café has tables out all year. It tends to be very lively on Sunday afternoons in winter and hot summer nights, and pleasantly quiet on spring evenings.

Chiosco di Ponte Milvio Off maps
Largo Diaz; bus 32, 69, 200, 232. **Open** *April–Nov daily 6pm–2am.*
A lovely place to have an *aperitivo* and relax out of doors, but it can get crowded in the summer after 10pm. Sometimes art exhibits hang from the trees. It's not a tourist place, and has to be reached by bus from the centre.

Down Under D2
Via E. Turba 34; bus 32, 69. **Open** *8.30pm–3am.*
Warm atmosphere in this Oz pub between the Vatican and Monte Mario, where you can play darts in a big lively room downstairs (but don't try using the decorative boomerangs).

Zodiaco Off maps
Viale Parco Mellini 90, **t** *06 3549 6744; bus 23, 30, 31, 69, 70, 88.* **Open** *10am–1am.*
Well off the beaten track, in the Parco Mellini on Monte Mario, with a marvellous view of the city. Look at the photos on the walls inside to get a glimpse of Rome as it was. Good ice cream.

Clubs and Discos

Rome's discos and clubs range from the exclusive, long-established haunts of the glitterati (where you're unlikely to get in unless you sparkle with money and fame too), through trendy discos where fashion victims bop to not-quite-the-latest House beats, to scruffy alternative venues where you don't need to worry if your clothes are crumpled or your hair unwashed. They are all expensive – you can pay €15–30 even in dismal places – with entrance prices reflecting the fact that Romans drink modestly: the owners can't count on profitable bar sales, even when the prices are outrageously inflated (as they often are). The main clubbing nights are Thursday, Friday and Saturday, and during the rest of the week entrance is usually cheaper. You'll also find lots of theme nights and special events (like fashion shows) laid on in an effort to attract the crowds.

Alien M4
Via Velletri 13–19, **t** *06 841 2212; bus 38, 63, 80, 86, 88, 92, 217, 313, 360, 490, 491, 495.* **Open** *Sept–May Tues–Sat 11pm–4am, June–July Sat 11pm–4am.*
Very hip (for Rome). House music, catwalk-style dress, and raised platforms for the show-offs to dance on. Very popular, especially on Tuesdays, with a mainly 25–35-year-old crowd. It's big, but has quite a selective door policy. One of the longer-running clubs in town. Do not plan to go there on a Sunday – it's the worst night.

Alpheus H15
Via del Commercio 36, **t** *06 574 7826; bus 23, 769.* **Open** *Sept–June Tues–Sun 10pm–4.30am, July–Aug Fri and Sat 10pm–4.30am.*
Concerts, live music, art events and gay evenings are held at this important and very big club in Ostiense. Girls get in free before midnight.

Blue Cheese (ex-Bocciodromo) G14
Via di Monte Testaccio 23, **t** *06 5728 8312; bus 95, 673.* **Open** *Tues–Sun 10pm–4am.*
A former bowling club, with a big underground atmosphere. It occasionally stages concerts, book launches and art exhibitions. Look out for Blue Cheese party nights.

Brancaleone Off maps
Via Levanna 11, **t** *06 820 0959; bus 60, 311, 342, 343, 344.* **Open** *Thurs–Sun 10.30pm–5am.*
With origins as a *centro sociale* (see below), Brancaleone is now officially a private venue, although it maintains an open-to-all door policy. It has a bar, cinema and art shows, concerts and European DJs on Friday nights.

Circolo degli Artisti Off maps
Via Casilina Vecchia 42, **t** *06 7030 5684; bus 85, 105, 157, 412, 810.* **Open** *Tues–Sun 9pm–3am.*
University student paradise with a disco, live music, art exhibitions, pay TV for football matches and, in summer, '5,000 metres under the stars' nights.

Classico Off maps
Via di Libetta 3, **t** *06 5728 8857; bus 23, 769.* **Open** *Tues–Sun 10pm–4am.*
In the heart of the Ostiense nightlife suburb, where it's hard to distinguish one place from another, Classico has an open space in front with video projections on one of the walls. Inside,

there are three different zones, with club, groove, loft music and sometimes live gigs. See also 'Gay and Lesbian', p.347.

Ex Magazzini Off maps
Via dei Magazzini Generali 8/bis, t 06 575 8040; bus 23, 769. Open daily 9pm–4.30am, Sun also 4.30am–9pm
Pulls mostly a student crowd with its concerts and DJs. On Sunday mornings there is a market (vintage records and books) in the club, with free brunch.

Gilda J6
Via Mario de' Fiori 97, t 06 678 4838; bus 117, 119. Open Sept–June Tues–Sun 11pm–4am.
Jacket required, tie obligatory. You might meet some of the local politicos here, at the piano bar or on one of the comfortable couches. If you can get an invitation, there are usually exhibits of some kind before the official opening hours. Elegant and stuck-up, Gilda is a Rome institution, with a tight door policy. The best and easiest way to get in is by calling in advance to book a table and order a bottle.

Piper M2
Via Tagliamento 9, t 06 841 4459; tram 3, 19, bus 63, 86, 92, 630. Open Thurs–Sat 11pm–4am.
Another institution, this one with a history. The first miniskirts in Rome were seen here in the 1960s. The Piper has survived two decades by revamping itself every season and laying on theme nights, fashion shows and gigs almost every night. Live music every Monday. A little passé now, with an enthusiastic pick-up scene. It's open in the afternoons for teenagers, and on Friday, Saturday and Sunday draws a young crowd.

Riparte Café F12
Via degli Orti di Trastevere 7, t 06 586 1816; tram 3, 8, bus H, 23, 44, 75, 280, 780. Open Mon–Sat 8pm–1am.
Trendy hangout of Rome's fashionistas, drawn by its stylish design and music. Loud and commercial, attracting those who are trendy enough to breach its tight door policy.

Zoobar G14
Via di Monte Testaccio 22, t 06 6537 3017; bus 95, 673. Open Sat and Sun 9pm–3am.
Pop and commercial selection. Great fun. Relaxed admission policy – anyone welcome.

Centri Sociali

Radical Romans squatted many disused forts and other buildings around Rome in the 1970s and 1980s. These squats still house alternative communities, who also welcome the not-so-alternative to concerts and parties. Food, prepared communally, is often available – generally cheap bowls of pasta, but at the Villaggio Globale you may find African dishes too. While elements of bourgeois opinion are, naturally, opposed to the squats, the *centri sociali* are welcoming, easygoing and entirely unthreatening. There may be a small charge for events, which goes towards the activities.

Forte Prenestino Off maps
Via Delpino, t 06 2180 7855; tram 5, 19, bus 114, 312. Open daily, times vary according to events.
Once a fort, this enormous occupied structure is an extraordinary place to visit. It hosts a multitude of activities including concerts, a tattoo and piercing salon, art events and a trattoria where you

can eat pasta on Sundays. Hosts a day-long party on 1 May.

Villaggio Globale G14
Ex-Mattatoio, Lungotevere Testaccio, t 06 5730 0329; bus 170, 781. Open daily, times vary according to events.
This former abattoir hosts an African restaurant on Friday nights, and frequent dance nights, often with live music. Check *Roma c'è* or *Trovaroma* for the programmes of this very active organization.

Towards Dawn

One favourite late-night activity is to make the *cornetti caldi* circuit, reminiscent of the sweet-tooth delirium that supports 24-hour doughnut shops in American suburbs. Join in the fun at the **Forno**, a bakery at Vicolo dei Cinque 40 (G10), the *gelateria* **M. Marcucci** at Piazzale Ponte Milvio 26 (off maps), or go to **Via Cernaia 47/a** (L6); brush sleeves with Rome's underworld at **Castellini** on Piazza Venezia (I8); or join the transvestites eating freshly baked pizza at **Pizzalandia**, Piazza del Risorgimento 46/a (D5–6). Real Romans know plenty of other places around the city and its suburbs where you can find *cornetti* all night, but you'll need a car for most of the rest. Other places to try are Piazza Cavour, Via Oderisi da Gubbio and around San Giovanni.

In the summer, watermelon and *grattachecche* – crushed ice with fruit-flavoured syrups – can be picked up all night at kiosks along the Lungotevere. There's one on Lungotevere Marzio, just by Ponte Umberto 1 (G7).

Entertainment

Compared with London, Paris, Berlin or New York, Rome's cultural offerings are pretty limited and provincial. Neither its orchestras nor the opera company are of international standard, it rarely attracts major international artists, and there's little sign of innovation in either theatre or ballet. The same goes for rock and pop: home-grown fare is pretty dire and visits by major US and UK bands are rare. There is, however, plenty of jazz, and enough Latin American music for you to salsa every night.

Listings & Tickets

The best source of what's on is *Trovaroma*, a weekly listings supplement which comes free with *La Repubblica* on Thursdays, although obviously it's in Italian. *Roma c'è*, a weekly magazine, also provides bundles of information about music, cinema, art exhibitions, shopping, restaurants and a section in English called 'Don't Miss', listing major events – also published weekly on Thursdays. *Wanted in Rome*, the newspaper of the English-speaking community, is issued on the 15th of every month, and has some information on what's on.

Tickets for concerts and other events go on sale weeks in advance, and can be purchased from agencies around town. A small charge (around €1.50–2) is made for this *prevendità* service.

Ticket Agencies
Anubis, Via Somalia 213, **t** 06 860 0719.
A.S.S.O. Card, Via Modena 30/a, **t** 06 487 1350.
Box Office Ricordi, Via del Corso 506, **t** 06 320 3790. Viale Giulio Cesare 88, **t** 06 375 0375.
Messaggerie Musicali, Via del Corso 473, **t** 06 6819 2349.
Orbis, Piazza Esquilino 37, **t** 06 474 4776.
w *www.ticketone.it*
w *www.ticketweb.it*.

Music

There are any number of live music venues, most of them given over to jazz and Latin American music, virtually all of them unpretentious places where the emphasis is on having a good time rather than cutting a *bella figura*. The more interesting concerts tend to be towards the weekend – check your *Trovaroma* or *Roma c'è* before setting out.

Because of Italian licensing laws, virtually all live music venues are private clubs, which means you sometimes have to become a member in order to attend even a single concert. Membership is usually in the order of €2.50–10 and lasts for a year and you have to pay for the concert tickets too. If you stay long enough there may be some free events as well. A club may offer a discount if you tell them you're only passing through the city.

Jazz, Blues and Latin American

Alexanderplatz C5
Via Ostia 9, **t** *06 3974 2171*; *metro Ottaviano, bus 49*. **Open** *Mon–Sat 8pm–1am*.
Well-established and very well known jazz and blues club with a restaurant and a sushi bar. In the summer the concerts move to Villa Celimontana, and are called 'Jazz & Image Alexanderplatz'. Concerts nearly every night. Popular, so reserve.

Big Mama G11
Vicolo San Francesco a Ripa 18, **t** *06 581 2451*; *tram 8, bus H, 44, 75, 780*. **Open** *Wed–Sun 9pm–2am*.
Hot crowded jazz and blues venue in Trastevere. A few 'names', but more often local bands playing covers. Smokers are segregated into a room on the side. Attracts a slightly older crowd of jazz-lovers.

Caffè Latino H14
Via di Monte Testaccio 96, **t** *06 5728 8384*; *bus 95, 673*. **Open** *Tues–Sun 8pm–2am*.

Jazz, soul and salsa pumped out in a small, sweaty room, with an interesting concert programme. Go early on Saturdays if you want to get in before it reaches its 400-person limit. The usual crowd of 25–35-year-olds. Admission €10.

Caruso H14
Via Monte Testaccio 36, **t** *06 574 5019*; *bus 95, 673*. **Open** *Tues–Sun 8pm–2am*.
Latin-American music in one of the caves hollowed into the side of Monte Testaccio.

Criscamngiù G8
Piazza della Cancelleria 87, **t** *06 6830 8888*; *bus 40, 46, 62, 64, 116, 116T*. **Open** *Tues–Sun 10am–2am*.
A brand new venue with promise. It's a simple and elegant bar during the day and plays live music in the evening. Check *Roma c'è* for gigs.

Folkstudio K9
Via Frangipane 42, **t** *06 487 1063*; *metro Cavour, bus 75, 84, 117, 204*. **Open** *Tues–Sun 7pm–1am*.
Acoustic, folk, blues, and occasionally avant-garde classical and contemporary music. Bring your own drinks.

Four XXXX Pub H13
Via Galvani 29–29/a, **t** *06 575 7296*; *metro Piramide, tram 3, bus 23, 30, 75, 95, 280, 673, 716, 719*. **Open** *9.30pm–2am*.
Tex-Mex bar with a room in the basement for music. Usually jazz, small live bands and singers, with a very cosy atmosphere. Check the programme for special events.

Gregory's J6
Via Gregoriana 54, **t** *06 679 6386*; *metro Spagna, bus 117, 119*. **Open** *10pm–3am*.
Jazzy and romantic, very small and atmospheric. A good quality selection of Italian and occasionally international jazz.

Gusto Wine Bar H5
Via della Frezza 23, **t** *06 322 6273*; *bus 81, 117, 119, 204, 590, 628, 926*. **Open** *daily 10am–midnight*.
This nicely designed bar holds jazz jam sessions in the evening. It's also a 'cigar bar' with pizzeria, restaurant and shop attached.

Il Locale G7

Vicolo del Fico 3, **t** *06 687 9075;* ***bus*** *116, 116T.* **Open** *daily 6pm–1am.*

In the heart of the Piazza Navona nightlife zone, this *locale* plays drum and bass, jazz and Italian music. It's a straight club with DJs on nights when there are no live musicians and it occasionally augments its musical offerings with photo exhibitions. Being so central, it can get very crowded, but it's pleasantly informal.

La Palma Off maps

Via Giuseppe Mirri 35, **t** *06 4359 9029;* ***metro*** *Tiburtina,* ***bus*** *71, 111, 168, 204, 211, 409, 490, 491, 492, 495, 545, 649.* **Open** *8pm–2am.*

One of the most interesting music venues in town, large, comfortable and informal, with open-air concerts in summer. Broad selection of jazz gigs – check *Roma c'è*. Also a restaurant.

Rock and Pop

The chances of your visit coinciding with a major rock or pop concert are low – most international groups bypass Rome in favour of the trendier northern cities. If you have the chance to be in Rome for your favourite band's gig, the major venues are **PalEUR** (the Palazzo dello Sport in EUR) and **Stadio Flaminio** (at Foro Italico). Ticket prices are on a par with those in Britain, but audiences tend to be more subdued.

Accademia 90 G10

Vicolo della Renella 90, **t** *06 6589 6321;* ***tram*** *8,* ***bus*** *H, 23, 280, 780.*

Live rock on three floors. There is a pizzeria on the top floor *terrazza,* an Italian variant on rock and roll.

Alpheus H15

Via del Commercio 36, **t** *06 574 7826;* ***bus*** *23, 769.* **Open** *Sept–June Tues–Sun 10pm–4.30am, July–Aug Fri and Sat 10pm–4.30am.*

Purpose-built complex in Ostiense, usually with three events happening simultaneously in its three halls. Some good rock concerts, events and parties – and a decent restaurant. Also holds a disco (*see* 'Nightlife', p.320).

Blue Night D7

Via delle Fornaci 8–10, **t** *06 630 0011;* ***metro*** *Ottaviano,* ***bus*** *64.* **Open** *Tues–Sun 8pm–1am.*

Rock, blues and pop, mostly acoustic, Italian.

Club Picasso H14

Via Monte Testaccio 63, **t** *06 574 2975;* ***bus*** *95, 673.* **Open** *Tues–Sat 9pm–2am.*

A Testaccio cellar with live indie, funk, blues, rock and occasionally jazz bands. Cabaret evening on Tuesday.

Riparte Café F12

Via degli Orti di Trastevere 7, **t** *06 586 1816;* ***tram*** *3, 8,* ***bus*** *H, 23, 44, 75, 280, 780.* **Open** *Mon–Sat 8pm–1am.*

Live music every evening in a stylish environment. Strict door policy, so dress up.

Classical Music and Opera

Accademia Filarmonica Romana H3

Via Flaminia 118, box office **t** *06 320 1752;* ***metro*** *Flaminio,* ***tram*** *2,* ***bus*** *88, 204, 231, 490, 495, 628, 926.*

The academy organizes concerts in various places around town, including the Giardino della Casina Vagnuzzi, Sala Casella and Teatro Olimpico, playing a range of popular works from the classical repertoire. Performances occasionally feature dance too.

Accademia Nazionale di Santa Cecilia E7

Via della Conciliazione 4 (auditorium); ***bus*** *30, 64; Via dei Greci (main seat); Via Vittoria 6 (box office),* **t** *06 361 1064;* ***bus*** *117, 119.*

For symphonic music, Rome's celebrated Accademia Nazionale di Santa Cecilia (the patron saint of music) offers regular orchestral performances in the auditorium in Via della Conciliazione. Smaller recitals are usually performed at the Accademia's headquarters in Via dei Greci, near the Spanish Steps. Music varies from Bach to Bruce Springsteen, for Rome's best orchestra. Also guest artists.

Associazione Musicale 'Il Tempietto'

t *06 8720 1523 for information.* *Performs at locations all over town, ask for details when you book your tickets.*

One of the most active classical music associations in town, with a very rich programme all year round. Features young artists performing classical music and, in the summer, some foreign choirs. Concerts take place in churches and archaeological sites.

Istituzione Universitaria Concerti P7

Aula Magna, Università La Sapienza, Piazzale Aldo Moro 5, **t** *06 6361 0051;* ***bus*** *C, 71, 204, 492.*

Concerts organized for students but open to everyone, with a wide range of genres. Concert calendar starts October and ends April.

Oratorio del Gonfalone F8

Via del Gonfalone 32/a, **t** *06 687 5952;* ***bus*** *23, 40, 46, 62, 64, 116, 116T, 280, 870.*

Medieval, baroque, chamber and choral music. Tickets may be more expensive for big name performances. Book at least a week in advance for this very central venue; reservations can be made by phone.

Teatro dell'Opera di Roma L7

Piazza B. Gigli, off Via del Viminale, **t** *06 481 7003,* **w** *www.opera.roma. it;* ***metro*** *Repubblica,* ***bus*** *H, 40, 60, 64, 70, 71, 116T, 170.* **Open** *for winter season Nov–May.*

Ranked among Italy's top five, the opera performs in winter; some tickets go on sale two days before each performance (when you may be able to get cheaper ones). In July and August the Opera moves to a variety of outdoor locations, including the Baths of Caracalla.

Teatro Sistina J6

Via Sistina 129, **t** *06 420 0711;* ***bus*** *49, 61, 62, 71;* *wheelchair accessible.*

The Concerti della Telecom Italia (formerly Concerti Italcable) is a series of concerts held between November and April; tickets are free but you'll need to reserve as long in advance as you can.

Cinema

As an English-speaking foreigner, your chances of taking in a good film in Rome are slim, as all films in Italy are dubbed, and the only regular English-language cinema is the Pasquino. Several cinemas, however, now have set days when the films are in their original language – *versione origi-nale*. All films are shown at 4, 6, 8.30 and 10pm – programme times are only altered for exceptionally long films – with an interval in the middle.

Alcazar G11
Via Cardinale Merry del Val 14, t 06 588 0099; tram 8, bus H, 23, 280, 780; wheelchair accessible.
Original language day is Monday in this slightly dilapidated cinema, which shows interesting films. You'll have to stand if you're late.

Greenwich G13
Via Bodoni 59, t 06 574 5825; tram 3, bus 23, 30, 75, 280, 95, 170, 280, 716, 781.
A nice little cinema in Testaccio, which shows films by Italian directors (hence no English-language night) that do not always get distributed elsewhere. Don't be put off by the queue, as everyone usually gets in.

Intrastevere F9
Vicolo Moroni 3, t 06 588 4230; bus 23, 280.
Shows films in *versione originale* when it can get them. Very small screens, but a good selection.

Nuovo Olimpia I7
Via in Lucina 16, t 06 686 1068; bus 117, 119.
Versione originale films when available. Good international and Italian independent films.

Nuovo Sacher G11
Largo Asciani 1, t 06 5811 8116; tram 3, bus 23, 44, 75, 280.
A cinema famously owned by Italian director Nanni Moretti (best known abroad for his 1994 film *Caro Diario*) and run according to his principles, with no interval during screenings.

Pasquino F10
Piazza San Egidio, t 06 580 3622; tram 8, bus H, 23, 280, 780.
Presents a different English-language film, usually recent second-run, every few days. Avoid screen 3. The international crowd meets here and hangs out in the restaurant and internet café.

Quattro Fontane K7
Via Quattro Fontane 23, t 06 474 1515; metro Barberini, bus 116T.
Four screens, showing films that do not get a wide distribution. Also a bar and small bookshop.

Quirinetta I7
Via M. Minghetti 4, t 06 679 0012; bus 62, 63, 81, 85, 95, 117, 119, 160, 175, 204, 492, 628, 630, 850.
Very near the Trevi Fountain, the Quirinetta has a big screen and Dolby surround sound – and shows films in *versione originale* every day.

Cinema Clubs

Cinema clubs are easy to join for a small fee at the door and usually show films in their original language. In the dog days of summer the colossal 'bread and circus' marathon outdoor film showings can be a lot of fun, even if in Italian (*see* 'Estate Romana', p.326).

Grauco Film Ricerca R10
Via Perugia 34, t 06 782 4167; bus 81, 105, 157, 412, 810.
Alternative programming in an intellectual, film-student atmosphere.

Il Labirinto F4
Via Pompeo Magno 27, t 06 321 6283; bus 70, 280, 913.
More experimental film in an underground cinema.

Theatre and Dance

Although there are scores of theatres for Italian speakers, there's little on offer if you only speak English. The theatre season runs from October to May, with some outdoor performances in summer (*see* 'Estate Romana', p.326). Rome is not a good dance city, but it's worth keeping an eye out for performances by visiting companies.

Teatro Argentina H8
Largo Argentina 52, t 06 687 5445; tram 8, bus H, 30, 40, 46, 62, 63, 64, 70, 81, 87, 186, 492, 628, 810, 916; wheelchair accessible. Try to book tickets 2–3 weeks in advance.
The most interesting and well-known theatre in Rome, with a beautiful interior. A modern and international programme.

Teatro India G15
Lungotevere Papareschi, t 06 6380 4601/2; bus 170, 766, 780, 781; wheelchair accessible.
Modern adaptation of an industrial space (rare for Rome), right on the river – very pleasant in spring. Avant-garde theatre, art shows and club nights too.

Teatro Olimpico Off maps
Piazza Gentile da Fabriano 17, t 06 326 5991; bus 204, 231, 910; wheelchair accessible. Some tickets available one week in advance.
International dance and theatre.

Teatro Parioli Off maps
Via G. Borsi 20, wheelchair accessible; t 06 6802 2329; bus 53, 168, 217. Call for tickets one week ahead.
The famous Maurizio Costanzo TV talk show is recorded live here every night – your chance to be on Italian television, participating in the best of studio-based light entertainment.

Teatro Politecnico GI
Via G.B. Tiepolo 13, t 06 361 1501; tram 2, bus 204.
A largely contemporary programme, mainly in Italian, with occasional performance art and live music.

Teatro Quirino I7
Via M. Minghetti 1, t 679 4585; bus 62, 63, 81, 85, 95, 117, 119, 160, 175, 204, 492, 628, 630, 850; stalls wheelchair accessible.
Classic Italian repertory theatre. High standards, but not much experimentation.

Teatro Sistina J6
*Via Sistina 129, **t** 420 0711; **metro**
Barberini, Spagna, **bus** 116, 116T, 117,
119, 590; wheelchair accessible.*
International and Italian musicals
and occasionally concerts.

Teatro Valle G–H8
*Via del Teatro Valle 23, **t** 6880 3794;
bus 30, 40, 46, 62, 64, 70, 81, 87, 116,
116T, 186, 204, 492, 628; wheelchair
accessible.*
One of the most beautiful old
theatres of the city (built in 1727).
Contemporary theatre is usually
included in its programme.

Teatro Vascello D–E12
*Via G. Carini 78, **t** 589 8031; **bus** 710,
44, 75, 870, 871; wheelchair accessible. Some tickets on the night.*
A good place for dance and festivals, such as the annual Roma
Europa Festival in September.

Teatro Vittoria H13
*Piazza San Maria Liberatrice, **t** 06
574 0598; **tram** 3, **bus** 23, 30, 75,
280, 716. Book tickets one week in
advance.*
Specializes in comedy. A historical
theatre of the city.

Estate Romana

The heat traditionally pushes
Romans to search for cooler places
in summer – *villeggiatura* – but
habits are changing. In the past
the city would have been deserted
in August, with shops, bars,
cinemas and theatres all closed
for the annual holidays. Now,
although families still make an
exodus, many young people stay
in town for the summer, and a
series of events is organized most
years by Rome's city hall, known as
the Estate Romana (Roman
Summer). The programme of
events is printed in *Roma c'è* or
Trovaroma (*see* p.323), or details
can be found through the
Comune di Roma (**w** *www.
comune.roma.it*). Events vary
annually (some years it doesn't
happen at all), but some of the by-
now almost regular features
include: **Fiesta**, on the Via Appia
Nuova (a 10-minute train ride
from Termini Station) – a reconstruction of a South-American
pueblo with 10 restaurants, 3
open-air clubs, salsa classes, pubs,
stalls selling costumes, hats and
accessories, and, if this all sounds
appalling, an interesting
programme of big-name concerts

from Latin America; **Cinema
Massenzio**, one of the original
events of the Estate Romana –
screenings of last season's big hits
under the stars, with views of the
Colosseum at night beyond;
Testaccio Village (G–H14) – a rather
commercial rock venue with
restaurants and bars, in the
middle of the Testaccio clubbing
area, the village is a rather
commercial rock venue with
restaurants and pubs; at **Villa Ada**,
'Roma Incontra il Mondo' (Rome
Meets the World) – theatrical
performances staged on an island
in a small lake in this park in the
north of Rome, with a good selection of international artists
invited to perform; **Villa
Celimontana** (K–L11) – a park on
the far side of the Colosseum that
plays host to fine jazz concerts,
as well as a sushi bar and an
elegant café.

Ironically, Rome's other major
summer draw was initiated by
Mussolini – opera staged in the
Baths of Caracalla. In recent years
it has been subject to the vicissi-
tudes of noise environmentalists,
who claim that the vibrations
created by certain sopranos as
they hit the high notes damage
the ancient walls. Once again,
check listings guides for details.

Shopping

'City where all is sold!' sneered Jugurtha, the North African rebel, who found the Romans in the imperial age ready to sell the catapult to flatten themselves. Modern Rome is one of Italy's most thrilling shopping cities, and will still sell you just about anything – from Castelli Romani wine to Piranesi prints, and the odd bit of Baroque bric-a-brac – if you pay enough for it. There are few bargains – most Romans buy their clothes and household goods at the markets or department stores, and these are more like Marks and Spencer or Woolworth than Selfridges or Macy's. Rome, alongside Milan, is the capital of off-the-peg designer fashions, as well as of *haute couture*. There are also a growing number of affordable local boutiques, which each year create their own unique home-made collections with an eye to comfort and good quality fabrics as well, of course, as looks.

Via Condotti, leading straight into the Spanish Steps, is Rome's most famous shopping street – its Bond Street or Fifth Avenue – although the whole area between Piazza di Spagna and the Via del Corso (once known as the 'English Ghetto' for its population of fleeceable milords) is full of fancy boutiques and shops. Nearly all of Italy's big-name designers have outlets here, many so plush that their customers feel obliged to put on the dog just to go in and buy more clothes. Other areas to try: Via Cola di Rienzo for less expensive clothes; Piazza Navona, the Pantheon and Campo de' Fiori for the trendy and off-beat, including overpriced used clothes that fascinate the French; Via dei Cestari, north of Corso Vittorio Emanuele, for monkish, priestly, and nunnish fashions, reliquaries (relics are Rome's most traditional souvenir, after all) or monstrances; for souvenir kitsch, Termini Station and the streets around the Vatican offer John XXIII barometers, papal flicker pictures, kooky scarves, and Colosseum ashtrays.

Shopping hours are from 9am (or 10am for high fashion) to 1 or 1.30pm, then 3.30 to 7.30, although most shops in the centre now stay open from Monday to Saturday, 10am straight through to 7pm. Most food shops, however, have stuck with the traditional siesta break, and are open 7.30–1.30 and 5–8; they close from October to May on Thursday afternoon, from June to September on Saturday afternoon, and all year round on Sunday. A few markets are open all day every day. Many other shops close all day on Sunday and on Monday morning. Hairdressers stay closed on Monday afternoons too. Travel agents shut for the weekend. Romans prefer to do their shopping in the late afternoon and early evening, so you'll find shops much less crowded in the morning.

A note on sizes: Italian clothes are lovely, but if you have a large-boned Anglo-Saxon build, you may find it hard to find a good fit, especially in trousers or skirts, and shoes are often narrower than the sizes at home. For a size conversion chart for clothes and shoes, see p.67.

Antiques

Trawl the shops in and off **Via del Babuino** (H4–I5) for luxurious furniture and paintings, *objets d'art* and Baroque Madonnas and crucifixes in search of a new home. Look for 20th-century 'antiques' and bric-a-brac on nearby **Via delle Carrozze** (I6). The shops around **Via dei Banchi Nuovi** (F7), **Via del Pellegrino** (G8) and **Via dei Coronari** (F7) are more fun, if a notch below Via del Babuino in prices and quality; the shopkeepers here try to make up for it by rolling out the red carpet, lighting torches and lining the street with kumquat bushes for a twice-yearly **Antiques Festival** in mid-May and mid-October.

Some of the shops to look out for: **Moretti**, at Via dei Coronari 95, with antique scientific and astro-

nomical instruments, and **Bottegantica**, Via di San Simone 70 (a dead-end alley just off Via dei Coronari) with antique majolica. Most of the antique shops, however, tend to a Baroque sensibility (and most of that is 18th- and 19th-century stuff). Some exceptions: **Fabrizio Lombardi**, Via dei Coronari 31, for kitschy collectables; **L'Art Nouveau** at no.221, offering what its name implies, and more of the same at no.8; the proprietors of both these places have a very good eye for the most artistic creations of the *belle époque* and beyond. For low-key late 19th-century and and early 20th-century antiques go to **Via del Boschetto** (K8), the closest Rome can get to New York's Greenwich Village.

Via Margutta (I5) is Rome's mainstream arty farty lane. In spring and autumn the street sponsors outdoor exhibits of some of the most blatantly commercial art you're likely to encounter outside Athena.

Prints, art books and old postcards are sold every day except Sunday at the market in **Largo della Fontanella Borghese** (H6) and every now and then at the *bancarelle* on **Largo dei Lombardi** (H5). It is a lament of young artists in Rome that Romans don't buy art like the foreigners do. If you do find something you like that's too large to carry home, antique shops are usually all too happy to take care of shipping.

Agostinelli Off maps
Via D. Bartolomeo 42, Ostia; train Ostiense–Acilia, then bus 04B.
An Ali Baba's cavern of antiques. The owner will be proud to show you his little museum upstairs.

Angel's Station K8
Via Panisperna 244; metro Cavour, bus H, 40, 60, 4, 70, 71, 75, 84, 117, 170, 204.
Porcelain, jewellery, paintings and pictures, all starring angels.

Comics Bazar F8
Via dei Banchi Vecchi 127–128; bus 40, 46, 62, 64, 116, 116T.
Trinkets and curiosities.

Estremi G7
Corso del Rinascimento 54–56; bus 30, 70, 81, 87, 116, 186, 204, 492, 628.
Colonial furniture and African clothes and instruments.

Gea G7
Via dell'Orso 82; bus 30, 70. 81, 87, 116, 116T, 186, 204, 492, 628.
For an authentic and certified piece of Italy's history; Roman, Etruscan and Greek finds.

Mercanzia I7
Via dei Bergamaschi 49; bus 62, 63, 81, 85, 95, 117, 119, 160, 175, 204, 492, 628, 630, 850.
Genuine American crud by the ton, from old Happy Meal toys to Elvis Presley dolls.

Books

Anglo-American Book Co. I6
Via della Vite 27; bus 52, 53, 61, 71, 80, 85, 116, 116T, 117, 119, 160, 590.
Run by a dour bibliophile. Small but densely packed with good books in English. The best place to look for anything unusual.

L'Angolo del Collezionista di Pileri C4
Via Giordano Bruno 51; metro Cipro, bus 490, 492, 913, 990, 991, 999.
Mostly old books for young children, but also many interesting Mussolini-era works in Italian.

The Corner Bookshop G10
Via del Moro 48; bus 23, 280.
Welcoming English bookshop in the heart of Trastevere.

Economy Book and Video Center L7
Via Torino 135/a; metro Repubblica, bus H, 16, 40, 60, 64, 70, 75, 84, 105, 116T, 157, 170, 204, 360, 590, 649.
American-run. Wide selection and lots of second-hand paperbacks.

ESIA N6
Via Palestro 30; metro Castro Pretorio; bus 38, 75, 86, 92, 217, 360.
Academically-orientated books, textbooks and journals in English.

La Grotta del Libro G8
Via del Pellegrino 169; bus 40, 46, 62, 64, 116, 116T, 916.
Discount and remaindered Italian-language books.

Herder H7
Piazza Montecitorio, bus 116, 116T.
Good and scholarly, mostly German but also English, Italian, and many children's books.

Libreria del Viaggiatore G8
Via del Pellegrino 78; bus 40, 46, 62, 64, 116, 116T, 916.
Travel books in Italian, French and English – including this one.

The Lion Bookshop I5
Via dei Greci 36; metro Spagna, bus 117, 119.
One of Rome's largest selections of books in English, including a big children's section.

Open Door Bookshop G10
Via della Lungaretta 25; bus 23, 280.
Cosy new and second-hand English bookshop in Trastevere.

Clothes
Designer and One-off

Armani I6
Via Condotti 76–77; metro Spagna, bus 117, 119.
Roman outlet of the celebrated Milanese designer; his Emporio (Via del Babuino 140) features younger, more casual styles.

Battistoni I6
Via Condotti 61/a; metro Spagna, bus 117, 119.
A luxurious boutique in the second courtyard of the Palazzo Caffarelli, long Rome's most fashionable tailor. Made-to-order shirts and suits; also cashmere sweaters, blazers, and coats with an English touch.

Bomba H4
Via dell'Oca 39; bus 81, 117, 119, 590.
Maria Cristina Bomba creates high-quality women's clothing that stands out for its comfort, style and femininity, all made in-house. Items range from silk and velvet evening dresses to scarves, bags, hats and hand-woven cotton stockings. A space is dedicated to emerging local fashion and jewellery designers. The shop also makes clothes to order.

Cenci, Angelo H8
Piazza della Rotonda 77; bus 116, 116T.
Classy shirts and suits for men. High quality and prices.

Cenci, Davide H7
Via di Campo Marzio 1–7; bus 116, 116T.
No relation of Angelo (above), Davide Cenci has dressed middle-aged ladies and gentlemen with conservative good taste for generations.

Conbipel B6
Via Anastasio II at Viale degli Ammiragli; metro Cipro, bus 490.
One of Rome's less expensive stores for machine-washable, basic knitwear for women, men, and children (although women get by far the largest selection).

Ermenegildo Zegna I6
Via Borgognona 7/e; metro Spagna, bus 117, 119.
The three-storey showcase for one of Italy's top designers of men's clothing, stocked with business, smart casual and weekend wear, as well as shoes and leather goods. Stunning silk ties. Suits and dress shirts made to measure.

Fendi I6
Via Borgognona 36/e; metro Spagna, bus 117, 119.
Roman-designed furs, fashions, bags, shoes and accessories, with a megastore on Via di Fontanella Borghese, beyond the Corso.

Le Gallinelle K8
Via del Boschetto 76; metro Cavour, bus H, 40, 60, 64, 70, 71, 117, 170.
Wilma Silvestri sits behind the counter of her little workshop, pedalling away on her antique sewing machine. Creative clothing for men and women plus deluxe vintage pieces.

Gucci I6
Via Condotti 8; metro Spagna, bus 117, 119.
One of the most famous Italian designers for style and quality.

Krizia I5
Piazza di Spagna 87; metro Spagna, bus 117, 119.
Another Milanese offering trendy, flattering clothes for women.

Missoni Donna I5
Via del Babuino 96; **metro** *Spagna,* **bus** *117, 119.*
Trademark colourful knits.

Missoni Uomo I6
Piazza di Spagna 78; **metro** *Spagna,* **bus** *117, 119.*
Men are catered for at this store.

Sorelle Fontana I5
Salita di San Sebastianello 6; **metro** *Spagna,* **bus** *117, 119.*
The 'Fountain Sisters' have been dressing smart women *all'italiana* since the '30s.

Le Tableau I5
Via Belsiana 96/a; **metro** *Spagna,* **bus** *117, 119.*
Long skirts and dresses, knitwear and suits. Quality and charm.

Valentino I6
Via Bocca di Leone 16; Piazza Mignanelli 27; **metro** *Spagna,* **bus** *117, 119.*
Piazza Mignanelli is *haute couture,* the 'Lion's Mouth' off-the-peg.

Valentino Uomo I6
Via Condotti 12; **metro** *Spagna,* **bus** *117, 119.*
Utterly insane, but worth a look.

Versace I5, I6
Via Bocca di Leone 26; Via Frattina 116; **metro** *Spagna,* **bus** *117, 119.*
Sister Donatella keeps the empire of the late lamented Gianni going.

Versace Uomo I6
Via Borgognona 25; **metro** *Spagna,* **bus** *117, 119.*
More sequins here.

Yves Saint Laurent I5
Via Bocca di Leone 34–5; **metro** *Spagna,* **bus** *117, 119.*
The Roman boutique of French fashion's biggest money maker.

Lingerie

Demoiselle I6
Via Frattina 93; **metro** *Spagna,* **bus** *117, 119.*
Stocks La Perla – lingerie elegant enough to wear to parties.

Simona H5
Via del Corso 82; **bus** *52, 53, 63, 80, 95, 116, 116T.*
All the best Italian brands, La Perla included, can be tried in comfortable dressing rooms. Helpful staff.

Shoes, Gloves and Bags

Domus I6
Via Belsiana 52; **metro** *Spagna,* **bus** *117, 119.*
Wide selection of women's shoes; what they don't have, you can order from them.

Gucci I6
Via Condotti 8; **metro** *Spagna,* **bus** *117, 119.*
Shoes, bags, suitcases (as well as clothes) needing no introduction.

Ibiz G9
Via dei Chiavari 39; **tram** *8,* **bus** *116.*
One of the best for wallets, handbags and suitcases.

Loco G8
Via dei Baullari 22; **bus** *116.*
'Crazy' in Spanish translates as trendy shoes in Rome.

Raphael Salato I5
Piazza di Spagna 456; **metro** *Spagna,* **bus** *117, 119. Via Veneto 104;* **bus** *52, 53, 63, 80, 95, 116, 116T.*
Rome's modern Raphael puts his masterpieces on your feet instead of the wall, and gets more money for them, too.

Second-hand and Alternative

Moon G8
Via del Governo Vecchio 89/a; **bus** *40, 46, 62, 64.*
Vintage classics – a miniature fashion museum, in fact.

Sempreverde G8
Via del Governo Vecchio 26; **bus** *40, 46, 62, 64.*
Trendy period clothes – from whichever era is in fashion. The stock is renewed every month.

Department Stores

Except for La Rinascente, these are all comparable to Debenhams or K-mart, asking reasonable prices for the kind of reasonable clothes that most people wear. Perfumes and cosmetics, however, are usually more expensive in these stores than in small *profumerie,* which often offer special discounts.

COIN E5, O11
Via Cola di Rienzo; **bus** *30, 70, 81, 186, 280, 590, 913. Piazzale Appio;* **metro** *San Giovanni,* **bus** *16, 85, 87, 117, 186.*
Good value for clothes and kitchen gear.

La Rinascente I7, M4
Piazza Colonna; **bus** *62, 63, 81, 85, 95, 116, 116T, 117, 119, 160, 175, 204, 492, 628, 630, 850. Piazza Fiume;* **bus** *63, 86, 88, 92, 217, 360, 490, 491.*
Six rather old-fashioned floors of clothes. The Piazza Fiume branch has kitchenware in the basement.

Standa G11, E5
Viale Trastevere 62–64; **tram** *8,* **bus** *H, 780. Via Cola di Rienzo 173;* **bus** *30, 70, 81, 186, 280, 590, 913. Also branches at Viale Oceano Atlantico 271, Corso Francia 124, Via dei Colli Portuensi, Viale Regina Margherita, Piazza Talenti and throughout the city.*
Very popular and economical. The Trastevere branch has a food supermarket in the basement. The Via Cola di Rienzo branch sells food only. All other branches stock good value clothing.

UPIM J6, M8
Via del Tritone 172; **bus** *52, 53, 61, 62, 63, 71, 80, 116, 116T, 119, 630. Piazza S. Maria Maggiore;* **bus** *70, 71, 75, 204. Other branches across the city.*
Italy's Woolworth's.

Food

Castroni E5, H4
Via Cola di Rienzo 196; **bus** *30, 70, 81, 280. Via Flaminia 28;* **metro** *Flaminio,* **bus** *88, 95, 204, 490, 491, 495. Branches at Via Ottaviano 55, Piazza della Balduina 1, Via di Boccea 173, Via Catania 54, Piazza Irnerio 73.*
If, unlike the Italians, you ever get tired of Italian food, this chain sells imported delights from all over the world – Marmite, fragrant Thai rice, hot Madras

curry paste, blueberry muffin mix, maple syrup and so on. It also sells a lot of top-quality Italian food: rice , pasta, olive oil, balsamic vinegar, jam, honey, nuts, chocolate, candied fruit, coffee and liquorice. The best branch is the Via Cola di Rienzo one.

Albero del Pane H9
Via Santa Maria del Pianto 1; bus 30, 40, 46, 62, 63, 64, 70, 81, 87, tram 8.
Organic food (although no fresh produce), vitamin and herb shop. Well worth a browse.

Ciavatta J7
Via del Lavatore 5; bus 71, 117, 119.
A neighbourhood shop near the Trevi Fountain with a small but choice selection of wines, cured meat and cheeses; top-quality canned tuna, coffee, pasta, etc.

Franchi E5
Via Cola di Rienzo 200–204, w www.franchi.it; bus 30, 70, 81, 280.
Top quality Italian-style deli, with stand-up meals served at the counter. An exceptional range of cheeses and cured meats from all over Italy, superb-quality pasta, truffles, and ready-made dishes such as braised artichokes (in winter) and tomatoes stuffed with rice (in summer). World-wide shipping available.

Supermercato Di Meglio H7
Via dei Giustiniani 18; bus 116, 116T.
An attractive supermarket, with two rare commodities for Rome: location a stone's throw from the Pantheon, and long opening hours (8am–10pm daily).

La Tradizione B5
Viale Cipro 8/e; metro Cipro, bus 490.
Another of Rome's top shops for cheese, with hard-to-find Italian cheeses and cured meat products as well as country bread, truffles, and some French imports.

Volpetti H13
Via Marmorata 47; tram 3, bus 23, 280.
Top-quality meats, cheeses and breads from every corner of Italy,

plus a good selection of pre-prepared foods. Free tastes, but watch the hard sell. Don't miss Volpetti Più, the cafeteria-style restaurant around the corner (*see* 'Eating Out', p.312).

Home

Art'è H7
Piazza Rondanini; bus 30, 31, 70, 87, 116.
Rome's headquarters for the height of high-tech gimcracks, creative kitsch, and Art Deco folly (clocks, kitchen décor, etc.). A great sense of design and a sense of humour (in Italy, would you really expect to see the Andrews Sisters appearing as kitchen canisters?).

L'Atelier F8
Via Sforza Cesarini 54; bus 40, 46, 62, 64.
Custom-made *trompe l'oeil* decoration on wood: doors, panels and mail boxes.

Cesari H4
Via del Babuino 195; bus 119.
Refined linen and bath towels, plus women's nightclothes.

C.U.C.I.N.A. I5
Via Mario dei Fiori 65; metro Spagna, bus 117, 119.
Everything for the kitchen, from imported pâté moulds to Italian copper pots and Indian mats. Stylish and pricey.

Cucinando B6
Viale degli Ammiragli 10; metro Cipro; bus 247, 492, 907.
Professional-grade cookware, including Agnelli pots and pans (aluminium & teflon) and handy plastic-handled paring knives by Victorinox.

La Galleria G10
Via della Pelliccia 29/a; bus 23, 280.
Decorative objects gathered from all over Italy.

Ikea Off maps
Via Agnanina 81; metro Anagnina, then a free shuttle service every 30 minutes from 10am to 8pm daily.
A showcase for the Swedish furnishing and design giant – useful if you're staying awhile.

Leone Limentani I9
Via del Portico d'Ottavia 47; bus 30, 40, 46, 62, 63, 64, 70, 81, 87, tram 8.
A dusty, maze-like basement store, Limentani has for generations sold china and crystal, dishes and cutlery made by the world's leading manufacturers – including Rosenthal and Ginori. Items do not have price tags (you wait in line to be given a price tour), but the savings can be significant.

Oriental Quality C3
Via della Giuliana 105, bus 23, 70.
Bargain oriental carpets. Machine-made, but with beautiful patterns and colours. From €100 for a medium-sized carpet.

Poignée J6
Via Capo le Case 34; bus 117, 119.
Brass handles in many different styles – or made to order – as well as brass accessories for your bathroom.

Sono un Autarchico K8
Via del Boschetto 92; metro Cavour, bus H, 40, 60, 64, 70, 71, 117, 170.
Aluminium pots, French-style tumblers, glass orange squeezers, and other objects for the kitchen.

Jewellery

Ashanti K8–9
Via del Boschetto 117; metro Cavour, bus H, 40, 60, 64, 70, 71, 117, 170.
Creative jewellery in coral, silver, copper, and hard stones with an ethnic flair. Custom orders taken.

Bulgari I6
Via Condotti 11; metro Spagna, bus 117, 119.
The king of jewellers, in the most palatial of Via Condotti's palatial shops, which in a previous incarnation was the *trattoria* where Severn bought the languishing Keats' daily take-away.

Georg Jenssen I6
Piazza di Spagna; metro Spagna bus 117, 119.
Gorgeous-looking jewellery and tableware in silver and stainless steel by the Danish designer famous for simple elegance.

Massimo Mario Melis H7

Via dell'Orso 57; bus 30, 70. 81, 87, 116, 116T, 186, 204, 492, 628.

Creations with an archaeological bent, using bits of old Roman glass and bronze.

Massoni I6

Largo Goldoni 48; metro Spagna, bus 81, 117, 119.

A long-established family firm much frequented by Italian and visiting Hollywood film stars.

Ourouboros

Via Sant'Eustachio 15; bus 116.

Exceptional hand-made jewellery, often following unique designs.

Markets

Rome's food and flower markets are a treat. Every last stall-holder could pass for a B-movie character actor, with a sarcastic wit to match, not to mention the fact that they sell fruit and vegetables of a freshness rarely seen these days. **Campo de' Fiori** (G8; *bus 40, 46, 62, 64, 116, 116T. Open Mon–Sat dawn–1*) has the added charm of being in the *centro storico*. There is a covered *mercato rionale* in every *rione* or neighbourhood *(see p.40)*, and there are good open-air markets at **Piazza San Cosimato** in Trastevere (G11; *tram 8, bus H, 23, 280, 780. Open Mon–Sat dawn–1*), **Piazza Testaccio** (H13; *tram 3, bus 23, 30, 75, 95, 170, 781, 280, 716. Open Mon–Sat dawn–1*) and **Via Andrea Doria** (C4; *metro Ottaviano. Open Mon–Sat dawn–1*), one of the most lavish, near the Vatican. The famous market in **Piazza Vittorio Emanuele II** has been moved to the nearby Caserma Pepe and along Via Turati (N8; *tram 5, 14, 19, bus 70, 71. Open Mon–Sat dawn–1*) as the result of a years-long fight between the city hall along with local residents, who wanted the market to move in order to restore Piazza Vittorio to its original beauty, and the sellers, who did all they could not to be moved. It still sells good fresh produce.

Rome's famous flea market, at **Porta Portese** in Trastevere (F13; *tram 3, bus 23, 44, 75, 280. Open*

Mon–Sat dawn–1), happens every Sunday morning from the crack of dawn until lunch time. The old *contessas'* genteel junk (chandeliers, Mussolini memorabilia and gilded stuccoes), which shoppers once sought, is now swamped by car parts, plastic buckets, pirated cassettes and smuggled lighters, but with luck and persistence you can still find early 20th-century furniture, brass lamps and attractive bric-a-brac. After 10am Porta Portese gets very crowded, so watch out for pickpockets. Also be wary of the clusters of people betting on cards – no one has ever been known to win

The morning new and used clothes market of **Via Sannio**, just outside Porta San Giovanni (O11; *metro San Giovanni, bus 16, 86, 87, 117, 186. Open Thurs and Sat mornings*), is a good hunting-ground for designer cast-offs – and the odd retro item.

There's a print market in **Piazza della Fontanella Borghese** (H6; *bus 81, 116, 116T, 117, 119, 590, 628. Open Mon–Sat 8am–1pm*). You could also visit the **Mercato de' Fiori**, Rome's wholesale plant and flower market in Via Trionfale (C4; *metro Cipro, bus 490, 492, 913, 990, 991. Open Tues 5am–1pm*).

Music

Disfunzioni Musicali P8

Via degli Etruschi 4–14; bus C, 71, 204, 492.

The hippest record shop in town, selling and exchanging new and second-hand discs, CDs and cassettes. Good selection of US alternative bands.

Metropoli Rock M7

Via Cavour 72; metro Termini, bus 75, 84, 117, 204.

An amazing number of recordings as well as some genuine collectors' items.

Ricordi I8, H5, D5

Via C. Battisti 120; bus 30, 40, 62, 63, 64, 70, 81, 87, 186, 492, 628, 810, 916. Via del Corso 506; metro Flaminio, bus 117, 119. Viale Giulio Cesare 88; metro Ottaviano,

Lepanto, *bus 51, 70, 590, 913, 991, 999.*

Rome's biggest selection of music CDs, DVDs, records, tapes etc.

Paper, Crafts and Stationery

Ecole de F8

Vicolo della Moretta; bus 40, 62, 64, 116, 116T.

One of the larger shops, with a wide and up-to-date selection.

Stilofetti H7

Via degli Orfani 82; bus 116, 116T.

Devoted to antique and modern fountain pens; will also repair your old favourite.

Vertecchi I5

Via della Croce 70/a and 38; metro Spagna, bus 117, 119.

Located in a *palazzo* guarded by telamones sculpted by Bernini's father, Pietro, this is Rome's best fine art and crafts shop; the branch at no.38 specializes in fine art papers.

Perfumes

Aveda J6

Rampa Mignanelli 9; metro Spagna, bus 117, 119.

The only Aveda shop in Italy, with lotions, make-up, beauty treatments, shampoos, hair dyes, and perfumes, all made from natural ingredients. Also visiting 'star' hair stylists (reservations essential), makeovers, make-up lessons, and aromatherapy. No smoking.

Ippoliti M4

Corso d'Italia 99; bus 490, 491, 495.

Well stocked with all the top-of-the-market scent brands.

Lush G9

Via dei Baullari 112; bus 40, 46, 62, 64, 116, 116T.

The soap and cosmetic chain store that looks more like a deli shop: lotions are refrigerated ice-cream style and sold by weight. Famous sayings about soap hang on the wall, including Napoleon's telegram to Paolina: 'I will return in three days. Don't wash yourself.'

Unusual and Offbeat

Eredi Baiocco H10
Via della Luce 3/a; **tram 8, bus** *H, 23, 280, 780.*
Chalk casts of Roman statues in all sizes, and various decorative pieces to hang on the wall. Custom orders.

Etnica G8
Via del Pellegrino 90; **bus** *40, 46, 62, 64, 116.*
Hand-made crafts imported from Africa, such as masks, carpets and tapestries.

In Folio F8
Corso Vittorio Emanuele 261; **bus** *40, 46, 62, 64.*
Retro fans and kitchen tools, plastic and stainless steel furniture.

Ai Monasteri G7
Corso del Rinascimento; **bus** *30, 70, 81, 87, 116, 116T.*
Monastic products from around Italy. Choose between a Trappist *rosé* and a Franciscan *amaro* from Umbria, along with holy chocolates and remedies to keep your hair on your head.

Profondo Rosso F5
Via dei Gracchi 260; **bus** *30, 70, 186, 280, 590, 913.*
Books, videos, masks, dolls and trinkets all related to horror. Small museum on the first floor.

Il Tucano I7
Via dei Crociferi 44; **bus** *62, 63, 81, 85, 492, 628.*
A big store selling an eclectic array of goods made in southeast Asia, including wooden toys, bags, lamps, cast-iron portable griddles, teapots, baskets and tableware at unbeatable prices.

Wines and Booze

La Bottega del Vino di Anacleto Bleve H9
Via Santa Maria del Pianto 9/a–11; **tram 8, bus** *H, 63, 630, 780.*
First-rate wine shop also offering a 'wine parking' service in its cellar. Also rare and fine whisky, champagne and rum. Doubles up as an informal restaurant at lunch time *(see p.307).*

Il Cantiniere F9
Via di Santa Dorotea 9; **tram 8, bus** *H, 23, 280, 780.*
In the heart of Trastevere, with three pretty rooms and (rare for a wine cellar) summer seating outside.

Enoteca Buccone H5
Via di Ripetta 19; **bus** *81, 117, 119, 204, 628, 926.*
A drinker's heaven; 20-year-old bottles of Scotch under an inch of dust.

Il Goccetto F8
Via dei Banchi Vecchi 14; **bus** *40, 46, 62, 64.*
A traditional neighbourhood hangout with great wines by the glass and a well stocked cellar. Cheese, cured pork and pickles.

Trimani M6
Via Goito 20; **bus** *38, 86, 92, 217, 360.*
Family-run for three generations, this is one of Rome's better stocked wine shops, with a range from Frascati Doc to Sassicaia 1989. Also runs a wine bar and restaurant round the corner *(see p.310).*

Al Vino Al Vino K8
Via dei Serpenti; **bus** *H, 40, 60, 64, 70, 75, 84, 117, 170.*
Attractive neighbourhood *enoteca* with a great choice of wines in the very low to moderate price range (€5–15).

Sports and Green Spaces

Sports

Bad luck those of you wanting to work off the excess pasta: participating in sports is virtually impossible in Rome without paying a hefty membership fee to join a club. You can, of course, jog or cycle most pleasantly in one of the parks, swim gratis on some of Rome's beaches and at Lake Bracciano, or join a group for a ramble outside the city.

The city is not brilliant for spectator sports, either, although there are of course, two top football clubs, Lazio and Roma, the Serie A (first division) winners in 2000 and 2001 respectively. There are also international horse and tennis championships.

The main sports complexes are listed below. For sport-by-sport listings see the following pages.

Foro Italico Off maps
*Lungotevere Marasciallo Diaz; **bus** 32, 48, 53, 186, 200.*
Built by Mussolini, now reserved for football, swimming competitions and water polo, and host to the prestigious international tennis championships in May.

Palazzetto dello Sport
Off maps
*Piazza Apollodoro 10; **tram** 2, **bus** 53, 217.*
Across from Flaminio, tennis, basketball, skating, gymnastics.

Palasport Off maps
*Viale dell'Umanesimo; **metro** EUR Palasport, EUR Fermi.*
EUR's Palazzo dello Sport is used for basketball, boxing, indoor tennis, and rock concerts. It also has an Olympic velodrome, a field hockey ground and a large pool.

Stadio Flaminio Off maps
*Via and Piazza Stadio Flaminio; **tram** 2, **bus** 53, 217.*
Rome's second stadium, just across the bridge from Foro Italico, is used for football and big events.

Stadio Olimpico Off maps
*Viale dei Gladiatori 2; **bus** 32, 48, 53, 186, 200.*
Rome's main football stadium, tacked on to the Foro Italico.

You can watch competitions and championships at two private sports complexes, too.

Acqua Acetosa Off maps
*Via dei Campi Sportivi 48; **bus** 231, 230.*
Up beyond Villa Ada, with fields for rugby, polo and football.

Complesso Sportivo Tre Fontane Off maps
*Via delle Tre Fontane 1; **metro** EUR Palasport, EUR Fermi.*
In EUR, with running tracks, a covered gym and skating rink.

Boating

There are many places in and around Rome where you can charter a boat for an outing in the Mediterranean.

Lake Bracciano is the main boating lake near Rome, with sailing dinghies for hire in most of its villages, and at many of the lakeside restaurants.

Rowing down the Tiber is a popular Roman pastime, but the rowing clubs are very expensive and, on the whole, have long waiting lists. As the clubs won't accept short-term members, it's not worth approaching them unless you're living in Rome.

Rigo Yachts Off maps
*Via Pindaro 50–59; **t** 06 509 0222, **e** rigoyachts@tin.it, **w** www.rigoyachts.com.*
Out towards the coast, this is a good place to contact for a sail down the coast. A 38ft sailing boat costs around €2,100 a week without skipper. Rigo also rents motor boats and smaller yachts.

Bowling

Bowling Brunswick Off maps
*Lungotevere Acqua Acetosa 10, **t** 06 808 6147, **w** www.brunswick.it; **bus** C, 217. **Open** Sept–July daily 10am–2am;*
This bowling alley may be slightly out of the way, but it also offers mini-golf, a restaurant and a bar. Come for cosmic bowling on Friday and Saturday night with strobe lights and fluorescent pins.

The cost of a game ranges from €2.50 a person on a weekday morning to €10.50 at weekends, including shoes.

TM Roma N3
*Viale Regina Margherita 181, **t** 06 855 1184; **tram** 3, 19. **Open** Sept–July Tues–Sun 10–midnight.*
Bowling, bar and ping pong. Video games too, for the less active.

Football

Rome has two football teams, Lazio (**w** www.sslazio.it) and Roma (**w** www.asroma.it). Both play at the Stadio Olimpico (*see* above). Matches happen once or twice a week: Italian League games take place from the last Sunday in August to mid-May on Sunday at 3pm or 8.30pm. Champions' League games take place from the end of August to mid-December and from late March to early May on Tuesday, Wednesday or Thursday at 8.30pm. Tickets range in price from €18–110 and are put on sale 10–14 days ahead. For the hottest matches the sooner you secure a ticket the better. Your hotel concierge might be able to get tickets in advance, but beware of *bagarini* (touts), who demand exorbitant prices for tickets that often turn out to be fake. The *curva* (the end sector behind the goal) has the cheapest tickets (about €18), but be aware that for safety reasons these tickets are not sold to supporters of the visiting team. The Tribuna Monte Mario is where VIPs sit (€75–110).

Ticket Vendors

AS Roma Stores IS
*Piazza Colonna 360, **t** 06 6920 0642; **bus** 62, 63, 81, 85, 95, 117, 119, 160, 175, 204, 492, 628, 630, 850.*
Tickets for AS Roma can be bought at this or any of the other 158 stores in the city (see the website for addresses). Some tickets go on sale in the week preceding the match (the rest are allocated to club members). The remaining tickets go on sale four hours before kick-off at a kiosk outside the Stadio Olimpico itself.

Lazio Point M8

Via Farini 34, **t** *06 6482 6688;* **metro** *Termini, Cavour,* **bus** *16, 70, 71, 75, 84, 105, 157, 204, 360, 590, 649, 714.*

Tickets for Lazio matches can be acquired here.

Orbis L8

Piazza Esquilino 37, **t** *06 474 4776;* **metro** *Termini, Cavour,* **bus** *16, 70, 71, 75, 84, 105, 157, 204, 360, 590, 649, 714.* **Open** *Mon–Sat 9.30–1 and 4–7.30.*

The handiest place to buy all tickets is from this agency.

Box Office Ricordi, Messaggerie Musicali, A.S.S.O. Card, Anubis, **w** www.ticketone.it and **w** www.ticketweb.it *(see p.323)* may be able to sell you tickets for football matches too.

Golf

Golf in Rome is a rich man's sport. During the week a round on the links costs €47–65. In addition, unless you are a *tesserato* (a card-carrying member of the International Golf Federation), most clubs will only allow you to play if you're accompanied by a member. If you prefer to watch, the championships take place from April to October.

Castel Gandolfo Country Club Off maps

Via di Santo Spirito 13 (2.7km on Via Nettunense, after Castelluccia), **t** *06 931 2301.* **Open** *daily 8–dusk;* **adm** *€47 Mon–Sat, €65 Sun, hols.*

The newest, most exclusive and most challenging course in Rome, designed by Robert Trent Jones in a volcanic basin, with an 18th-century Chigi villa beautifully converted into a club house.

Circolo Golf Roma Off maps

Via Appia Nuova 716, **t** *06 780 3407;* **metro** *Arco di Travertino.* **Open** *Tues–Sat 8.30–dusk;* **adm** *€65 Mon–Fri, €76 Sat–Sun.*

It's nearly impossible to play at weekends as this is when championships take place.

Federazione Italiana Golf Off maps

Via Flaminia 388, **t** *06 323 1825,* **w** *www.federgolf.it;* **tram** *2.*

For information on anything to do with championship golf in Italy, contact the federation.

Golf Club Olgiata Off maps

Largo dell'Olgiata 15 (19.5 km on Via Cassia), **t** *06 3088 9141.* **Open** *Tues–Sun 7.30–dusk;* **adm** *€47 Tues–Fri, €65 Sat–Sun.*

Twenty-seven holes, 20 km from the centre.

Golf Club Parco dei Medici Off maps

Viale Parco de'Medici 165 (off the Roma–Fiumicino road), **t** *06 655 3477.* **Open** *Wed–Mon 7–dusk;* **adm** *€47 Mon and Wed–Fri, €65 Sat–Sun.*

The only club within the Grande Racordo Anulare (ring road).

Gyms

As with pools and tennis clubs, gyms and fitness centres are rarely open to non-members.

Roman Sport Center J4

Viale del Galoppatoio 33 (entrance in Via Veneto), **t** *06 320 1667;* **bus** *88, 95, 116, 116T, 204, 490, 491, 495.* **Open** *Nov–May daily 9am–10pm, June–Oct Mon–Sat 9am–10pm;* **adm** *€26 per day.*

A notable exception is the Roman Sport Centre, right in the centre , which sells daily passes to non-residents. Swimming pool, gym, aerobics, heart machines and private instructors.

Strike Music Club Off maps

Via Conca d'Oro 352, **t** *06 812 4903;* **bus** *88, 343, 344.* **Open** *Sept–July Mon–Sat 10–10;* **adm** *€6.50.*

Body-building gym in Montesacro. Lockers available, and an extra fee of €1 for a towel.

Riding and Racing

The time for horse-lovers to visit is May, when the International Horse Show takes place on the Piazza di Siena in the Villa Borghese. Events include cavalry charging as well as jumping.

For keen riders, there are loads of riding clubs, but none accept short-term members. From Sept to May check out *Roma c'è* for riding tours in Lazio and Umbria. Lessons are around €20.

Centro Ippico Fioranello Off maps

Via di Fioranello 101 (near Ciampino), **t** *06 7135 5570.*

One of the only places you can ride in the summer, this riding school offers lessons at €12.50 per hour, and plans to offer excursions too in the future.

Centro Ippico Roma Ovest Off maps

Via Casetta Mattei 322, **t** *06 6615 5013;* **bus** *98, 786.*

Follow country trails and rest in the club house.

Centro Ippico Talenti Off maps

Via Dario Niccodemi, **t** *06 8713 3209;* **bus** *335, 341.*

Take riding lessons in Montesacro, except in August.

Ippodromo Roma Capannelle Off maps

Via Appia Nuova 1255 (12km, before Ciampino), **t** *06 716 771,* **w** *www.capannelle-galoppo.it.*

If you can't get on a horse's back, this is Rome's most famous course to watch show jumping and racing, known as Le Capannelle.

Roma Polo Club Off maps

Via dei Campi Sportivi 43, **t** *06 807 0907;* **bus** *C, 230, 231.*

Lessons given from November to March.

Swimming

The best chance for a swim is to go to the coast – the further away from the Tiber mouth the better – or head up to Lake Bracciano. Rome's pools are only open to members. In summer, however, a couple of sports centres and hotels with pools open them up to the public on a daily rate. There's a pleasant outdoor pool at EUR.

If you want to join a swimming centre, expect to pay €25–50 membership plus €50–70 per month and be prepared to present a medical certificate.

Bear in mind that the hours set aside for free swimming are very limited; check that the pool isn't taken up by a club training session.

AS Urbe Nuoto C5
Via Tunisi, t 06 3972 0797. Open Sept–July Mon–Sat 7–7.
A swimming school with Spartan looks. No lockers.

Centro Sportivo Aventino I13
Via Marmorata 14, t 06 574 0637. Open Sept–June Mon–Sat 8am–10pm.
Pool membership includes free stretch classes three times a week. No lockers.

CSI Off maps
Lungotevere Flaminio 55, t 06 323 4732; wheelchair accessible. Open June–Sept daily, Oct–May Mon–Sat only, 6.30am–8pm.
Swimming school and masters' training alongside free swimming sessions. From June to mid-Sept it opens to non-members. Garden, bar and lockers.

Hilton Off maps
Via Alberto Cadlolo 101, t 06 3509 2040; shuttle bus runs to and from Piazza Barberini once an hour. Open June–Sept Mon–Fri 7–10, Sat–Sun 9–7; adm Mon–Sat €36 a day, Sun and hols €52 a day.
Glass-domed indoor pool with garden, bar, a shallower second pool for children, sauna, Turkish baths, gyms, yoga classes etc.

Piscina Comunale SS. Lazio Nuoto Off maps
Via di Villa di Lucina 82, t 06 541 5522. Open Mon–Sat 6am–8pm; adm Mon–Sat €5, Sun, hols €6.50.
Cheaper, but slightly less central, than the Piscina delle Rose.

Piscina delle Rose G25
Viale America 20, t 592 6717. Open June–mid-Sept daily 9am–7pm, Tues and Thurs until 10pm; adm €10.50.
This Mussolini-era pool in EUR is one of Rome's nicest.

Villa Flaminia Sport Off maps
Via Donatello 20, t 06 322 2019. Open Sept–June 6am–10pm; adm €6.50.
A decent pool, but no lockers.

YMCA Sport Centre Off maps
Viale Libano 68, t 06 592 3595. Open Nov–May 8am–9.30pm.
At EUR. Also a gym.

Tennis

In Italy, tennis is usually played in private clubs, open to members only. In large towns such as Rome, clubs are often way out of the centre. If you would like to join a club, a good central one is the CSI (*see above*), or you can get a list of clubs from the Italian and Lazio region tennis federations.

Federazione Italiana Tennis Off maps
Viale Olimpico 1, t 06 3263 8599.

Federazione Italiana Tennis Comitato Regionale del Lazio Off maps
Via delle Tre Fontane, t 06 592 2551.
One club generously open its courts to the plebs in summer.

Circolo Tennis Belle Arti Off maps
Via Flaminia 158, t 06 322 6529; tram 2. Open to non-members July–Aug; adm €10.50 per hour.
A 10-minute ride from the centre, this club opens its courts to the wider public when its wealthy Roman members escape to the seaside for the summer.

For those who prefer to watch, Italy's annual International Tennis Championships are in May.

Walking

Many cultural associations organize rambles, hikes, treks, bike and cross-country skiing excursions outside Rome. Check the 'Fuoriporta' section of *Roma c'è*, or try one of the following groups.

Four Seasons
t 06 2780 0384, w www.fsnc.it.
Country rambles.

Natura e Avventura
t 06 4288 0810, w www.naturaavventura.it.
Adventures in nature.

Il Sentiero degli Elfi
t 06 8632 0876, w www.tiscalinet.it/sentieroelfi.
Follow the elves down their path.

Green Spaces

Botanical Gardens F9
Entrance on Largo Cristina di Svezia, t 06 4991 7107; bus 23, 280. Open Mar–Oct Tues–Sat 9.30–6.30, Nov–Feb until 5.30 only; adm €2.
Rome's **Orto Botanico** is a tranquil haven sheltering beneath the Janiculum. Here you can see 3,500 species of plants from all over the world, from ancient trees to carnivorous and aquatic specimens. Interesting sections are the Giardino dei Semplici (medicinal plants); the Giardino Giapponese (Japanese); the Giardino per Non Vedenti (for the blind), with herbs and scented flowers labelled in Braille; and the Giardino della Flora Mediterranea. Toilets.

Colle Oppio L9–M10
Entrances on Via Labicana, Viale Monte Oppio, Via Mecenate; metro Colosseo, tram 3, bus 85, 87, 117, 204. Open 8–sunset.
Just opposite the Colosseum, the Colle Oppio or Parco Traiano is now most famous for housing Nero's Golden House, but the prominent walls actually belong to the Baths of Trajan. The park is also popular with dog-walkers and picnicking refugees from the Forum. Bar and *fontanelle* (drinking water fountains).

Giardinetti del Quirinale K7
Entrances on Via del Quirinale, Via Piacenza; bus 71, 117. Open 8am–sunset.
A tiny garden which comes in handy if you need a rest in this very built-up central area.

Giardino degli Aranci I12
Entrances on Via di S. Sabina, Piazza Pietro d'Illiria, Clivio di Rocca Savella; bus 175. Always open.
Perched on top of the Aventine Hill, this is a tiny orange grove, which most Romans don't even know about. It's a steepish walk up, but once at the top there's a scent of orange blossom and good views back over the city, or it's just a short walk further to the famous view through the keyhole to St Peter's (*see* p.169).

Janiculum E8–10

Entrances on Via G. Garibaldi, Via di Porta San Pancrazio, Piazzale Aurelio, Piazza della Rovere; **bus** *44, 75, 870.* **Open** *all days, hours.*

The Janiculum is most popular with Roman *pomicioni* (snoggers) at night. They congregate by their hundreds in cars, on mopeds and Vespas, and even occasionally on foot – summer and winter alike – to admire the views over the city and, more importantly, each other. There are usually refreshment stands selling soft drinks.

Palatine Hill J10

Entrance through the Roman Forum or from Via di San Gregorio; **metro** *Colosseo,* **tram** *3,* **bus** *84, 85, 87, 117, 175.* **Open** *daily 9 until one hour before sunset;* **adm** *€6.*

The groves of the Palatine gardens are a fine refuge from the after-noon sun. *See p.151 for details.*

Villa Ada Off maps

Entrances on Via Salaria, Via di Ponte Salario, Via Panama; **tram** *3, 19,* **bus** *53, 168, 360.* **Open** *daily 8am–sunset.*

Parioli is the name for the huge area north of Villa Borghese, home to Rome's nouveaux riches, their sports-car driving, Barbour-jacket-clad offspring and Filipina maids. It's a residential district of villas surrounded by tiny gardens and curving boulevards lined with oleander trees. The large Villa Ada borders it to the east, formerly Villa Savoia, a hunting preserve for King Vittorio Emanuele III. It is now partly a public park, popular with jugglers, and partly the Egyptian Embassy, housed in the ex-Palazzina Reale (the former royal hunting lodge). Century-old oak trees and redwoods are the

home of squirrels, rabbits and birds, including many protected species. You'll need three hours to explore Rome's wildest park fully, climbing through thick groves, picking up pine cones, or resting by its three lakes. The Egyptians had a lot to do with the building of Rome's first and only **mosque** nearby, designed by postmodern architect Paolo Portoghesi. It's on Via della Moschea, near the **Acqua Acetosa**, a fountain ascribed to Bernini.

Villa Borghese I3–K4

Entrances on Viale Trinità dei Monti, Via di Porta Pinciana, Via Raimondi, Via di Villa Giulia, Piazzale Flaminio, Piazzale del Brasile; **metro** *Spagna, Flaminio,* **tram** *2, 3, 29,* **bus** *52, 53, 95, 116, 490, 491, 495.*

The beautiful gardens of the Villa Borghese, where the pines of Rome seem their most pinishly Roman, are well worth a walk in any season. In autumn for the spectacular red and yellow shades of the falling leaves. In winter for a rest on a sun-kissed bench with a view of the city roofs. In spring, when flower beds and Judas trees explode in a symphony of colours. In summer to catch the breeze and the luxurious scent of magnolias along the shady Viale delle Magnolie. On a Sunday, all of Rome's families with children seem to be out strolling, and a puppet theatre sets up on the Pincio. Villa Borghese also boasts a café, the Casina dell'Orologio – a very pleasant place for a cup of tea. You can rent a bike from the car park between 9am and 7pm daily for €5 a day (**t** *06 322 5240*). *See p.229 for other attractions.*

Villa Celimontana K–L11

Entrances on Piazza SS. Giovanni e Paolo, Piazza della Navicella; **metro** *Colosseo, Circo Massimo,* **tram** *3,* **bus** *62, 63, 81, 8, 95, 117, 160, 175.* **Open** *7am–sunset.*

An attractive, rather hidden park with a wooded area and good play areas for children. In summer it hosts jazz concerts as part of the Estate Romana (*see p.326*). It's a two-minute from the park to Piazza San Gregorio, a popular venue for weddings – always a good spectacle at the end of a Saturday afternoon stroll. Toilets, *fontanelle.*

Villa Doria Pamphili A11–C12

Entrances on Via Aurelia Antica, Via Leone XIII, Via della Nocetta, Via di Porta San Pancrazio, Via Vitellia; **bus** *31, 791.* **Open** *8am–sunset.*

Villa Doria Pamphili, Rome's largest public park, was originally laid out by sculptor Alessandro Algardi for one of the insatiable kinsmen of Innocent X, in the first half of the 17th century. It perches on the Janiculum, stretching along the Via Aurelia, the main road along Italy's coast into Gaul. It's a pretty place full of tall parasol pines and palm groves, with fine views over Rome and a natural lake, almost large enough to get lost in. There are *fontanelle*, playgrounds, a bar, toilets and a roller-skating area. Underneath it is riddled with catacombs, although only the catacombs of San Pancrazio are open for visits (**t** *06 581 0458*).

Children and
Teenagers' Rome

Children's Rome

Italians love children and if you travel in the company of a toddler or two you'll get plenty of smiles and understanding, which might make up for a general lack of facilities and amenities. Most children love Rome and most Romans love children too. The trouble is that the little monkeys never want to see what you want to see, and if you aren't careful your holiday will become a sordid journey into ice cream and pizza blackmail. If your offspring have arrived at the age of reason, a good strategy for a happy holiday is to lay your cards on the table from the beginning: ask them what they'd like to do, and tell them what you want to do, and split the days accordingly (somehow it always works out best if the adults do their bit first).

You can make Rome come alive for your children with a little homework: read your Livy before a trip to the Forum, so you can recite inspiring tales of noble Romans in the very spot where they took place. A good read for the kids is *Asterix the Gladiator*, which takes place in the Rome of Julius Caesar, with fine scenes of Roman baths, apartment houses and the Circus Maximus (although whether or not Rome had Gaulish restaurants is debatable).

Most children enjoy the Colosseum, Castel Sant'Angelo with its dungeons, a trip to the catacombs, the Trevi Fountain, the Villa d'Este at Tivoli, the Monster Park at Bomarzo, and racing up to the top of St Peter's dome (but poor parents!). You could also have your child's portrait (or caricature) drawn in Piazza Navona, or just keep them occupied by letting them sit in cafés with crayons and paper. If money's no object, there are horse and carriage rides around the *centro storico*, leaving from the Spanish Steps (make sure to agree on the fare before you set foot in the carriage).

For letting off steam, see 'Sports and Green Spaces', pp.335–8.

Baby-sitting

Most of the four- or five-star hotels listed in the 'Where to Stay' chapter offer baby-sitting, but do enquire about availability and rates when you reserve your room. Otherwise try one of the agencies (*see* below), or look at the ads in *Wanted in Rome*. There are also 'baby parking' clubs (crèches) in Rome, most out of the centre.

Alpha Communication H6
Via Tomacelli 103, *t 06 6880 2615*.
An established baby-sitting agency with good credentials.

Baby Club P5
Via Baglivi 12, *t 06 4423 0082*.
One reasonably central crèche, with large playgrounds and baby-sitting, day and evening.

Pronto Baby L4–M3
Via Po 22, *t 06 841 3433*.
Another well-recommended baby-sitting agency.

Eating Out

Children's menus and high-chairs in restaurants are more the exception than the rule in Italy, but this does not mean that your two-year-old cannot happily participate in your banquet. He or she will be propped on a pile of cushions by an adoring waiter, and most restaurants will have no problem making simple dishes *fuori menu*, such as *pasta con olio e parmigiano* (pasta with olive oil and parmesan) or *al pomodoro* (with tomato sauce), *minestrina in brodo* (tiny bits of pasta in broth sprinkled with parmesan), *pesce lesso* (steamed fish), *riso al burro* (boiled rice with butter), *verdura lessa* (boiled vegetables), *uova* (eggs) and so on. You should ask for a *mezza porzione* upon ordering and expect a discount (around 30 per cent) on the full portion price. Young Italian kids get a lot of fun out of spaghetti-eating by picking up the 'worms' with their hands, but unles you have a change of clothes for every meal it's a good idea to chop the spaghetti up first. In Rome, a small piece of chewy *pizza bianca*, sold at *pizza al taglio* bakeries, goes a long way as a pacifier, and an ice-cream cone can be a powerful way to head off approaching tantrums. Roman fountains (*fontanelle*), scattered all over the city, spout excellent drinking water which is also fun to 'catch'. Show your children how to close off the spigot from below with a finger, forcing the water to come of the top in a tame stream.

Baby food (*omogeneizzati*) and nappies or diapers (*pannolini*) are available from general stores and supermarkets and, at a steeper price, from pharmacies.

Entertainment

Rome is not particularly well-off for children's theatre, although it is always worth scanning the pages of *Roma c'è*, but there are a few venues for puppetry, mime and child-orientated cinema or virtual reality shows – such as the puppet show on the Passeggiata del Gianicolo on the Janiculum Hill, with outdoor shows in the afternoon. Some other options are listed below.

English Puppet Theatre G8
Piazza dei Satiri, *t 06 589 6201*; *bus 40, 46, 62, 64, 116, 116T*.
There are usually shows on Sunday afternoons between September and Easter, but ring ahead to make sure that day's show really is in English.

Teatro Don Bosco Off maps
Via Publio Valerio 63, *t 06 7158 7612*; *metro Giulio Agricola*.
If your kids speak Italian, are learning the language or just fancy a multilingual experience, they might enjoy this theatre with music, puppets and mimes.

Teatro Mongiovino Off maps
Via G. Genocchi 15, *t 06 513 9405*; *bus 30, 160, 670, 671, 714, 715, 716*.
Another kids' theatre, in the Garbatella district.

Time Elevator I8
Ex-Majestic movie theatre, Via SS. Apostoli 20, *t 06 699 0053*,

w www.time-elevator.it; bus 62, 63, 81, 85, 95, 117, 119, 160, 175, 204, 492, 628, 630, 850. **Open** daily 9am–midnight; **adm** €10.

For a full immersion in English in the history of Rome from its foundation in 880 BC to the present day, you can treat your children to a 45-minute, 3D movie.

Kids Cinema Cola di Rienzo F5
Piazza Cola di Rienzo 88–90, t 06 323 5693; **bus** 30, 70, 81, 186, 280, 590, 913.

A cinema with decoration inspired by well-known fables, which shows only kids' movies and cartoons – but not in English.

Festivals

At Christmas, Piazza Navona (G8) fills with stalls selling calze della befana – the Italian equivalent of Christmas stockings – candies packed in an old sock which young children believe is hung on the chimney by the befana – a witch on a broomstick – on the night of 5–6 January. According to tradition, naughty children get a sock filled with coal instead of sweets and toys, but now the coal is made of sugar and is a treat for good children too. Pastry shops sell special stockings, and stalls on Piazza Navona sell tacky ones. It's still an appealing spectacle around dusk, and is immensely popular with the Romans.

Museums and Attractions

Museo delle Cere J8
See p.116.
Good for a laugh on a rainy afternoon; spot the Seven Dwarfs, Cinderella and the dinosaurs.

Museo di Roma in Trastevere F10
See p.195.
The museum displays six full-scale reconstructions of popular scenes: a street game called saltarello (hopscotch), a pharmacy, a wine wagon, an osteria, a public bill board and a group of roaming flute players.

Castel Sant'Angelo F6
See p.223.
The popes' prison and torture chamber for centuries, the Castel Sant'Angelo is sure to appeal to the gory-minded innocents.

Colosseum K–L10
See p.149.
More accessible to the imagination than the dusty remains of the Forum and the Palatine, especially if that imagination is fed with tales of gladiatorial combat and lions. Don't forget that it was opened in the year AD 80 with a gala massacre of 5,000 animals, roughly one every 10 seconds; the Romans' appetite for such sport led to the extinction of the native elephant and lion of North Africa and Arabia. If this is all too violent and nasty, it's still good fun for kids to climb up to the top.

Catacombs

For reasons mysterious to most adults, the underground holds a particular allure for children.

Catacombs of Priscilla Off maps
See p.234.
The largest and oldest of all catacombs. On the eastern side of Villa Ada, they can be combined with a picnic lunch in the park. Look for frescoes of Jonah and the Whale.

Catacombs of San Sebastiano
Appian Way walks map
See p.249.
Most of the other catacombs are clustered around the Appian Way, including these, where you might want to pause in the chapel on the right to see the original set of the Domine Quo Vadis? footprints.

Circuses

One way to wear out any child is racing around a Roman circus, but don't mention the word as you won't find any trapeze artists.

Circus of Maxentius Appian Way walks map
See p.250.
Maxentius incorporated all the latest circus technology of its era in the construction of his circus, such as the starting stalls for

chariots arranged at an angle to make the race as fair as possible. It's a quarter of a mile long.

Circus Maximus J11
See p.167.
It's not much of a looker, but it still provides a good open space for a vivid imagination fired by racing chariots and horses.

Outside Rome

Monster Park of Bomarzo Day trips map
See p.266.
An unusual day trip, where you can picnic in the company of grotesque monsters carved out of the rock.

Etruscopolis Day trips map
Via delle Pietrare, Tarquinia, t 0766 855 175; see also 'Tarquinia', p.263.
If you plan to visit the Etruscan necropolis of Tarquinia, don't miss this underground historical park with everyday scenes of Etruscan life and seven reconstructed tombs to creep around.

Parks and Playgrounds

Among Rome's many parks, **Villa Ada** (off maps; see p.338) has the largest children's playground, featuring merry-go-rounds, a train, climbing frames and swings, a lake with ducks and, in the warm season, riding lessons on ponies.

Villa Borghese (H3–K4; see p.229), on the Galoppatoio side, has slides (scivoli) and swings (altalene). At the latter, you can rent a bike, roller blades or a boat to paddle on the lake.

Villa Celimontana (K–L11; see p.338) has a playground too.

Zoo J–K2
See p.232.
Rome's once rather fusty zoo is undergoing a slow eco-friendly renovation, and is now called the Bioparco. Elephants, camels, hippos, monkeys, snakes, tigers and panthers are currently on view, and children can visit the Fattoria dei Bambini, a petting zoo with sheep, rabbits and hens.

Shopping

Age d'Or Off maps
Piazza Santiago del Cile 3–4;
bus *53, 168, 217.*
Elegant clothes for children,
custom-made for special events.
Quite expensive.

Berté G8
Piazza Navona 108; **bus** *30, 70, 81,*
87, 116, 116T.
High-quality toys for babies,
clothes and beds as well.

La Casa di Flora G9
Via San Salvatore in Campo 53;
tram *8,* **bus** *H, 40, 46, 62, 64, 63.*
A toy workshop specializing in
dolls' houses.

Cir I5
Via del Babuino 103; **metro** *Spagna,*
bus *117, 119. Piazza Barberini 11;*
metro *Barberini;* **bus** *52, 53, 61, 62,*
63, 80, 95, 116, 116T,119, 204, 492.
Classic baby clothes from Florence
with lace and embroidery, at
surprisingly affordable prices.

La Città del Sole H7
Via della Scrofa (at Largo Toniolo);
bus *116, 116T.*
A small chain, and nothing less
than the most charming and
innovative toy shops in all Italy;
everything clever and creative
from €3 to €160.

Herder H7
Piazza Montecitorio; **bus** *116, 116T.*
Many children's books.

Leonardo Coiffeur Off maps
Via F. Gai 12, **t** *06 324 0340;* **tram** *2,*
bus *C, 53, 200, 201, 204, 222.*
A long-established hairdresser for
children only.

The Lion Bookshop I5
Via dei Greci 36; **metro** *Spagna,*
bus *117, 119.*
Rome's largest selection of children's books in English.

Mel-Giannino Stoppani I8
Piazza SS. Apostoli 65; **bus** *30, 40,*
46, 62, 63, 64, 70, 81, 87, 186, 492.
Specialist children's bookshop,
with activities and workshops for
children in Italian, advertised in
the *Roma c'è* listings magazine.

Pergioco F4
Via degli Scipioni 109–111; **metro**
Lepanto, **bus** *30, 70, 81, 186, 280.*
Video games.

Piccadilly J6
Via Sistina 92; **metro** *Spagna,*
bus *117, 119.*
One of the cheapest places to find
quality baby and infant clothes.

Rachele G8
Vicolo del Bollo 6; **bus** *40, 46, 62,*
64, 116, 116T.
Has its own line of clothing for
children up to 6 years old. Also
takes custom orders.

Rocco Giocattoli Off maps
Viale Libia 46; **bus** *36, 60, 62, 84.*
Good for children's things, all at
discount prices.

Summer Camp

**American Overseas School
of Rome** Off maps
Via Cassia 811, **t** *06 3326 4841,*
f *06 3326 2608;* **shuttle bus.**
Runs a summer day camp (all in
English) for children aged 3–15.
Activities include soccer, volley-
ball, basketball, tennis, swimming
and computer classes. A shuttle
bus picks kids up for the day.

Water Sports

Water Parks

Acquapiper Off maps
*Via Maremmana Inferiore
(29.3km), località Guidonia-
Montecello,* **t** *0774 326 538.*
You'll see huge posters every-
where advertising this water park.

Hydromania Off maps
*Vicolo Casal Lumbroso (Grande
Racordo Anulare, exit 33 to
Pescaccio-Lumbroso),* **t** *06 6618
3183,* **w** *www.hydromania.it;* **bus**
906. **Open** *daily 9–6;* **adm** *€11.50
Mon–Fri, € 13.50 Sat, Sun and hols.*
The nearest to Rome. It has water
slides, a children's lagoon with
floating castles, a large jacuzzi tub
for adults, a wave pool, countless
water games, a poolside disco etc.

**Sporting Club Il Faro
Acquasplash** Off maps
Via Palo Laziale 63, Ladispoli,
t *06 991 2942.* **Open** *daily 10–6;*
adm *€10.*
Waves, slides, galore near the
beach at Ladispoli, north of Rome.

Beaches

Rome's main beaches are at the
Lido di Ostia (Day trips map; *take
the Roma–Ostia road, the Ostiense
– about 30 minutes from EUR – or
the metro to Piramide and a train
from the Stazione Ostiense to Ostia
Lido*) and, heading north, the more
salubrious beaches of **Fregene**,
Maccarese and **Ladispoli** (Day trips
map; *take the Via Aurelia – 20–40
minutes from St Peter's*). The water
is not especially inviting at any of
these places, but it will cool you
down. Many of the beaches are
private. Daily admission costs
around €6–8, which usually
includes beach loungers and
umbrellas. There are plenty of
cafés and refreshment stands.

Maccarese is home to the **Bau
Beach**, a stretch of sand reserved
for dogs to run free (local law
doesn't allow them anywhere else
for a swim and a roll in the sand).
Dogs outnumber humans here –
there's even a fast-food kiosk for
them alongside a restaurant
cooking fish and organic food.

Transport

In Rome, children under 10
travel for free on trams, buses and
the metro. In Italy, children under
four travel for free in FS trains and
children under 12 pay 50 per cent
of the adult fare. Be ready to show
a document proving their age.

Where to Stay

Almost every Italian hotel will
add a children's bed on request,
but it rarely comes free of charge;
expect to pay 35 per cent extra.
Babies and infants may be able to
share their parents' room for
nothing; enquire when you book.

Teenagers' Rome

In many ways Rome is a perfect city for teenagers, large but not too large, with a safe *centro storico* where it's possible to walk and enjoy a vibrant nightlife until 2 or 3am, and plenty of trendy boutiques geared to young shoppers. In the summer, beaches and water parks are a short drive, or in some cases train or bus ride, from town, and the **Estate Romana** (*see* p.326) offers a constant flow of outdoor concerts, movies, theatre performances and discos. **Football** dominates Sunday afternoons from late August through May, punctuated by honking car horns to celebrate victory. AS Roma, one of the two teams of the city, won the Italian Championship in 2001; sales at the club's stores on Piazza Colonna and Corso Vittorio Emanuele went through the roof.

All Roman teenagers aspire to be scooter riders. Visitors can try a moped out at **Scoot a long** (K9; *Via Cavour 302, t 06 678 0206*), at **Scooters for Rent** (J–K6; *Via della Purificazione 84, t 06 4885485*), **I bike Rome** (H3; *in the garage under Villa Borghese, t 06 322 5240*), **Happy Rent** (M8; *Via Farini 3, t 06 481 8185*) or **St Peter Motor Rent** (E6; *Via di Porta Castello 43, t 06 687 5714*) for around €45 a day including two helmets.

Trastevere, Campo de' Fiori and the web of streets around Piazza Navona and Piazza della Rotonda are where teenagers go for pizza, ice cream, beer, wine and night caps. In particular the **Drunken Ship**, on Campo de' Fiori (G8; *bus 116, 116T*), is popular with young Americans studying in Rome and a fixture on pub crawls organized for English-speaking kids – largely to the disgust of Roman teenagers, who are not heavy drinkers. If you wish to join the beer-swilling, contact **Walks of Rome** (L8; *Via Urbana 38, t 06 484 853, e info@walksofeurope.com, w www.walksofeurope.com; metro Cavour, bus 75, 84, 204*).

On a hot Roman night, many a teenager makes a detour to one of the kiosks selling *cocomero* (water melon slices) or *grattacchecca* (crushed ice mixed with fruit-flavoured syrup). Two of the most popular *grattaccheccari* are on Lungotevere Anguillara (H10; *left as you cross Ponte Garibaldi; bus 23, 280*), or Lungotevere Sanzio (G10; *to the right; bus 23, 280*), where there's also a *cocomeraro*.

Close to the Spanish Steps are two major teenagers' attractions. **McDonald's**, on Piazza di Spagna (I5; *metro Spagna, bus 117, 119*), which features ancient Roman décor in its basement dining room, and comes complete with a pasta and salad bar, is one. **Gilda**, on Via Mario de' Fiori (I6; *see* p.321), is the other: a disco that caters to the rich and famous most nights, on Saturday afternoons it opens its doors to tribes of girls in platform shoes and mini skirts escorted by boys in jeans and sportswear.

Teenagers' favourite shopping street in the centre is **Via del Corso** (H4–I8; *see* p.328), which is now closed to traffic and has the feel of a half-mile long school playground. Most shops sell low-quality clothing and shoes styled to impress, but it's also possible to find the odd bargain. For sportswear, go to **Cisalfa**, at the corner of Piazza Augusto Imperatore (H6; *bus 81, 204, 590, 628, 926*). Across the piazza is **Messaggerie Musicali**, well stocked with CDs of the latest sugary Italian pop. **Disfunzioni Musicali** (P8; *see* p.332) is a much more sound music store. The chain stores **Expensive**, **Avant!**, **Etam** and **Intimissimi** (all with branches on the Corso and in every other popular shopping area) sell outer and under clothes for girls, and are all worth a quick look. Better quality clothes for girls can be found at **Baloon**, on Piazza di Spagna (I5; *metro Spagna, bus 117, 119*), which sells good value silk garments (hand washable) and offers a rare, for Rome, customer service: items can be exchanged without a fuss.

The ethnic look is still going strong among Rome's teenagers. At **Fabindia** (F7; *Via del Banco di Santo Spirito 40; bus 40, 46, 62, 64*), you can find original Indian wear for both sexes. **La Chiave** (H8; *Largo delle Stimmate 92; bus 30, 46, 62, 62, 64, 70, 81, 87, 492, etc.*) sells hand-made and exotic gifts, jewellery and scarves. Another ethnic treasure trove is **Il Tesoro** (K8; *Via dei Serpenti 135; bus 117*), with a fast turnover of goods and a great choice of cheap trinkets from pocket mirrors to drawer knobs, furniture and clothes.

If you can't live without a US-style shopping mall, there is **Cinecittà 2** (off maps; *metro Anagnina*), one of the few places where stores are open on Sunday.

Culture-orientated teenagers may like the **Palazzo delle Esposizioni** (K7; *see* p.182), Rome's major venue for temporary photo exhibits and obscure contemporary art and design. The museum hosts international art house film (*film d'autore*) seasons, often in their original language (*versione originale*) with Italian subtitles. See *Roma c'è* for programme details. There is also a café-bar and gift shop (*entrance on Via Milano*), with an arty atmosphere.

The **Pasquino** cinema shows films exclusively in English (F10; *see* p.325). Several other cinemas show *versione originale* (often English) films one night a week. See 'Entertainment', p.325 for cinema details, and check *Roma c'è* for programme details.

344

Gay and
Lesbian Rome

Rome is home to a thriving gay and lesbian community, but gays and lesbians are less visible here than in cities like San Francisco or Amsterdam, so unless you know where to go, you won't notice anything queer about the city. Apart from Via Monte Caprino (next to the Campidoglio), gay cruising grounds are mainly outside the centre, and can only be reached by car.

The best way to touch base with the city's gay and lesbian scene is to go to the **Libreria di Babele** (*see* below) and pick up the magazine *Aut* and a map of gay Rome, both free. The monthly *Time Out* has a Gay & Lesbian section (in Italian), with updated information about parties and special events. If you have internet access, check out w *www.getout.it*, a gay site with glamour, chat, travel, shopping, services and news. For any kind of assistance and information in English, contact the ever-helpful **Circolo Omosessuale Mario Mieli** (*see* below).

Although the Gay Jubileum Day was not part of the Vatican's Holy Year 2000 programme, the Pope at one point conceded that homosexuals are all God's children, too – as long as they remain chaste. Straight Italians tend to be of two minds about the gay community. In the most general sense, in Italy as elsewhere, leftwingers tend to support gay rights, while rightwingers do not. The Italian language has many derogatory words for homosexual, and a widespread Catholic-inspired belief persists that homosexuality prevents people from making anything good of their life.

Rome's present (left-wing) city government, elected in 2001 and serving through at least 2005, is gay-friendly, but the latest (right-wing) national government is not: Silvio Berlusconi's Forza Italia, also elected in 2001, and its political allies are all sadly engaged in a moral campaign against homosexuality. Being homosexual is not, however, a crime under Italian law, and couples – gay or straight – who have lived together for five years or more obtain comparable legal status to married couples. Gay or lesbian couples cannot legally adopt children in Italy.

Associations

Gay

Archivio Massimo Consoli Off maps
Via Dario Bellezza (località Frattocchie), t 06 935 47567. Europe's most important archive (open to the public) for the history and culture of the gay community.

Circolo di Cultura Omosessuale Mario Mieli Off maps
Via Efeso 2/a, t 06 541 3985, f 06 541 3971, e info@mariomieli.it, w www.mariomieli.it; metro Basilica San Paolo, bus 23, 128, 761, 766, 769, 770. A cultural association that has become legendary since its founding in Rome in 1983. A staff of volunteers keeps it among the most active groups of its kind in southern Europe, planning cultural events, administering HIV tests and providing counselling, legal aid and home care for people with AIDS. The group organized the first International Gay Pride Festival in Rome on 8 July 2000.

Gay & Geo
t (mobile) 339 223 9253. Organizes weekly excursions and hiking around Rome (call by Thurs to join them on Sun).

Gruppo Pesce Roma Off maps
Nuova Olimpiclub, Lungotevere di Pietra Papa, t (mobile) 340 525 1157; bus 128, 170, 766, 791.

A sports-orientated association for gay swimmers.

Nuova Proposta G6
Via Marianna Dionigi 5, t (mobile) 347 810 0824, e nuovaproposta@ katamail.com; bus 34, 48, 87, 926. An association bringing together gays who believe in God.

Lesbian

Arci-lesbica Roma Off maps
Via dei Monti di Pietralata 16, t 06 418 2211, e arcilesbica_romana@ hotmail.com, w www.women.it/ arciles/roma; metro Tiburtina, then bus 211.
Runs a helpline Tues–Wed 6pm–9pm. The website also has links to numerous other lesbian and gay groups and events.

Centro Femminista Separatista E9
Via San Francesco di Sales 1/b, t 06 686 4201; bus 23, 280. The Coordinamento Lesbiche Italiane (CLI) and Coordinamento Lesbiche Romane (CLR), which meet on Monday at 8.30pm and Tuesday at 7pm, are based here.

Beaches

Il Buco Day trips map
Off the Ostia-Torvaianica coastal road (7–8km), near Ostia Lido. A well-known gay beach with a very lively, cruisey scene, lots of bars and good sound systems.

Spiaggia sull'Aurelia Off maps
Off the Via Aurelia (42km). Also a favoured haunt of the gay beach scene.

Bookshops

Libreria di Babele F8
Via dei Banchi Vecchi 116, t 06 687 6628, e babelecla@tiscalinet.it. Open Tue–Sat 10–2 and 3–7.30, Mon 3–7.30 only; bus 40, 46, 62, 64. Well stocked with free brochures and the whole gamut of gay and lesbian literature, from literary gems like Marguerite Yourcenar's *Life of Hadrian* to hardcore cartoons and magazines. Most of the stock is in Italian.

'La Bancarella'
di Handy Capp M4
Piazza Alessandria 2, **t** *06 8530*
3071, **e** *andy.capp@tiscalinet.it;*
bus *62, 84, 90, 490, 491, 495.*
Videos, porn magazines and sado-
masochistic cartoons. Mail order.

Libreria delle Donne G10
Via dei Fienaroli 31/d, **t** *06 518 7724;*
tram *8,* **bus** *H, 23, 280, 780.*
A selection of books pertinent to
women. A good place to find out
about about women's groups.

Queer K8
Via del Boschetto 25, **t** *06 474 0691;*
bus *H, 40, 60, 64, 70, 117, 170.*
Books, magazines, videos and
gadgets are sold at this tiny new
bookshop in the centre of town.

Cruising

Many of Rome's gay cruising
grounds are hard to reach without
a car. **Monte Caprino** (I9; **bus** *30,*
44, 63, 81, 95, 204, etc.), on the
Campidoglio; **Piramide Cestia** (I14;
metro *Piramide*); along the walls
of the **Protestant Cemetery** for
trans (H14; **metro** *Piramide*); **Colle**
Oppio (L9–M10; **metro** *Colosseo,*
tram *3,* **bus** *85, 87, 117, 204 etc.*), near
the Colosseum; and the park
around the **Palazzo della Civiltà**
del Lavoro at EUR (F23; **metro** *EUR-*
Magliana), can all be reached on
foot or by public transport. If you
have wheels, you can also reach
the further-flung hunting grounds
on the **Via Appia Antica,** near the
GRA ring road; in the **Parco di**
Montesacro, off Via Nomentana;
at the **Esso petrol station** on the
GRA between the Casilina and
Prenestina; and the **Mattatoio,** Via
Palmiro Togliatti (trans only).

Saunas

Apollon M9–10
Via Mecenate 59/a, **t** *06 482 5389;*
metro *Colosseo,* **tram** *3,* **bus** *85, 87,*
117, 204. **Open** *daily 2pm–11pm.*
Men only. Also jacuzzi-style tubs,
Turkish bath and private rooms.

Europa Multiclub L5–6
Via Aureliana 40, **t** *06 482 3650;*
metro *Repubblica,* **bus** *16, 30, 60,*
61, 62. **Open** *Mon–Thurs 2pm–2am,*
Fri–Sat 2pm–6am.
Italy's largest sauna, offering
solarium, giant jacuzzi-style pool
with a cascade, Turkish bath,
dressing rooms with massage,
beauty salon, gym, video bar and
movie theatre.

Eating Out

Asinocotto H11
Via dei Vascellari 48, **t** *06 589 8985;*
tram *8,* **bus** *H, 23, 280, 780.* **Open**
Feb–Dec Tues–Sun 12–4 and 8–12.
Moderate.
Posts the gay-friendly rainbow
flag outside. Italian creative food
and an acceptable wine list.

Giardino dei Ciliegi G10
Via dei Fienaroli 4, **t** *06 580 3423;*
tram *8,* **bus** *H, 23, 280, 780.* **Open**
Oct–May Mon–Fri 6pm–2am;
Sat, Sun and hols 5pm–2am;
June and last 2 weeks of Sept daily
8pm–2am. **Inexpensive.**
Tea room and salad bar.

Nerone L9
Via delle Terme di Tito 96, **t** *06 481*
7952; **metro** *Colosseo,* **bus** *117, 204.*
Open *Sept–July Mon–Sat 1–3.30*
and 7.30–12.30. **Inexpensive.**
A favourite gay hang-out with
traditional Roman cuisine.

Le Sorellastre E9
Via S. Francesco di Sales 1/b,
t *718 5288;* **bus** *23, 280.* **Inexpensive.**
The sisterhood at this exclusively
lesbian joint prepares Italian and
international cuisine.

Entertainment

There aren't any venues that
specialize in gay or lesbian
cinema, theatre or dance. Check
the listings in *Trovaroma* or *Roma*
c'è, pick up one of the publications
or contact one of the associations
listed on p.345, for special events.
There is, however, one museum
that has become something of a
gay pilgrimage sight.

Museo Andersen G–H3
Via P.S. Mancini 20, **t** *06 321 9089;*
metro *Flaminio,* **tram** *2,* **bus** *82,*
204. **Open** *Tues–Sun 9–7;* **adm** *€4.*

Housed on the ground floor of a
pretty early 20th-century
building, it was once the private
apartment and atelier of
Norwegian sculptor Hendrik
Christian Andersen, the man loved
by Henry James.

Nightlife

Bars

Garbo G10
Vicolo di Santa Margherita 1/a,
t *06 5832 0782;* **tram** *8,* **bus** *H, 23,*
280, 780. **Open** *daily noon–2am.*
A gay and lesbian pub with snacks
and cocktails, in Trastevere.

Glance N4
Via Nomentana 145, **t** *(mobile) 347*
430 1881; **tram** *3, 19,* **bus** *62, 84, 90.*
Open *noon–10pm.*
Half pub, half delicatessen. Also
serves non-alcoholic drinks.

Hangar H11
Via in Selci 69, **t** *06 488 1397;*
metro *Cavour,* **bus** *75, 84, 204.*
Open *Tues–Sat 5pm–2am.*
Rome's most popular gay bar, but
nowhere near hangar size – when
it fills up at night it can become
almost unbearably suffocating.

Shelter H11
Via dei Vascellari 35, no phone;
tram *8,* **bus** *H, 23, 280, 780.* **Open**
9pm–late.
Hetero-friendly gay and lesbian
meeting place.

Side Meeting Point M10
Via Labicana 50, **t** *(mobile) 348*
0692 9472; **tram** *3,* **bus** *85, 87, 117,*
186, 204, 810, 850.
A mainly gay pub.

Clubs and Discos

Alibi G14
Via di Monte Testaccio 39–44,
t *06 574 348;* **bus** *95, 673.*
Rome's classic gay disco.

Apeiron L8
Via dei Quattro Cantoni 5, **t** *06 482*
8820; **metro** *Cavour,* **bus** *75,*
84, 204.
Gay pub and sex club on two
floors. Dark room, videos on
Tuesday and strippers on Friday.

Goa Off maps
*Via di Libetta 13, **t** 06 574 8277;*
***bus** 23, 769.*
One of Rome's hottest discos, with Goan-style décor. Hosts disco parties between October and May for men (**Gorgeous Goagay**, every Tuesday) and for women (**Venus Rising**, last Sunday of the month). The rest of the year the two nights join and move to the **Classico** (*Via di Libetta 3, **t** 06 5728 8857*). Drag Queen shows in the hetero-friendly garden. Also women-only and men-only areas, and a dark room (every Saturday).

Halloween 08
Piazzale Tiburtino 31, no phone;
***bus** C, 204, 492.*
The disco venue of Arci-lesbica Roma (*see above*) on the first and third Tues of every month.

K Men's Club Off maps
*Via Amato Amati 6, **t** (mobile) 374 622 0462; **bus** 553.*
Leather bar with dark rooms, hard core films and a labyrinth.

Qube Off maps
*Via di Portonaccio 212, **t** 06 541 3985; **metro** Tiburtina.*
Made famous by vampish trans-vestite Vladimir Luxuria, the

creator of **Muccassassina** ('Murdering Cow'), considered to be Rome's most transgressive event (held here from October to May, every Friday night).

Skyline Club P8
*Via degli Aurunci 26–28, **t** 06 444 0817; **bus** C, 71, 204, 492.*
Trendy American-style gay club with cool jazz and soul from Tuesday to Saturday. Open to all on Thursday. Leather nights 2nd Saturday of every month.

Travel Agents

Queer Nation Holidays
*Via del Moro 95/r, Firenze, **t** (055) 265 4587, **f** (055) 265 4560, **e** info@queernationholidays.com, **w** www.queernationholidays.com*
Based in Florence, but deserves a mention. Arranges holidays and Italian language classes with gay or lesbian teachers.

Zipper M5
*Via Castelfidardo 18, **t** 06 488 2730, **e** zipper.travel@flashnet.it, **w** www.zippertravel.it; **metro** Termini.*
Organizes gay and lesbian package holidays.

Where to Stay

Appennini O2–3
*Via Appennini 32, **t** 06 855 1262, **f** 06 860 8113, **e** appennini@hotmail.com; **tram** 3, 19, **bus** 36, 60, 62, 84, 90. **Moderate**.*
Fairly central and quiet B&B, with a garden.

Bologna Q4
*Piazza Bologna 6, **t/f** 06 4424 0244, **e** d.pajella@tiscalinet.it; **metro** Piazza Bologna, **bus** 61, 62, 309, 310. **Moderate**.*
Another hospitable place to stay; a gay-run, gay-friendly B&B.

Gayopen M9
*Via dello Statuto 44, **t** 06 482 0013, **e** orsogrigio@hotmail.com, **w** www.angelfire.com/com/mo/riclaudioholidays. **Inexpensive**.*
Welcoming B&B, whether you're travelling alone or as a couple.

Festivals

In the 19th century, Rome's traditional Holy Week customs had lapsed through inertia. 'Holy Father,' someone asked. 'Should we not restore the solemn rites of the past?' 'Why not?' replied Pius IX. 'It will amuse the English.'

For details of Rome's excellent summer calendar of concerts, cinema, dance and outdoor festivity, the Estate Romana, *see* 'Entertainment', p.326.

January

New Year's Day
1 January
Candlelit procession in the Catacombs of Priscilla.

Festa della Befana
6 January
Last day of the toy fair in Piazza Navona and yet another chance for children to hang up their stockings – for the *befana* (witch) to leave sugared coal (*see* p.341).

Festa di Sant'Agnese
21 January
Shearing of lambs to gather wool for the bishops' palliums at S. Agnese fuori le Mura.

February

Candelora
2 February
Blessing of candles in Testaccio.

Festa di San Biagio
3 February
Free anti-sore-throat bread, blessed and drizzled with olive oil (good for one year), is distributed at the church of S. Biagio, known as the Chiesa della Pagnotta, next to the Aracoeli stairs.

Carnival
Until the start of Lent
Rome, once famous for its mad carnival, now celebrates at private parties, where everyone spends a small fortune to pose in elegant costumes (*see* p.103).

March

Festa di San Giuseppe
19 March
In the Trionfale neighbourhood (between the Vatican and Monte Mario), bars serve *frittelle* (fried pastries, often with cream inside) along with the usual *cornetti*. Market and bright lights near the church of S. Giuseppe.

April

There are so many **Holy Week** events that the Tourist Office publishes a booklet in English listing them all. On **Good Friday** evening the Pope leads the candlelit Procession of the Cross at the Colosseum. On **Easter Sunday** he gives his traditional blessing from the balcony in St Peter's Square. Over Easter masses of pink azaleas decorate the Spanish Steps.

Sagra del Carciofo Romanesco
Early–mid April
The festival of Roman artichokes in Ladispoli includes artichoke floats, folk dancing and fireworks.

Rome's Birthday
21 April
Celebrated with free entrance to some of the city's museums (a different selection every year – ask the Tourist Office) and fireworks.

Santa Caterina da Siena
29 April
The patroness of Italy is celebrated at the church of S. Maria sopra Minerva, where her tomb is.

May

Throughout the month, Via Margutta, near the Spanish Steps, holds an **outdoor art exhibition**. For two weeks from mid-May, the antique shops in Via dei Coronari spice up trade with an **antiques fair**, during which the street is carpeted and torch-lit. As long as the petals stay on the flowers, the city **rose garden** is on show on Via di Valle Murcia, near the Aventine. The **International Horse Show** takes place in Villa Borghese's Piazza di Siena in early May, with jumping events and cavalry charging (*see* p.336). **International Tennis Championships** are held at the Foro Italico in May (*see* p.337).

June

Festa della Repubblica
2 June
Visit the military barracks or follow the civilian parade for Italy's Republic day.

Sunday after Corpus Christi
Flowers in various designs carpet the main street of Genzano in the Castelli Romani.

Festa di San Giovanni
23–24 June
At S. Giovanni in Laterano. Market stalls and lotsof snails and *porchetta* (whole spit-roast suckling pig) to eat.

Festa dei Santi Pietro e Paolo
29 June
Major religious celebration in St Peter's.

Strawberry Festival
All month
At Nemi in the Castelli Romani.

July

The **Estate Romana** gets in full swing during July and August, with open-air cinema, rock, dance and opera performances.

Festa de' Noantri
Third week
The festival of 'We Others' in Trastevere was once Rome's most authentic, popular festival, with food, wine, and dancing. The city is now trying to poison it with the usual commercial rubbish.

August

The **Estate Romana** continues until the end of the month for the few Romans left in the city.

Festa della Madonna della Neve
5 August
A release of white flowers at S. Maria Maggiore to symbolize the miraculous snow (*see* p.186).

Ferragosto
15 August
The peak of the summer holidays for Italians, when only tourists are left in Rome; everything closed.

Anniversary of the Great Fire under Nero
23 August
Not celebrated, oddly enough.

September
Another **outdoor art exhibition** in Via Margutta and a **craft fair** on Via dell'Orso.

Santa Rosa
3 September
Features the Macchina di S. Rosa, which is carried through the streets of Viterbo in procession (*see p.268*).

October
Yet another **antiques fair** on Via dei Coronari, mid-month for two weeks, and the **craft fair** continues in Via dell'Orso.

Ottobrata Romana
All month
Musical events in Trastevere.

Sagra dell'Uva
1st Sunday
White wine is offered at the wine festival in the main square of Marino, in the Castelli Romani (traditionally it flows in the fountains, but the *comune* no longer stretches to such luxury).

November
All Soul's Day
1 November
Everyone goes to the cemetery to light candles for the dead.

December
The Piazza Navona toy fair (*see* January, Festa della Befana) begins in the first week – lots of bright lights and a chance to buy sweets or handmade Christmas crib figures. Bagpipe players from the Abruzzi play their strange wailing melodies. Elaborate *presepi*, or cribs, appear in most churches and in front of St Peter's. The jewel-encrusted Santo Bambino of S. Maria in Aracoeli (*see p.123*) is relocated to a *presepio* to receive the homage of Rome's children in little speeches and poems.

Festa della Madonna Immacolata
8 December
In Piazza Mignanelli, firemen place a wreath on the head of the Madonna's statue (*see p.107*) to celebrate her immaculate conception. The Pope usually attends for prayers.

Christmas Eve
24 December
Midnight mass at S. Maria Maggiore.

Christmas
25 December
The Pope gives his 'Urbi et Orbi' blessing from St Peter's balcony at noon.

Festa di San Silvestro
31 December
The Pope visits the church of the Gesù for the feast of S. Silvestro and sings the ancient Te Deum. The Mayor of Rome presents a silver chalice (arrive by 5pm to get a good view). Meanwhile, Romans wolf down sausages and lentils for good luck and stuffed pig's foot (*zampone*), drink a *spumante* toast, set off a few sparklers, hurl one or two old plates out of the window (watch out if you're in the street, and don't leave your car anywhere near human habitation) then go to bed, in a relatively subdued celebration of the pagan New Year's Eve.

Language

The fathers of modern Italian were Dante, Manzoni and TV. Each did, or has done, their part in creating a national language from an infinity of regional and local dialects. Dante, a Florentine, the first 'immmortal' to write in the vernacular, did much to put the Tuscan dialect in the foreground of Italian literature with his *Divina Commedia* (Divine Comedy). Manzoni's revolutionary novel, *I Promessi Sposi* (The Betrothed), heightened national consciousness by using everyday language all could understand in the 19th century. TV in the last decades has performed an even more spectacular linguistic unification; although the majority of Italians still speak a dialect at home, school, work and their TV idols insist on proper Italian.

Perhaps because they are so busy learning their own beautiful language, Italians are not the most adept at learning others. English lessons, however, have been the rage for years, and at most hotels and restaurants in Rome there will be someone who speaks English. The words and phrases below should help you out in most situations, unless you come up against the roughest of *romanaccio* dialect. The ideal way to come to Rome is with some Italian under your belt – your visit will be richer, and you're more likely to make Italian friends.

Pronunciation

Italian words are pronounced phonetically. Every vowel and consonant (except 'h') is sounded. Consonants are the same as in English, except 'c' which, when followed by an 'e' or 'i', is pronounced like the English 'ch' (*cinque* thus becomes 'cheen-quay'). Italian 'g' is also soft before 'i' or 'e' as in *gira* ('jee-ra'). The letter 'z' is pronounced like 'ts'.

The consonants 'sc' before the vowels 'i' or 'e' become like the English 'sh' as in *sci*, pronounced 'shee'; 'ch' is pronouced like a 'k' as in Chianti, 'kee-an-tee'; 'gn' as 'ny' in English (*bagno*, pronounced 'ban-yo'); while 'gli' is pronounced like the middle of the word 'million' (Castiglione, for example, is pronounced 'Ca-steely-oh-nay').

Vowel pronunciation is: 'a' as in English father; 'e' when unstressed is like 'a' in 'fate' (*mele*), when stressed it can be the same or like the 'e' in 'pet' (*bello*); 'i' is like the 'i' in 'machine'; 'o', like 'e', has two sounds, 'o' as in 'hope' when unstressed (*tacchino*), and usually 'o' as in 'rock' when stressed (*morte*); 'u' is pronounced like the 'u' in 'June'.

The stress usually (but not always) falls on the penultimate syllable. Accents indicate if it falls elsewhere (as in *città*). Also note that, in the big northern cities, the informal way of addressing someone as you, *tu*, is widely used; the more formal *lei* or *voi* is commonly used in provincial districts, *voi* more in the south.

Basic Vocabulary

yes/no/maybe *sì/no/forse*
I don't know *Non (lo) so*
I don't understand (Italian) *Non capisco (l'italiano)*
Does someone here speak English? *C'è qualcuno qui che parla inglese?*
Speak slowly *Parla lentamente*
Could you assist me? *Potrebbe aiutarmi?*
Help! *Aiuto!*
Please *Per favore*
Thank you (very much) *Grazie (molte/mille)*
You're welcome *Prego*
It doesn't matter *Non importa*
All right *Va bene*
Excuse me *Permesso/Mi scusi*
Be careful! *Attenzione!/Attento!*
Nothing *Niente*
It is urgent! *È urgente!*
How are you? *Come sta?* (formal)/ *Come stai?* (informal)
Well, and you? *Bene, e Lei?/e tu?*
What is your name? *Come si chiama?/Come ti chiami?*
Hello *Salve/Ciao (both informal)*
Good morning *Buongiorno*
Good afternoon/evening *Buonasera*
Good night *Buona notte*
Goodbye *ArrivederLa (formal)/ Arrivederci/Ciao (informal)*
What do you call this in Italian? *Come si chiama questo in italiano?*
What?/Who?/Where? *Che cosa?/ Chi?/Dove?*
When?/Why? *Quando?/Perché?*
How? *Come?*
How much (does it cost)? *Quanto (costa)?*
I am lost *Mi sono perso*
I am hungry/thirsty/sleepy *Ho fame/sete/sonno*
I am sorry *Mi dispiace*
I am tired *Sono stanco*
I feel unwell *Mi sento male*
I am ill *Sono malato*
Leave me alone *Lasciami in pace*
good/bad *buono/cattivo*
well/badly *bene/male*
hot/cold *caldo/freddo*
slow/fast *lento/rapido*
up/down *su/giù*
big/small *grande/piccolo*
here/there *qui/lì*

Travel Directions

One (two) ticket(s) to Naples, please *Un biglietto (due biglietti) per Napoli, per favore*
one way *solo andata*
return *andata e ritorno*
first/second class *prima/ seconda classe*
I want to go to... *Desidero andare a...*
How can I get to...? *Come posso andare a...?*
Do you stop at...? *Si ferma a...?*
Where is...? *Dov'è...?*
How far is it to...? *Quanto è lontano...?*
What is the name of this station? *Come si chiama questa stazione?*
When does the next bus leave? *Quando parte il prossimo autobus?*
From where does it leave? *Da dove parte?*
How much is the fare? *Quant'è il biglietto?*
Have a good trip! *Buon viaggio!*

Public Transport

airport *aeroporto*
bus stop *fermata*
bus/coach *autobus/pullman*
customs *dogana*
platform *binario*
train *treno*
railway station *stazione ferroviaria*
seat (reserved) *posto (prenotato)*
taxi *tassì/taxi*
ticket *biglietto*

Orientation

near/far *vicino/lontano*
left/right *sinistra/destra*
straight ahead *sempre diritto*
forward/backwards *avanti/indietro*
north/south *nord/sud*
east *est/oriente*
west *ovest/occidente*
crossroads *bivio/incrocio*
street/road *strada/via*
square *piazza*
bridge *ponte*

On Wheels

car hire *autonoleggio*
motorbike/scooter/moped *motocicletta/Vespa/motorino*
bicycle *bicicletta*
petrol/diesel *benzina/gasolio*
garage *garage*
This doesn't work *Questo non funziona*
mechanic *meccanico*
map/town plan *carta/pianta*
Where is the road to...? *Dov'è la strada per...?*
breakdown *guasto*
driving licence *patente di guida*
speed *velocità*
danger *pericolo*
parking *parcheggio*
no parking *sosta vietata*
narrow *stretto*
toll *pedaggio*
slow down *rallentare*
one-way *senso unico*

Shopping and Sightseeing

I would like... *Vorrei...*
Where is/are... *Dov'è/Dove sono...*
How much is it? *Quanto costa?*
open/closed *aperto/chiuso*
cheap/expensive *a buon prezzo/caro*

bank *banca*
beach *spiaggia*
bed *letto*
church *chiesa*
entrance/exit *ingresso/uscita*
hospital *ospedale*
money *soldi*
newspaper *giornale*
pharmacy *farmacia*
police station *commissariato*
policeman *poliziotto*
post office *ufficio postale*
sea *mare*
shop *negozio*
room *camera*
tobacco shop *tabaccaio*
WC *toilette/bagno/servizi*
men *Signori/Uomini*
women *Signore/Donne*

Days

Monday *lunedì*
Tuesday *martedì*
Wednesday *mercoledì*
Thursday *giovedì*
Friday *venerdì*
Saturday *sabato*
Sunday *domenica*
Weekdays *feriali*
Holidays *festivi*

Numbers

one *uno/una*
two/three/four *due/tre/quattro*
five/six/seven *cinque/sei/sette*
eight/nine/ten *otto/nove/dieci*
eleven/twelve *undici/dodici*
thirteen/fourteen *tredici/quattordici*
fifteen/sixteen *quindici/sedici*
seventeen/eighteen *diciassette/diciotto*
nineteen *diciannove*
twenty *venti*
twenty-one/twenty-two *ventuno/ventidue*
thirty *trenta*
forty *quaranta*
fifty *cinquanta*
sixty *sessanta*
seventy *settanta*
eighty *ottanta*
ninety *novanta*
hundred *cento*
one hundred and one *centouno*
two hundred *duecento*
one thousand *mille*
two thousand *duemila*
million *un milione*

Time

What time is it? *Che ore sono?*
day/week *giorno/settimana*
month *mese*
morning/afternoon *mattina/pomeriggio*
evening *sera*
yesterday *ieri*
today *oggi*
tomorrow *domani*
soon *fra poco*
later *dopo/più tardi*
It is too early/late *È troppo presto/tardi*

Hotel Vocabulary

I'd like a double room please *Vorrei una camera matrimoniale, per favore*
I'd like a twin room please *Vorrei una camera doppia, per favore*
I'd like a single room please *Vorrei una camera singola, per favore*
...with bath, without bath *...con bagno, senza bagno*
...for two nights *...per due notti*
We are leaving tomorrow morning *Partiamo domani mattina*
May I see the room, please? *Potrei vedere la camera, per cortesia?*
Is there a room with a balcony? *C'è una camera con balcone?*
There isn't (aren't) any hot water/soap... *Manca/Mancano acqua calda/sapone...*
...light/toilet paper/towels *...luce, carta igienica, asciugamani*
May I pay by credit card? *Posso pagare con carta di credito?*
May I see another room please? *Per favore, potrei vedere un'altra camera?*
Fine, I'll take it *Bene, la prendo*
Is breakfast included? *E' compresa la prima colazione?*
What time do you serve breakfast? *A che ora è la colazione?*
How do I get to the town centre? *Come posso raggiungere il centro città?*

Restaurant Vocabulary

Do you have a table for two (three/four)? *C'é una tavola per due (tre/quattro)?*

Menu Vocabulary

Antipasti (Starters)

antipasto misto mixed starters
bruschetta garlic toast (with olive oil and tomatoes)
carciofi (sott'olio) artichokes (in olive oil)
frutti di mare seafood
funghi (trifolati) mushrooms (with anchovies, garlic, lemon)
gamberi ai fagioli prawns (shrimps) with white beans
mozzarella (in carrozza) soft cow/buffalo cheese (fried with bread in batter)
prosciutto crudo (con melone) Parma ham (with melon)
salsicce sausages

Minestre (Soups) and Pasta

agnolotti meat-stuffed pasta parcels
cappelletti small stuffed pasta parcels, often served in broth
crespelle crêpes
frittata omelette
orecchiette ear-shaped pasta
panzerotto crescent-shaped pastry filled with tomato and tuna or tomato and mozzarella
pasta e fagioli soup with beans, bacon and tomatoes
pastina in brodo tiny pasta in broth
polenta cake or pudding of corn semolina
ravioli flat stuffed pasta parcels
spaghetti all'amatriciana spaghetti with spicy bacon, tomato, onion and chilli sauce
spaghetti alle vongole spaghetti with clam sauce
stracciatella broth with eggs and cheese
tortellini crescent-shaped stuffed pasta parcels

Carne (Meat)

agnello/abbacchio lamb
anatra duck
arrosto misto mixed roast meats
bollito misto meat stew
braciola chop
brasato di manzo braised beef with vegetables
bresaola dried raw meat

bucatini thin pasta tubes
carpaccio thinly sliced raw beef
cervella brains
cervo venison
coniglio rabbit
costoletta/cotoletta chop
guanciale pork cheek
lumache snails
manzo beef
osso buco veal knuckle stewed in its own marrow
pajata veal intestine
pancetta bacon
piccione pigeon
carne alla pizzaiola beef in tomato and oregano sauce
pollo chicken
polpette meatballs
rognoni kidneys
saltimbocca rolled veal, prosciutto and sage, in wine
scaloppine thin slices of veal sautéed in butter
stufato beef and vegetables braised in wine
tacchino turkey
trippa tripe
vitello veal

Pesce (Fish)

acciughe/alici anchovies
anguilla eel
aragosta lobster
baccalà dried salt cod
bonito small tuna
calamari squid
cape sante scallops
cozze mussels
fritto misto mixed fried fish
gamberetti shrimps
gamberi prawns
granchio crab
insalata di mare seafood salad
merluzzo cod
ostriche oysters
pesce spada swordfish
polipi/polpi octopus
sarde sardines
sogliola sole
squadro monkfish
stoccafisso wind-dried cod
tonno tuna
vongole small clams
zuppa di pesce fish soup or stew

Contorni (Vegetables)

aglio garlic
asparagi asparagus
carciofi artichokes
cavolo cabbage
ceci chickpeas
cetriolo cucumber
cicoria green chicory
cipolla onion
fagiolini French (green) beans
fave broad beans
funghi (porcini) mushrooms (cep)
insalata (mista/verde) salad (mixed/green)
lenticchie lentils
melanzane aubergine
patate potatoes
patatine potato chips
peperoncini hot chilli peppers
peperoni sweet peppers
peperonata stewed peppers in tomato and herb sauce
piselli peas
pomodoro(i) tomato(es)
porri leeks
puntarelle stripped curled stalks of cicoria catalogna
rucola rocket
spinaci spinach
verdure greens/vegetables
verza Savoy cabbage
zucca pumpkin
zucchine courgettes

Formaggio (Cheese)

bel paese soft white cow's cheese
burrata mozzarella-like cheese with a creamy centre
cacio/caciocavallo pale yellow, sharp cheese
caprino goat's cheese
parmigiano parmesan cheese
pecorino sharp sheep's cheese
provolone sharp, tangy cheese; **dolce** is less strong
stracchino soft white cheese

Frutta (Fruit, Nuts)

albicocche apricots
ananas pineapple
arance oranges
banane bananas
ciliegie cherries
cocomero watermelon
fragole strawberries
frutta di stagione fruit in season
lamponi raspberries
limone lemon

macedonia di frutta fruit salad
mandorle almonds
mele apples
more blackberries
nocciole hazelnuts
noci walnuts
pesca peach
pesca noce nectarine
pompelmo grapefruit
prugna/susina prune/plum
uva grapes

Dolci (Desserts)
amaretti macaroons
crostata fruit flan
gelato (produzione propria) ice cream (home-made)
granita (con panna) flavoured ice (with cream), usually lemon or coffee
panettone cake with candied fruit and raisins
semifreddo refrigerated cake
spumone a soft ice cream
tiramisù tiramisù
torta cake, tart
zabaglione creamy dessert of egg yolks and Marsala
zuppa inglese trifle

Bevande (Beverages)
acqua minerale mineral water
  gasata/non gasata with/without fizz
aranciata orange soda
birra (alla spina) beer (draught)
caffè coffee
caffè macchiato (freddo/caldo) espresso with a drop of milk (cold/hot)
caffè ristretto extra-short black coffee
cappuccino frothy milky coffee
espresso short black coffee
latte (intero/scremato) milk (whole/skimmed)
latte macchiato milk with a drop of coffee
succo di frutta fruit juice
tè tea
tè freddo sweet iced tea
tisana herbal tea
vino (rosso, bianco, rosato) wine (red, white, *rosé*)

Cooking Terms
aceto (balsamico) vinegar (balsamic)
affumicato smoked
bicchiere glass
burro butter
conto bill
coltello knife
cucchiaio spoon
forchetta fork
forno oven
fritto fried
ghiaccio ice
griglia grill
in bianco plain/without tomato
marmellata jam
menta mint
miele honey
olio (di olivo) olive oil
pane (tostato) bread (toasted)
panini sandwiches (in roll/ciabatta/focaccia etc.)
panna cream
pepe pepper
ripieno stuffed
rosmarino rosemary
sale salt
salvia sage
tavola table
toast toasted sandwich, usually ham and cheese
tovagliolo napkin
tramezzini sandwiches (in sliced bread)
uovo/uova egg/eggs
zucchero sugar

Index

Numbers in **bold** indicate main references. Numbers in *italic* indicate maps.
Except for St Peter's, Christian basilicas and churches are listed under 'churches'.

Rome Street Maps

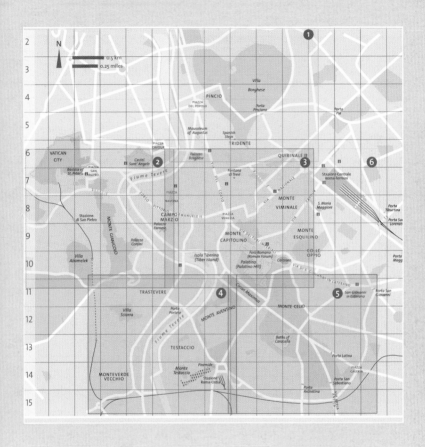

Key

			Pedestrianized Road
i	Information		Park
★	Place of Interest	✝	Cemetery
Ⓜ	Metro Station		River
	City Wall/Ruin		Place of Interest
			Public Building

N

250 m

220 yards

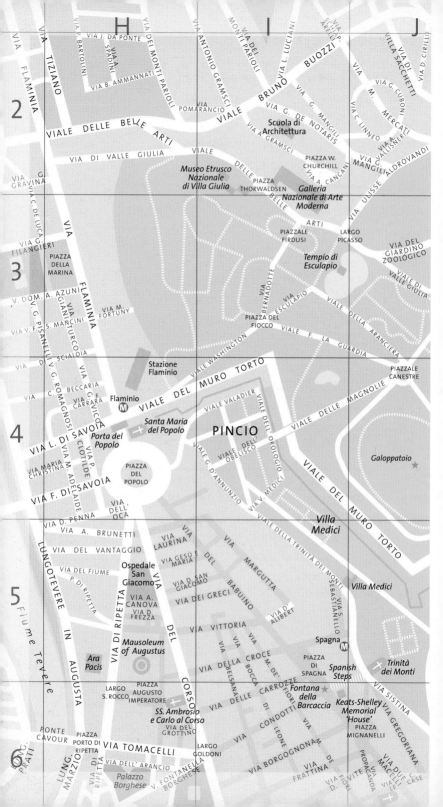

H I J

VIA FLAMINIA
VIA TIZIANO
VIA P. BARTOLINI
VIA J. DA PONTE
VIA A. SPADINI
VIA DEI MONTI PARIOLI
VIA B. AMMANNATI
VIA ANTONIO GRAMSCI
VIA DEI MONTI PARIOLI
VIA L. LUCIANI
BRUNO BUOZZI
VIA P. ARETINO
VIA DI VILLA SACCHETTI
VIA D. CIRILLO

2

VIALE DELLE BELLE ARTI
VIA DI VALLE GIULIA
VIALE POMARANCIO
VIALE
VIALE
VIA G. MANGILI
VIA G. DE NOTARIS
Scuola di Architettura
VIA A. GRAMSCI
PIAZZA W. CHURCHILL
VIA C. LINNEO
VIA M. G. CUBONI
VIA A. VALISNERI
VIA MERCATI
VIA G. GRAVINA
VIA C. DE LUCA

Museo Etrusco Nazionale di Villa Giulia
DELLE
PIAZZA THORWALDSEN
Galleria Nazionale di Arte Moderna
VIA A. CANCANI
VIA ULISSE ALDROVANDI
VIA MANGILI
VIA DEL GIARDINO ZOOLOGICO

3

VIA G. FILANGIERI
PIAZZA DELLA MARINA
VIA FLAMINIA
V. DOM. A. AZUNI
V. G. PISANELLI
VIA TURCO
VIA C. MANCINI
VIA M. FORTUNY
V. V. SCIALOIA
BELLE
ARTI
PIAZZALE FIRDUSI
LARGO PICASSO
VIA BERNADOTTE
Tempio di Esculapio
VIA ESCULAPIO
PIAZZA DEL FIOCCO
VIALE DELLA ARANCIERA
VIALE DI VALLE GIULIA
VIALE F. LA GUARDIA

4

VIA DI SCIALOIA
VIA G. ROMAGNOSI
C. BECCARIA
VIA G. F. CARRARA
VIA L. DI SAVOIA
VIA M. ADELAIDE
VIA P. CLOTILDE
VIA MARIA CHRISTINA
VIA F. DI SAVOIA
Stazione Flaminio
Flaminio M
Santa Maria del Popolo
Porta del Popolo
PIAZZA DEL POPOLO
VIALE WASHINGTON
VIALE DEL MURO TORTO
VIALE VALADIER
VIALE DELL' OROLOGIO
PINCIO
VIALE DELL' OBELISCO
VIA G. D'ANNUNZIO
VIALE DELLE MAGNOLIE
PIAZZALE CANESTRE
Galoppatoio ★
VIALE DEL MURO TORTO

5

LUNGOTEVERE IN AUGUSTA
Fiume Tevere
VIA D. PENNA
VIA A. BRUNETTI
VIA DEL VANTAGGIO
VIA DEL FIUME
P. DI RIPETTA
VIA DI RIPETTA
VIA A. CANOVA
VIA D. FREZZA
VIA DELL' OCA
VIA LAURINA
VIA GESÙ E MARIA
Ospedale San Giacomo
VIA D. SAN GIACOMO
VIA DEI GRECI
VIA DEL BABUINO
VIA MARGUTTA
VIA VITTORIA
VIA D. ALIBERT
VIALE DELLA TRINITÀ DEI MONTI
VIA V. MEDICI
Villa Medici
Villa Medici
VIA S. SEBASTIANELLO
Spagna M
Trinità dei Monti

6

Ara Pacis
Mausoleum of Augustus
LARGO S. ROCCO
PIAZZA AUGUSTO IMPERATORE
SS. Ambrosio e Carlo al Corso
VIA DEL GROTTINO
LARGO GOLDONI
VIA DELLA CROCE
VIA DELLA BELSIANA
VIA BOCCA DI LEONE
VIA DELLE CARROZZE
Fontana della Barcaccia
PIAZZA DI SPAGNA
Spanish Steps
Keats-Shelley Memorial 'House'
PIAZZA MIGNANELLI
VIA DEL CORSO
VIA MARIO DE' FIORI
VIA CONDOTTI
VIA BORGOGNONA
VIA FRATTINA
VIA DELLE CONVERTITE
VIA DI PROPAGANDA
VIA SISTINA
VIA GREGORIANA
VIA DUE MACELLI
PONTE CAVOUR
LUNG. PRATI
LUNG. MARZIO
PIAZZA PORTO DI RIPETTA
VIA DI RIPETTA
VIA TOMACELLI
VIA DELL' ARANCIO
Palazzo Borghese
V. FONTANELLA BORGHESE
VIA DELLE VITE
V. DI FIORI
LE CASE

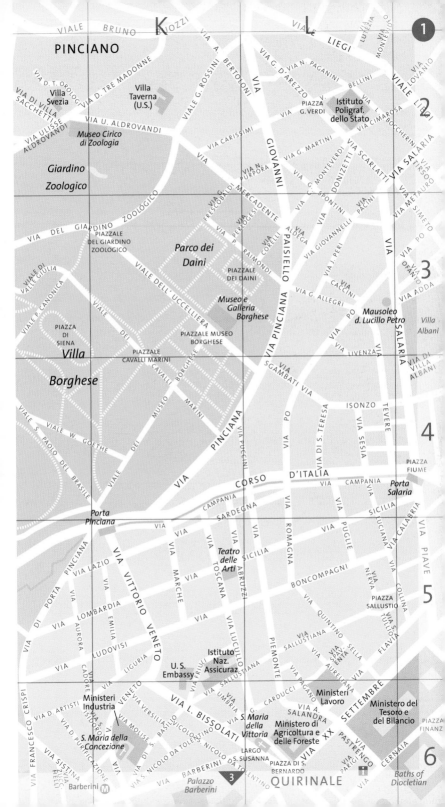

VIALE BRUNO BUOZZI

VIALE LIEGI

1

PINCIANO

VIA VENEZIA TRIPOLI

VIALE LIEGI

VIA G. D'AREZZO

VIA A. BERTOLONI

VIA G. ROSSINI

VIA N. PAGANINI

VIA BELLINI

VIA MONTEVIDEO

VIA GIOVANNI

VIA D. T. OROLOGIO

VIA D. TRE MADONNE

Villa
Svezia

Villa
Taverna
(U.S.)

PIAZZA
G. VERDI

Istituto
Poligraf.
dello Stato

VIA L. BOCCHERINI

VIA L. CIMAROSA

2

VIA DI VILLA SACCHETTI

VIA U. ALDROVANDI

Museo Cirico
di Zoologia

VIA CARISSIMI

VIA G. MARTINI

VIA C. MONTEVERDI

VIA DONIZETTI

VIA SCARLATTI

VIA SALARIA

VIA TIRSO

VIA ULISSE ALDROVANDI

Giardino

Zoologico

VIA N. PORPORA

VIA G. SPONTINI

VIA J. PERI

VIA PACINI

VIA METAURO

VIA SIMETO

VIA PO

VIA DEL GIARDINO ZOOLOGICO

PIAZZALE
DEL GIARDINO
ZOOLOGICO

VIA G. FRESCOBALDI

VIA MERCADENTE

VIA PERGOLESI

VIA PAISIELLO

VIA GIOVANNELLI

VIA OFANTO

VIA ADDA

Parco dei
Daini

VIA G. ALLEGRI

VIA ADDA

3

VIALE DI VALLE GIULIA

VIALE P. CANONICA

VIALE DELL'UCCELLIERA

PIAZZALE
DEI DAINI

VIA RAIMONDI

VIA CORELLI

VIA G. CACCINI

Villa
Albani

Museo e
Galleria
Borghese

VIA PINCIANA

VIA SALARIA

Mausoleo
d. Lucillo Petro

VIA DI
VILLA
ALBANI

PIAZZA
DI
SIENA

VIALE DEI

PIAZZALE MUSEO
BORGHESE

VIA PO

VIA LIVENZA

Villa

Borghese

PIAZZALE
CAVALLI MARINI

VIA SGAMBATI VIA

VIALE S. PAOLO DEL BRASILE

VIALE W. GOETHE

VIA DEI

VIA MUSEO

VIA CAVALLI

MARINI

VIA PUCCINI

VIA PINCIANA

VIA PO

VIA DI S. TERESA

ISONZO

VIA SESIA

TEVERE

4

CORSO

D'ITALIA

PIAZZA
FIUME

Porta
Pinciana

VIA CAMPANIA

SARDEGNA

VIA CAMPANIA

Porta
Salaria

VIA DI PORTA PINCIANA

VIA PINCIANA

VIA LAZIO

VIA VITTORIO VENETO

VIA TOSCANA

VIA SICILIA

VIA ROMAGNA

VIA PUGLIE

VIA SICILIA

VIA CALABRIA

VIA PIAVE

Teatro
delle
Arti

VIA ABRUZZI

BONCOMPAGNI

VIA LUCIANA

VIA NERVA

5

VIA MARCHE

VIA EMILIA

VIA LOMBARDIA

VIA AURORA

VIA LIGURIA

VIA LUDOVISI

VIA VENETO

VIA FRIULI

VIA LUCULLO

VIA PIEMONTE

VIA QUINTINO SELLA

PIAZZA
SALLUSTIO

VIA COLLINA

VIA S. TULLIO

VIA FLAVIA

VIA CADORE

VIA SALLUSTIANA

VIA AV. SELLA

VIA SALLUSTIANA

VIA AURELIANA

Istituto
Naz.
Assicuraz.

U.S.
Embassy

VIA VERSILIA

VIA UMBRIA

VIA PACANO

Ministeri
Lavoro

SETTEMBRE

Ministero del
Tesoro e
del Bilancio

PIAZZA
FINANZ

6

VIA FRANCESCO CRISPI

Ministeri
Industria

VIA D. ARTISTI

S. Maria della
Concezione

VIA BASILIO

VIA MOLISE

VIA NICOLO DA TOLENTINO

VIA L. BISSOLATI

VIA G. CARDUCCI

S. Maria
della
Vittoria

VIA SALANDRA

Ministero di
Agricoltura e
delle Foreste

VIA XX

PASTRENGO

VIA PARIGI

CERNAIA

Baths of
Diocletian

VIA SISTINA

VIA DI PURIFICAZIONE

Palazzo
Barberini

3

LARGO
S. SUSANNA

PIAZZA DI S.
BERNARDO

QUIRINALE

Barberini Ⓜ

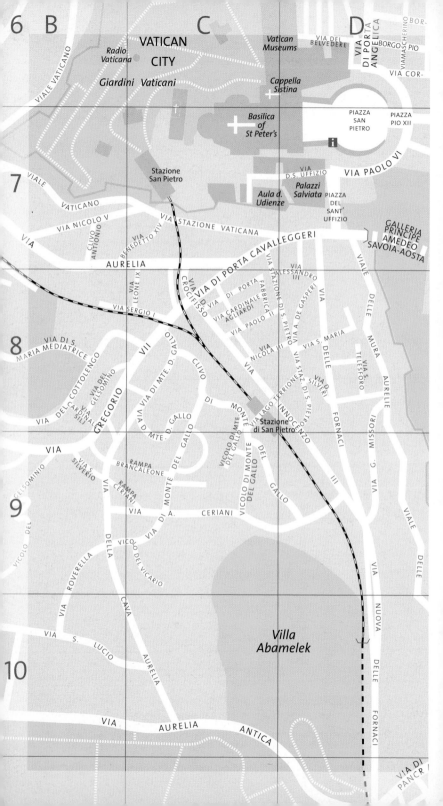

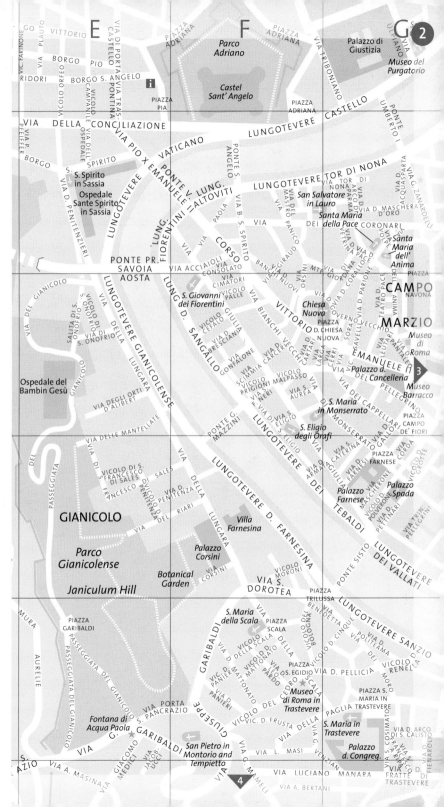

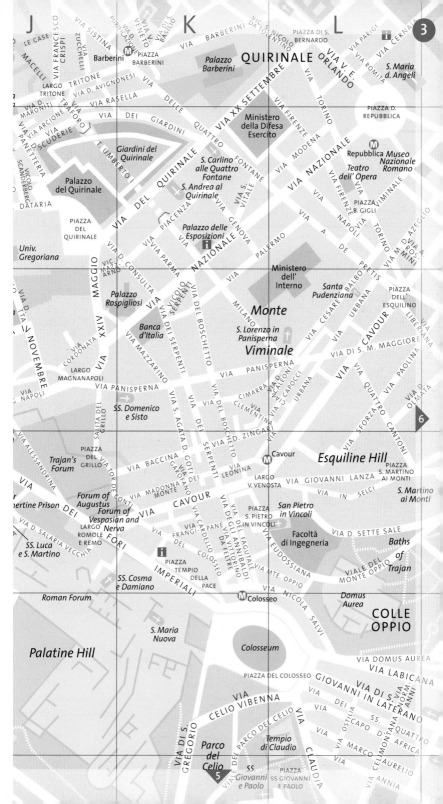

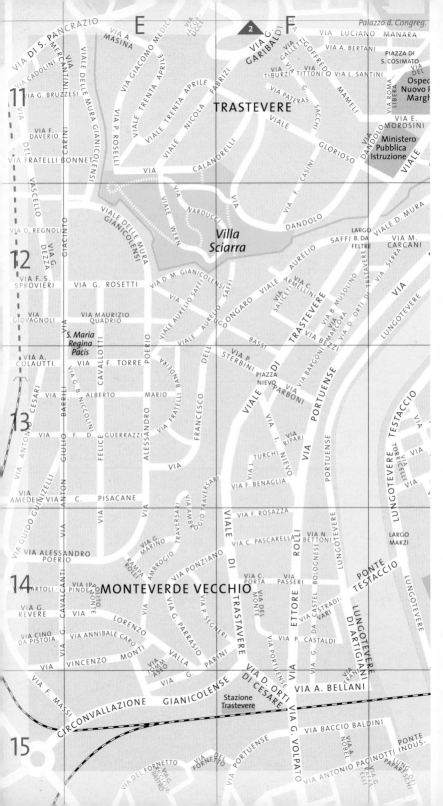

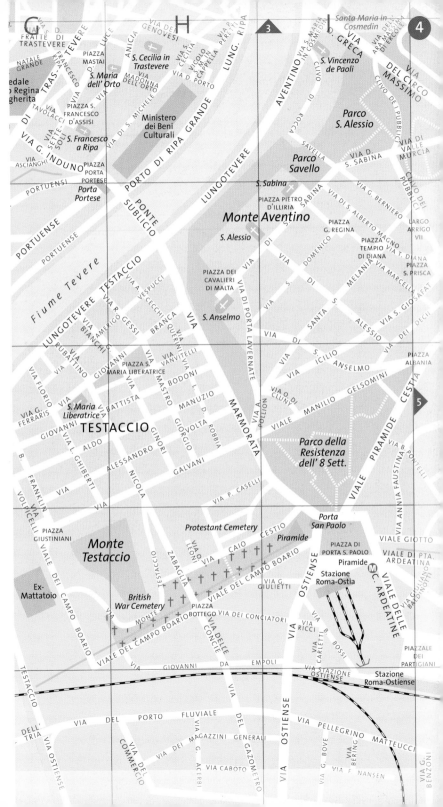

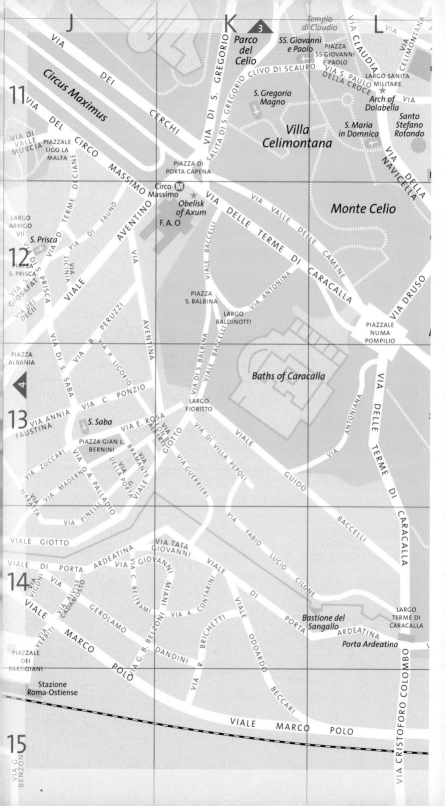

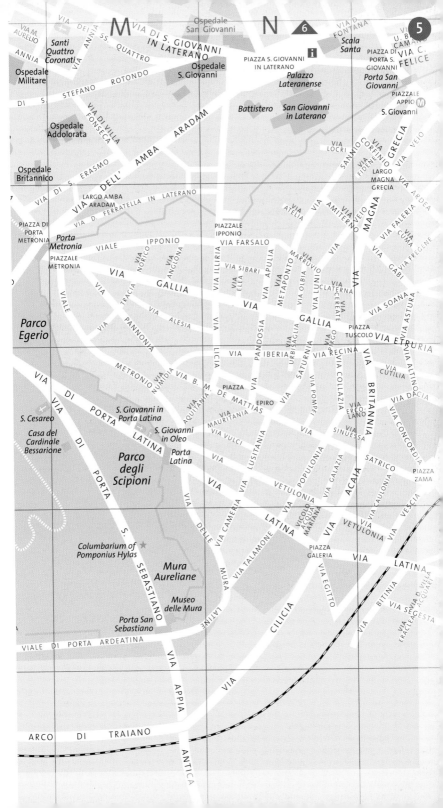

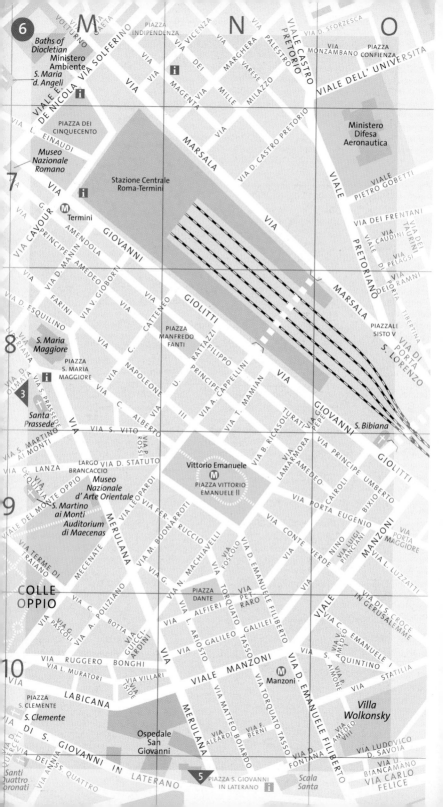

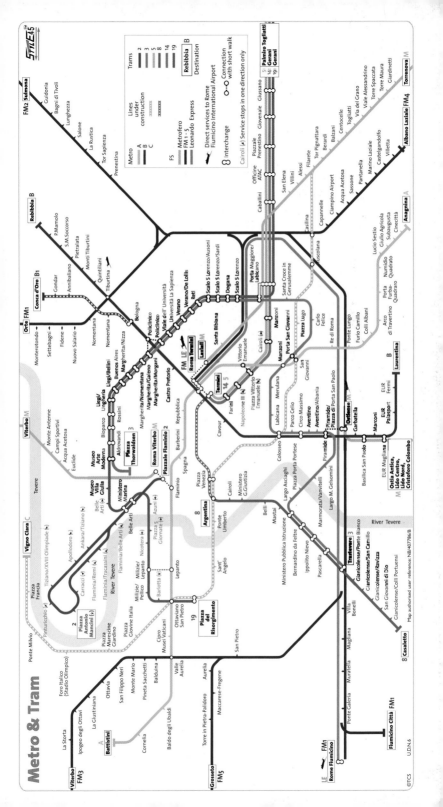

MADRID
Dana Facaros & Michael Pauls

CADOGANguides

BRUSSELS
Antony Mason

CADOGANguides

LONDON
Andrew Gumbel

CADOGANguides

Also available
Amsterdam
Barcelona
Brussels
Madrid
Paris

Available June 2002
Bruges
Florence
London
Prague
Sydney

Cadogan City Guides...
the life and soul
of the city

CADOGANguides
well travelled well read

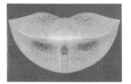